MW01625657

Joel Shapiro

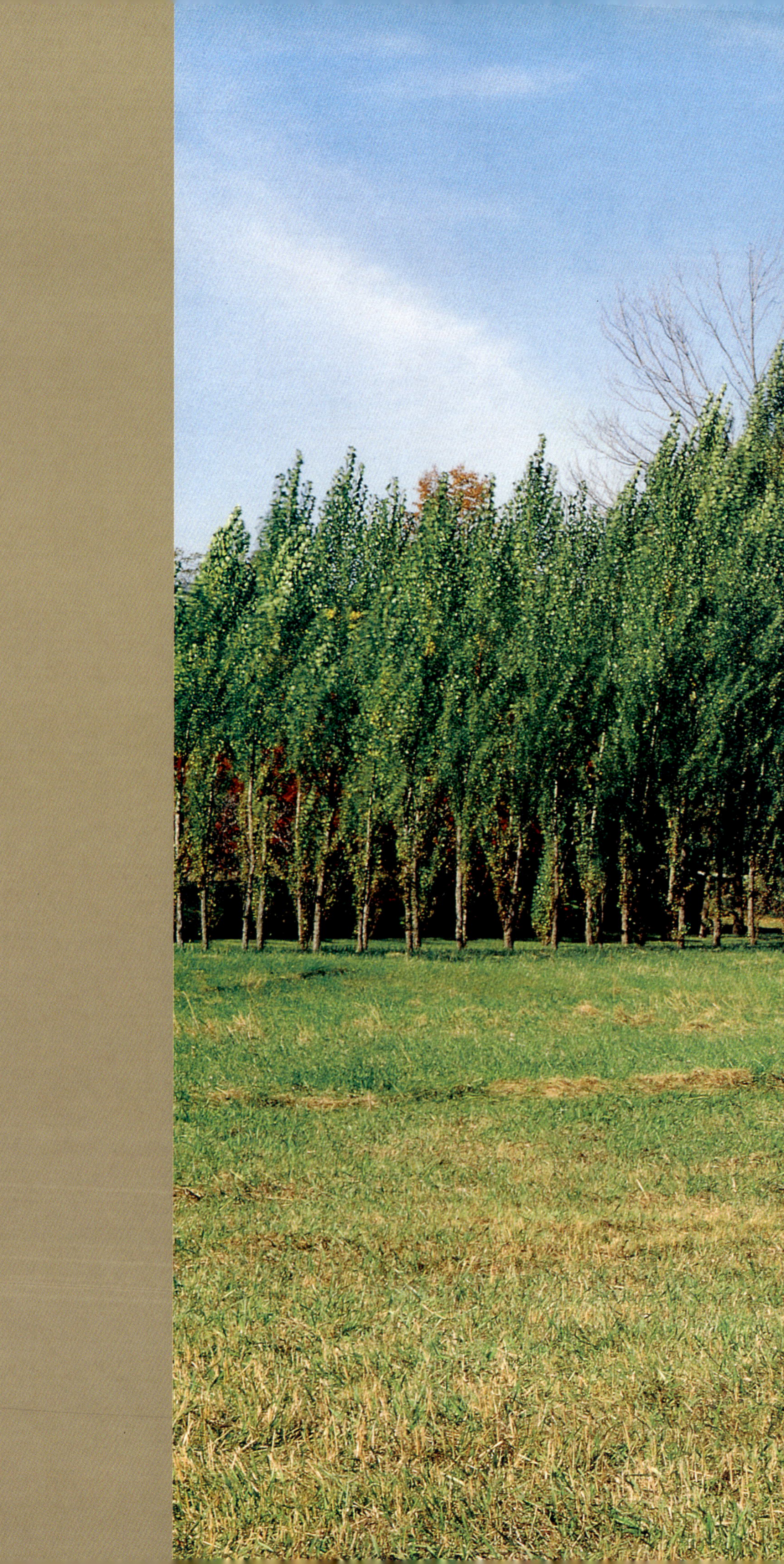

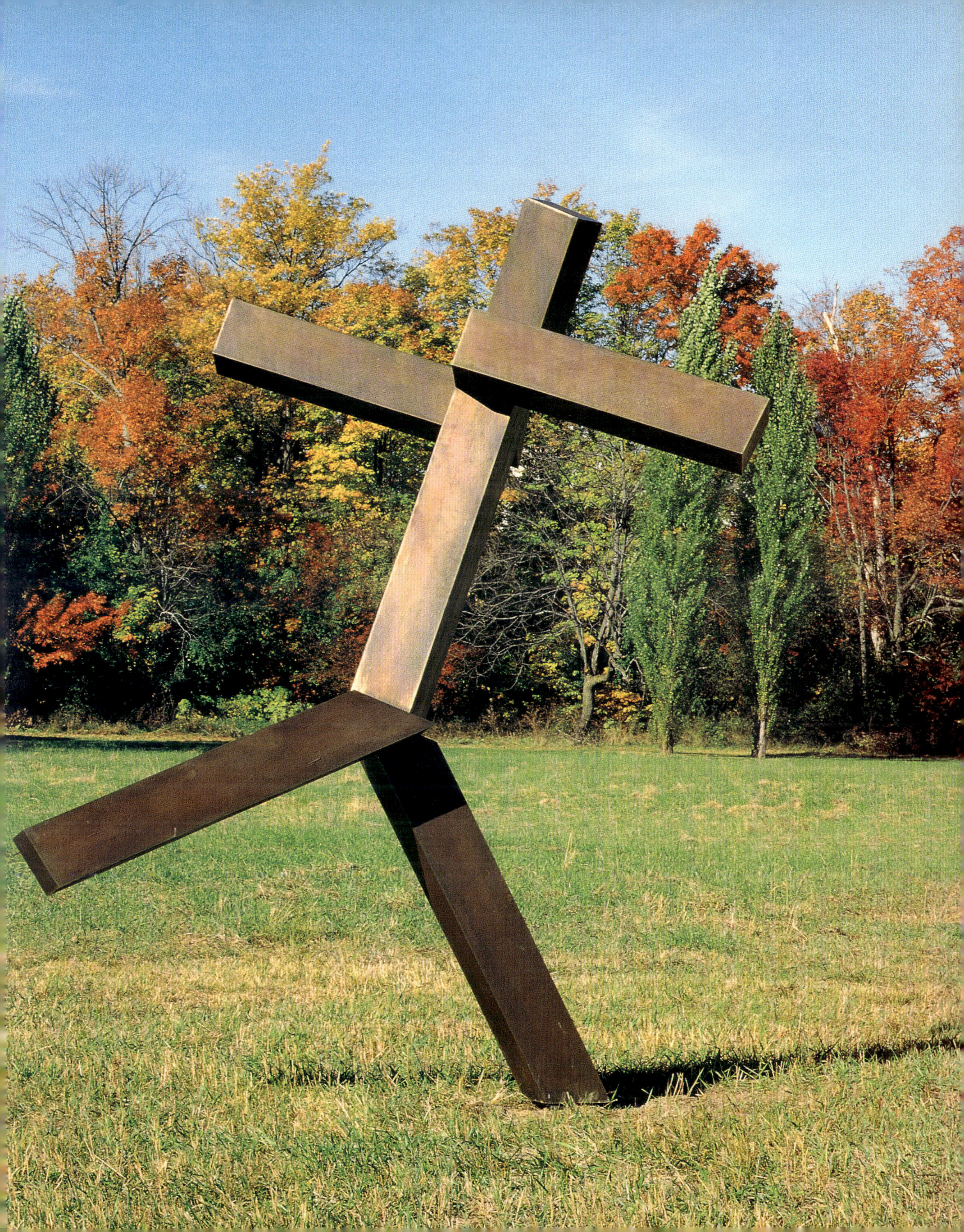

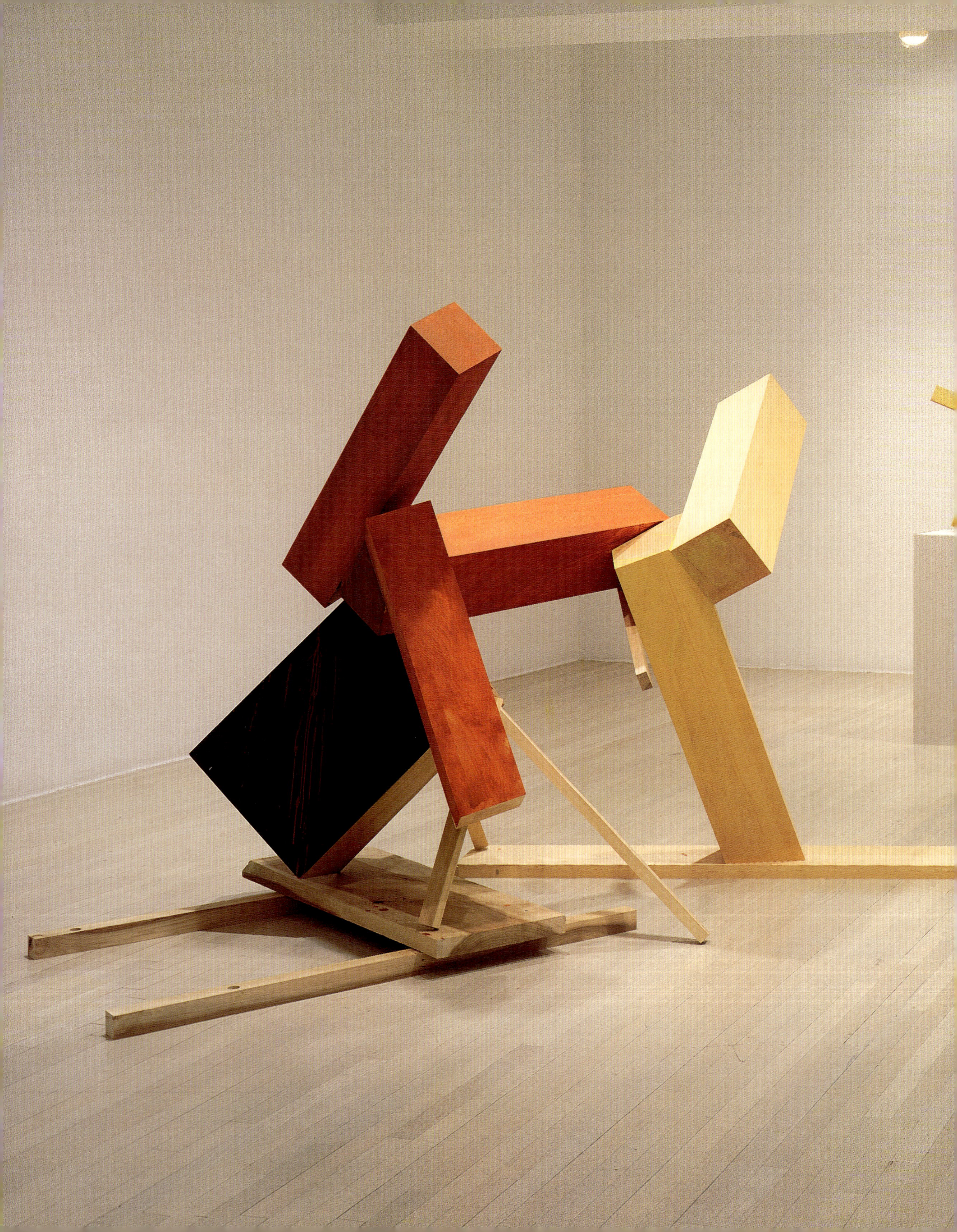

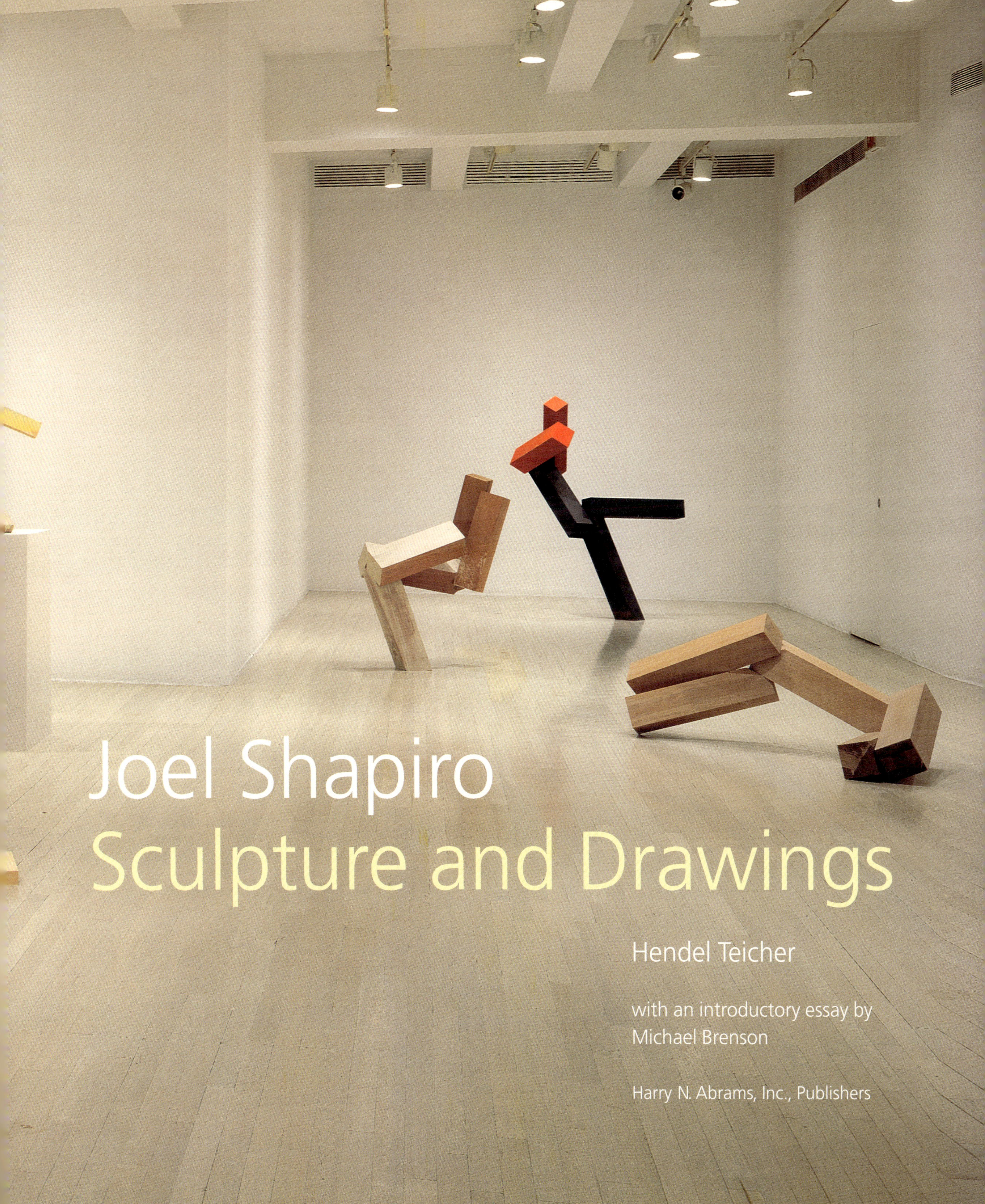

Joel Shapiro
Sculpture and Drawings

Hendel Teicher

with an introductory essay by
Michael Brenson

Harry N. Abrams, Inc., Publishers

Editor: James Leggio
Designer: Judith Hudson

Rights and Permissions:
Roxana Marcoci and Catherine Ruello

LIBRARY OF CONGRESS CATALOGING-IN-PUBLICATION DATA
Teicher, Hendel.
Joel Shapiro : sculpture and drawings / Hendel Teicher ; with an introductory essay by Michael Brenson.
p. cm.
Includes bibliographical references.
ISBN 0-8109-4178-3 (clothbound)
1. Shapiro, Joel—Criticism and interpretation. 2. Human figure in art. I. Brenson, Michael. II. Title.
N6537.S522T45 1998
709' .2—dc21 97-29141

Printed and bound in France

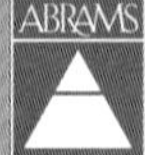

Harry N. Abrams, Inc.
100 Fifth Avenue
New York, N.Y. 10011
www.abramsbooks.com

ILLUSTRATED PAGES 2–3:
Untitled. 1989. Bronze (edition 0/4), 7'5" x 6'4" x 2'3" (226.1 x 194.3 x 68.6 cm). Collection the artist

ILLUSTRATED PAGES 4–5:
Installation view of the exhibition "Joel Shapiro: Painted Wood Sculpture and Drawings," PaceWildenstein, New York, 1995

Contents

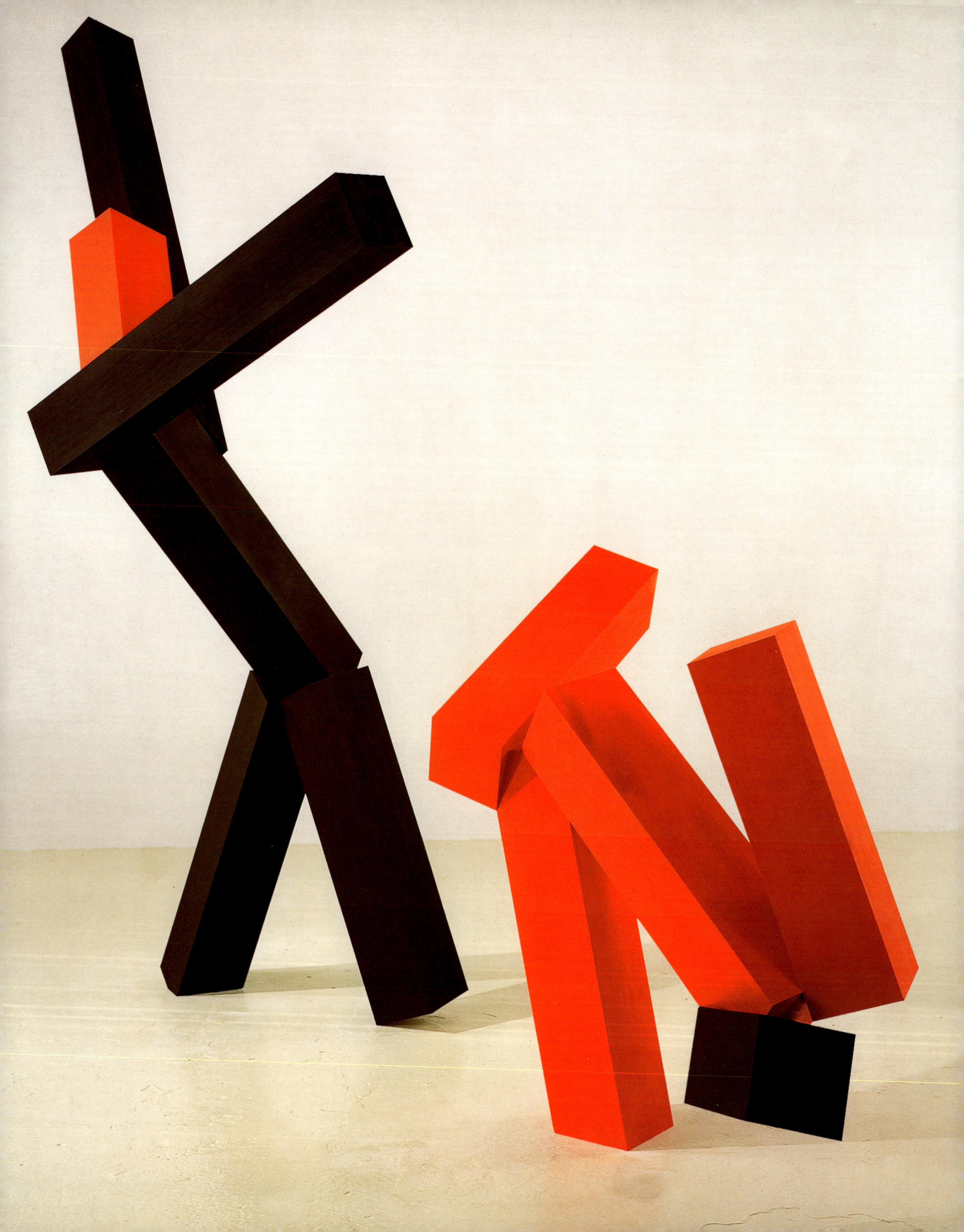

Joel Shapiro and Figurative Sculpture

Michael Brenson

OPPOSITE:
Untitled. 1995–97. Oil on wood, two parts, 9'1" x 6'5" x 46" (276.9 x 195.6 x 116.8 cm) and 51 x 62 x 28" (129.5 x 157.5 x 71.1 cm). Courtesy PaceWildenstein

Joel Shapiro is passionate about modernist figurative sculpture. He speaks with open admiration about Auguste Rodin, Henri Matisse, and Pablo Picasso. He describes Alberto Giacometti as "the sculptor of the century."[1] In response to a question about Marcel Duchamp, he makes clear that it is with these figurative sculptors that he feels he belongs. "He's a brilliant artist," Shapiro says. "I mean, his work is phenomenal, but it's not a vein that I'm interested in. I have no choice. I'm involved in a more humanist pursuit, for better or worse. There's such history behind figurative sculpture. So many brilliant people have been doing it. Geniuses. Giacometti. Matisse. Picasso. It's not a question of whether you think they're good or not; they're beyond good. They're consummate, profound artists."

The connections between the figurative tradition in modernist sculpture and the sculptures Shapiro has been creating during the past fifteen years are unmistakable. Shapiro's materials are wood, plaster, and bronze, which were staples of modernist sculpture in the late nineteenth and early twentieth centuries. His constructions and assemblages of rectangles carry with them the memory of the startling sculptural equilibrium of Matisse's *Large Seated Nude* (figure 1) and the gestural originality of his *Serpentine* (figure 2). They suggest the playfulness and the openness to process essential to the creativity and content of Picasso's work, as well as the freedom with which Picasso erected a core of volume and then affixed objects to it or embedded them in it. Shapiro's figures are equally hard to imagine without Giacometti's modesty and intimacy and ability to make standing, walking, sitting, or running seem at once the most common, dignified, and revealing of acts.

Like each of these modernists, and like another modernist sculptor he admires, Constantin Brancusi, who made the dialogue between abstraction and figuration so fertile that many sculptors continue to explore it, Shapiro believes deeply in form. He is fully attentive to surface, edge, shape, and volume and makes the viewer's attentiveness to the language of sculpture essential to the experience his sculpture offers. He finds inexhaustible sources of insight and movement in the interrelationships of gravity and flight, expansion and contraction, stability and precariousness. He values each step of the working process, from the rough sculptural sketch in which a few small strips of wood are slapped together; to the refinement of proportions and shape and the enlargement of scale to the life-size or larger works bolted into or sprawled across the floors of galleries; and now, increasingly, to the huge cast and welded Shapiros the non-art public can encounter on a busy street, in a corporate lobby, or outside a museum.

One of the most important distinctions between modernist figurative sculpture and other prominent modernist developments, such as Constructivism, Suprematism, and de Stijl, is that the sculptures of Rodin, Matisse, Giacometti, and Picasso are not utopian. Even if one or more of these artists were drawn to ideas of social progress and transformation, they did not put their sculpture in the service of them. They were very much concerned with the here and now – with the physical and psychological vibrations of people close to them, with spatial and psychological pressure, with the elegance and sensuality of a face or flower, with the feeling and structure of a head or back, with the ability of the human body to communicate responses and feelings so basic that almost anyone in the presence of their images could find in them echoes of their own situation.

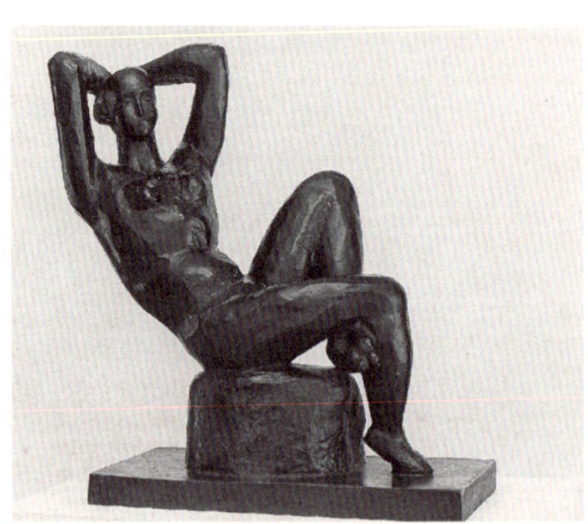

Fig. 1 Henri Matisse. *Large Seated Nude*. 1923–25. Bronze, 31¼ x 30½ x 13¾" (79.4 x 77.5 x 34.9 cm). The Museum of Modern Art, New York. Gift of Mr. and Mrs. Walter Hochschild (by exchange)

Shapiro's sculptures are not instruments of a cause. They are conceived apart from any social, political, or ideological uses to which human beings can be put. They acknowledge context but are not contextual. The rectangular boxes of which they are composed incorporate the surrounding architecture into the figures rather than demanding that the figures be understood in terms of their surroundings. Their emphasis is not on how the environment determines the individual but on how the individual shapes the environment. They reflect an aversion to hard-core ideology and group thinking that is characteristic of Shapiro's Post-Minimalist generation, born during World War II and the Holocaust, when totalitarian destruction was fueled by obedience and generalization. Shapiro offers a vision of the human body as a physical and spiritual organism that changes so constantly and has so many sides that it can never be definitively categorized or controlled. Shifting identity is an essential part of its nature. So is movement. So is rootlessness. Shapiro's figures are architectural building blocks that could be adjusted to any occasion: they are their own homes. Camouflage and self-defense are part of their nature as well. They may pull viewers in through the intensity of their delight or pain, but they can also hold them at bay through their projecting volumes and indifference to touch. Unlike Giacometti's figures, which are at times besieged by space, Shapiro offers a vision of the individual body as an organism with such powers of metamorphosis and self-reliance that it can clearly hold its own against politics and history. His figures are what they are and where they are completely, but they are also, always, something and somewhere else. It is their capacity for transformation – not in the future, although this is an important part of their potential, but in the moment, and from moment to moment – that endows them with the capacity for survival and revelation.

So despite his unapologetic enthusiasm for Matisse, Picasso, and Giacometti, Shapiro resists as much as he accepts the modernism he loves. With all his affection for Giacometti, his work is not concerned with ultimate questions, ultimate meanings. With all his respect for Brancusi, he does not make objects for prayerful contemplation. And while he may feel at ease with the word genius, which was part of the romance of modernist criticism and which makes postmodernists cringe, he has the postmodern aversion to the idea of a masterpiece. "The idea of a single piece that's *the* great piece is nonsense," he says. And he has the postmodern distrust of the heroic, although he frequently flirts with heroic associations, both in the size of his public commissions and in his sculptural rhetoric, which can suggest an unconquerable stride or man triumphing over death.

In addition, while Shapiro uses early modernist materials, he uses them in decidedly nonmodernist ways. There is no mystique of materials in his figurative work – no alluring tactility, no monolithic core that draws viewers in. Nor is there truth to materials. Plaster can be shaped by wood. Plaster can resemble wood. Three kinds of wood – fir, poplar, and pine – can be combined in one sculpture, and it is hard to tell the difference between them. It can also be hard to tell the difference between his wood and bronze surfaces. Bronze is used not to develop indestructible commodities, although they may become that, but rather, most of the time, to insist upon form. In Shapiro's approach to materials, as in his approach to imagery, everything is at all times capable of emerging from and flowing into something else.

One of the clearest distinctions between the idea of the individual in Shapiro and the idea of the individual in Rodin and Giacometti lies in Shapiro's resistance to the idea of an immutable essence. His figures have multiple selves. Because they are usually a composite of several distinct and equally forceful psychological responses and physical states, they may acknowledge, but they always resist, the notions of tragedy and fate that run through Rodin and Giacometti and so much other European art. Even when it is clear that something irrevocable has been done to them, Shapiro's figures change course, enter another state, and, by so doing, leave destiny, which may have thought it had them in its grip, behind.

In short, with all its respect for tradition and the individual, Shapiro's work is consistently surprising. It is also complex in ways that have barely begun to be investigated. And there is a radical dimension to it, one shaped by Jewish memory of the Holocaust and a particularly American notion of democracy and freedom. I want this essay to locate where that radicality is.

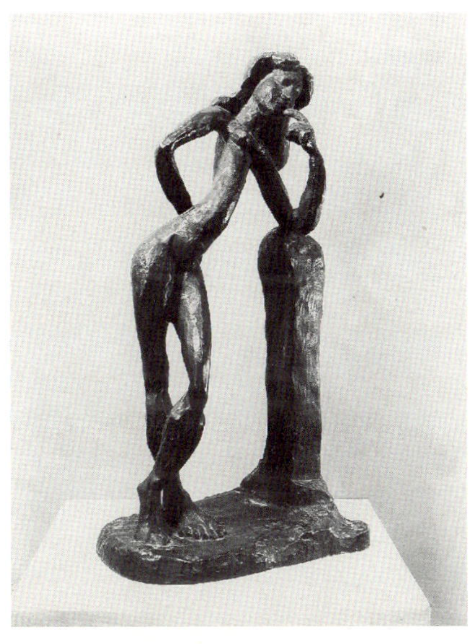

Fig. 2 Henri Matisse. *La Serpentine*. 1909. Bronze, 22¼ x 11 x 5½" (56.5 x 28 x 19 cm), including base. The Museum of Modern Art, New York. Gift of Abby Aldrich Rockefeller

II

What is a Shapiro figure? How does it work? How are its meanings communicated by its sculptural language?

The vocabulary is basic. Shapiro works with rectangular boxes, usually substantially elongated. They are entirely assembled, that is to say, the four rectangular and two square sides are cut and worked separately and then joined. The flat pieces of wood are so plain that they could not seem more ordinary, more matter-of-fact, but when they assume their place in boxes joined to other boxes they become evocative. They can suggest the limbs, torso, and head of a body. They can suggest both architectural and children's building blocks. They can bring to mind, as well, the trunks and limbs of trees. Because of their hint of boys' toys, and the absence of softness and curves, the figures usually seem male, but most of their gestures and emotions belong to women as well as men, and there is occasionally a sense of a man and woman locked together in the same configuration.

The rectangular boxes are essential to one of the key aspects of the work, the fluid relationship between figuration and abstraction. The boxes enable Shapiro to build sculptures that are clearly figurative, and they enable him to build sculptures that seem figurative but whose exact shapes and movements are hard to define. The rectangles make clear that the sculptures never pretend to be what they suggest or represent. Their geometry acknowledges the Minimalism that was the main force in sculpture as Shapiro was coming of age, even as the joining of rectangular boxes into figurative constructions asserts his wish to make sculpture that is more supple and referential. The constructions of rectangles also encourage viewers to consider the process by which each sculpture was made, including the formal decisions so important to its energy and content.

If the vocabulary is elementary yet loaded with feeling and information, so is the movement the rectangles suggest. Walking, running, dancing, falling, tripping, and tumbling are some of the basic actions Shapiro explores. Invariably, however, there is more than one action in the same construction, sometimes within the same point of view. A figure is on its feet, firmly on the ground, but it may also be standing on its head, its feet spread in the air. The same figure may pull back or hurl itself forward. Sometimes the same movement or gesture evokes different, even conflicting, responses. A figure's legs are splayed and one arm raised like a singer in a triumphant moment, but the arm also suggests a call for help by a dying man. In Shapiro's world, up can become down; front, back; legs, arms; and foot, head. Victory can become inseparable from defeat, entrapment from release, exuberance from melancholy. Elementary movements and basic shapes become human and poetic mysteries.

This multi-sidedness and interconnectedness would not be so compelling without Shapiro's ability to immerse his figures in each emotion or action. Whatever their responses or movements, they are engaged in them so totally that nothing else matters; nothing else even exists. Shapiro has a special understanding of the mechanics of the body and, most notably, of its spasmodic intensity when consumed by a particular emotion or event. Whatever activities or feelings his figures express, they have lurched or launched into them with such finality that their entire bodies are expressions of them. In a Shapiro sculpture each emotion or action seems so absolute that it is a condition, even as it flips into another emotion or action and reveals itself to be just one of the complex states that constitute a human being.

The conviction of these figures also depends upon Shapiro's incorporation of many experiences of time. For example, a vertical or diagonal rectangle may seem to have been positioned with great deliberation. But a diagonal attached to it may have emerged and been joined a little more quickly. And a diagonal rectangle attached to that may have taken its place even faster. Finally, a rectangle at shoulder or neck height may have been rammed into the construction so that its presence adds a note of impulsiveness, even rashness. Very rarely do all the rectangles in a Shapiro construction suggest the same timing. This differentiation within the sculptural process strengthens the identity of each part as it becomes part of the whole.

Just as important is Shapiro's ability to build into his figures an awareness of different ages. His surfaces may be pristine, cut slowly or quickly, or marked by the whorls of a circular saw that can make the wood seem etched by history. The smooth or worn surfaces suggest, along with the associations of the building blocks with architecture and with games, both a child's and an adult's experience. So do the movements, which can range from a child's carefree running, to an adolescent's self-conscious performing, to an adult's methodical laboring. So does the way the sculptures point both toward the ground and up into space and therefore reach out to different sizes of people. So does the sense of a child's hypnotic absorption communicated by a body that is adolescent or adult in size.

How to combine finality with fluidity has been one of the prevailing issues of twentieth-century sculpture. Clearly, Shapiro wants to make sculpture that has the kind of inevitability that so much great sculpture has had and yet still insists upon the human dynamism and velocity of change that are facts of a technological age. Clearly, too, he wants the experience of dynamism and change to be grounded in the physical and psychological life of the body. His determination to keep rooting this experience in the concreteness of the body, and in the texture of everyday life, is part of what gives his sculpture its moral urgency and weight.

III

While it is impossible in a brief essay to explore adequately the meanings of Shapiro's work, it is important to consider some of the other implications of the ways in which it is put together and unfolds. Particularly those that suggest a kind of progressive thinking that does not sacrifice individualism, that does not let anyone off the hook, and that does not bow to any party line.

Shapiro's sculpture is fundamentally populist. Its imagery is familiar. The gestures and feelings it embodies are everyone's and no one's property. There is no emotion or action in it to which the vast majority of people cannot relate. Its movements cross borders, pointing toward a physical and spiritual soil that different races, classes, genders, and nations share.

The states of feeling and being that are honored by Shapiro's sculptures do not exist in a hierarchical relationship to one another. Sadness, joy, depression, exhilaration, all coexist in a way that makes it clear that they are all inescapable and valid. The human capacity for delight, ecstasy, and nobility is unequivocally acknowledged by Shapiro's figures; but so is the capacity for conflict, violence, and domination. In Shapiro's world, each individual has the potential to be or do anything. No human response or movement can be seen in isolation; each gains meaning in relation to another. Grace and despair, anxiety and delight, cruelty and tenderness are all part of the life of the body. To deny any one of them is to be blind to history and to the fullness and complexity of the self. It is also to limit the possibilities of the creative imagination.

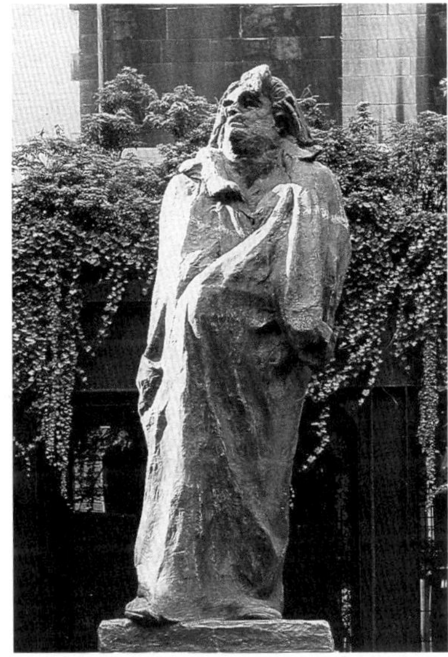

Fig. 3 Auguste Rodin. *Monument to Balzac*. 1897–98. Bronze (cast 1954), 9'3" x 48½" x 41" (282 x 122.5 x 104.2 cm). The Museum of Modern Art, New York. Presented in memory of Curt Valentin by his friends

Because Shapiro's figures are forever in flux, moving from action to action, emotion to emotion, they resist traditional notions of monumentality, which tend to rely, like Rodin's great *Monument to Balzac* (figure 3), on a monolithic presence. In Shapiro's work, sculptural conviction derives from the eccentric yet irrefutable joining of multiple selves. The Shapiro figure is often disjunctive. Sometimes it is hard to imagine how the body coheres, with its limbs pulling it this way and that. Shapiro does extol the individual, but it is an individual that is unsettled and in perpetual transition. The fact of fluidity and the gift of concentration may or may not produce a sense of monumentality. They are capable of producing a sense of grandeur that Rodin and Giacometti surely would have recognized even though they knew it was not their own.

It is just as essential to recognize that in Shapiro's figures the body can always be reimagined. Shapiro is a highly kinesthetic sculptor. He does not just show bodily states. He wants viewers to experience them: he wants the marching and tumbling and fighting and praying to be known by the viewer's body. He is exceptionally good at projecting a thrust or dropping a volume so that the body of the viewer feels itself being thrown outward or collapsing. He has the keenest sculptural sense since Matisse of the body's center of gravity in the hip and pelvic area, and he can play off it in ways that argue that a conventional experience of the body is not inevitable. He may be the only contemporary sculptor who can join a vertical or diagonal rectangle to the legs in such a way that the unexpected movement of the hip in relation to the legs is experienced as both dislocated and natural.

Shapiro encourages viewers to experience parts of their bodies both in terms of where they are known to be and in terms of where they might be in another time and space. He creates a kinesthetic identification with legs and shoulders as they are joined in fact; but by enabling viewers to experience offbeat and unpredictable joinings of limbs to trunk, and trunk to head, he also uses this kinesthetic identification to challenge the normal experience of the body. He makes unexpected relationships within the body seem essential to an understanding of sculptural and human freedom.

This is individualism of a thoughtful and challenging kind. It depends upon attentiveness to the physical and psychological mechanisms of the individual body and a commitment to the body as a site and source of freedom. It encourages empathy, concentration, and openness to the child in the adult and the adult in the child and to all sides of the human whole. During a period in which the individual tends to be either dumbly mythified or all but drowned in a sea of context and determinism, it throws its weight toward the complexity and mobility of the self and the lyricism and drama of the embodied soul. And even if Shapiro does not want his sculpture to be put in the service of ideas of social progress and transformation, the presence of a wide-open and unimaginable future is alive and well in it. The ability to make people think about the individual in thoughtful and challenging ways was among the achievements of Rodin, Matisse, and Giacometti. It may be that it is only by working within the tradition of figurative sculpture that such a challenge can be formulated in contemporary art with comparable intelligence and flair.

1 All quotations in this essay are from Peter Boswell's interview with Joel Shapiro printed in *Joel Shapiro: Outdoors* (Minneapolis: Walker Art Center; Kansas City, Mo.: Nelson-Atkins Museum of Art, 1995), pp. 27–40.

Plates

Text by Hendel Teicher

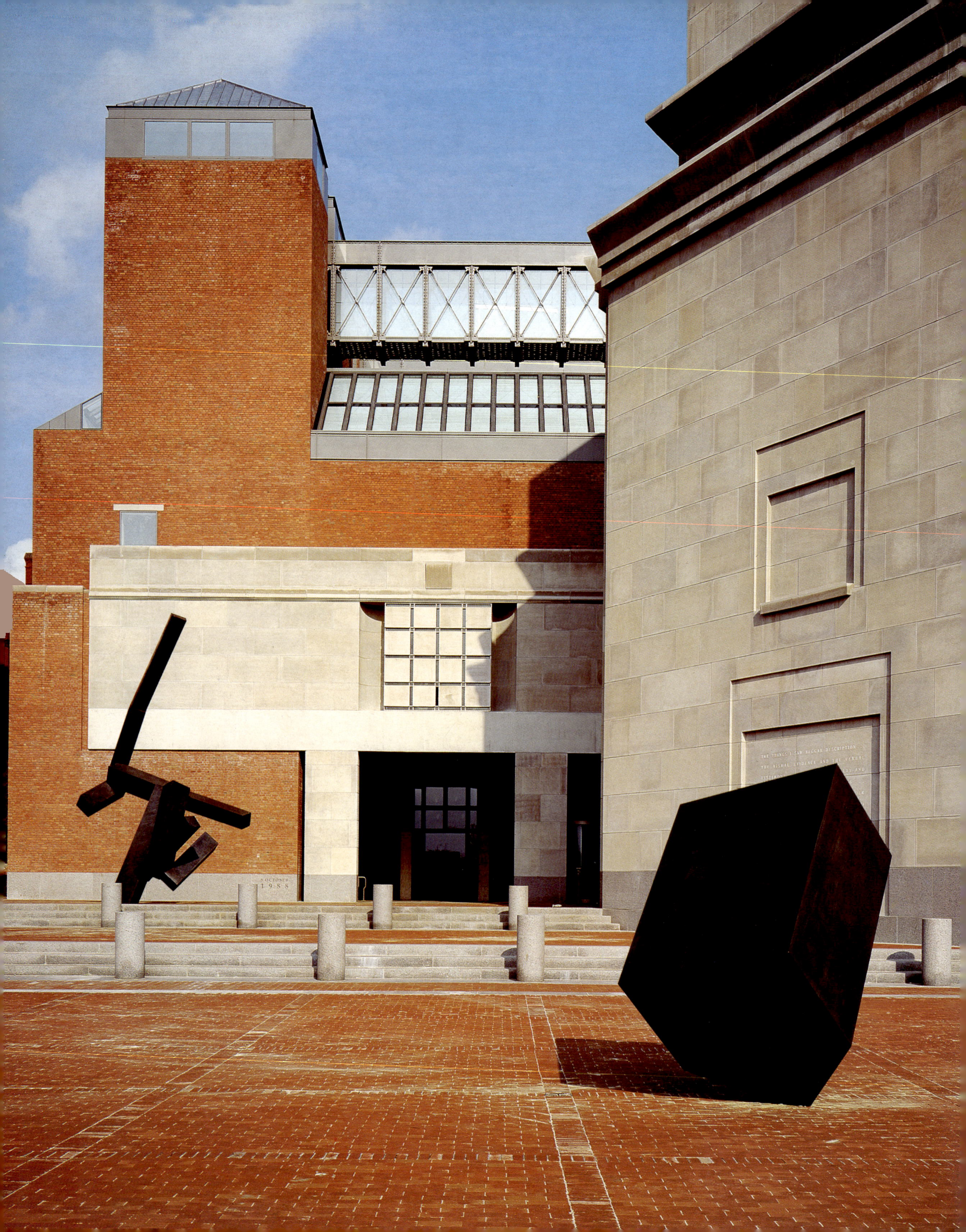
THE THINGS I SAW BEGGAR DESCRIPTION
THE VISUAL EVIDENCE AND THE VERBAL
OCTOBER
1988

Memory

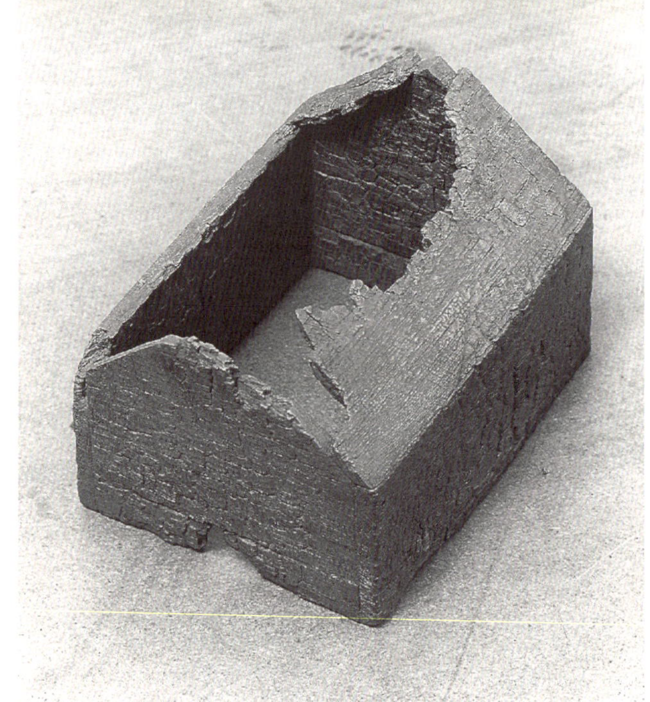

2 Untitled. 1989. Cast iron, 7¾ x 10¾ x 8 5/16" (19.7 x 27.3 x 21.1 cm). Collection Ivy Shapiro

PREVIOUS SPREAD:

1 *Loss and Regeneration*. 1993. Bronze, figure: 25'9" x 17'8" x 7'8" (784.9 x 538.5 x 233.7 cm); house: 9' x 7'8" x 7'8" (274.3 x 233.7 x 233.7 cm). The United States Holocaust Memorial Museum, Washington, D.C. Gift of Ruth and Albert Abramson and Family, In Memory of the Children Who Perished in the Holocaust. See also plates 6, 7, 9.

Joel Shapiro's inspiration is drawn from the realm of memory, private as well as collective. Perhaps nowhere is this clearer than in his commission for the United States Holocaust Memorial Museum in Washington, D.C. Opened in November 1993, the museum commemorates the eleven million people – among them Jews, Gypsies, political dissidents, homosexuals, and the disabled – murdered by the Nazis before and during World War II. The museum's purpose, to bear witness to the Holocaust, transforms the building and its surroundings into a site of profound contemplation. And for this memorial commission, appropriately, Shapiro has created his most monumental work to date (plate 1). Conceived as a permanent installation, the sculpture stands outside an entrance to the museum.[1]

In 1989, Shapiro was invited to participate in a competition for the creation of another Holocaust memorial, this one sponsored by the city of Düsseldorf.[2] For that project he proposed a small, burnt house, cast in iron (plate 2), to be placed in the center of the residential courtyard (plate 5) designated as the site for the memorial. Under the heading "Mechanism" on the competition application form, he wrote in capital letters simply "MEMORY," and under the heading "Intention and Scale," he explained: "The sculpture is intentionally not large since I do not want to glorify or 'monumentalize' the period. The house is a symbol of human life and community. The burning of the house signifies loss. Its smallness in relation to the size of the bare courtyard signifies the vulnerability and fragility of civilization. Its ruined state is a mnemonic of destruction."[3] This statement points directly to the meaning of the Washington

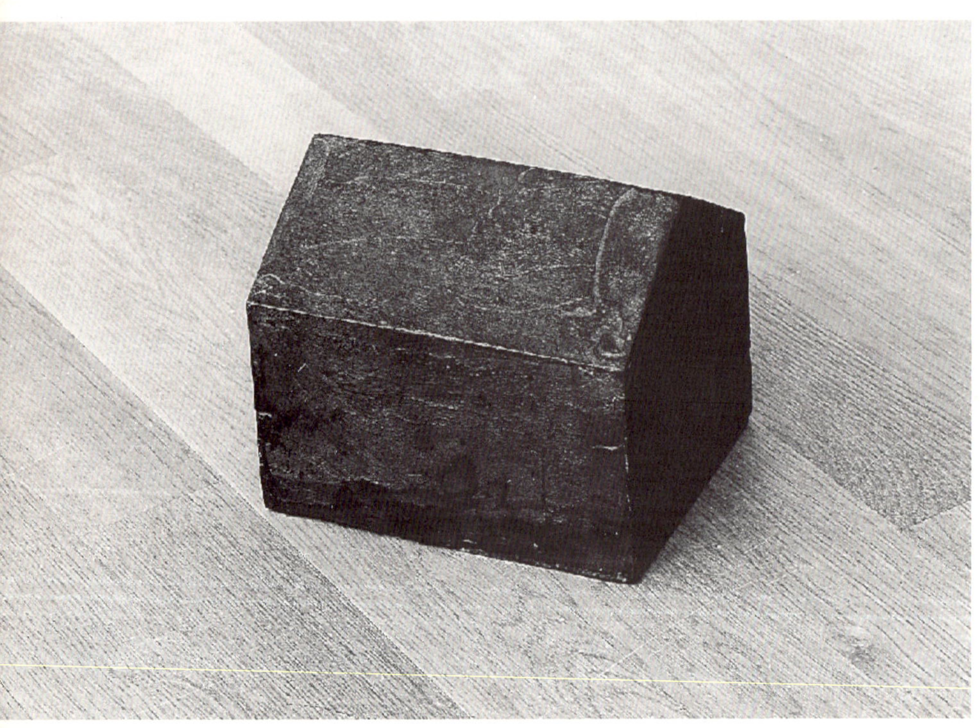

3 Untitled. 1973–74. Cast iron, 5½ x 6⅝ x 5" (14 x 16.8 x 12.7 cm). Private collection

sculpture. But there, Shapiro would revise his intentions regarding the implications of scale, and use the large size of the Holocaust sculpture to communicate the same feelings of fragility and loss.

The house is one of the artist's major themes. Since 1973, Shapiro's small, solitary house (plate 3) has appeared and reappeared under multiple metaphorical guises. His obsession with it reached a critical moment in the demolished and incinerated houses of 1989 (plate 4), one of which was submitted for the Düsseldorf competition. Shapiro was struggling with his own complex feelings about the image and admitting more openly to vulnerability and doubt. "I was interested in disrupting the image," he recalls. "I was trying to cut into it, rip it up, but that house kept creeping back into my work."[4] Some of his most dramatic attempts to free himself of the image can be seen in his wood or cast-iron houses (plates 2, 4). The appearance of these works bears witness to the violence that has torn them open and exposed their ravaged interiors. Destructive acts frozen in time, they are profoundly moving and disturbing.

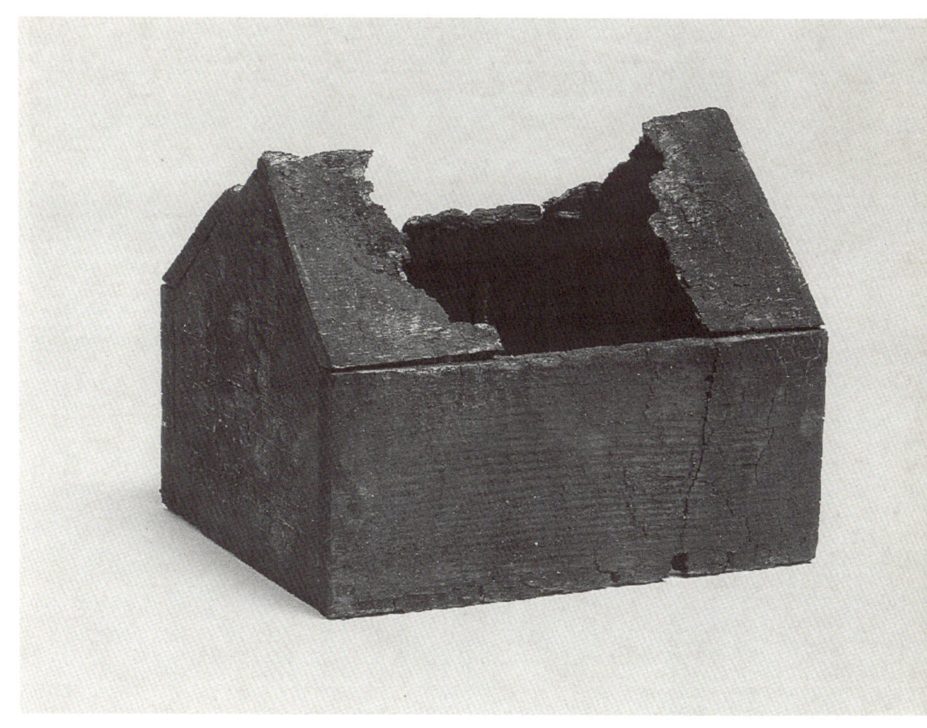

4 Wood study for a memorial in the inner courtyard of the Stadthaus, Düsseldorf, Mühlenstrasse 29. 1989. Burnt wood, 6⅞ x 9⅛ x 7⅛" (17.5 x 23.2 x 18.1 cm). No longer extant

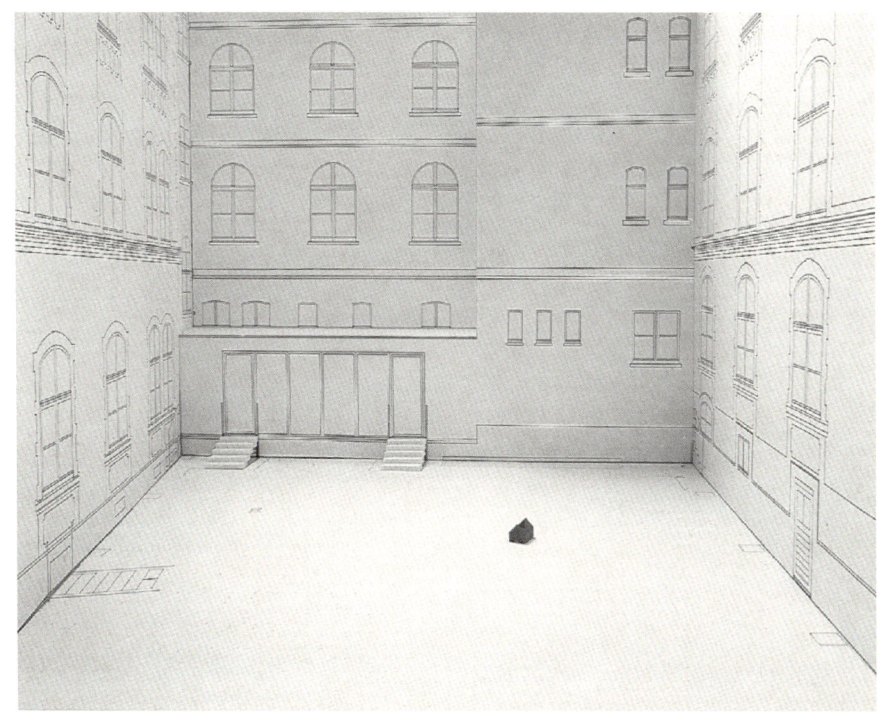

5 Model of view from north of site with proposed sculpture and location for the Stadthaus, Düsseldorf, Mühlenstrasse 29. 1989. Burnt wood, 6⅞ x 9⅛ x 7⅛" (17.5 x 23.2 x 18.1 cm). No longer extant

The archetypal geometry of the house gives Shapiro's work an emotional reach related to the art of Tony Smith. Both sculptors respect geometric rationality as well as intuitive feeling, as can be seen by comparing Shapiro's upside-down house (plate 6) and Smith's *Black Box* (figure 1). Of his own work, Smith once commented: "All my [sculptures are] on the edge of dreams, they come close to the unconscious in spite of their geometry. On one level my work has clarity. On another it is chaotic and imagined."[5] A persistent ambivalence locates Shapiro's work, too, like that of Smith, between abstract thought and latent figurative representation. In Shapiro's sculpture, however, the symbolism of the house as shelter and safe haven is deliberately subverted by the instability of a structure turned over on its roof, made inaccessible, and sealed by a black patina that absorbs all light. In place of a house as shelter, we are given a resonant mental image of one – a *memory* of a house – and this conveys the core of Shapiro's subject: the reality of absence and loss. It is for this reason that Shapiro's investigation of the archetypal house led him inevitably to its inhabitant, the figure. It is the human body that has been the focal point of his mature work; and like the house, his other principal theme, the body contains memories.

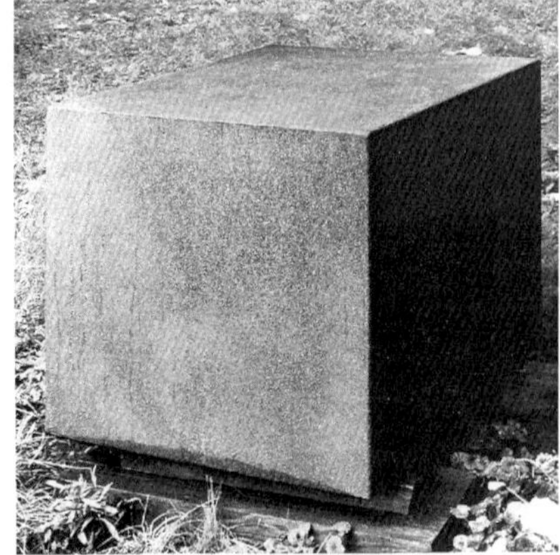

Fig. 1 Tony Smith. *The Black Box*. 1962. Steel (edition of 3), 22½ x 33 x 25" (57.2 x 83.8 x 63.5 cm). Collection Joel Shapiro, New York

The Washington commission represented a major challenge and an important new stage in Shapiro's work. For the first time, he combined his two main themes in a single work. Yet the work's difficulty lay not only in the thematic content, but also in the demands of the site. Shapiro had to address the relationship of scale between his sculpture and the formidable architecture of James Ingo Freed. (Within the museum and without, Freed has hauntingly combined the formal vocabulary of industrial modernism with the psychological claustrophobia of the camps.) Despite its unprecedented dimensions – these are the largest house and the largest figure Shapiro has made so far – he still wanted the sculpture to retain a sense of "human scale." The question of scale was noted by the sculptor himself: "I don't think it was possible until the Washington sculpture for me to do a big piece outdoors that would retain my hand in it. Now I had the will and the means to do it." That is, the large figure's division into smaller segments keeps the viewer engaged with human-scale elements. At the same time, their complex joining assumes a constantly changing perspective of possible readings. (Indeed, in this regard it is interesting to note that Shapiro resists naming his works, unwilling to lock them into a single interpretation. When urged to title the Washington sculpture, he only reluctantly offered the provisional wording "For the Dead and Surviving Children," which he subsequently revised to the much less specific title *Loss and Regeneration*.)

In developing the commission over the course of two years, beginning in 1991, Shapiro systematically experimented with his two most frequently recurring images. All the studies and related sculptures, varied as they may be in color, composition, scale, and placement, feature the encounter between figure and house. A bronze of 1991 (plate 8) that opened the way to the memorial sculpture is distinguished by the precarious position of the house, mounted dangerously by its corner, high on a wall. Compact, dark, and heavy, it is on the verge of falling. The viewer must actively shift between looking up at the house, isolated on the wall, and looking down to the floor, where a headless figure also seems to be falling. The figure is brighter in color; light plays on its edges and on the junctures of its five rectangular forms. The dynamic juxtaposition of the two components invites us to read the house as the head of the falling figure. This visual complementarity unifies the work both spatially and conceptually.

The finished project in Washington (plate 1) is graver and more dramatic. The monumental figure stands near the facade of the museum, and the overturned house, more human in height, is a few steps away on the plaza facing a green lawn; the real-life scale relationship between the two components has been disturbingly reversed. The figure, detached and tree-like, seems to be falling but also pulling itself up; turned on its end, the house is likewise unbalanced, resting on a corner of the roof. As a result, although they are separated physically, figure and house thus have a visual and a symbolic bond. The viewer, moving between them, can imagine a time and place shared by both.

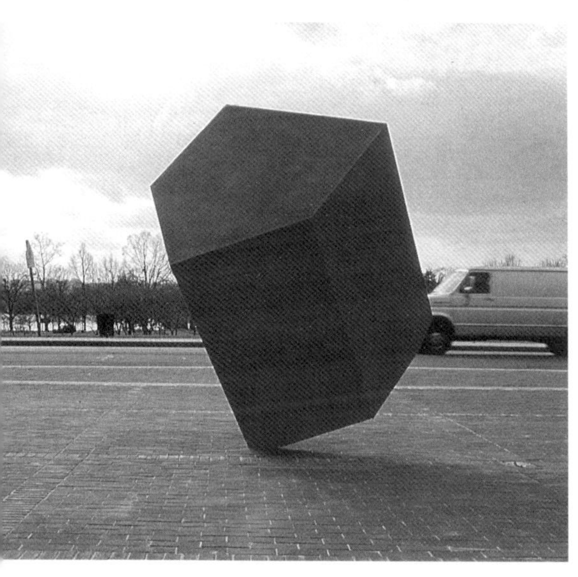

The distinctive form that is a hybrid of tree and human figure emerged early in Shapiro's work. Used almost representationally, the form made its first appearance lying on the ground in a bronze from 1976–77 (plate 225). This untitled work was created during a very difficult period, marked by the suicide of Shapiro's sister, and it evokes a painful personal event. As the sculptor observes: "It is adamant and complicated. It's dead and sexual." Shapiro has increased the emotional resonance of the figure-tree in the Washington sculpture. Perceived as a human figure, it is caught between rising and falling, immobilized in the midst of its own movement. Seen as a tree, one that reaches to more than twenty-five feet and topples with the weight of its limbs, the form suggests both the process of growth and its sudden interruption.

Shapiro's Holocaust sculpture is installed within sight of the Washington Monument. It is illuminating, therefore, to compare Shapiro's work to another tragic, modern sculpture, one that makes a direct comment on the Washington Monument – Barnett Newman's *Broken Obelisk* (figure 2). Newman wrote that his work was "concerned with life, and I hope I have transformed its tragic content into a glimpse of the sublime."[6] For Newman, according to Harold Rosenberg, the sublime arose from the transformation of geometric shapes – the magic of numbers, angles, and locations. Newman's search is not unlike Shapiro's: abstract shapes become what Newman called a "living thing, a vehicle for an abstract thought complex, a carrier of awesome feelings."[7]

In his imposing work for the Holocaust Museum, Shapiro has merged the abstract and representational aspects of the house and the figure. In the geometries of these powerful archetypes, viewers find evocative human qualities raised to the level of the monumental.

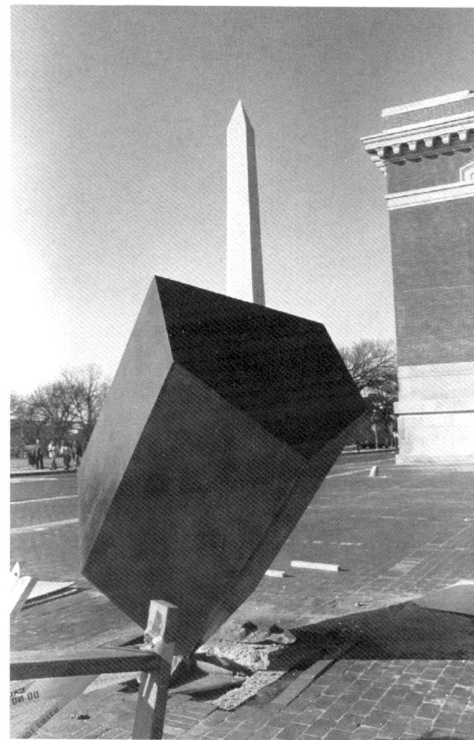

6, 7 Component of *Loss and Regeneration*, during installation and as permanently installed. 1993. See also plates 1, 9.

Fig. 2 Barnett Newman. *Broken Obelisk.* 1963–67. Cor-ten steel, 26' x 10'6" x 10'6" (792.5 x 320 x 320 cm). Institute of Religion and Human Development, Houston

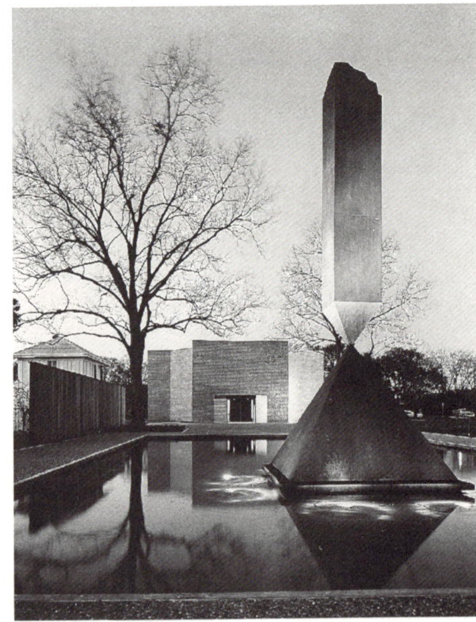

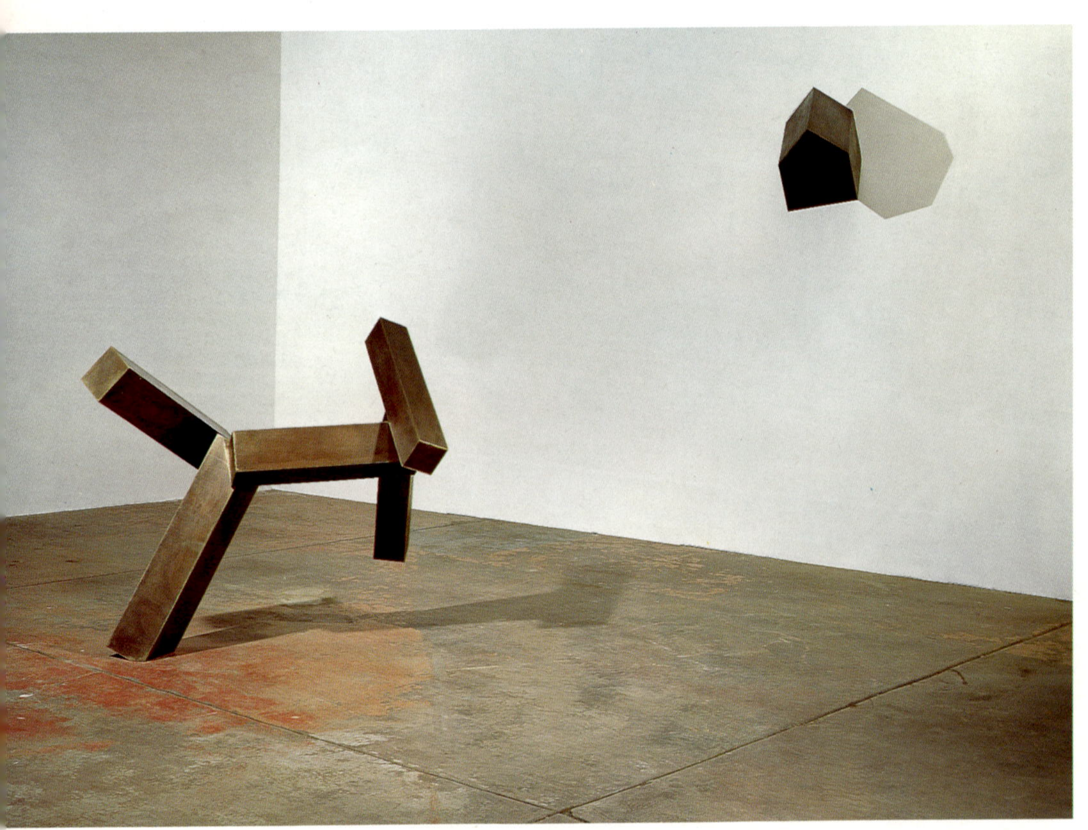

8 Untitled. 1991. Bronze (edition 3/3), figure: 66 x 72 x 36" (167.6 x 182.9 x 91.4 cm); house: 21 x 26 x 36"(53.3 x 66 x 91.4 cm). Tel Aviv Museum of Art. Acquired through the contribution of Pierre and Maniusia Estate, with the assistance of the British Friends of the Art Museums of Israel, 1995

OPPOSITE:

9 Component of *Loss and Regeneration.* 1993. See also plates 1, 6, 7.

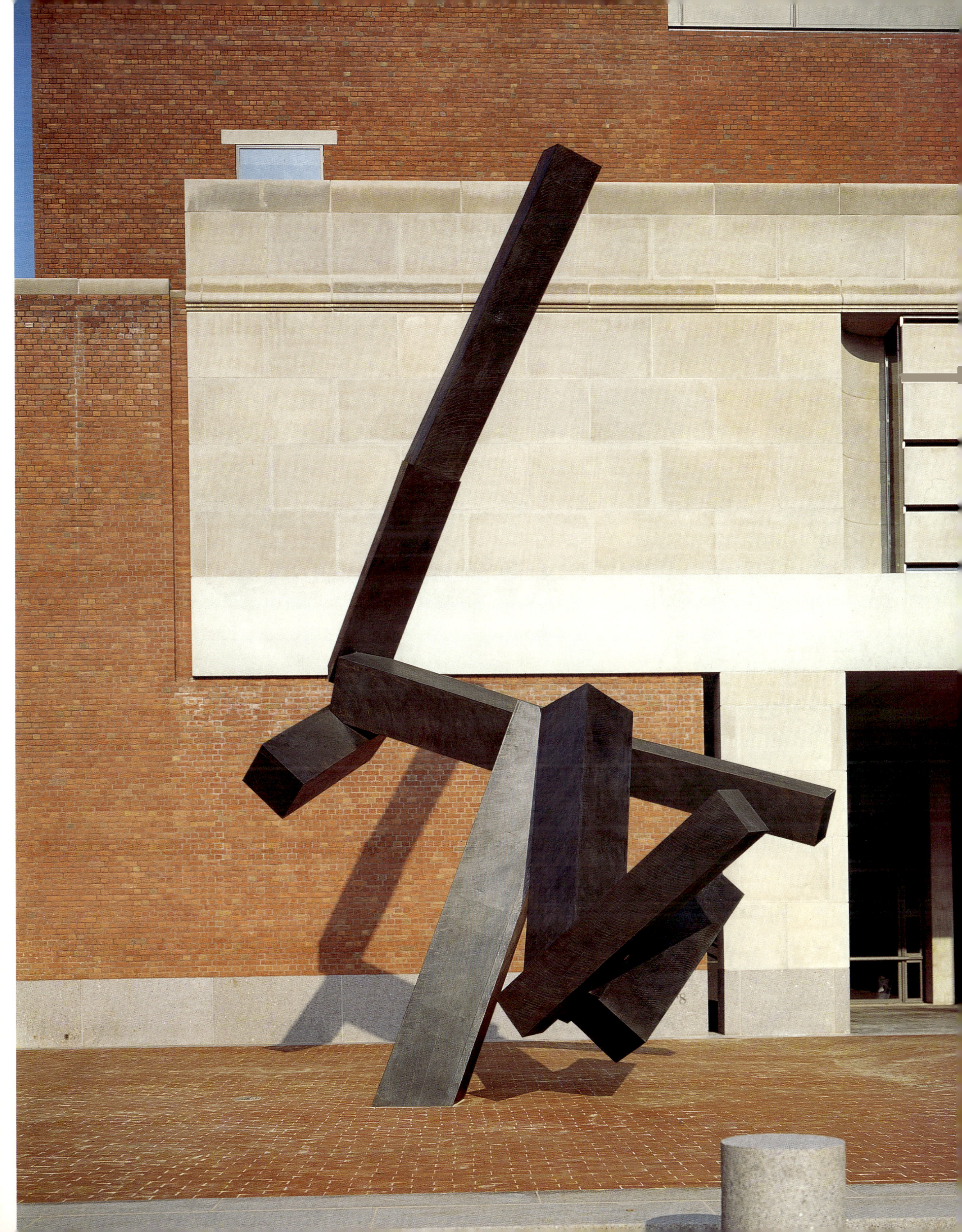

Structures

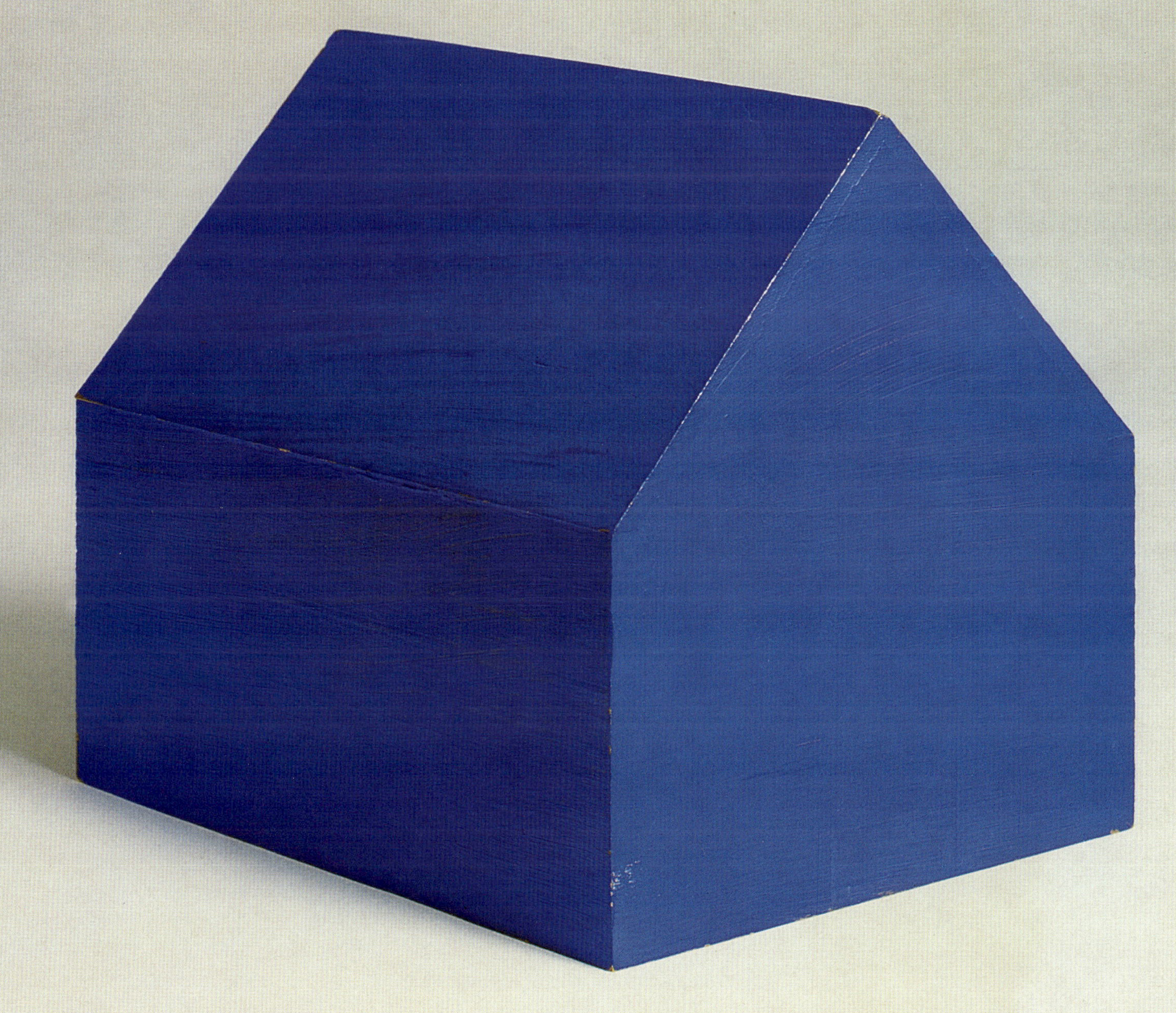

In 1965, Shapiro, then twenty-four, joined the Peace Corps and traveled to India. This experience would change his life more than he could have anticipated, for during the course of his two years of service he firmly resolved to become an artist.

As a youngster, Shapiro was often taken to the Metropolitan Museum of Art, where he was captivated by the Egyptian galleries and the medieval armor collection, and to the Museum of Modern Art, where as a teenager he took painting classes. He and his sister, Joan, shared an enthusiasm for the arts, and Manhattan was a rich resource. As adolescents they developed an appetite for jazz. Shapiro remembers how Joan, a year older and much more outgoing than he, sneaked him into clubs: "[She] took me to Birdland once. I thought that was great. That was life, that was really exciting."[8] Today, he still speaks with deep regard about the "abstract" qualities of the great jazz artists; Thelonious Monk and Duke Ellington remain favorites.

Art was encouraged at home – his mother, Anna Shapiro, a microbiologist, dabbled in sculpture – and the children often received art materials as gifts. But art was not seen as a legitimate profession. Shapiro recalls that his father, Joseph Shapiro, a doctor, was "a very dominant individual, and the idea of my being an artist didn't seem possible to him." His parents wanted a medical career for their son. Shapiro accommodated them by taking pre-medical courses, but without much enthusiasm.

Shapiro's decision to join the Peace Corps reflected this ambivalence about the direction of his career, as well as a desire for adventure. In addition, the Peace Corps seemed to provide a meaningful alternative to the Vietnam War, which was intensifying at that time. And since Shapiro already had some connection to India – his sister, married to an Indian citizen, lived in Bombay – he requested an assignment there.

In India, Shapiro worked as a teacher, and he helped farmers to organize their production and become self-sufficient, following the guidelines of Mahatma Gandhi's agricultural programs. Shapiro lived in rural areas, where he encountered traditional Indian arts and developed a deep interest in them. He became friends with a number of people who shared his passion for these arts and were dedicated to their preservation. Among them were members of the Sen family. Shapiro would often join them on excursions to archaeological sites, including the caves of Ellora and Ajanta, and to museums and temples in the southern states. He was struck especially by Indian sculpture. Despite its reliance on naturalism, it seemed both abstract and psychological in its impact. And the sculptures seemed almost Baroque in their multiplicity and sense of endless addition. Their sheer number was overwhelming, and the way they activated space in temple and home, in public square and in open landscape, made a profound impression on Shapiro. He remains passionate about the art of India, and he has added many objects to his personal collection. Moreover, the vibrant physicality and warmth of south Indian bronzes, and their extravagant sense of movement, have influenced his approach to his work.

PREVIOUS SPREAD:

10 Untitled. 1985–86. Oil on bronze, 6 x 7 x 5½" (15.2 x 17.8 x 14 cm). The Eli and Edythe L. Broad Collection

Even with his Peace Corps responsibilities, Shapiro found time to take countless photographs, to collect books on Indian art, and to make his first serious attempt at painting. "Being outside my own culture permitted me to look at the idea of culture," he says. "It's easier to be an observer than a participant." And indeed, his interest in craftsmanship in his own work can be traced to the experience of India. Whether creating an everyday utensil or a sacred bronze, the craftsman approaches fabrication in the same way – with an acute sensitivity to material. It is the working process of the artisan that Shapiro would bring to his own modernist concerns. To some extent, Indian art became a model for his sculptural strategies. Both New York City and India would remain living sources of Shapiro's inspiration. His sojourn in Asia was a period of apprenticeship and an initiation into a wider world.

Early Works (1968–72)

Upon his return to New York from India in early 1967, Shapiro was intent on making up for lost time and anxious to start his artistic career. He was combative and competitive, and his first works are marked by a restless experimentation; the artist facetiously comments that at the time he was "going through an idea a week."

This turbulent activity was paralleled by the changing circumstances of his personal life. While studying for his master's degree at New York University, Shapiro supported himself by working at the Jewish Museum and doing odd jobs. And at this time, he married Amy Snider, an art educator whom he had met before entering the Peace Corps. Their daughter, Ivy, was born in 1969. After five years of marriage, the two decided to separate in 1972. Shapiro moved into his studio on Leonard Street in lower Manhattan.

The New York art world at the time was becoming somewhat more inclusive than it had been in the preceding, male-dominated decades. Shapiro's circle counted many ambitious women artists. Sympathetic to their sensibilities, he developed friendships with Elizabeth Murray, Jennifer Bartlett, and the dealer Paula Cooper, among others. Cooper, committed to new art, opened the first gallery in SoHo in 1968.

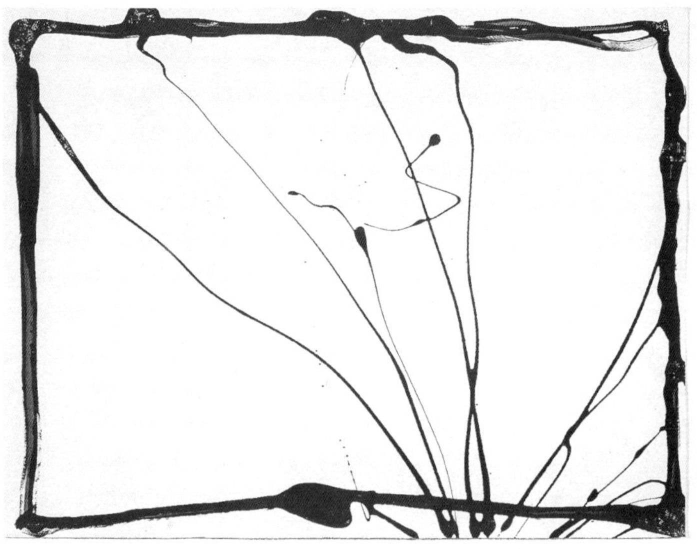

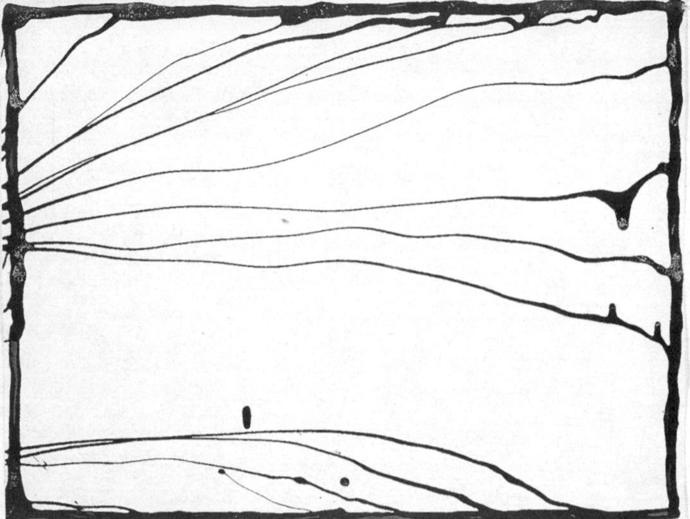

11 Untitled. 1968–69. Enamel on paper, 22¼ x 29¾" (56.5 x 75.6 cm). Collection the artist

12 Untitled. 1968–69. Enamel on paper, 22¼ x 30" (56.5 x 76.2 cm). Collection the artist

13 Untitled. 1971. Oil on canvas, 14 x 18" (35.6 x 45.7 cm). Collection the artist

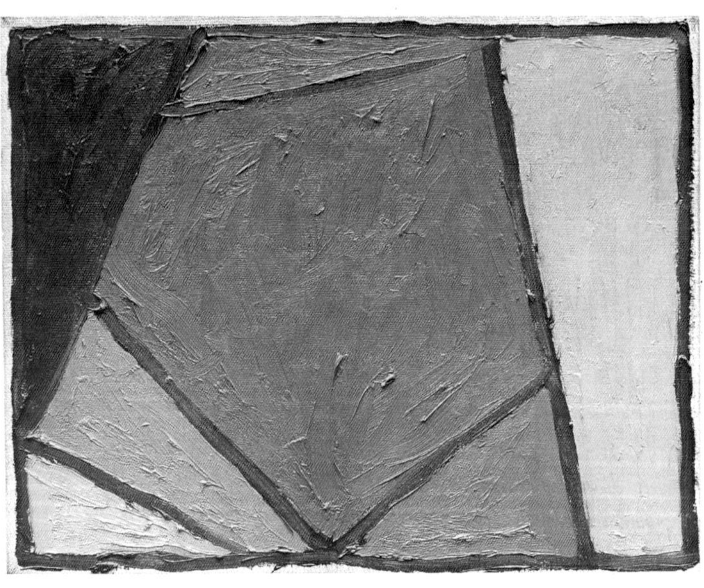

Wall Pieces

Shapiro began his career by experimenting with painting, and although that has not been his primary medium, his approach has always been "painterly." Among his first paintings were works on paper (plates 11, 12). Here, gleaming black lines demarcate open fields. The strokes form thick traceries and are almost calligraphic. Shapiro reframes the sheet while creating fluted shapes out of liquid paint. He uses the paint as a record of its own movement; the gestures are left in a state of suspended animation.

A small, dense oil from 1971 (plate 13) stands in contrast to these earlier works. The edges of the canvas are emphasized and redefined, but now vigorous, nearly expressionistic strokes build geometric shapes whose deep green surfaces are thickly worked with a palette knife.

In 1968 and 1969, Shapiro was also making three-dimensional works with nylon filaments in varying sizes and shapes – squares and rectangles, balls and braids (plates 14, 15). He would dye the material in buckets and nail or staple it to the wall at eye level. A modest material and a modest gesture were given new life as art. Skeins of nylon offered Shapiro the possibility for both indeterminacy and flexibility. Some of these sculptural reliefs, his only soft constructions, were included in a 1969 Whitney Museum exhibition, "Anti-Illusion: Procedures/Materials," which focused on current aesthetic issues. Most of the twenty-four participating artists had similar concerns – whether with processes and procedures, simple repetitive structures, or the use of unconventional materials.

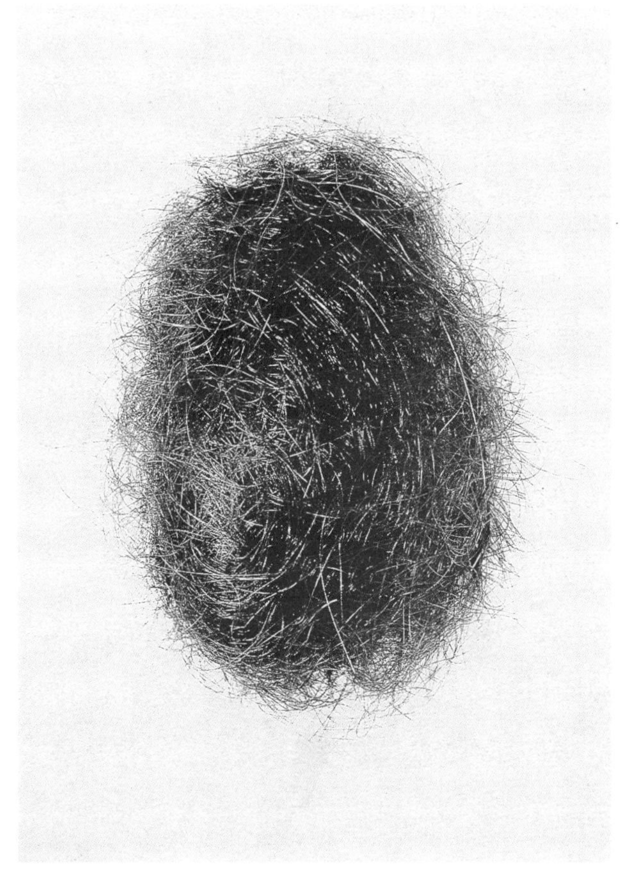

14 Untitled. 1968. Dyed nylon stapled on wall, 13 x 8 x 2½" (33 x 20.3 x 6.4 cm). No longer extant

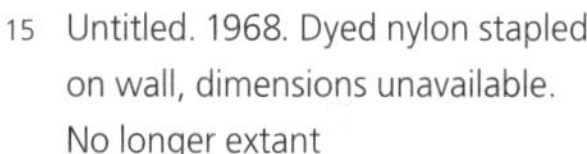

15 Untitled. 1968. Dyed nylon stapled on wall, dimensions unavailable. No longer extant

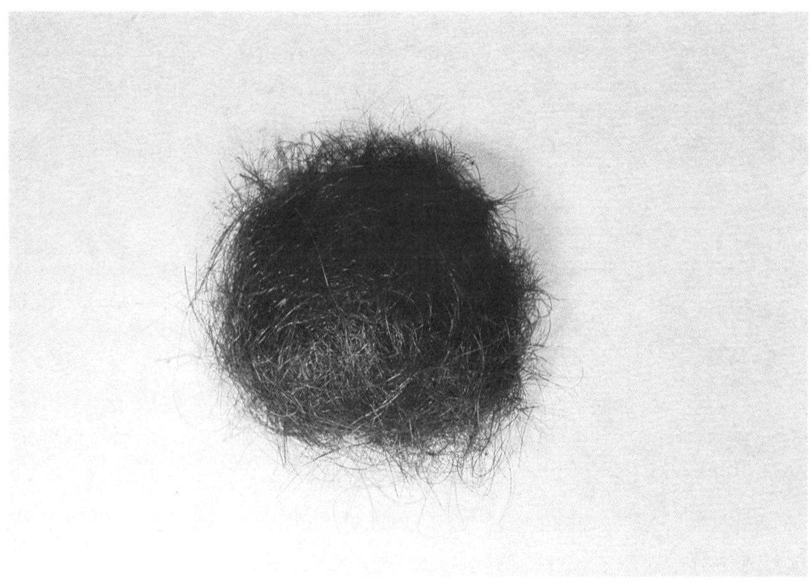

16 Untitled. 1969. Dyed nylon stapled on wall, 66 x 66" (167.6 x 167.6 cm). No longer extant

One of Shapiro's exhibited works (plate 16) was a square of deep red in which the nylon fibers form thick, flowing curls that absorb light and create an impenetrable surface. The intensely tactile qualities of this hairlike material give the work a sexual connotation. The process of shaping the piece was essentially a mixing and tangling of the fibers on the surface. Dense and mysterious, the work's convolutions record the duration of its own making. In her catalogue essay, Marcia Tucker, the show's organizer, stressed Shapiro's interest in "physical decision-making processes that have no functional necessity."[9]

A large drawing from 1969 (plate 18) features the repeated imprint of the tip of the artist's index finger; points of equally dense black ink generate parallel lines crossing the entire surface. Like the process just seen, the act of stamping, too, marks time, so to speak. And the repetition could easily extend beyond the limits of the paper on either side, implying a past and a future. The drawing represents a slice of time as well as a slice of space.

A smaller drawing from 1968 (plate 19) employs graphite and grease worked with the fingers. Its intense concentration of intertwining lines recalls the nylon fiber reliefs. Another drawing from 1968 (plate 20) takes the same gestural approach, this time using graphite and beeswax on a gesso ground to register nervous activity. The agitated center is surrounded by a border area that is lighter in tone. This softly drawn "frame" has been cut down with a razor to limit the size of the drawing. The way he uses borders, edges, and other framing devices helps Shapiro not only to focus attention but to contain turbulence. Both of these drawings are, indeed, visualizations of energy.

17 Untitled. 1969–70. Ink on paper, 14 x 16⅞" (35.6 x 42.9 cm). Collection Sarah-Ann and Werner H. Kramarsky

18 Untitled. 1969. Ink on paper, 64⅜" x 11'3¼" (163.5 x 343.5 cm). The Museum of Modern Art, New York. Gift of Mr. and Mrs. Alfred R. Stern

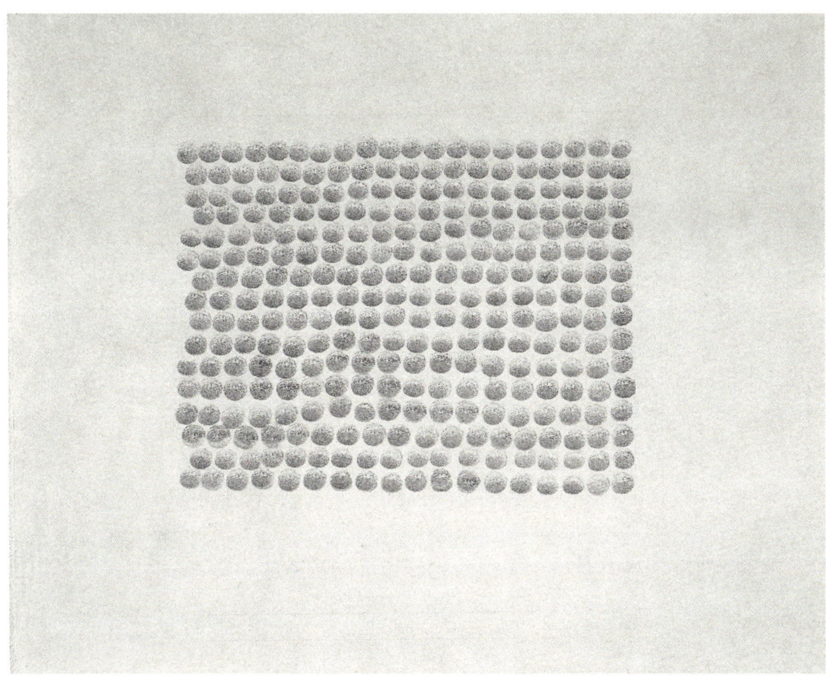

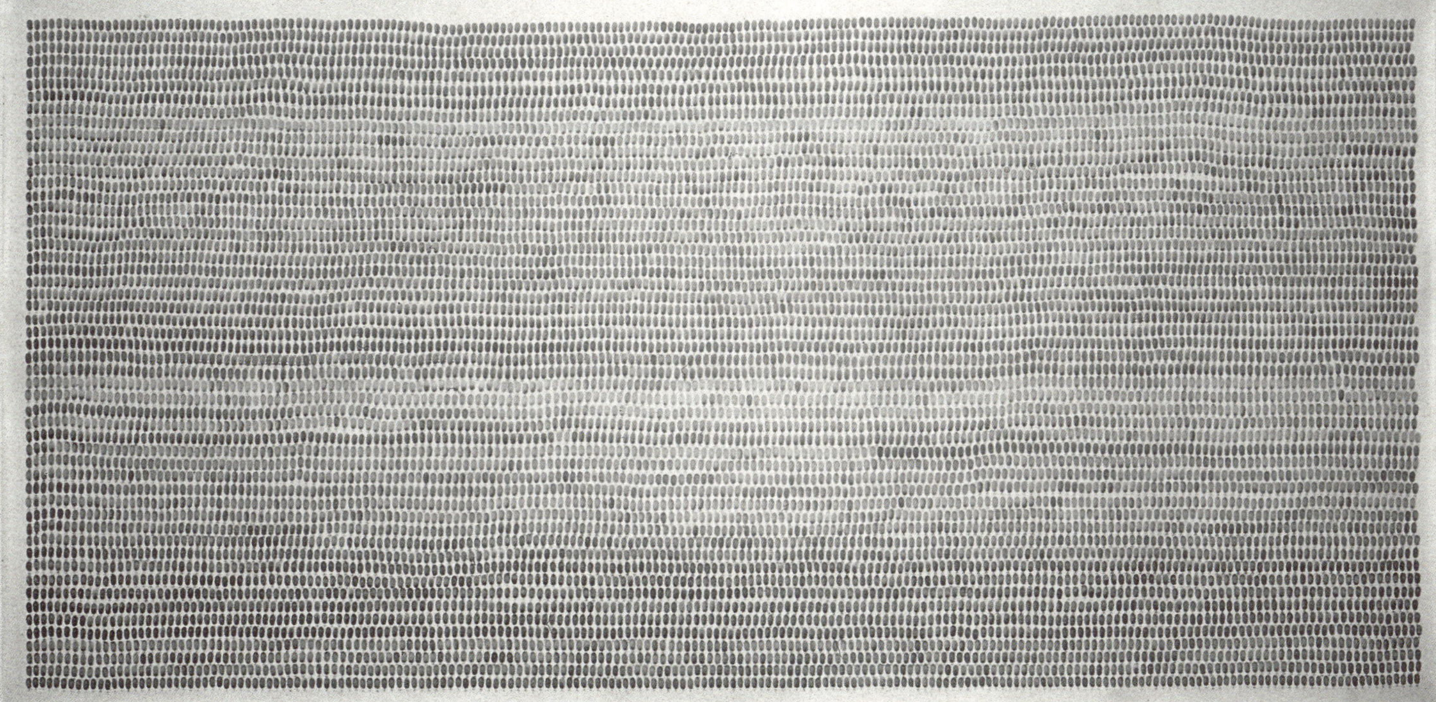

Materials and Processes

Shapiro had his first solo show in March 1970, at the Paula Cooper Gallery. The event marked the beginning of an affiliation that was to last for more than twenty years. For the show, Shapiro installed a work designed specifically for the gallery's space, using two adjoining walls. The installation had an almost theatrical quality. From a distance, only a thin horizon of materials was visible at eye level; the viewer had to cross the vacant gallery to really "see" the sculpture. Shapiro had built small, wood shelves, identical in size and placed at regular intervals, each unit of this horizontal frieze fixed to the wall with two short metal brackets (plates 21, 22). The different shelves presented a palette of various materials: steel, plaster, glass, paraffin, slate, lead, plexiglass, concrete, wood, felt, gum rubber, aluminum, tar, marble, homosote, and copper. This suite of identically sized objects shown in a uniform and repetitive sequence is rare in Shapiro's work. He would later favor the autonomous singularity of each sculptural object. Even when part of a series, each piece would be resolved as an entity in itself.

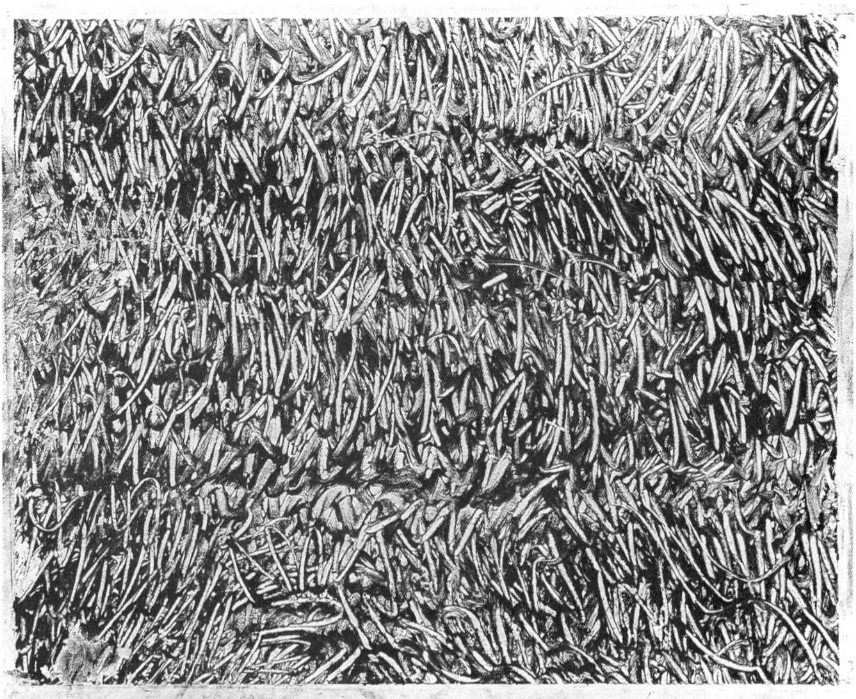

19 Untitled. 1968. Grease and graphite on paper, 18 x 23" (45.7 x 58.4 cm). Collection Jean and Joel Levin, Buffalo

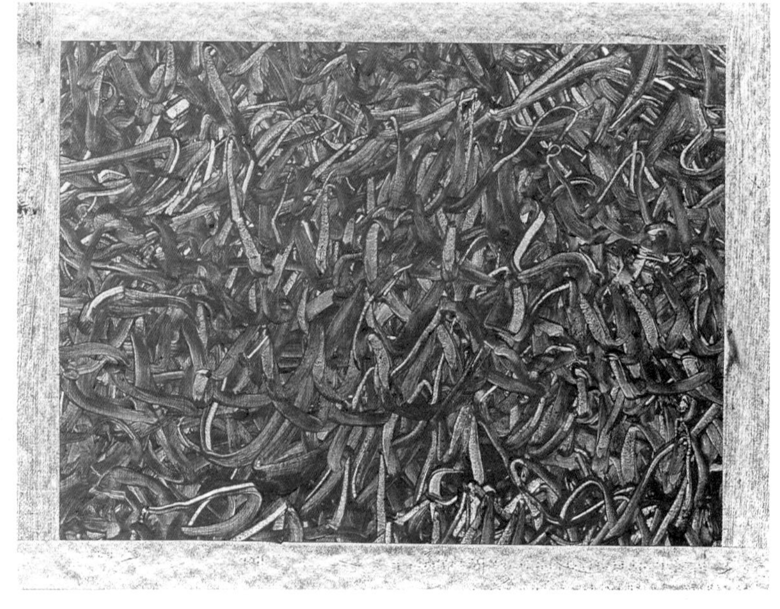

20 Untitled. 1968. Gesso, beeswax, and graphite on paper, 14 x 18" (35.6 x 45.7 cm). Museum Overholland, Amsterdam

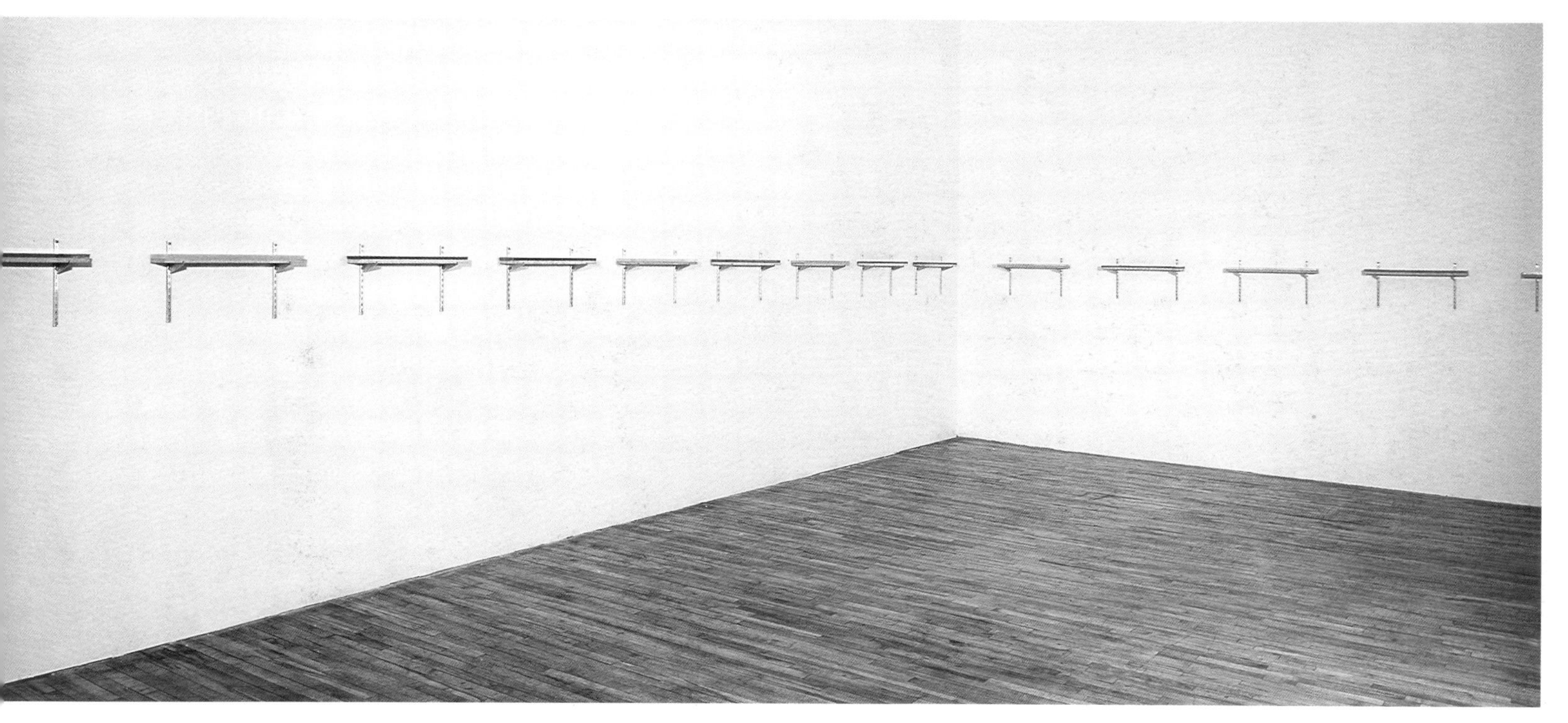

21, 22 Untitled. 1969–70 (installed in the exhibition "Joel Shapiro," Paula Cooper Gallery, New York, 1970). Mixed media, 12 x 23⅞ x 5" (30.5 x 60.6 x 12.7 cm) each unit, 59" x 49'8" (149.6 x 1513.8 cm) overall. Collection the artist

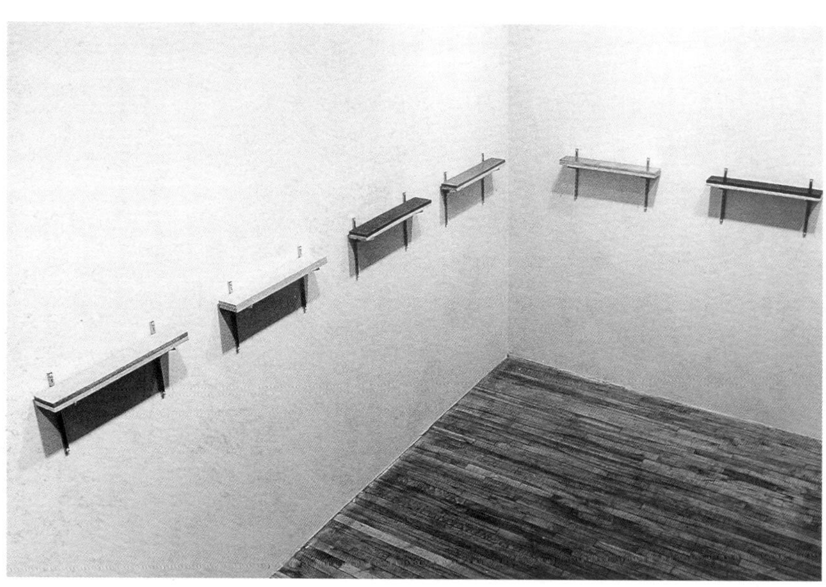

This later direction is perhaps seen in the fact that, after positioning his materials transversely, Shapiro reduced the assembly to a single, stratified arrangement (plate 23). The solitary unit held an unruly accumulation. Shapiro's approach is one of trial and error, and this was an early example of the constant questioning and testing of prior work that are essential to his art.

Shapiro would continue to concentrate on the presentation of physical evidence. A sculpture of 1970 titled *75 lbs.* (plate 24) consists of a bar of lead abutting a larger bar of magnesium. In another piece, *122 lbs.* (plate 25), a cylinder of iron meets a length of tree trunk. The corporeal quality of the fallen trunk would later absorb him. In both works, identical weights of dissimilar materials are juxtaposed, and their differences – of dimension and of density – are underscored. These materials are presented matter-of-factly, directly on the floor. In Carl Andre's work, the formal problem of the base had been solved by doing away with it altogether. By simply arranging industrial elements on the floor, as in *64 Zinc Square* (figure 3), Andre placed his work in a one-to-one relationship with the viewer, unencumbered by a separating base.

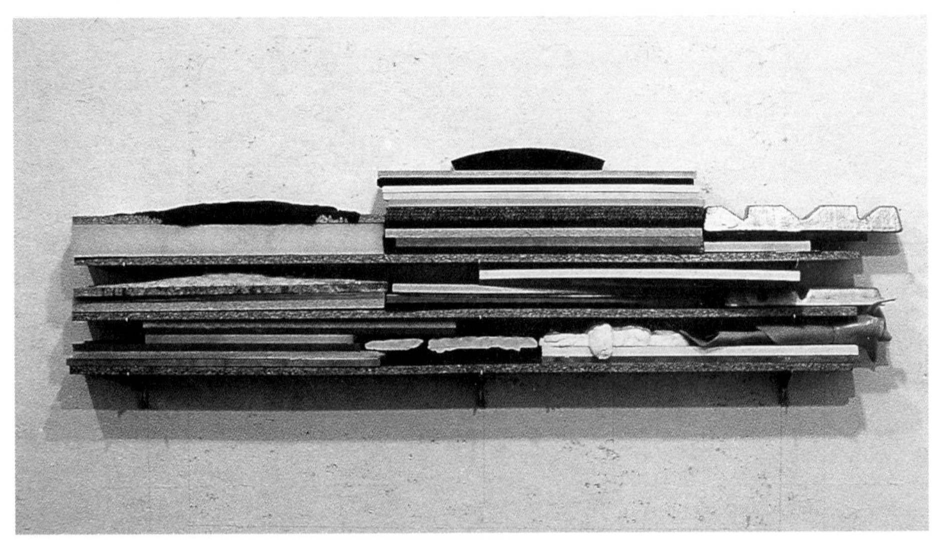

23 Untitled. 1969–70. Mixed media, approx. 60 x 20 x 5" (152.4 x 50.8 x 12.7 cm). No longer extant

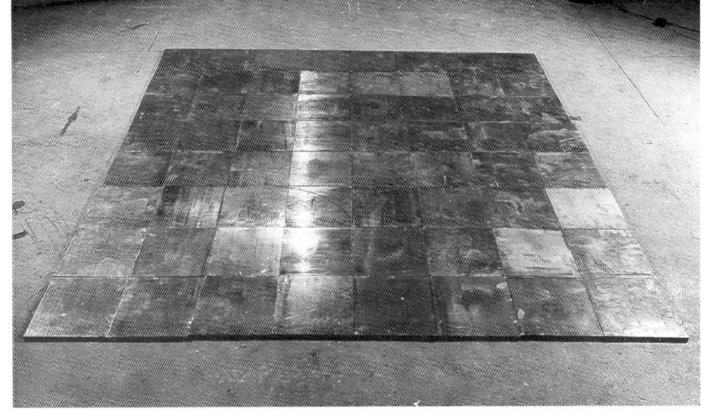

Fig. 3 Carl Andre. *64 Zinc Square*. 1969. Zinc, ⅜ x 8 x 8" (.9 x 20.3 x 20.3 cm) each, ⅜ x 64 x 64" (.9 x 162.6 x 162.6 cm) overall. Courtesy Paula Cooper Gallery, New York

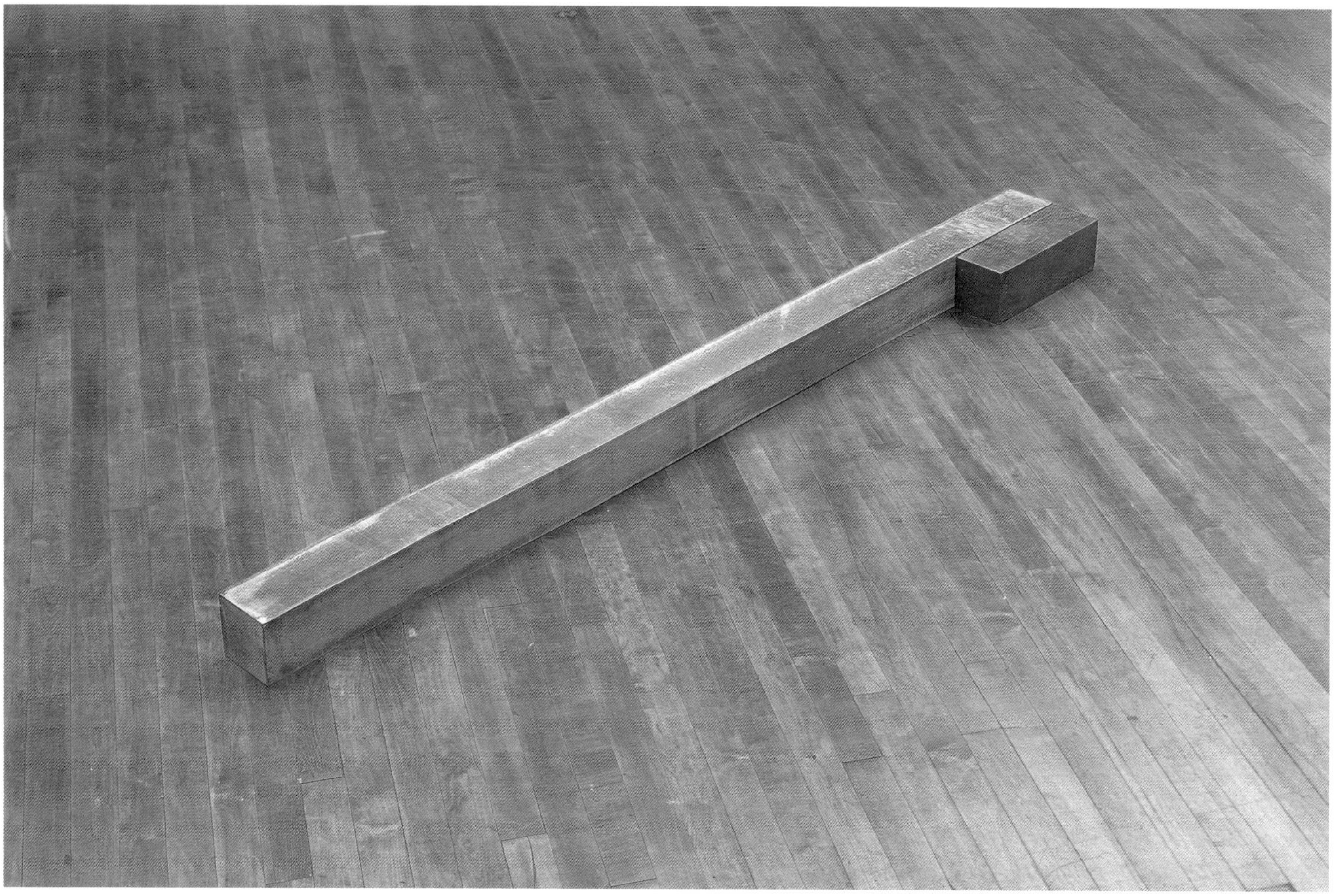

24 *75 lbs.* 1970. Magnesium and lead, 4" x 6'1¼" x 8" (10.2 x 186.1 x 20.3 cm). Private collection

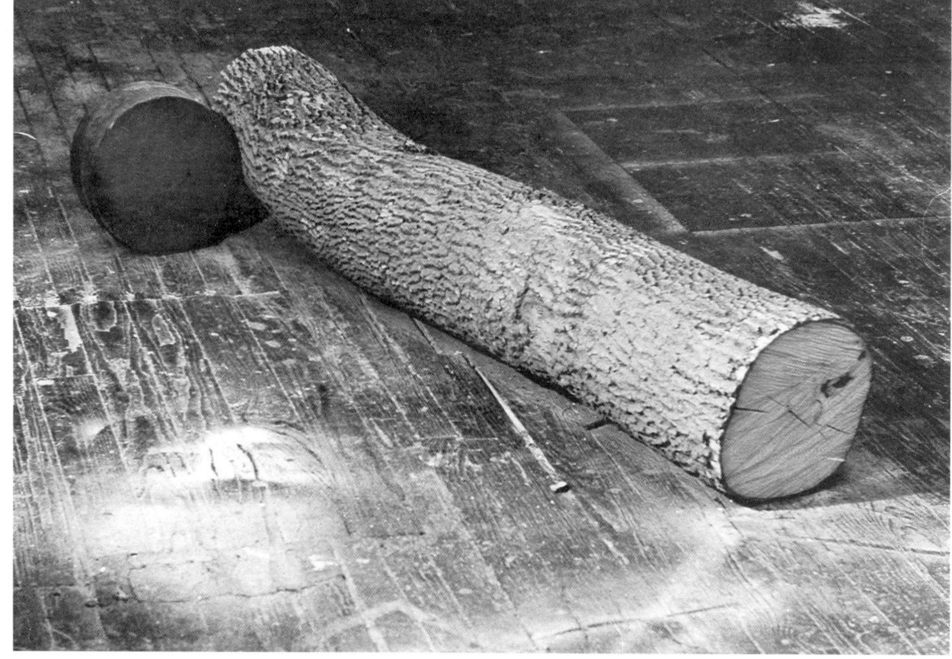

25 *122 lbs.* 1970. Wood and iron, 12 x 20 x 68" (30.5 x 50.8 x 172.7 cm). No longer extant

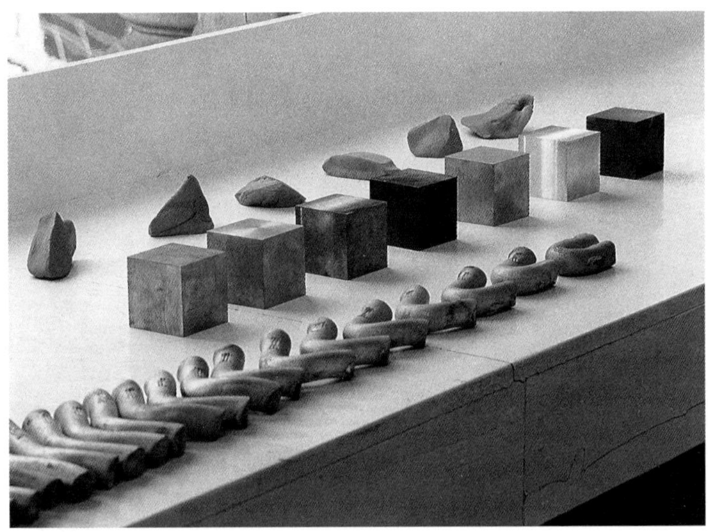

26 Installation view of the exhibition "Joel Shapiro," Paula Cooper Gallery, New York, 1970

Another group of sequential works, made over a two-year period, Shapiro chose to exhibit on an extant countertop (plate 26) that was related to the height of the worktable on which the pieces had been made. This accumulation of elements can be seen as halfway between a wall piece and a freestanding sculpture in conception; the countertop was a base in disguise, holding three parallel rows of objects. The middle row, which recalled Shapiro's first shelf installation, was a sequence of solid metal cubes, each cast from a different metal; their sizes were the same, but the weight of each cube was different. The back row consisted of roughly formed pieces of clay. And in the front row, lengths of zinc rod progressed from straight to curved and gradually decreased in size. Originally the same dimensions, they were forged into new shapes by increasing numbers of blows from a hammer.

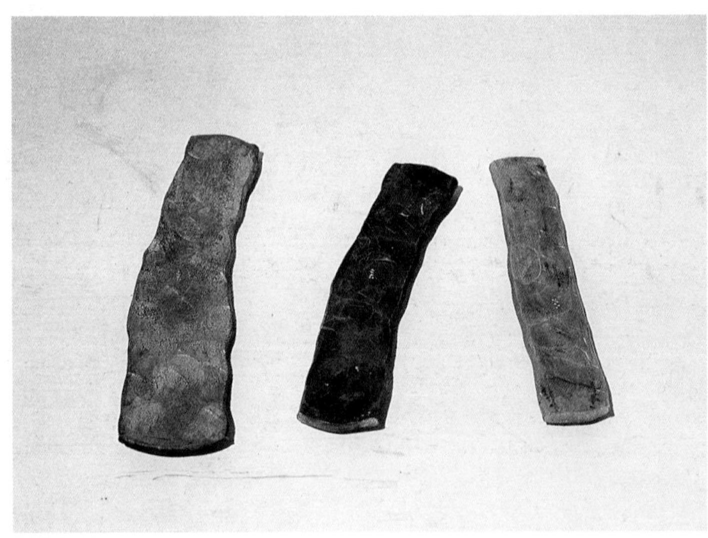

27 *200 Blows*. 1971. Copper, bronze, and zinc; copper: ¼ x 9¼ x 2¼" (.6 x 23.5 x 5.7 cm); bronze: ⅜ x 8⅛ x 1¾" (1 x 20.6 x 4.4 cm); zinc: ⅜ x 8 x 1⅛" (1 x 20.3 x 3.8 cm). Collection James F. Duffy, Grosse Pointe, Michigan

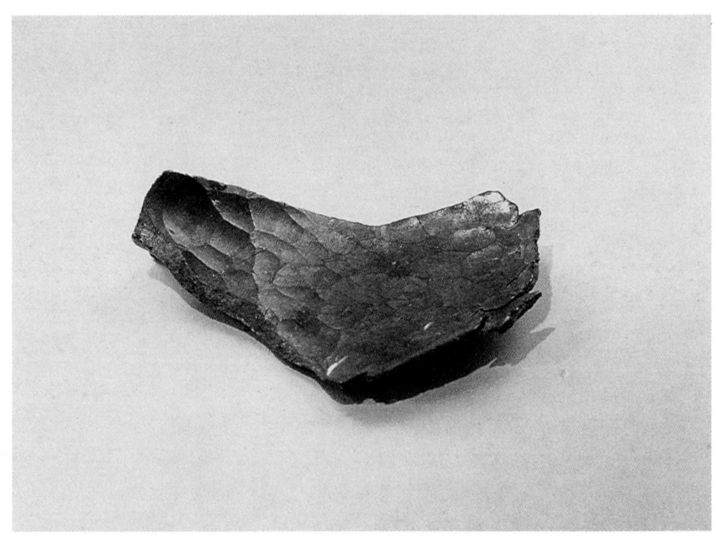

28 *600 Blows*. 1971. Lead, 1⅜ x 6 x 4½" (3.5 x 15.2 x 11.4 cm). Collection the artist

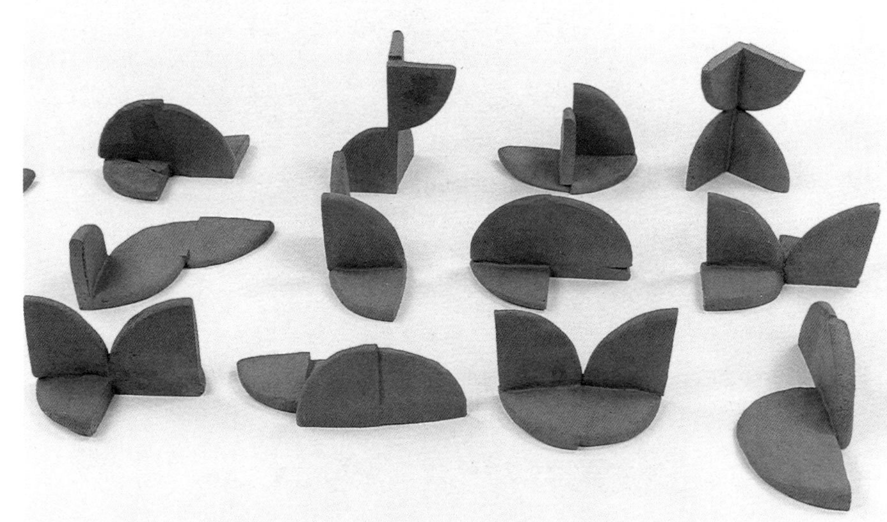

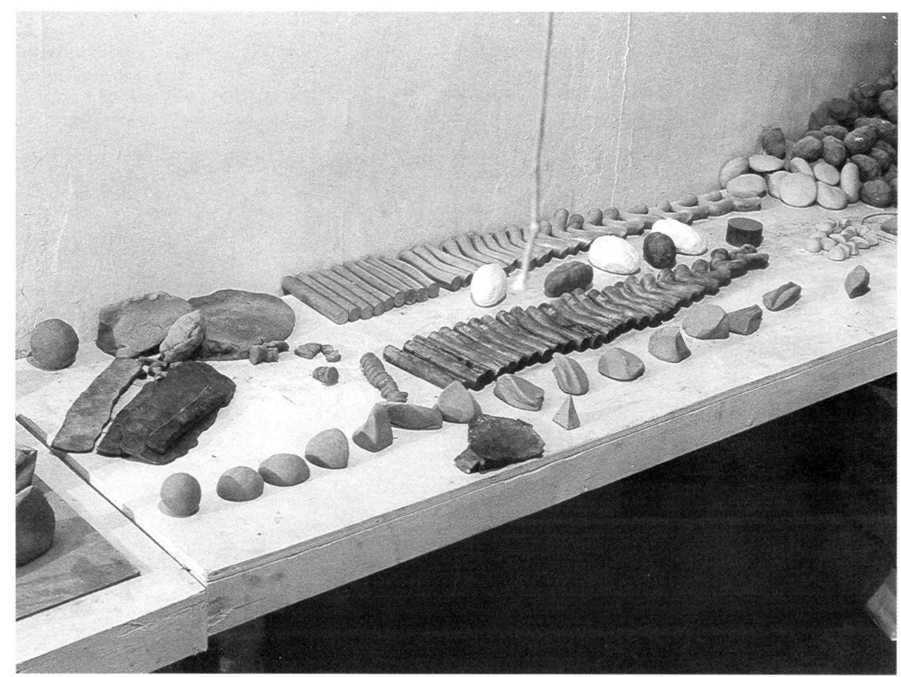

In these and other works, Shapiro introduced elements that were handmade and intuitively formed. He concentrated on irregular forms of clay to register direct gestures. And sometimes, in confronting an object's physical density, he literally came to blows with his materials. That physical activity was quantified with the descriptive titles *200 Blows* and *600 Blows* (plates 27, 28). The flattened pieces of copper, bronze, zinc, and lead in these works reveal a variety of markings and shapes. The differing formal results are a consequence of the relative hardness of each metal.

Other elements of Shapiro's emerging vocabulary can be seen in a terra-cotta sculpture made up of fifty-one components (plate 29). These animated and playfully figurative arabesques, formed by cutting and joining flat, circular pieces of clay, point toward later developments in his work.

A 1970 photograph of the artist's studio shows a group of objects, in a wide range of forms and materials, scattered or stacked in an apparently random order (plate 30). Shapiro was treating his work as an accumulation of artifacts. The way that groups of elements were organized was no longer so didactic; instead, it began to look as if their arrangement had resulted from the play of emotional or psychological factors. Indeed, Shapiro says that he was now "structuring the work so possibilities could occur, rather than working in some preconceived vein."[10] He was shaping things on the basis of his own visual experience.

29 Untitled. 1971. Terra-cotta, up to 51 components, longest dimension approx. 5" (12.7 cm) each component; overall dimensions variable. Collection the artist

30 View of the artist's studio, New York. 1970

Handmade

Shapiro's continuing exploration led his work in many directions, and he had few inhibitions about exhibiting his experiments. He has acknowledged that Paula Cooper created a stimulating, experimental atmosphere for artists in her gallery: "Paula was an admirable dealer. She was measured and made very few demands. . . . She absolutely encouraged development and change."[11]

Shapiro's increasingly personal and complex vocabulary was revealed in 1972 with his second solo show (plate 31). This time, all the works were placed on the floor. The support had been eliminated, and the sculptures were distributed on the floor throughout the gallery, whereas earlier they had been placed across a shelf or tabletop. This radical change, of both scale and perspective, meant that the viewer now inhabited the same space as the sculptures.

The objects were handmade from clay, or carved from stone, or welded in metal. Three basic shapes were probed: the sphere, the cylinder, and the cone. *One Hand Forming* and *Two Hands Forming* (plate 32) are titles that describe Shapiro's procedures. He shaped balls of clay, a primordial and pliable material, and built each sculpture out of these hand-size elements, modeling with repetitive movements. Each of the sculptures is composed of modular units of either spheres or rolled cylinders (plates 33, 34). The abutting or stacked elements constitute the shape of the final work.

OPPOSITE:

32 *One Hand Forming* (background) and *Two Hands Forming* (foreground). Both 1971. Fired clay, *One Hand Forming*: 77 units, 1½" (3.8 cm) diameter x 3½" (8.9 cm) each; *Two Hands Forming*: 93 units, 3" (7.6 cm) diameter each. Collection the artist

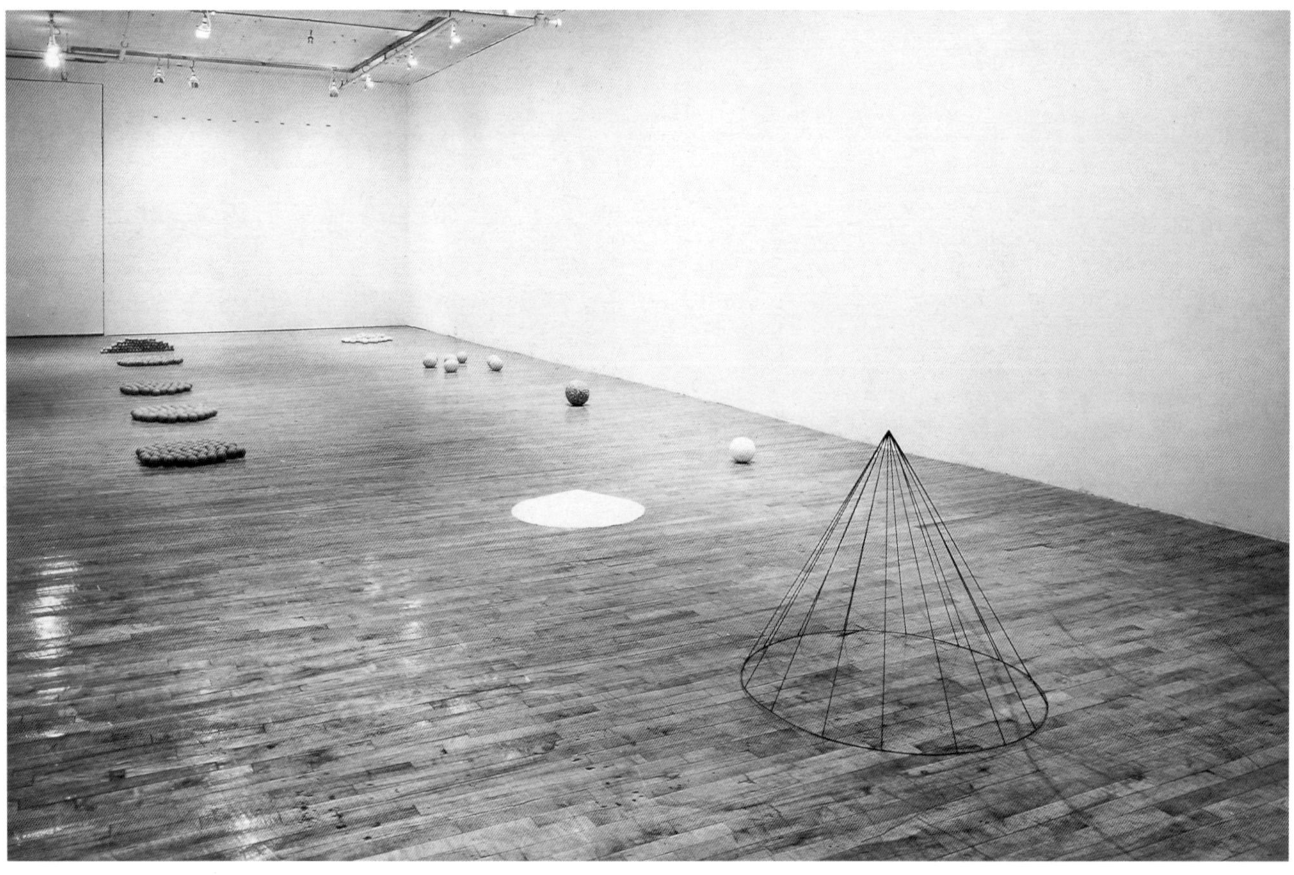

31 Installation view of the exhibition "Joel Shapiro," Paula Cooper Gallery, New York, 1972. Works shown here also appear in plates 32, 34–37.

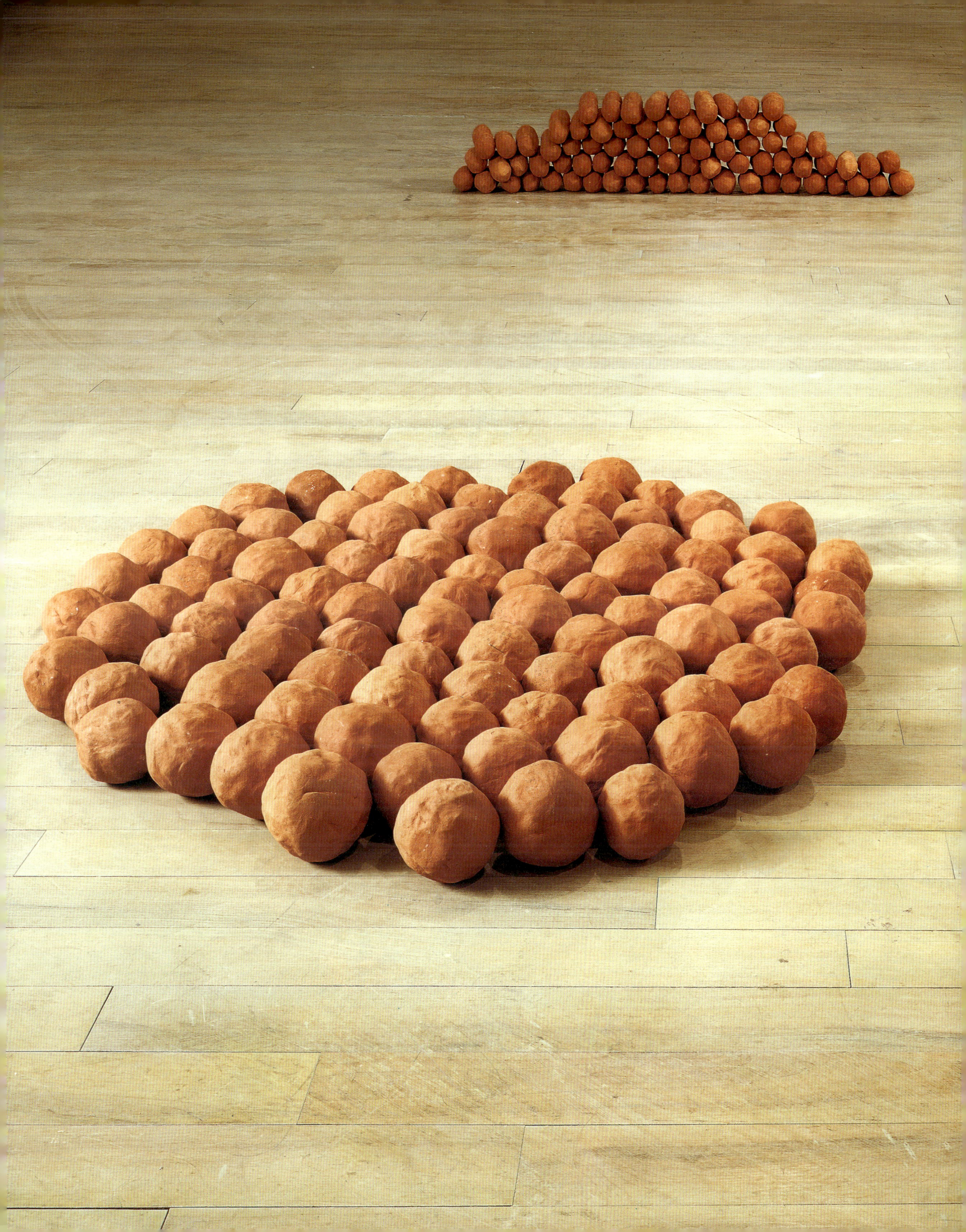

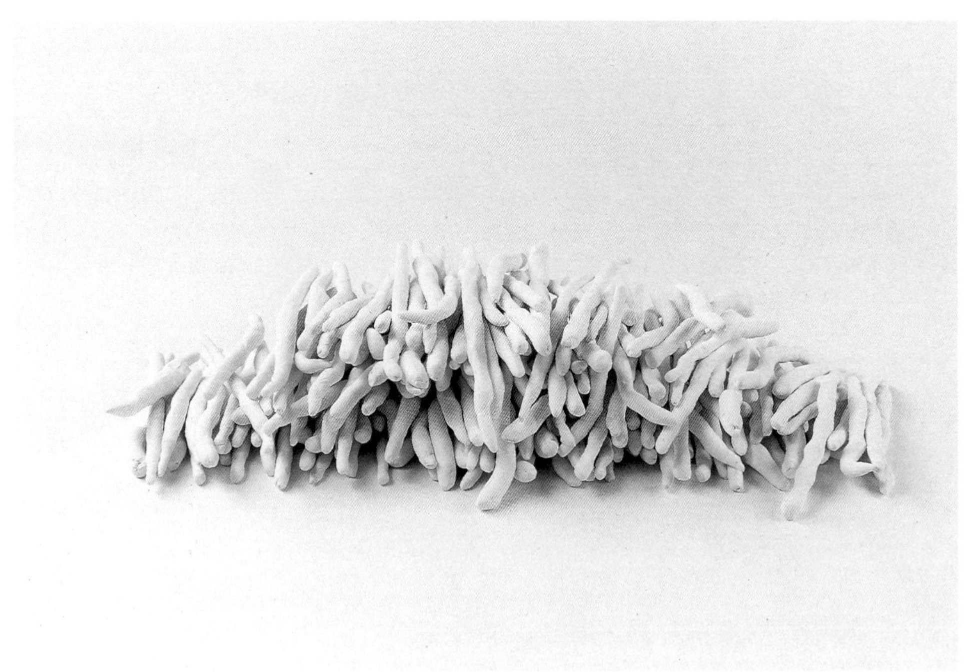

33 Untitled. 1972. Fired clay, 203 units, ½" (1.3 cm) diameter x 5" (12.7 cm) each. Collection the artist

34 *One Hand Forming*. 1971. Fired clay, 77 units, 1½" (3.8 cm) diameter x 3½" (8.9 cm) each, 34 x 9 x 4" (86.4 x 22.9 x 10.2 cm) overall. Collection the artist

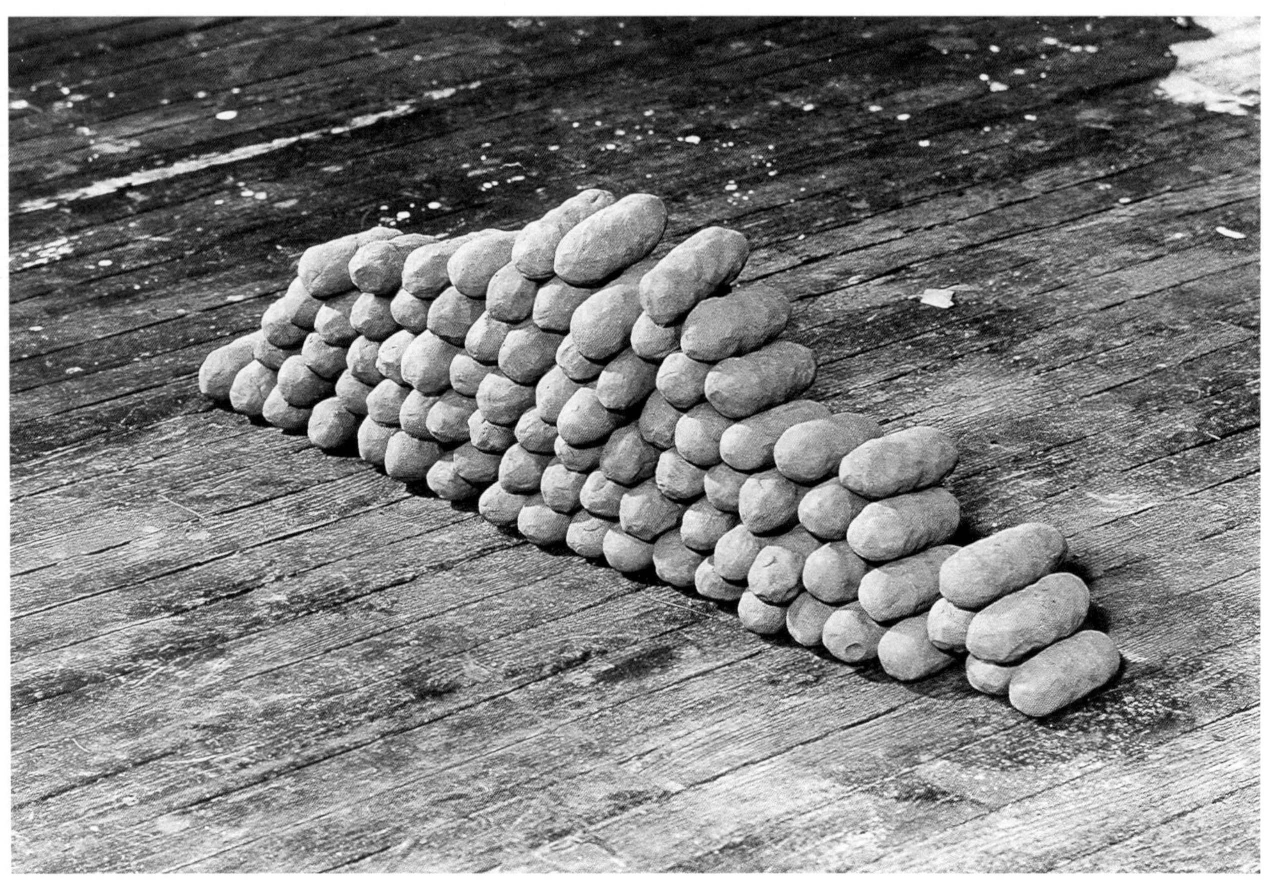

The soft clay records every mark made by the artist, and one senses that modeling is a pleasurable activity for Shapiro. He has a long familiarity with clay. He attended ceramics classes as a child; later, in India, he helped construct cooking ovens, and he recalls that it was "fun to build [them] out of mud and cow dung."[12] Modeling possesses sexual and scatological associations; it is linked with the body and bodily functions.

At the same time, Shapiro had been carving stone sculptures. These pieces contain fewer elements than do the works in clay, and the spheres here are larger (plates 35, 36). The obdurate quality of the stone forced Shapiro to employ another shaping device; the rock has been chiseled. Whereas an additive process lay behind the clay works, now Shapiro cut away to reveal form.

The accumulation of individual components seen in works such as these was a strategy of much Post-Minimalist art. In *Sequel* (figure 5), for example, Eva Hesse unified disparate parts on a latex field. Shapiro's installations exhibit a variety of compositional devices, affected by whether the components are seen individually or as a group. Their emotional characteristics, too, can change according to how their physical nature is affected by grouping. When viewed singly, they seem heavy and offer a grave countenance. When in a group and thus less monolithic, they can seem almost playful.

The cone, the third geometric figure tested in the 1972 show, had broad implications for Shapiro. A welded wire construction (see plate 31) asserted itself against the other sculptures in the exhibition. Assembled and joined, it was the tallest freestanding object. This peaked form would appear in other guises: in *Pariscraft No. 2* of 1971 (plate 37)[13] and, as a triangle, in a charcoal-and-crayon drawing of 1972 (plate 38). Each of these three works maps out a geometric form in a different way. With the wire piece, space remains open, measured by the repetition of metal spokes. In *Pariscraft No. 2,* the volume described by the cone is hidden, while the surface records evidence of its construction. In the drawing, the interior of the triangle is measured with a graduated series of short, horizontal strokes. These three works presage the insistence on the vertical in Shapiro's subsequent sculpture.

Shapiro was of course not alone in exploring materials and processes. His earlier works sought to find their place within current sculptural discourse. He had interests in common with his immediate contemporaries, artists such as Richard Serra, Bruce Nauman, and Eva Hesse: the grammar of process, the use of unconventional materials, the idea of sculpture as site-specific installation, and a workmanlike, hands-on approach to fabrication. Shapiro was occupied also with questions raised by the Minimalists somewhat earlier. The works of Donald Judd and Carl Andre in particular helped him define positions he could either accept or reject. Their attention to issues of scale, specificity, and sequencing challenged him. Shapiro admired the simple geometry of works by the Minimalists, whose sculptures were often arranged in neat rows or grids. These artists eliminated the need for the traditional base by locating their work directly on the floor, and this notion of "grounding" was most significant for Shapiro. Regarding his own work, he says, "Once on the floor, you couldn't refute it. You couldn't deny its presence, its factualness."

This early phase of Shapiro's career had been characterized by a feverish, all-consuming production of works. It laid the foundation for his future art.

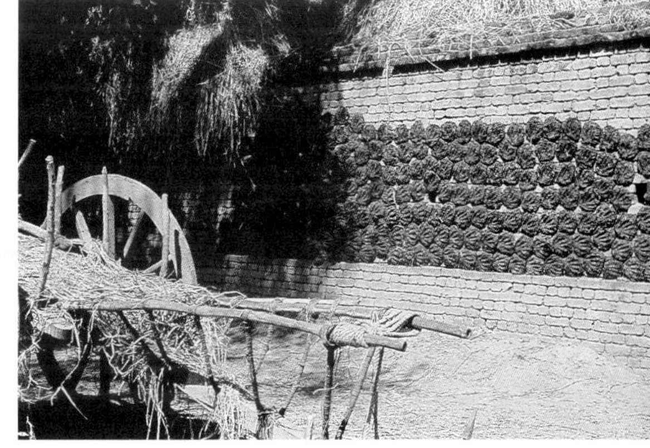

Fig. 4 Village in India. 1966. Photograph by Joel Shapiro

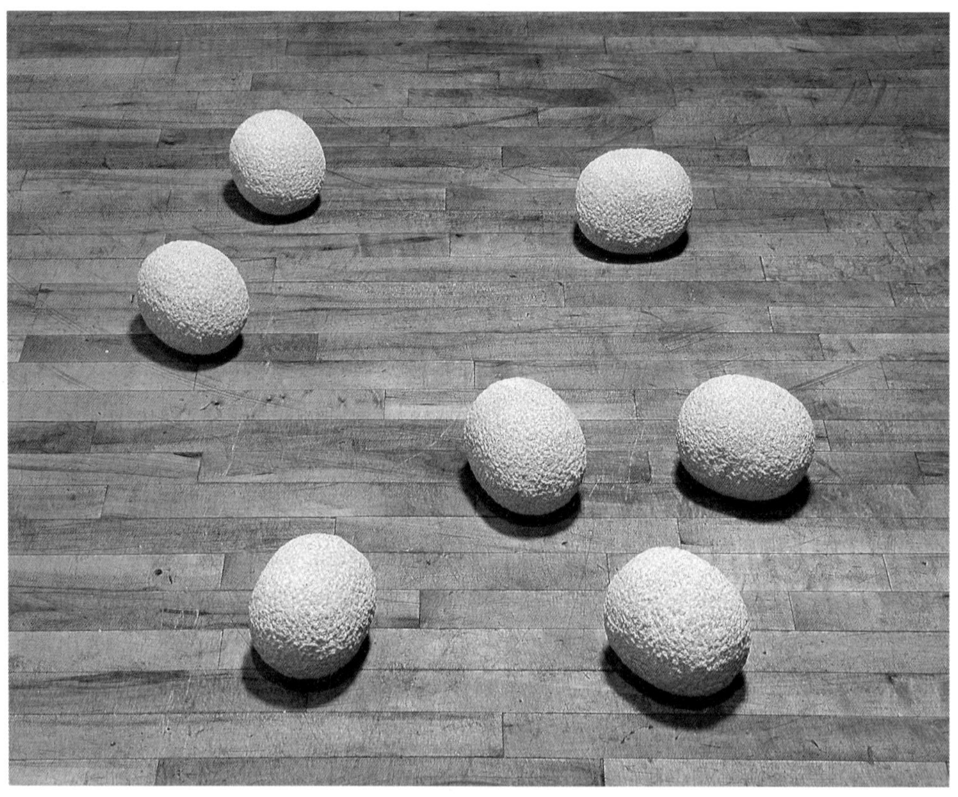

35 Untitled. 1971. Carved limestone, 7 units, 5½ x 4½ x 6" (14 x 11.4 x 15.2 cm) each. Museum of Contemporary Art, Chicago. Gift of the Lannan Foundation

36 Untitled. 1971. Carved granite, 8½ x 8½ x 7½" (21.6 x 21.6 x 19.1 cm). The Museum of Contemporary Art, Los Angeles. Gift of the Lannan Foundation

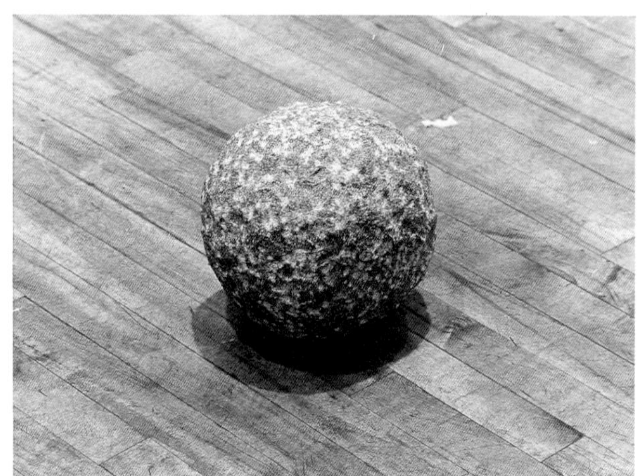

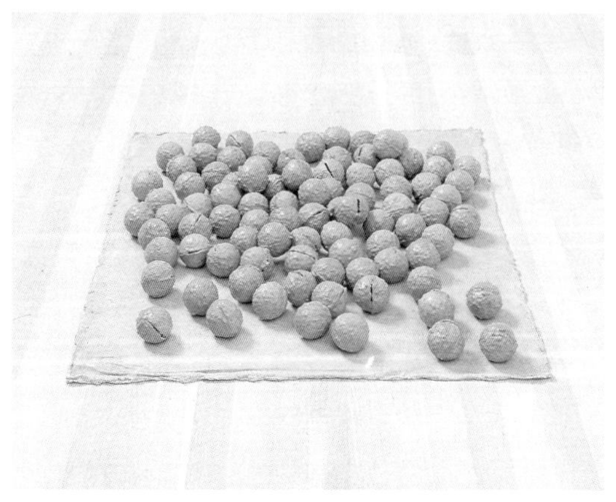

Fig. 5 Eva Hesse. *Sequel*. 1967–68. Latex mixed with powdered white pigment, 91 spheres, approx. 2⅝" (6.7 cm) diameter each, 30 x 32" (76.2 x 81.3 cm) overall. The Art Institute of Chicago

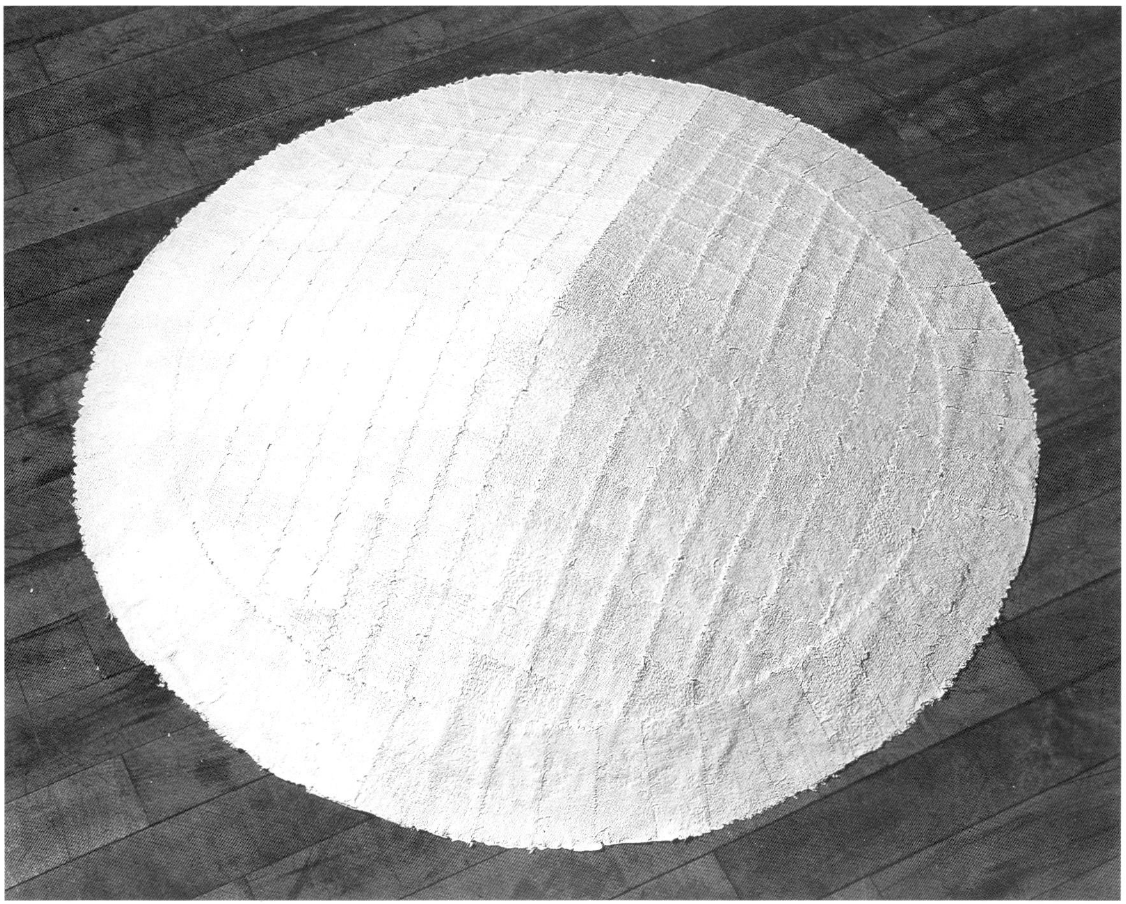

37 *Pariscraft No. 2.* 1971. Plaster and gauze, 5" (12.7 cm) high x 36" (91.4 cm) diameter. Collection the artist

38 Untitled. 1972. Charcoal and crayon on paper, 38 ¼ x 24" (97.1 x 61 cm). Collection Sanford Schwartz and Carole Obedin

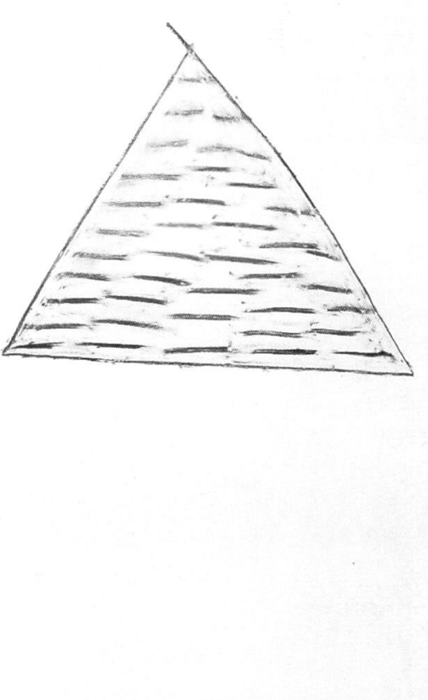

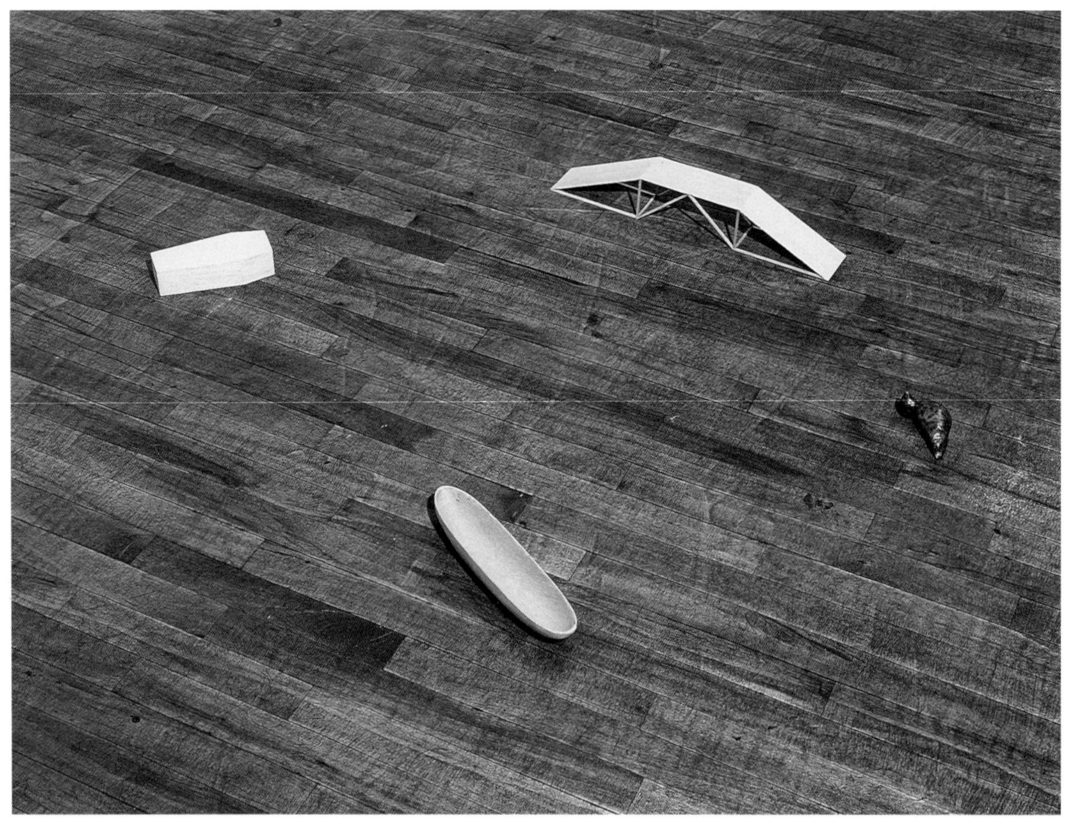

39 Untitled. 1972. Four units: balsa-wood bridge, 3 x 20¼ x 3" (7.6 x 51.4 x 7.6 cm); basswood boat, 1⅝ x 11⅝ x 2⅝" (4.1 x 29.5 x 6.7 cm); balsa-wood coffin, 1¾ x 7 x 2¾" (4.4 x 17.8 x 7 cm); bronze bird, 1¾ x 3¾ x 2¾" (4.4 x 9.5 x 7 cm). Collection the artist

Metaphors (1971–75)

Shapiro's work explores two seemingly opposing realms, as he cultivates the ambiguity between abstract and figurative form. He structures the abstract elements of his formal vocabulary to convey the emotional resonance of the figurative.

The untitled floor installation from 1972 (plate 39) is an important example of his drive at this time to create works that were more personal. Shapiro acknowledges that he wanted to express something "more internal – more about myself – which was frightening."[14] The piece is composed of four representational objects – a bridge, a coffin, a boat, and a bird. Small and placed close to one another, these vulnerable elements are held together in an intimate relationship. Their association recalls Alberto Giacometti's *The Palace at 4 A.M.* (figure 6), a mise-en-scène in which abstract objects perform an enigmatic drama within a fragile architecture. Giacometti is the modernist with

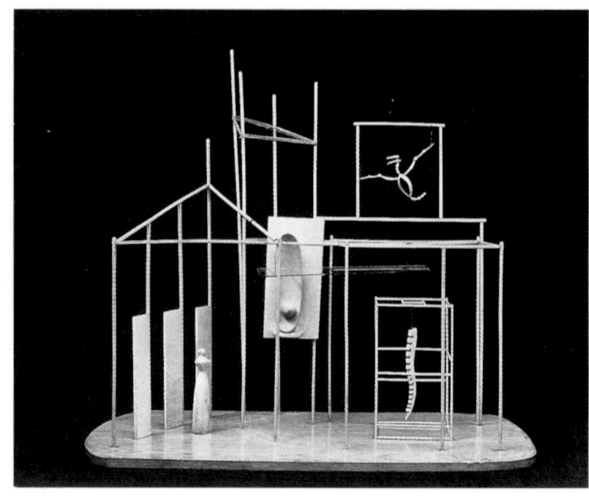

Fig. 6 Alberto Giacometti. *The Palace at 4 A.M.* 1932–33. Construction in wood, glass, wire, and string, 25 x 28¼ x 15¾" (63.5 x 71.8 x 40 cm). The Museum of Modern Art, New York. Purchase

whom Shapiro shares, throughout his work, the greatest number of concerns. They both allow humanistic ideals and "life and its complications" to shape their sculptural form. But compared to the Giacometti work, with its proscenium space, Shapiro's work engages the viewer in a much more physically direct dialogue: possibly influenced by sculptures he had seen in India (figure 7), he avoids the isolating distance of the pedestal and places his work at the viewer's feet. Shapiro puts the viewer onstage with the sculpture and forces the viewer to play an active role within the sculptural drama below. The floor is conceived as a pictorial "ground" with low-lying elements, and we move among them with an overhead view. Rosalind Krauss noted how the observer thus crosses into the fictive world, through mental participation: "We are at one with its scale; our intimacy with the object is a function of our ability to erase the disparity between its actual size and ours."[15]

The four objects of this untitled work interact not only formally but also narratively. Shapiro was constructing images that conveyed his state of mind. Unlike earlier works, these objects were not simply the evidence of physical actions; they allude to archetypal forms, and they therefore trigger imaginative and affective associations. Each element evokes a different kind of movement or passage: the bridge is a means of crossing from one point to another; the boat is a vehicle; the bird once flew freely in space; and the coffin, finally, suggests the passage from life to death. The ritualistic aspect of these constructions is not incidental.

The four objects constitute a metaphor of mortality. The bird, which lies the most heavily on the floor, is the only object of the four – and the first ever – that Shapiro chose to cast in bronze, and its very weight and density emphasize its immobility. "As long as the wood was balsa wood or [the piece was] made out of clay or. . . a material that was not permanent," he observed, "I was on safe ground."[16] With bronze, however, he was forced to work in a more declarative way, and this obligation challenged his tentative gestures into becoming more solid structures.

Working in bronze also addressed Shapiro's long-standing concern with process, with how to capture and record the successive stages of sculptural development. On a technical level, the mold used for casting is simply a device for capturing a "physical memory" – that of the wood or plaster prototype. Moreover, Shapiro's final casts record each state, as the cast surfaces come to evidence the history of their construction. And, evoking another kind of memory, every cast can be seen as recalling the art-historical tradition of the medium. For all of these reasons, Shapiro confirms that "casting had a memory and a connection with the past."

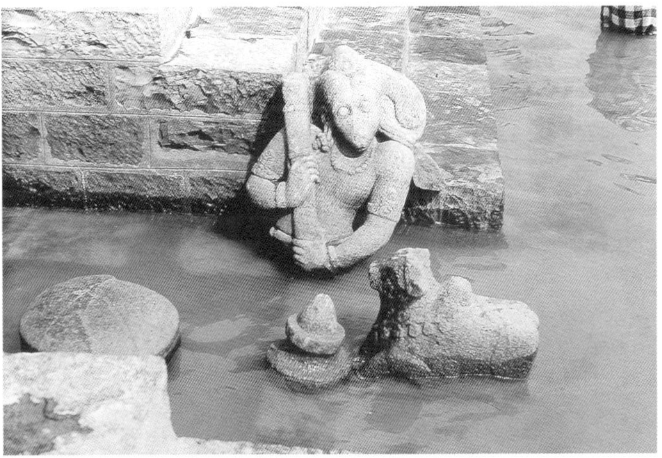

Fig. 7 Alampur, India. 1966. Photograph by Joel Shapiro

In a group of related individual works, Shapiro further explored the components and themes of the 1972 installation. The mirror images of *Two Bronze Birds* (plate 40) were made, respectively, with the artist's right and left hands. Here, Shapiro combined his earlier interest in process and his new concern with image making: the construction of the two birds, as well as their size and shape, make them surrogates for the artist's own hands. And Shapiro again used the image of a bridge (plate 42). *Bridge* was milled from a solid piece of cast iron (in this case, milling served as a surrogate for carving). This small, solitary sculpture was first shown, in the vastness of the Clocktower's exhibition space, in 1973 (plate 41). Shapiro then lived within sight of the Brooklyn Bridge; it was the dominant feature in the immediate landscape. Yet the particular power of his bridge image came from his compression of it into this unexpected size.

Also shown in the Clocktower exhibition was *Ladder* (plate 43). This tiny, fragile construction of lightweight basswood leaned against a very high wall. Obviously functionless and impossible to climb, the minute apparatus made the room a Swiftian confusion of proportions.

An untitled work of 1971–74 (plate 44) resembles a capsized boat. Closed, and offering the viewer no means of passage, it seems a combination of the boat and the coffin from the 1972 installation (plate 39). Here as elsewhere, Shapiro was refining a few elementary forms, and making them his own.

Despite their apparent reticence, these works sometimes betray the artist's turmoil. Many of them describe a fascination with physical features that have sexual connotations: openings, closings, penetrations. In 1974, in an attempt to express such themes more directly, Shapiro made a renewed effort to represent the human figure. After considerable struggle, a piece emerged in an outburst of frustration (plate 45). "I was furious, feeling wounded and threatened. I was trying to work with a figure, and it didn't work, so I just took these mannequins I'd found and ripped them apart and threw them on the ground." The dismantled pieces sprawled on the floor bear a certain resemblance to another of Giacometti's early Surrealist works, *Woman with Her Throat Cut* (figure 8). Shapiro's treatment of the mannequins, his rage, stemmed from his inability to find meaning in the representation of the figure. The result was dismembered body parts strewn about the gallery floor.

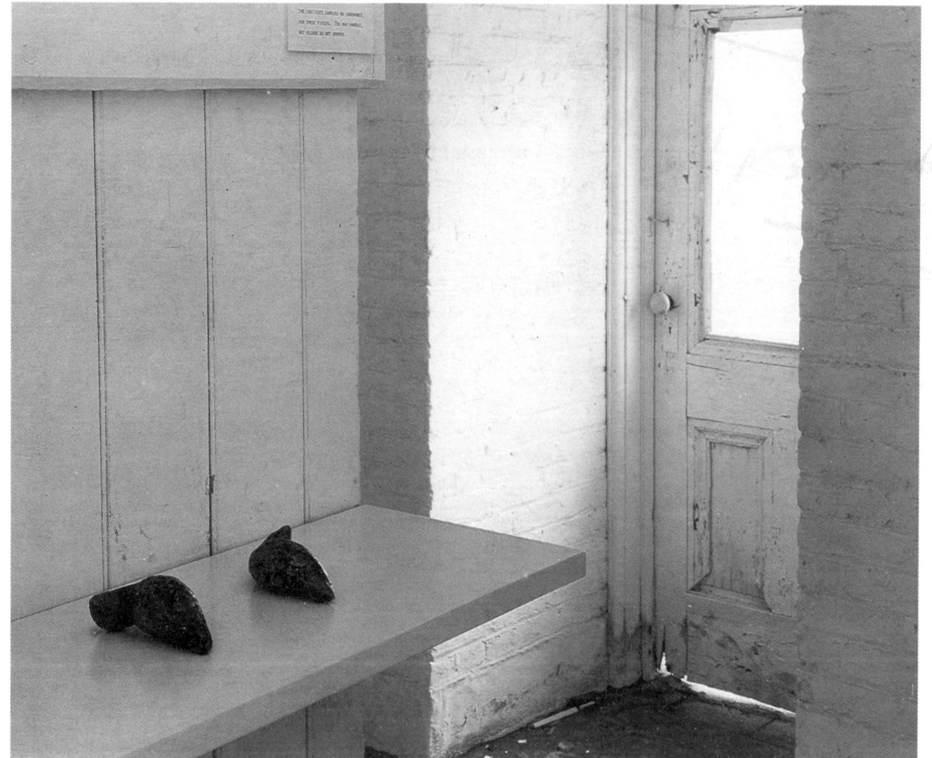

40 *Two Bronze Birds*. 1972–73 (installed in the exhibition "Joel Shapiro," The Clocktower, Institute for Art and Urban Resources, New York, 1973). Bronze, 1 ¾ x 3 ¾ x 2 ¾" (4.4 x 9.5 x 7 cm). Collection Bryan Montgomery, London

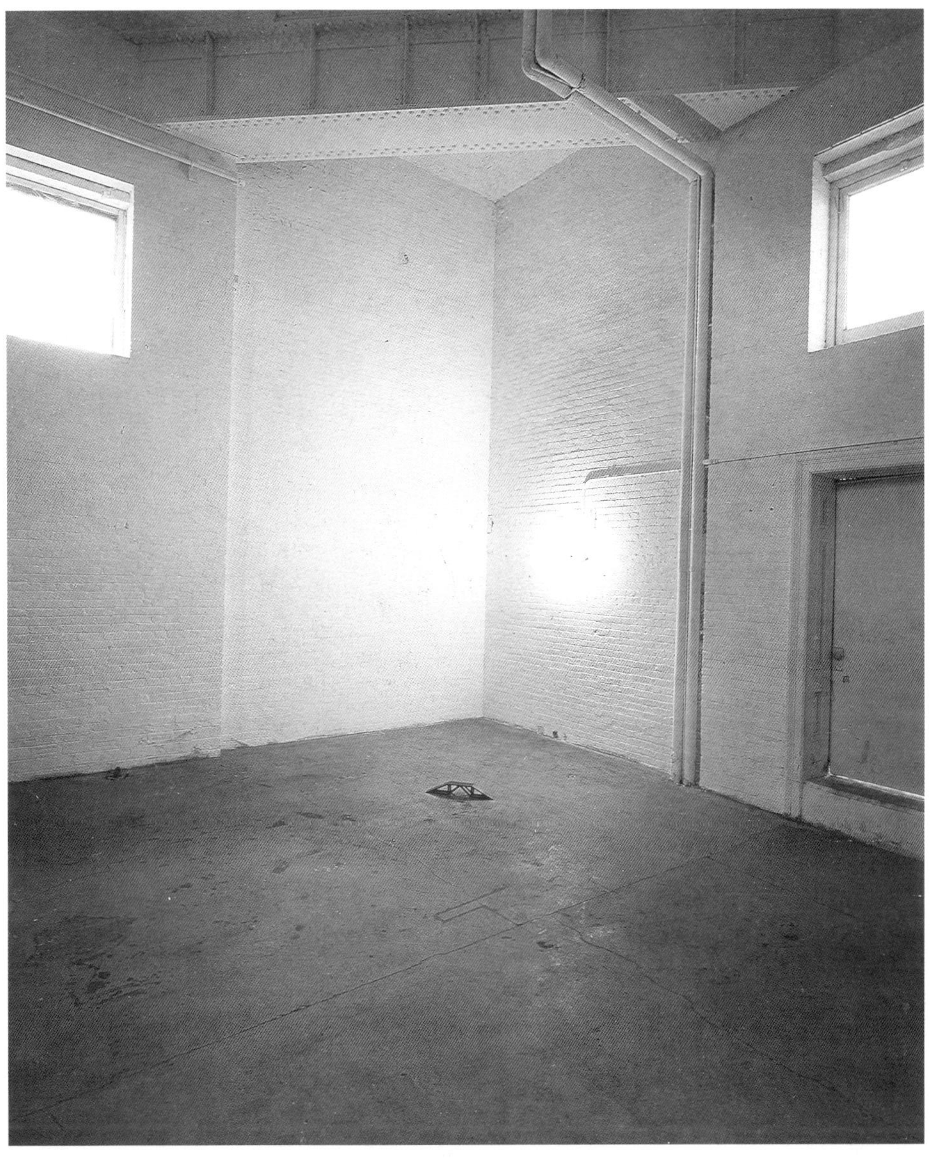

41 *Bridge*. 1973 (installed in the exhibition "Joel Shapiro," The Clocktower, Institute for Art and Urban Resources, New York, 1973). The work shown here also appears in plate 42.

42 *Bridge*. 1973. Milled cast iron, 3½ x 22½ x 3" (8.9 x 57.2 x 7.6 cm). Collection James F. Duffy, Grosse Pointe, Michigan

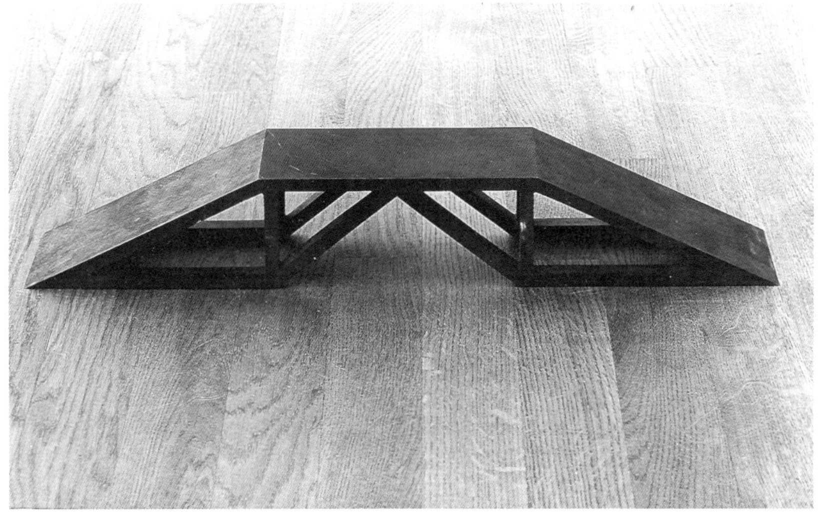

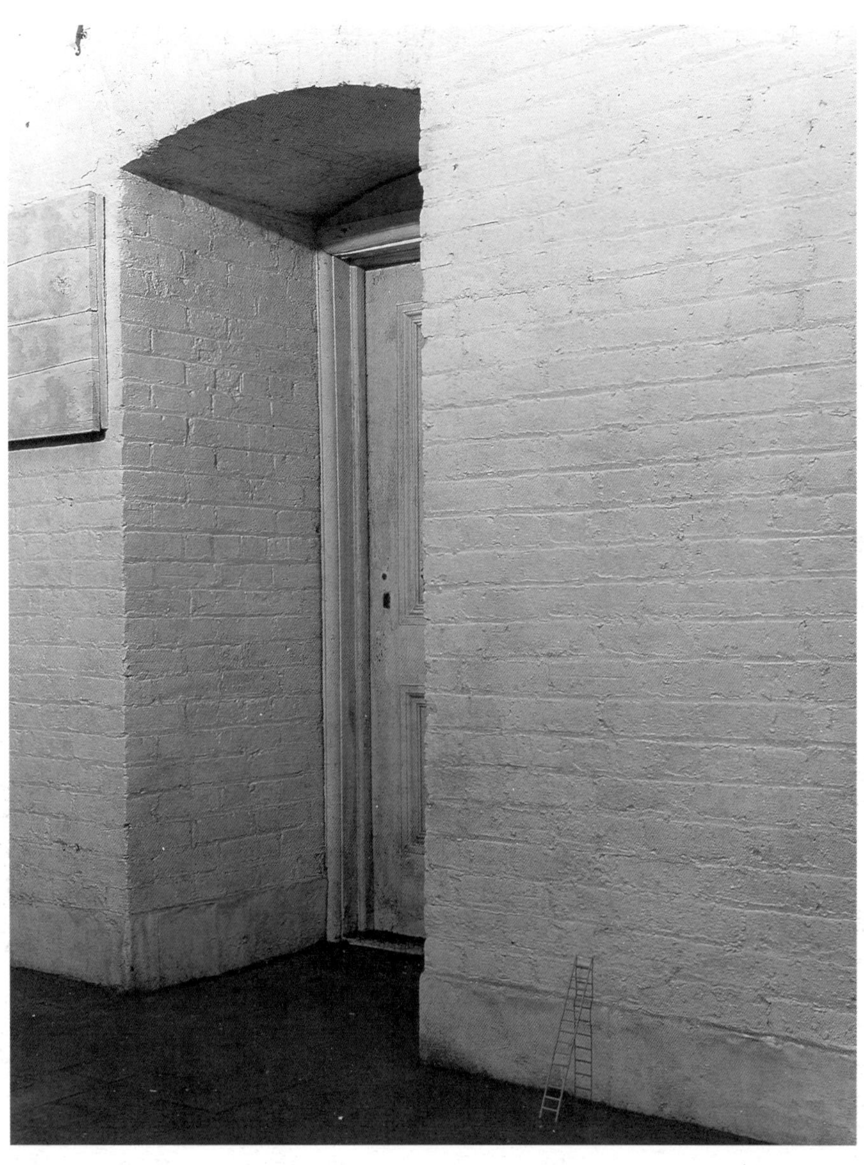

43 *Ladder*. 1973 (installed in the exhibition "Joel Shapiro," The Clocktower, Institute for Art and Urban Resources, New York, 1973). Basswood, 11¼ x 1½ x ⅛" (28.6 x 3.8 x .1 cm). Collection Sarah-Ann and Werner H. Kramarsky

44 Untitled. 1971–74. Cast iron (edition 2/3), 2¾ x 11 x 4¼" (7 x 27.9 x 10.8 cm). Collection Paula Cooper

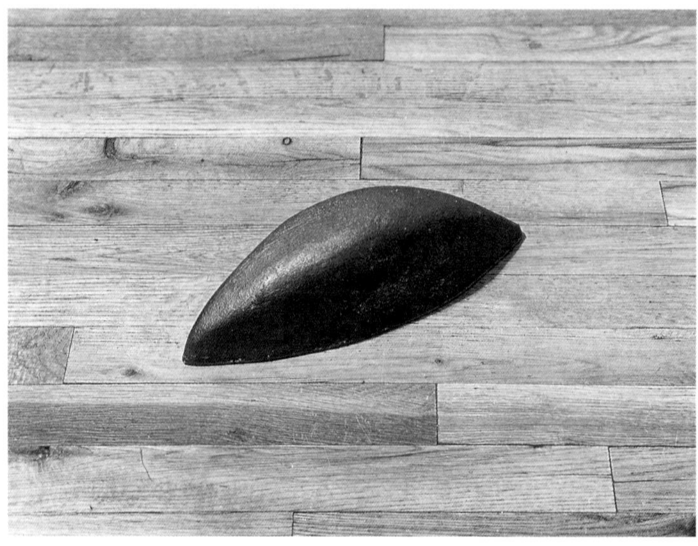

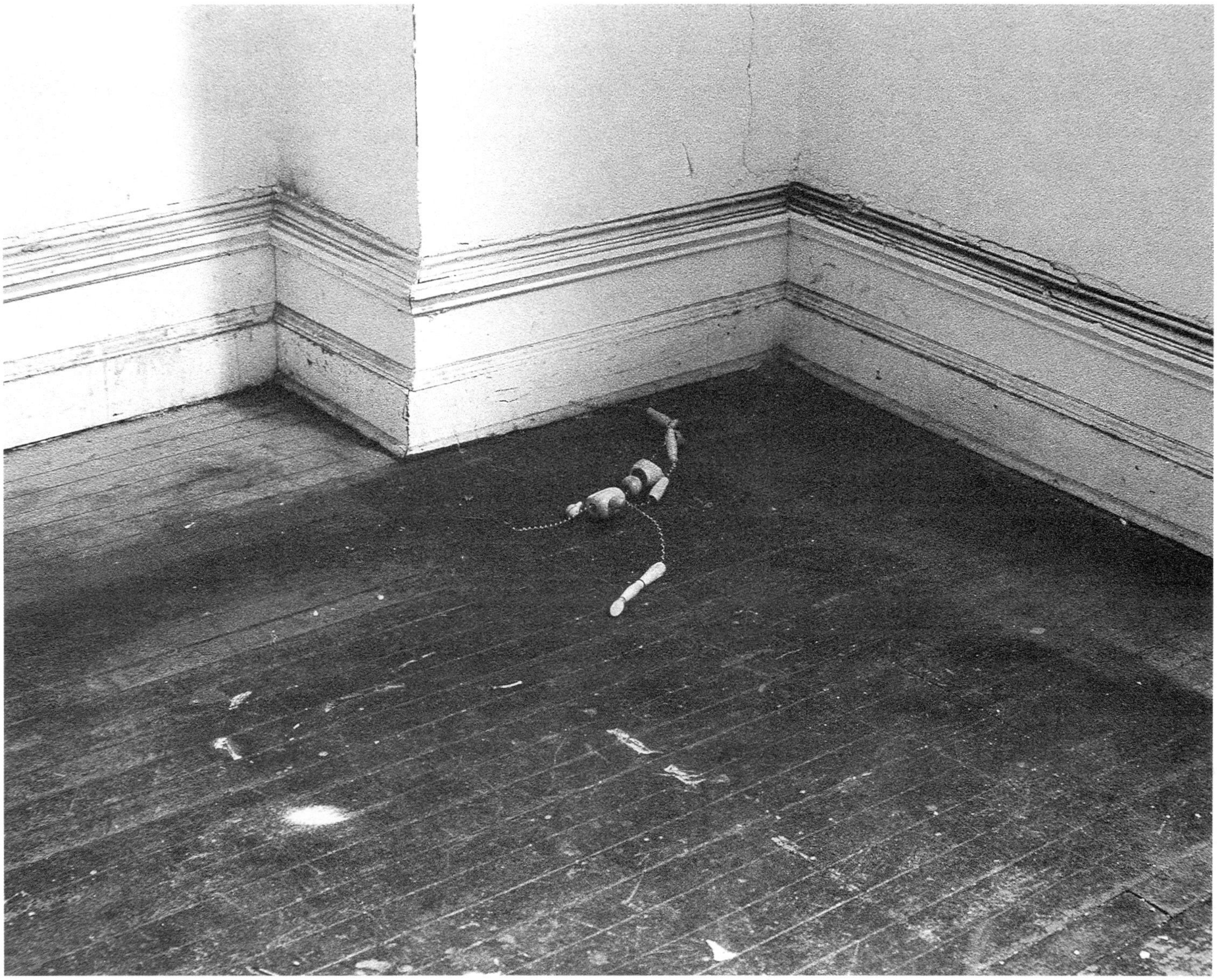

45 Detail of Untitled. 1974 (installed in the exhibition "Figuratively Sculpting," The Clocktower, Institute for Art and Urban Resources, New York, 1974). Mannequins, 2" x 8'10" x 8'4" (5.1 x 269.2 x 254 cm) variable. Collection the artist

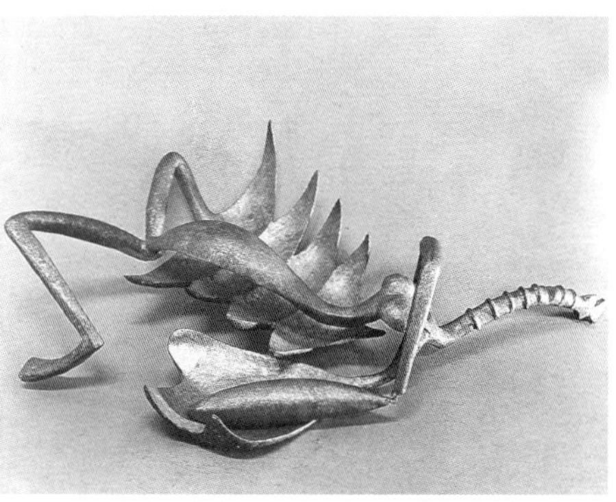

Fig. 8 Alberto Giacometti. *Woman with Her Throat Cut*. 1932. Bronze (cast 1949), 8 x 34½ x 25" (20.3 x 87.6 x 63.5 cm). The Museum of Modern Art, New York. Purchase

Shapiro looked for another subject that could substitute for the figure. On a trip to Vermont, he had taken photographs of horses. One of these pictures (plate 46) was used as the announcement for his exhibition at Paula Cooper's new gallery in early 1974. The cropped image focuses on the horse's powerful, muscular frame. In contrast, an untitled sculpture of 1973–74 (plate 47) presents a tiny bronze creature with simplified contours; it stands iconically rigid atop a small shelf on four long legs, with its tail straight out. Unassuming, almost shy, it is a distant relative of the heroic equestrian sculptures of public squares. The model for this work appears to have been another photograph (plate 48), in which the horse stands still, in the center of deep pictorial space. Another work (plate 49), made from pieces of wood glued together, depicts a rider as well as a horse. The horseman sits backwards in the saddle; he looks away and seems lost. Indeed, the work itself almost disappears: in an act of self-effacement, Shapiro sprayed the piece and the wall simultaneously with dark green enamel.

Shapiro was also developing another group of works with more abstract concerns. Specifically, he was interested in how abstract formal elements could nonetheless be read as recognizable objects – shelf, chair, couch, table. Depiction remained a particular taboo of Minimalism, and what Shapiro wanted to define was a new position between abstraction and representation. Characteristic works (plates 50–54) create simple geometries suggestive of furniture and other utilitarian objects. Despite their spareness, these works use a variety of methods to describe space: volumes can be either open or closed, for example, and walls vary in size and thickness.

In the mid-seventies, Shapiro devoted a good deal of attention to the subject of the chair (plate 55). Through a series of works in a range of materials, he sought to fix the "physical memory"[17] of sitting. His chairs try to capture the experience of the mind as well as that of the body. In contrast to Giacometti's figurative works of the 1940s, where the reduction in size corresponds to some optical or perceptual reality, Shapiro's diminutions instead activate the conceptual imagination of the viewer – the part of the mind that says "chair." That is, the images are reduced so as to fit comfortably "inside" one's head, like visual memories. In this sense, they are not small scaled. The scale of a piece is determined not by its size per se, but by what Shapiro calls its "viability in that size": its ability to "function as sculpture."[18] The placement of these small objects on the floor is crucial to their perceptual effect as sculpture. The geometries of the sculptures echo the architecture of the rooms they occupy, giving them a sense of belonging there, but their vulnerability and their isolation within the space charge the environment with a theatrical energy.

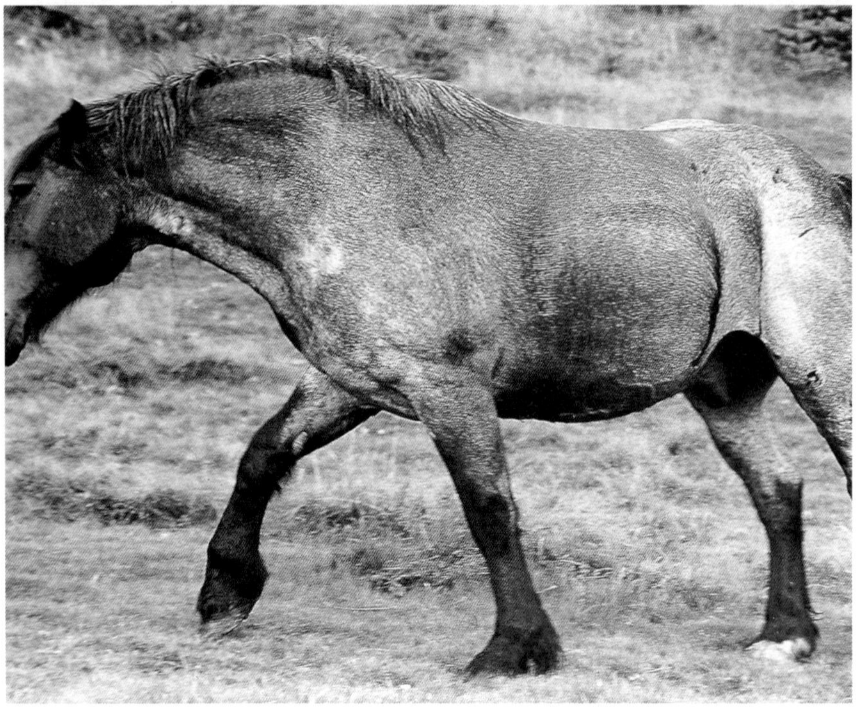

46 Photograph. 1973. Black-and-white print, 8 x 10" (20.3 x 25.4 cm). Collection the artist

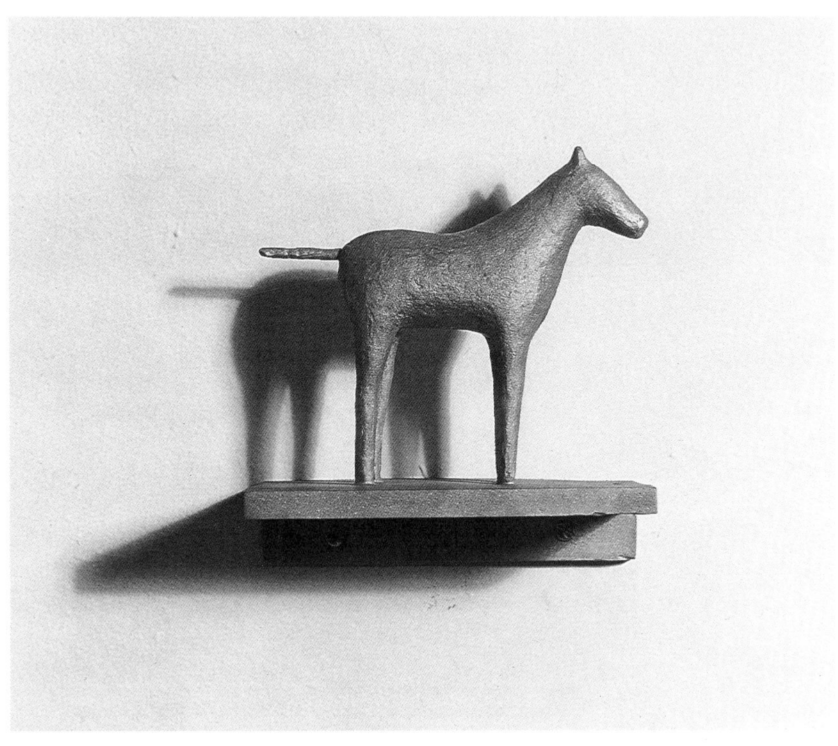

47 Untitled. 1973–74. Bronze, 4¾ x 5 5/16 x 3¼" (12.1 x 13.6 x 8.2 cm). Collection Carol O. Selle

48 Photograph. 1973. Black-and-white print, 8 x 10" (20.3 x 25.4 cm). Collection the artist

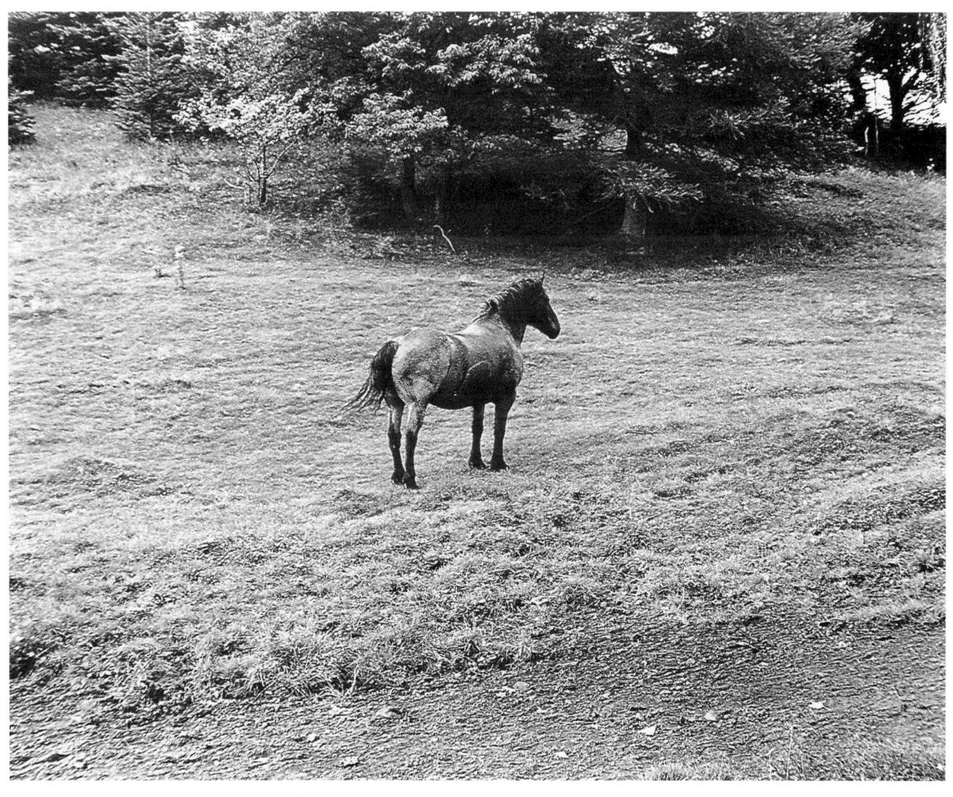

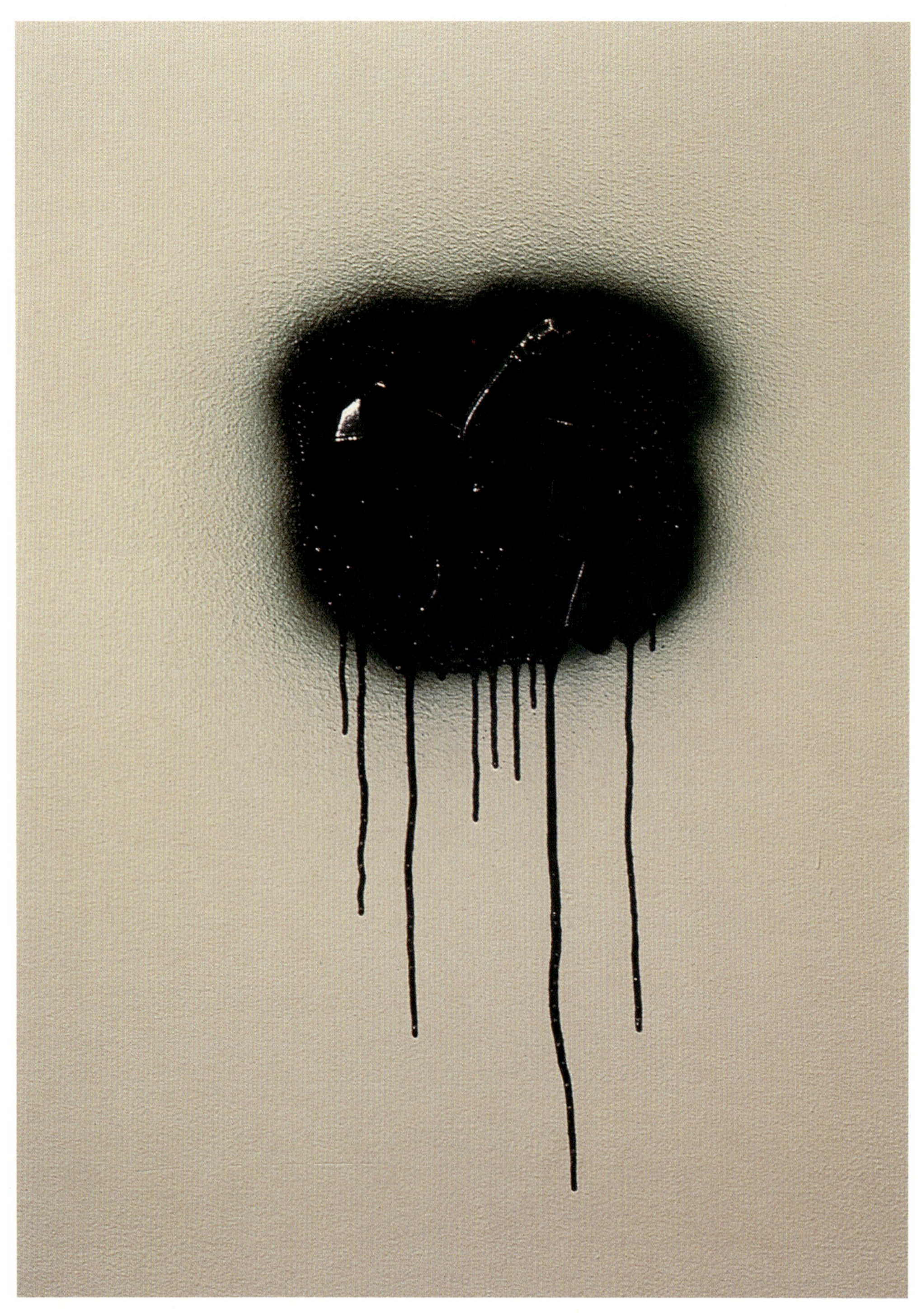

49 Untitled. 1973. Enamel on wood, 6 ½ x 6 ½ x 1⅛" (16.5 x 16.5 x 2.9 cm). Collection Michael Goedhuis

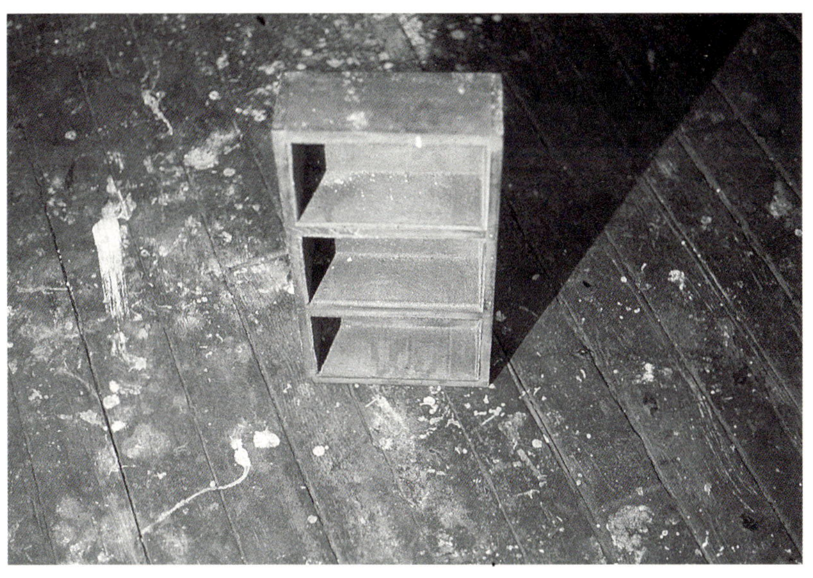

50 Untitled. 1973–74. Cast iron, 16 7/8 x 8 1/8 x 3 1/2" (42.9 x 20.6 x 8.9 cm). Collection the artist

51 Untitled. 1975. Casein on rag paper, mounted on casein on rag paper, 42 x 48" (106.7 x 121.9 cm). Collection the artist

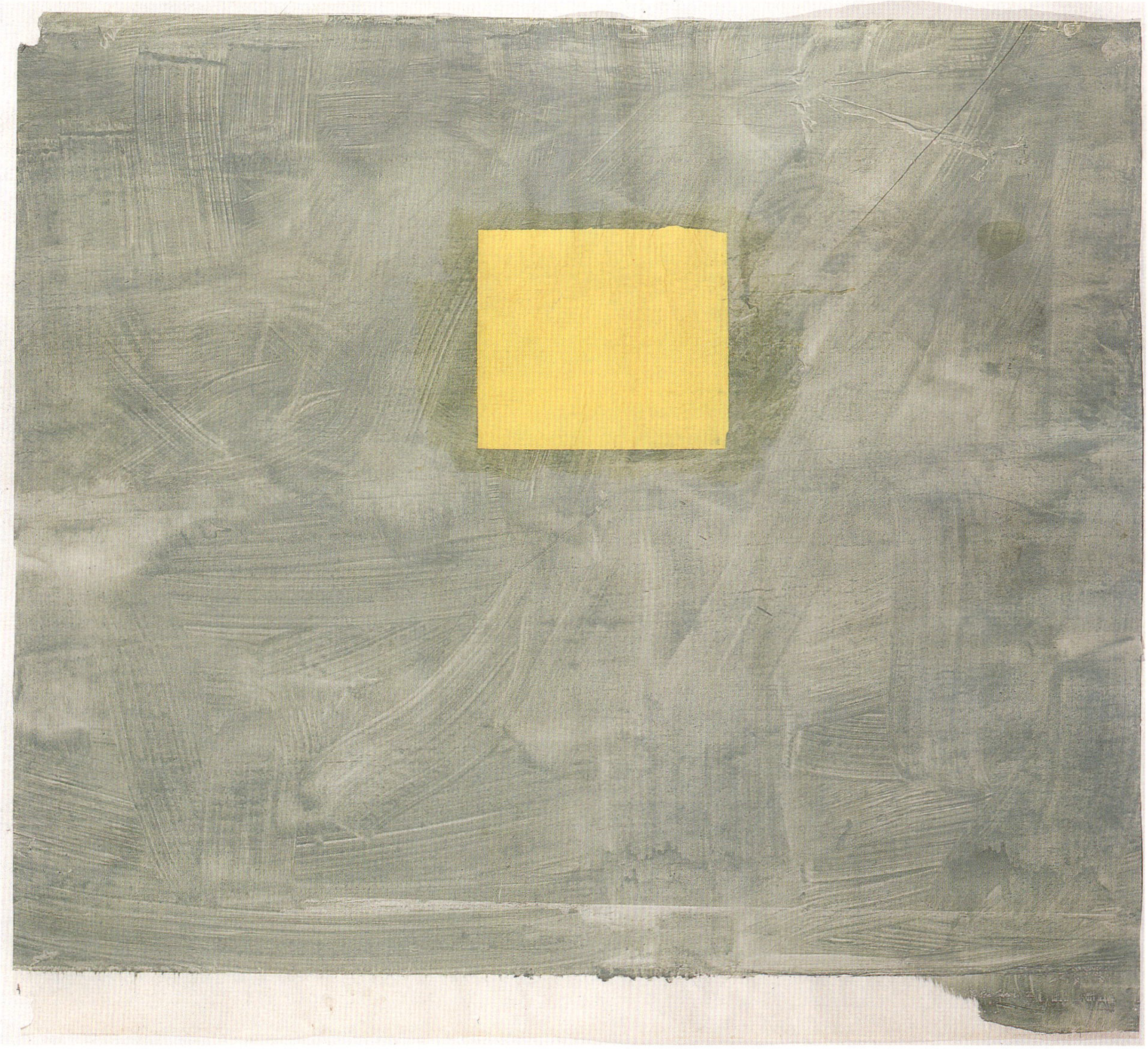

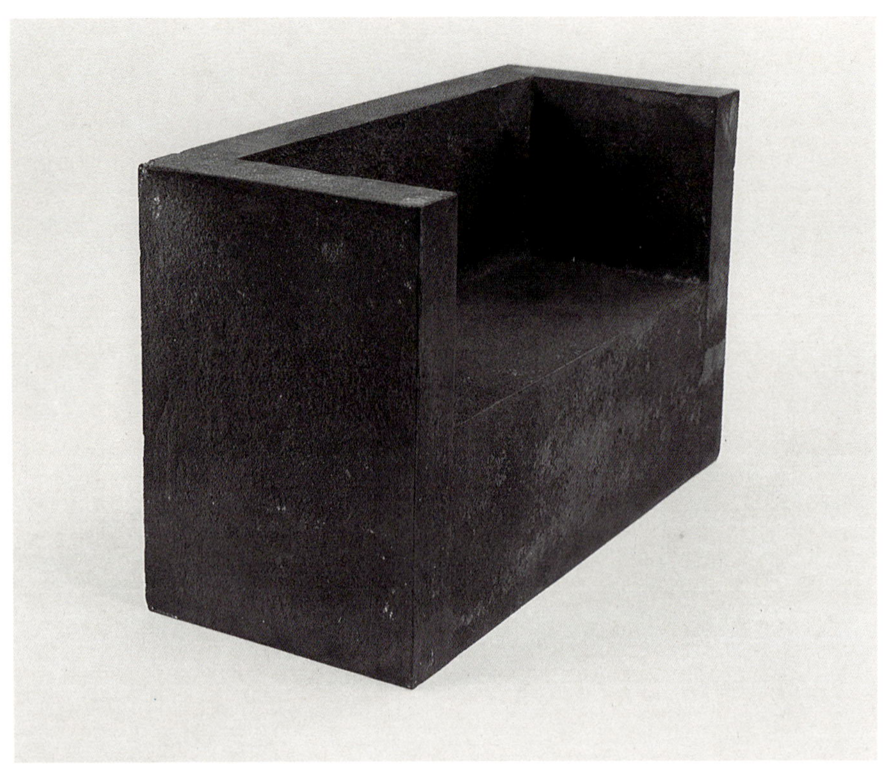

52 Untitled. 1973–74. Cast iron, 4⅛ x 9⅝ x 5 13/16" (10.5 x 20.6 x 8.9 cm). Collection the artist

53 Untitled. 1974. Cast iron, 5⅜ x 6 x 4⅞" (13.6 x 15.2 x 12.4 cm). Solomon R. Guggenheim Museum, New York. Panza Collection, extended loan

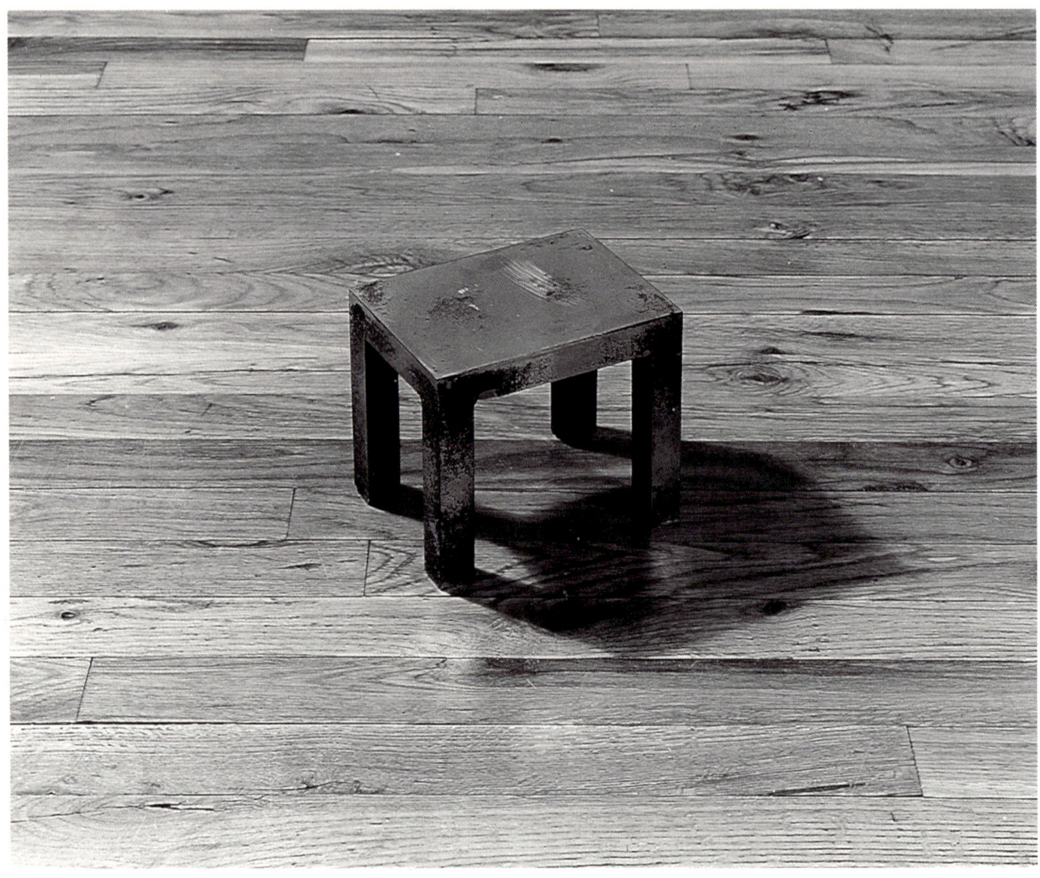

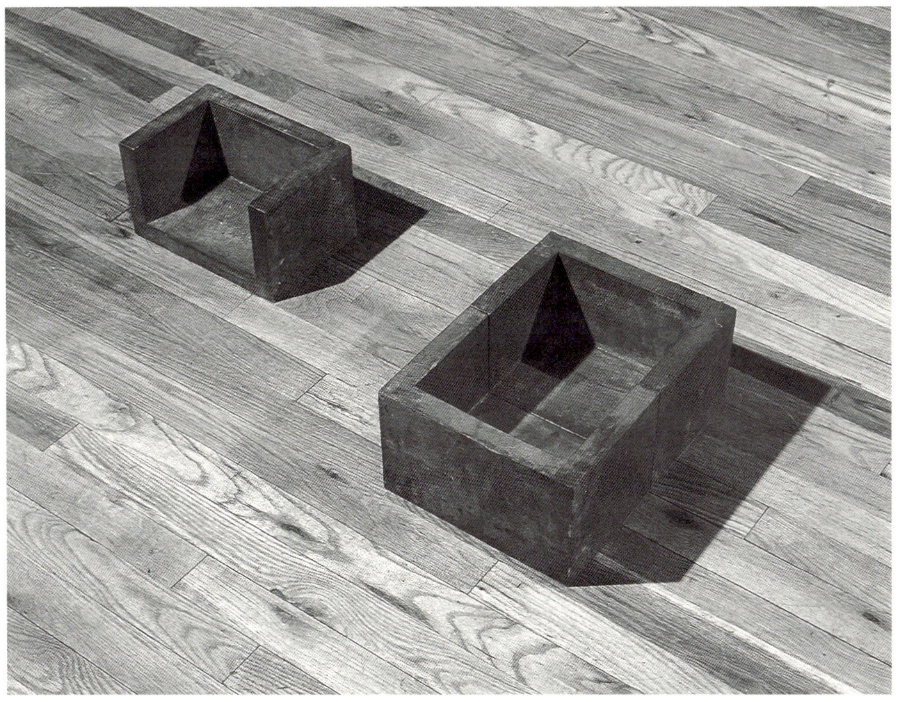

54 Untitled. 1975. Cast iron, 3 units, 5½ x 6½ x 9½" (14 x 16.5 x 24.1 cm) each. Collection the artist

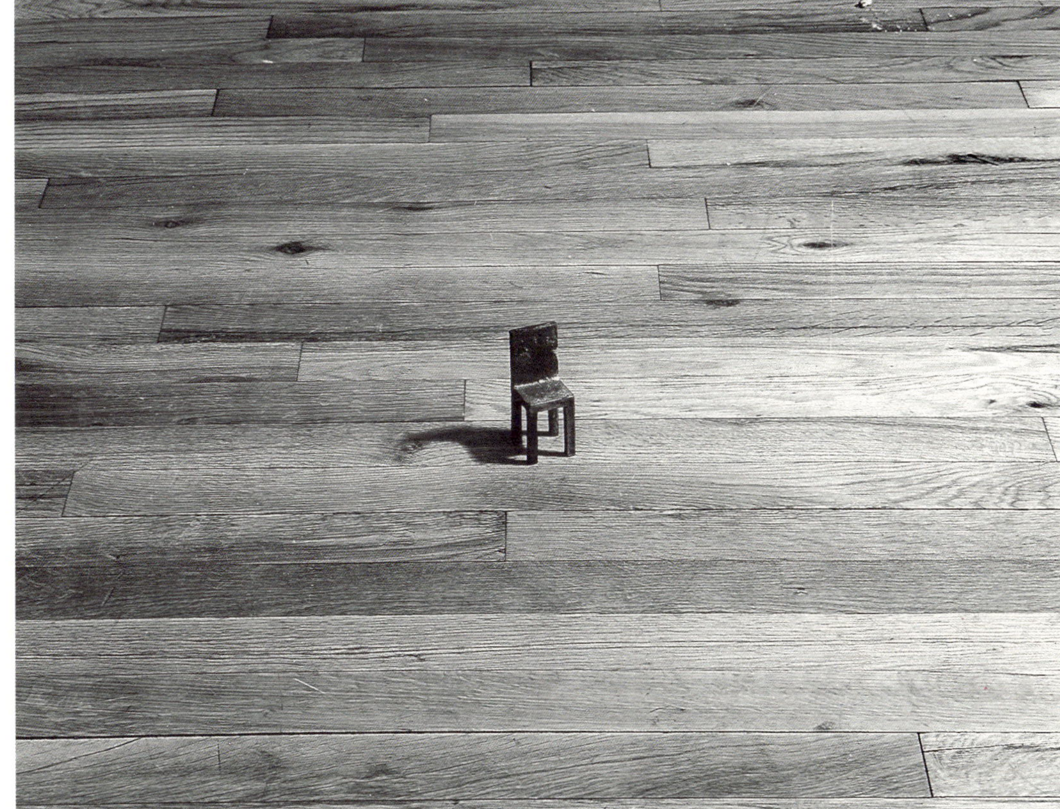

55 Untitled. 1973–74. Cast iron, 3 x 1¼ x 1¼" (7.6 x 3.2 x 3.2 cm). Solomon R. Guggenheim Museum, New York. Panza Collection, extended loan

In a three-part work titled *Family Portrait* (plate 56), Shapiro charts a different dynamic. Describing at once his own and all family relationships, the piece is an anomaly for him. His periodic deviations from a "logical" line of development in his work have been described by the critic Roberta Smith: "His aberrant pieces show that in certain situations or moods, when he's trying to express a new subject or feeling, or outline an ambition before he can make good on it, almost nothing is beneath his dignity." These "aberrant" works point "insistently to the emotional source of Shapiro's art."[19] So too with the small, enigmatic *Family Portrait*. The work is composed of three oil paintings on masonite. The smallest, on the left, is built up with strong brushstrokes of blue, dark gray, and black; a succession of rectangles painted along the edges acts as a frame and occupies most of the painting. The central panel, a square, is composed of black and white painted bands around a white ground. A small, dark spot and the inscription "MOTHER" occupy the white field. The third painting, a smaller square with a gray frame, contains the inscription "SISTER." This triple portrait continues Shapiro's formal investigation of boundaries – borders that limit or affirm identity, and which function as markers between inside and out. It also invokes the complex psychological implications of "boundaries" within the mechanics of family relations. The salient relationship here is between the two larger, lighter, and cleaner "female" elements and the dark, painterly "male" panel. Perhaps Shapiro was trying to locate his own position with respect to the territories occupied by these two "others" – the family's female components.

By 1973, when he painted the triptych, Shapiro had lived through, in less than ten years, a number of major personal events: a marriage, the birth of his only child, and a divorce. And in that year, he met the painter Ellen Phelan, who would become his wife. It is apparent from *Family Portrait* that his female relations were already central to Shapiro's conception of himself as an artist. Now Phelan would play a pivotal role in the formation of a new family structure. Moreover, although Phelan is a painter, both artists would share common values and interests, within a sustaining and critical relationship.[20]

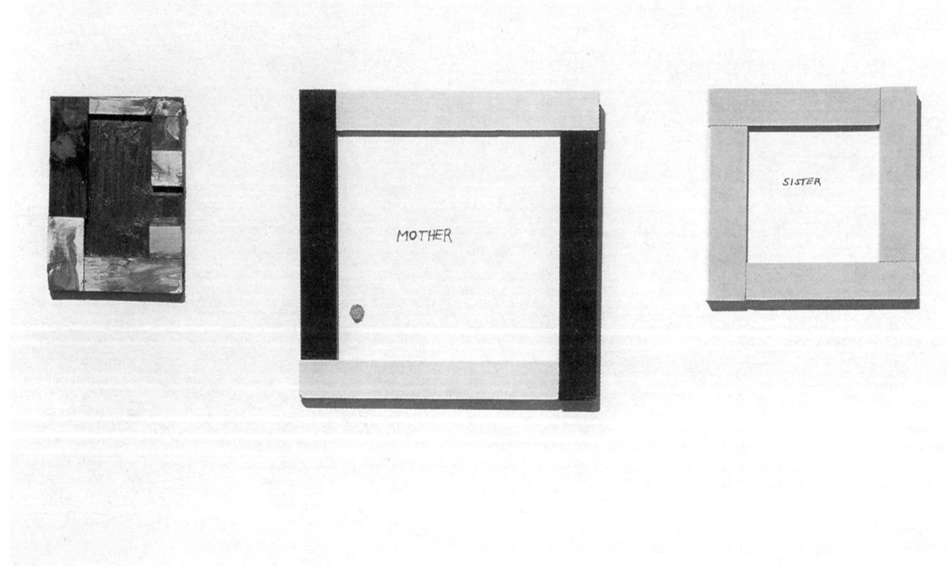

56 *Family Portrait*. 1973. Oil on wood and masonite; 5 x 3½ x ⅜" (12.7 x 8.9 x 1 cm); 8 x 8 x ⅜" (20.3 x 20.3 x 1 cm); 5½ x 5½ x ⅜" (14 x 14 x 1 cm). Collection Jean Pigozzi, Geneva

Houses (1973–97)

"All great simple images reveal a psychic state," Gaston Bachelard has written. "The house, even more than the landscape, is a 'psychic state,' and even when reproduced as it appears from the outside, it bespeaks intimacy."[21] Shapiro's choice of the house as a major theme allowed him to explore a full range of emotions through a simple image – one of the most personal and familiar.

Perhaps recalling the siting of Indian temples, and in keeping with the Minimalist approach, each of Shapiro's houses is presented within a complete unity. Yet the small structures, positioned on seemingly immense floors, inevitably carry with them associations from the domestic realm. Shapiro's houses are psychological models situated in a dynamic space.

Solitary Houses

A small house from 1973–74 (plate 57) poses, even in its apparent simplicity, a multitude of questions. Is it just a seven-sided object, or is it a house? And if it is a house, what is its meaning? This solitary structure, sealed in a heavy mass of cast iron, asserts its presence in the world by charging the space around it. Through its dark compression into such a small size, it creates its own gravitational field. A much less impenetrable, less daunting house (plate 10) is covered with a coat of intense blue paint through which the bronze surface occasionally emerges. By painting it, Shapiro brought out its pictorial and imaginary qualities, awakening the magic, and the fright, associated with strange houses in childhood fairy tales.

As he developed the theme, Shapiro made small-scale structures that correspond to psychological space. Mostly set on the floor, the elementary geometric forms become more urgent. Shapiro conducts his formal and spatial inquiry by combining different materials and their colors in one work (plate 58), extending or subtracting parts of the house form (plate 59), and otherwise varying size and scale. The houses range from the basic, simple house (plate 60) to the more expansive (plate 61). A more complex pairing of solitary houses (plate 62), one sitting on the floor and the other projecting from the wall, emphasizes their illusionistic and conceptual aspects.

Drawings of the seventies (plates 63, 64) speak of similar procedures: questioning sizes, emptying or filling shapes, measuring effects of colors, experimenting with positions. Curiously, these drawings are larger than the sculptures they are related to; the sheet of paper receives the forms, as the floor does in Shapiro's three-dimensional work.

57 Untitled. 1973–74. Cast iron, 5½ x 6⅝ x 5" (14 x 16.8 x 12.7 cm). Private collection. For another view of this work, see plate 3.

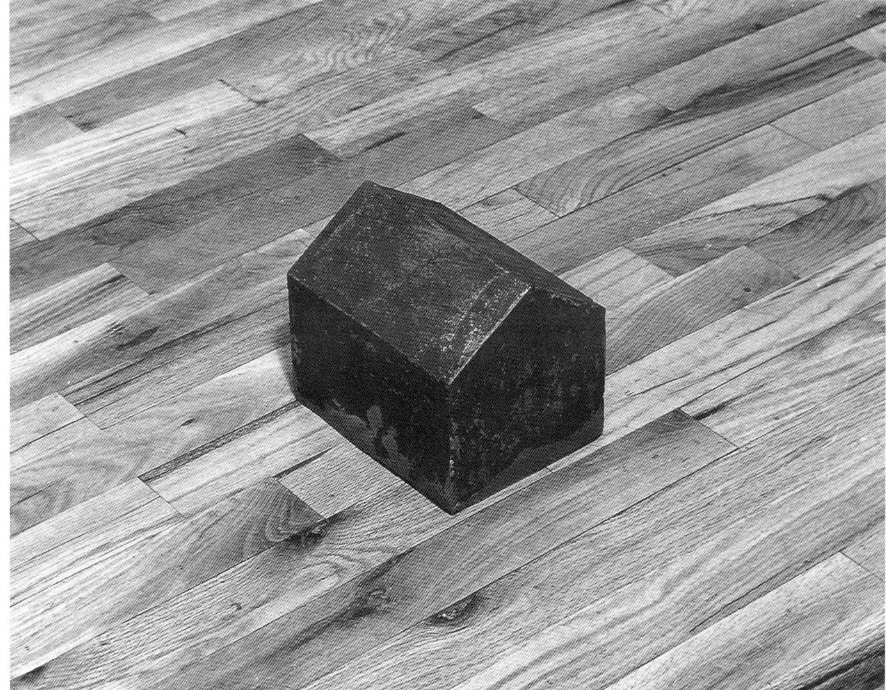

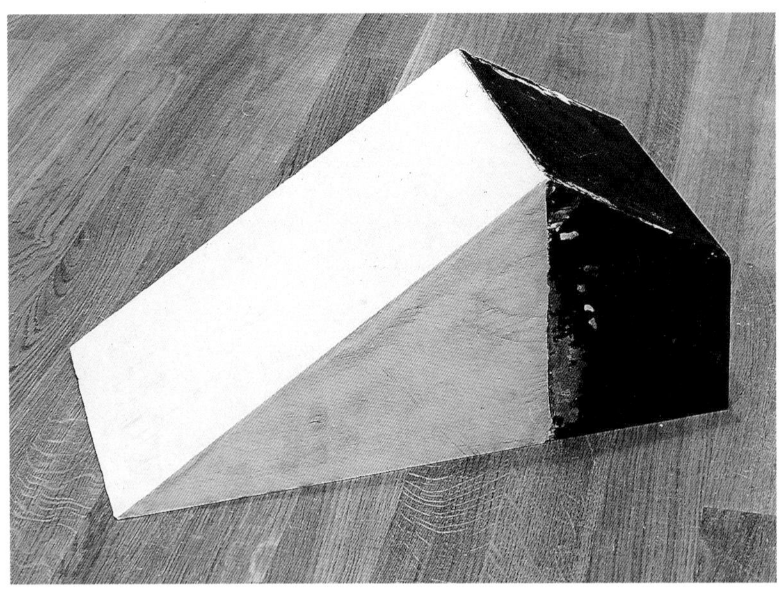

58 Untitled. 1976. Plaster and cast iron, 7¾ x 17⅜ x 8⅝" (19.7 x 44.1 x 21.9 cm). Collection the artist and Paula Cooper

59 Untitled. 1974. Bronze, 9½ x 14¾ x 14⅝" (24.1 x 37.5 x 37.1 cm). Private collection

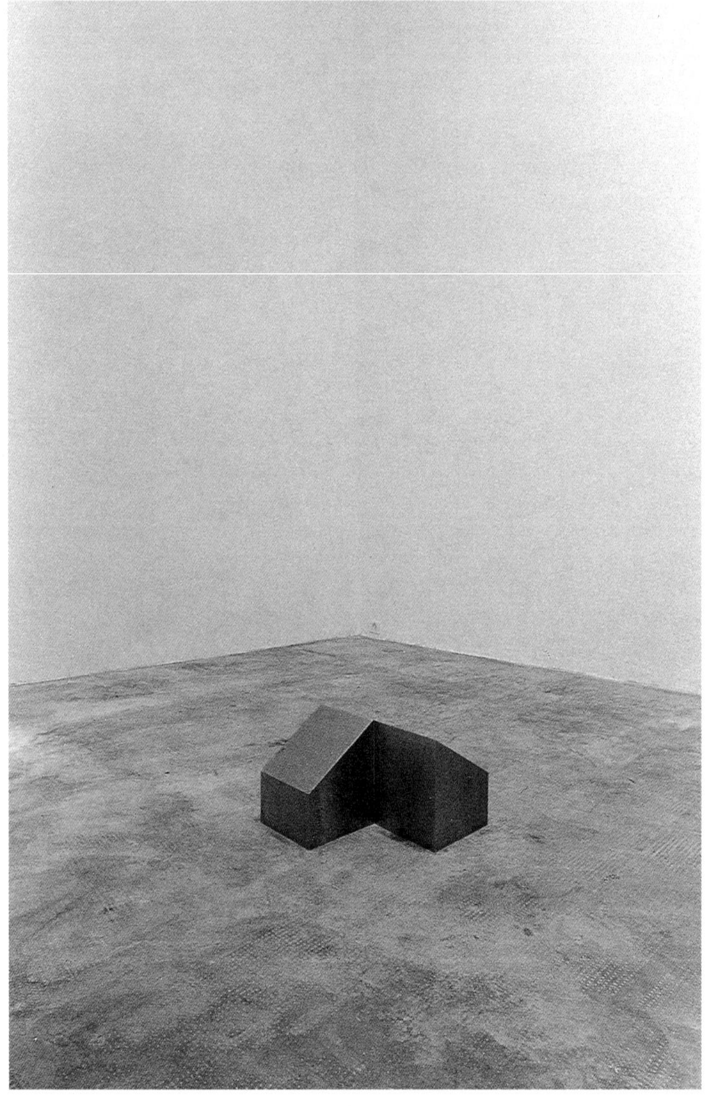

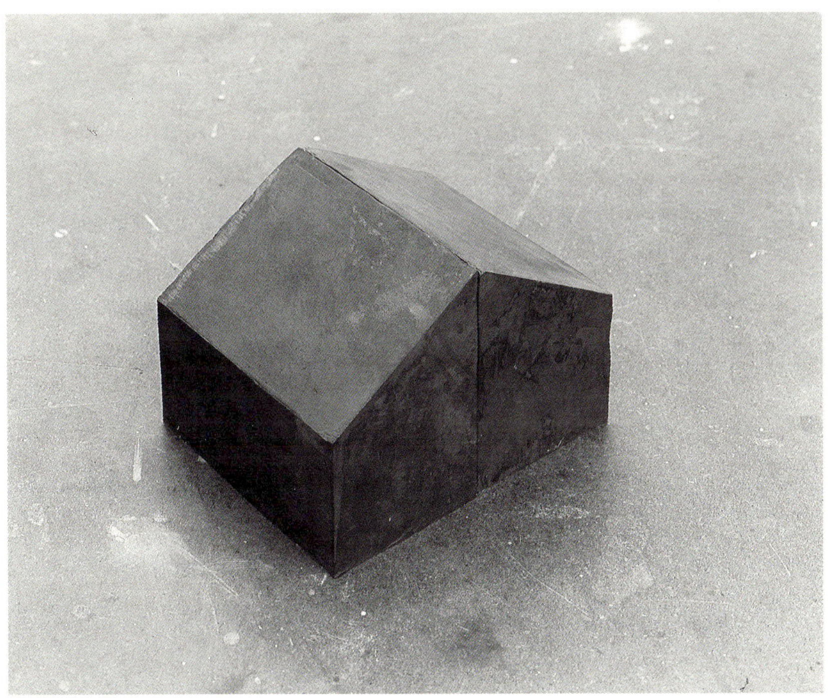

60 Untitled. 1975. Cast iron, 7 ½ x 10 ¾ x 8 ½" (19.1 x 27.3 x 21.6 cm). The Museum of Contemporary Art, Los Angeles. The Barry Lowen Collection

61 Untitled. 1974. Cast iron, 6 ⅝ x 16 x 15 ¾" (16.8 x 40.6 x 40 cm). Collection the artist

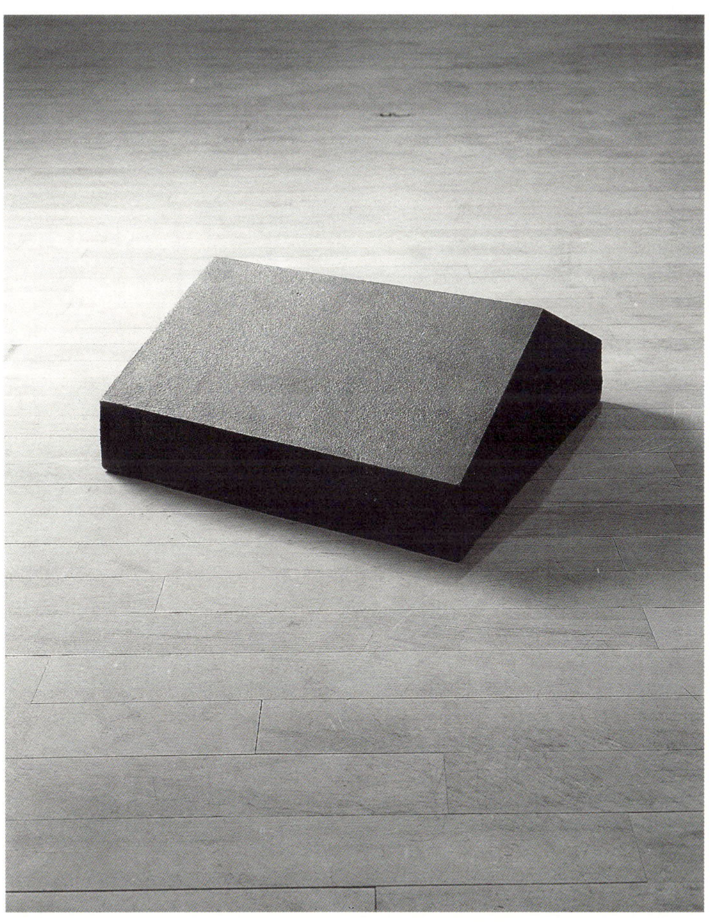

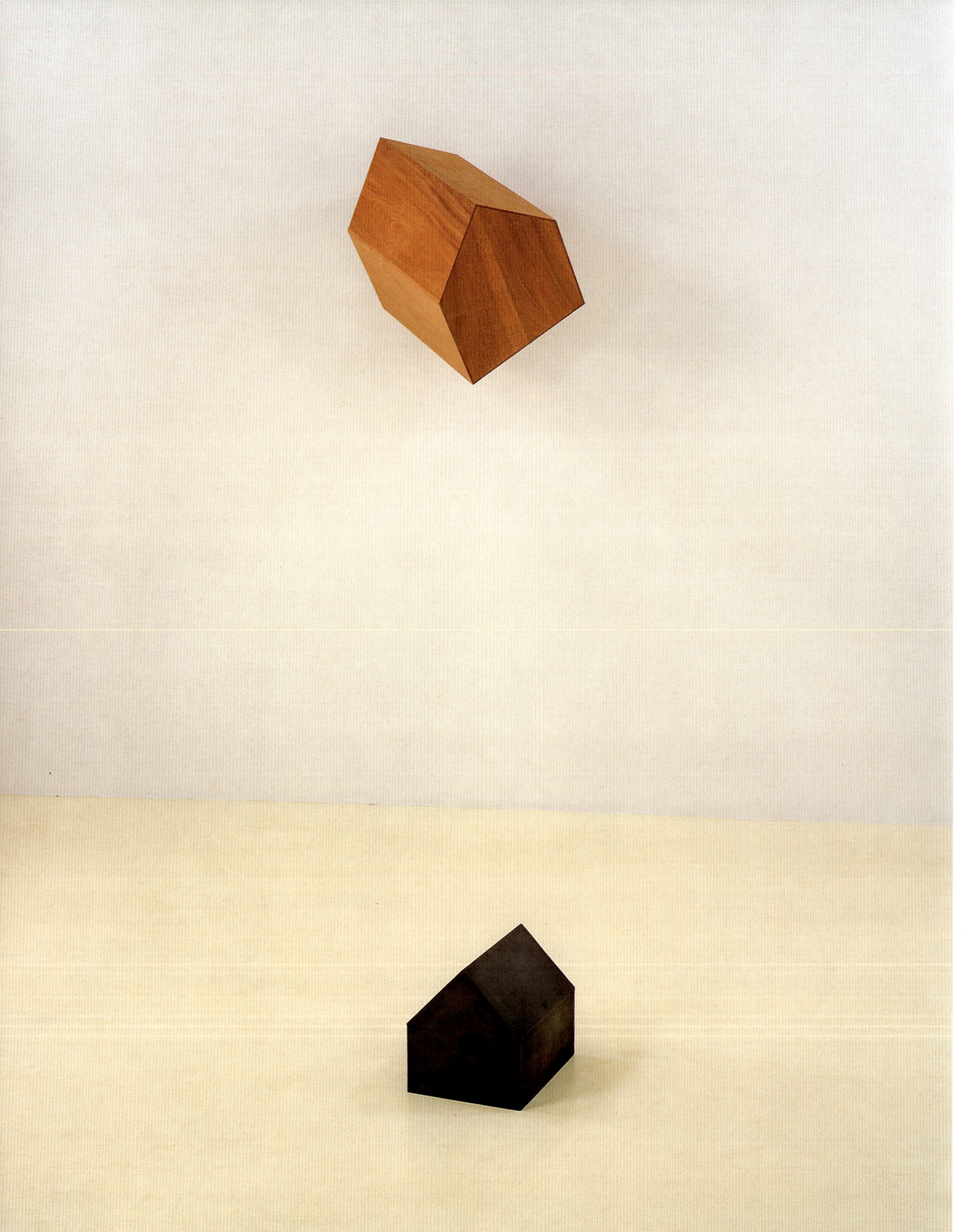

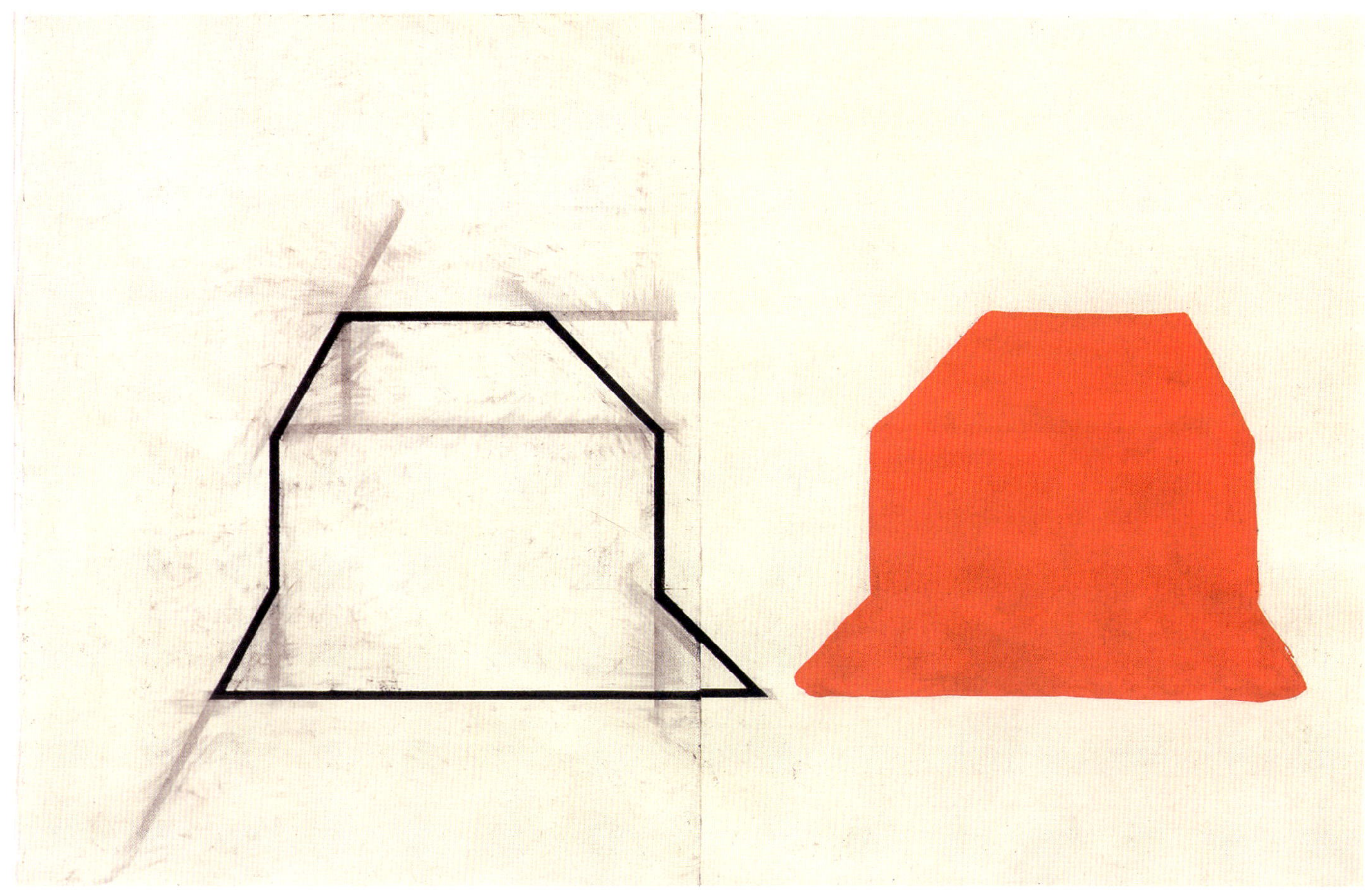

63 Untitled. 1979. Charcoal and gouache on paper, 23 1/16 x 36 1/2" (58.6 x 92.7 cm). Private collection

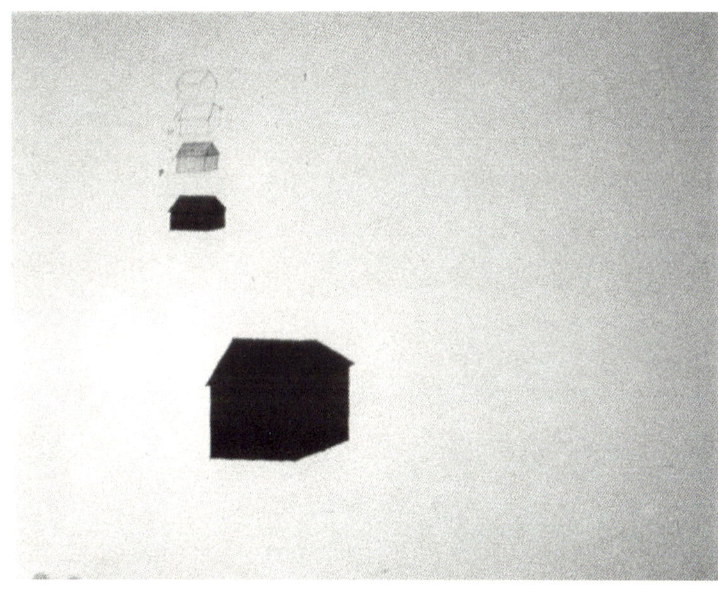

64 Untitled. 1973. Ink, pencil, and color pencil on paper, 15 1/4 x 19 1/2" (38.7 x 49.5 cm). Private collection

OPPOSITE:

62 Untitled. 1996–97. Cast iron and wood, 10 3/4 x 13 1/4 x 10 1/4" (27.3 x 33.7 x 26.0 cm) and 31 x 29 1/4 x 31 3/4" (78.7 x 74.3 x 80.6 cm). Collection the artist

65 Untitled. 1973–74. Cast iron, shelf: 1¼ x 6¾ x 4" (3.8 x 17.1 x 10.2 cm); house: 2⅞ x 3⅜ x 2⅜" (7.3 x 8.6 x 10.2 cm). Collection Robert and Meryl Meltzer

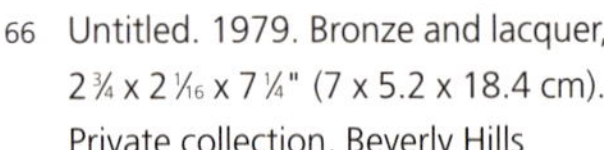

66 Untitled. 1979. Bronze and lacquer, 2¾ x 2 1/16 x 7¼" (7 x 5.2 x 18.4 cm). Private collection, Beverly Hills

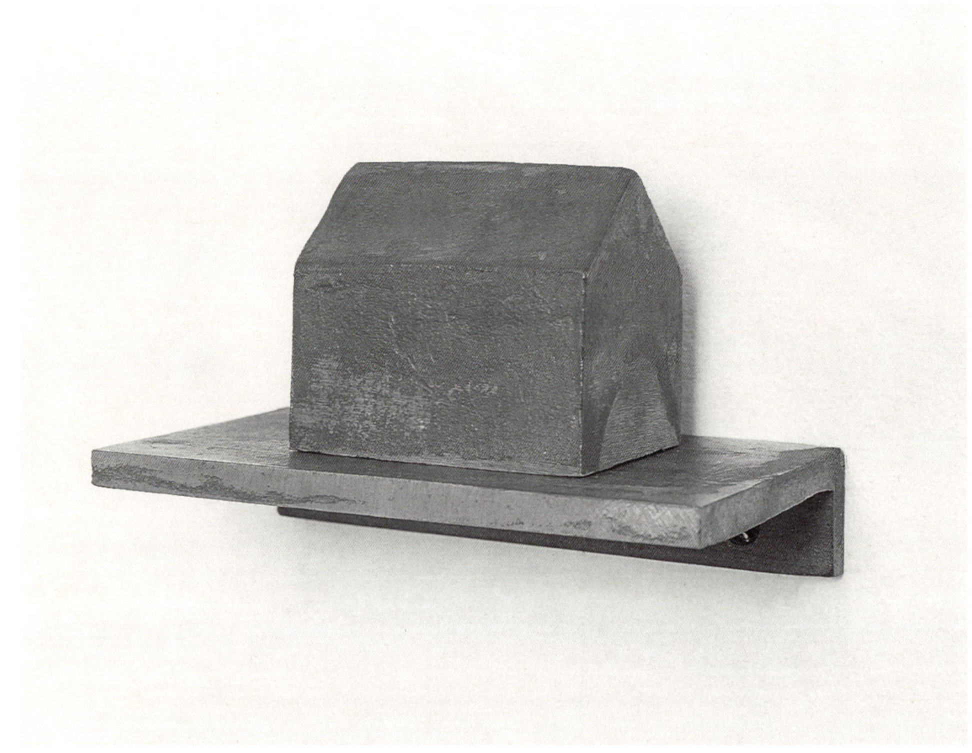

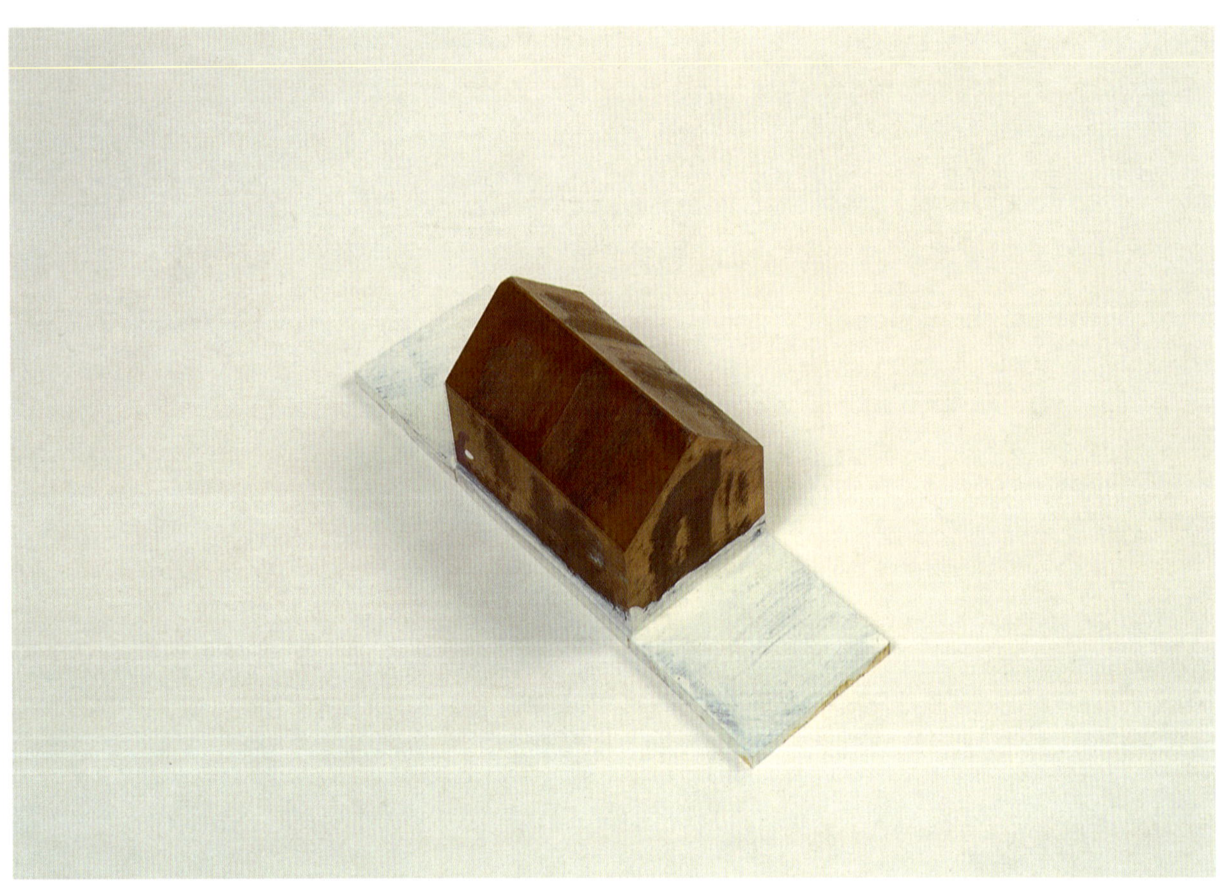

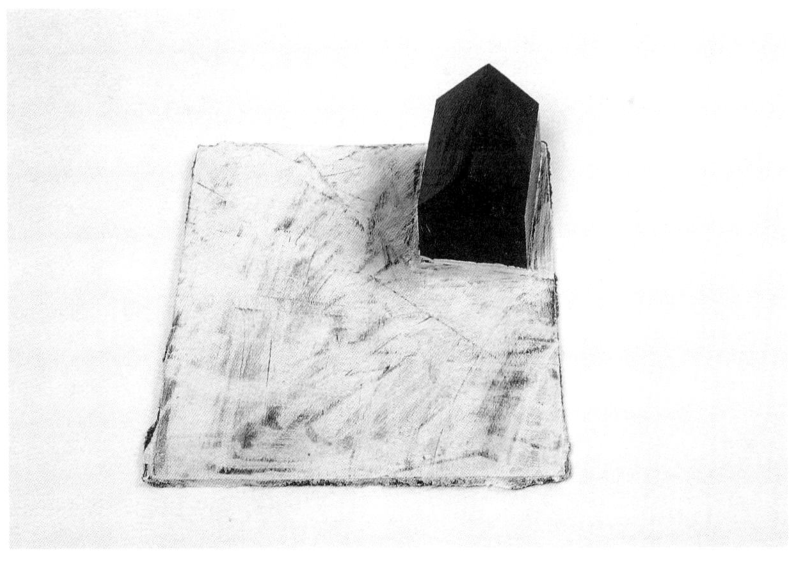

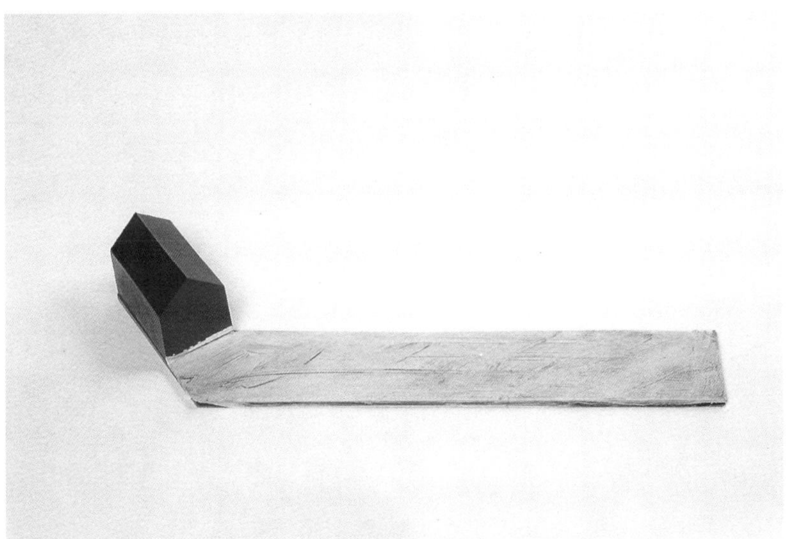

Houses and Fields

Alone or in sets, some houses are placed on surfaces that extend the house forms themselves and grow to become fields or passageways. These serve as low bases and hence offer an opportunity for new formal development.

Here, we should recall Shapiro's earlier use of the shelf as the simplest way to create a base, and thus a sense of distance. In that respect, the diminutive house from 1973–74, on a small shelf (plate 65), generates considerable psychological tension: it appears immediate and close, being placed at eye level; and yet at the same time it seems distant, because of its small size and its elevated position, like a house on the horizon.

In a group of four sculptures from 1979 (plates 66–69), a field around the house becomes a substitute for the floor. Solitary bronze houses are placed in the center, in a corner, or at the end of a colored plane. They sit, slightly elevated from the floor, atop white or black lacquered surfaces. The large, expressive strokes of paint on these fields, and sometimes on the houses, propel these works toward the pictorial.

67 Untitled. 1979. Bronze and lacquer, 2½ x 7⅝ x 8½" (6.4 x 19.4 x 21.6 cm). Collection Richard Artschwager

68 Untitled. 1979. Bronze and lacquer, 2¾ x 2¾ x 16½" (7 x 7 x 41.9 cm). Collection Ivy Shapiro

69 Untitled. 1979. Bronze and lacquer, 2¾ x 5⅝ x 8¼" (7 x 14.3 x 21 cm). Courtesy Barbara Mathes Gallery, New York

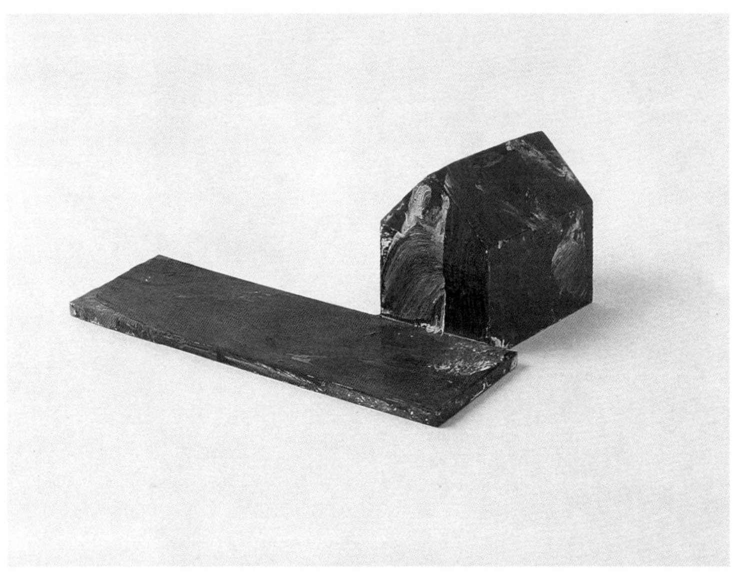

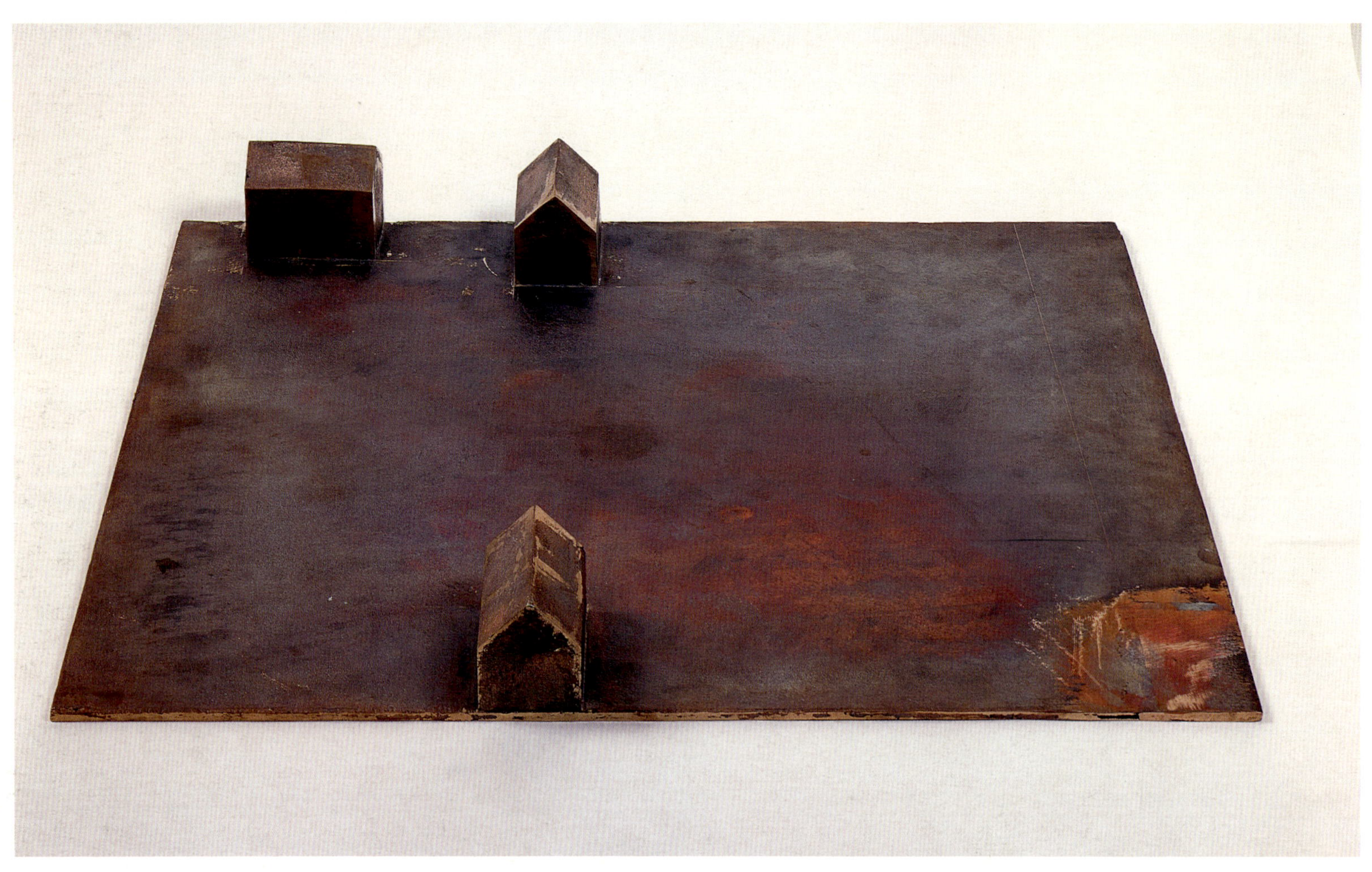

70 Untitled. 1979. Bronze (edition 1/3), 3 1/8 x 24 3/8 x 19 3/8" (7.9 x 61.9 x 49.2 cm). Collection Vera G. List

OPPOSITE:

71 Untitled. 1975–76. Bronze on wood base (edition 1/2), 3 1/2 x 28 3/4 x 21 1/2" (8.9 x 73 x 54.6 cm). Whitney Museum of American Art, New York. Purchase, with funds from Mrs. Oscar Kolin

Other works convey a "painterly" attitude toward the surface without actually being painted. In some cases, such as the work shown in plate 70, there is an actual marking of the field's surface that results from the artist removing a house and shifting it to another location. In addition, amid the same work's configuration of three small houses, the variegated expanse of unpainted bronze provides its own color field. In another bronze (plate 71), a small house occupies the center of a large field, which is placed on a wood table. This elevation frees the house from the horizontal grip of the floor, isolating and magnifying it. At the same time, the surrounding plane is a celebration of dense, fluctuating, brown metallic color, a voluptuous, viscous surface.

Shapiro's elaboration of these flat surfaces suggests the importance of drawing within his creative method. He turns to drawing when he encounters certain formal problems. The pictorial path is faster, more flexible and controlled, and it is therefore one of his major tools for inventing solutions and developing his sculptural work. Shapiro's confidence in drawing may come simply from the fact that a sheet of paper is more circumscribed and manageable than space in the round. Shapiro's own physical engagement in the process of drawing is, moreover, less demanding than it is with sculpture. Drawing can thus be a means to clarify visual ideas; it is a more direct "record of [his] thought,"[22] an informative counterpart to his three-dimensional work, and its indispensable companion.

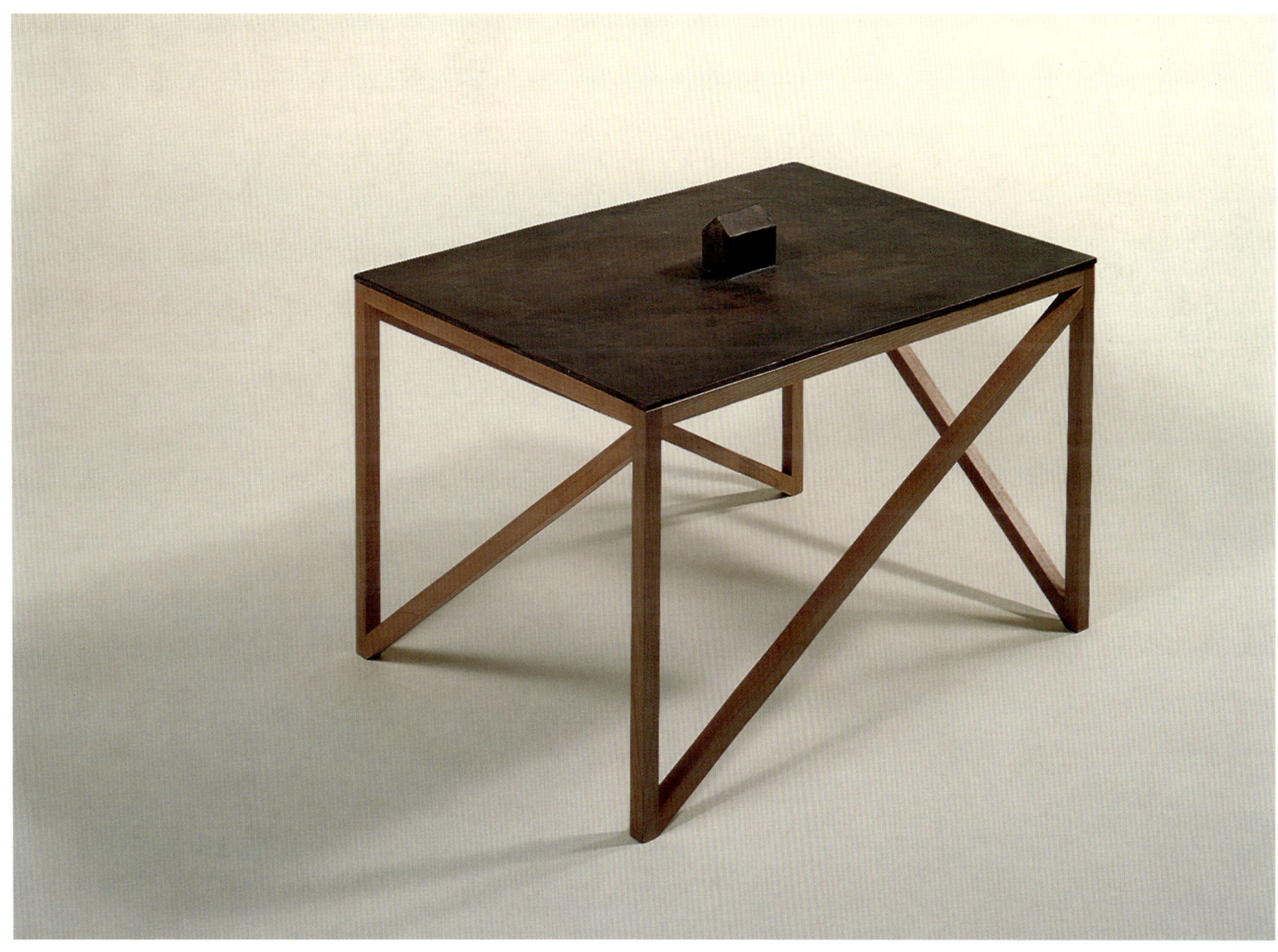

Houses with Openings

Another series of structures introduces a new configuration: the surfaces are broken by apertures, and the interiors are excavated by partly hidden passageways (plates 72–76). Here, the interior, negative space is emphasized. The openings, varying in size and location, offer entry into a previously impenetrable mass. Through them the viewer is invited to make inquiries into the psychological implications of the void within.

One heavy, cast-iron sculpture (plate 72) is like a bunker, protecting its interior from view. The opening of another cast-iron house (plate 74), in contrast, leads one to look inside, at a dark interior with two small openings that admit light, like windows. Indeed, the difference in scale between the large, central opening and the two smaller ones beyond creates an illusion of deep space within. A related plaster house (plate 75) is a simple white box with two dark apertures. However, another plaster form (plate 76) has its interior laid open – a white stillness of underground rooms and corridors, seemingly dead and frozen. It is tempting to interpret such works as representational, but their focus on space, material, and form affirms them as essentially abstract sculptures.

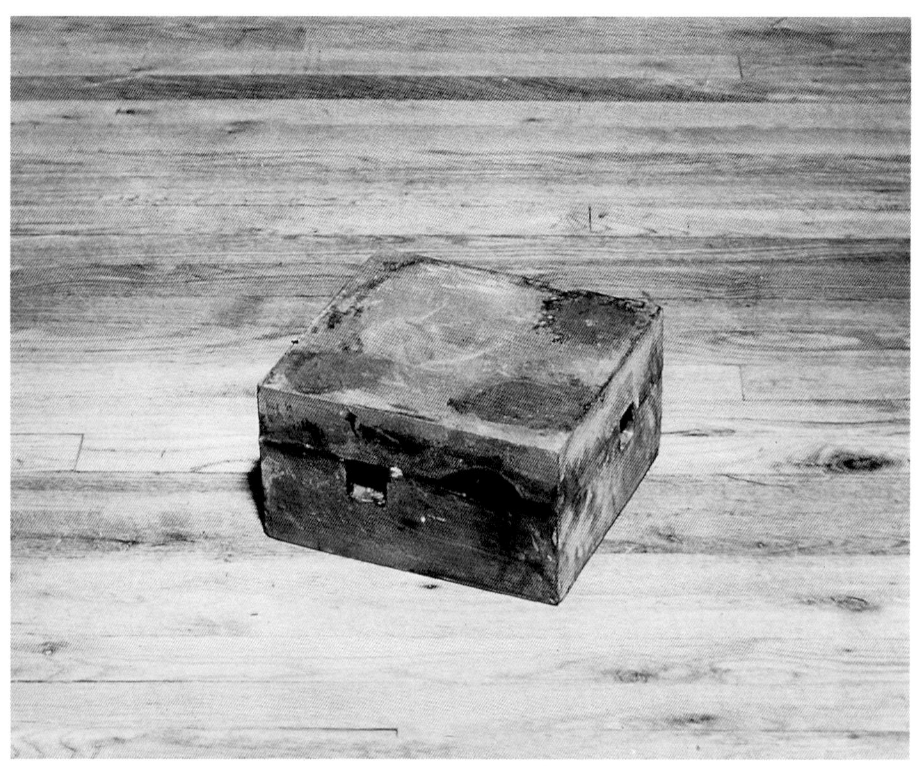

72 Untitled. 1975. Cast iron, 5¼ x 10 x 9⅜" (13.3 x 25.4 x 23.8 cm). No longer extant

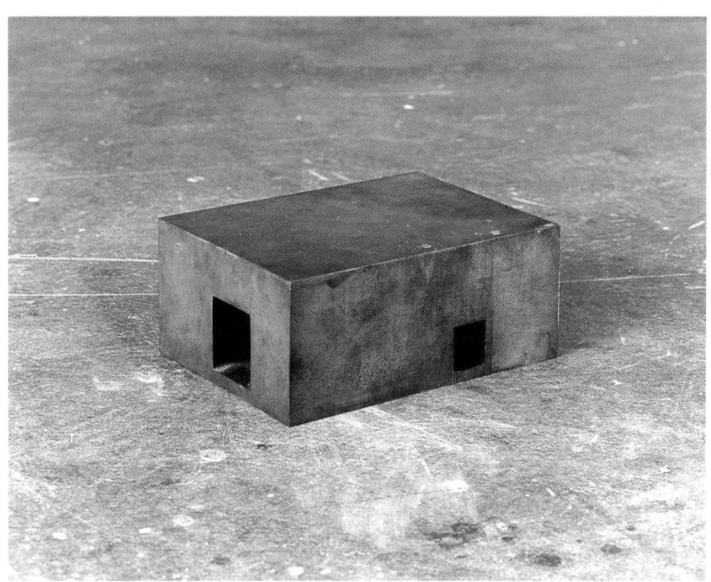

73 Untitled. 1975. Cast iron (edition 1/2), 2⅝ x 4¾ x 6¼" (6.7 x 12.1 x 15.9 cm). Dallas Museum of Art. Matching grants from the National Endowment for the Arts and The 500, Inc.

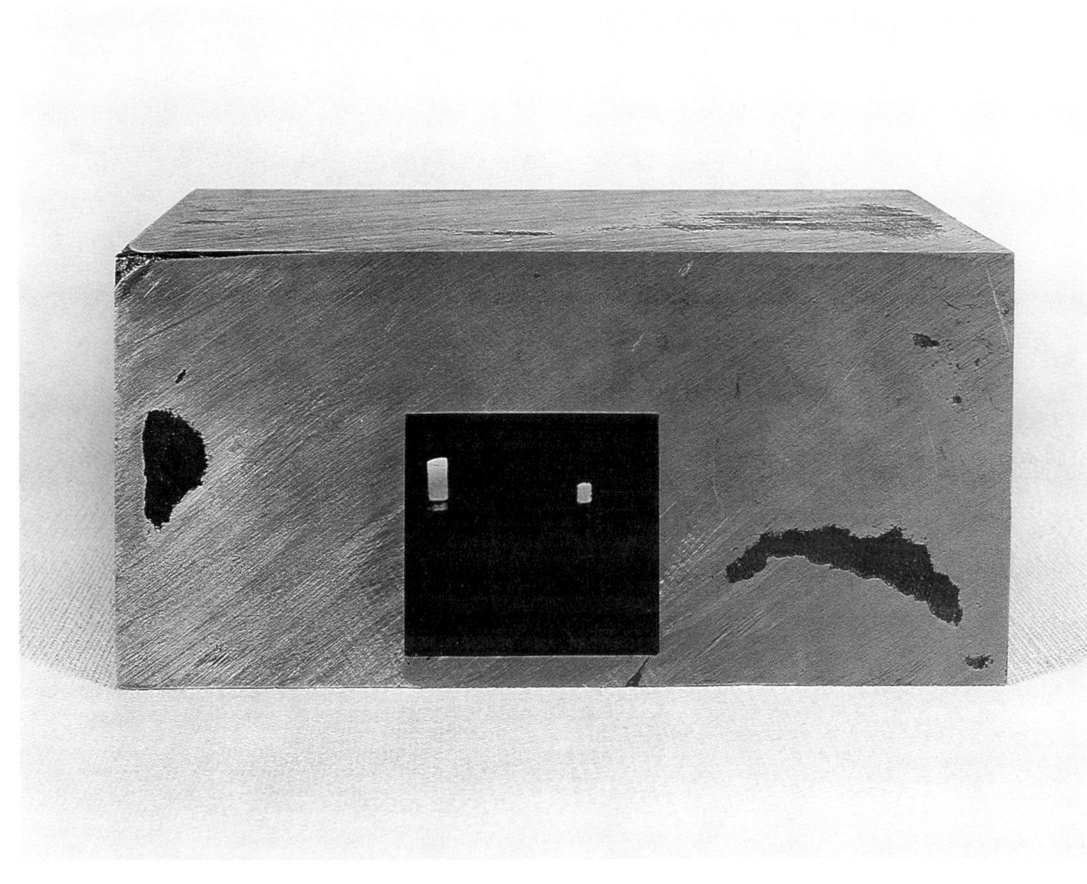

74 Untitled. 1975. Cast iron (edition 0/1), 2⅝ x 4³⁄₁₆ x 5⅝" (6.7 x 10.6 x 14.3 cm). Collection the artist

75 Untitled. 1974–75 (reconstructed 1992). Cast plaster, 5¼ x 9½ x 10" (13.3 x 24.1 x 25.4 cm). Collection the artist

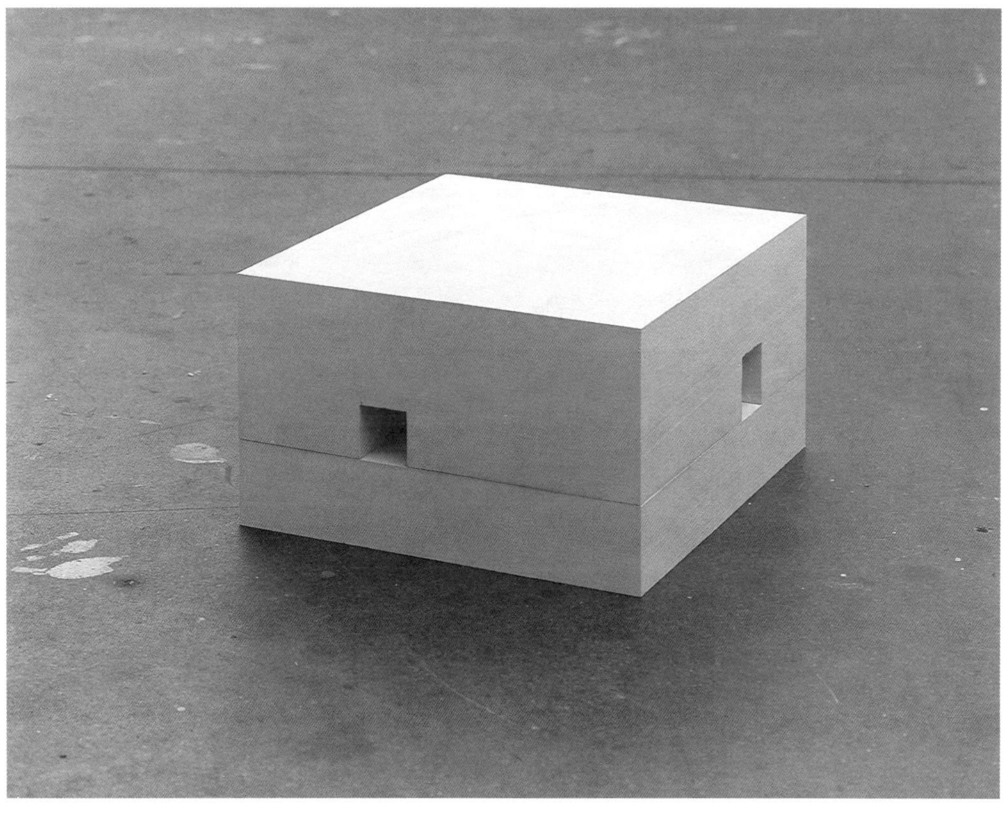

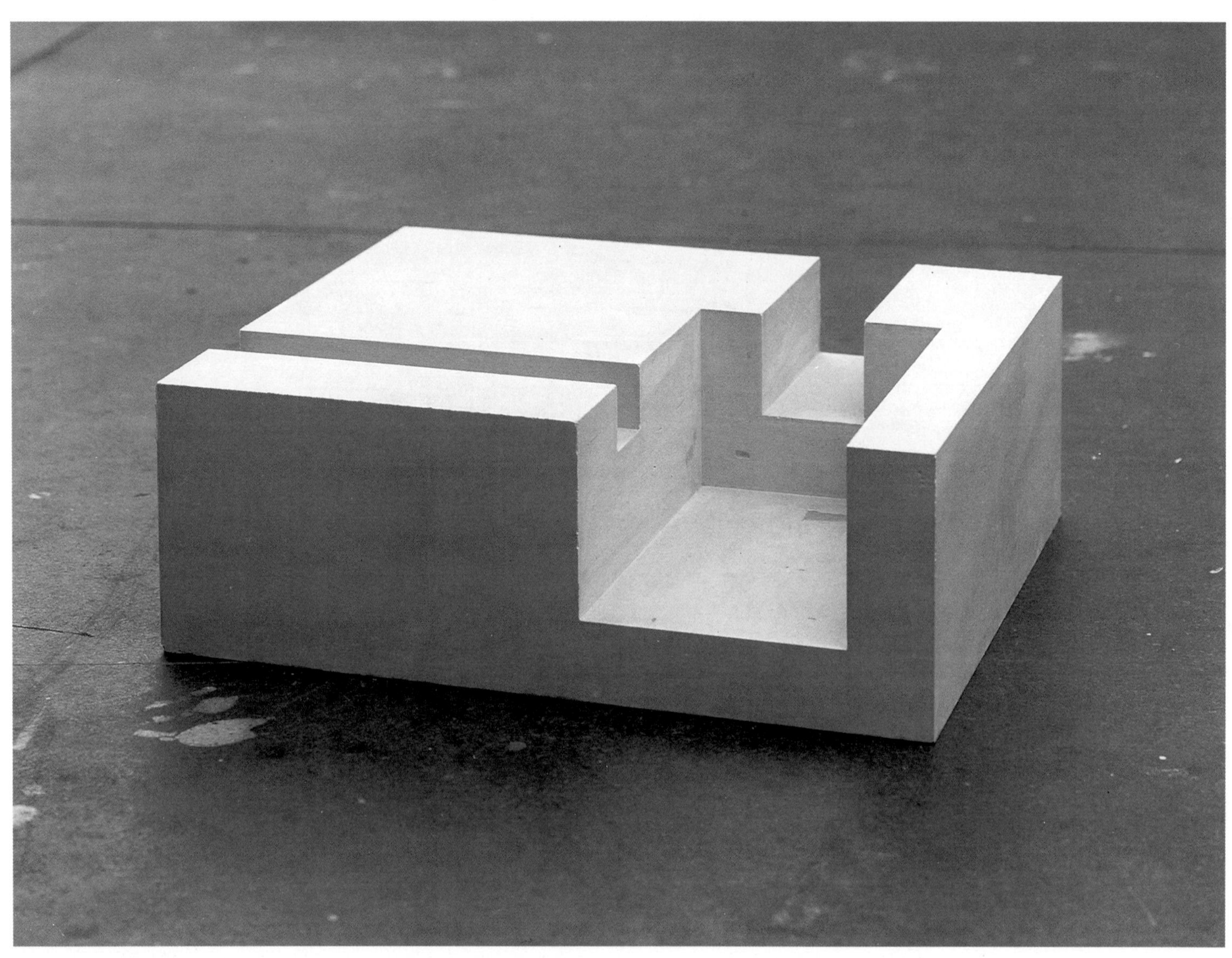

76 Untitled. 1975 (reconstructed 1992). Cast plaster, 4¾ x 12⅛ x 14¼" (12.1 x 30.8 x 36.2 cm). Collection the artist

Sight Lines

A very small work of glued and pinned wood from 1972–73 (plate 77) elaborates Shapiro's idea of passageways as routes for the pursuit of thoughts. Two identical open triangles, facing in opposite directions, abut each other at the edge of a doorway, to which they are pinned horizontally. This unusual installation permits a double reading: one a frontal vision of a largely closed object, and the other a side view into an object with a fragile, open passage. The viewer must stand in the doorway – another passage – to see the work fully.

In another sculpture with the passageway as a focus (plate 79), two mute bronze houses face each other from either end of a long wood beam. They are confined to a one-track, back-and-forth exchange.

A bronze house from 1974 on a long shelf (plate 78) responds to the artist's need to go beyond the image of the house and turn his thoughts in a new direction. The path leading away from the house stops where it intersects with the projected line of the roof's slope, however, and drops straight down. Shapiro's use of a projected line to mark off the limits of real space evokes Giacometti's powerful *Pointe à l'oeil* (figure 9) and *The Nose,* both conceptually and formally, especially if one reads the house as a surrogate head and visualizes the path as a projection of thought or speech. The long shelf, unusual in Shapiro's work, beckons the viewer to follow it back to the house/head at its other end. This passage is both physical and mental, and it can thus be at once precise and unbound. Paradoxically, this and other works making use of sight-line ideas depend on such rigid structures as rods, shelves, and bases to facilitate the free passage of thought.

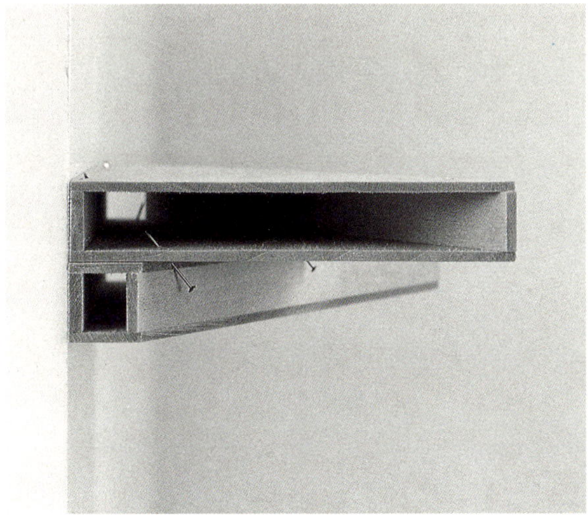

77 Untitled. 1972–73 (reconstructed 1992). Basswood, 1 x 3 x 4" (2.54 x 7.6 x 10.2 cm). Collection the artist

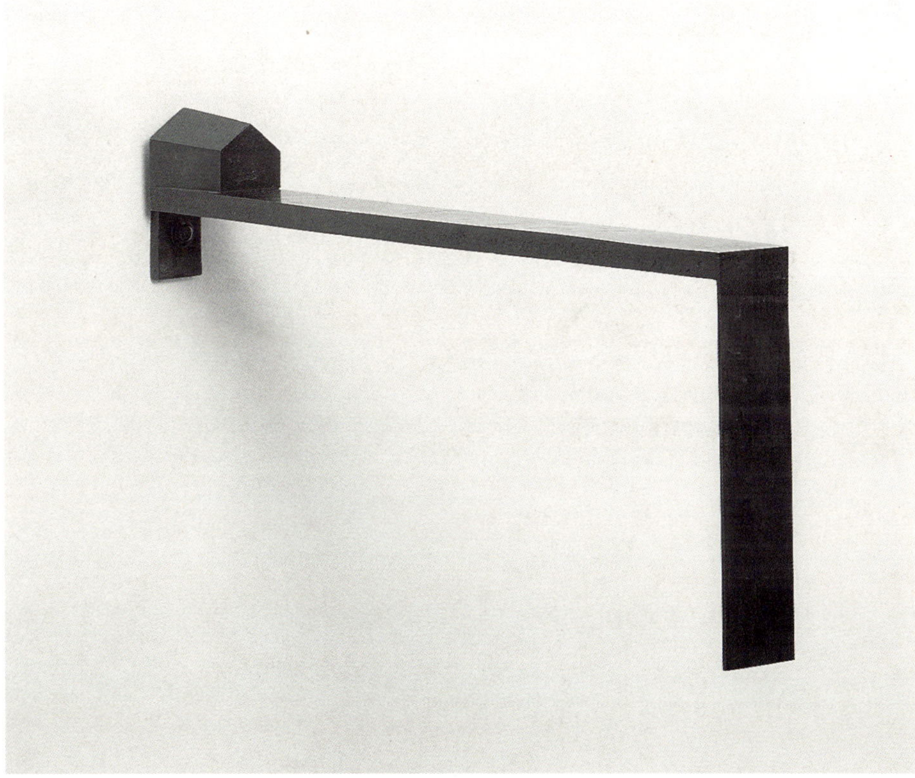

78 Untitled. 1974. Bronze (edition 2/3), 12⅞ x 2½ x 28⅛" (32.5 x 6.4 x 71.5 cm). The Museum of Modern Art, New York. Purchased with the aid of funds from the National Endowment for the Arts and an anonymous donor

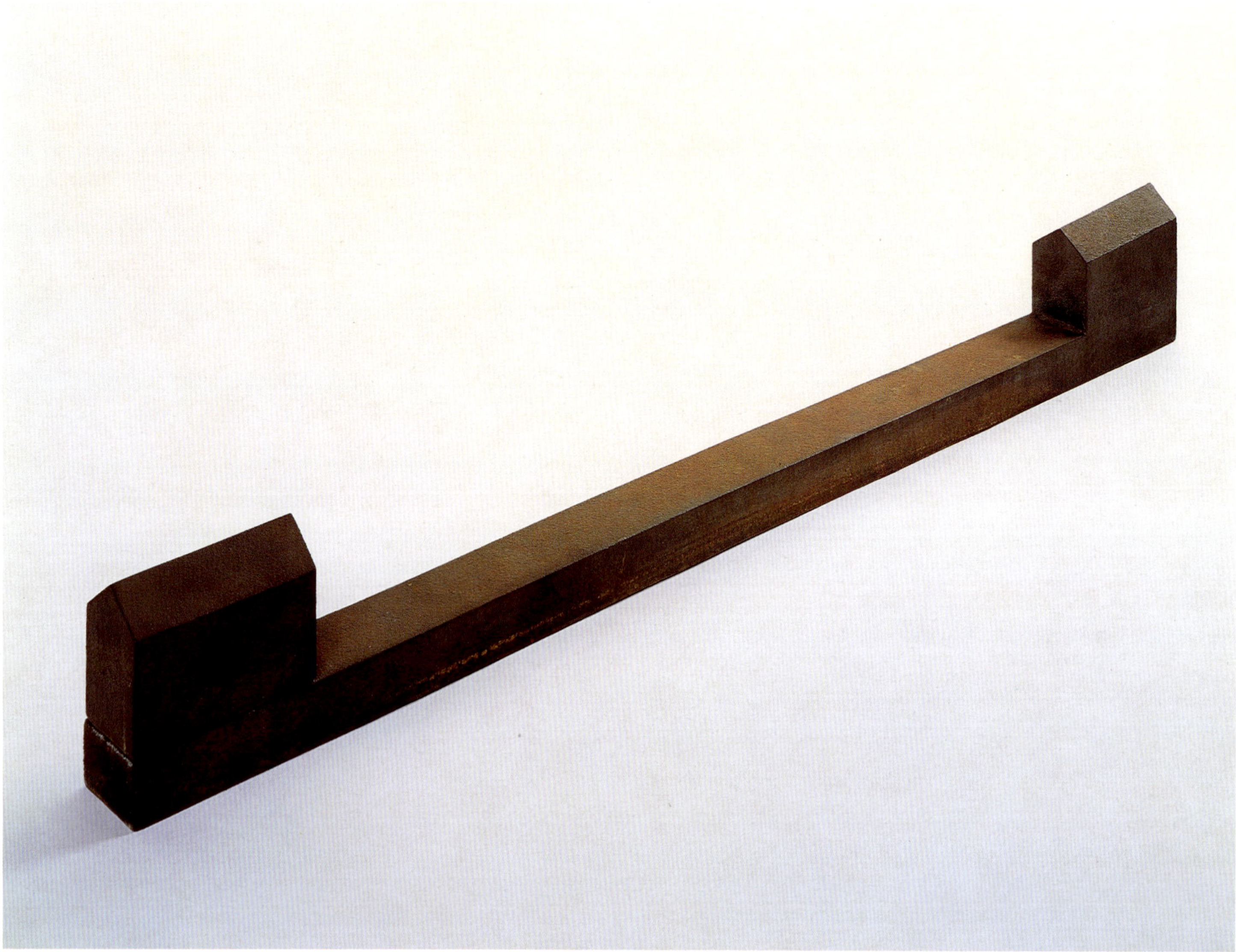

79 Untitled. 1974. Cast iron on wood base, 4 ½ x 35 x 2 ¼" (11.4 x 88.9 x 5.7 cm). The Eli and Edythe L. Broad Collection

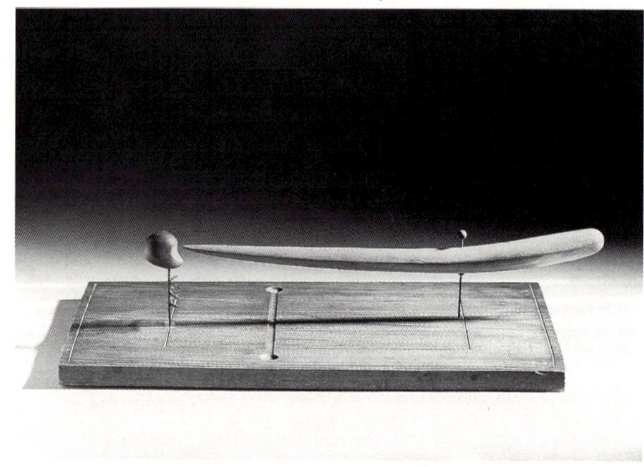

Fig. 9 Alberto Giacometti. *Pointe à l'oeil*. 1932. Wood and metal, 4 ⅞ x 22 ⅞ x 11 ⅝" (12.5 x 58.1 x 29.5 cm). Musée National d'Art Moderne, Centre Georges Pompidou, Paris

Extensions (1974–81)

As Shapiro continued his investigation of passages and openings, they became more complexly associative in their meanings, as in the 1976 work *Chasm* (plate 80). Four thick walls create a narrow shaftway open on two sides, the entrance to a cul-de-sac. At the same time, the use of iron gives the angular forms a sense of masculine aggressiveness. The sexual force animating this sculpture results from the ambiguity of its shape, which the artist says is "about entering and being entered."[23]

Another sculpture featuring a hollow shaft (plate 81) also invites a dual reading. Shapiro has described this work as "androgynous. The inside and outside share the same space."[24] The rectangular bronze slab, installed as a shelf at eye level, is punctured at the back by a dropped shaft that comes to a dead end. The view into the elevated shaft being hidden, our attention is drawn instead to the complex relationship between interior and exterior spaces. Years later, the idea of hidden space is reinterpreted in a related work (plate 82), a table whose four corner legs are, again, hollow shafts.

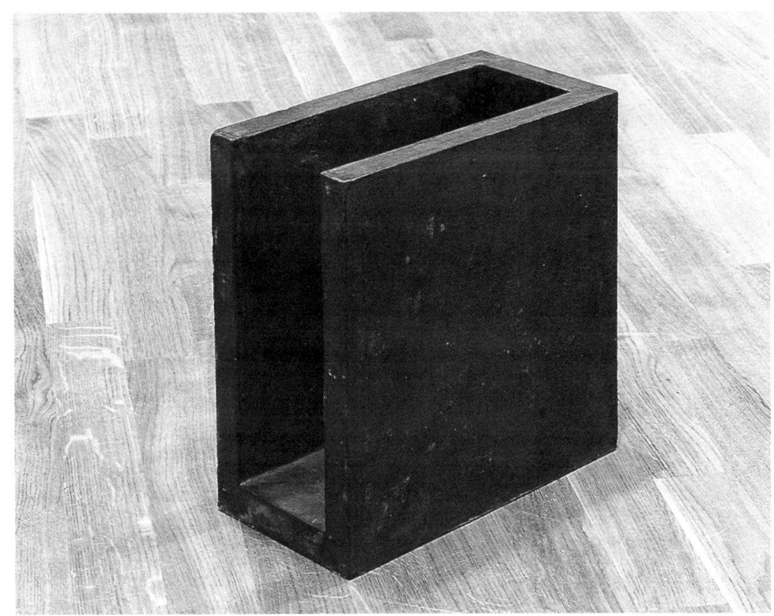

80 *Chasm*. 1976. Cast iron (edition 2/3), 12 x 12 x 6¼" (30.5 x 30.5 x 15.9 cm). Private collection

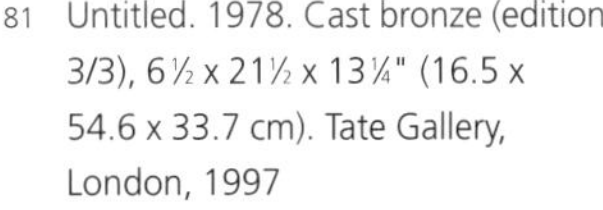

81 Untitled. 1978. Cast bronze (edition 3/3), 6½ x 21½ x 13¼" (16.5 x 54.6 x 33.7 cm). Tate Gallery, London, 1997

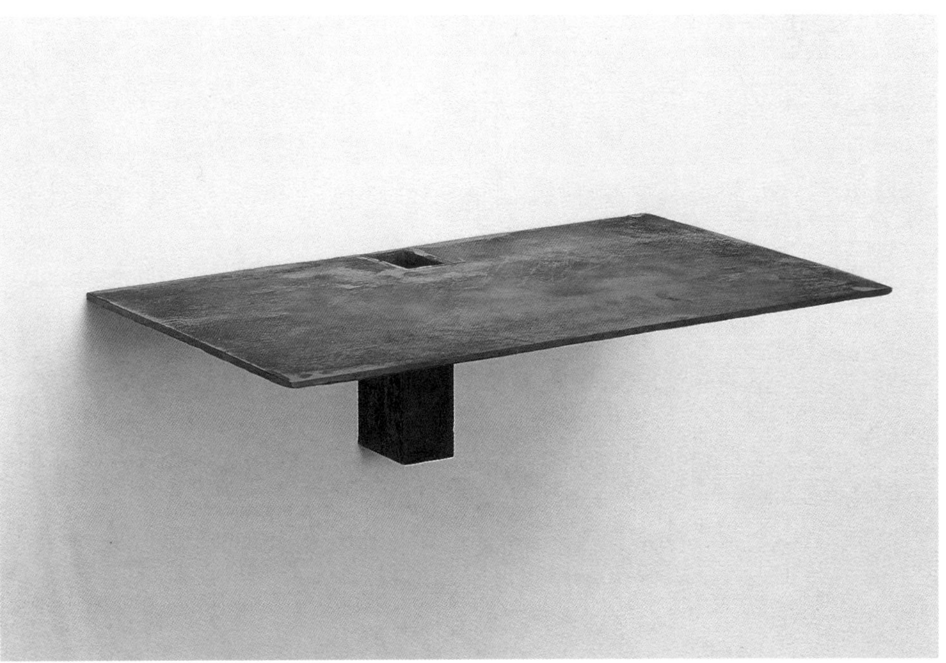

Shapiro reworks the relationship between positive and negative space in both drawing and sculpture. In charcoal and chalk drawings from 1978 and 1979 (plates 83–85), spaces are defined by frames, demarcated zones, and stepped patterns. The white surfaces of the large sheets of paper are heavily marked by the intense manipulations to which the forms have been subjected. The boundaries that delimit space produce different rhythms, according to the length, breadth, and intensity of the drawn lines.

Shapiro's sculptures, meanwhile, increased significantly in size and confirmed his drive to break with monolithic form. Two bronzes from 1977 (plates 86, 87) recline along the floor. The center of each is a constructed articulation, a "knot" from which walls extend to interact with real space. The heavy, dark masses imply the possibility of a contracting and an unfolding movement. Another work placed on the ground (plate 88) widens and narrows to reveal hollow and solid areas. This eccentric sculpture, recalling the houses with openings, has an elaborate, angular corridor. A plaster study (plates 89, 90) shows how the empty space of such a passageway can be transformed into a solid structure, continuing the dialogue between positive and negative space.

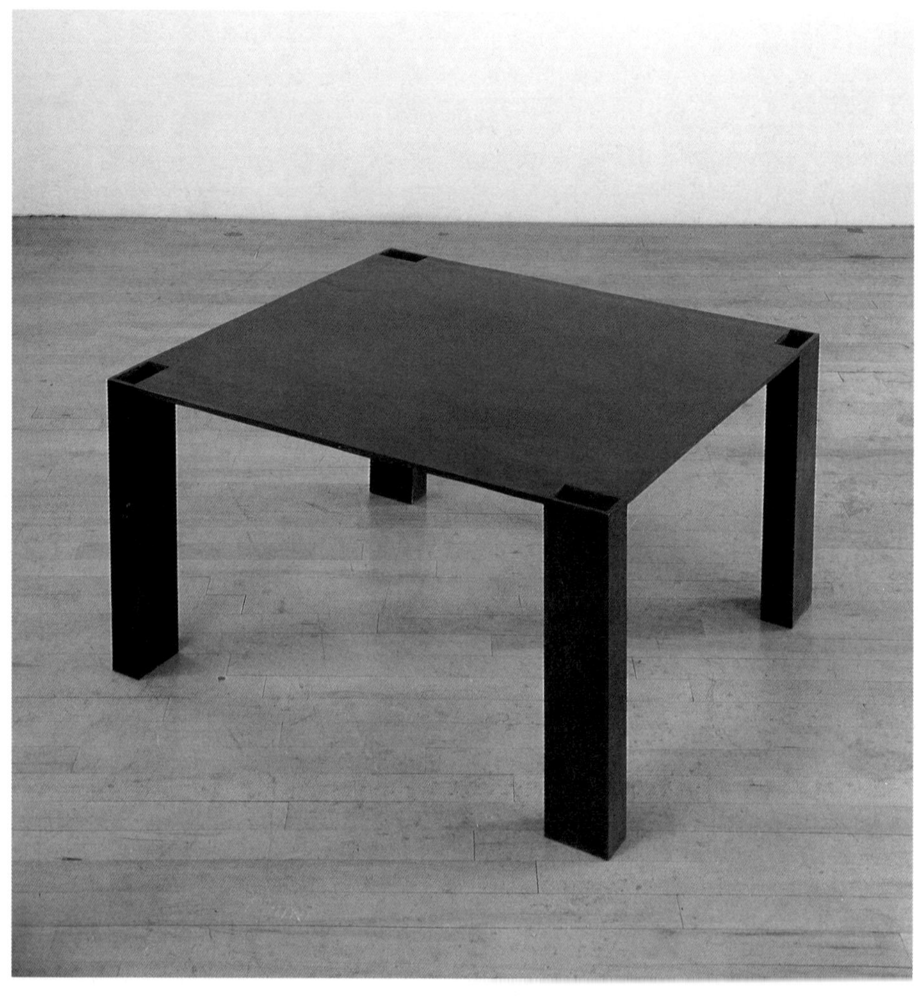

82 Untitled (table). 1994. Bronze (edition of 8 with 1 prototype), 17 x 31½ x 29" (43.2 x 80 x 73.7 cm). Collection Michael and Judy Ovitz, Los Angeles

83 Untitled. 1978. Chalk on paper, 30 x 22 ¼" (76.2 x 56.5 cm). The Metropolitan Museum of Art, New York. Purchase, Friends of the Department Gifts and matching funds from the National Endowment for the Arts

84 Untitled. 1979. Charcoal on paper, 16 ⅞ x 22 ¼" (42.9 x 56.5 cm). Collection Sarah-Ann and Werner H. Kramarsky

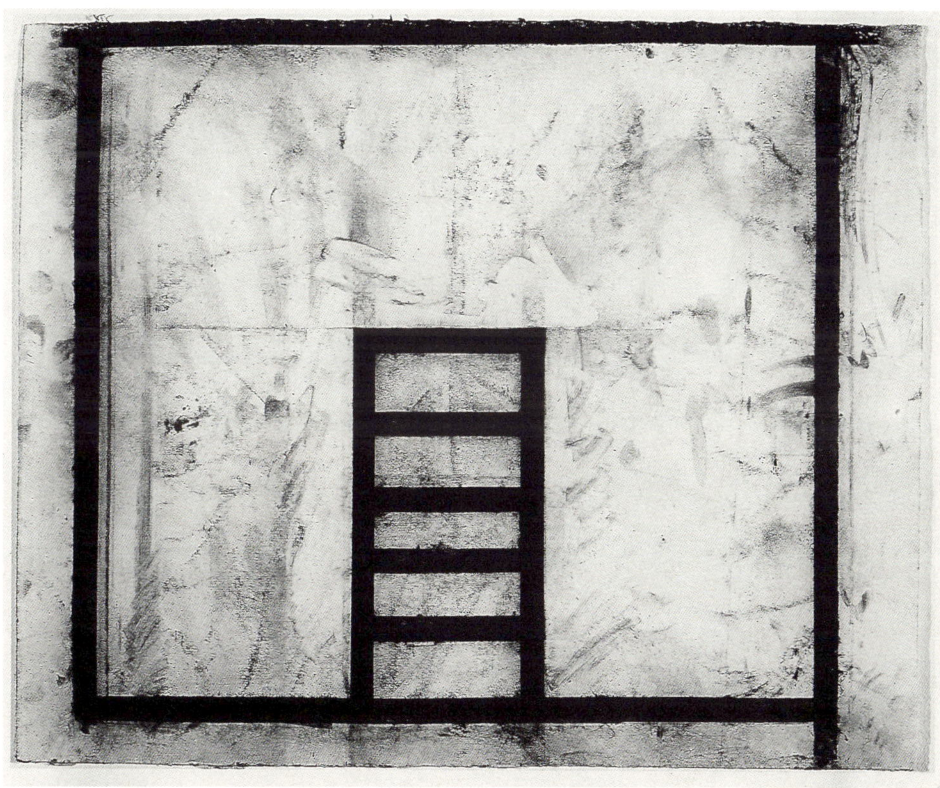

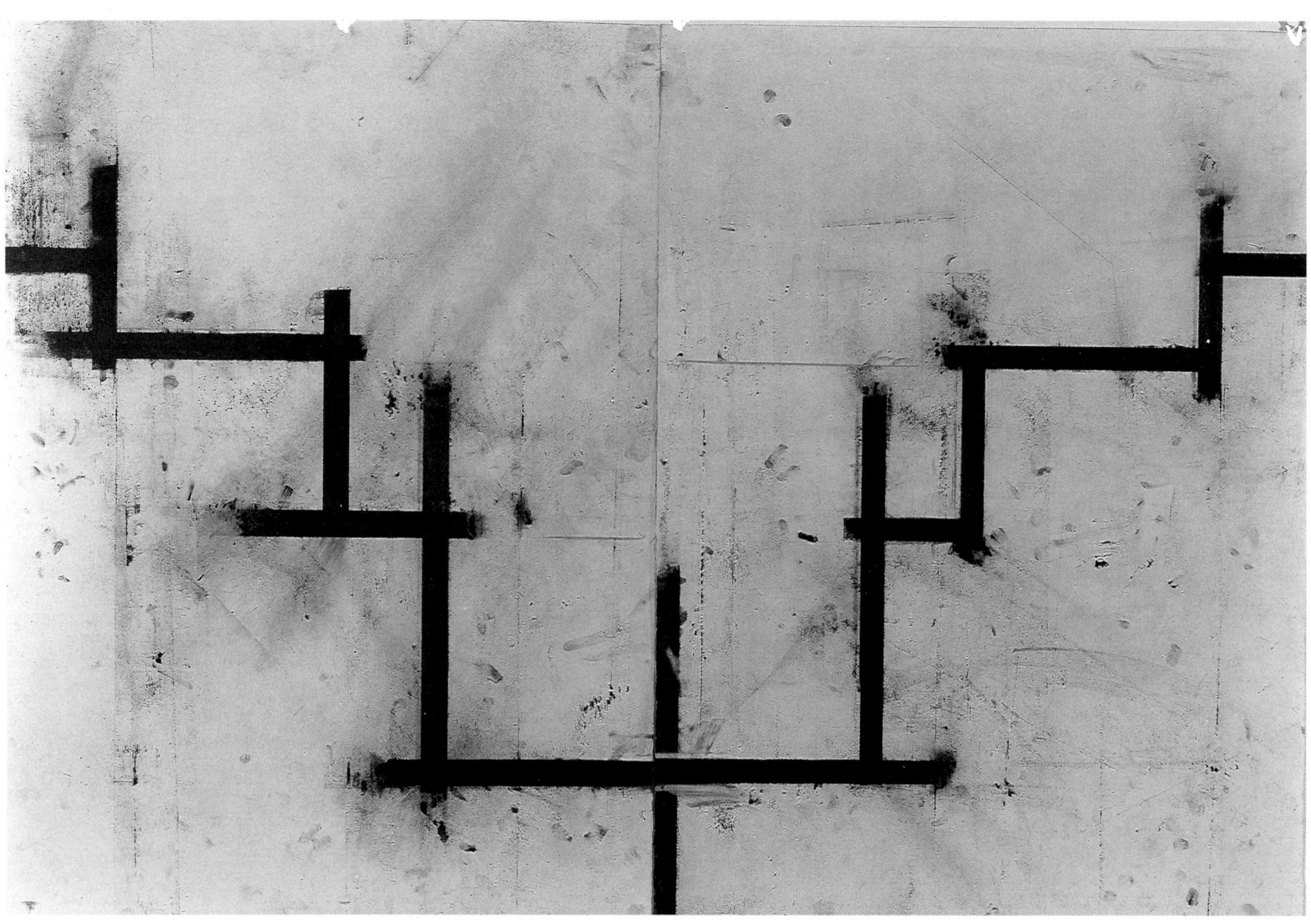

85 Untitled. 1978. Charcoal on paper, two sheets, 30 x 22 ¼" (76.2 x 56.5 cm) each sheet, 30 x 44 ½" (76.2 x 113 cm) overall. The Metropolitan Museum of Art, New York. Purchase, Friends of the Department Gifts and matching funds from the National Endowment for the Arts

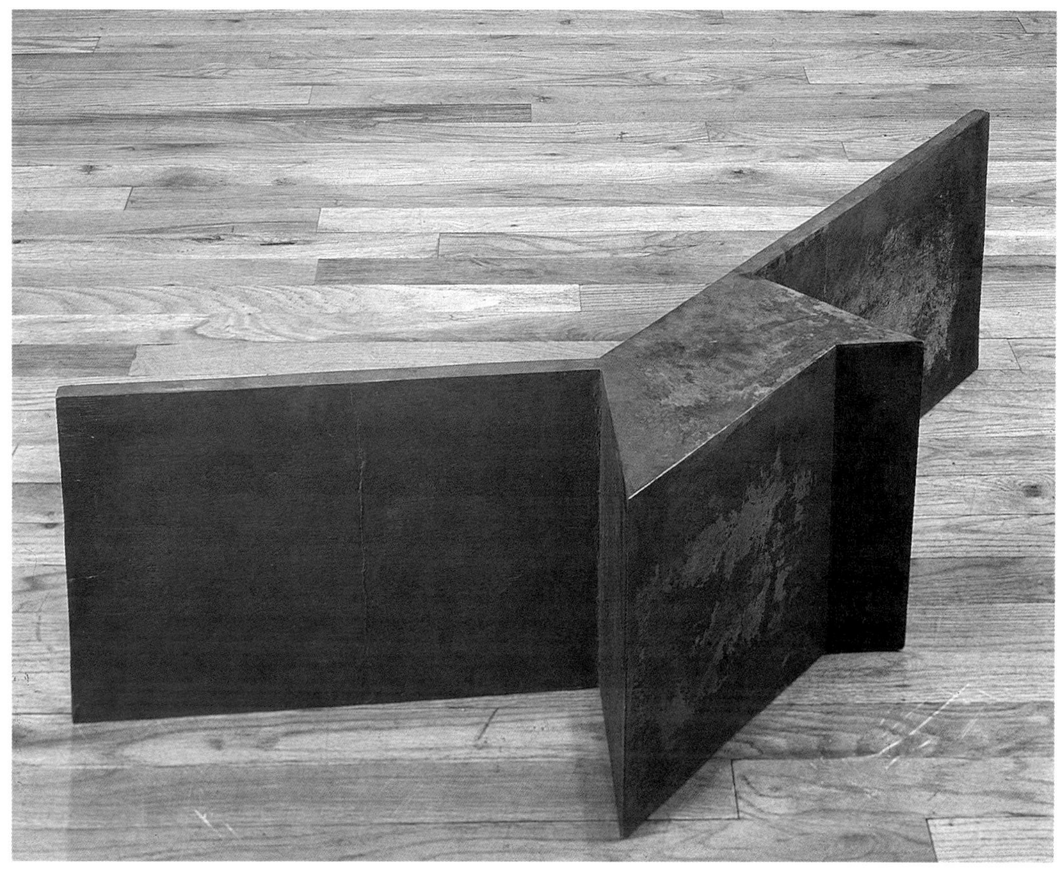

86 Untitled. 1977. Bronze (edition 3/3), $10\frac{9}{16}$ x $25\frac{1}{2}$ x $36\frac{3}{8}$" (26.8 x 64.8 x 92.4 cm). Albright-Knox Art Gallery, Buffalo. National Endowment for the Arts Purchase Grant and Gift of Mr. and Mrs. Armand J. Castellani, 1978

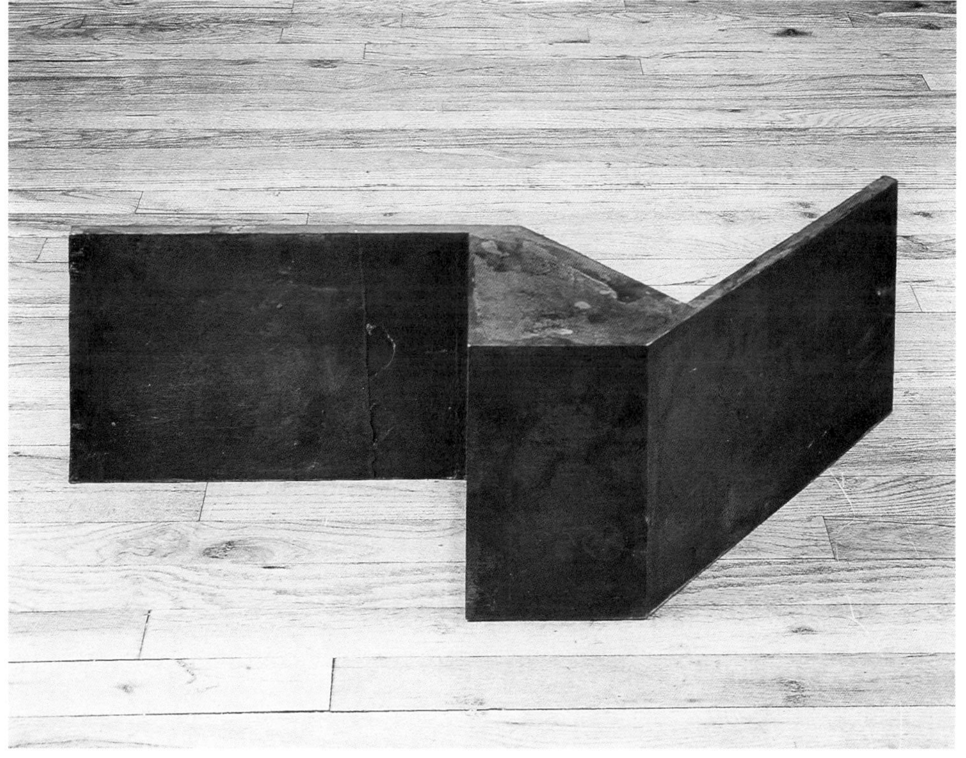

87 Untitled. 1977. Bronze (edition 1/3), $9\frac{15}{16}$ x $32\frac{9}{16}$ x $11\frac{3}{4}$" (25.2 x 82.7 x 29.8 cm). Stedelijk Museum, Amsterdam

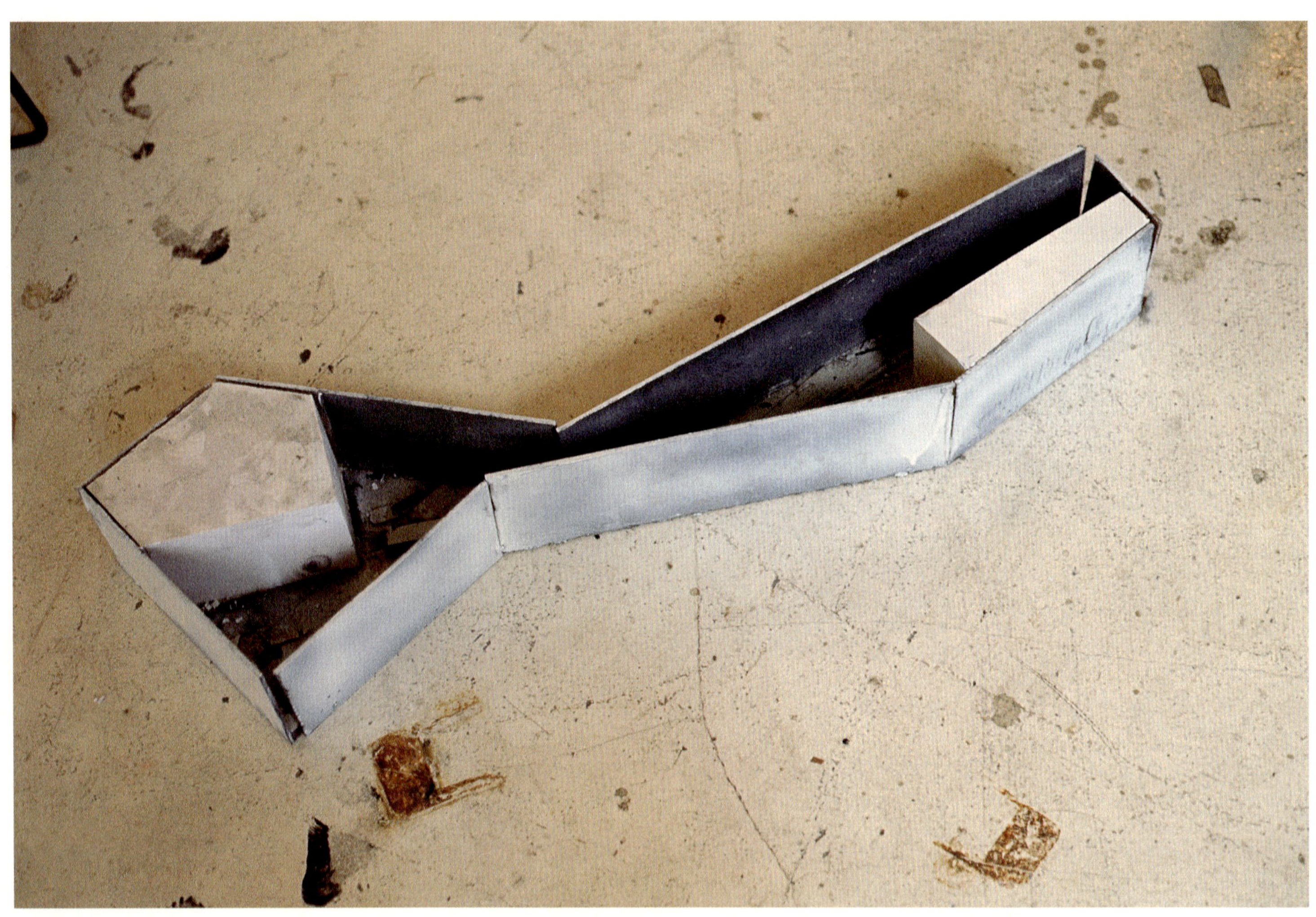

88 Untitled. 1977. Steel and plaster, 4¼ x 33¼ x 10⅜" (10.8 x 84.5 x 26.4 cm). Collection the artist

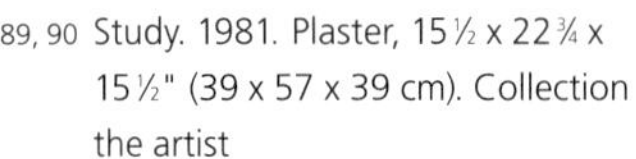
89, 90 Study. 1981. Plaster, 15½ x 22¾ x 15½" (39 x 57 x 39 cm). Collection the artist

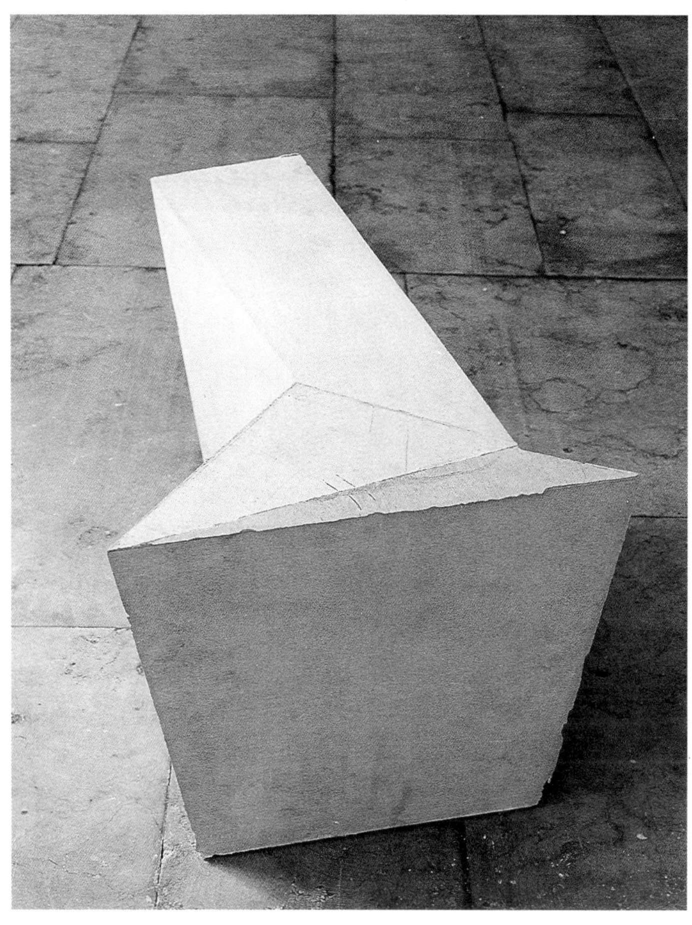

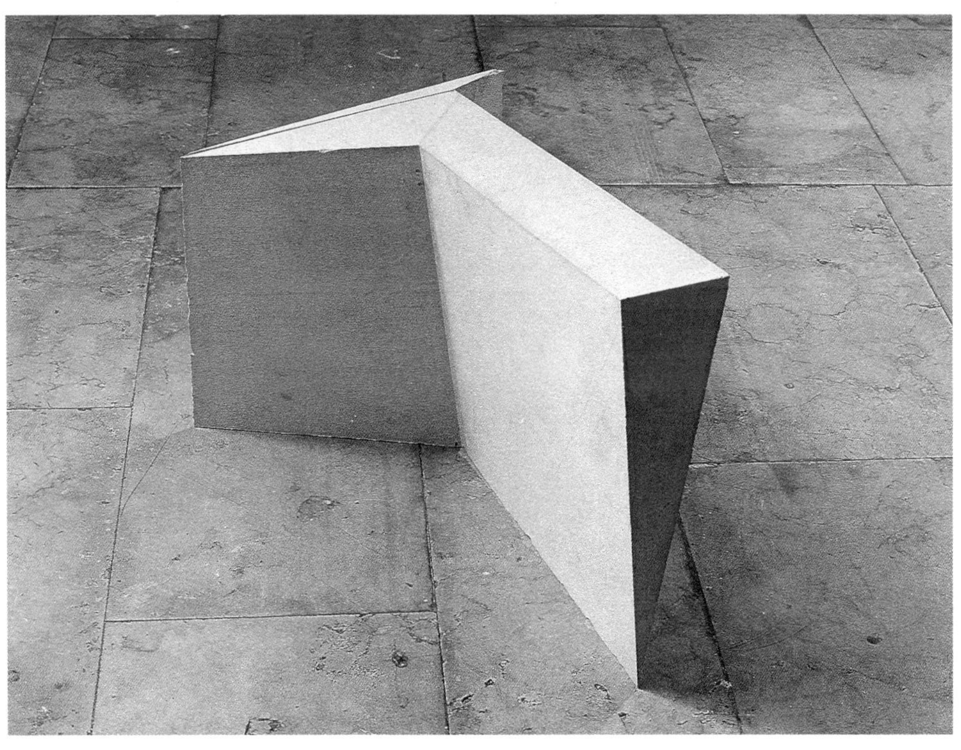

Shapiro has forcefully used the device of a slant cut to create ambiguous shapes that allow for multiple interpretations. Two floor sculptures (plates 91, 92), one cast plaster and the other cast bronze, are both hollow, with six visible contiguous facets; each sculpture can suggest, depending on position, an abstract form, a house, or a head. Shapiro's analogy between a geometric shape and the human head again recalls Giacometti, who asked that his works *The Cube* and *Head of a Man (Cubist Head)* be reproduced on the same page of the review *Minotaure* (figure 10).[25] Shapiro's two sculptures assert themselves in their stillness and concentration. Each form seems like a fallen fragment – a head on the ground.

Shapiro's forms open up over time, extending into and increasingly interacting with the space around them. A very long, narrow, milled-iron sculpture from 1979 (plate 93) recalls earlier works devoted to the juxtaposition of different materials, but now it is space that is the primary concern. An extended hollow shaft provides passage here; one's view slides along the narrow, dark corridor, which is unobstructed but leads nowhere.

The wide opening of a cast plaster from 1981 (plate 94) affords easy entry. At the same time, its rugged interior contrasts with the much smoother exterior, whose surface reveals only the grain of the plywood mold. A small opening in another cast plaster from the same year (plate 95) intimates a deep inner space. While their openings have an obvious bodily connotation, and while they hint at deep interiors, these sculptures also track a definitive development in Shapiro's work toward the external. They are released from an absorption in intimacy and given spatial autonomy in the real world.

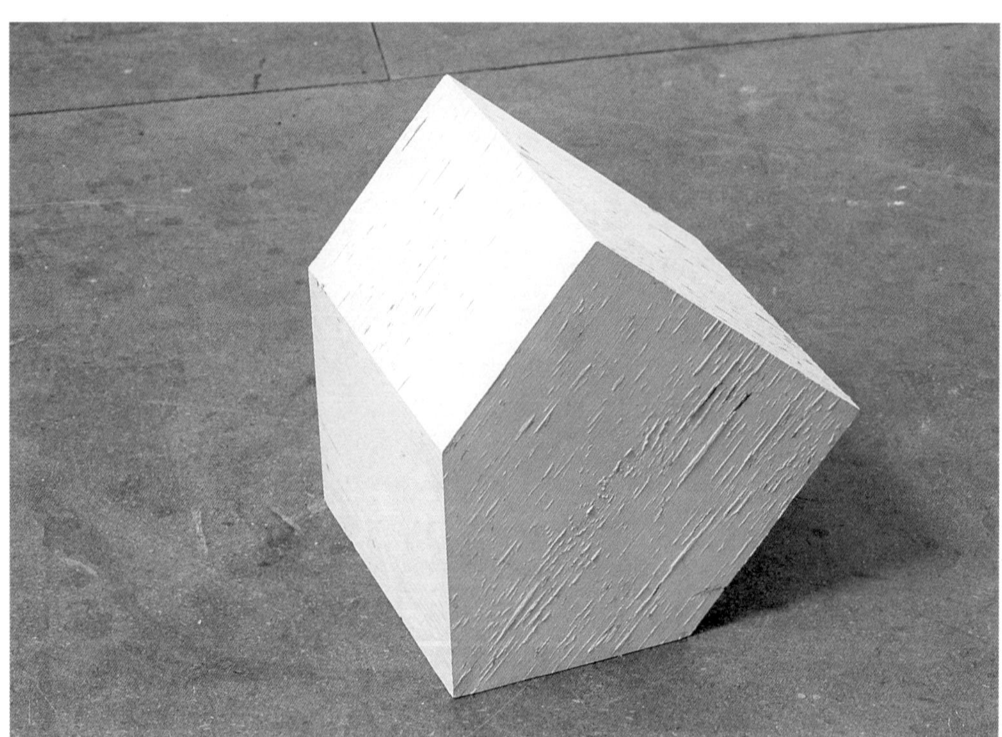

91 Untitled. 1980. Plaster, 12 x 10¼ x 11⁹⁄₁₆" (30.5 x 26 x 29.4 cm). Collection the artist

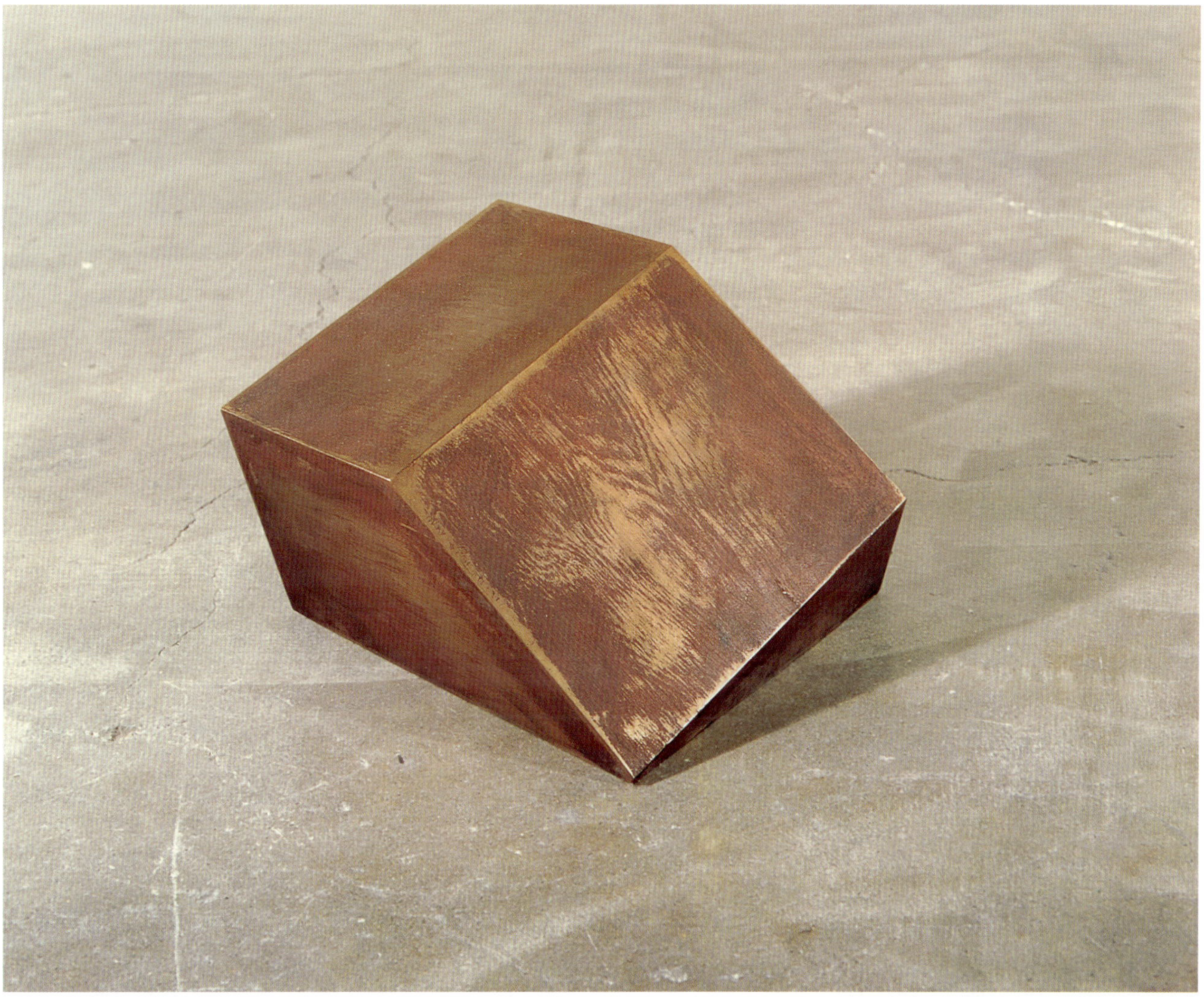

92 Untitled. 1980. Bronze (edition 3/3), 8⅝ x 12 x 12¼" (21.9 x 30.5 x 31.1 cm). The High Museum of Art, Atlanta. Museum purchase with funds from Edith G. and Philip A. Rhodes and the National Endowment for the Arts, 1981.112

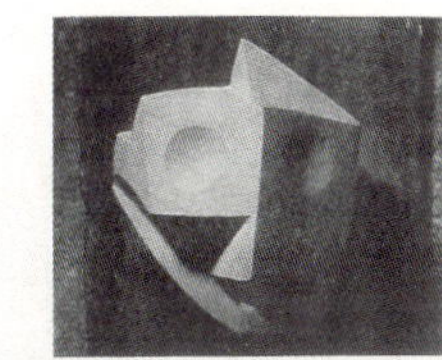

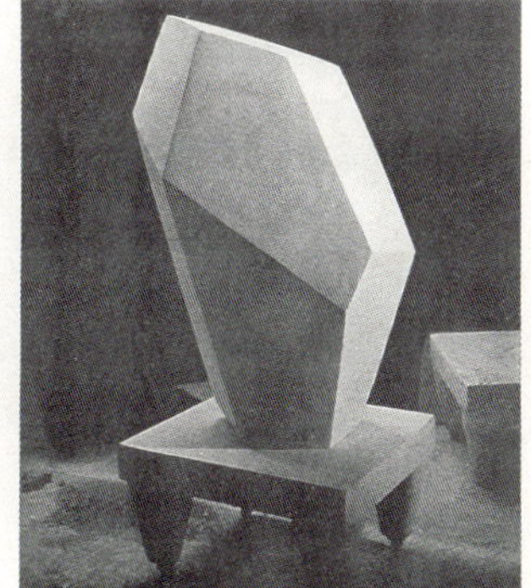

Fig. 10 Alberto Giacometti. *Head of a Man (Cubist Head)* and *Pavillon Nocturne (The Cube)*, as reproduced in *Minotaure*, 5 (May 12, 1934), p. 42

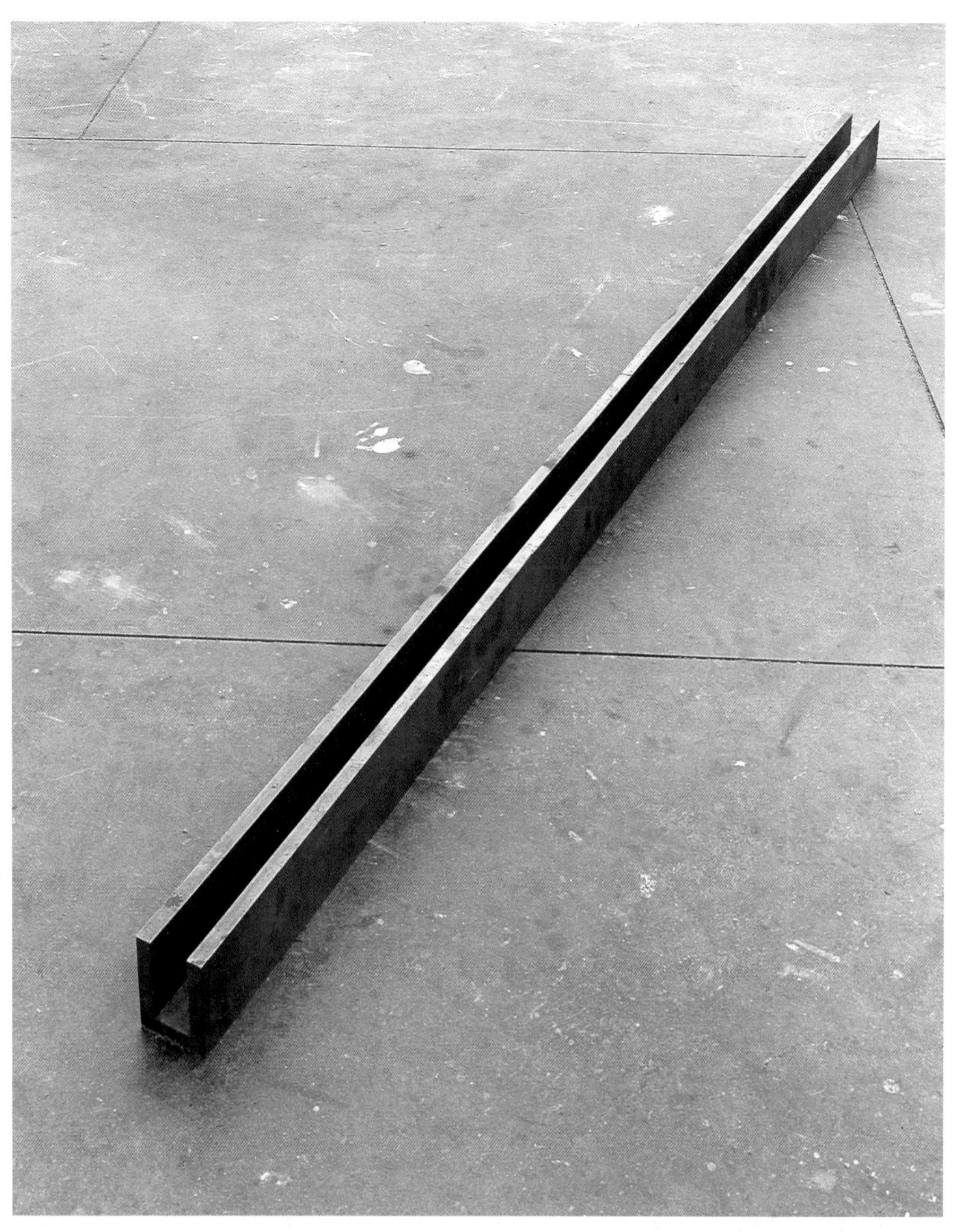

93 Untitled. 1979. Milled cast iron, 3 3/16 x 72 15/16 x 2 5/16" (8.1 x 185.3 x 5.9 cm). Collection the artist

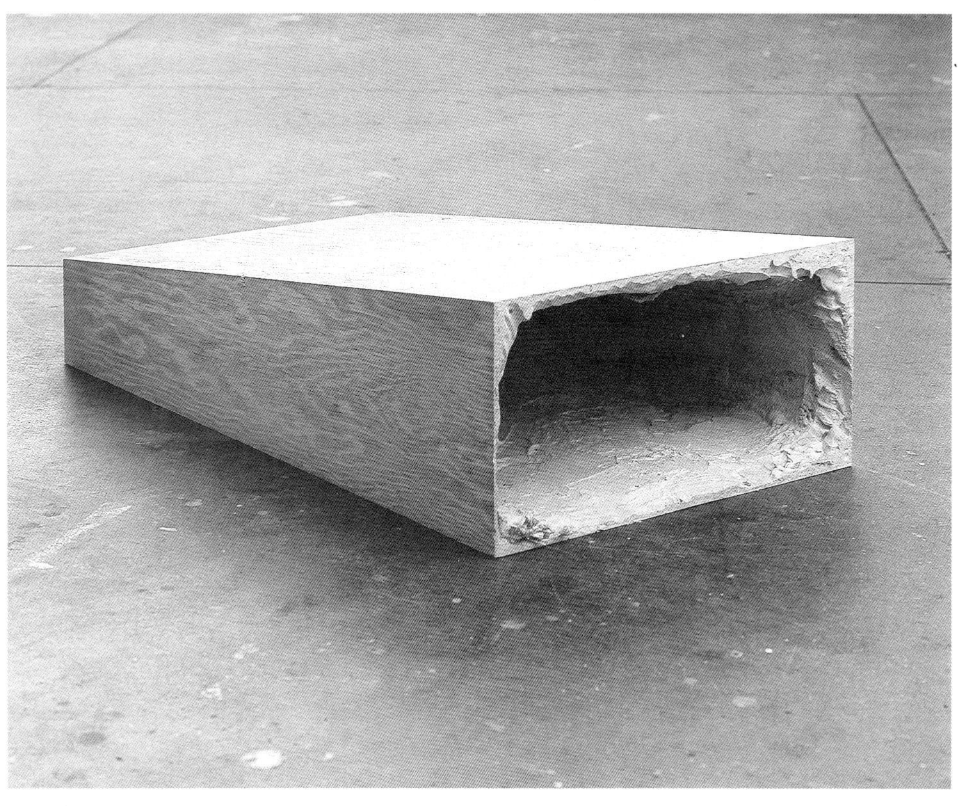

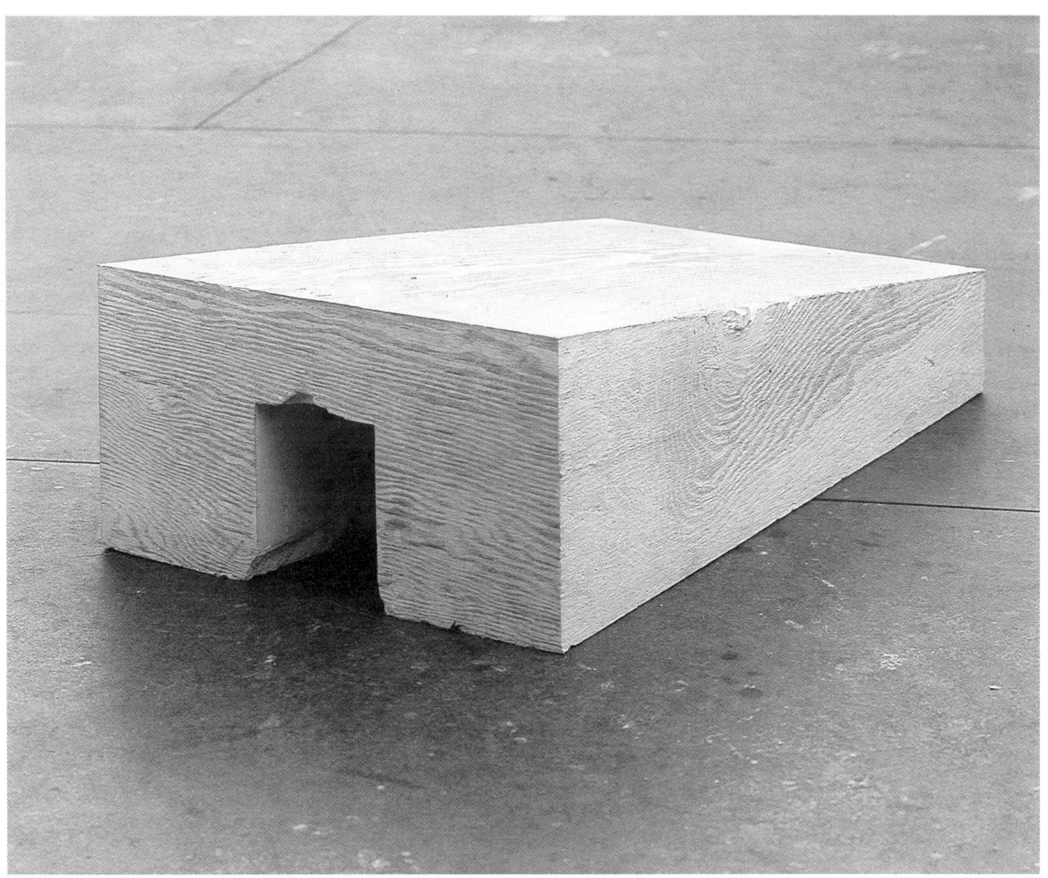

94 Untitled. 1981. Cast plaster, 6½ x 13⅜ x 24" (16.5 x 34 x 61 cm). Collection the artist

95 Untitled. 1981. Cast plaster, 6½ x 13⅜ x 24" (16.5 x 34 x 61 cm). Collection the artist

96 Untitled. 1978 (installated in the exhibition "Joel Shapiro," Gallery m, Bochum, Germany, 1978). Pine, 14½ x 12¼ x 2¾" (36.8 x 31.1 x 7 cm). Private collection

97 Untitled. 1976–77. Bronze (edition 1/3), 16⅝ x 13½ x 2¼" (42.2 x 34.3 x 5.7 cm). Private collection

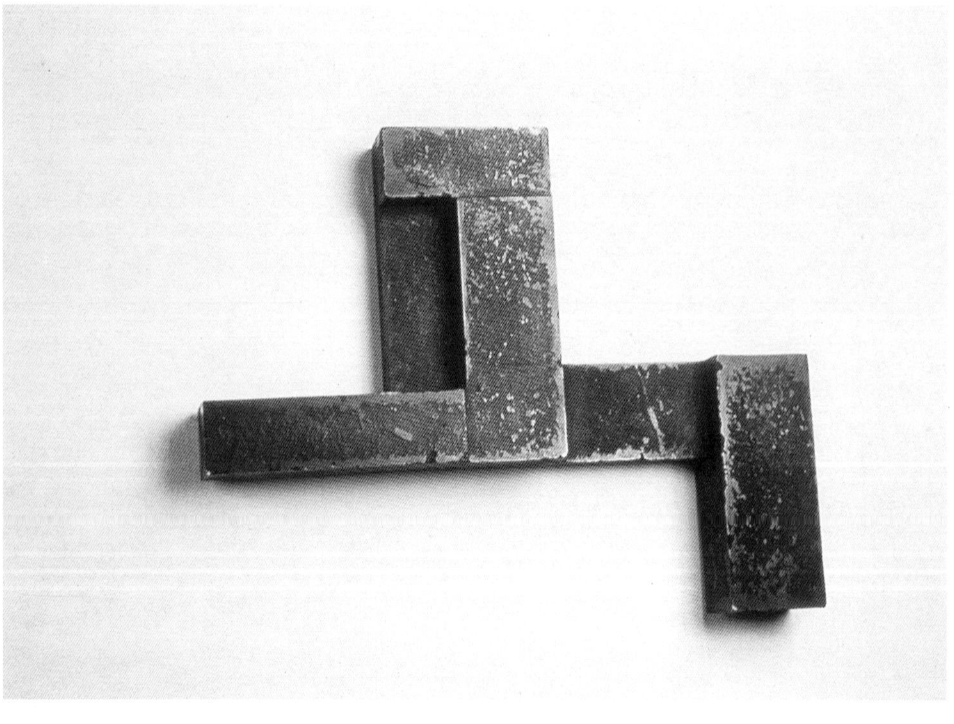

Reliefs and Drawings (1974–80)

For several years, Shapiro concentrated on a series of abstract reliefs, many of them painted, and on related gouaches. The reliefs are clearly an outgrowth of his earlier shelf pieces. Most of them are made of wood. Shapiro uses this, his preferred and primary sculptural medium, as naturally as he does pencil, and points out the similarity: "If I had to build anything, I would use wood, which is the most expedient, most easily manipulated material." Likewise, he is comfortable with drawing "because of its immediacy. It is direct, fast, and emphatic. How I draw is not that different from how I make sculpture."

In one group of reliefs from 1976–79 (plates 96, 97), rectangular shapes in varying thicknesses are placed flat against the wall at eye level. These dark bronze and raw wood pieces display the natural colors of their materials. They belong in part to the pictorial realm, by virtue of their frontality, and in part to the sculptural realm, by virtue of their thickness. In each, the austere branching and especially the central knot from which the contracted mass is extended recall floor pieces done around the same time. Like the floor pieces, the reliefs speak of movement and use the extension of boundaries to generate new spaces.

Other reliefs, from 1978–80 (plates 98, 99), composed of simple geometric shapes and angular cutouts, are built up by superimposing separate formal elements. This layering, along with the obvious saw marks, makes the construction process more evident. When such works are painted (plate 101), the delicate colors – clear blue, luminous red, pale pink – coat the reliefs uniformly but still permit a glimpse of the underlying wood. The effect of translucency has certain precedents in the work of the Constructivists. Shapiro was interested in the 1979 Guggenheim exhibition "The Planar Dimension,"[26] which explored the formal innovations of the Constructivists.

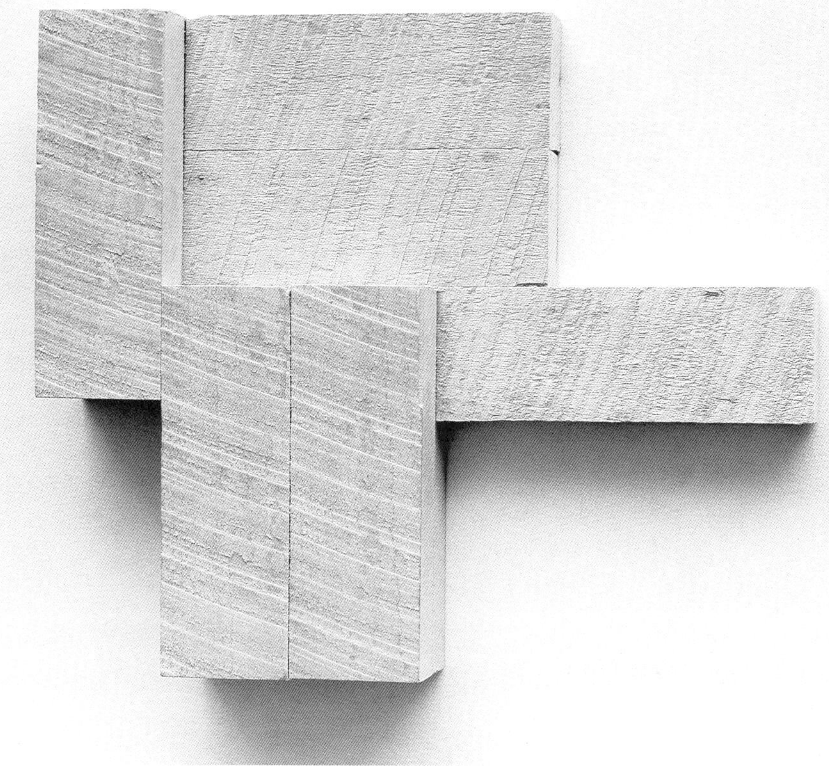

98 Untitled. 1978. Wood, 12⅜ x 14⅞ x 2¾" (31.4 x 37.8 x 7 cm). Courtesy the LeWitt Collection; Wadsworth Atheneum, Hartford

For Shapiro, the act of painting wood creates numerous possibilities. It can render a work more abstract. But the resulting smoothness can also destroy or negate the surface texture of planes. Color may also affect our perception of structure, as in a 1979 relief (plate 100), which is enriched by the thin veil of blue that unifies the different shapes. In a relief from 1980 (plate 102), color plays a didactic role, pinpointing the exact sequence of construction from the wall out into space.

Two reliefs in particular foreshadow future work. A frail, unpainted wood construction from 1974 (plate 103) starts timidly at the wall, then extends abruptly outward. The work's abstract reaching out suggests organic growth. In a construction from 1979 (plate 104), white-painted wood planes project from the wall – a hint of the radical figuration that is to come.

A painted relief from 1979–80 (plate 105) shares with a group of gouaches from the same time (plates 106–8) a more biomorphic form. These are lighter and more sensuous than previous works, and are almost joyous. The more fluid and expansive shapes play with color, weight, and space. Shapiro was preoccupied with color, as these reliefs and gouaches show. Color, obviously, constitutes an additional layer of emotion and can amplify meaning; it has, Shapiro notes, "an intrinsic metaphorical quality. It is not only perceptual but can have cultural connotations as well."

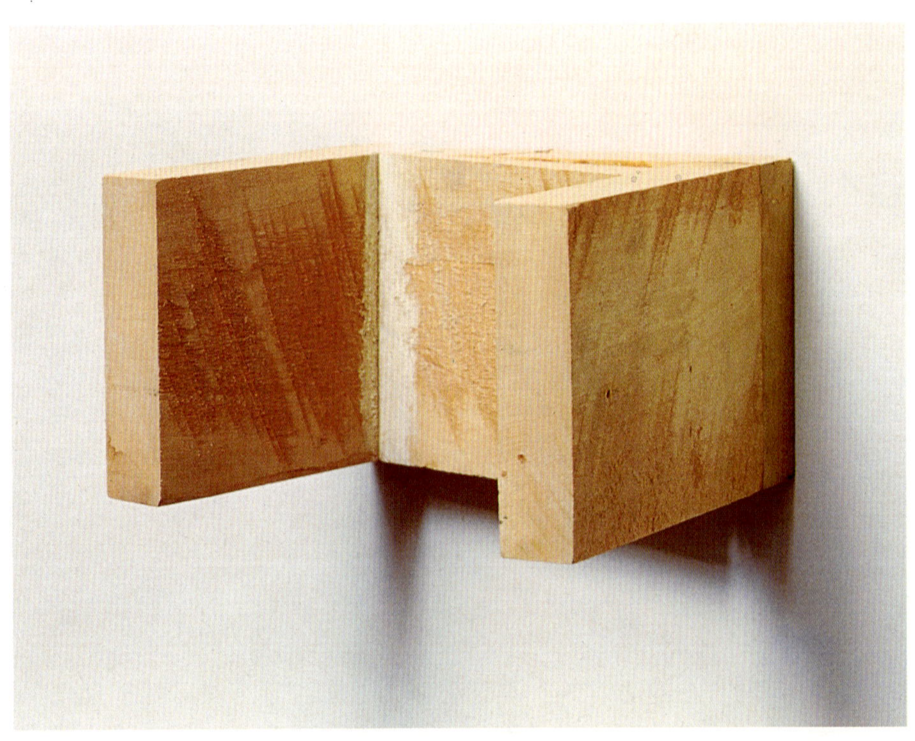

99 Untitled. 1979–80. Wood, 5½ x 10¼ x 8½" (14 x 26 x 21.6 cm). Collection the artist

OPPOSITE:
100 Untitled. 1979. Gouache on wood, 6½ x 5⅜ x 3¼" (16.5 x 13.7 x 8.3 cm). The Corcoran Gallery of Art, Washington, D.C. Gift of the Women's Committee of The Corcoran Gallery of Art with the aid of funds from the National Endowment for the Arts

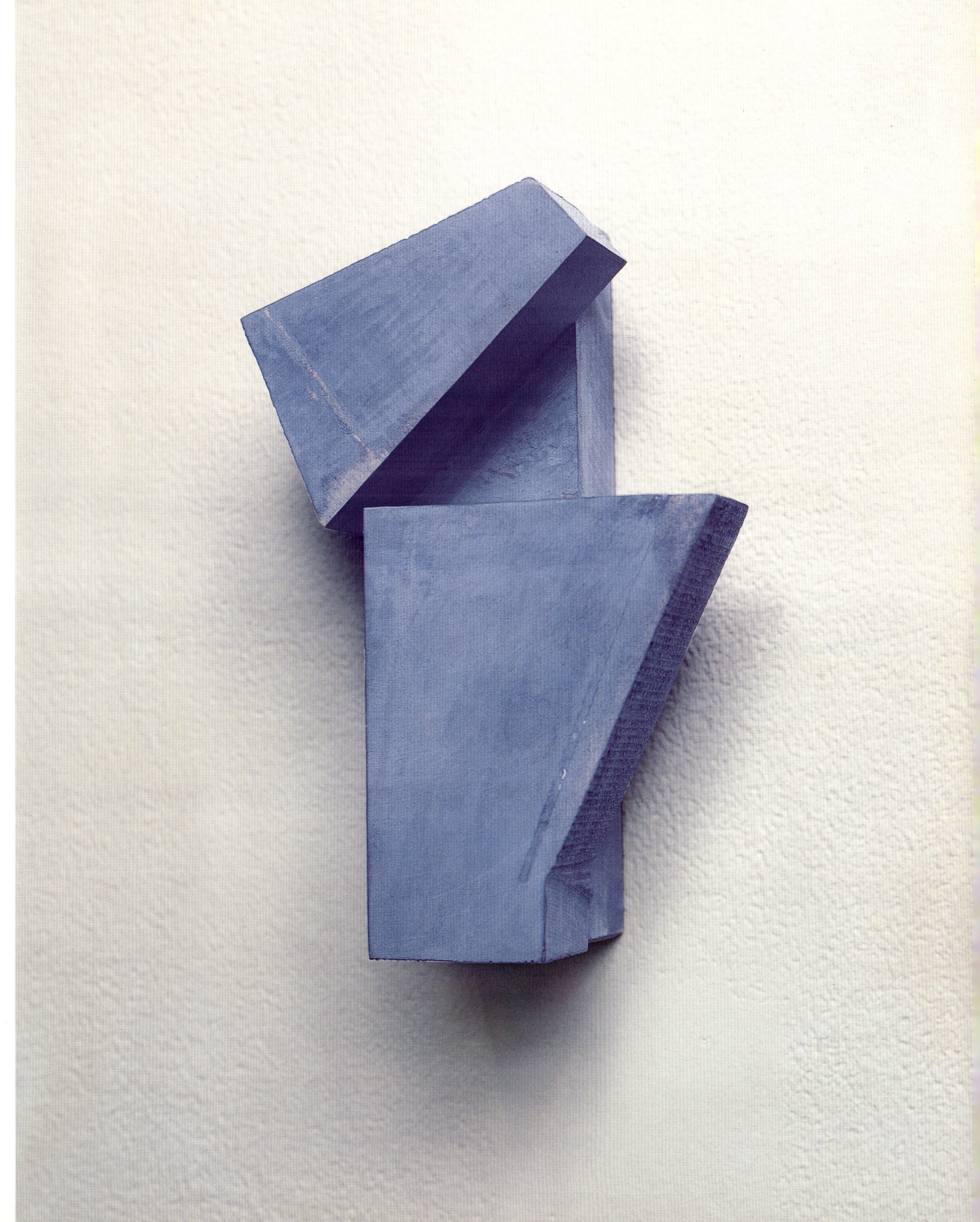

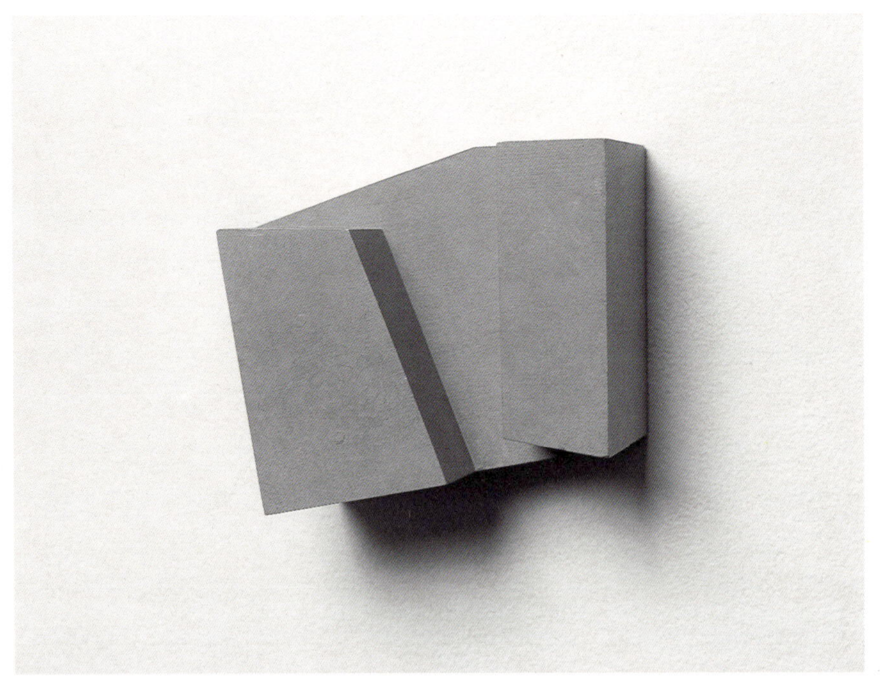

101 Untitled. 1978–79. Gouache on wood, 4¼ x 5 x 3" (10.8 x 12.7 x 7.6 cm). Collection the artist

102 Untitled. 1980. Oil on wood, 11¼ x 11¼ x 3⅝" (28.6 x 28.6 x 9.2 cm). Collection the artist

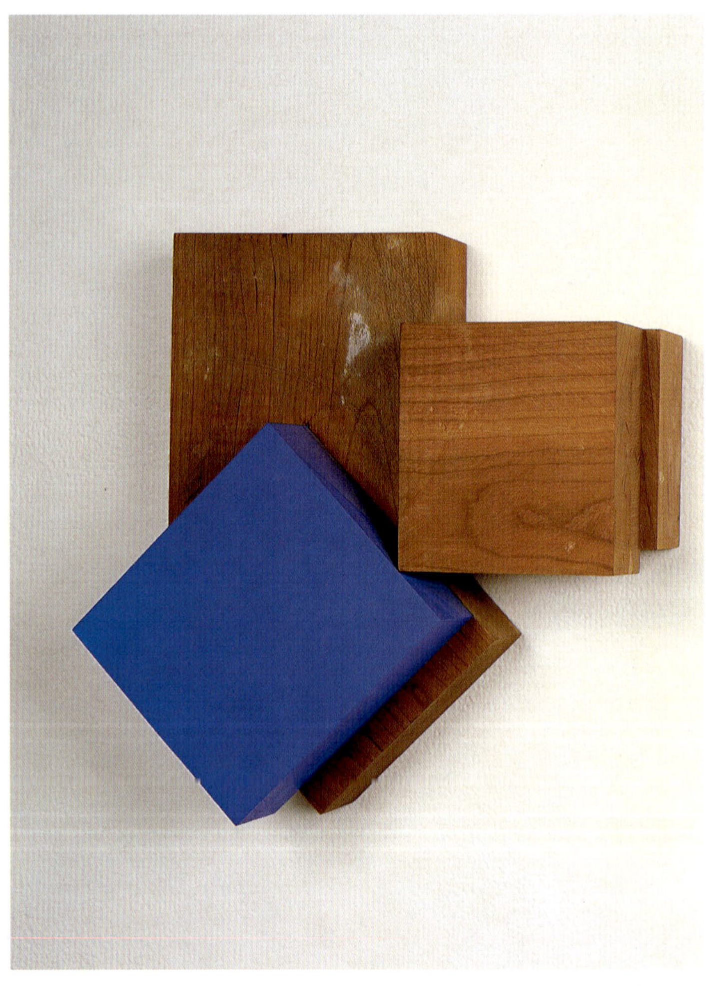

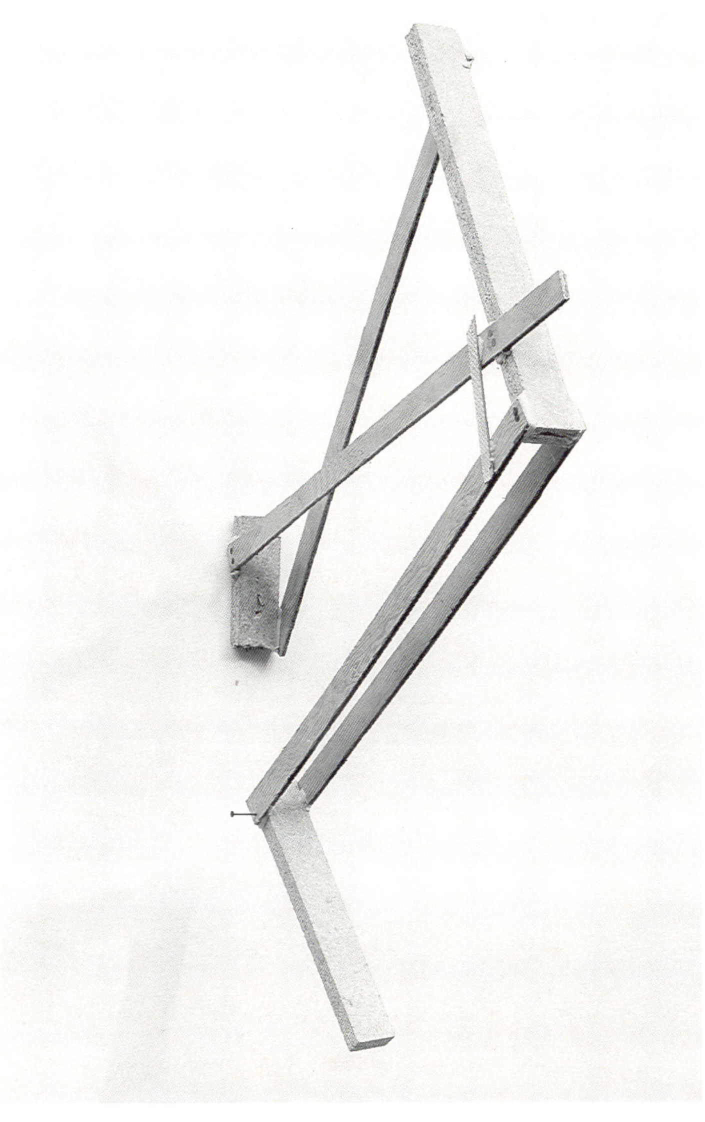

103 Untitled. 1974. Wood and nails, 20¼ x 2¾ x 35¾" (51.4 x 7 x 90.8 cm). Collection the artist

104 Untitled. 1979. Wood and white primer, 9½ x 3 x 7" (24.1 x 7.6 x 17.8 cm). Collection the Grinstein Family

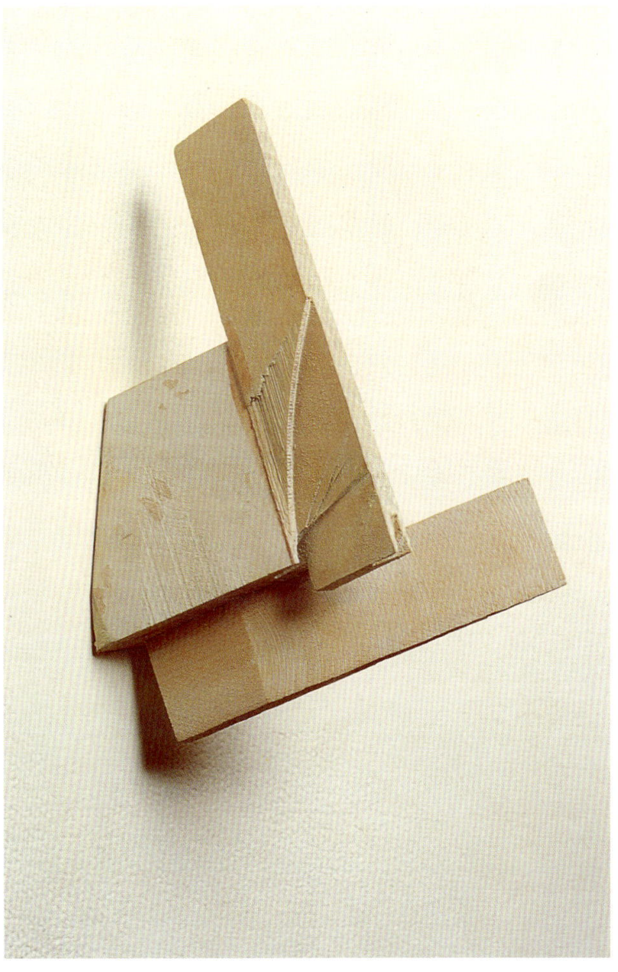

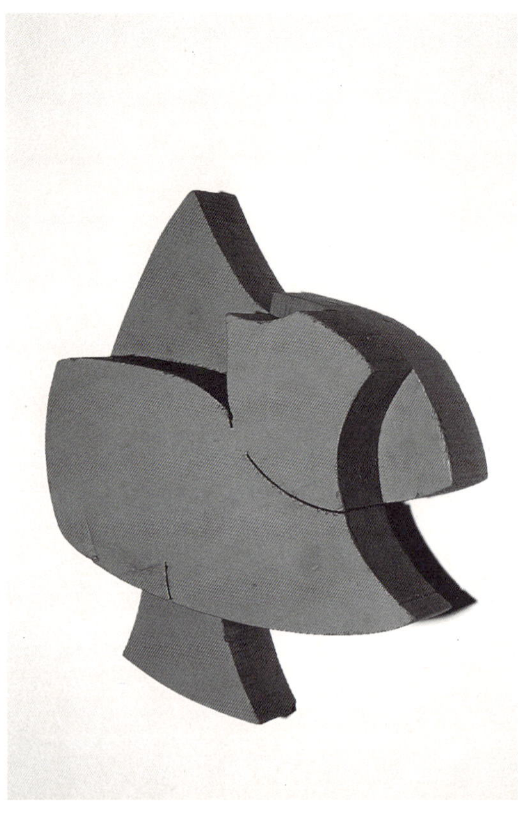

105 Untitled. 1979–80. Oil on wood, 9¼ x 7¾ x 3 1/16" (23.5 x 19.7 x 7.8 cm). Collection Martin Sklar

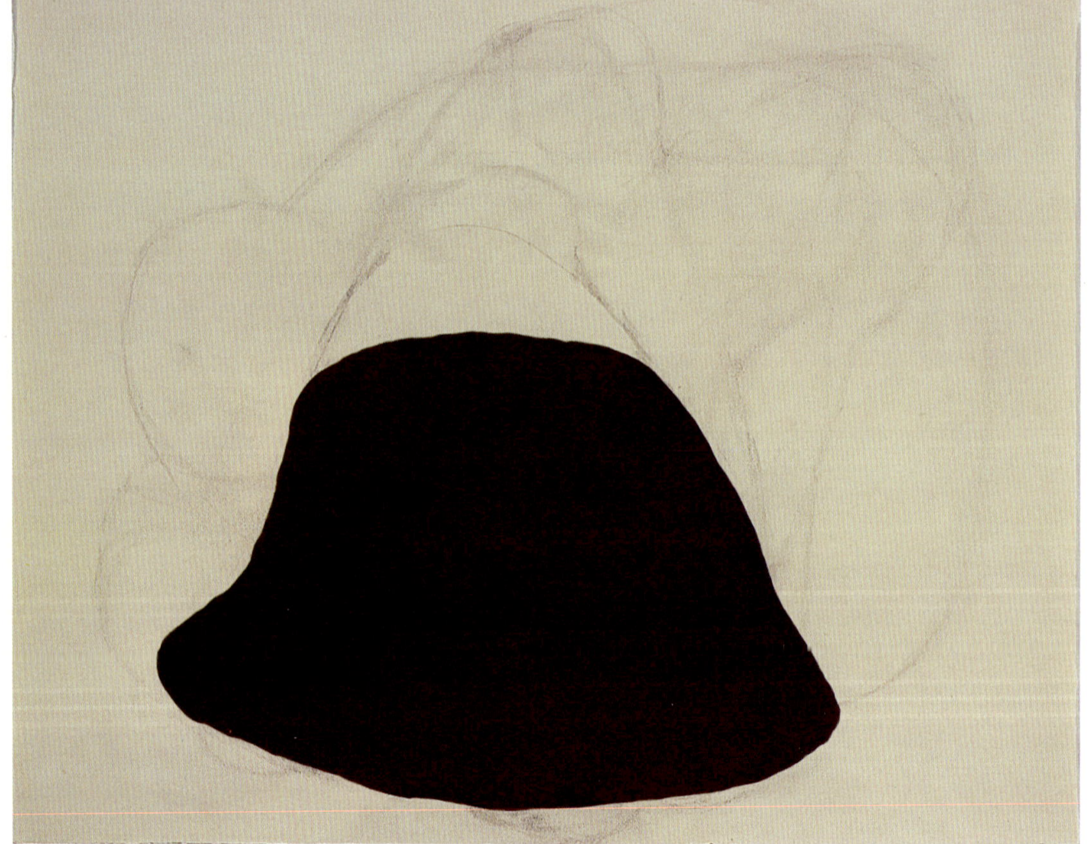

106 Untitled. 1979. Gouache on paper, 18⅛ x 23" (46 x 58.4 cm). Collection the artist

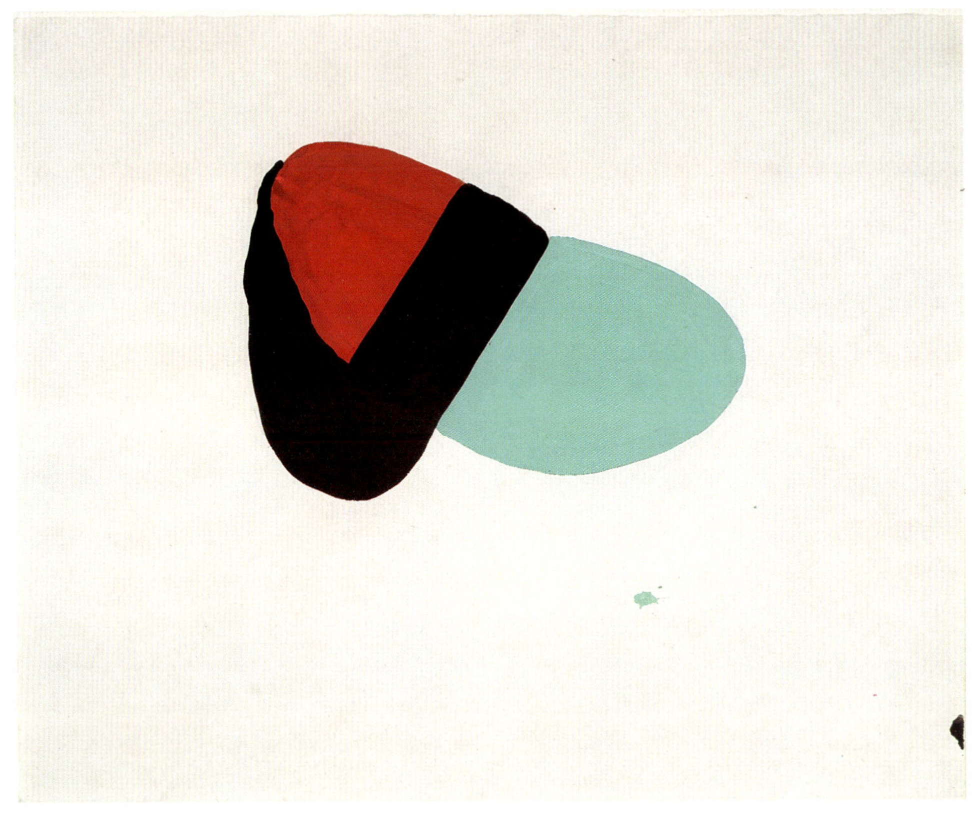

107 Untitled. 1980. Gouache on paper, 20¼ x 25" (51.4 x 63.5 cm). Collection the artist

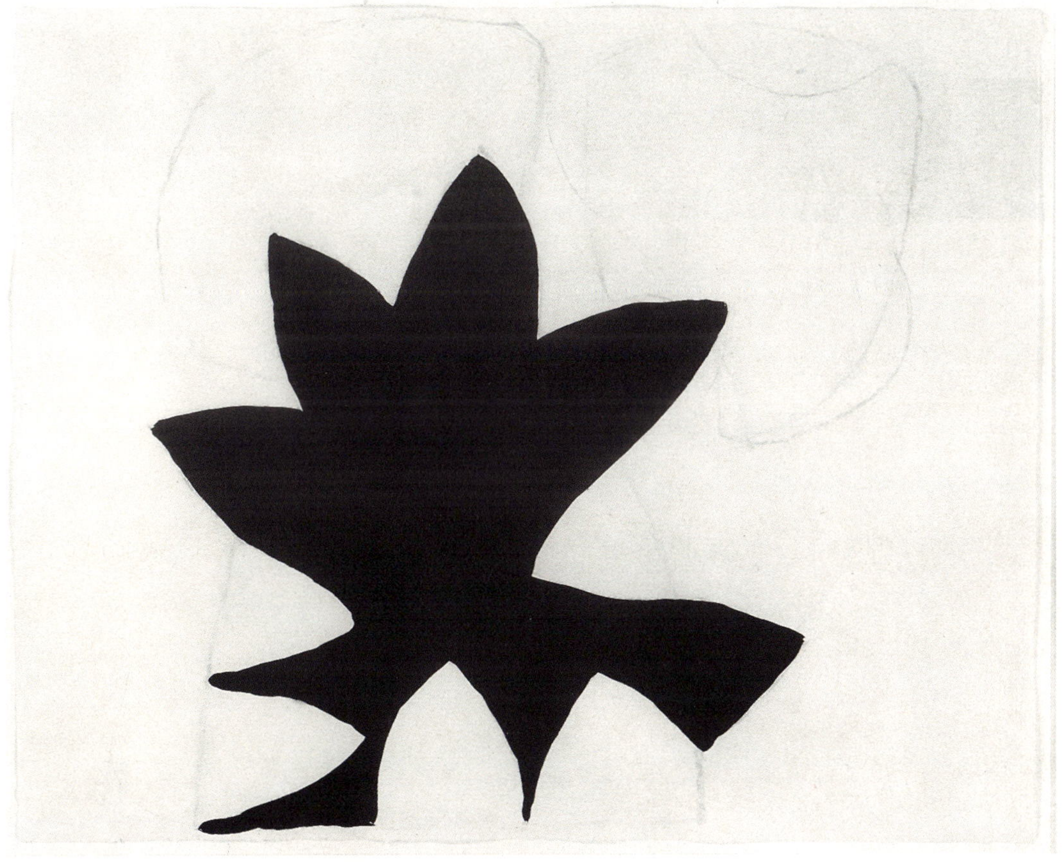

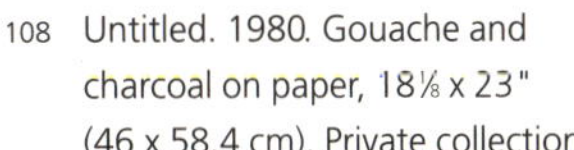

108 Untitled. 1980. Gouache and charcoal on paper, 18⅛ x 23" (46 x 58.4 cm). Private collection

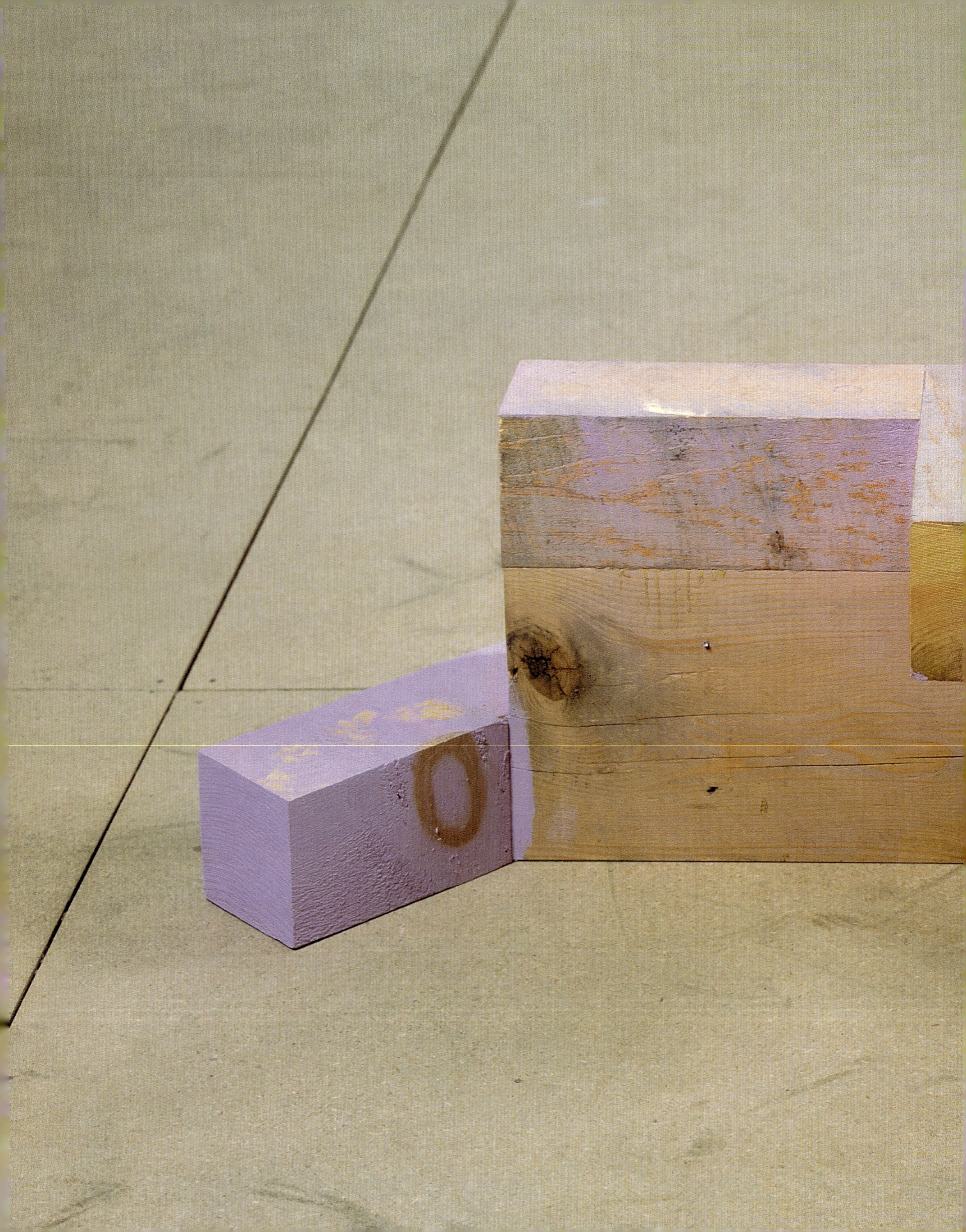

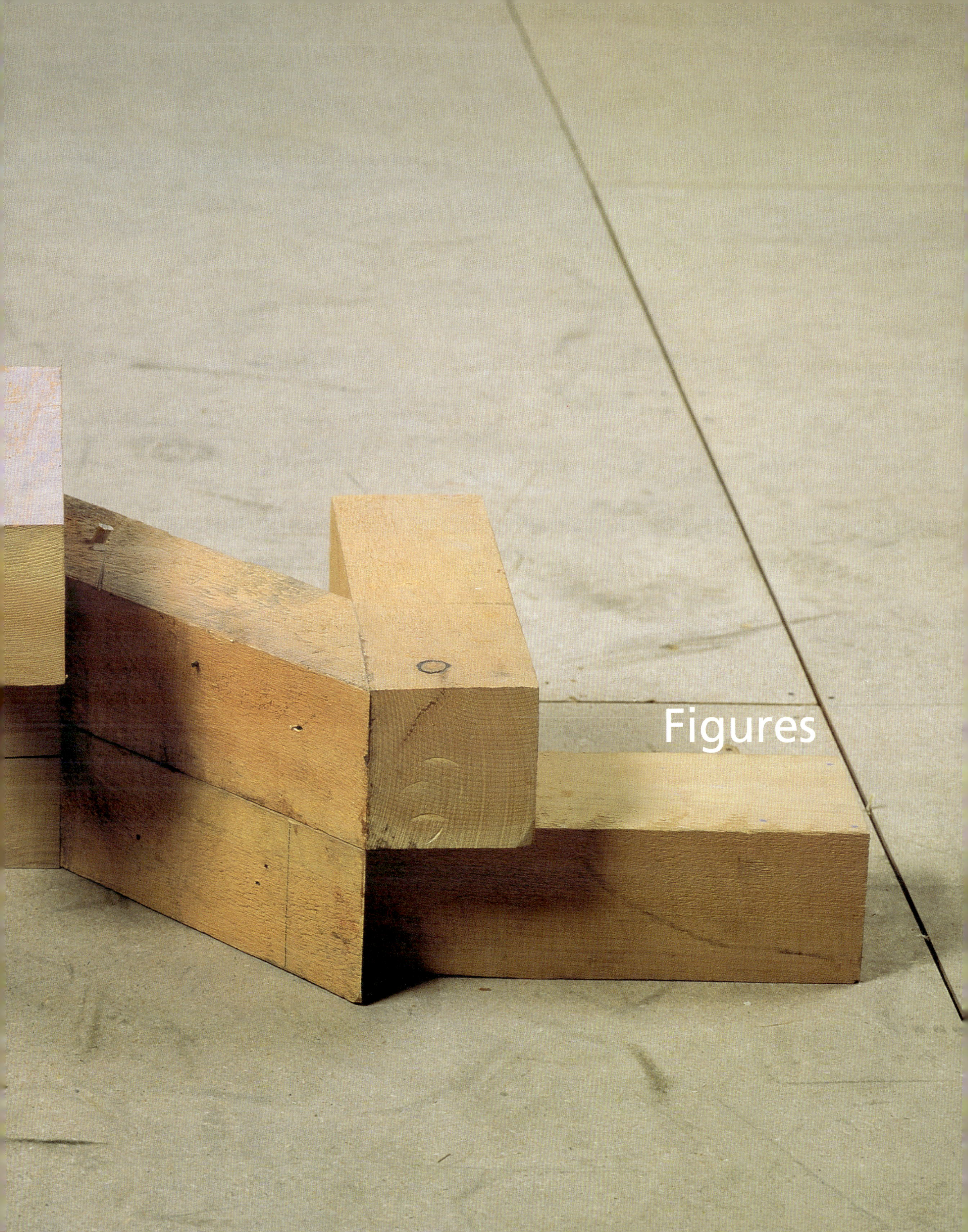

Figures

The Emergence of the Figure (1975–84)

Shapiro first depicted the human figure in a group of six etchings from 1975 (see plates 110–12).[27] He chose etching to introduce the theme. This difficult medium offered a useful degree of resistance against which Shapiro could work, and it also afforded the opportunity to see his imagery develop in an unfamiliar way. Conceived as rapid notations in black and white, these etchings narrate turbulent domestic dramas. Buildings, shoes, hats, frying pans, and figures animate the center of otherwise vacant pictorial surfaces. The active gesticulations of the figures contrast sharply with the stable architecture. The figure's central placement and its diagonally outstretched arms (see plate 110) energize a field in which representational and abstract shapes are combined. Whenever Shapiro's work leans toward representation, his figures give rise to a larger, more spacious sense of movement.

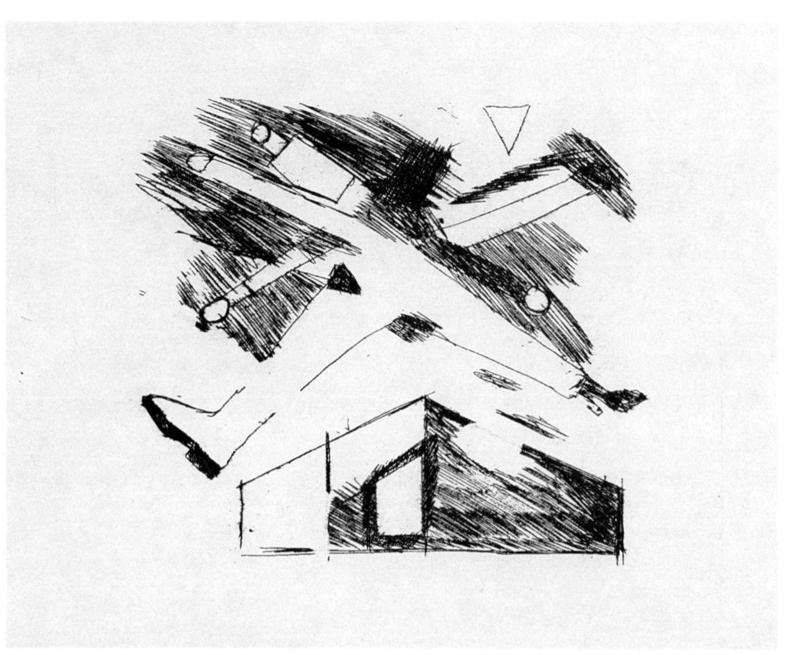

110 Untitled. 1975. Etching, 12½ x 17½" (31.8 x 44.5 cm). Published by the artist and Catherine Mosley, New York

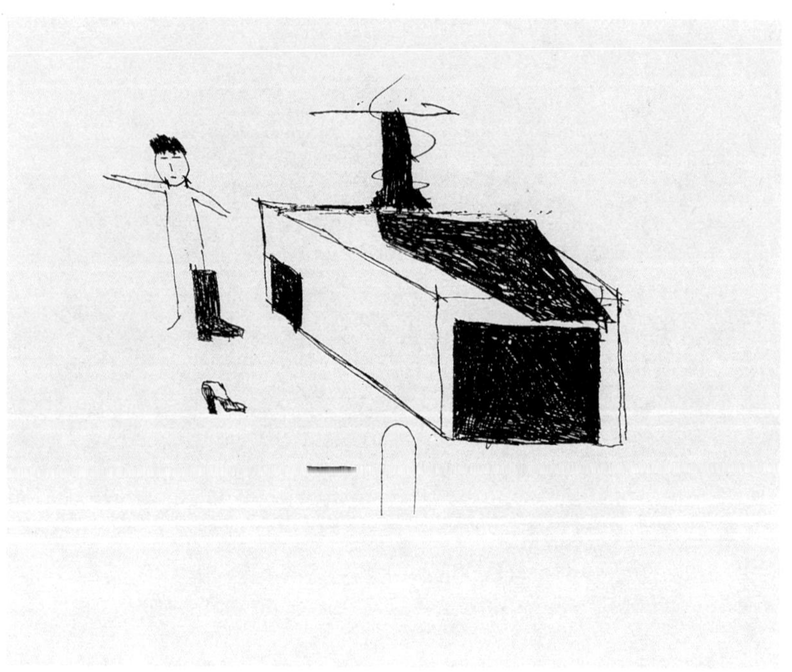

111 Untitled. 1975. Etching, 12½ x 17½" (31.8 x 44.5 cm). Published by the artist and Catherine Mosley, New York

PREVIOUS SPREAD:

109 Untitled. 1982. Wood and oil, 12⅜ x 43¼ x 13¼" (31.4 x 109.9 x 33.7 cm). Collection Douglas S. Cramer

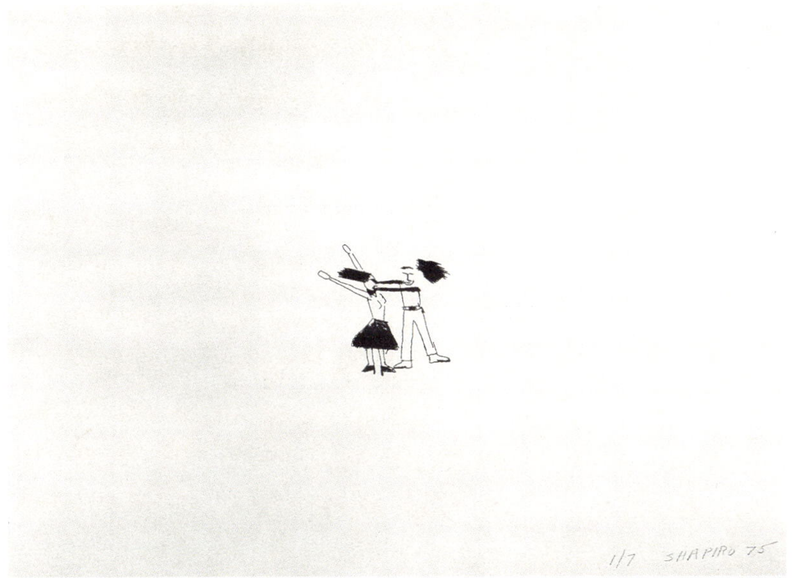

112 Untitled. 1975. Etching, 12½ x 17½" (31.8 x 44.5 cm). Published by Catherine Mosley, New York

In his sculptural development of the figure, a bronze representing a running man (plate 113) plays a pivotal role. Completely painted in red and black, the sculpture brings to mind a Lego toy assemblage with its clear-cut geometric shape. The man, conceived in silhouette as if for a relief, lifts one leg while remaining firmly rooted to the ground with the other. Shapiro used a spotlight when painting the sculpture, to emphasize the separate parts of the interlocking construction. Even though the man, Shapiro's first autonomous figure, is running, he seems stiff, as if trapped in a confined space; the impression is heightened by his diminutive size and the areas of black. Nonetheless, this figure represented a liberation for Shapiro. The work seemed to him to be much "more about a sense of possibility rather than a sense of impossibility."

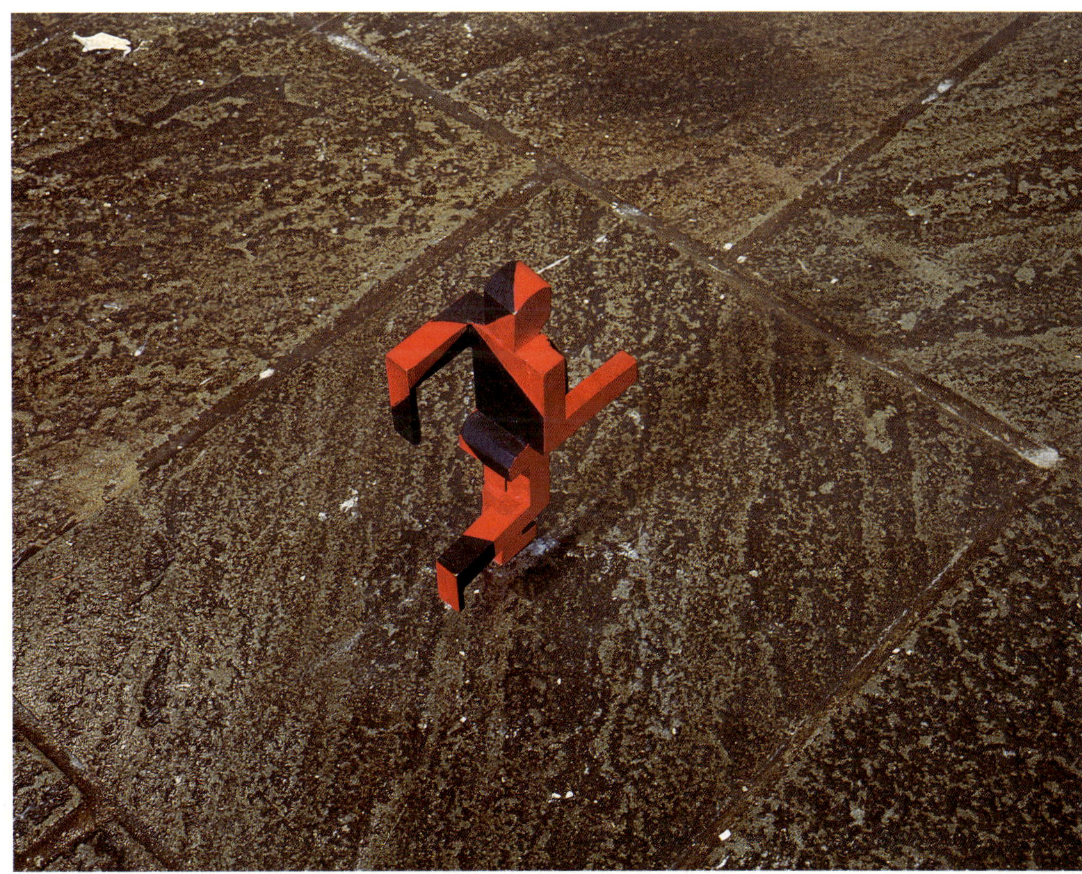

113 Untitled. 1976–77. Oil on bronze, 9¾ x 2⅝ x 5" (24.8 x 6.7 x 12.7 cm). Collection Elizabeth M. Petrie

The figure continued to evolve in two small wood studies from 1979. A study of a reclining figure (plate 114) and one of a seated figure grasping its legs (plate 115) were born of the simplest means: rectangular pieces of raw wood nailed together. The process and intention are clear, as are the sources of the materials – the hardware store and the lumberyard. These rough yet vulnerable pieces would be transformed a few years later into larger, more vibrant works. In 1982, the reclining figure becomes larger and more complex (plate 109). The rectangular beams of head and arm are now covered with a wash of lavender. The layer of color adds a layer of meaning. The tinted elements are perceived as both part of and independent from the recumbent body; they are more delicate and refined, while the unpainted wood elements are more blunt.

Likewise, the seated figure from 1979, though remaining small, would undergo a metamorphosis a few years later (plate 116). Now cast in bronze, the figure has been rolled over onto its knees with its head bowed; it appears more unified, its limbs drawn tighter, its shape more condensed. The alteration is not just formal; as with all of Shapiro's reconfigurations, here the change in posture is psychologically charged.

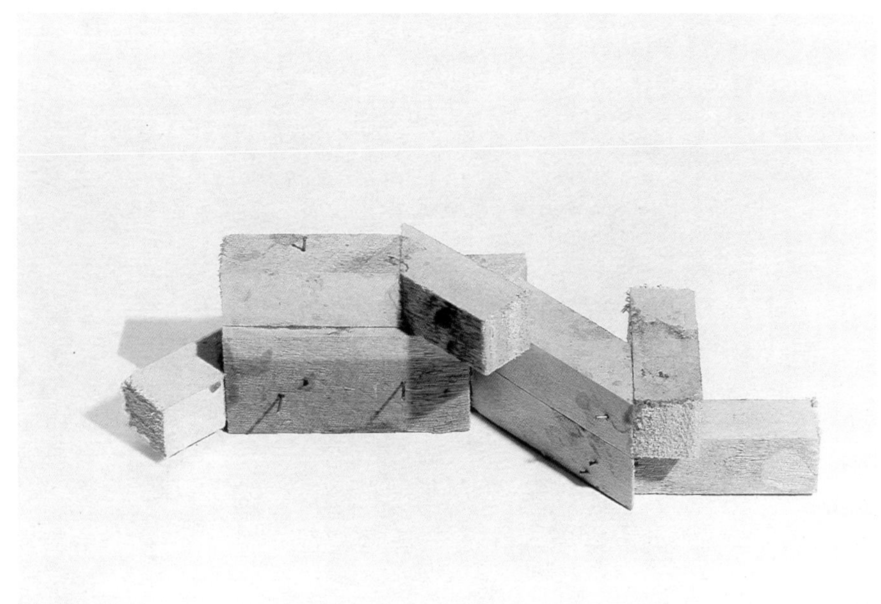

114 Study. 1979. Wood and nails, 2⅜ x 2⅝ x 8¼" (6 x 6.7 x 21 cm). No longer extant

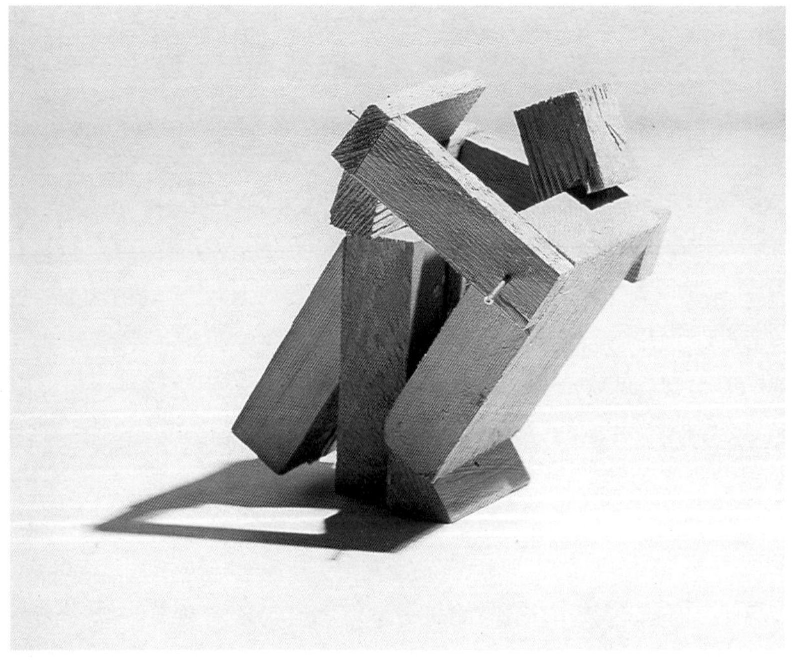

115 Study. 1979. Wood and nails, 4½ x 3¾ x 4½" (11.4 x 9.5 x 11.4 cm). No longer extant

Shapiro's inquiry into the representation of the human figure encompasses a number of visual strategies. Among them is the use of the shelf, which he employed in 1979 for the last time. Isolated on a shelf against a wall, a female figure, frontally positioned, is constructed around a vertical axis (plate 118). The vertical axis is significant, for from it – as torso or tree trunk – Shapiro will develop his personages. The components of this sculpture are crude and angular, and the handwork process of their fabrication is clear from the excess glue oozing from the joints. Evidence of this "soft," organic material will remain, and even be emphasized, in a bronze version (plate 117), where the bronze "overflow" at the junction of legs and torso has an almost anatomical correctness. Shapiro's early travel to India and Europe now makes itself felt in his work. The figure's stance on one leg, hip out, recalls the sensuous sculptures on the facades of Indian temples (figure 11), positioned against an architectural wall. At the same time, the figure's *contrapposto* and proportions, as well as its base, indicate Shapiro's interest in the classical tradition of Western sculpture (figure 12). And as so often in Shapiro's work, the play of ambient light on the bronze surface creates a lively sense of the sculpture in its surroundings.

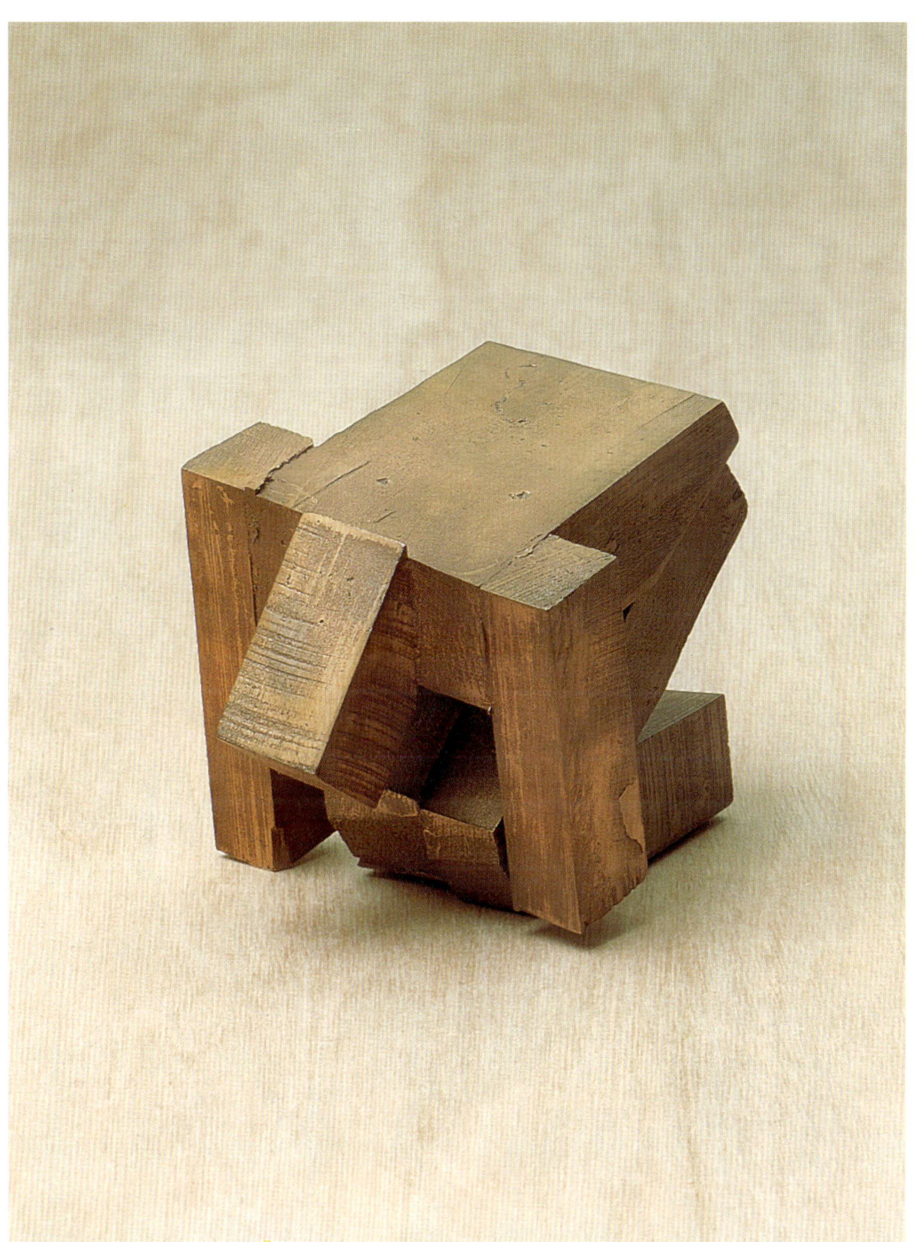

116 Untitled. 1982–84. Bronze, 4¼ x 5½ x 4" (10.8 x 14 x 10.2 cm). Collection Ivy Shapiro

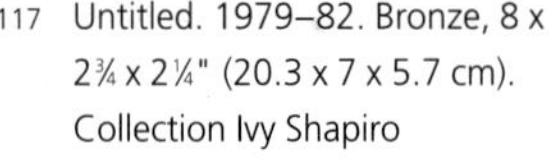

117 Untitled. 1979–82. Bronze, 8 x 2¾ x 2¼" (20.3 x 7 x 5.7 cm). Collection Ivy Shapiro

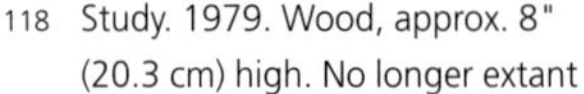

118 Study. 1979. Wood, approx. 8" (20.3 cm) high. No longer extant

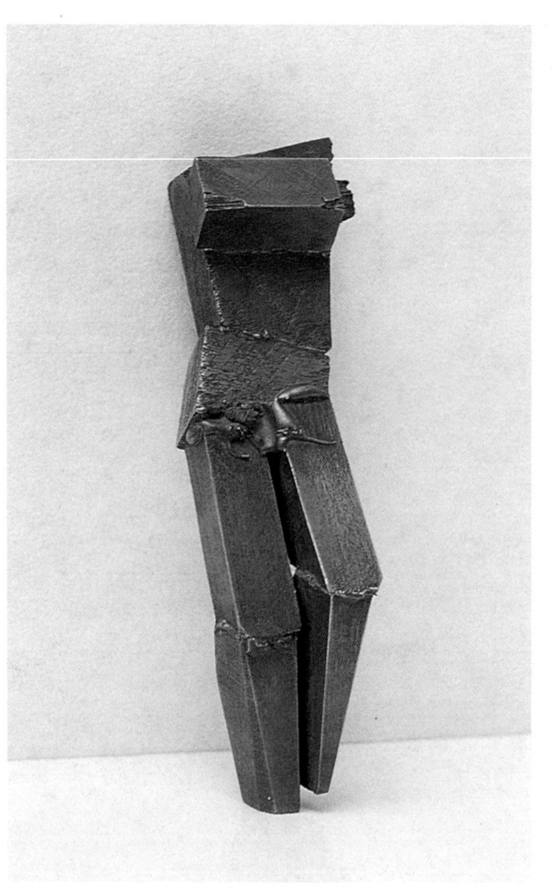

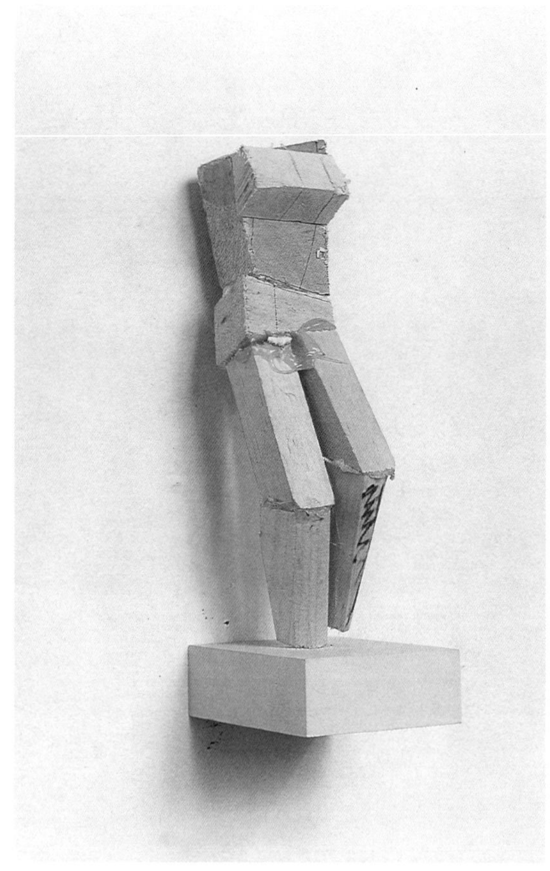

Fig. 11 Sculpture on the facade of Rajrani Temple, Bhubaneswar, Orissa, India. c. 1000. Photograph by Joel Shapiro

Fig. 12 *Aphrodite of Melos* (also called *Venus de Milo*). c. 150 B.C.E. Marble, 6'10" (2.1 m) high. Musée du Louvre, Paris

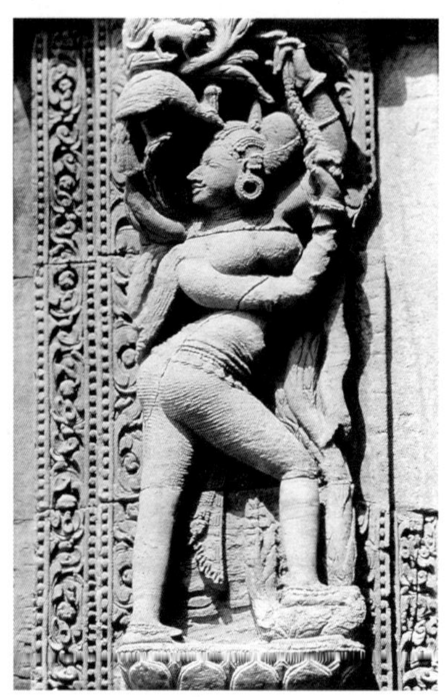

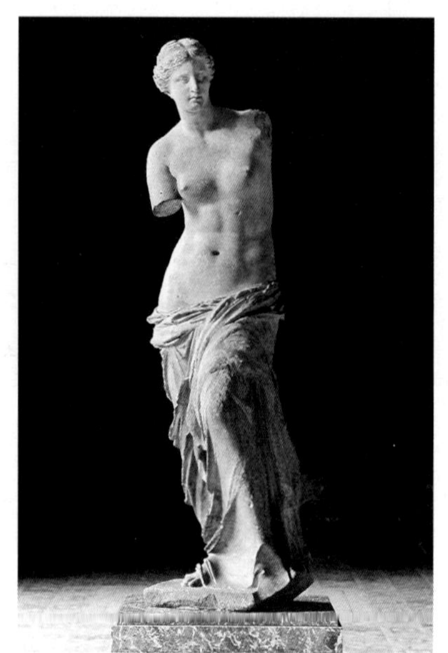

In two works from 1980 (plates 119, 120), Shapiro uses the idea of grafting to achieve a feeling of movement and growth. With the main part of the sculpture placed on the ground like a torso or a fallen tree trunk, smaller elements angle out like arms or branches. The process of separation seems slow in the painted wood sculpture (plate 119), where dark tones increase the sense of weight and struggle. The selective use of color – black torso, red arm – draws attention to the separate geometric parts and to the way they are joined. The grafting of arms to torso is abrupt, even forced.

The bronze sculpture (plate 120) is more dynamic in its urge to free itself from the ground. The torso is poised on a corner and leans on one arm: the slender, elongated limbs suggest two propeller blades, rotating the work into imbalance. Modeling was employed to graft the arms to the torso, creating rounded, organic junctures. The golden surface of the bronze unifies the sculpture while revealing the texture of the original wax and wood.

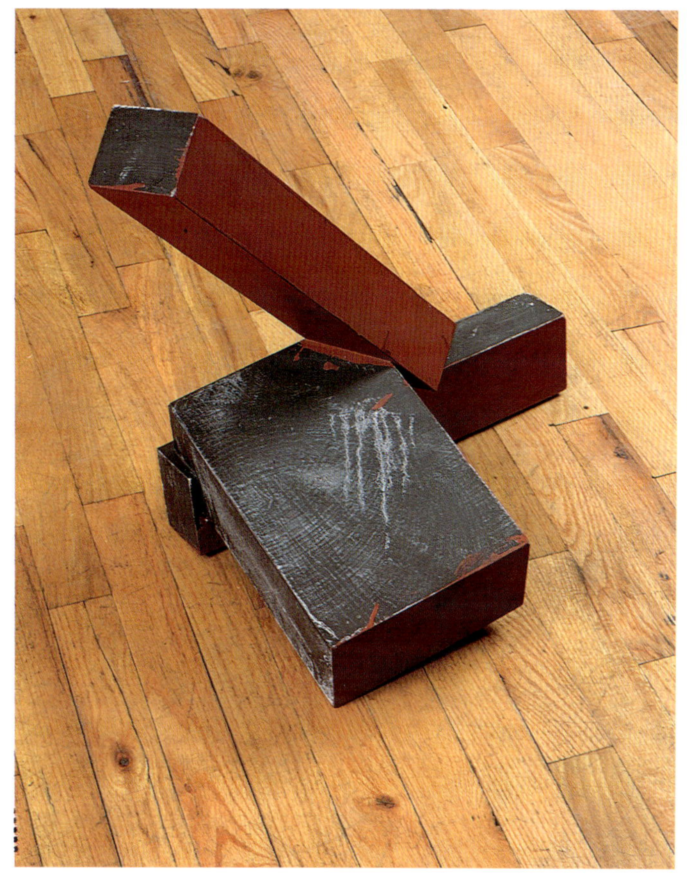

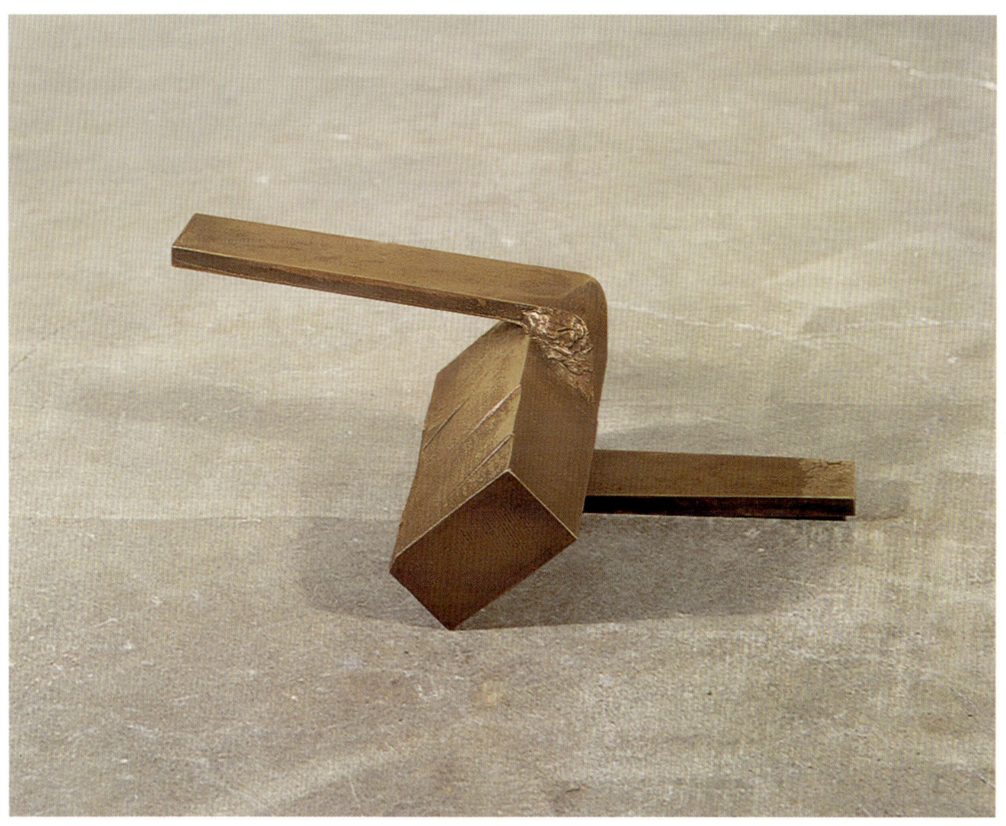

119 Untitled. 1980. Wood, casein, and oil, 18¼ x 16½ x 12½" (46.4 x 41.9 x 31.8 cm). Private collection

120 Untitled. 1980. Bronze (edition 1/3), 6 x 7¾ x 16" (15.2 x 19.7 x 40.6 cm). Private collection

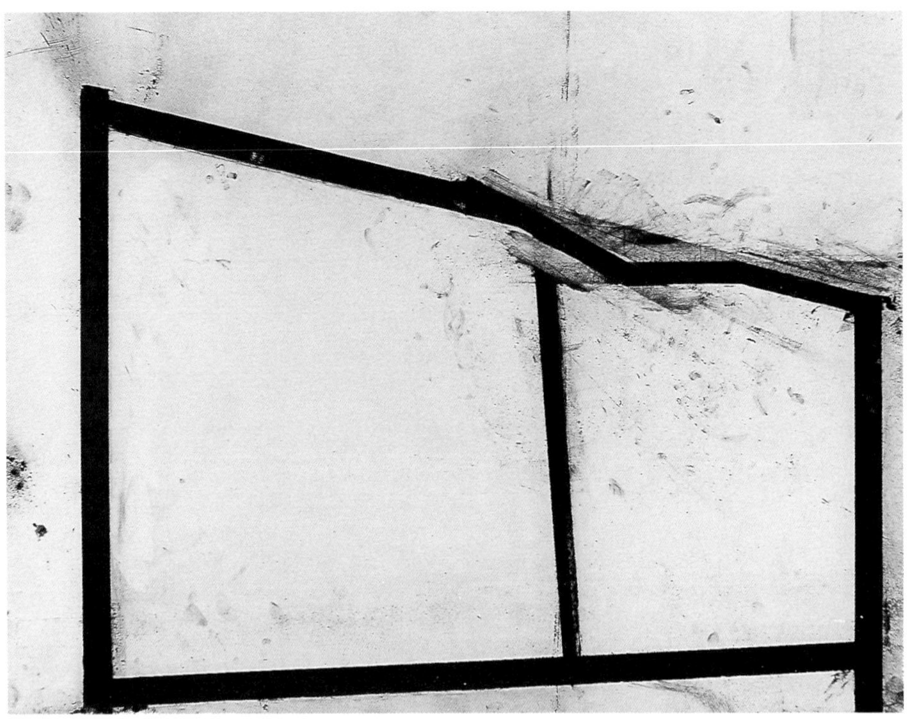

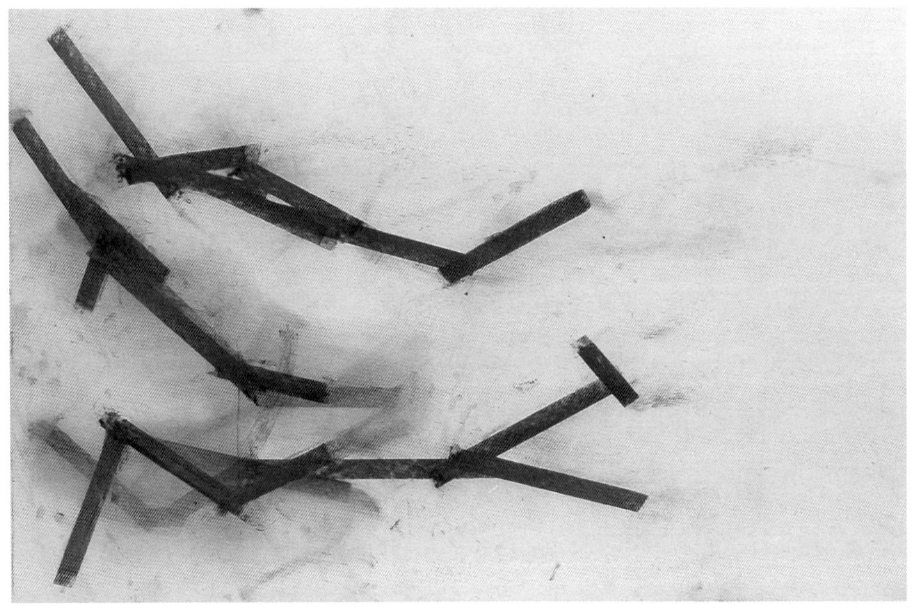

121 Untitled. 1981. Charcoal on paper, 22¼ x 30½" (55.5 x 76.5 cm). Collection Elizabeth Murray and Bob Holman

122 Untitled. 1981. Charcoal on paper, 26⅛ x 40¾" (66.4 x 103.5 cm). Collection Sherry Fabrikant

The location of the joints and the means of their articulation are crucial in conveying "how the form comes together by joining disparate elements," as Shapiro says. His absorption with ways of joining expresses itself also in works on paper, such as a charcoal drawing from 1981 (plate 121). Thick lines define two squarish zones that share an inner border, which at its top is interrupted by a slight gap. The central vertical is as much a joint linking the two zones as a border separating them.

In another drawing from the same year (plate 122), sequences of short segments come together to form three more or less horizontal lines running from the left toward the center. The joining of the segmented lines alludes to organic growth, or to the torsos and limbs of reclining figures. The zigzag configurations emerge from a smudgy and diffuse pictorial ground.

Freestanding Figures (1980–82)

Shapiro's freestanding figure of 1980 (plate 123) is a declaration of intent. In this almost life-size sculpture he embraces the human form in all its multiple possibilities, at the same time endowing it with a poetic singularity of its own. A new sense of excitement is discernible in this phase of his work, and it is manifested in the many inventive configurations that revel in their ambiguity. Shapiro is in fact driven by the possibility of producing alternative readings – "moments when it appears that a figure is a figure, and other moments when it looks like a bunch of wood stuck together – moments when it simultaneously configures and disfigures."[28]

His figures, like most of his sculptures, start with wood. The 1980 figure is an assemblage of standard four-by-fours from a lumberyard. It stands on one leg with the other lifted behind. One arm points frontwards; the other, pointing to the side, is considerably longer, suggesting a later grafting. These beams are indeed "a bunch of wood stuck together," but they also speak a refined language of posture and equilibrium. The significant action is always focused around the torso – the fulcrum – from which a multitude of movements emerges. The simplicity of Shapiro's geometric forms does not belie the complexity of emotions they can trigger; the viewer is presented with a range of subjective associations.

Shapiro's initial configurations led him to explore changes in material, size and scale, and shape. The 1980 figure was succeeded by larger, more complicated pieces. The complexity of the sculptures, their greater height and weight, required the use of assistants. Patrick Strzelec, also a sculptor, began working with Shapiro in the foundry in 1979. He has spoken of how difficult and unorthodox Shapiro's requirements are when he casts bronze. Shapiro works with traditional methods, but also against them. His insistence on retaining the extensive markings of the saw blade, for instance, presents especially complex technical problems at the foundry. Ichiro Kato, who assists Shapiro with his wood sculptures, has described similar demands, particularly in the assembling of the more massive and precarious works.

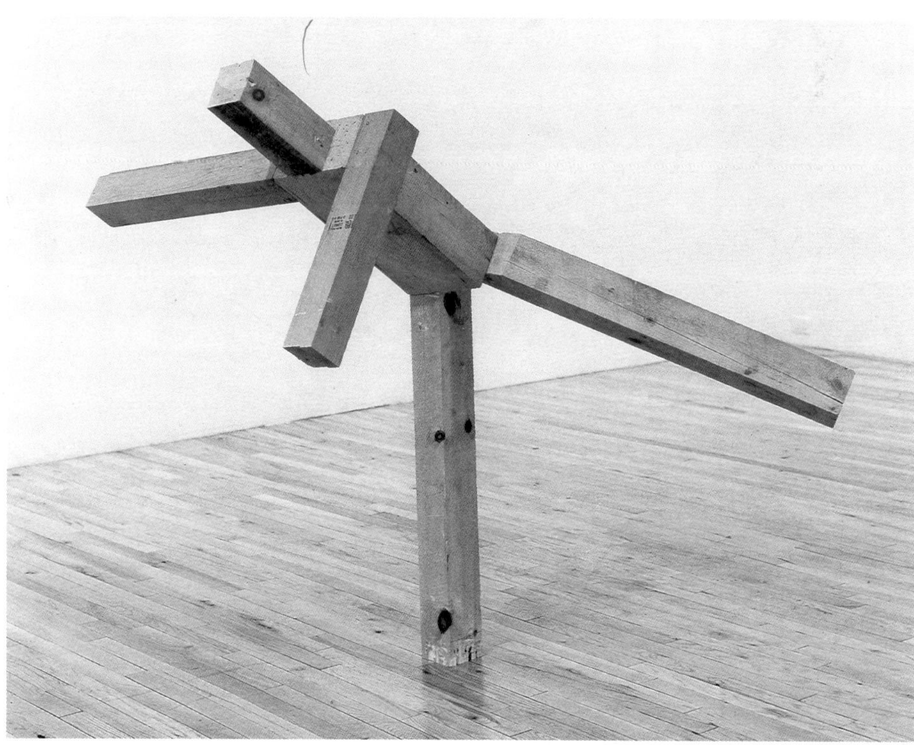

123 Untitled. 1980. Wood, 52⅞ x 64 x 45½" (134.3 x 162.6 x 115.6 cm). The Edward R. Broida Trust, Palm Beach, Florida

A bronze version of the 1980 figure (plate 124) seemed "so permanent" to Shapiro that he "wanted to break it up."[29] He translated it back into wood (plate 126) and gave it two heads, one of which he painted blue. Another version in wood, with an altered stance, has a single, blue head (plate 125). A bronze rendition (plate 128) features a bowed head with a supplementary limb (or head?) above it. A wood figure from 1982 (plate 127) has been altered by subtraction, its arms abruptly truncated and neck severed.

Shapiro's figures are rarely made as isolated pieces; instead, a single original configuration engenders other renditions, immediately or over a longer period. One such "family" of figures performs simultaneous acts of rising and falling. Corresponding wood and bronze sculptures from 1982 (plates 129, 130) are at the same time leaping and landing: arms and legs, as well as head and posterior, reverse positions. A wood figure that falls on its yellow head (plate 131) is all the more vulnerable because of its delicate, splayed limbs. A related drawing (plate 132) offers a view of another cinematic action.

Identifying members of the same family of figures depends on a memory of form. Shapiro stresses the extent to which form and memory combine in his art: "My work has to do with the memory of experience. It is an attempt to locate experience in form." For him, a form such as the figure is essentially a locus of remembered emotion, a repository in which past and present feelings are recorded. For this reason the figure remains, like memory, an abstraction, impossible to specify. As Shapiro puts it, "The figure is the source of abstraction."

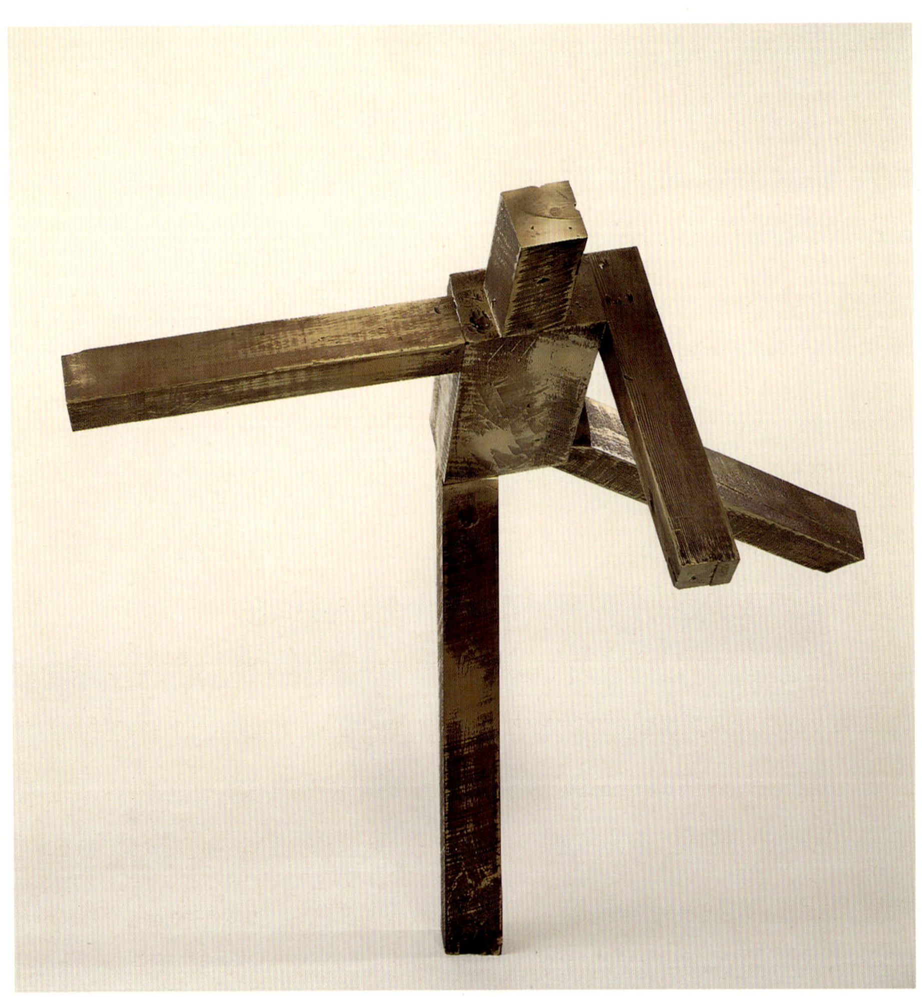

124 Untitled. 1980–81. Bronze (edition 0/3), 52⅞ x 64 x 45½" (134.3 x 162.6 x 115.6 cm). Whitney Museum of American Art, New York. Purchase with funds from the Painting and Sculpture Committee

OPPOSITE:

125 Untitled. 1981. Oil on wood, 54 x 30 x 30" (137.2 x 76.2 x 76.2 cm). Levi Strauss & Co. Art Collection

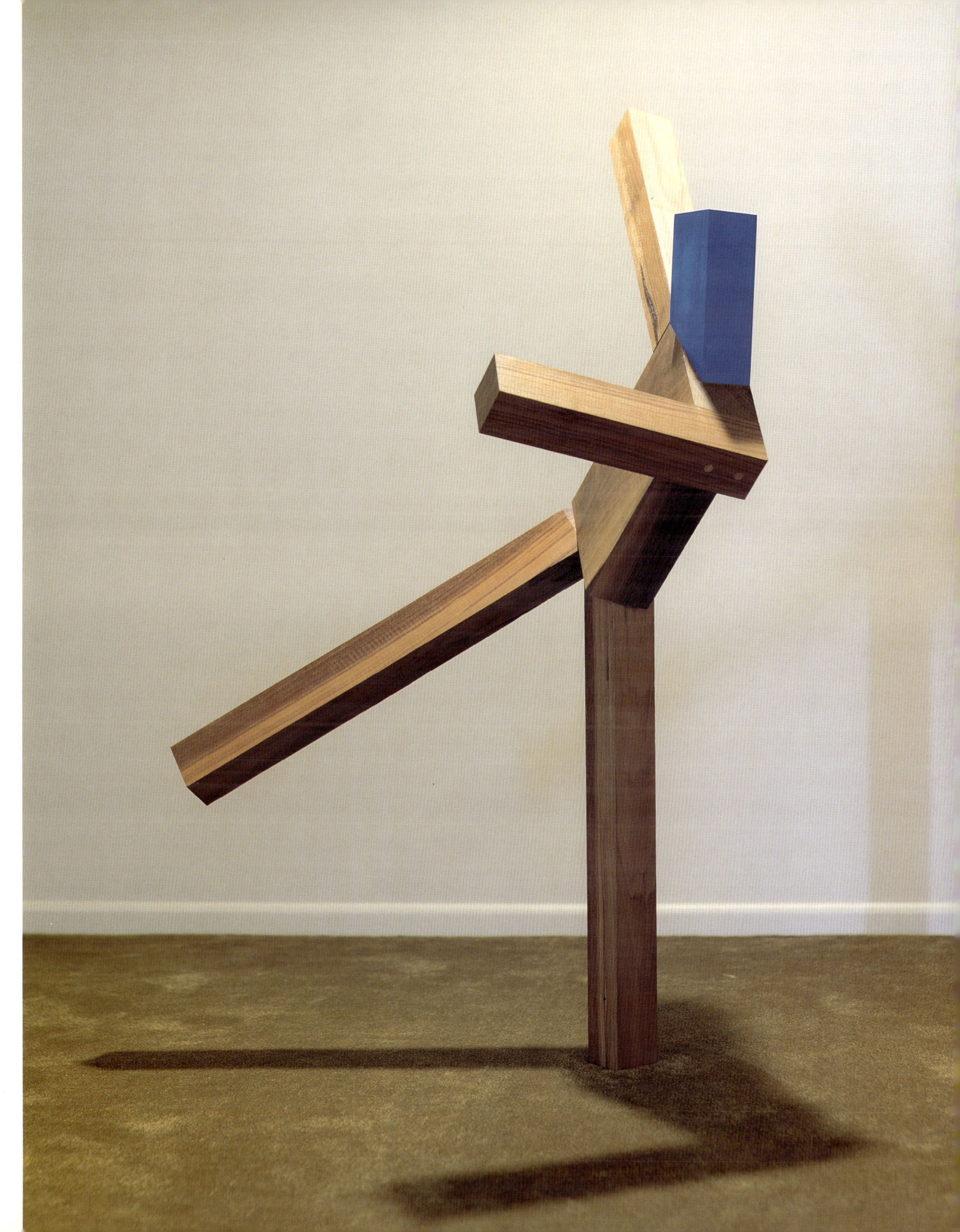

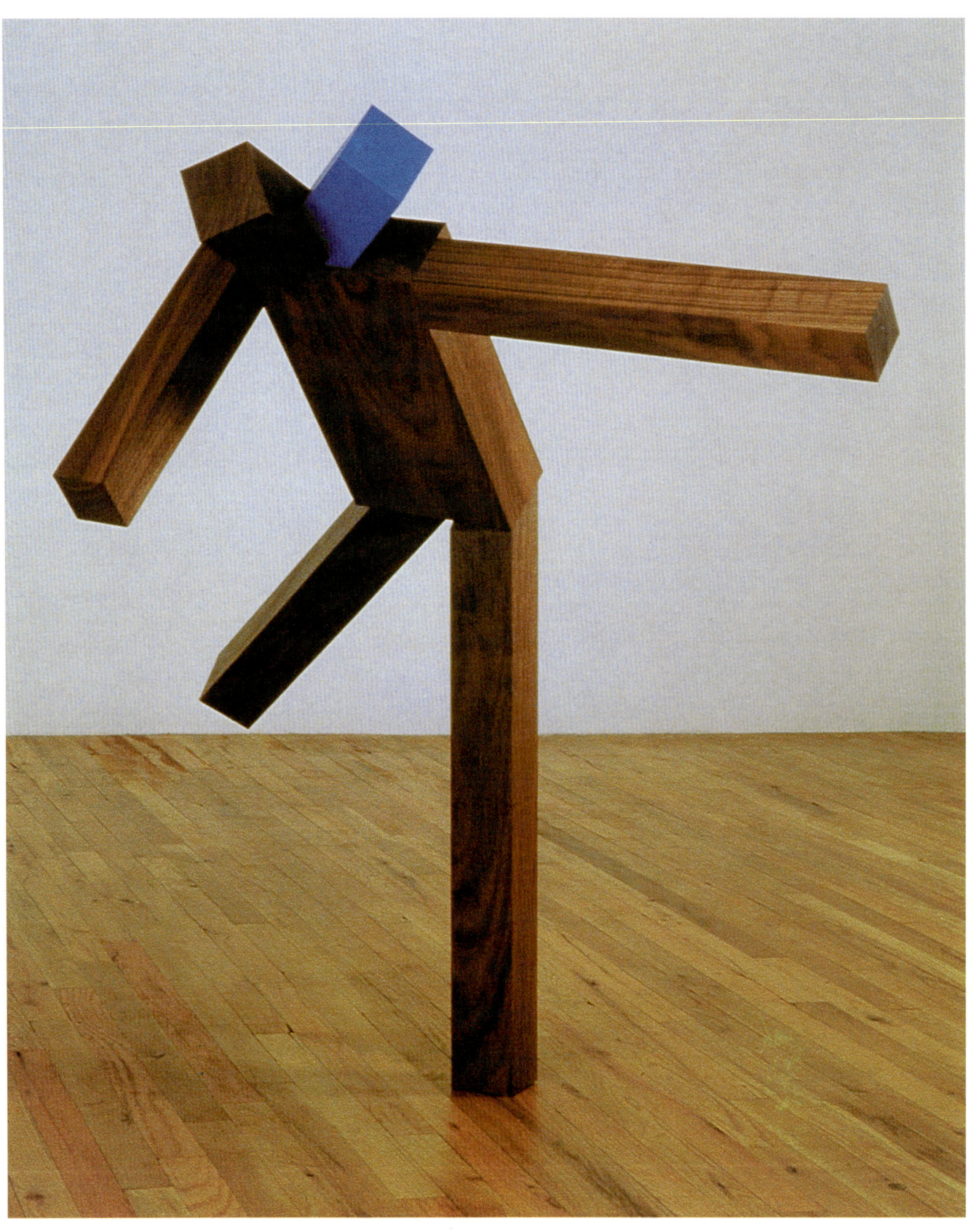

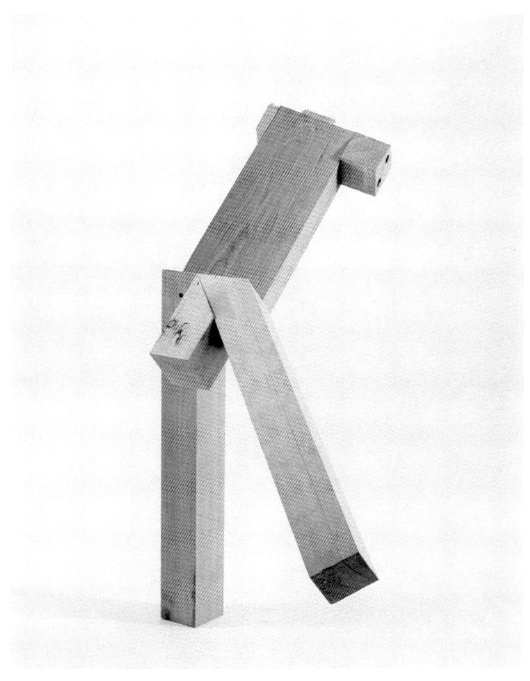

127 Untitled. 1982. Wood, 43½ x 28½ x 35" (110.5 x 72.4 x 88.9 cm). Private collection

128 Untitled. 1982. Bronze (edition 3/3), 6'1" x 70" x 30" (185.4 x 177.8 x 76.2 cm). Statens Konstmuseer – The National Swedish Art Museums; Moderna Museet, Stockholm

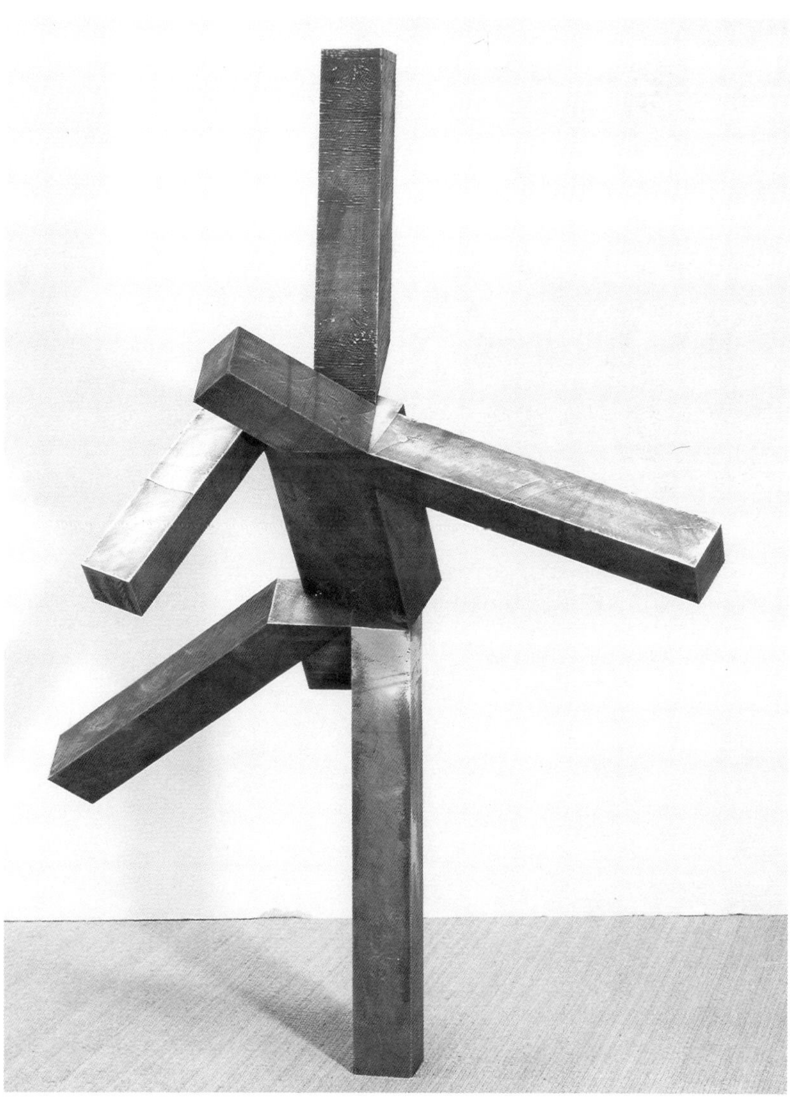

OPPOSITE:

126 Untitled. 1981. Oil on wood, 45 x 53¼ x 39½" (114.3 x 135.3 x 100.3 cm). Private collection, San Francisco

129 Untitled. 1982. Bronze (edition 1/3), 46½ x 50 x 45" (118.1 x 127 x 114.3 cm). Collection Michael and Judy Ovitz, Los Angeles

130 Untitled. 1982. Wood, 48 x 45 x 52" (121.9 x 114.3 x 132.1 cm). Collection Paula Cooper

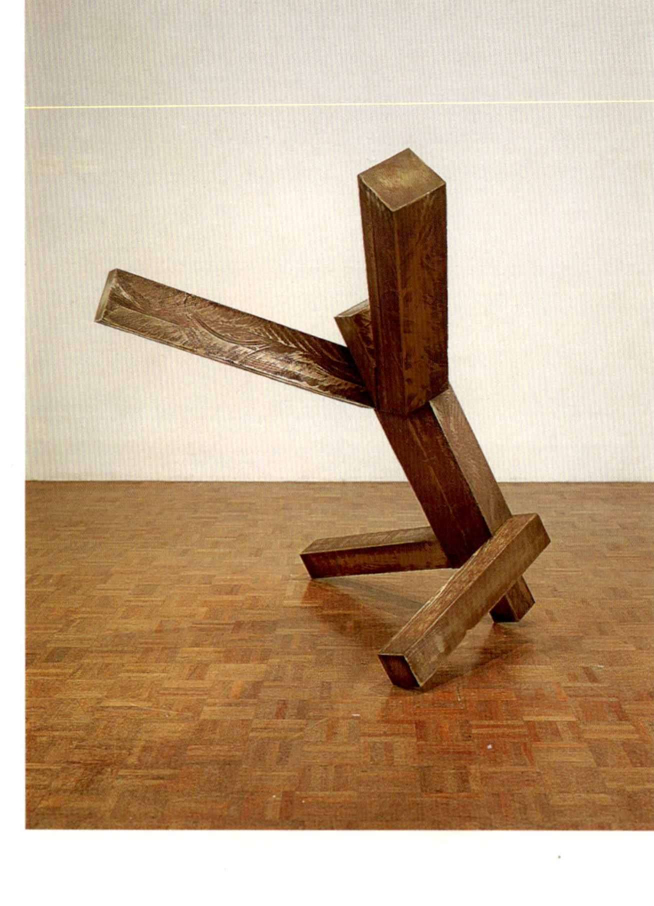

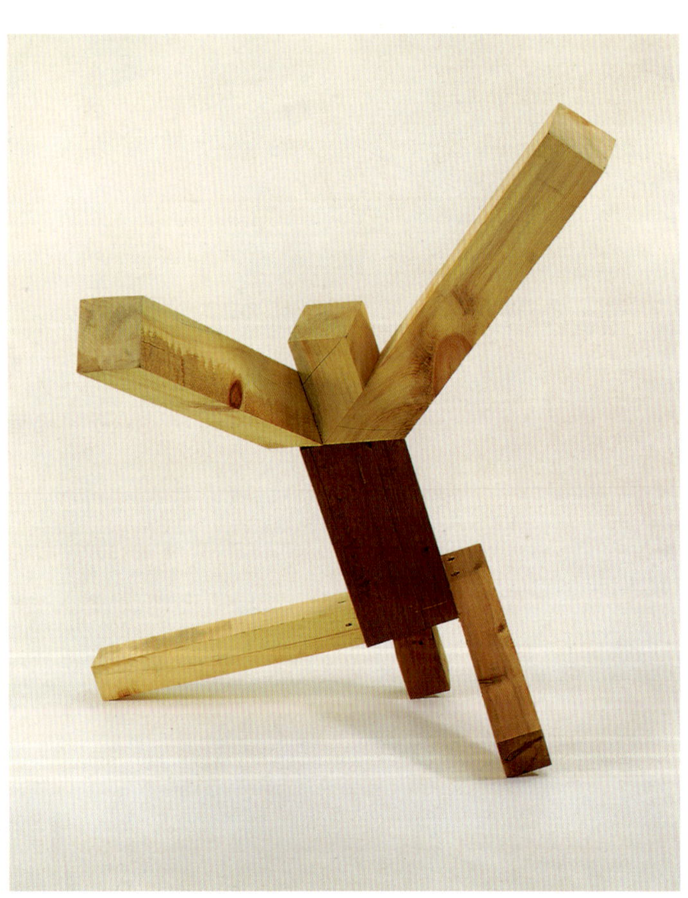

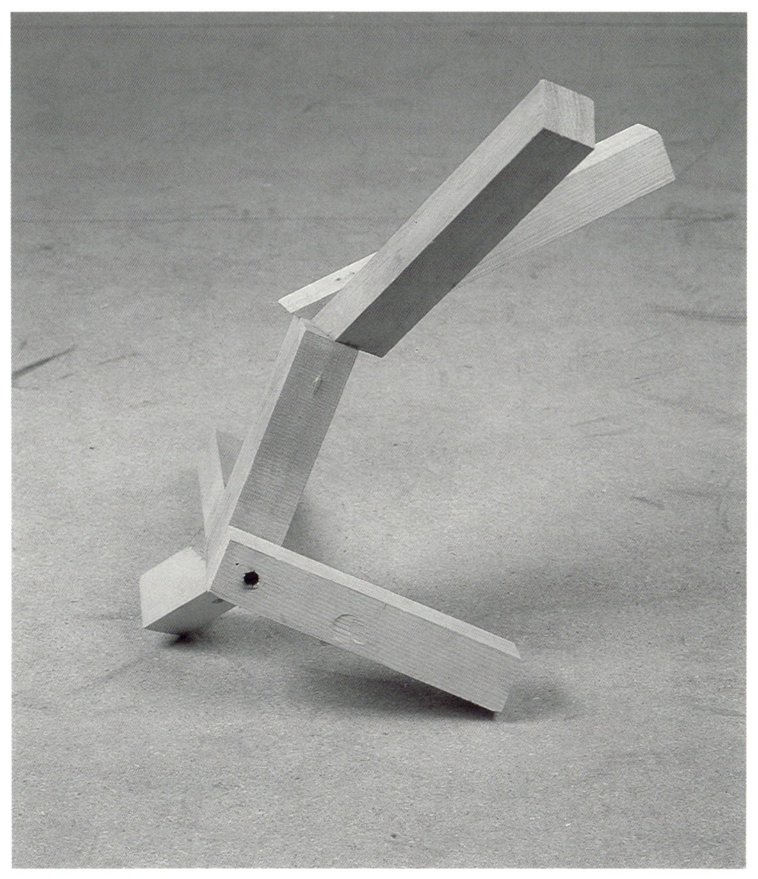

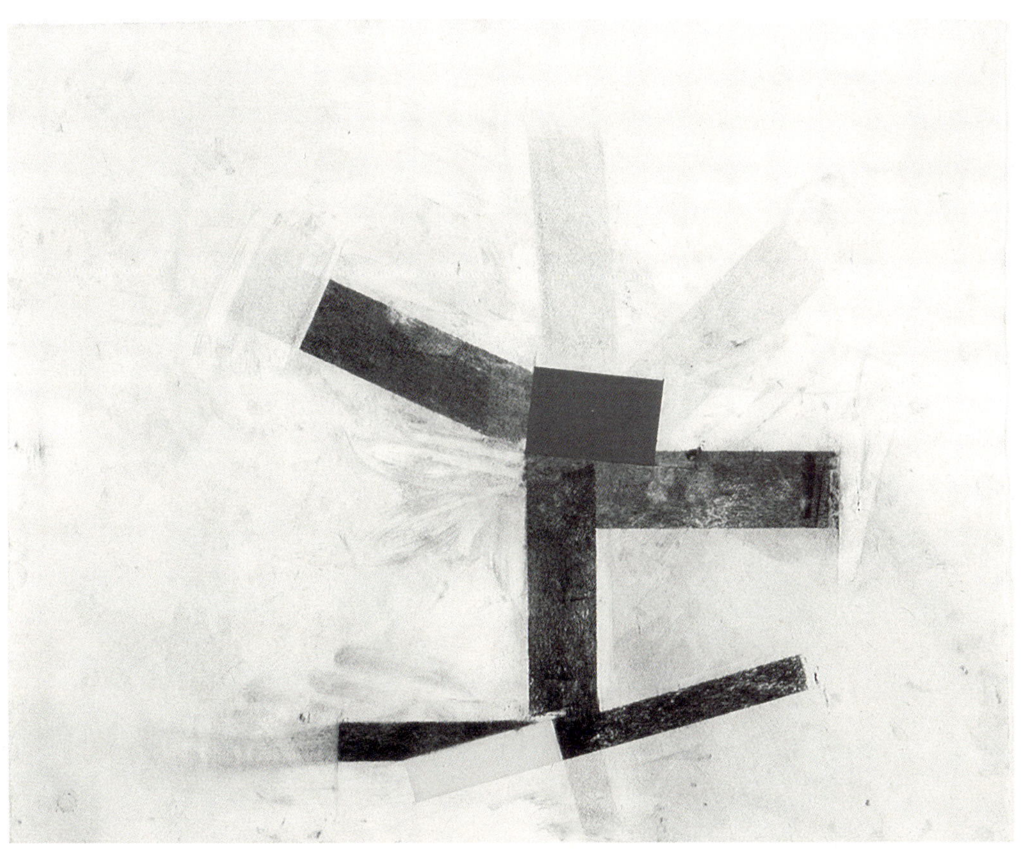

131 Untitled. 1982. Enamel on wood, 21 x 22 x 21" (53.3 x 55.9 x 53.3 cm). Collection Anne and William J. Hokin, Chicago

132 Untitled. 1982. Charcoal and gouache on paper, 19 7/16 x 24 3/8" (49.4 x 61.9 cm). Collection Joel and Anne Ehrenkranz

Choreography (1980–87)

Shifting moods and rhythms – now more expansive, now more grave – characterize the next phase of work. Some figures are fragmentary or lie close to the ground; others are dynamic and dominate their environment.

A group of figures from 1982–85 (see plate 133) seems caught in the act of dancing: they reach out (plate 135), balance on one leg (plate 136), or spin with arms and legs in a pinwheel (plate 134). These extreme movements activate the surrounding space. At times, the choreography expands to include daring acts that challenge gravity (plate 137).

In critical discussions of Shapiro's work, reference has often been made to the sculpture of David Smith, since both artists share the abstracted figure as a subject and use geometric forms and large scale to describe it. The differences between them are, however, profound. In *Cubi VI* (figure 13), for example, Smith employed geometric elements to outline a man walking. Shapiro's angular figures, in contrast to Smith's composed silhouettes, seem to grow from the inside out and twist or rotate in space. Smith, furthermore, used stainless steel, an impenetrable, reflective material; Shapiro uses bronze, a warmer, richer medium, whose surface intimately records his working process. The traces of process, of his constant trial-and-error approach, are always visible in his sculptures; the surface is a register of operations, summoning up and revealing the history of the finished work.

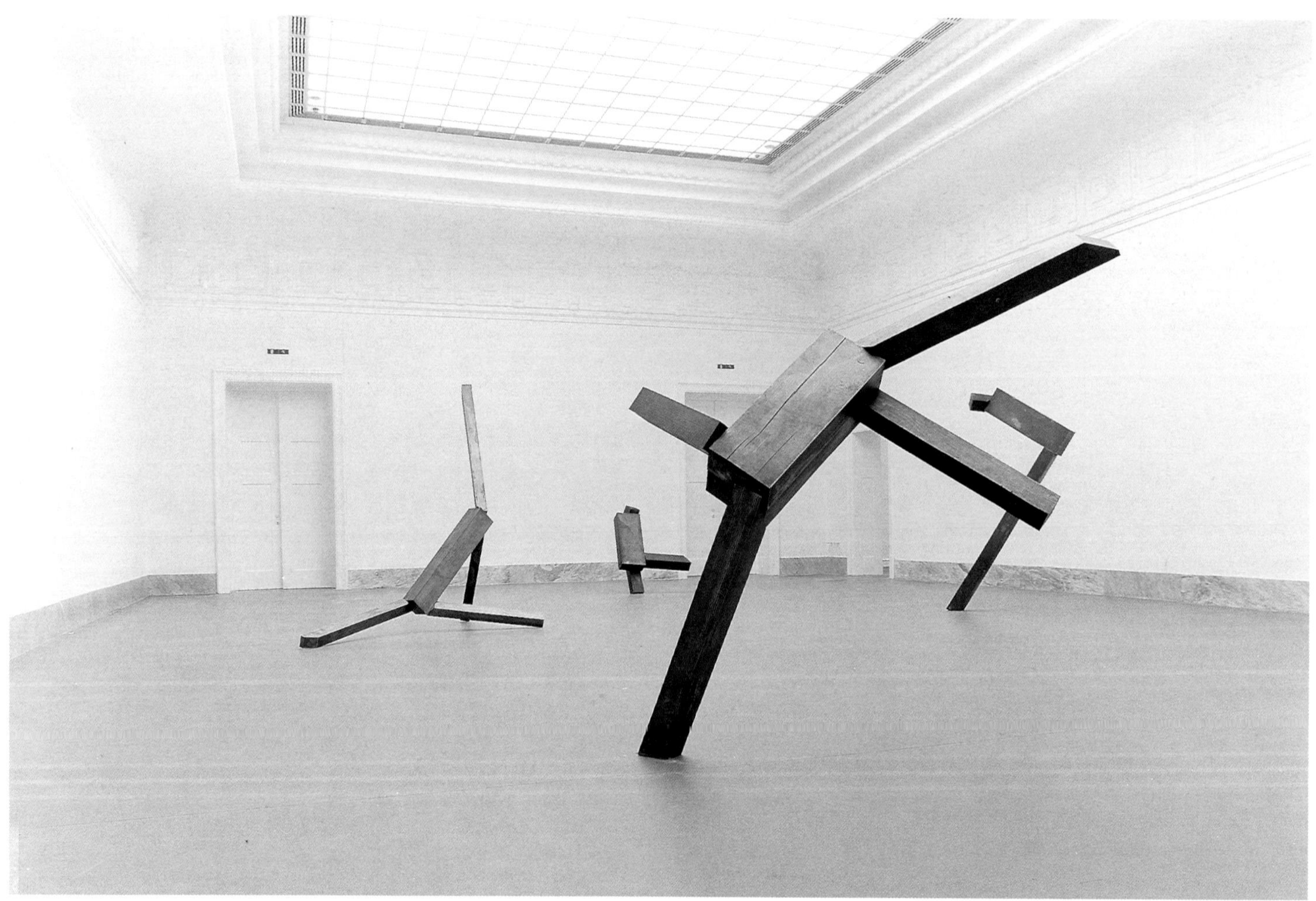

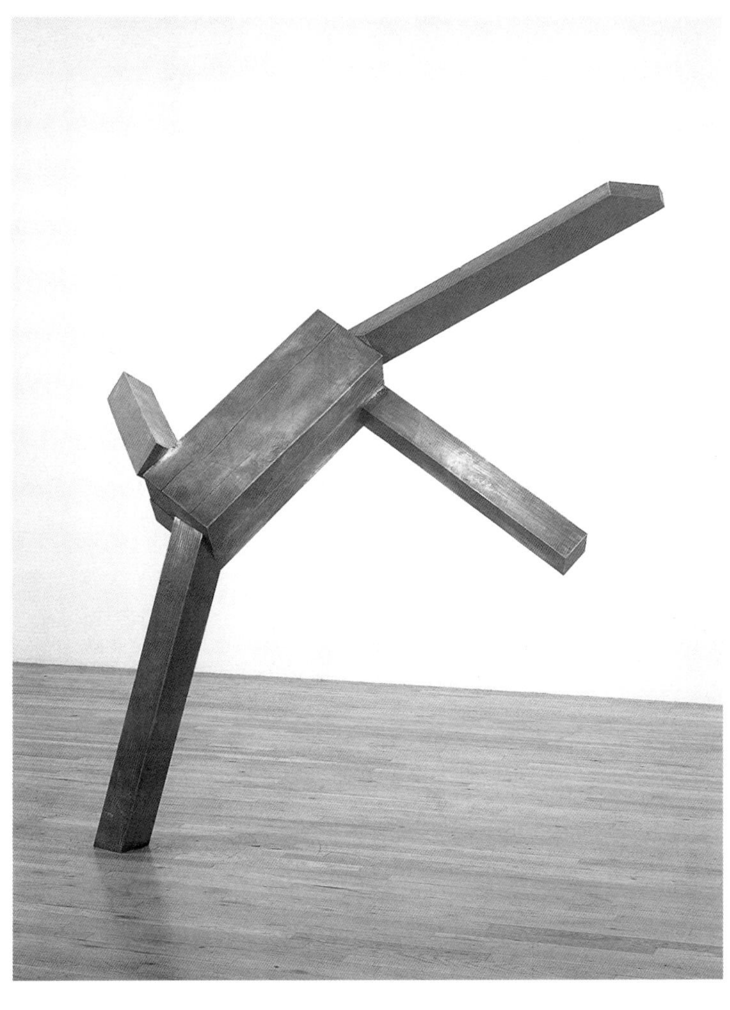

134 Untitled. 1983–84. Bronze (edition 1/3), 6'8¾" x 6'8" x 52" (205.1 x 203.2 x 132.1 cm). The Saint Louis Art Museum. Gift of Mr. and Mrs. Barney A. Ebsworth

135 Untitled. 1985. Bronze (edition 0/3), 7'6¼" x 7'5¾" x 52½" (229.2 x 228 x 133.4 cm). Hakone Open-Air Museum, Hakone-machi, Japan

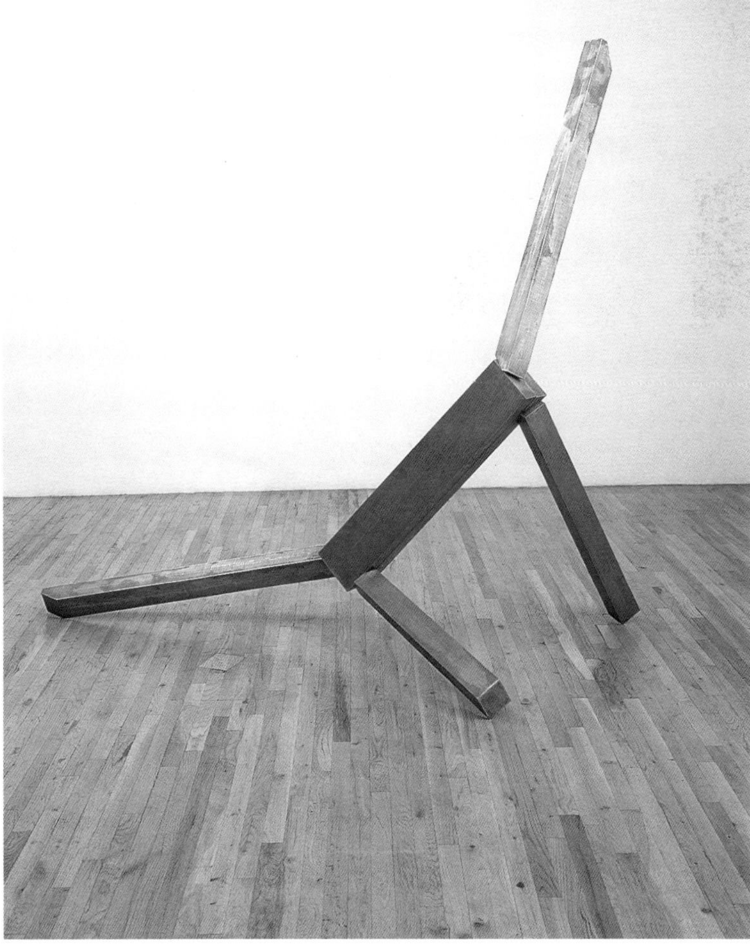

OPPOSITE:

133 Installation view of the exhibition "Joel Shapiro," Staatliche Kunsthalle, Baden-Baden, 1986. Works shown here also appear in plates 134–36.

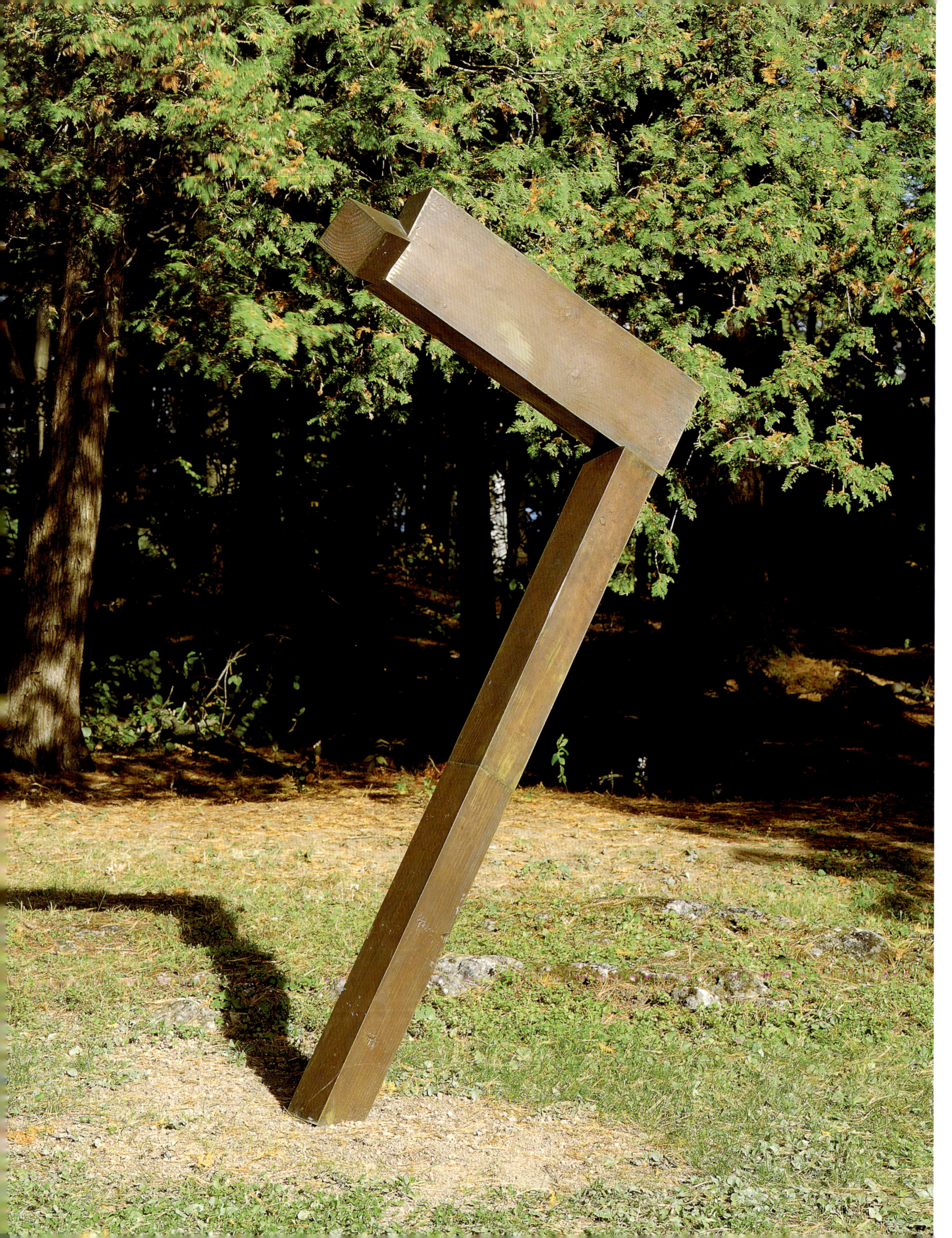

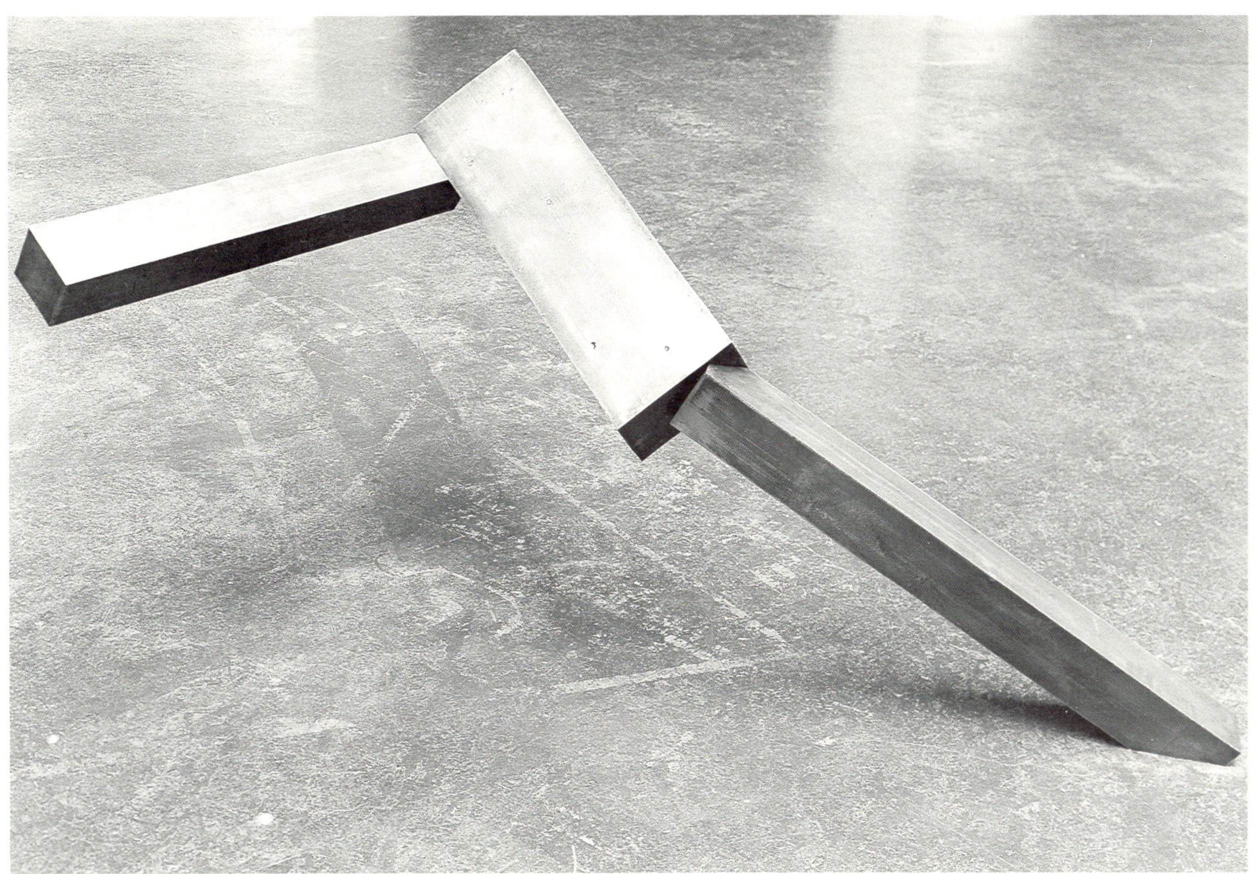

137 Untitled. 1982–83. Bronze (edition 1/3), 55" x 7'6" x 25" (139.7 x 228.6 x 63.5 cm). Private collection

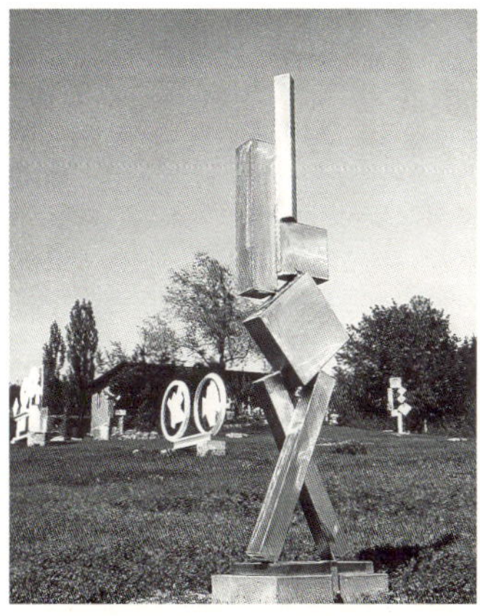

Fig. 13 David Smith. *Cubi VI*. 1963 (photographed by the artist, Bolton Landing, New York, c. 1963). Stainless steel, 9'10⅛" x 29½" x 21¾" (300 x 74.9 x 55.2 cm). Israel Museum, Jerusalem

OPPOSITE:

136 Untitled. 1983. Bronze (edition 0/3), 6'1" x 39½" x 14" (185.4 x 100.3 x 35.6 cm). Collection the artist

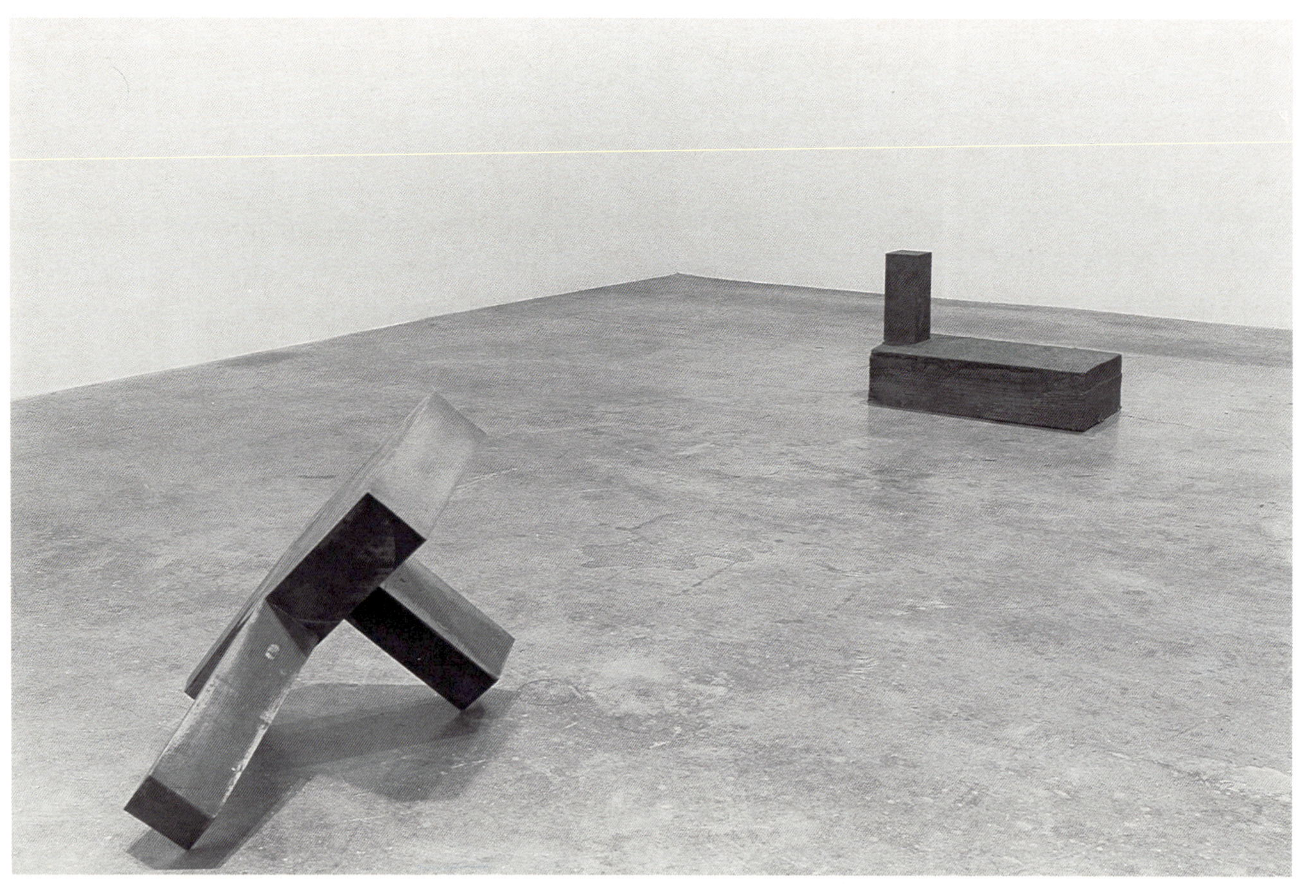

138 Installation view of the exhibition "Joel Shapiro: Sculpture and Drawings," Asher/Faure, Los Angeles, 1983. Works shown here also appear in plates 139, 140.

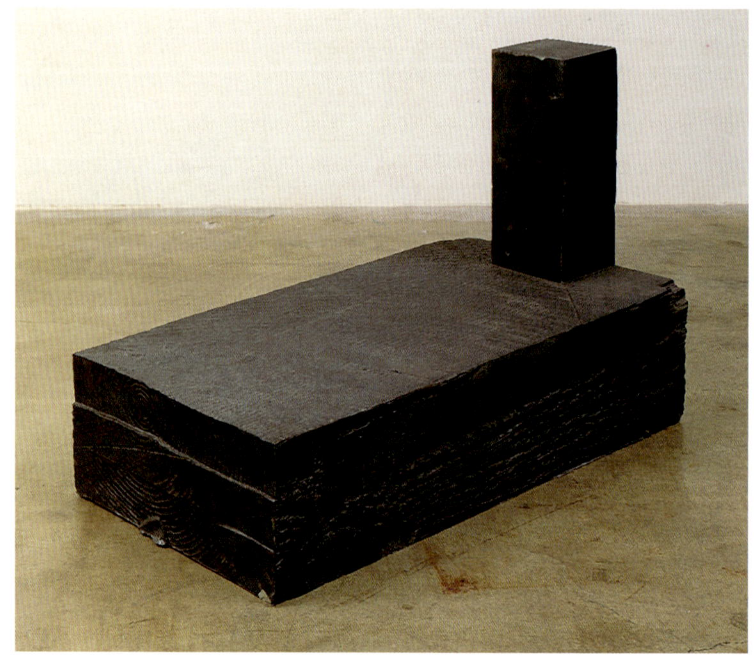

139 Untitled. 1982–83. Cast iron, 14½ x 11¼ x 23" (36.8 x 28.6 x 58.4 cm). Collection the artist

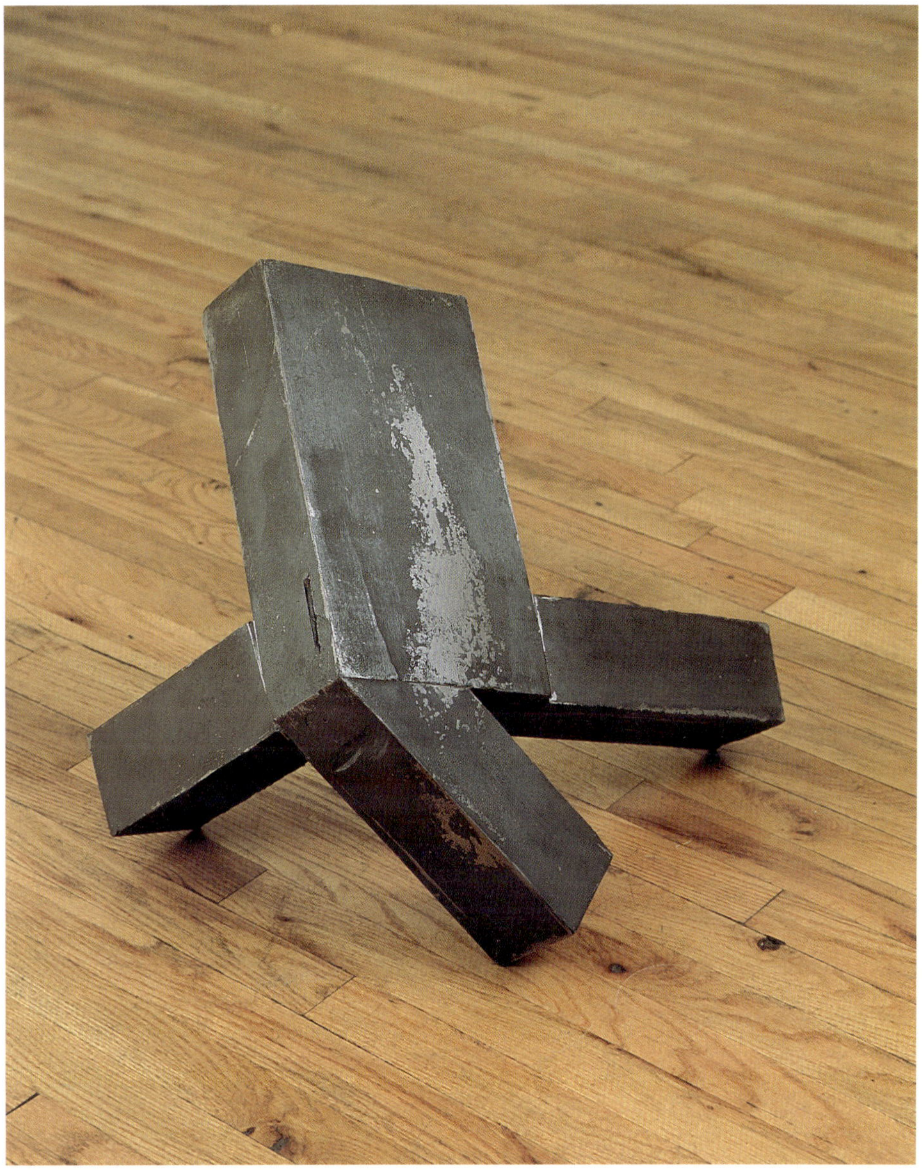

Simple but varied geometric forms – the essential structures of Shapiro's process – develop in a slow-motion choreography in works from 1982–86 (see plates 138–40, 143, 145). This group of sculptures consists of fragmentary figures, with torsos and truncated limbs. The torso, to which the limbs are grafted, and where an imagined whole is conceived, is the focus.[30] The appearance of the limbs is equivocal; they seem at once lopped off and budding. These muted configurations close in on themselves. The surface is articulated for the sake of abstract form; the flat planes are larger, the skin of the sculptures more exposed.

The horizontal beam of a plaster figure on the floor (plate 141) recalls the two houses joined by a passageway, from 1974 (plate 79). There is a considerable difference, though, between the two works, not only in scale and dimension, but also in mode of representation: the later work refers directly to the human figure, just as the earlier work did to houses, but now the subject is conveyed by abstracted form. In addition, the earlier, intimate psychological space has been transformed into a public domain. The volumes of the plaster figure impose on the viewer with their thick presence.

140 Untitled. 1982–83. Cast iron (edition 1/3), 17¼ x 18½ x 16¾" (43.8 x 47 x 42.5 cm). The Edward R. Broida Trust, Palm Beach, Florida

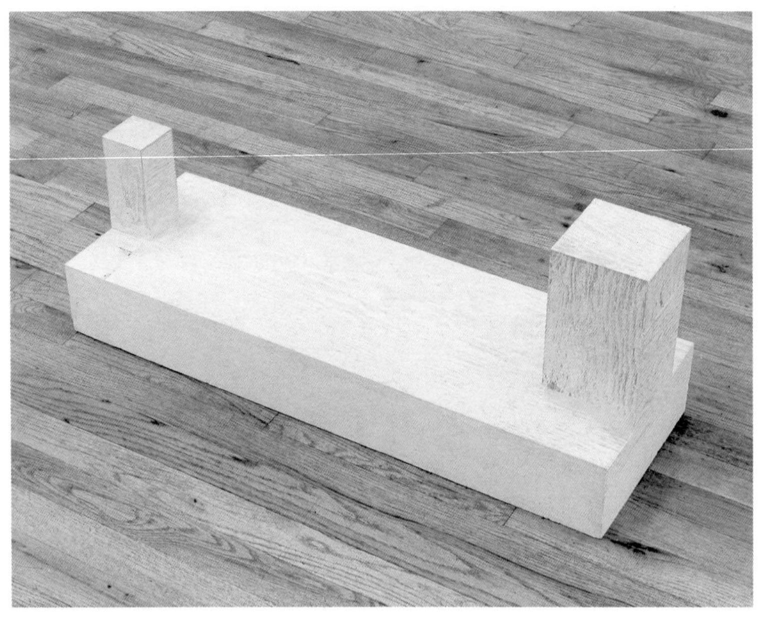

141 Untitled. 1983–84. Plaster, 12⅛ x 30⅛ x 10⅛" (30.8 x 76.5 x 25.7 cm). The Museum of Contemporary Art, Los Angeles. Gift of Margo H. Leavin

142 Untitled. 1984. Burnt wood and pencil, 37¾ x 14 x 11" (95.9 x 35.6 x 27.9 cm). Dr. Donald Kay, San Francisco

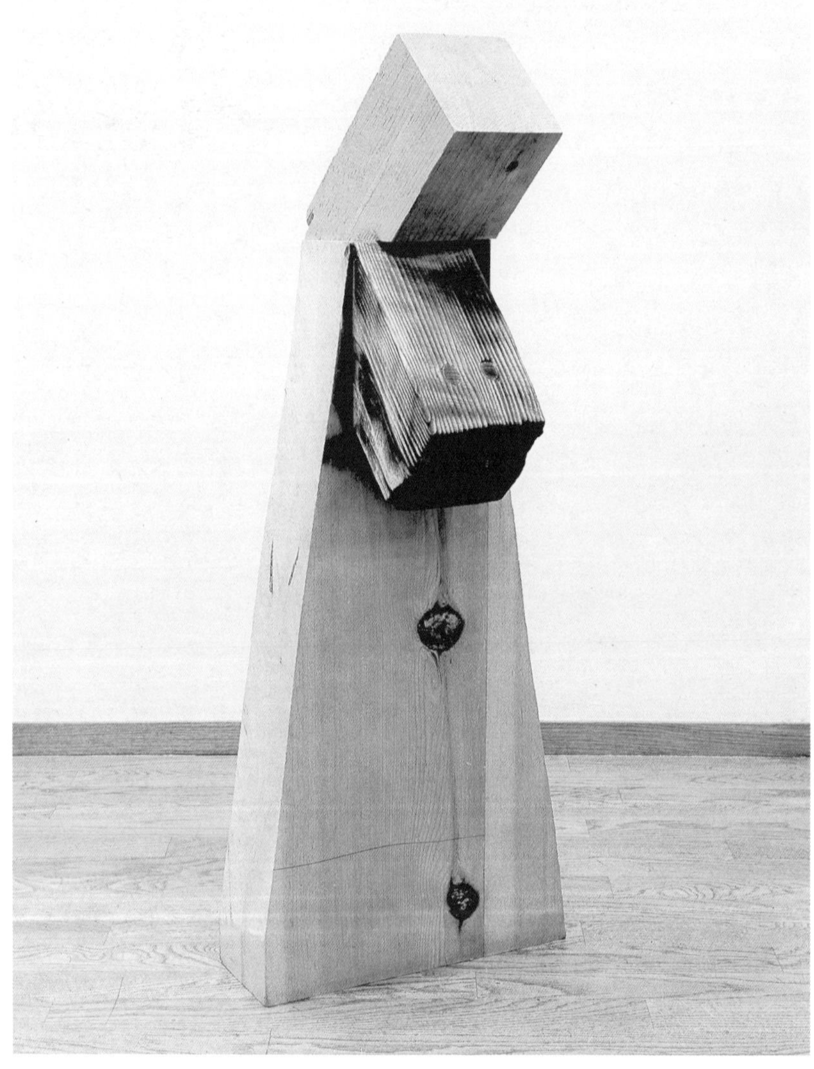

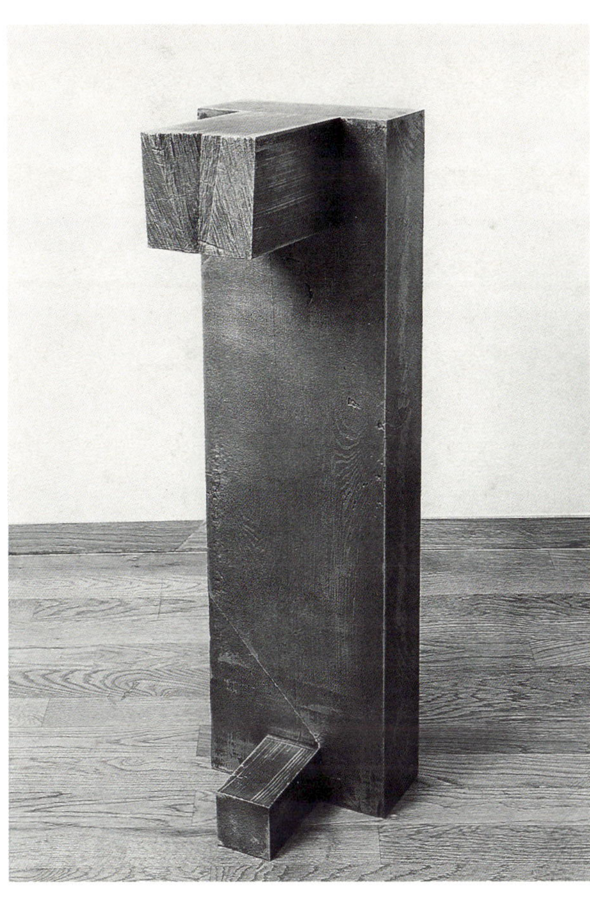

143 Untitled. 1983–84. Bronze (edition 1/2), 30 x 11½ x 8½" (76.2 x 29.2 x 21.6 cm). The Newark Museum. Purchase 1984, The Members Fund

144 Untitled. 1987. Charcoal, chalk, pencil, and pastel on paper, 43 x 30¾" (109.2 x 78.1 cm). Collection Ivy Shapiro

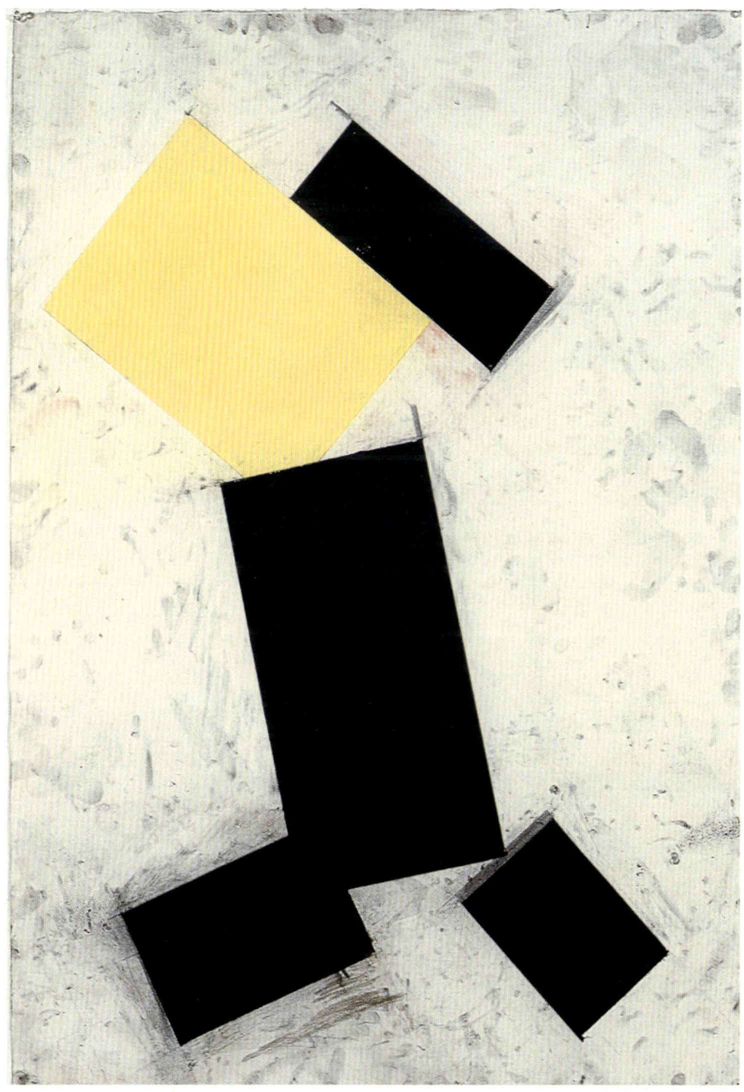

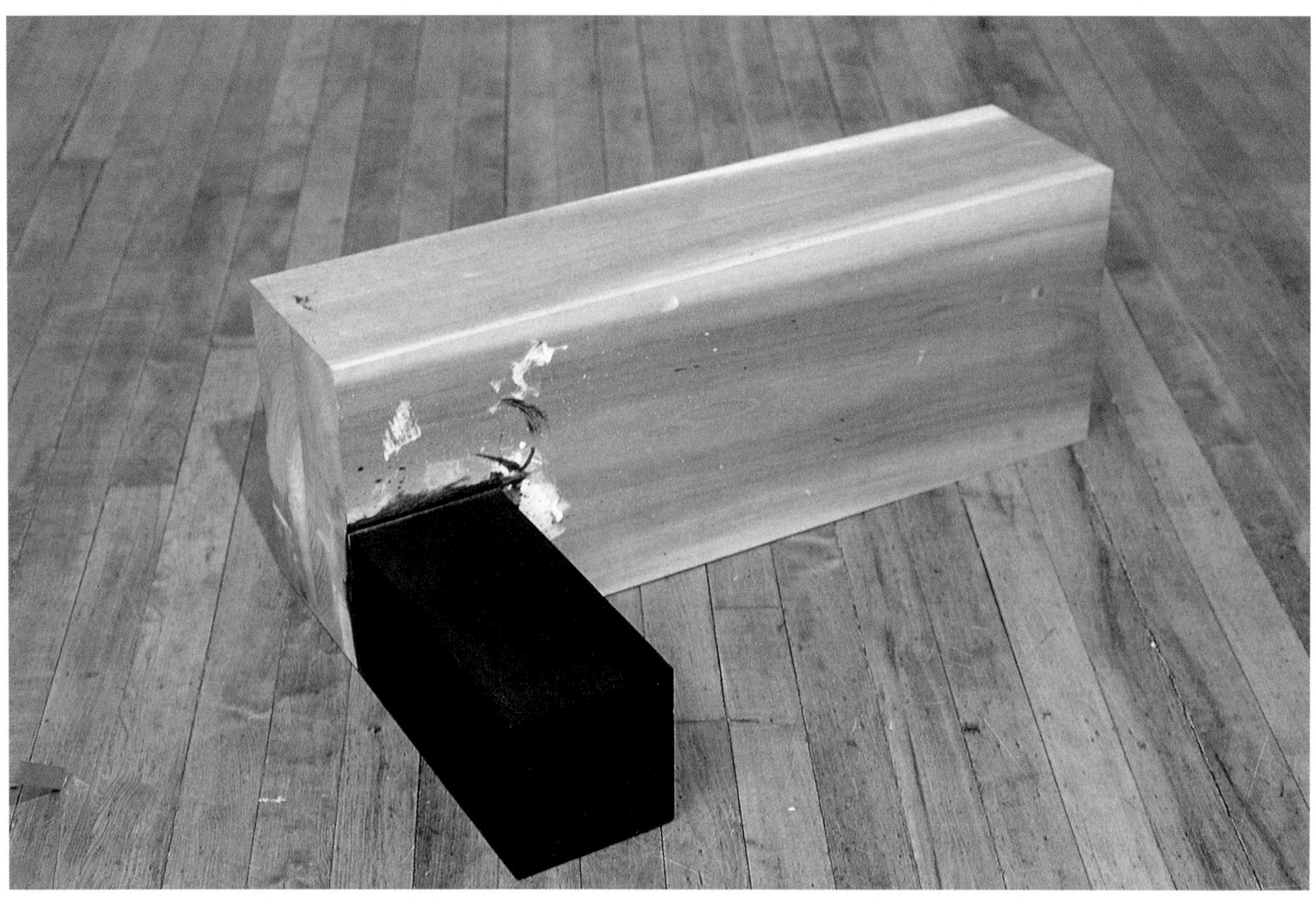

145 Untitled. 1985. Oil on poplar, 10 x 28 x 17 ¼" (25.4 x 71.1 x 43.8 cm). Collection the artist

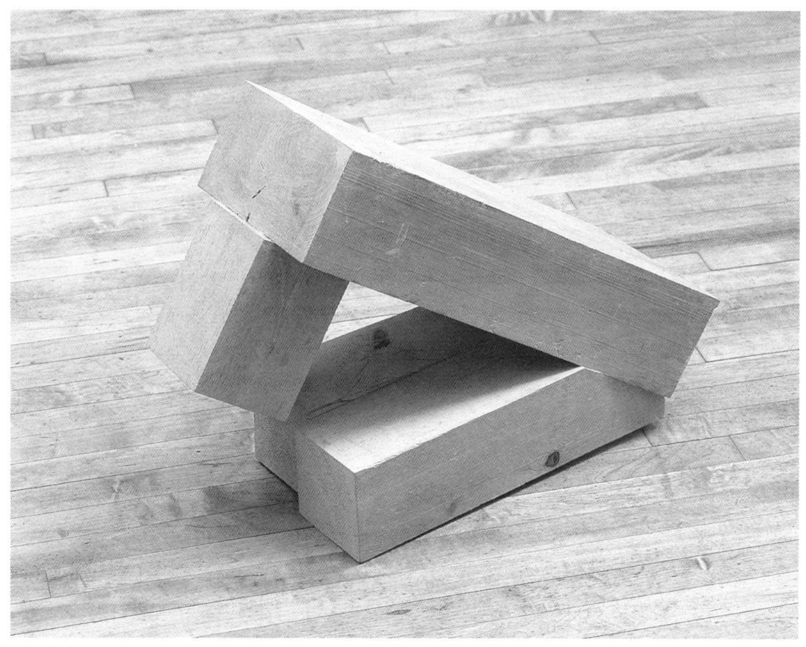

146 Untitled. 1982–86. Oil on wood, 18¾ x 28½ x 12½" (47.6 x 72.4 x 31.8 cm). Collection the artist

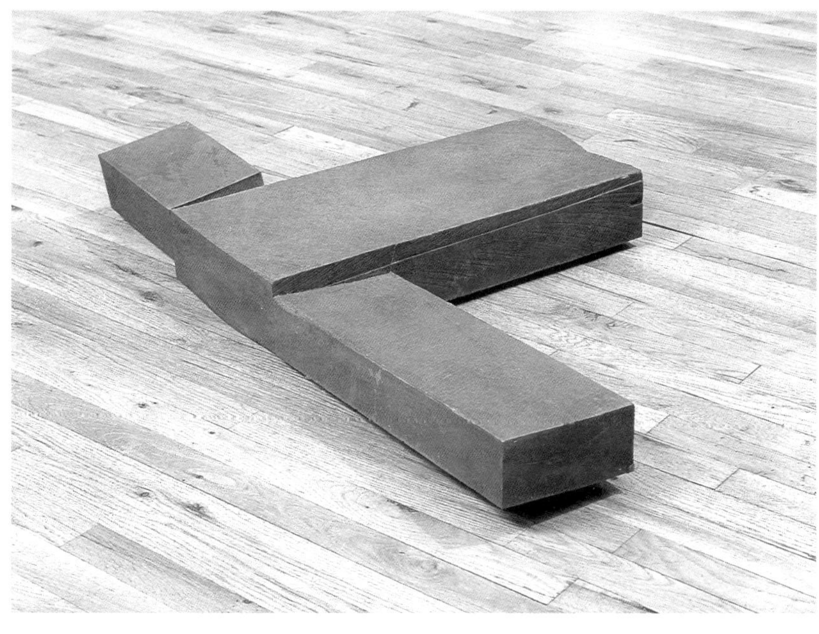

147 Untitled. 1984. Cast iron, 5¼ x 24¼ x 46¾" (13.3 x 61.6 x 118.7 cm). Private collection

148 Untitled. 1984. Bronze (edition 3/3), 43 x 43¾ x 35" (114.3 x 111.1 x 88.9 cm). Tate Gallery, London

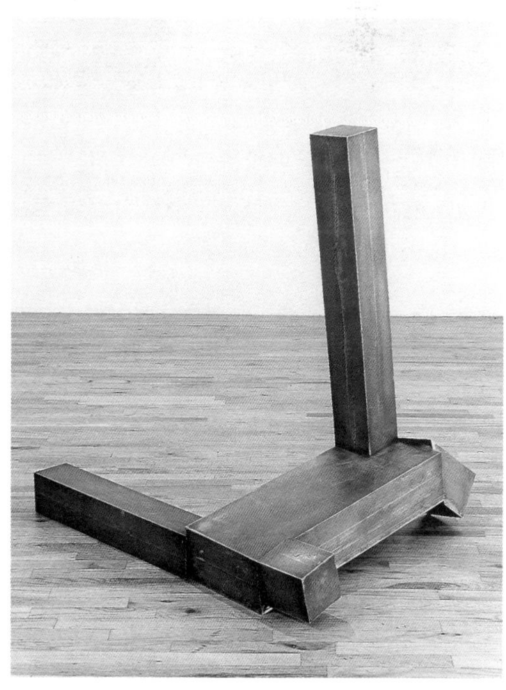

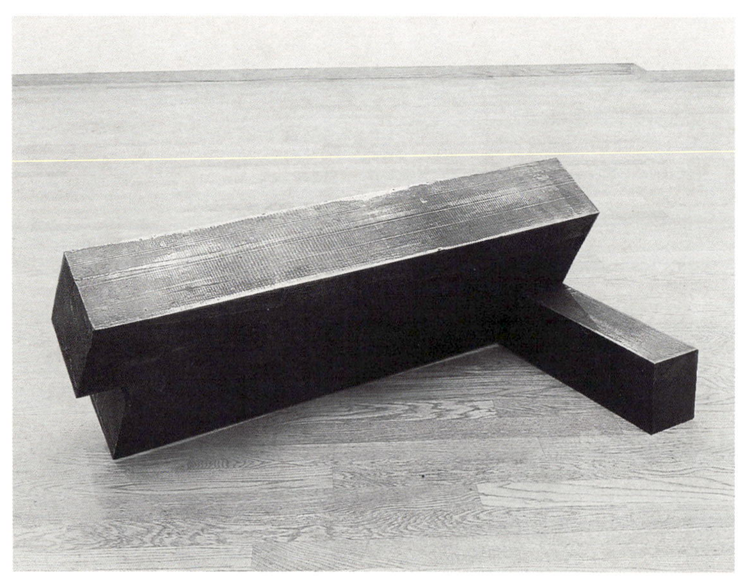

149 Untitled. 1983–84. Cast iron, 14¼ x 21 x 38⅜" (36.2 x 53.3 x 97.5 cm). Collection the artist

150 Untitled. 1987. Charcoal and chalk on paper, 54½ x 49½" (138.4 x 125.7 cm). Collection Paul F. Walter

151 Installation view of the exhibition "Joel Shapiro," Staatliche Kunsthalle, Baden-Baden, 1986. Works shown here also appear in plates 143, 152, 161.

152 Untitled. 1985. Bronze (edition 3/3), 38½ x 28½ x 14" (97.8 x 72.4 x 35.6 cm). The Detroit Institute of Arts

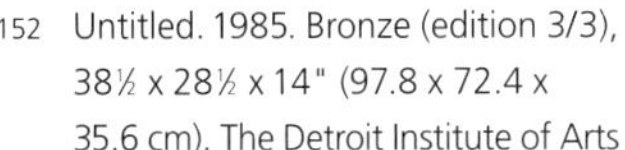

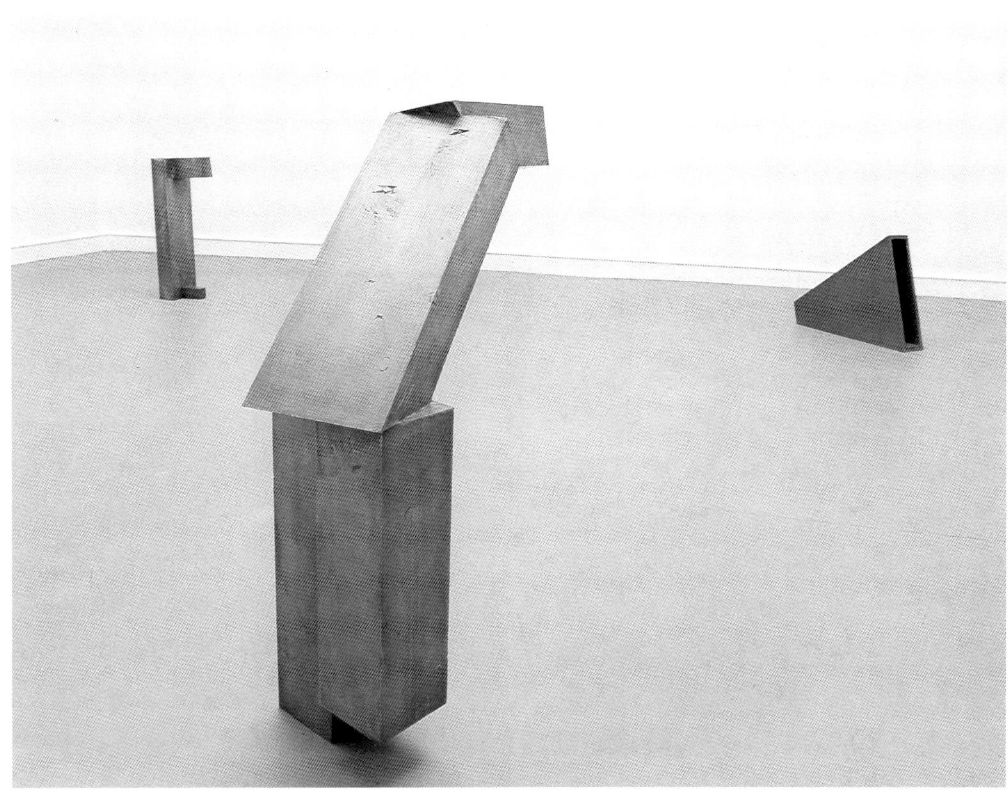

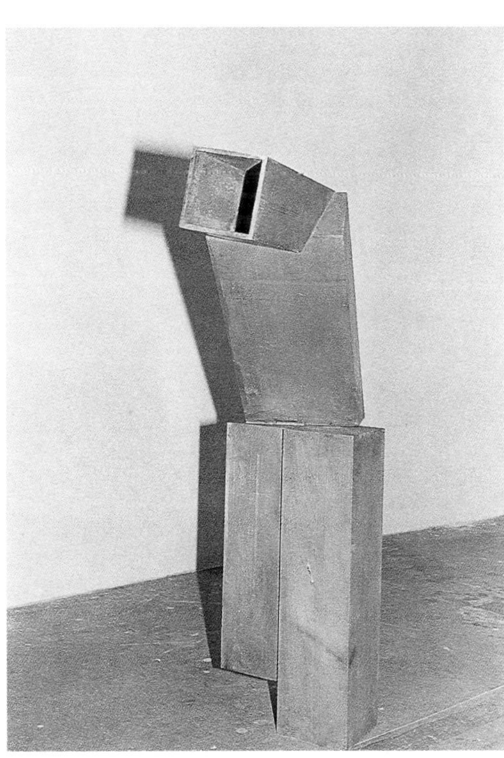

A standing bronze from 1985 (plate 152) is made of blocks – two legs, a torso, a head – one atop the other but unaligned, so that the figure leans slightly forward, giving the impression of slow, heavy movement. As the open "head" tips forward, though, we see into the depth of the body, and the hollow interior contradicts the evident weight of the figure.

Perched on a short, thick pole, a bronze from 1985–86 (plate 154) positions the torso at a diagonal and punctuates it with splayed arms and crossed legs. To an apparently simple and direct monumentality is added a complex treatment of the limbs – which are angled and which vary in size and position – while the bronze surface catches light in its minute striations. Shapiro has acknowledged that "originally the joints had very much to do with the geometry of the form, so they were right-angled, blunt, flat onto flat. Then I began to cut them and used forty-five-degree angles. Now the geometry is less proscriptive."[31] This allowed for a greater freedom of expression.

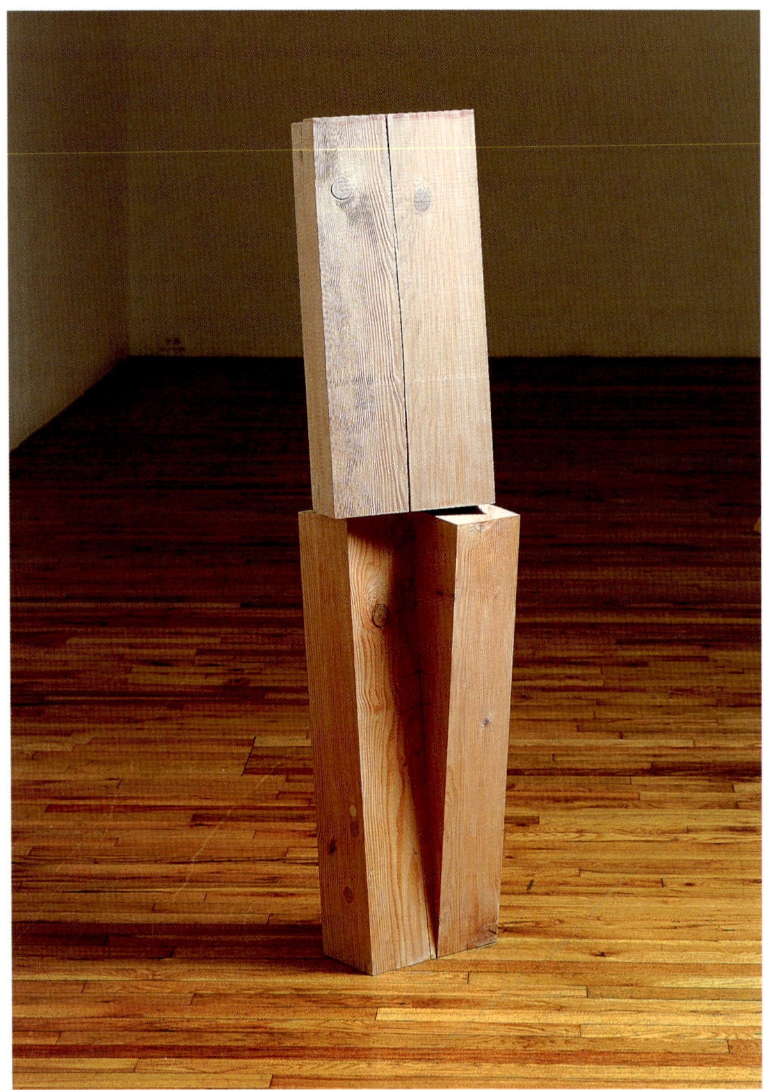

An unusual figure from 1986 (plate 155) extends its head to the ground, like a trunk, to find a new point of support. (The arms were ripped off and stuck under the head to provide this support.) This head/trunk might be read also as a large post, independent of the body, against which the face buttresses itself. With its bending contour, this linear sculpture draws attention to the negative space it creates. The work insists on its ambiguity – is it an animal, a human figure, or an abstract construction? – and resists either a predominately horizontal or vertical reading. Works of Tony Smith, especially *Willy* (figure 14), come to mind, for both their visual and emotional similarities, and for what Smith called "the inscrutability and mysteriousness of the thing."[32]

153 Untitled. 1986. Fir wood and oil, 54 x 12 x 10" (137.2 x 30.5 x 25.4 cm). Private collection

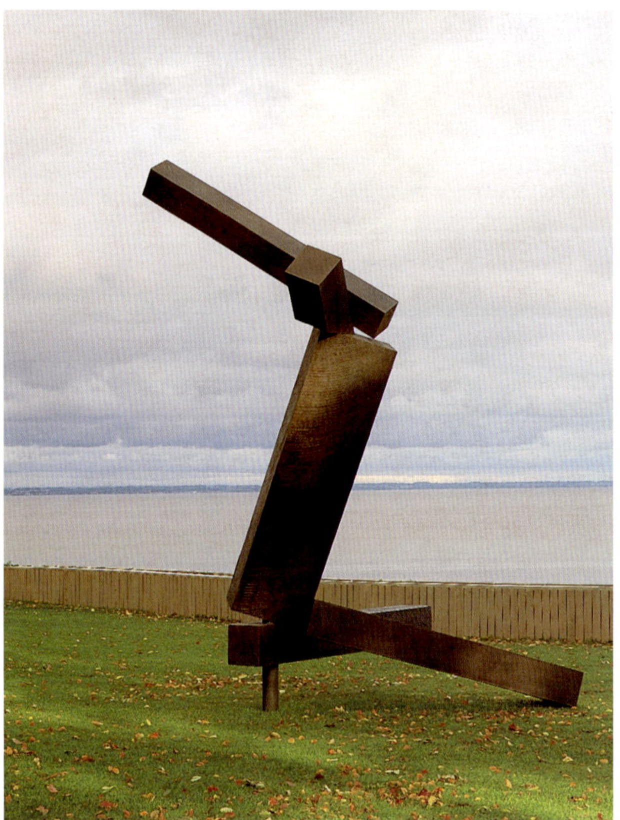

154 Untitled. 1985–86. Bronze (edition 1/3), 14' x 12' x 10'10" (426.7 x 365.8 x 330.2 cm). Louisiana Museum for Moderne Kunst, Humlebaek, Denmark. Donation, The New Carlsberg Foundation

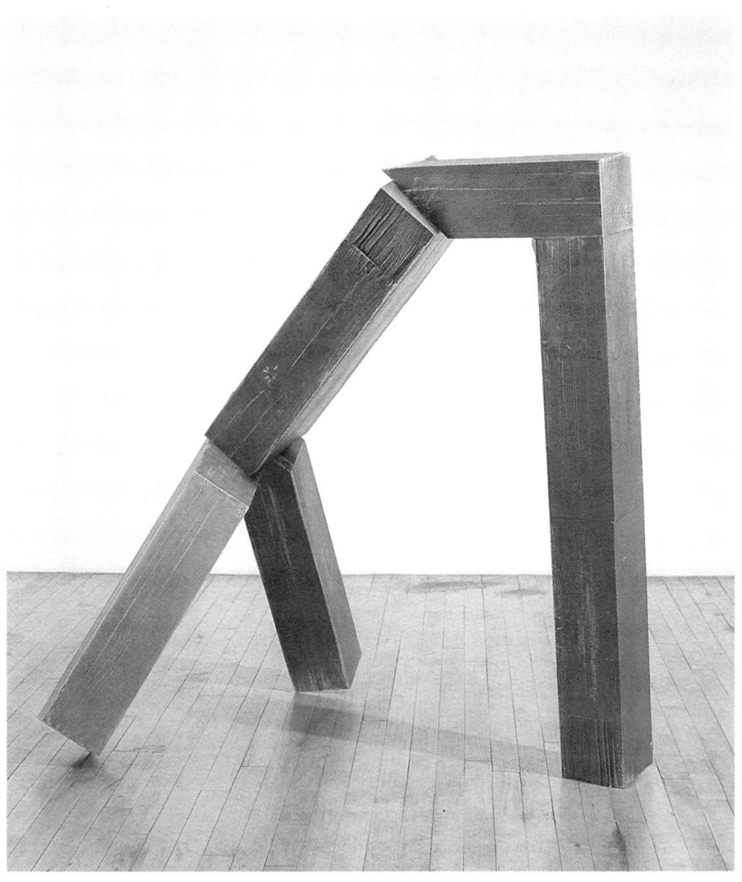

155 Untitled. 1986. Bronze (edition 3/3), 48⅜ x 51 x 34¼" (122.9 x 129.5 x 87 cm). Collection Paula Cooper

156 Untitled. 1985. Charcoal on paper, 43 x 30¾" (109.2 x 78.1 cm). Private collection

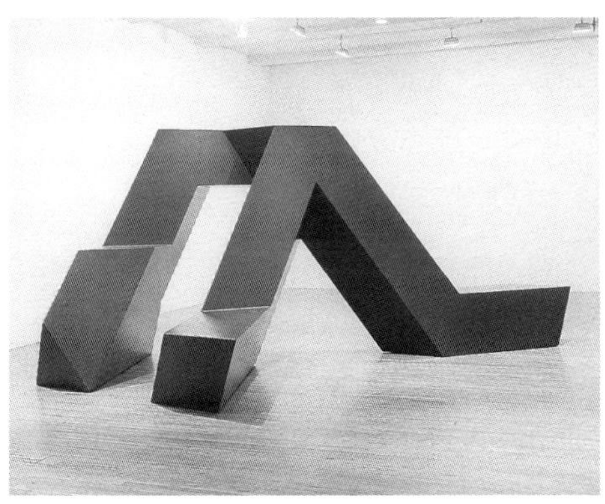

Fig. 14 Tony Smith. *Willy*. 1962. Steel, painted black, 7'7¼' x 11'3" x 18'8" (231.7 x 342.9 x 569 cm). Courtesy Paula Cooper Gallery, New York

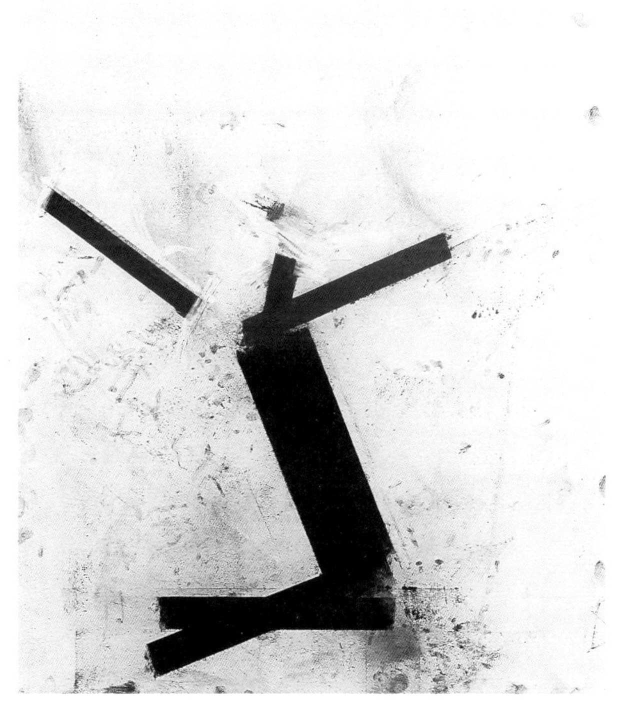

Experiments with the idea of mutation characterize a group of forward-leaning figures from the eighties. A study in wood and wax from 1980–81 (plate 157) is the first member of a new family identifiable by the peculiarities of supplementary body parts. Its descendants in bronze undergo dramatic changes in material (plate 158) or in both material and size (plate 160), and they display second heads, lengthened arms, double torsos. The rhythms – rapid or slow – of these new body parts are reinforced by changes in color and texture, the result of expressive modeling of the original wax. And every view of the sculptures allows at least a double reading. The keys to Shapiro's sculpture are transformation and movement; his work, as Shapiro himself has stated, is "about animating the inanimate."[33]

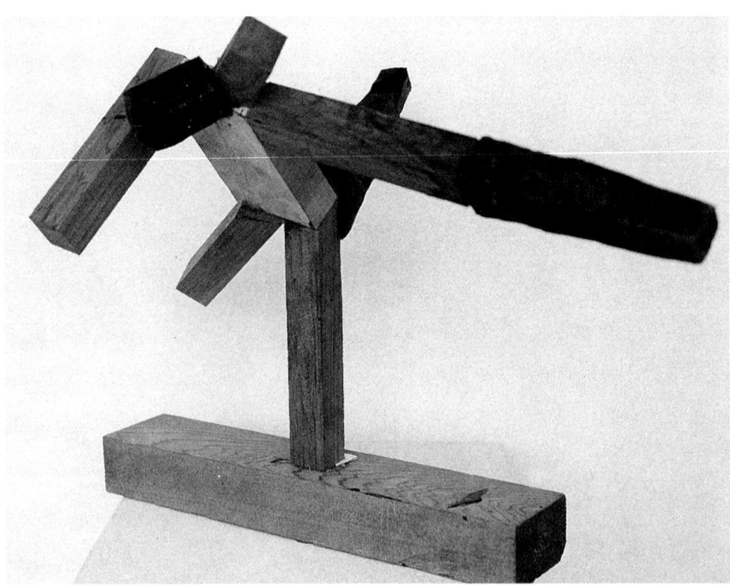

157 Study. 1980–81. Wood and wax, 12 x 16½ x 10¼" (30.5 x 41.9 x 26 cm). No longer extant

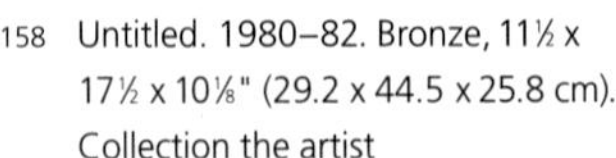

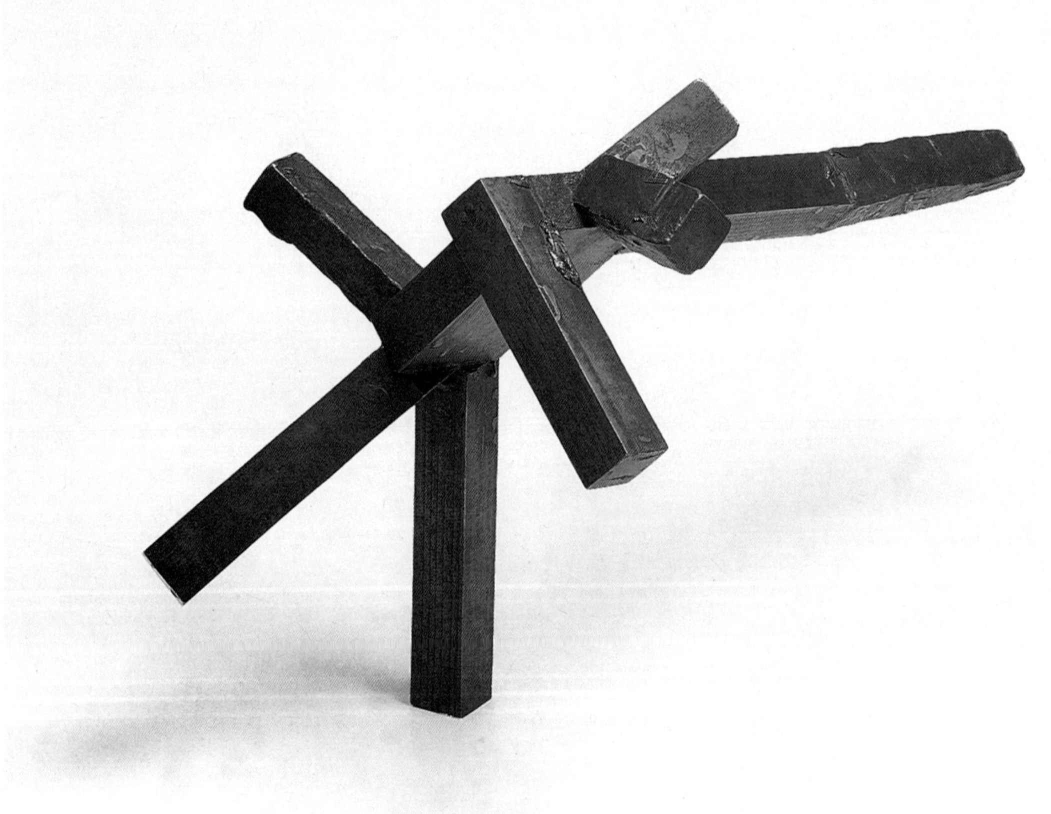

158 Untitled. 1980–82. Bronze, 11½ x 17½ x 10⅛" (29.2 x 44.5 x 25.8 cm). Collection the artist

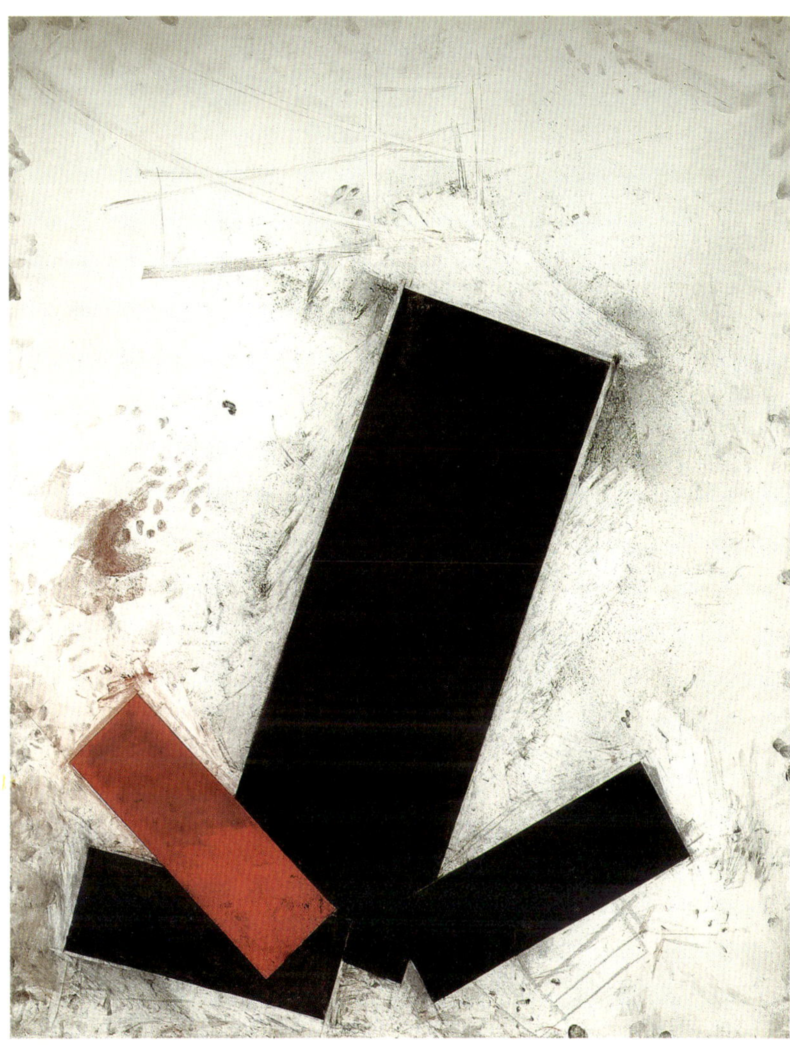

159 Untitled. 1987. Charcoal and chalk on paper, 53 x 42 ½" (134.6 x 108 cm). Whitney Museum of American Art, New York. Purchase, with funds from Mrs. Nicholas Millhouse and the Drawing Committee

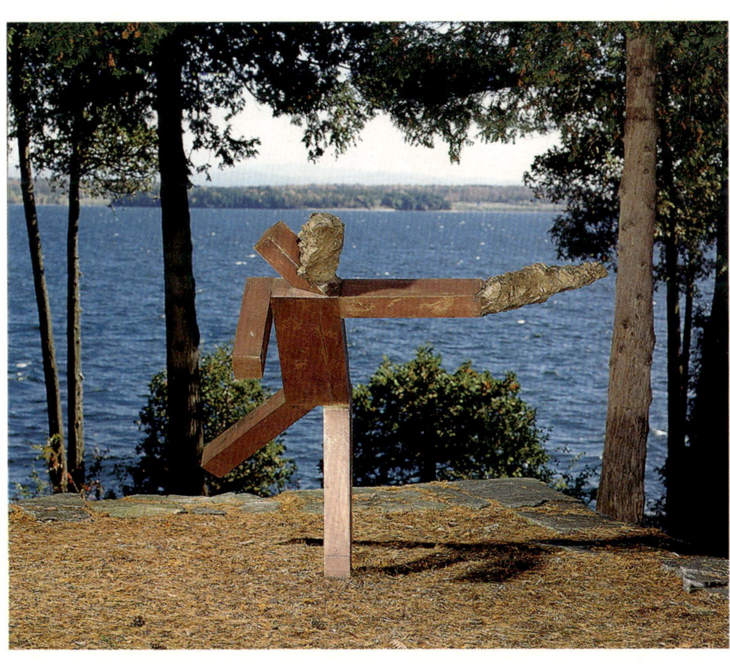

160 Untitled (G.E.). 1986–87. Bronze (edition 0/3), 64½ x 69½ x 49" (163.8 x 176.5 x 124.5 cm). Collection the artist

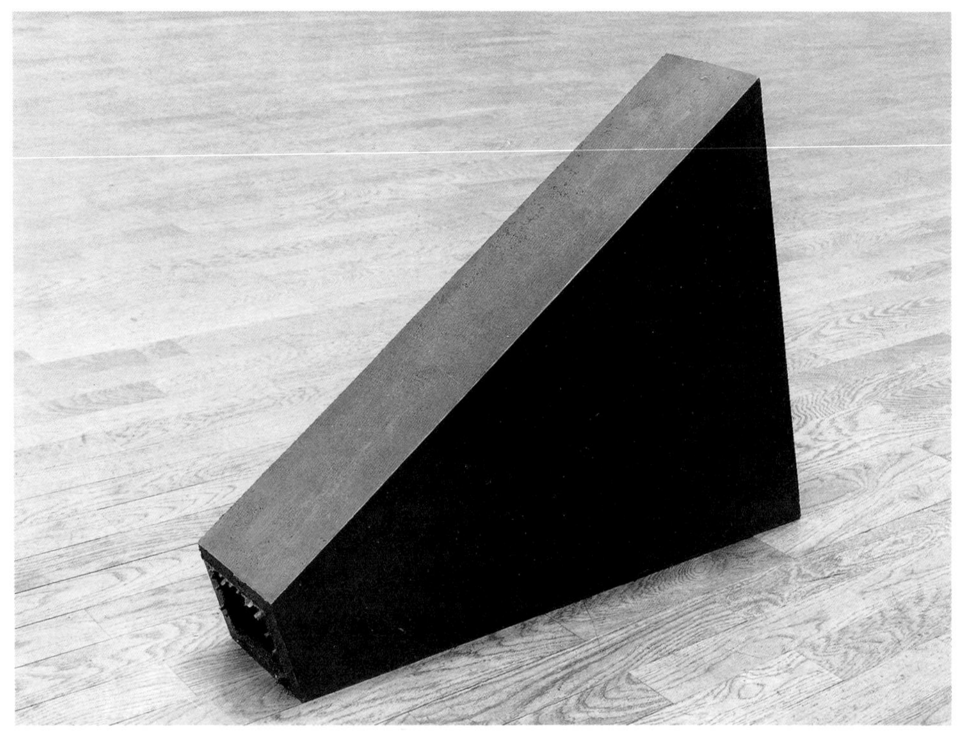

161 Untitled. 1984. Cast iron, 21½ x 29½ x 5¾" (54.6 x 74.9 x 14.6 cm). Colby College Museum of Art, Waterville, Maine. Museum Purchase from the Jere Abbott Acquisitions

162 Untitled. 1984–85. Plaster (edition 1/2), 36½ x 42½ x 39¼" (92.7 x 108 x 99.7 cm). Collection Paula Cooper

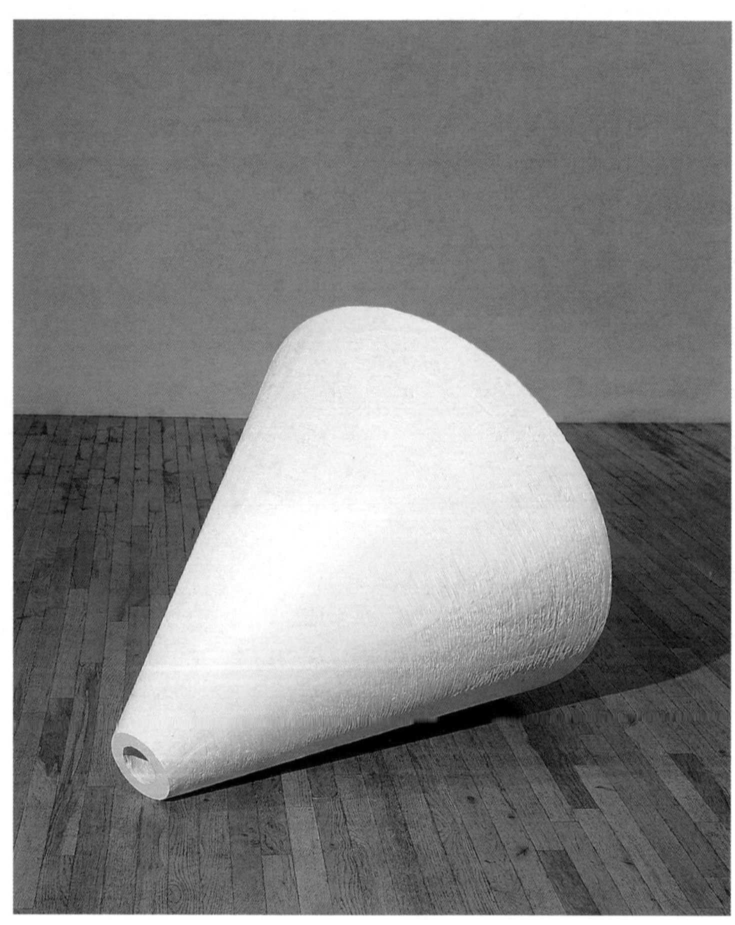

Solitary Forms (1984–87)

Shapiro does not always work in series. Sculptures from the eighties demonstrate his experimentation with single works.

Certain works with triangular shapes can be understood in several ways: as the abstraction of a torso or back, for instance, or as a directional passageway through space. The black, cast-iron wedge shape of a floor sculpture from 1984 (plate 161) has a broad opening at one end and a smaller, tighter one at the other. These contrasting openings suggest a change occurring somewhere along the internal corridor between them. The inner edges of the narrow opening reveal jagged traces of molten iron, unlike the rest of the sculpture, which is smooth.

A white plaster funnel (plate 162) has a thick, ridged skin, rough with deposits. Both its larger and its smaller openings have been cut cleanly. The overall form is balanced and neutral: the full, rounded cone describes a volume with equal pressure inside and out.

Still, there is a sexual intimation to that cone, which is made more explicit in a 1987 work in plaster (plates 163, 164). This latter sculpture can be installed in either of two ways: lying on the ground or standing. Its tapered shape is vaguely phallic, but also resembles a funerary urn (figure 15); sexuality and death are thereby linked. The fullness of the vessel connotes both potency and interment.

A plaster torso from 1987 (plate 165) is made up, essentially, of two flattened funnels joined like an hourglass and placed at eye level at the top of a metal pole. This "female" icon is conceived in planar terms. Shapiro's handling of the wet plaster has left imprints, especially at the waist, as if a lover were repeatedly discovering the pleasure of touch. The play of light brings out the worked surface texture. The torso developed from a form in a delicate blue gouache of 1979 (plate 166). The pole, a mechanical necessity for the sculpture, takes on its own life as an extended base, and also as a record of the accumulating deposits of plaster as the piece was built up.

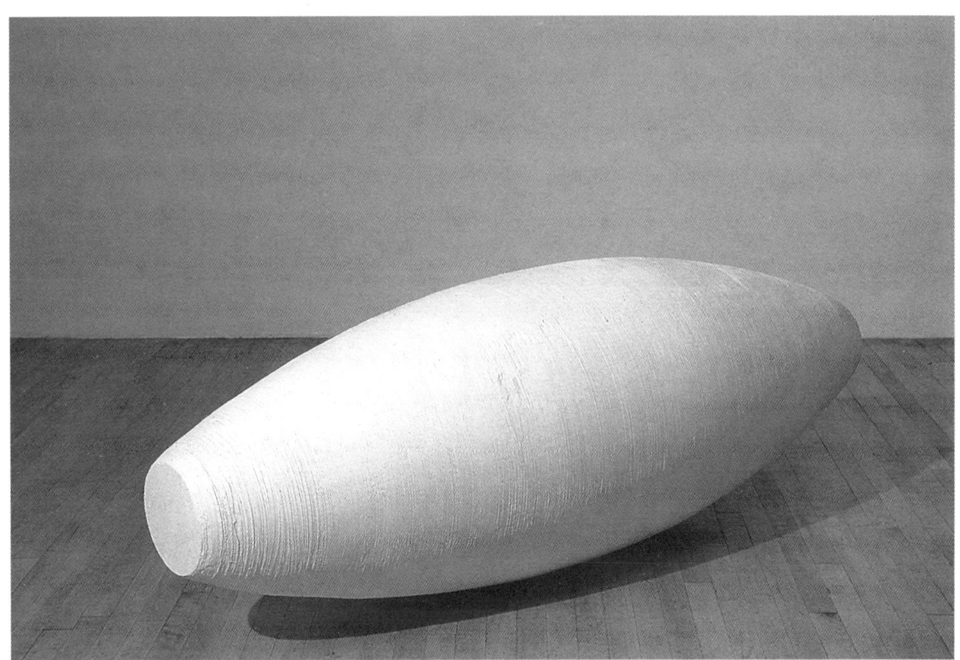

163 Untitled. 1987. Plaster, 24¾ x 71 x 24¾" (62.9 x 180.3 x 62.9 cm). Collection Yoshio Kojima

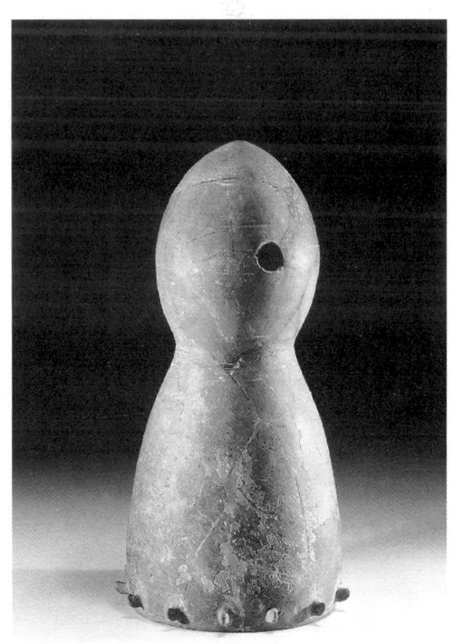

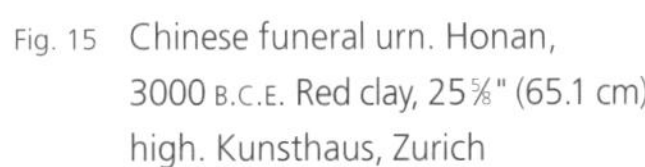

Fig. 15 Chinese funeral urn. Honan, 3000 B.C.E. Red clay, 25⅝" (65.1 cm) high. Kunsthaus, Zurich

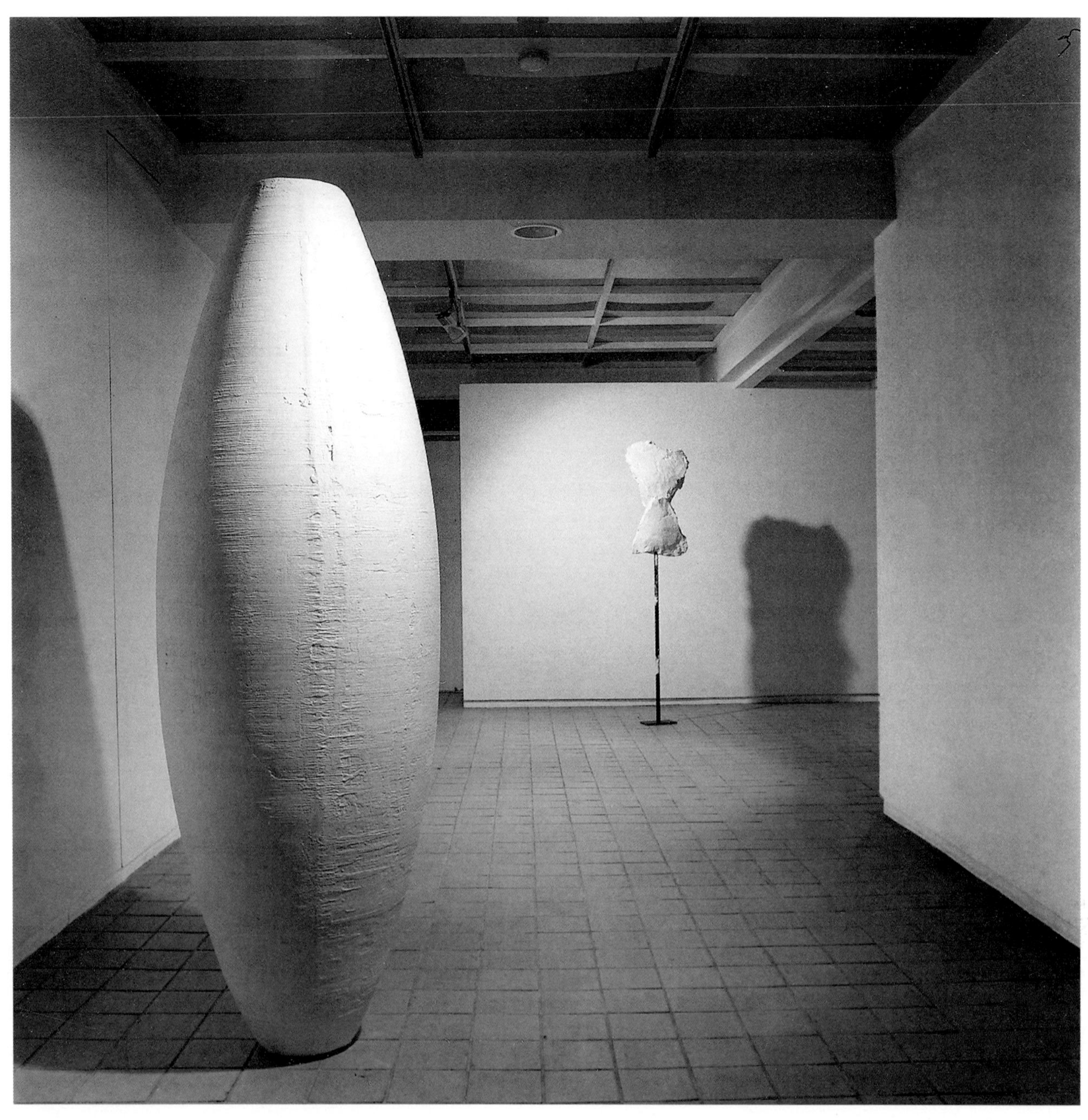

164 Installation view of the exhibition "Joel Shapiro," Gallery Mukai, Tokyo, 1988. Works shown here also appear in plates 163, 165.

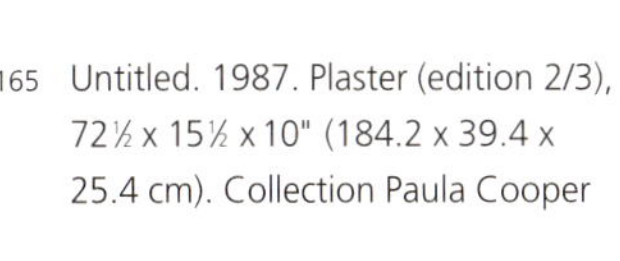
165 Untitled. 1987. Plaster (edition 2/3), 72½ x 15½ x 10" (184.2 x 39.4 x 25.4 cm). Collection Paula Cooper

166 Untitled. 1979. Gouache on paper, 18⅛ x 23" (46 x 58.4 cm). Collection the artist

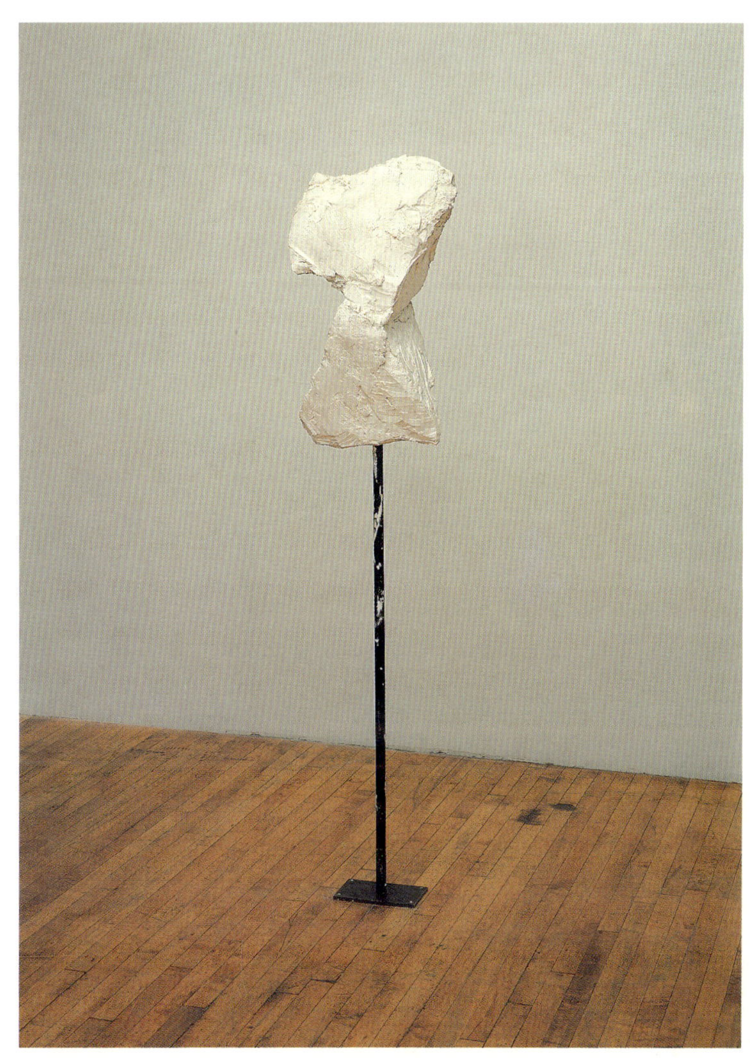

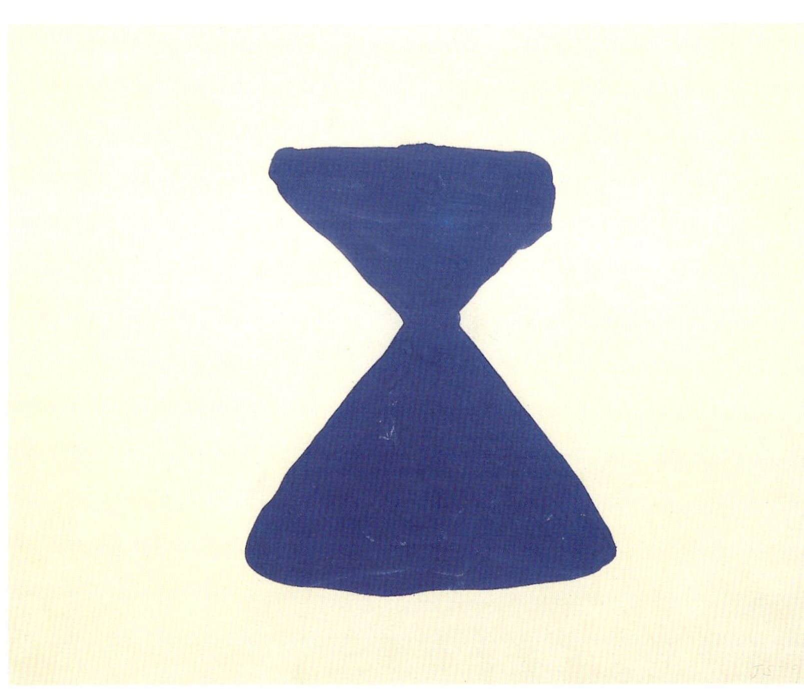

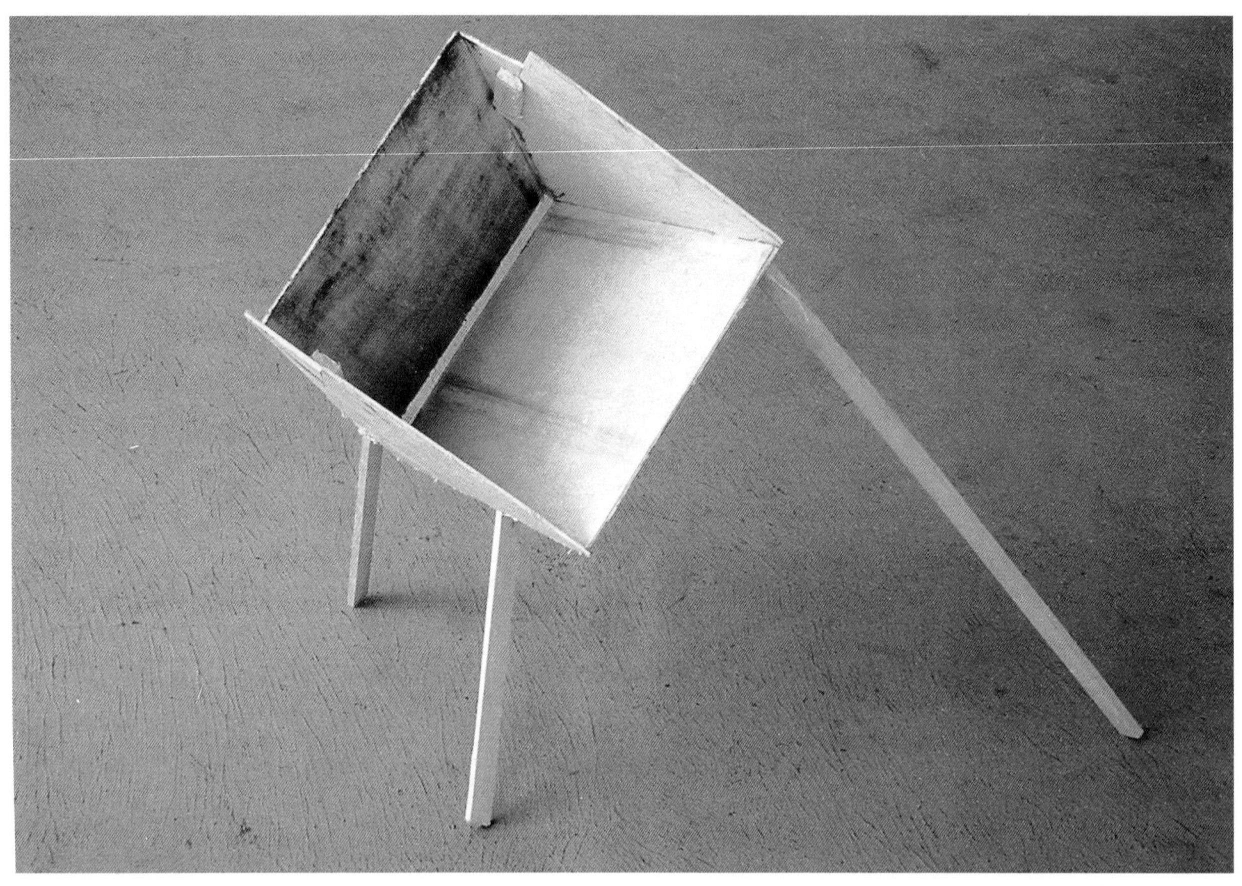

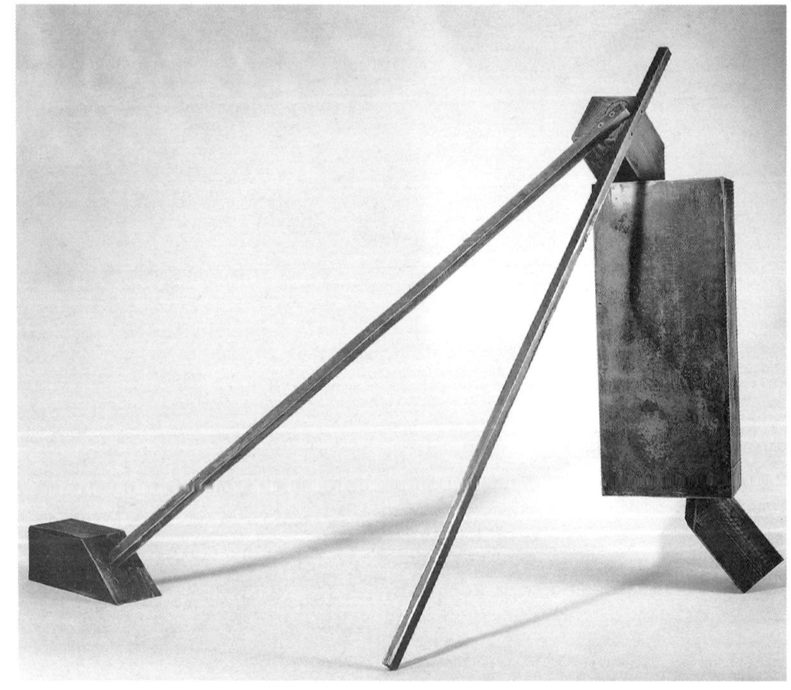

167 Study. 1985. Wood, approx. 31 x 28 x 13" (78.7 x 71.1 x 33 cm). Collection the artist

168 Untitled. 1986. Bronze (edition 2/3), 52¼" x 6'2" x 32¼" (132.7 x 188 x 81.9 cm). Hirshhorn Museum and Sculpture Garden, Smithsonian Institution, Washington, D.C. Museum Purchase, 1987

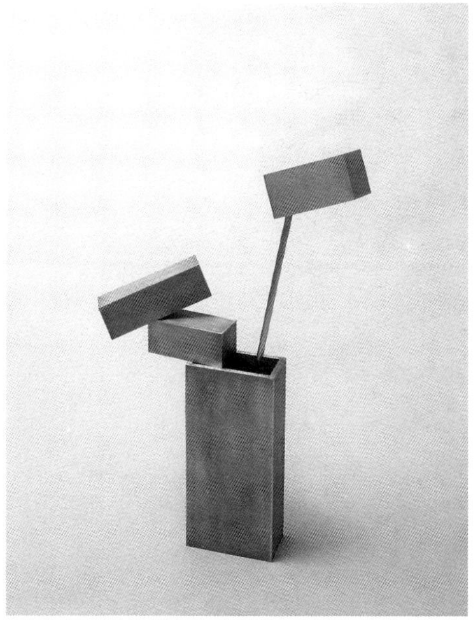

169 Untitled. 1986–87. Bronze (edition 1/3), 43 x 11 x 21" (109.2 x 27.9 x 53.3 cm). Collection the Chase-Manhattan Bank

170 Study. 1988–90. Wood and metal, 21½ x 12¾ x 7" (54.6 x 32.4 x 17.8 cm). Collection the artist

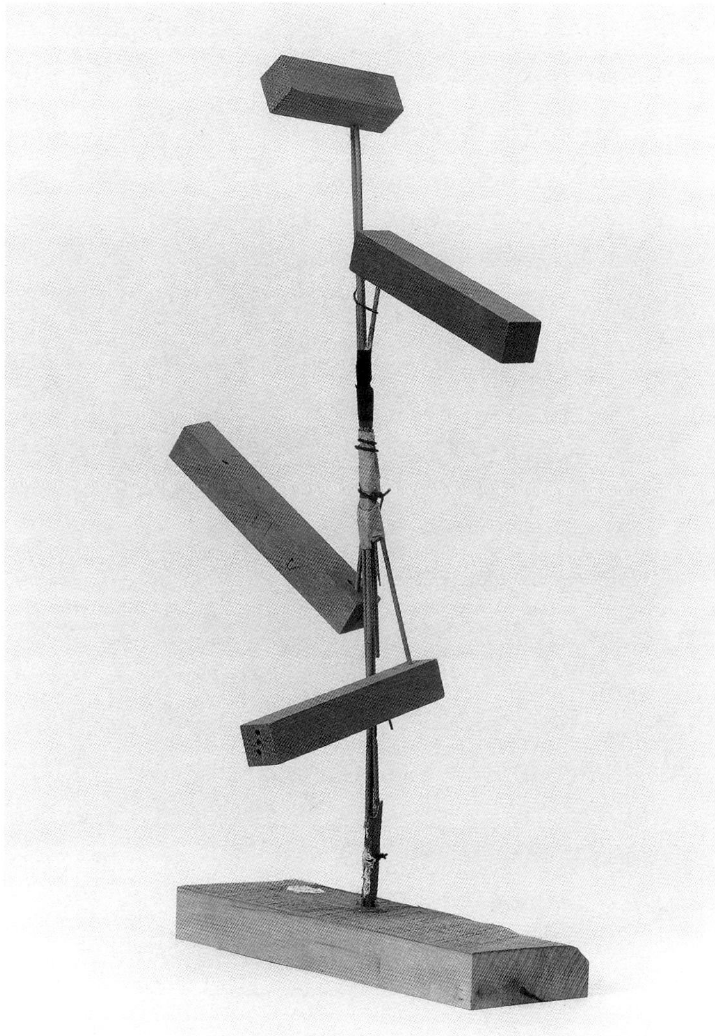

Poles (1984–89)

During a stay at the American Academy in Rome in late 1984 and early 1985, Shapiro worked on a number of studies in wood in which the pole first appears. He may have been inspired in the use of this device by Baroque architecture, which articulates space through a combination of heavy and light formal elements. The linear pole functions as a drafting device, a means of drawing in space. In one of the Roman studies (plate 167), three thin bars barely support an open triangular shape as it frees itself from the dominating influence of the ground.

In two bronzes from 1986–87 (plates 168, 169), hollow torsos extend and at the same time retract blocky appendages by means of poles. This paradoxical dynamic energizes the figures. The interplay between upright rectangular torsos and skewed, variable body parts heightens the contrast between interior stability and exterior mobility.

In a lively study from 1988–90 (plate 170), discrete body parts are attached to a single vertical pole placed on a stand. The pole becomes the spinal column of an implied figure. At the same time, its verticality and the elements freely branching from it suggest a tree. In another sculpture in which mass is dislocated (plate 171), poles and blocky segments alternate as they project themselves vigorously into the air.

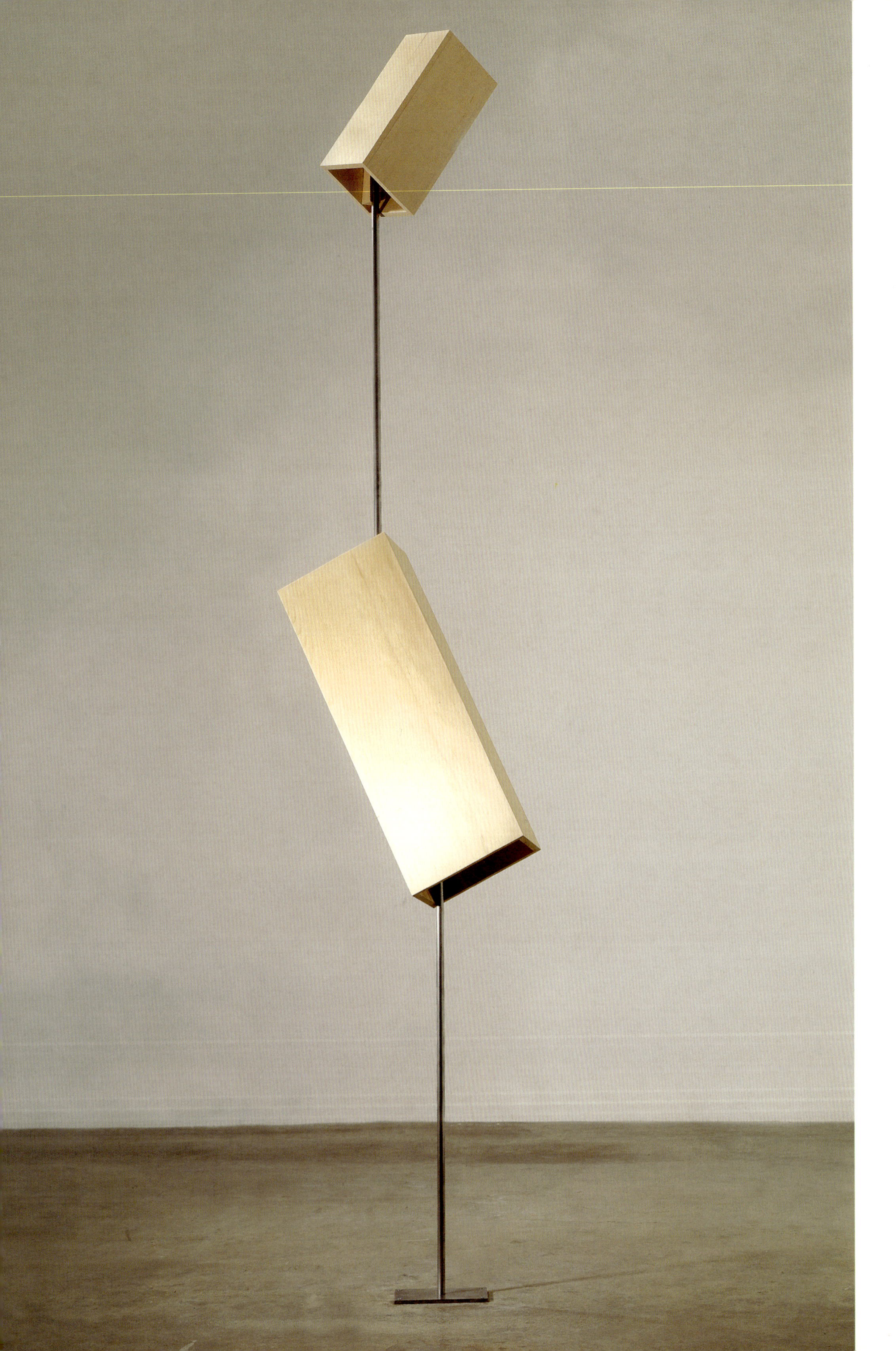

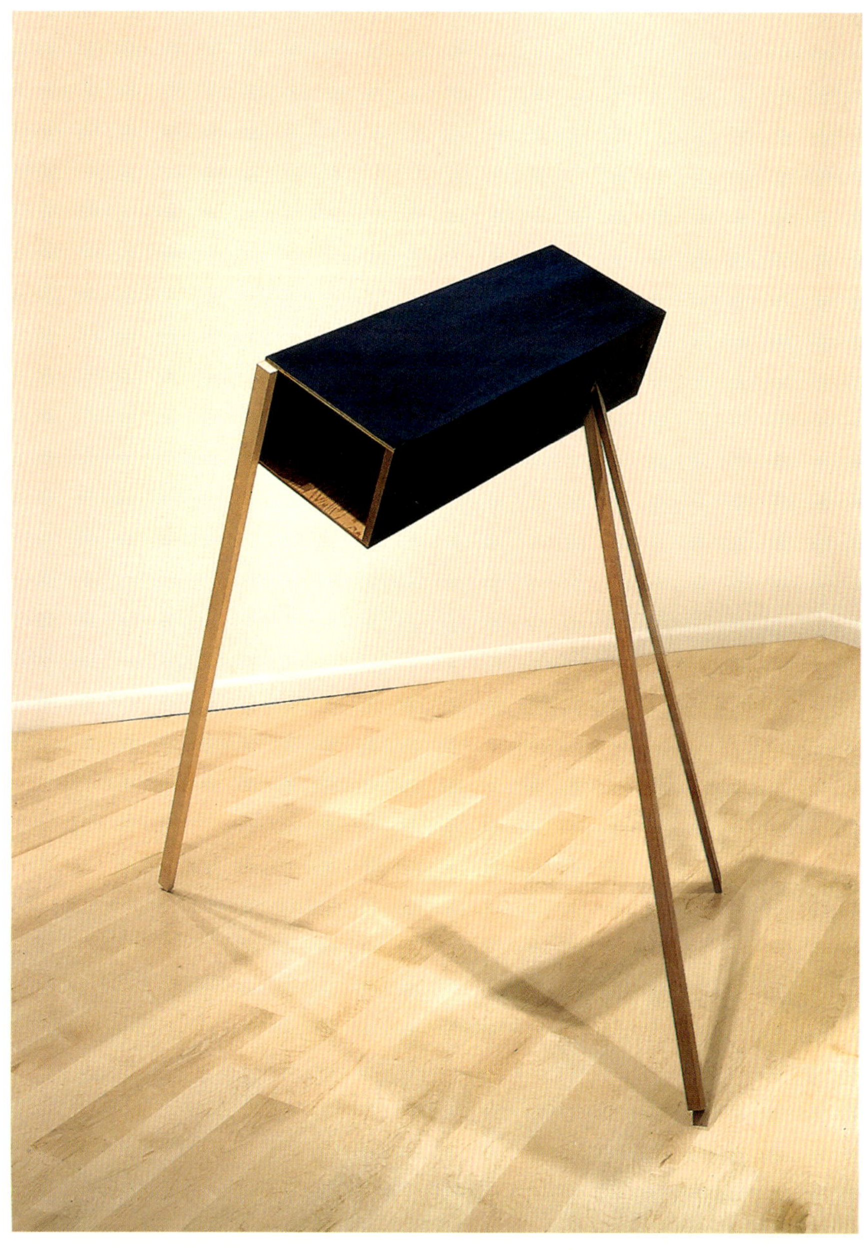

172 Untitled. 1986. Plywood and paint, 65 x 55 x 62" (165.1 x 139.7 x 157.5 cm). The Patsy R. and Raymond D. Nasher Collection, Dallas

Between 1987 and 1989, the poles and bars multiply and lengthen (plates 173–75). They lift up a single body and suspend it aloft. Their diagonal surge of energy divides and activates the space the poles occupy. A somewhat similar effect can be seen in the eight monumental verticals animating Jackson Pollock's *Blue Poles* (figure 16), where the sequence of angled lines marks and calibrates the intricately woven field.

A small study for an outdoor sculpture includes eight diagonal rods to which are attached four geometric elements. The full shapes and fine lines cast themselves into a lively occupation of space, and they create a spirited sense of alternating slow and rapid rhythms.

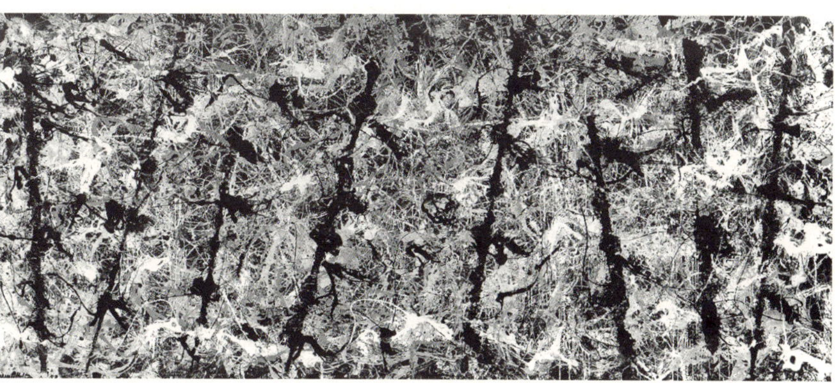

Fig. 16 Jackson Pollock. *Blue Poles*. 1952. Oil, enamel, and aluminum paint on canvas, 6'11" x 15'⅝" (210.8 x 458.8 cm). Australian National Gallery, Canberra

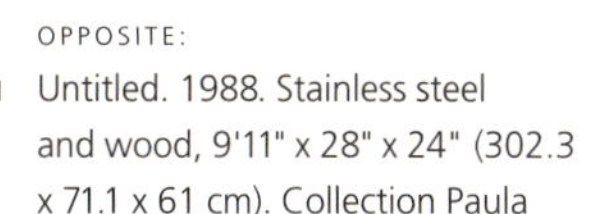

OPPOSITE:

171 Untitled. 1988. Stainless steel and wood, 9'11" x 28" x 24" (302.3 x 71.1 x 61 cm). Collection Paula Cooper

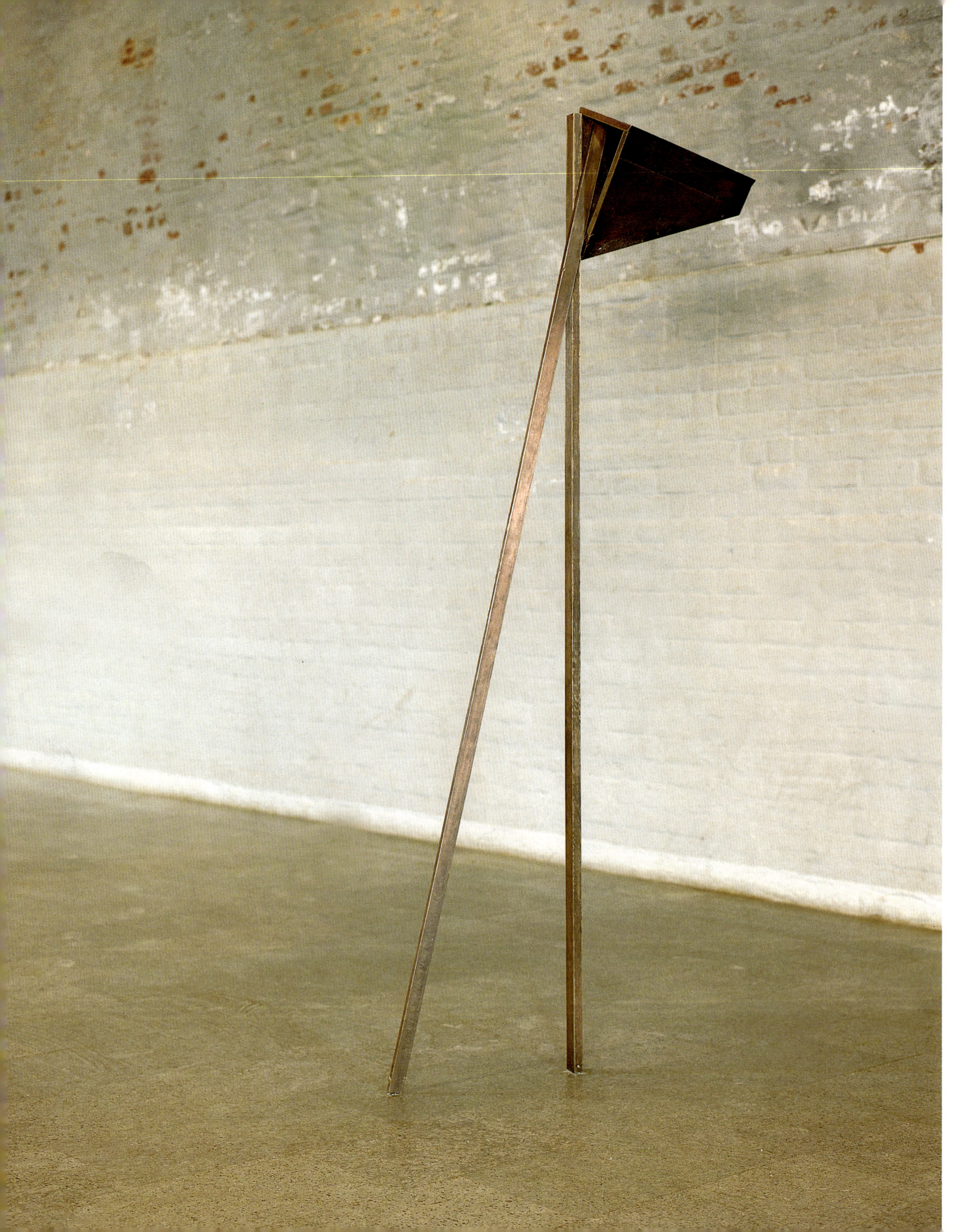

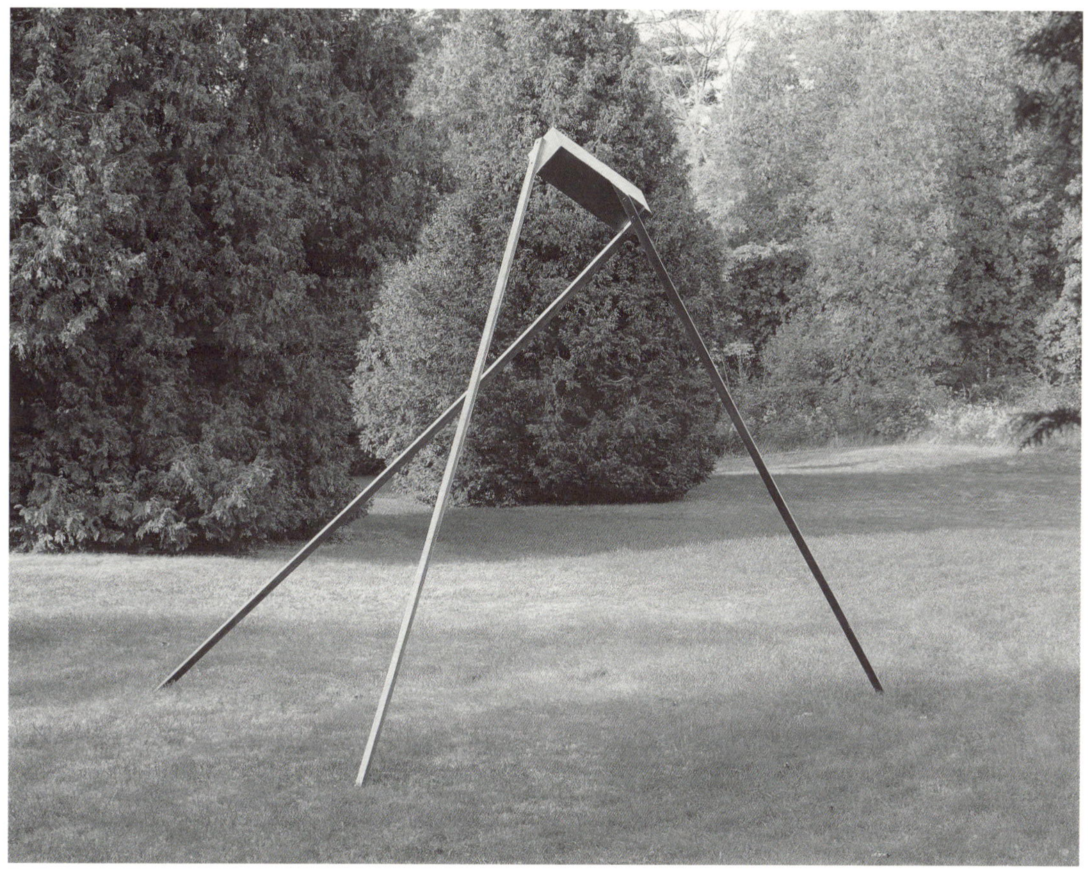

174 Untitled. 1987. Bronze (edition 1/3), 11'3¼" x 15'1" x 11'1½" (343.5 x 459.7 x 339.1 cm). The Museum of Modern Art, New York. Gift of Douglas S. Cramer in honor of Agnes Gund and Ronald S. Lauder, 1997

175 Untitled. 1987–88. Bronze (edition 2/3), 9'10" x 12'4" x 55" (299.7 x 375.9 x 139.7 cm). Fine Arts Museums of San Francisco. Gift of the John Berggruen Gallery, 1996.163-2a–e

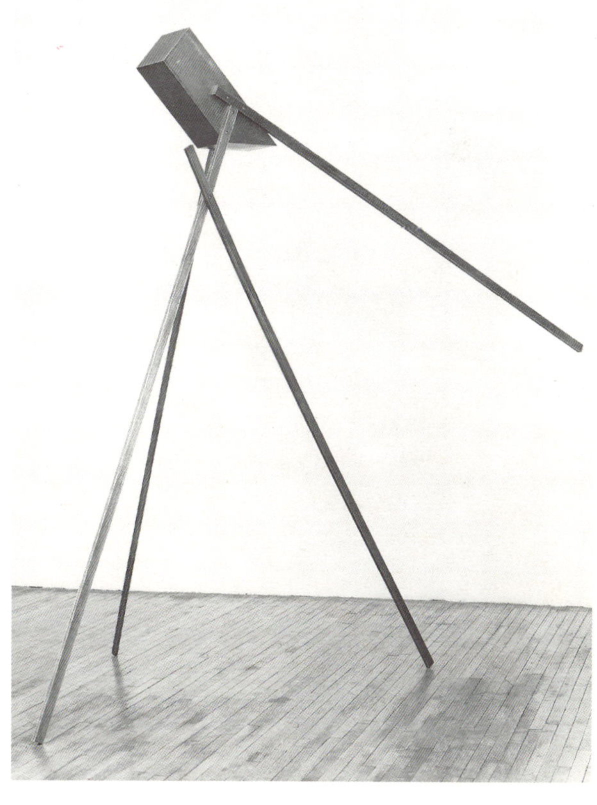

OPPOSITE:

173 Untitled. 1989. Bronze (edition 2/4), 8'1¾" x 38½" x 21½" (247.3 x 97.8 x 54.6 cm). Collection Paula Cooper

Doubles (1988–95)

Shapiro's sculptures are the result of constant questioning and probing. His investigations never follow a single path: after the lighter, almost airborne works on poles, he shifted to developing earthbound works of more monumental scale. These latter sculptures are more bluntly physical and confrontational, and the viewer is challenged, more than before, to step into their arena.

At the same time that he set up this confrontation, Shapiro doubled the figure. This simultaneous act of division and reinforcement involved a more complicated fabrication, as well as a more complicated emotion, and it demands from the viewer a slower reading. For example, two torsos may abut each other and become one, as in a bronze from 1988–90 (plate 177). Or a second torso may collide with the principal one, as in another bronze from the same years (plate 176). This configuration mutates further when each of the doubled torsos is joined by an arm (plate 178), producing the appearance of a whirling couple. The brusque arrival of a second torso in these two "running" configurations reinforces their heavy movement. And in a weighty bronze from 1989–90 (plate 179), a concentrated mass delivers a blow that knocks the figure off balance.

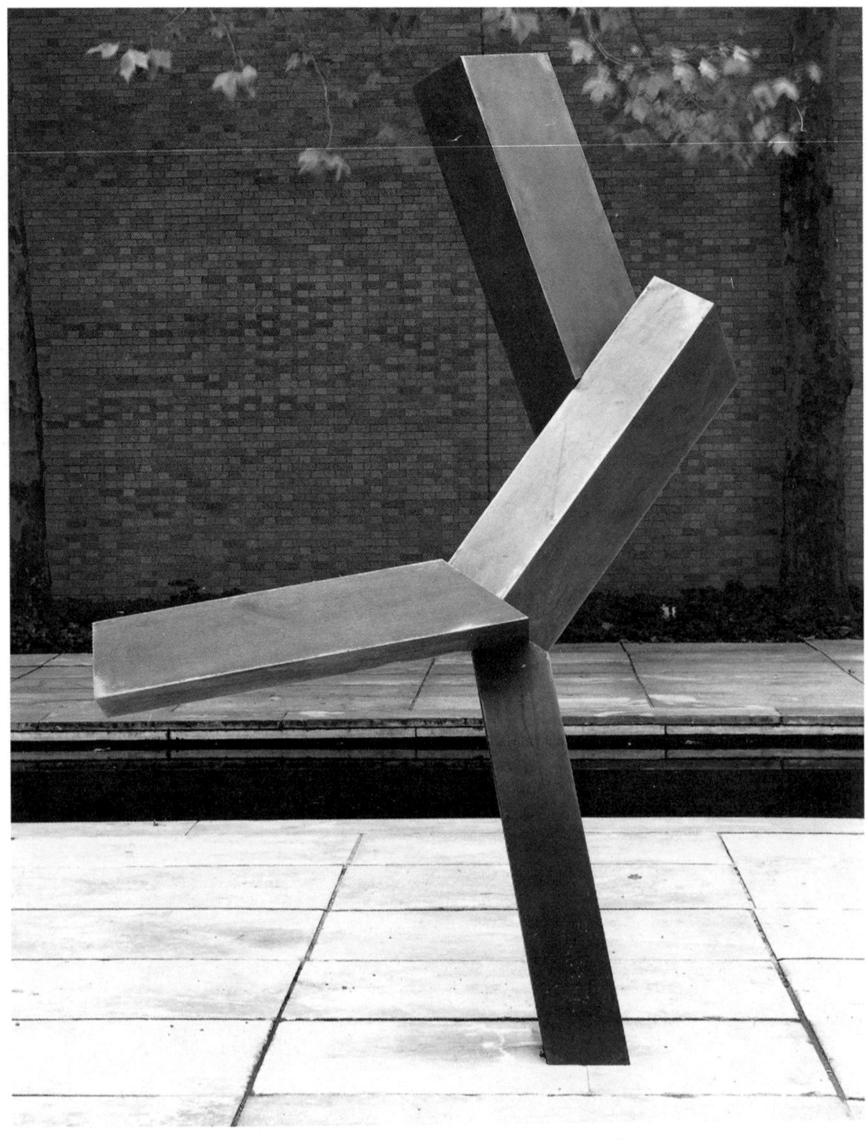

176 Untitled. 1989–90. Bronze (edition 4/4), 8'6½" x 43" x 6'6" (260.4 x 109.2 x 198.1 cm). The Museum of Modern Art, New York. Sid R. Bass Fund; gift of Jeanne C. Thayer, Robert F. and Anna Marie Shapiro, Agnes Gund, and William F. Bernhard; President's Fund Purchase (1990), Donald B. Marron, President; Jerry I. Speyer Fund; Emily and Jerry Spiegel Fund

OPPOSITE:

177 Untitled. 1988–90 (temporarily installed in Central Park, New York, August 1990). Bronze, 10'11½" x 7'7½" x 44" (334 x 232.4 x 111.8 cm). Collection G.S.A., Federal Building and Courthouse, Los Angeles

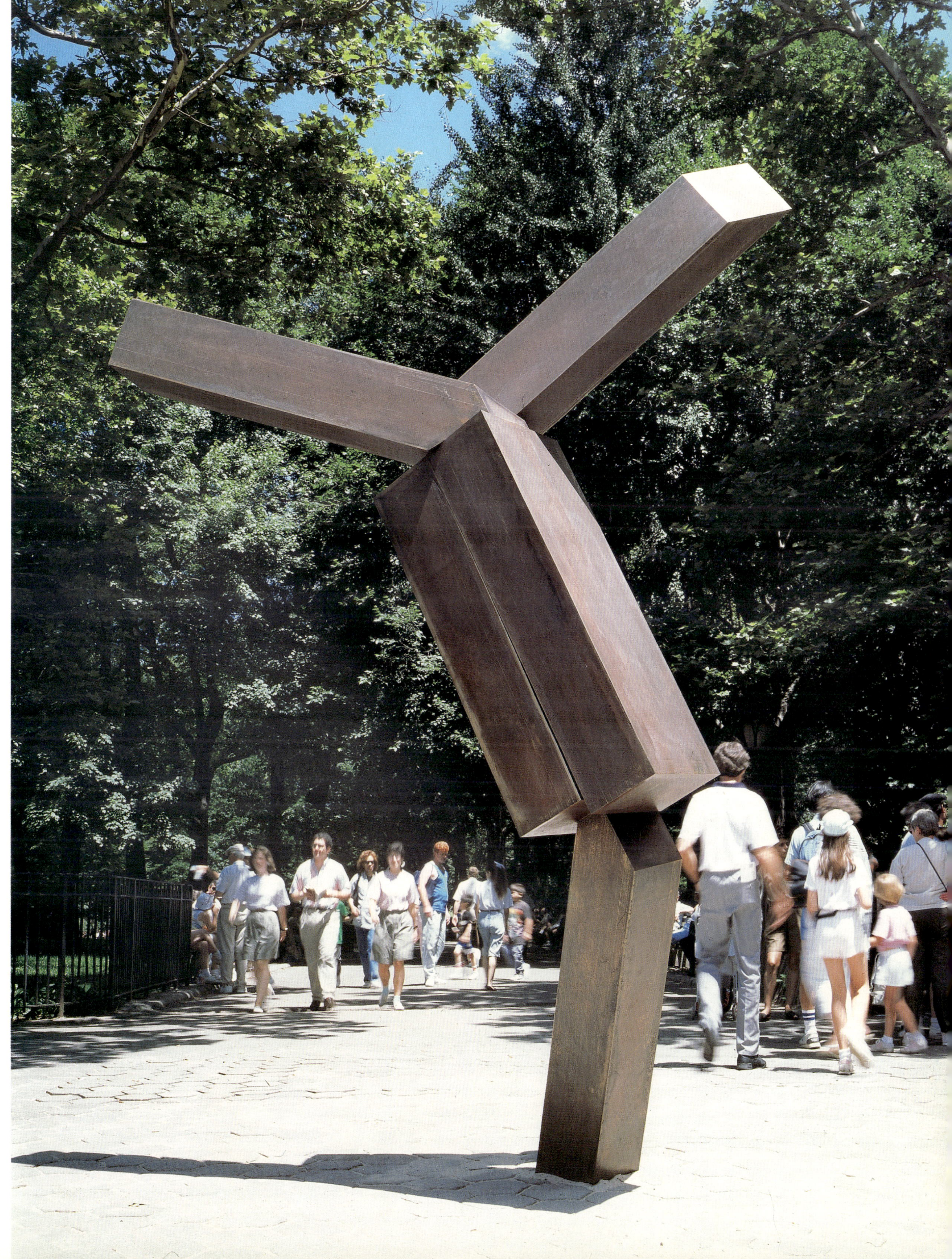

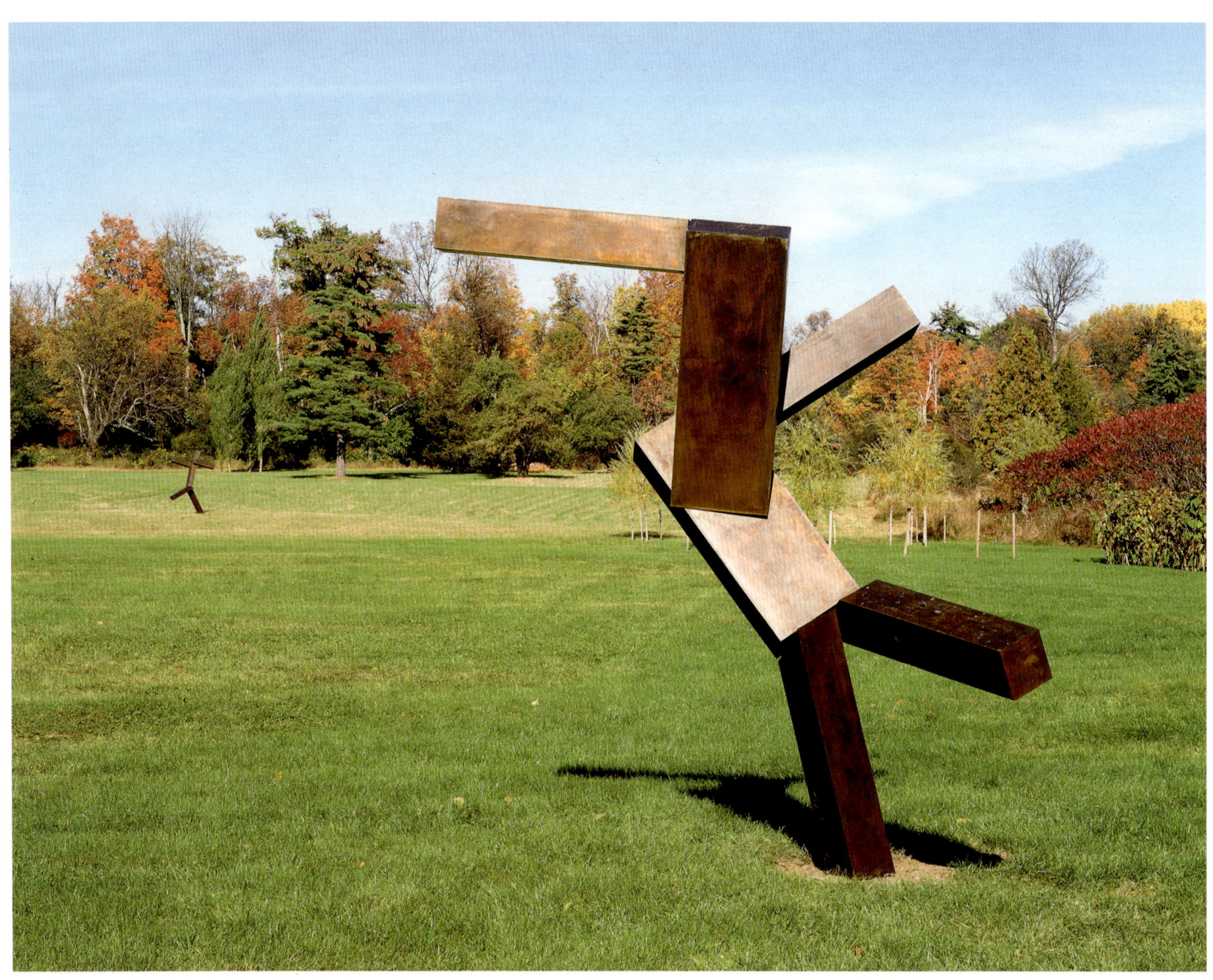

178 Untitled. 1988–89. Bronze (edition 0/1), 8'7" x 7'7" x 5'5" (261.6 x 231.1 x 165.1 cm). Collection the artist

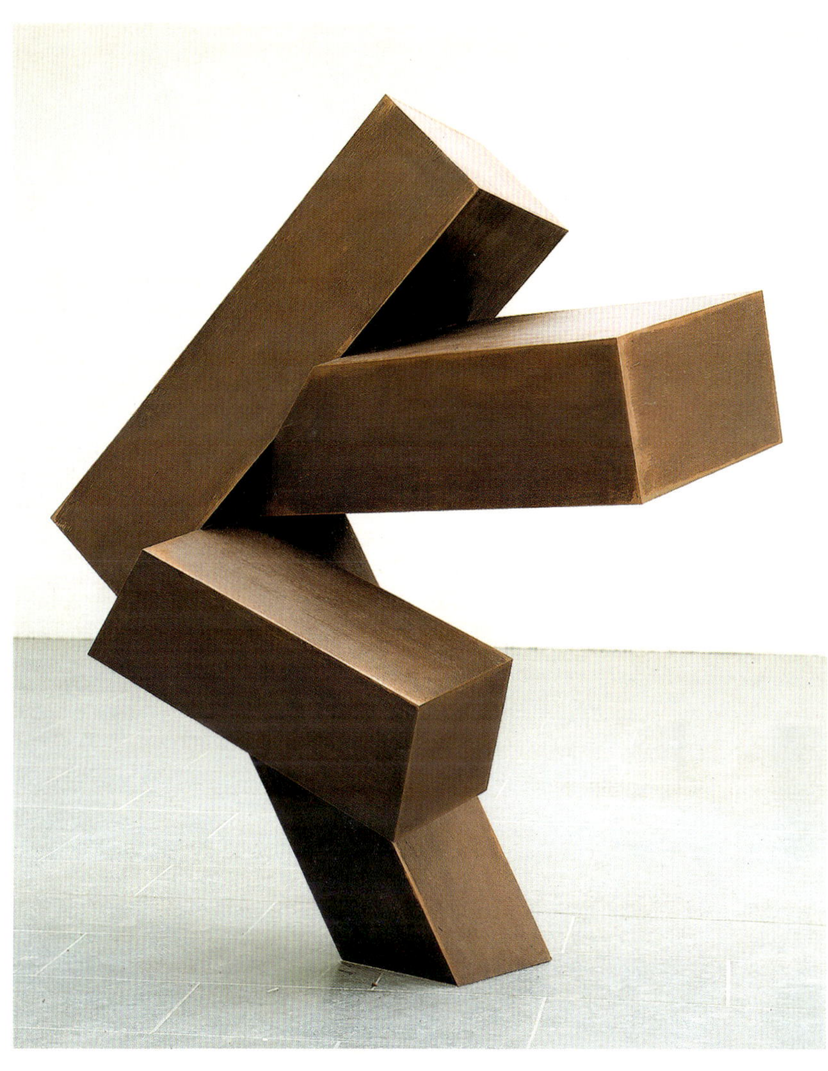

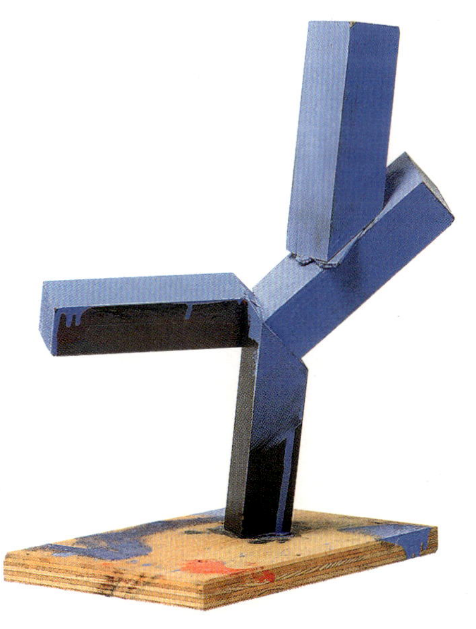

179 Untitled. 1989–90. Bronze (edition 1/3), 7'1¾" x 46¼" x 27" (149.2 x 117.5 x 68.6 cm). Collection Jane M. and David R. Davis, Medina, Washington

180 Untitled. 1989. Paint and wood, 13⅞ x 11¾ x 4½" (35.2 x 29.8 x 11.4 cm). Private collection

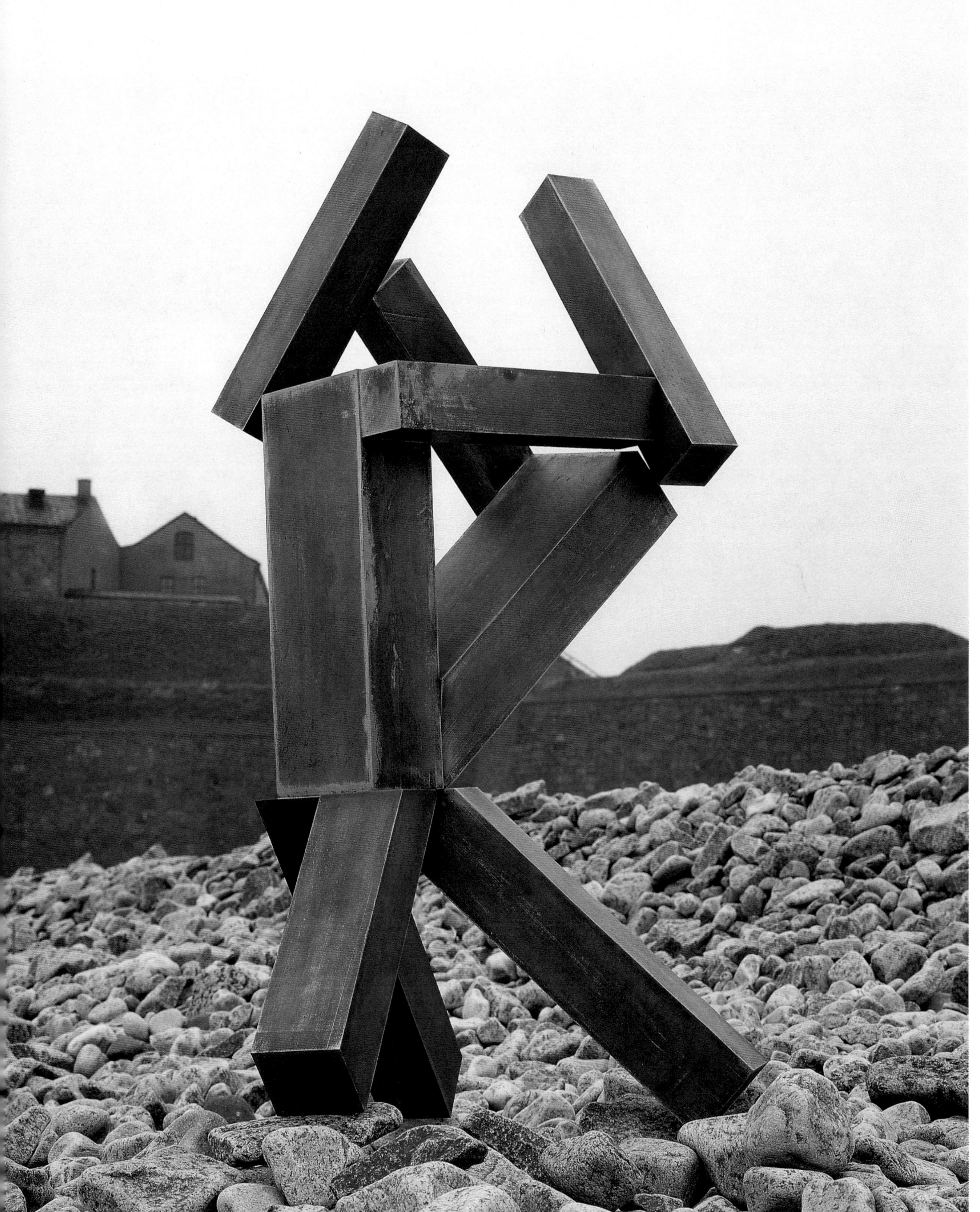

Some configurations develop into full-fledged couples, enacting what may seem to be particular moments and events. Even on this large scale, the works remain intimate. An untitled sculpture from 1987–88 (plate 181), with its multiple, active limbs and two torsos facing each other, suggests an impassioned encounter – a dance, or perhaps a fight. The imposingly simple composition of a bronze from 1989–90 (plate 182) unexpectedly draws the viewer to the work's subtleties: the heavy, interlocking volumes of the two torsos and two legs exhibit a delicate handling of surface, on which the color of the bronze ranges from reddish brown to yellow-gray.

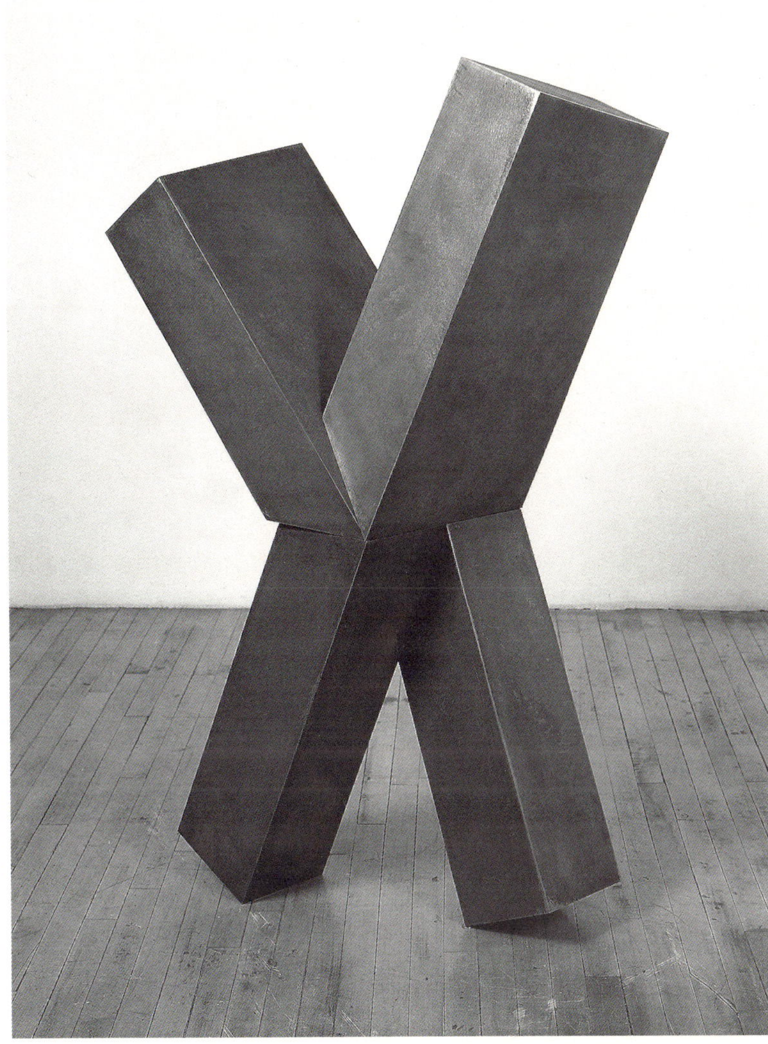

182 Untitled. 1989–90. Bronze (edition 1/4), 58 x 23 x 31¾" (147.3 x 58.4 x 80.6 cm). Private collection, New York

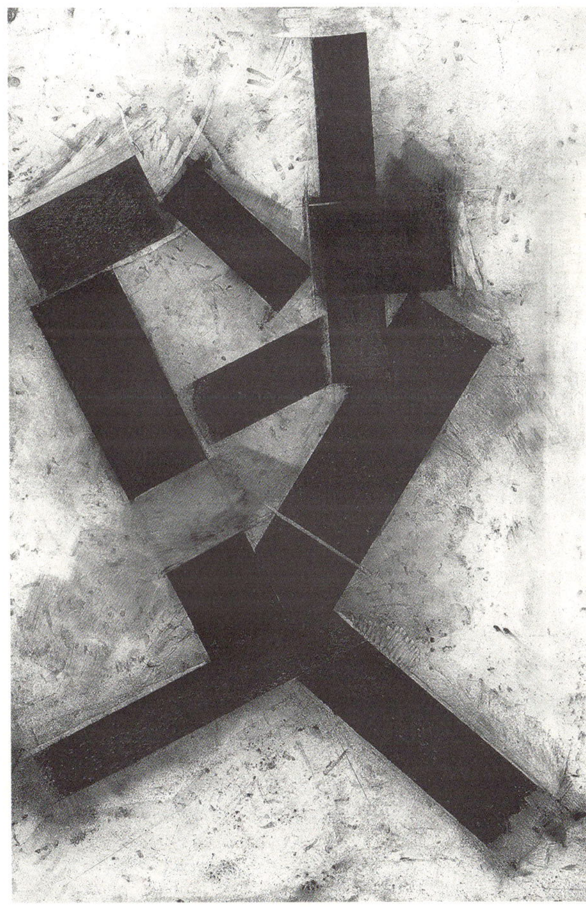

183 Untitled. 1988. Charcoal and chalk on paper, 59½ x 39¼" (151.1 x 99.7 cm). Collection Joan and Jay Topkis

OPPOSITE:

181 Untitled. 1987–88. Bronze (edition 0/4), 57½ x 34 x 35" (146.1 x 86.4 x 88.9 cm). Private collection

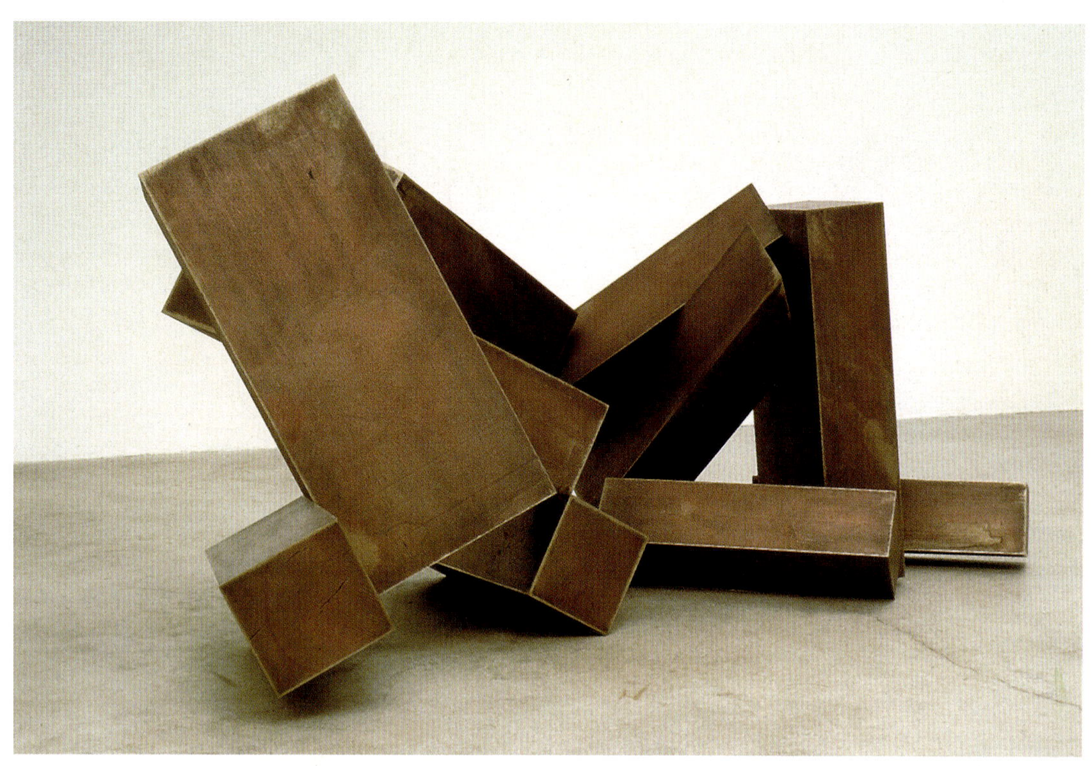

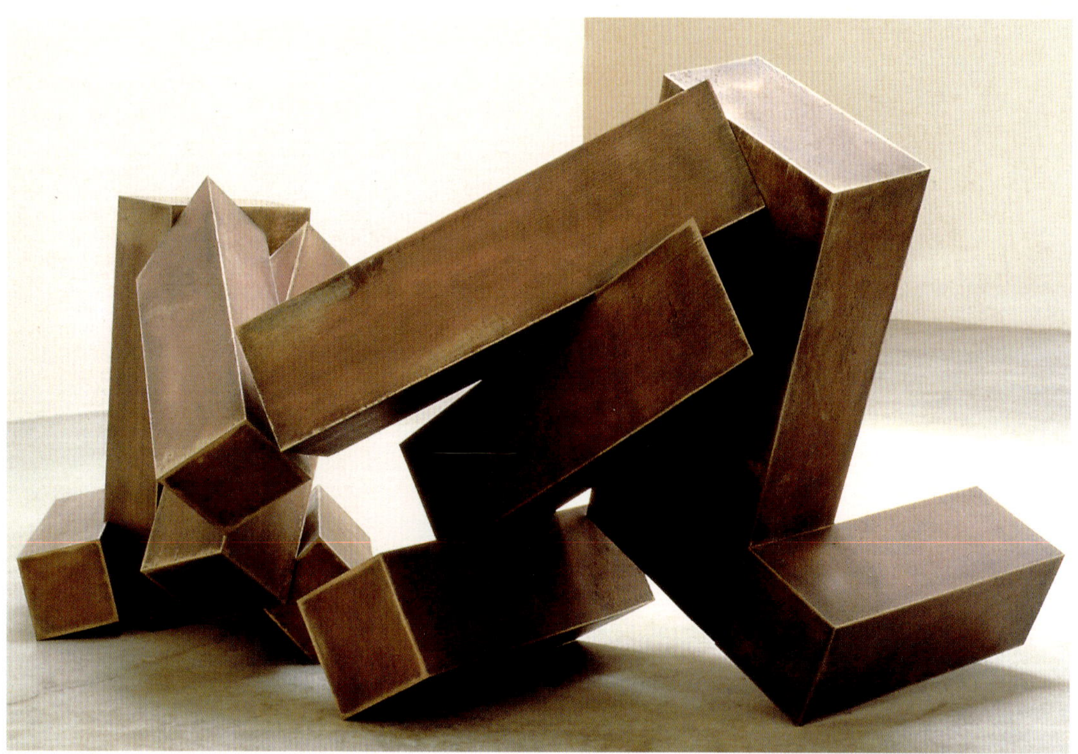

184, 185 Untitled. 1990–91. Bronze (edition 2/4), 35 x 72 x 37" (84 x 182.9 x 94 cm). Collection Douglas S. Cramer

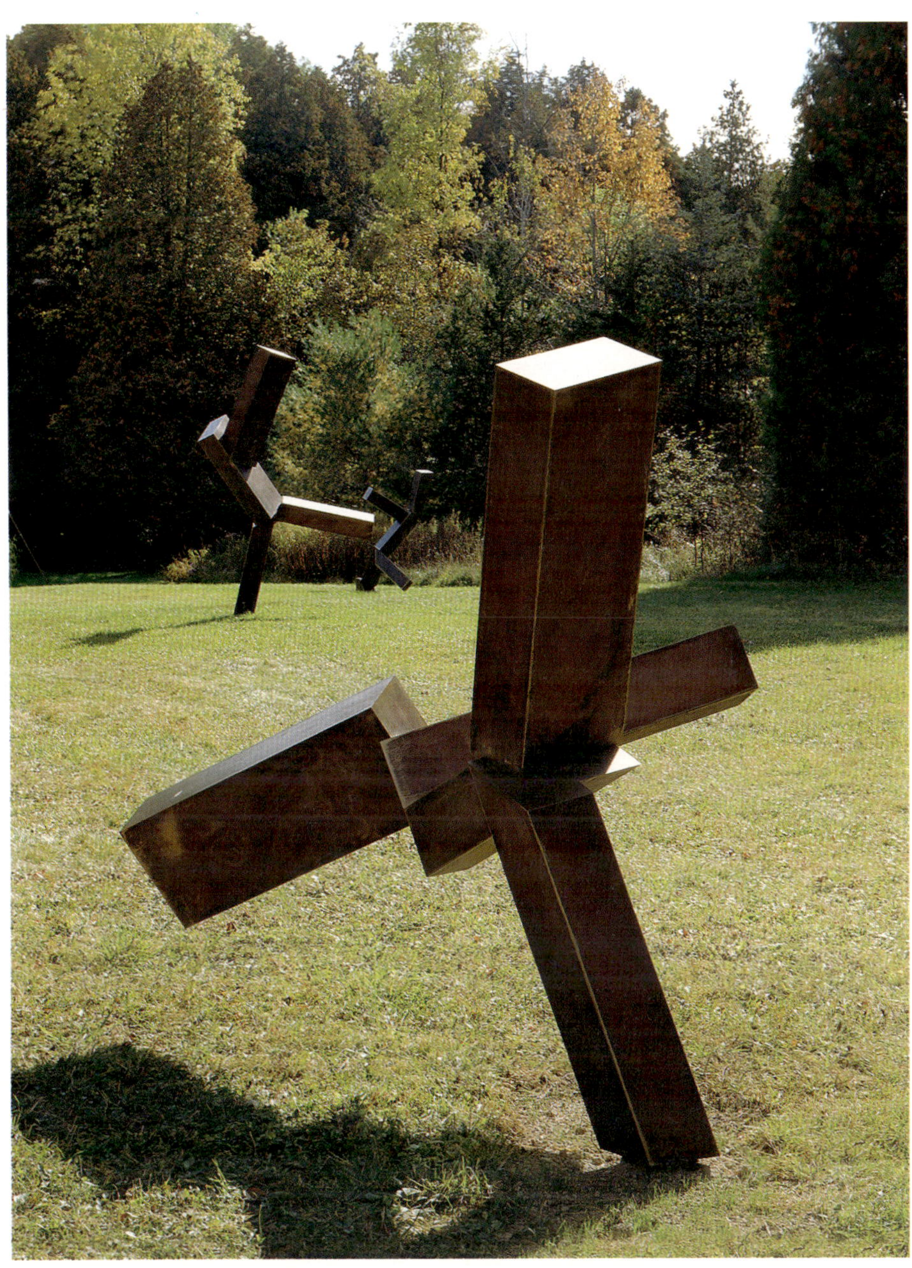

186 Installation, Westport, New York. Works shown here also appear in plates 176, 195.

Figures that remain separate may nonetheless be captured in close proximity. Various mise-en-scènes in which each figure plays a distinct role articulate Shapiro's expanding vocabulary. The thick, paired figures from 1990–91 (plates 184, 185) are combative, close to each other, heavy on the ground; they freeze in confrontation. In contrast, the slender, aerial dancers of 1995 (plates 188–90) cavort and swing their limbs expansively. Linear, light figures, they move buoyantly through space.

The double torsos are generated also as figures joined by a common leg. Rising and falling elements in bronzes from 1988 (plates 186, 195) speak of division, in time as well as personality. The falling figure in each of these sculptures could represent the past, the rising figure the present. Shapiro shows them wavering in the moment that divides ascent from descent. Despite their wavering, however, Shapiro's way of opening up new formal possibilities implies an affirmation.

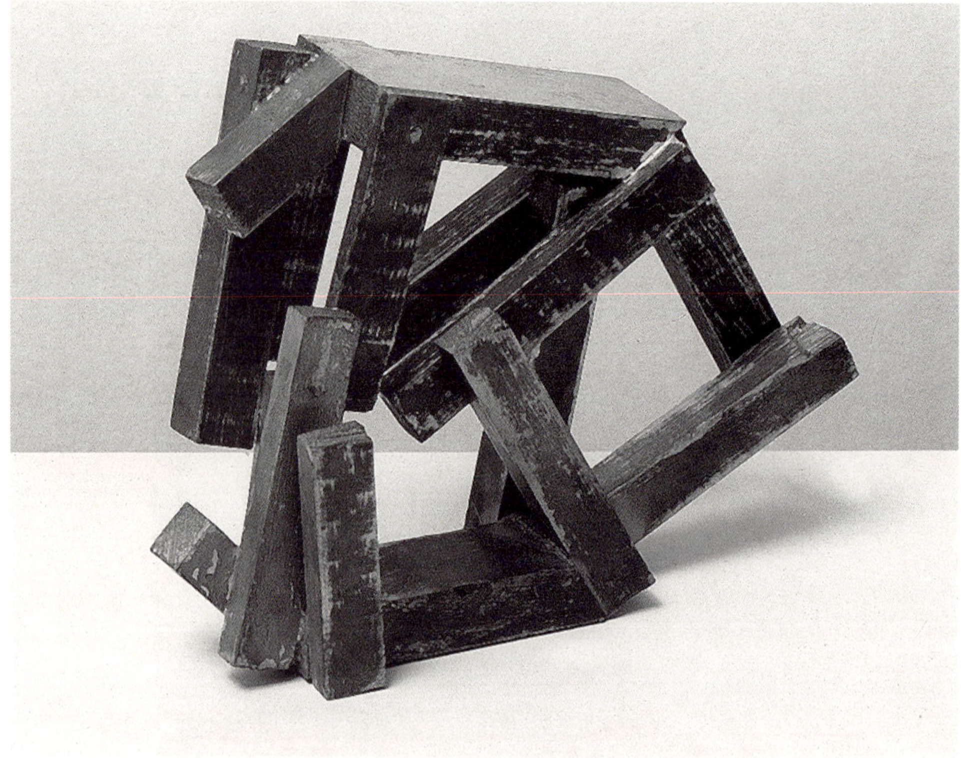

187 Untitled. 1984. Bronze, 6½ x 8⅝ x 3" (16.5 x 21.9 x 7.6 cm). Private collection

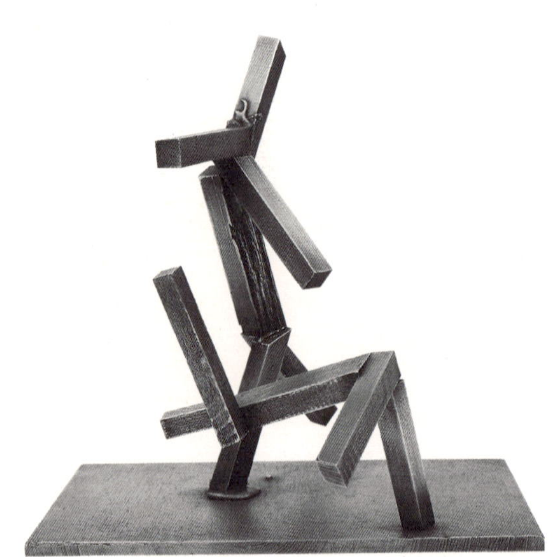

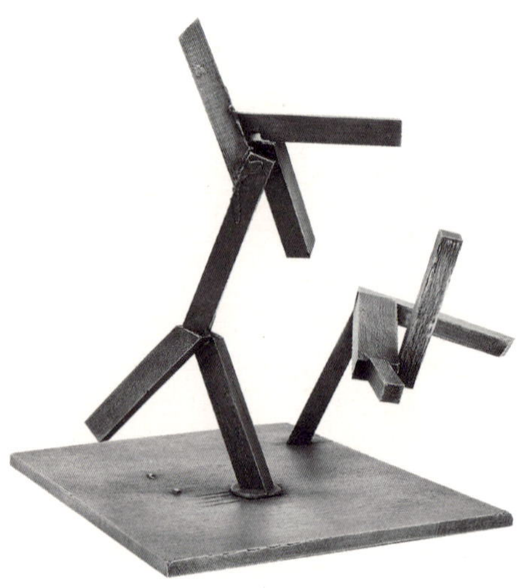

188–90 Untitled, PEN Award. 1995. Bronze, 10 x 10 x 11" (25.4 x 25.4 x 27.9 cm). Private collection

191 Untitled. 1994. Charcoal, pastel, and pencil on paper, 27½ x 19" (69.9 x 48.3 cm). Collection the artist

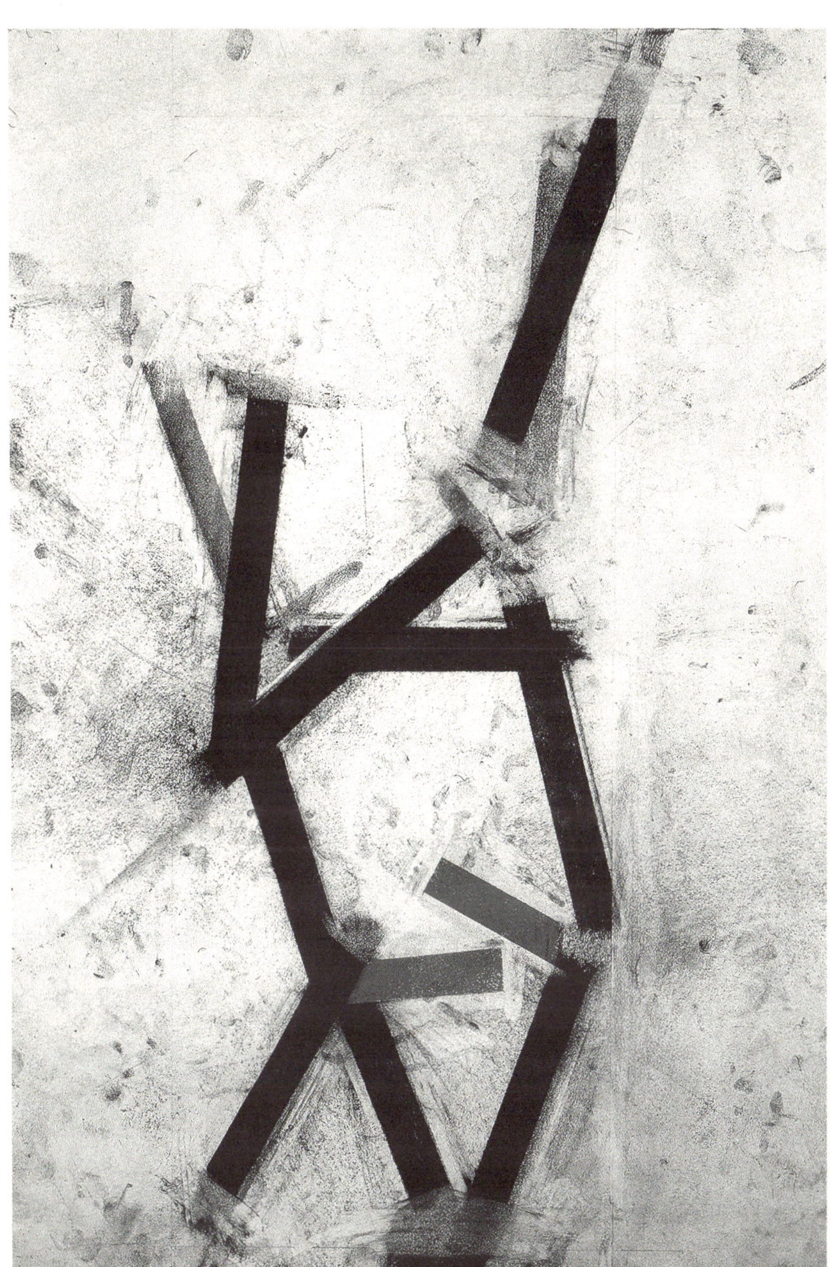

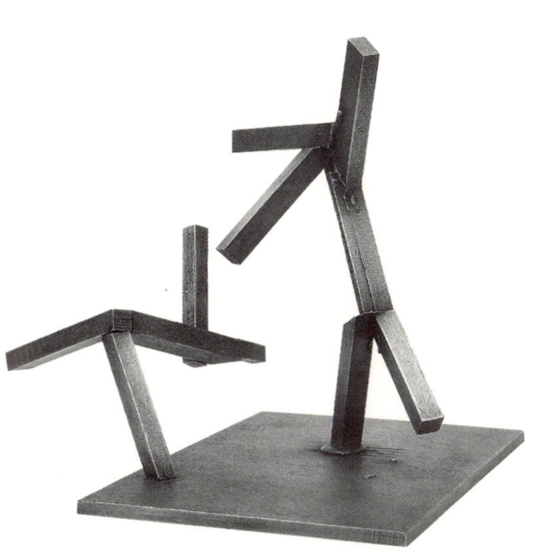

OPPOSITE:

193 Untitled. 1989. Bronze (edition 4/4), 70" x 6'8" x 30" (177.8 x 203.2 x 76.2 cm). Private collection

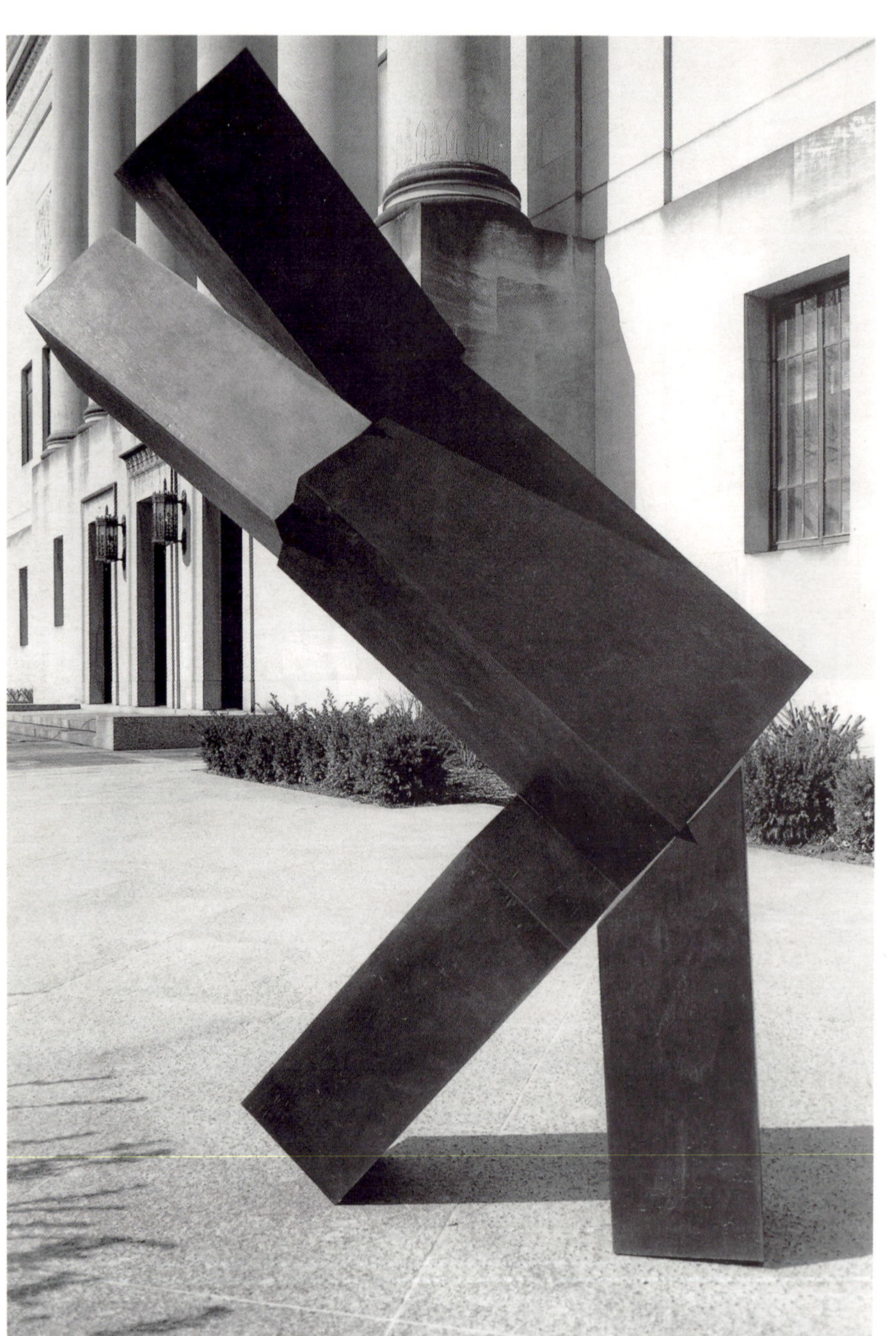

192 Untitled. 1991. Bronze (edition 2/4), 6'6½" x 59" x 27" (199.4 x 149.9 x 68.6 cm). On long-term loan to the Nelson-Atkins Museum of Art, Kansas City, Missouri, from the Hall Family Foundation

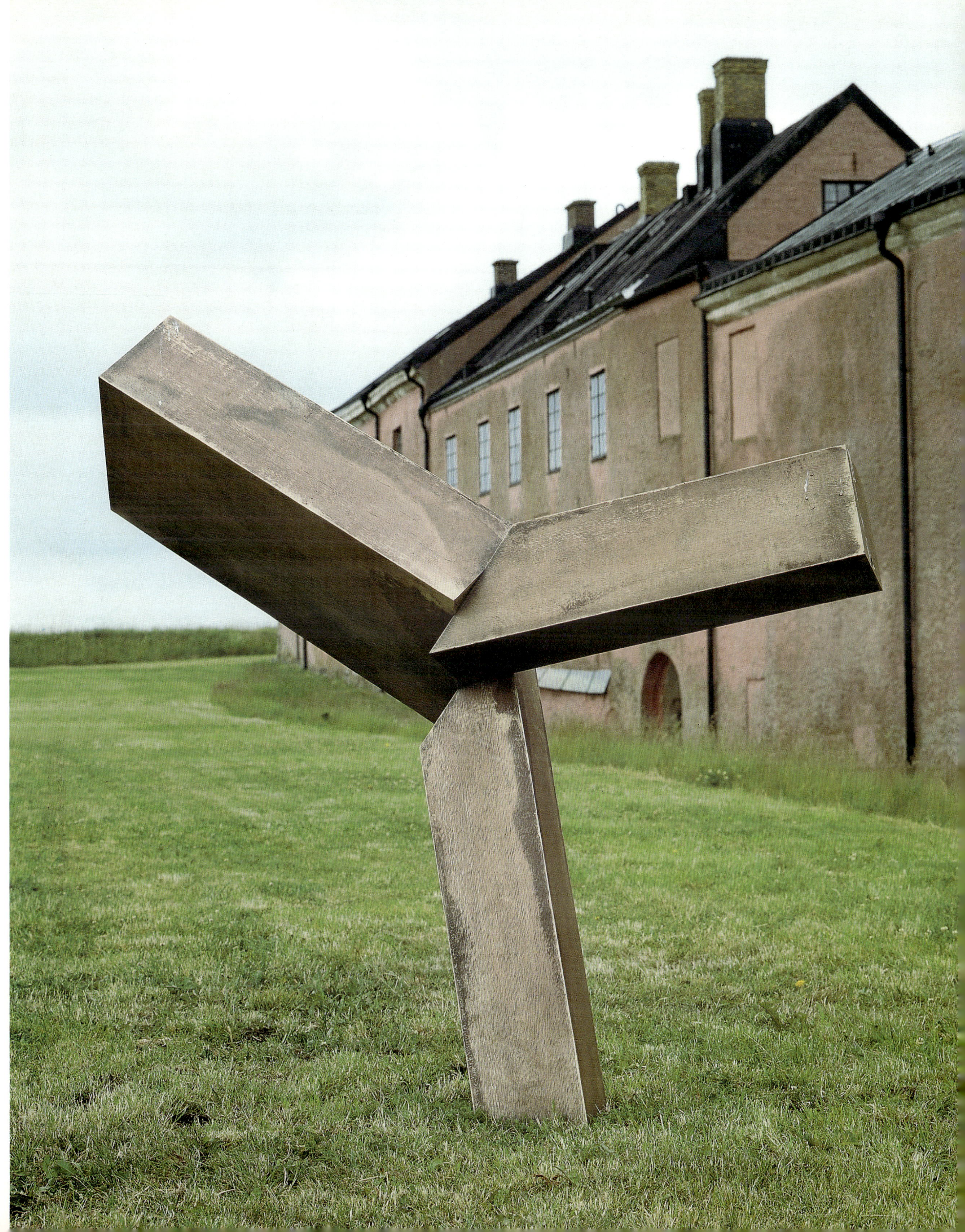

194 Untitled. 1988. Charcoal and chalk on paper, 7'4" x 60" (223.5 x 152.4 cm). The Museum of Modern Art, New York. Acquired with matching funds from the Robert Lehman Foundation, Inc., and the National Endowment for the Arts

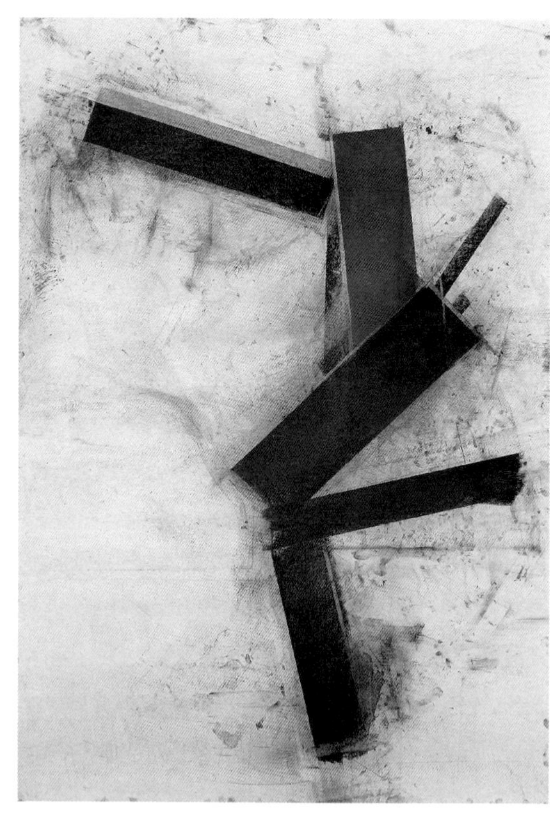

195 Untitled. 1989 (installed in the exhibition "Twentieth-Century American Sculpture at The White House, Exhibition V," Washington, D.C., 1996–97). Bronze (edition 4/4), 65 x 77 x 62½" (165.1 x 195.6 x 158.8 cm). National Gallery of Art, Washington, D.C.

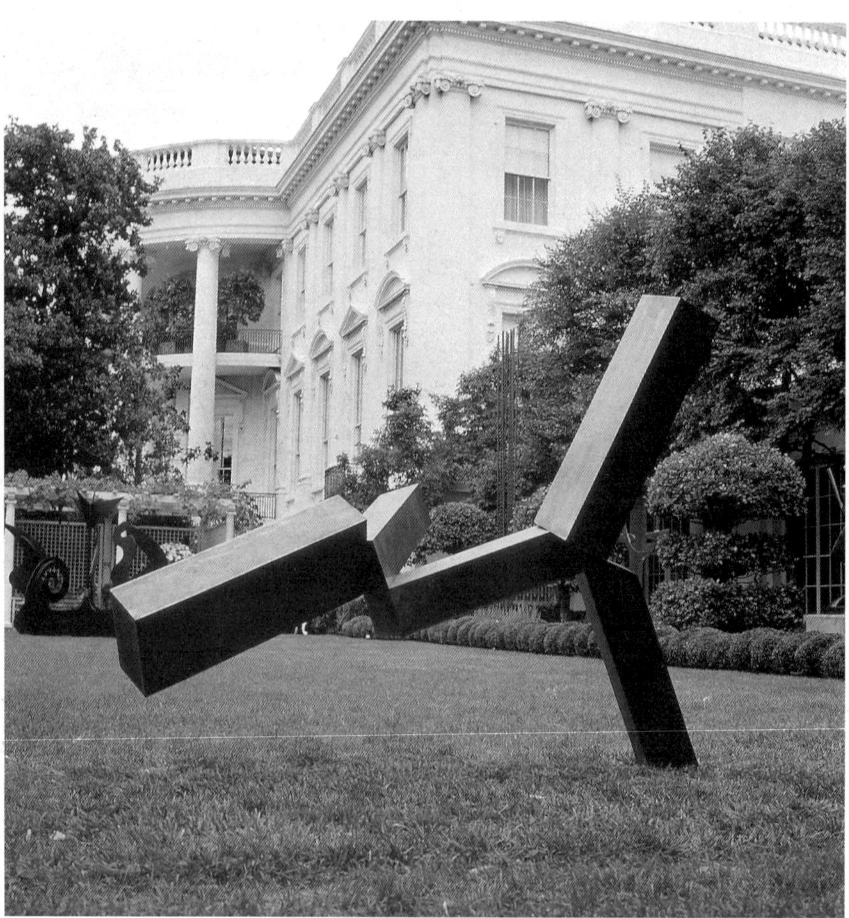

OPPOSITE:

196 Untitled. 1988. Bronze (edition 1/4), 56 x 68 x 60" (142.2 x 172.7 x 152.4 cm). Private collection

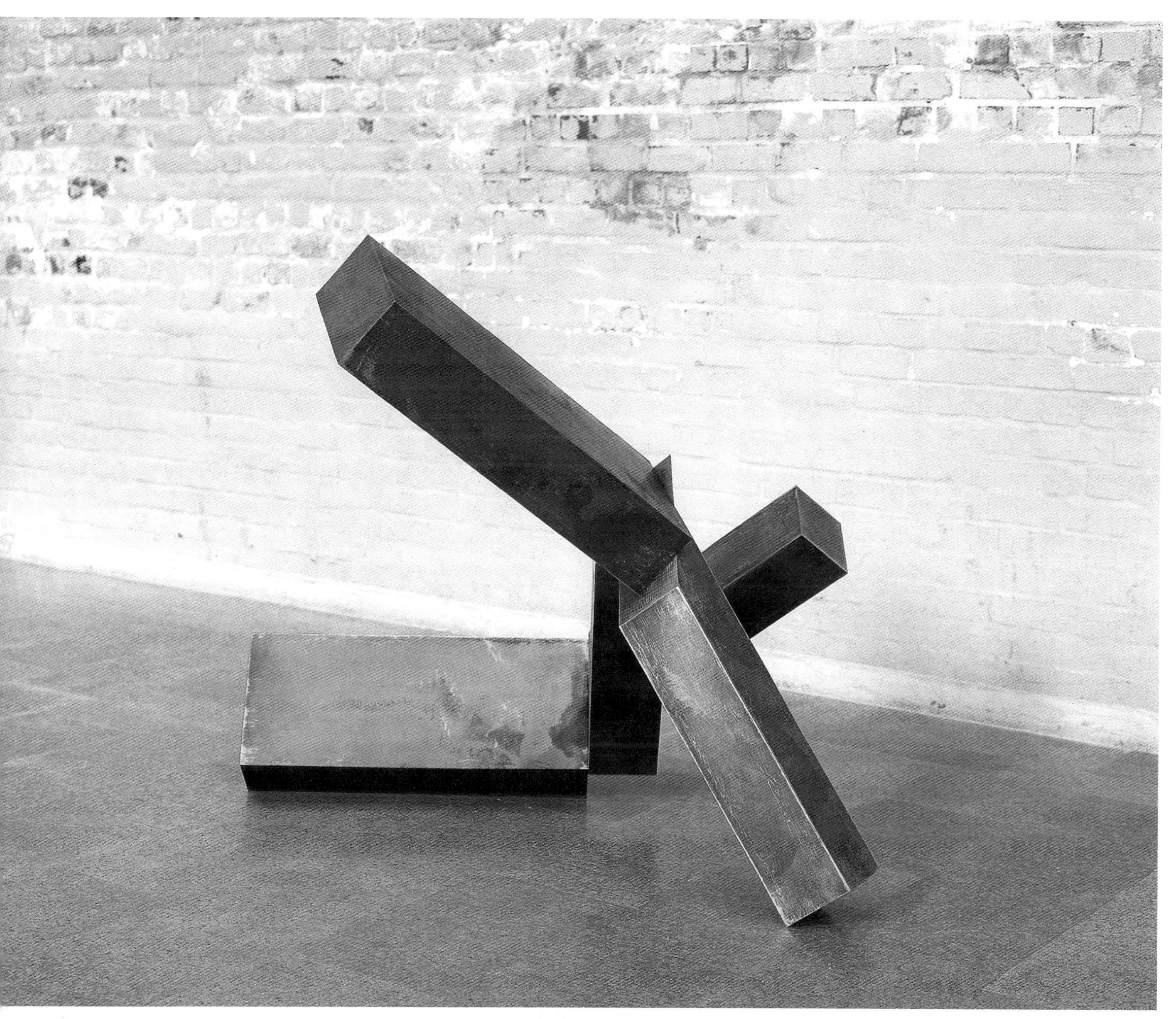

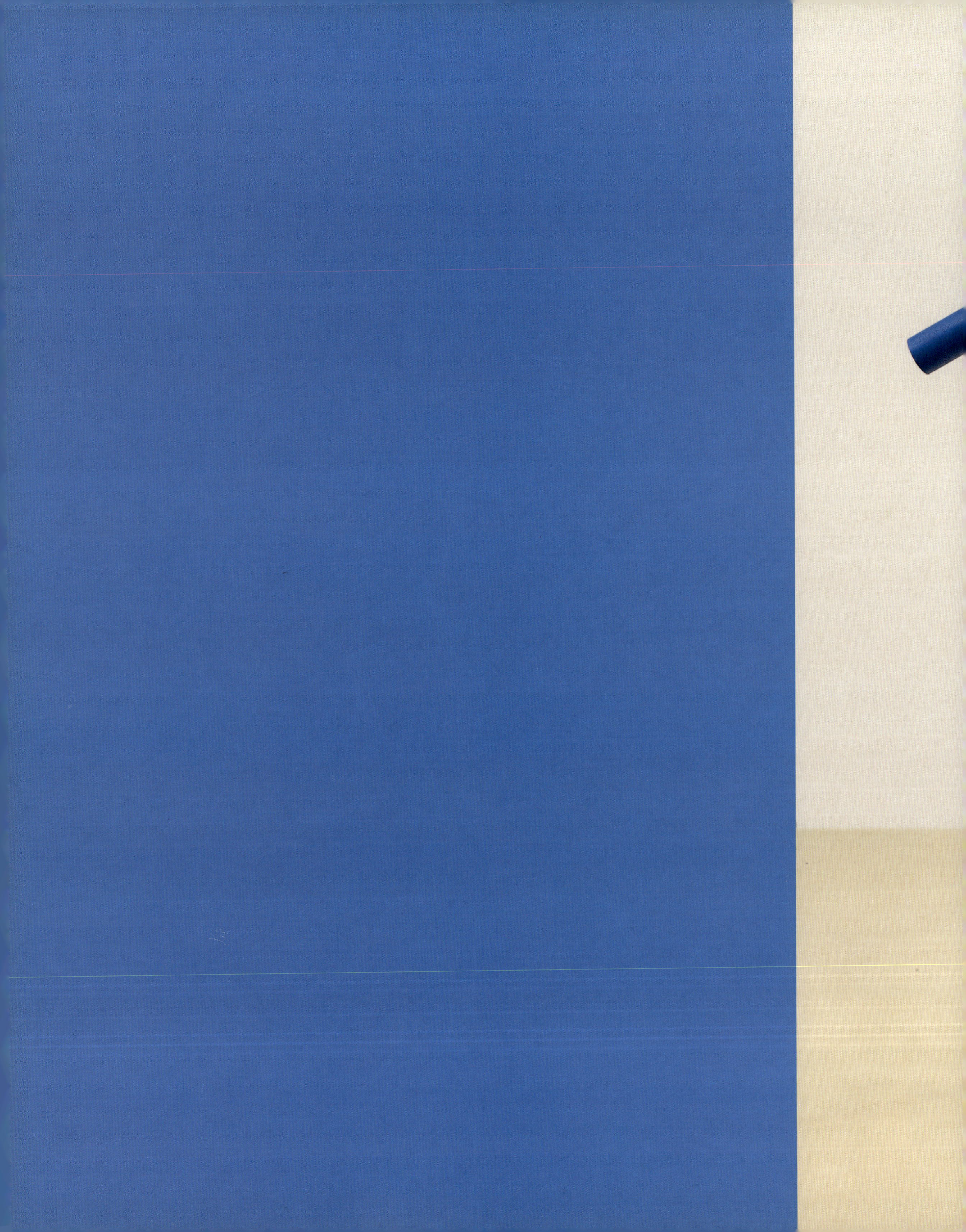

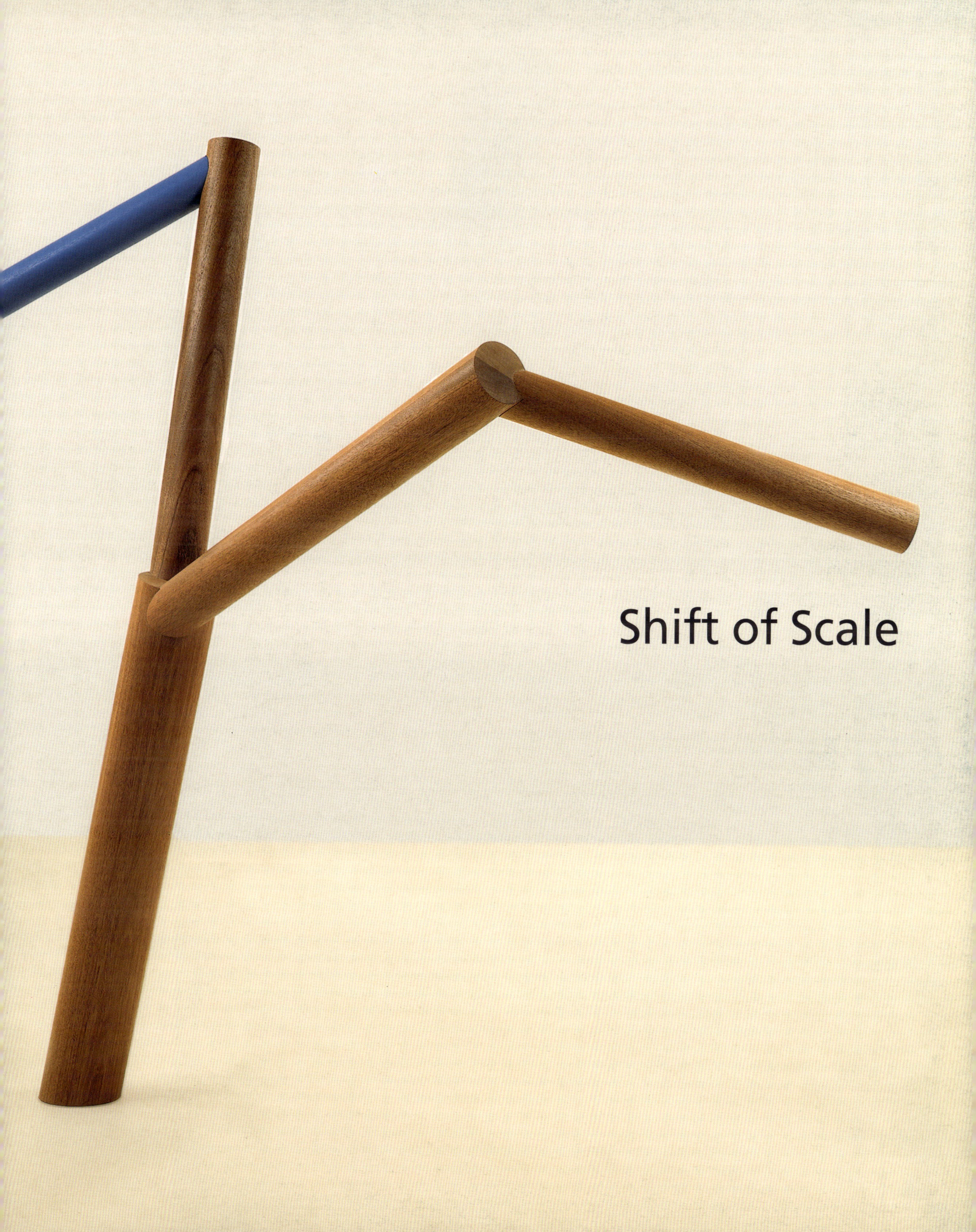
Shift of Scale

Addition and Subtraction (1989–92)

Shapiro's sculptures rely on a remarkable economy of means. Though employing relatively few geometric forms, they nonetheless convey an abundance of expressive possibilities. They even hint at what could be called a cinematic dimension: Shapiro's work as a whole can be seen as an ongoing succession of movements in which each individual work represents one significant moment. Time is stopped, an instant suspended. The viewer is permitted to imagine a sculpture's possible past and future, and to piece together a speculative narrative.

A group of works completed between 1989 and 1992 (plates 198, 199, 204, 206) illustrates this near-cinematic quality. Variations in color, along with the use of animated stances, extreme shifts of weight, and dramatic projections of the extremities, especially the head, distinguish these works. Their dynamism is reinforced by their greater scale – an increase not only in size per se but in psychological power.

These large-scale works are the result of a working process that follows an almost classical procedure. Shapiro's sculptures start as studies, and, like his drawings, the three-dimensional studies can be executed quickly, thereby maintaining his sense of gesture and touch. It is the intimacy of these preliminary, hands-on activities that preserves his impulses in an expressive form.

Drawings and sculptural studies from 1990–91 (plates 200–3) disclose Shapiro's additive and subtractive methods. The final image or form is built incrementally, and each step along the way is left as a record of this creative computation. Shapiro's drawing method is direct, almost diagrammatic: colors indicate the distribution of weight and the interlocking of distinct formal elements. The free use of metal, glue, wood, and paint in the three-dimensional studies enlivens forms and makes them more direct instruments for plastic thought. When a study is ultimately transformed into a larger sculpture, the process of enlargement beyond a certain size necessitates changes in material, in proportion, and sometimes in structure.

PREVIOUS SPREAD:
197 Untitled. 1993. Oil on wood, 59" x 6'2" x 36" (149.9 x 188 x 91.4 cm). Collection the artist

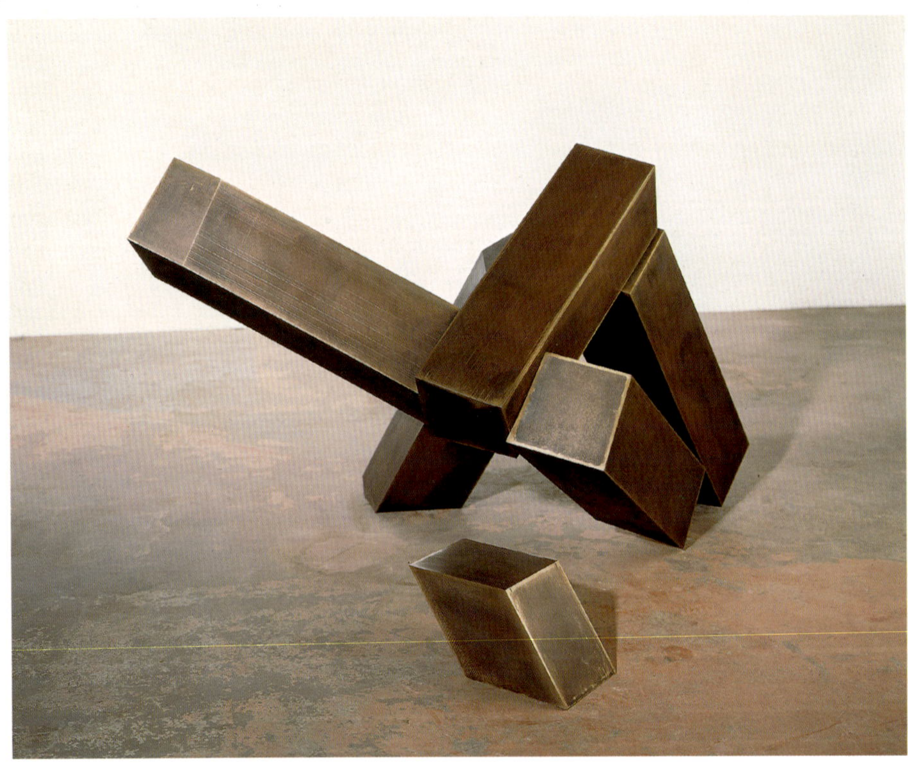

198 Untitled. 1992. Bronze (edition 0/3), 40" x 6'2" x 39" (101.6 x 188 x 152.4 cm). Collection the artist

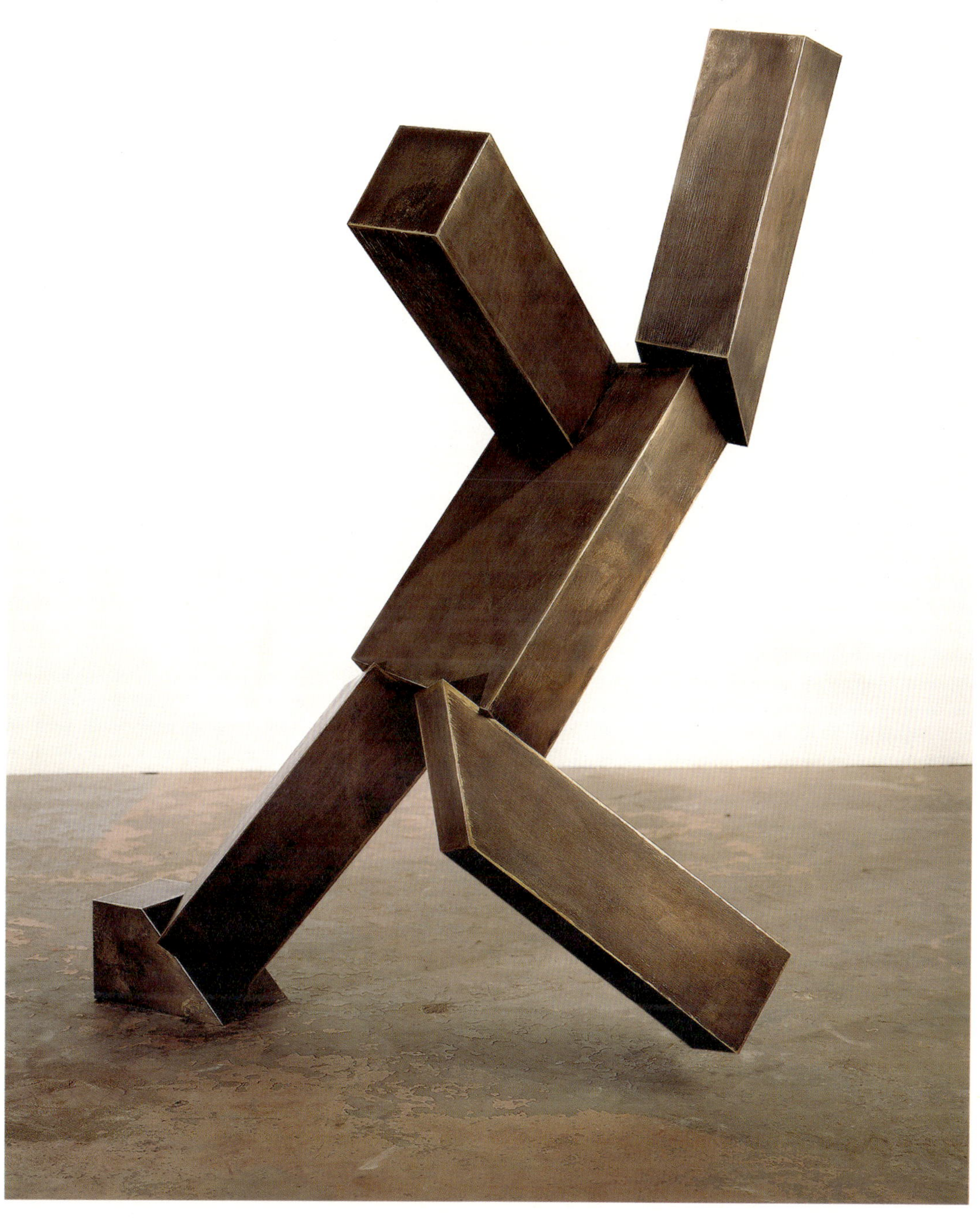

199 Untitled. 1991. Bronze (edition 1/3), 6'3" x 65" x 39" (190.5 x 165.1 x 99.1 cm). Collection Mitzi and Warren Eisenberg

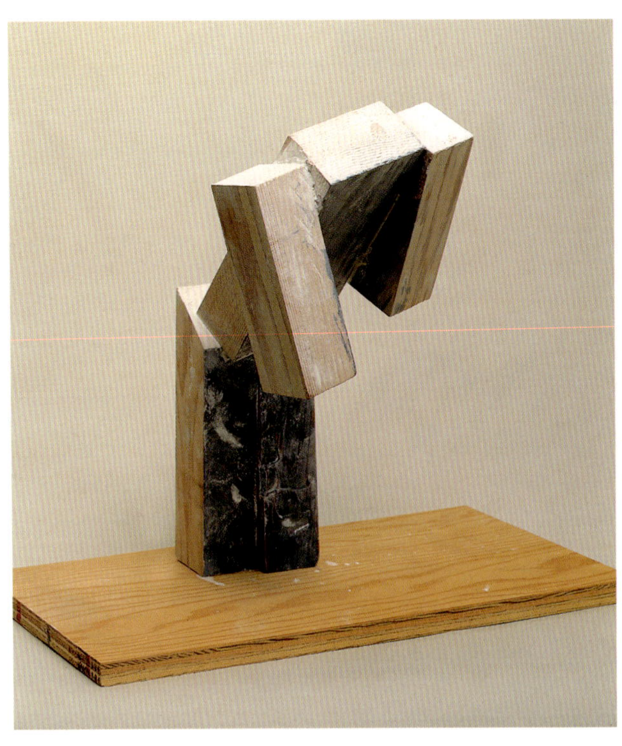

200 Untitled. 1990. Oil on wood, 13½ x 7¼ x 7⅜" (34.3 x 18.4 x 18.7 cm). Private collection

201 Untitled. 1990–91. Oil on wood, 23 x 21½ x 18" (58.4 x 54.6 x 45.7 cm). Instituto Valenciano de Arte Moderno, Valencia

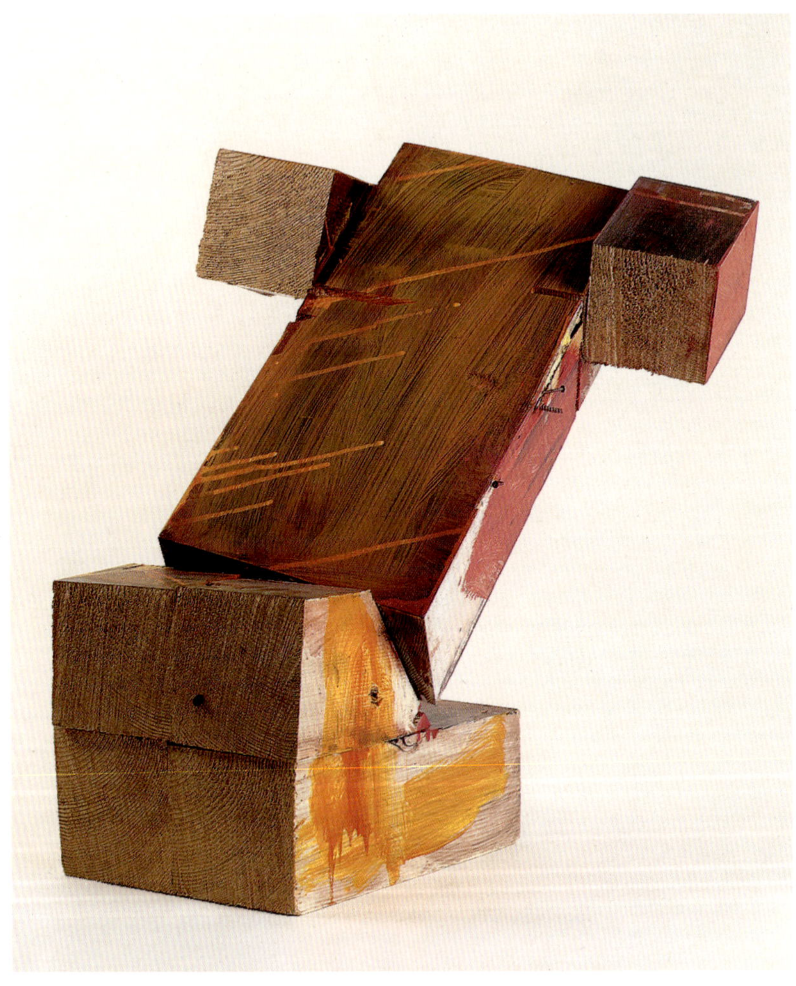

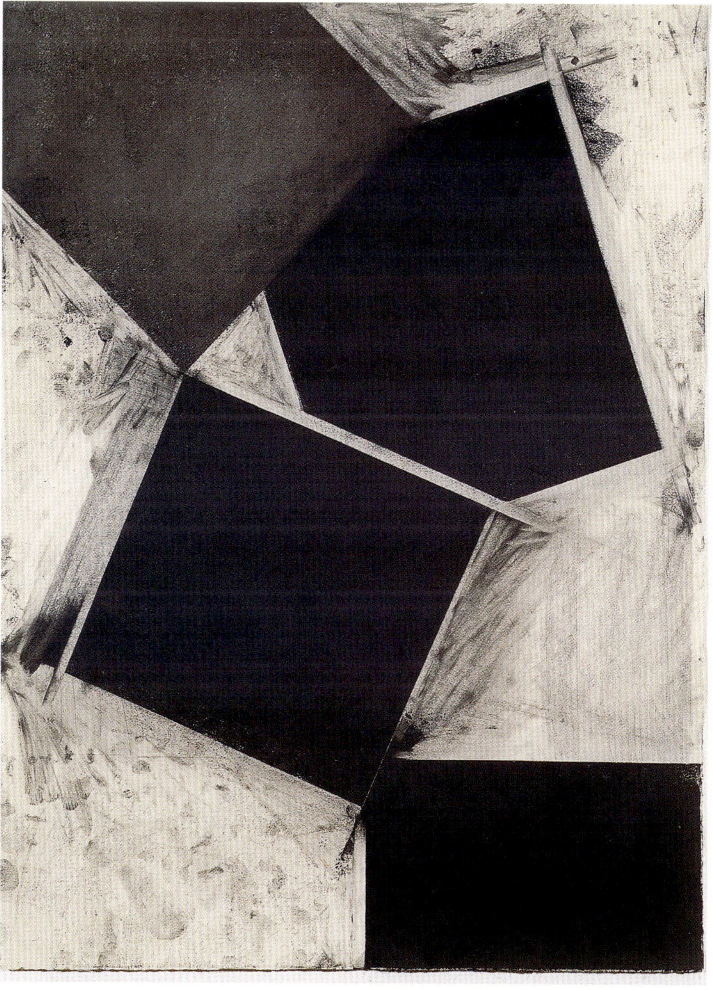

202 Untitled. 1990. Charcoal and chalk on light blue paper, 41½ x 28½" (105.4 x 72.4 cm). Collection Sarah-Ann and Werner H. Kramarsky

203 Untitled. 1990. Charcoal and chalk on paper, 30½ x 22¾" (77.5 x 57.8 cm). Private collection

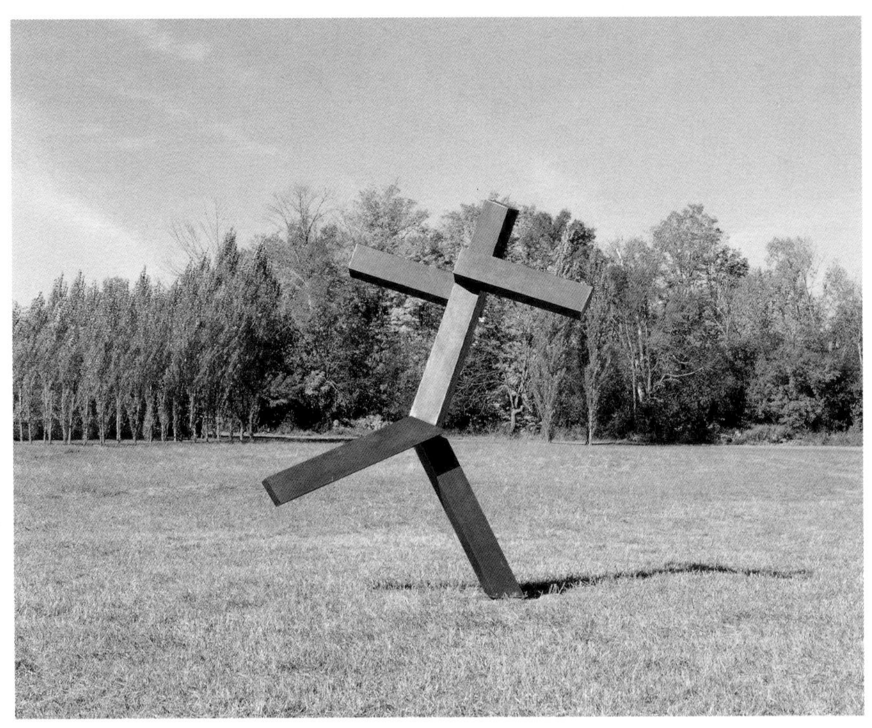

204 Untitled. 1989. Bronze (edition 0/4), 7'5" x 6'4" x 27" (226.1 x 194.3 x 68.6 cm). Collection the artist. Reproduced in color on pages 2–3.

205 Untitled. 1991. Bronze (edition 4/4), 7' x 10'5" x 54" (213.4 x 317.5 x 137.2 cm). Courtesy PaceWildenstein

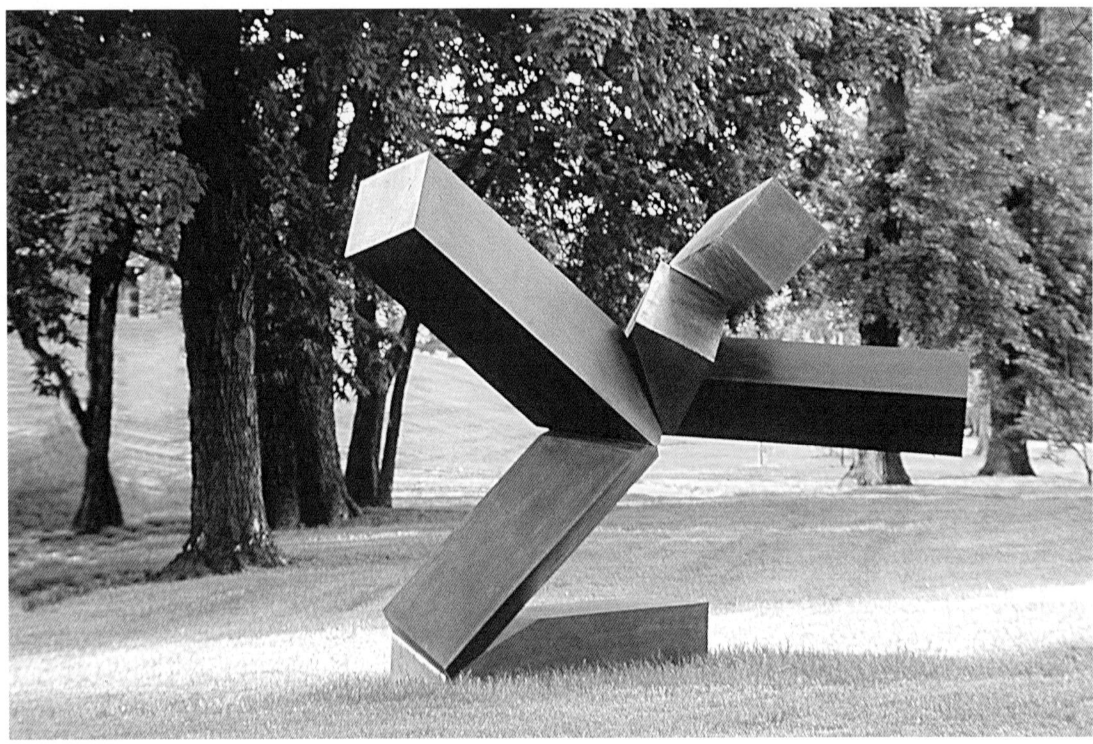

Shapiro's active involvement in this step-by-step process is evident in the choice of casting as a process. Itself the product of transformation, the cast metal records the sequential procedures of each sculpture's production. The original wood structure, the choice of hard- or softwood, the cut of the beams, the relative roughness of the grain – all this is imprinted on the bronze surface. Moreover, at the foundry there is ample choice of patinas and casting techniques. Shapiro seeks to preserve something of the raw material within the finished product and tries to remain as close as possible to his initial vision. He creates a form that records on its surface the process of its own making; and then, as another level of the creative process, he transforms it through casting. "If the work weren't layered," Shapiro says, "it would lose a lot." Part of what would be lost might be the *pentimenti,* so to speak, of the emotional process.

"Le plus profond, c'est la peau," Paul Valéry wrote. For Shapiro, too, there is nothing so deep as the skin of his sculptures. The surface – be it bronze, iron, wood, plaster, or paint – receives and brings to light the emotions from which a sculpture has originated.

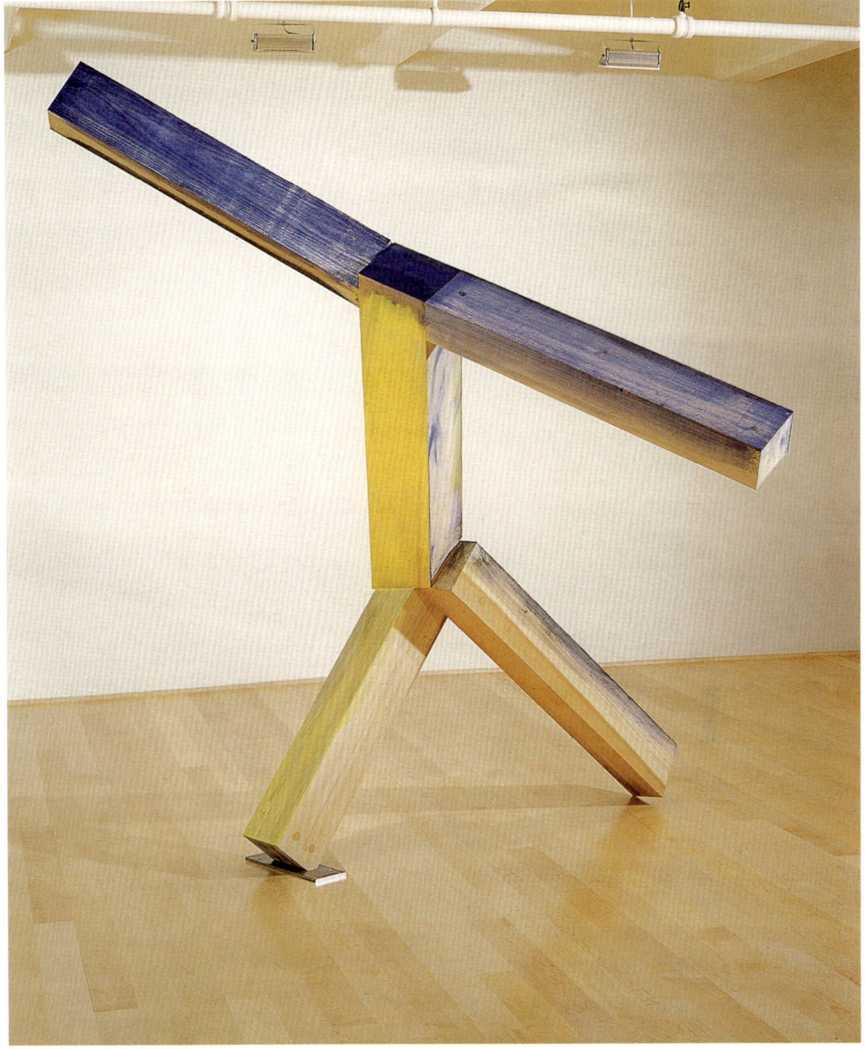

206 Untitled. 1989–90. Oil on wood, 7'7" x 7' x 7' (231.1 x 213.4 x 213.4 cm). Private collection

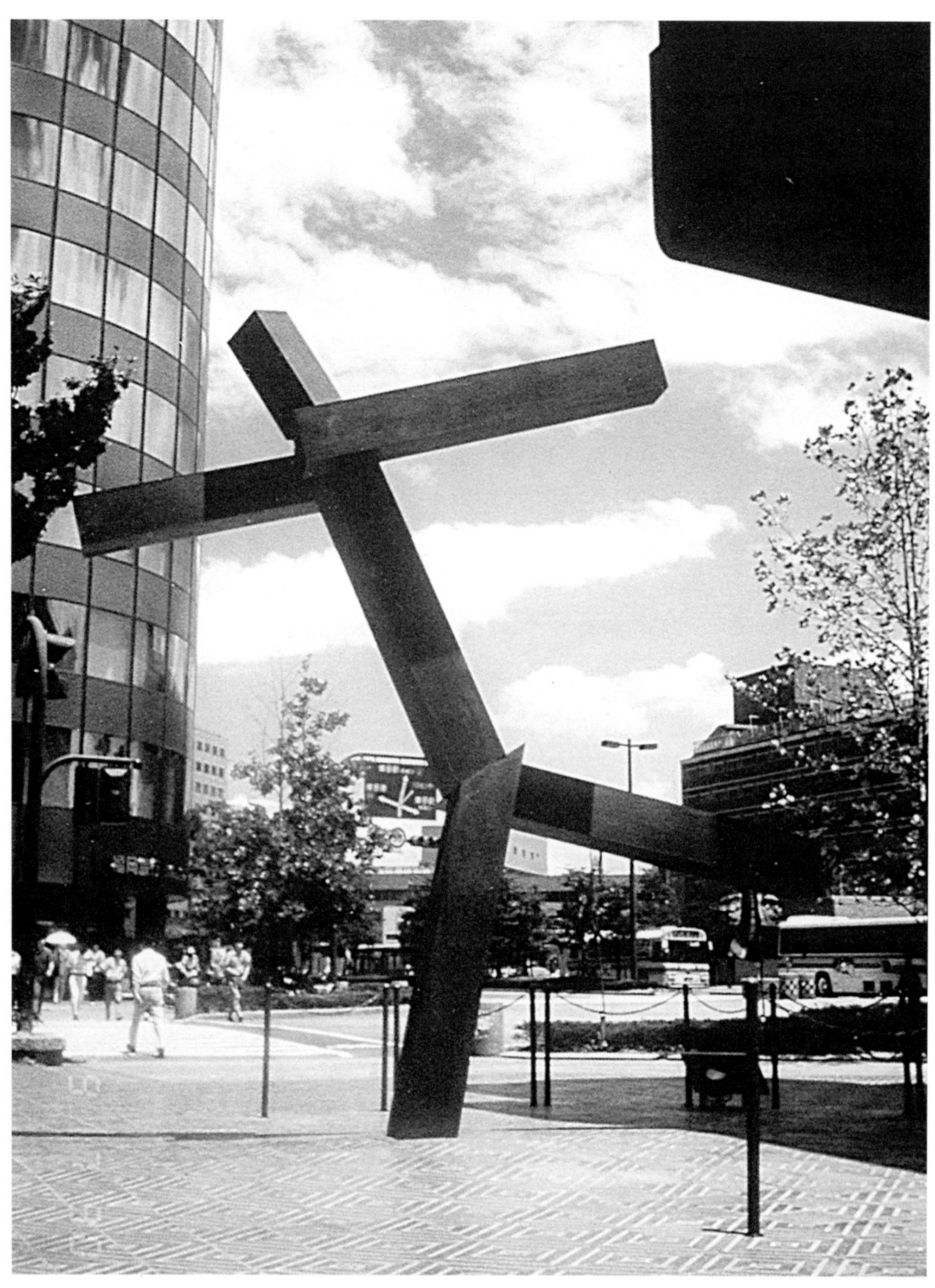

207 Untitled. 1988. Bronze, 15'6" x 46" x 15' (472.4 x 116.8 x 457.2 cm). Collection the Fukuoka City Bank, Ltd.

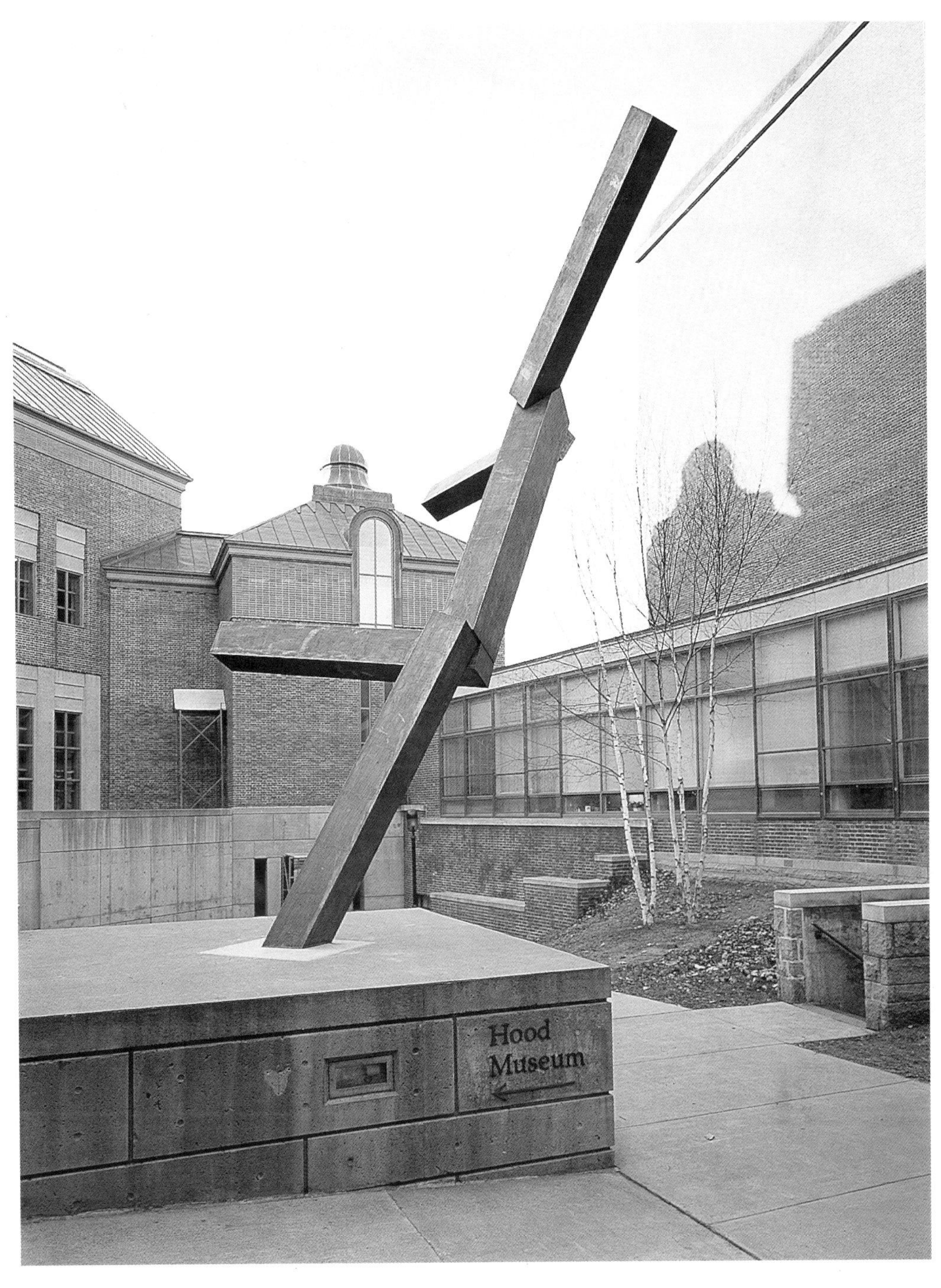

208 Untitled. 1989–90. Bronze (edition 1/4), approx. 20' (609.6 cm) high. Hood Museum of Art, Dartmouth College, Hanover, New Hampshire. Museum purchase

Spheres (1989–92)

In the late eighties, after a lengthy absence, the sphere returned to Shapiro's repertoire. Almost two decades before, it had figured in such pieces as *One Hand Forming* and *Two Hands Forming* (plate 32), conglomerations of hand-made clay balls. In shifting his emphasis and selecting this seemingly forgotten form, Shapiro again renewed himself. The reintroduction of the sphere, as in a plaster from about 1990 (plate 209), was also a way to refer to the full, volumetric form that he admires in Indian sculpture, such as the figure of the goddess Marichi from Shapiro's personal collection (figure 17).

Rounded shapes appear as well in pastels and woodcuts (plates 210–15).[34] Shapiro has a particular affinity with the latter medium. Wood is fundamental to his sculpture, as we have seen, and the woodcut offered another opportunity for him to investigate its expressive possibilities. The particular textures of walnut, cherry, butternut, mahogany, pear, sassafras, and oak are identifiable on the surface of the paper.

In contrast to his earlier, sculpted spheres, amassed or scattered on the ground, these pastel and woodcut orbs float weightlessly. In the empty spaces of the paper, spheres meet, cluster, and disperse; their choreography and their colors – pink, yellow, and red – suggest a lighthearted sexuality. This comfortable, exultant environment recalls Alexander Calder's *Calderberry Bush* (figure 18). Behind the playful simplicity, however, both artists demonstrate an exactitude in placing shapes and a keen formal intelligence.

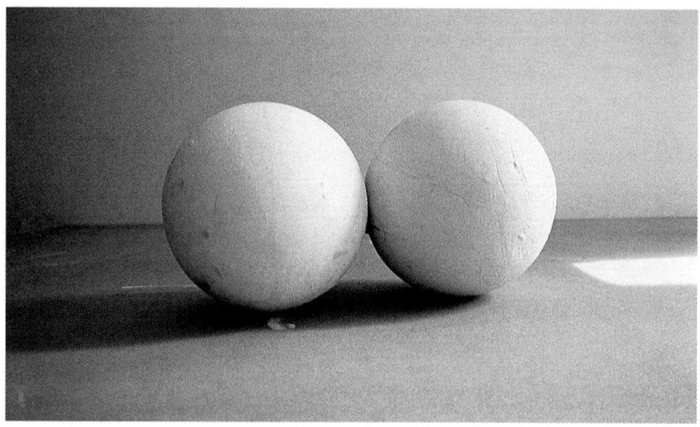

209 Study. c. 1990. Plaster, 7 x 13¾ x 7" (17.8 x 34.9 x 17.8 cm). Collection the artist

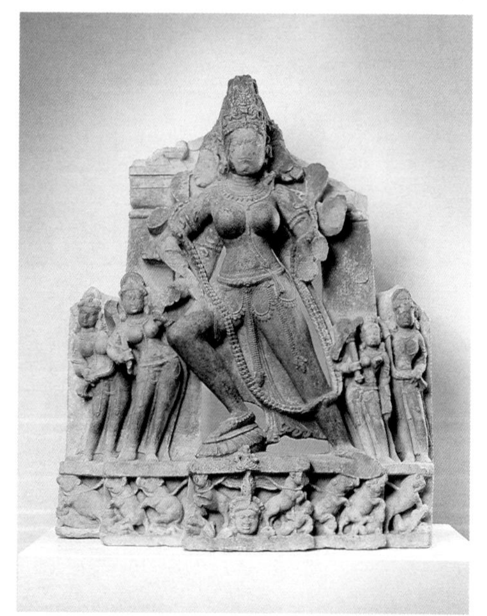

Fig. 17 *The Goddess Marichi.* Central India, 11th century. Stone, 37¾ x 31¾ x 10⅛ (95.9 x 80.6 x 25.7 cm). Collection Joel Shapiro, New York

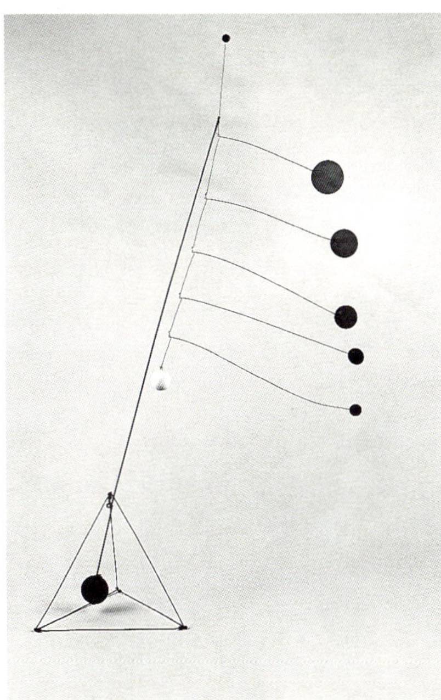

Fig. 18 Alexander Calder. *Object with Red Disks (Calderberry Bush)*. 1932. Painted steel rod, wire, wood, and sheet aluminum, dimensions variable; with base, 7'4½" x 33" x 47½" (224.8 x 83.8 x 120.7 cm). Whitney Museum of American Art, New York. Purchase, with funds from the Mrs. Percy Uris Purchase Fund

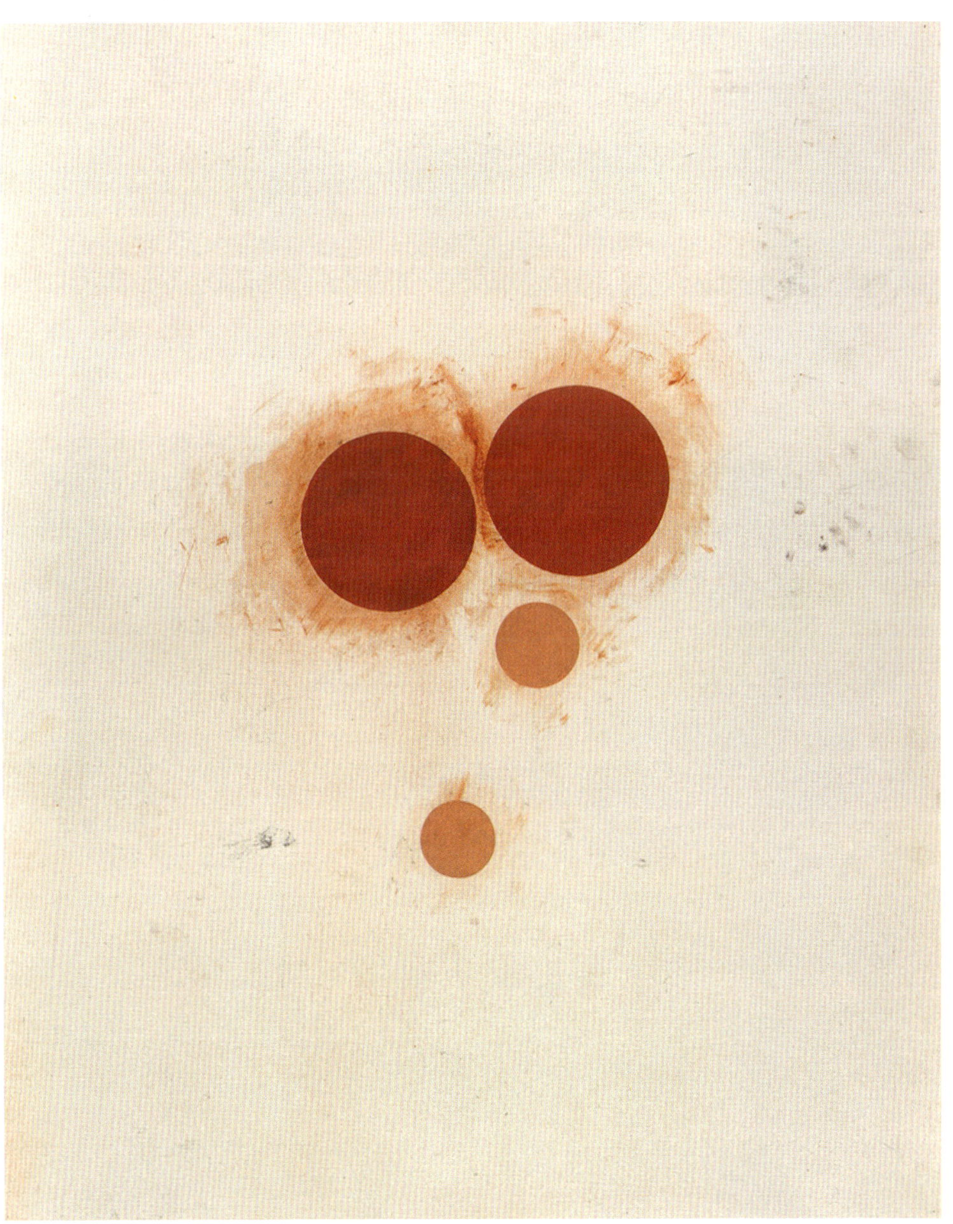

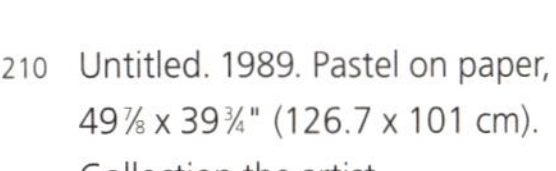

210 Untitled. 1989. Pastel on paper, 49⅞ x 39¾" (126.7 x 101 cm). Collection the artist

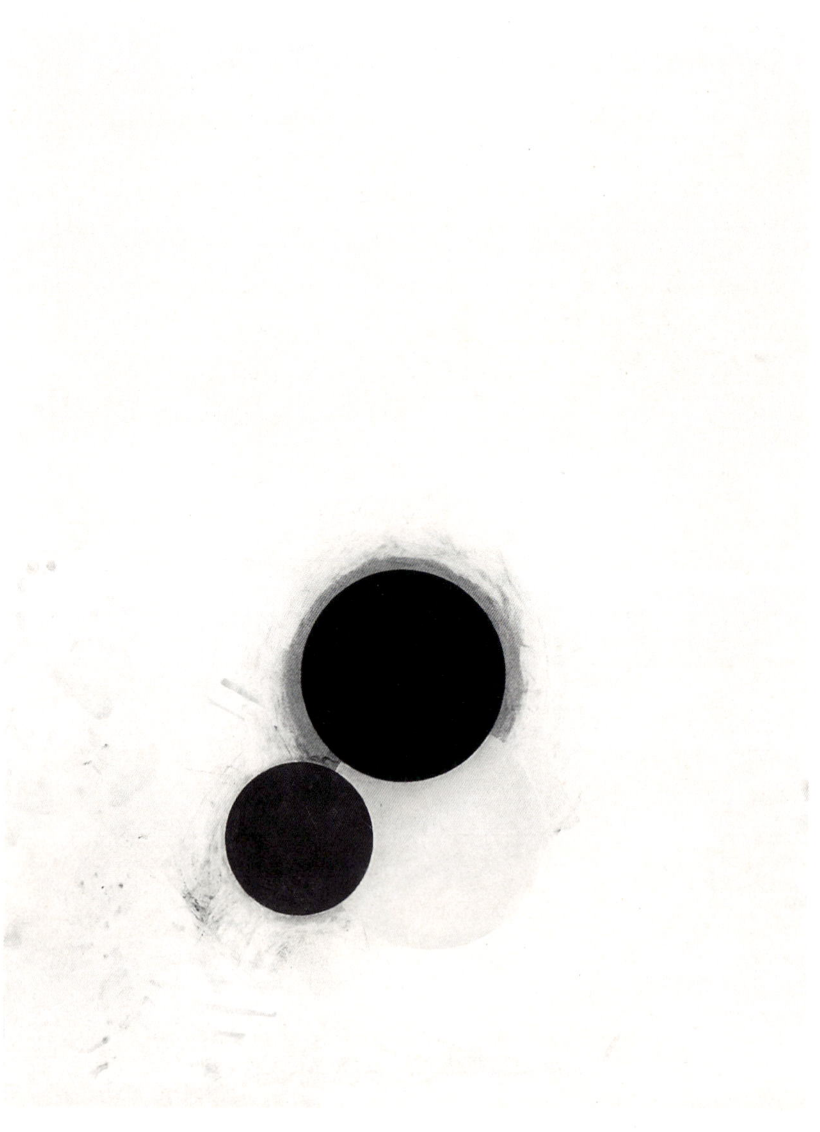

211 Untitled. 1989. Pastel, chalk, and charcoal on paper, 49⅞ x 36" (126.7 x 91.4 cm). Collection the Chase-Manhattan Bank

212 Untitled. 1990. Woodcut, 26 x 19" (66 x 48.3 cm). Published by the artist and Grenfell Press, New York

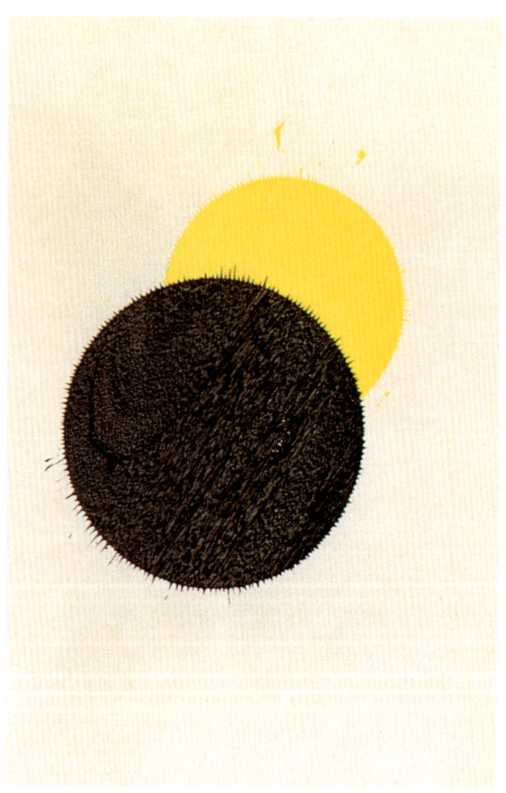

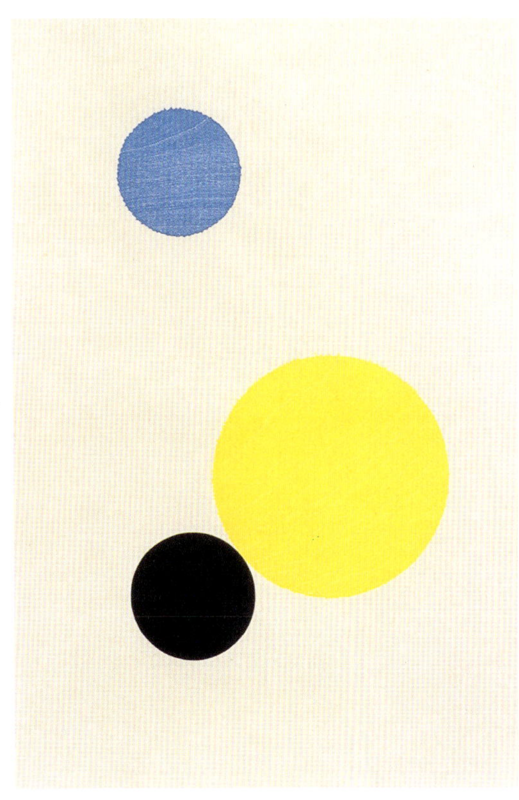

214 Untitled. 1990. Woodcut, 26 x 19" (66 x 48.3 cm). Published by the artist and Grenfell Press, New York

215 Untitled. 1990. Woodcut, 44¼ x 30½" (112.4 x 77.5 cm). Published by the artist and Grenfell Press, New York

213 Untitled. 1990. Woodcut, 44¼ x 30½" (112.4 x 77.5 cm). Published by the artist and Grenfell Press, New York

Spheres meet, cluster, and disperse also in floor sculptures. Earlier, the floor was a solid base; now, the relationship between the spheres and the ground is more dynamic. The floor is treated like a sheet of paper, a surface on which the spheres can act and react (plates 216, 218). Congregating spheres (plates 217, 219) lift themselves with the help of short poles or are suspended with wires. Each sculpture becomes a system of planetary spheres responding to gravitational forces.

In the studies for these floor sculptures (plates 209, 220), Shapiro experimented with wood, plaster, and wax balls and wood rods. The final bronze casting gives these disparate materials uniformity and the spheres a concentrated solidity. Because of the sculptures' smooth, round shapes, the irregularities of the joints become especially apparent; they catch the light and animate the bronze patina.

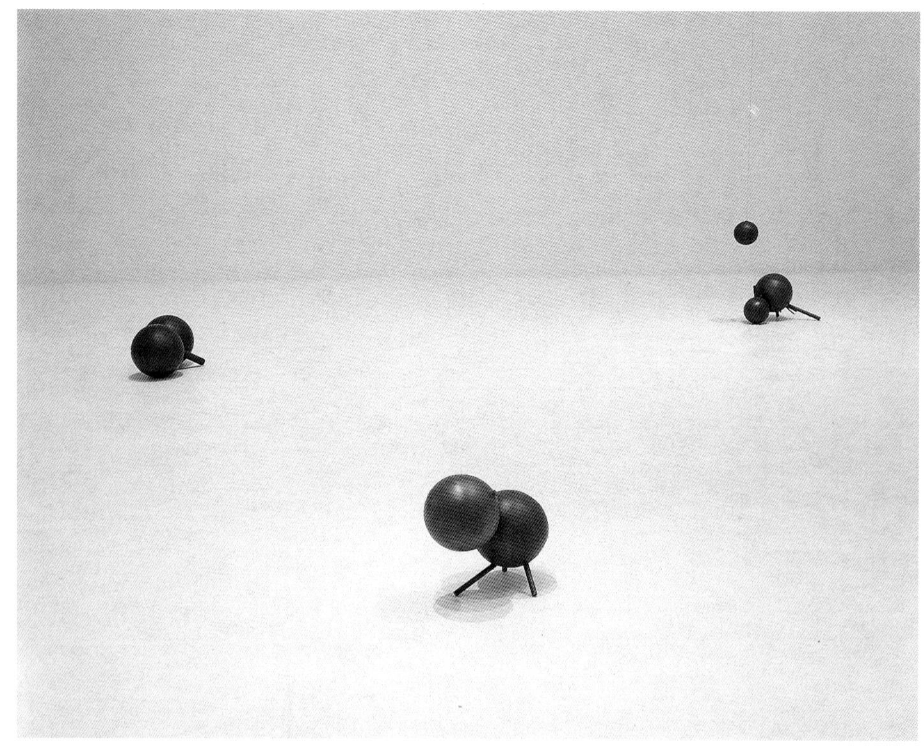

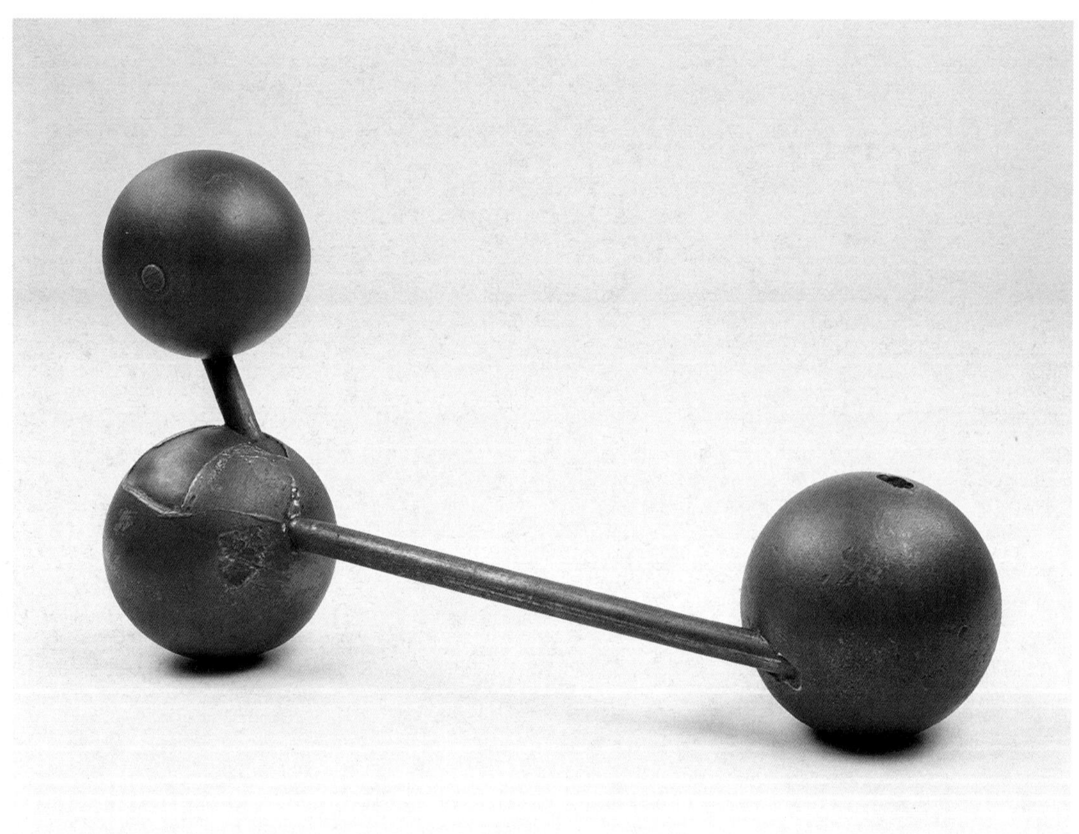

217 Untitled. 1992. Bronze (edition 1/3), 9½ x 17½ x 4½" (24.1 x 44.5 x 11.4 cm). Collection the artist

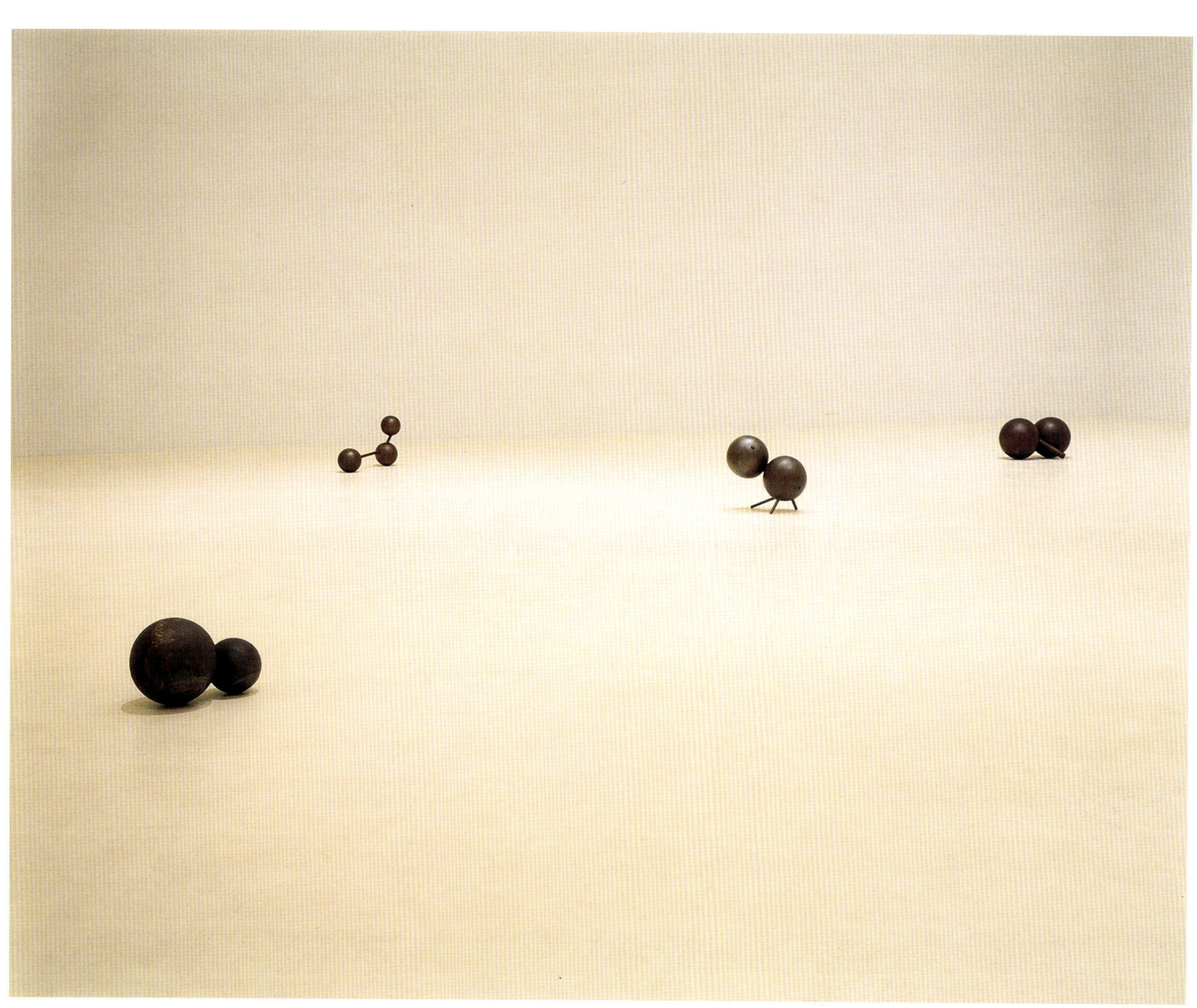

ABOVE AND OPPOSITE ABOVE:

216, 218 Installation views of the exhibition "Joel Shapiro: Sculpture and Drawings," The Pace Gallery, New York, 1993. Works shown here also appear in plates 217, 219.

219 Untitled. 1992. Bronze (edition 2/3), 19½ x 20½ x 11" (49.5 x 52.1 x 27.9 cm). Collection Mr. and Mrs. Frank Rothman

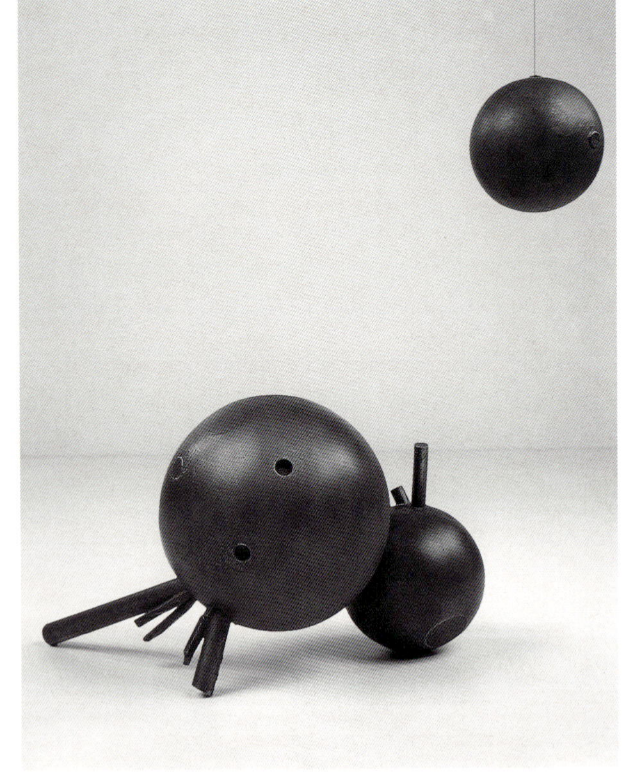

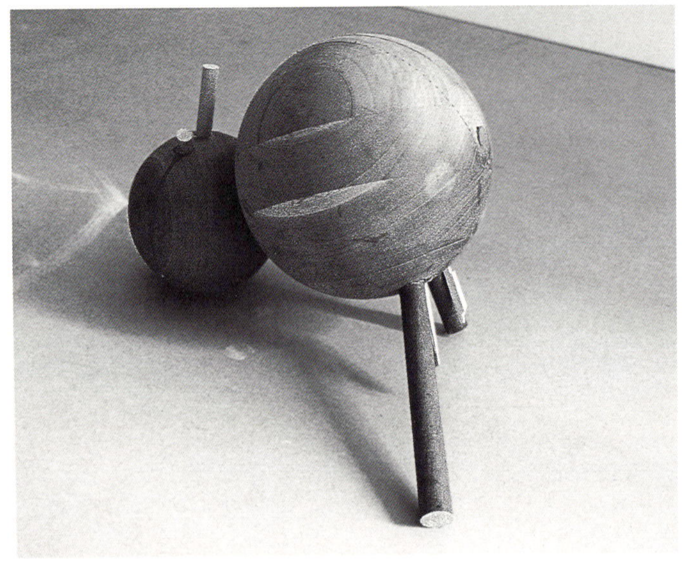

220 Study. 1990. Wood, dimensions unavailable. No longer extant. The work shown here is a study for the sculpture illustrated in plate 219.

221 Untitled. 1990. Bronze, 8¼ x 14 x 11½" (21 x 35.5 x 29.2 cm). Collection Douglas S. Cramer

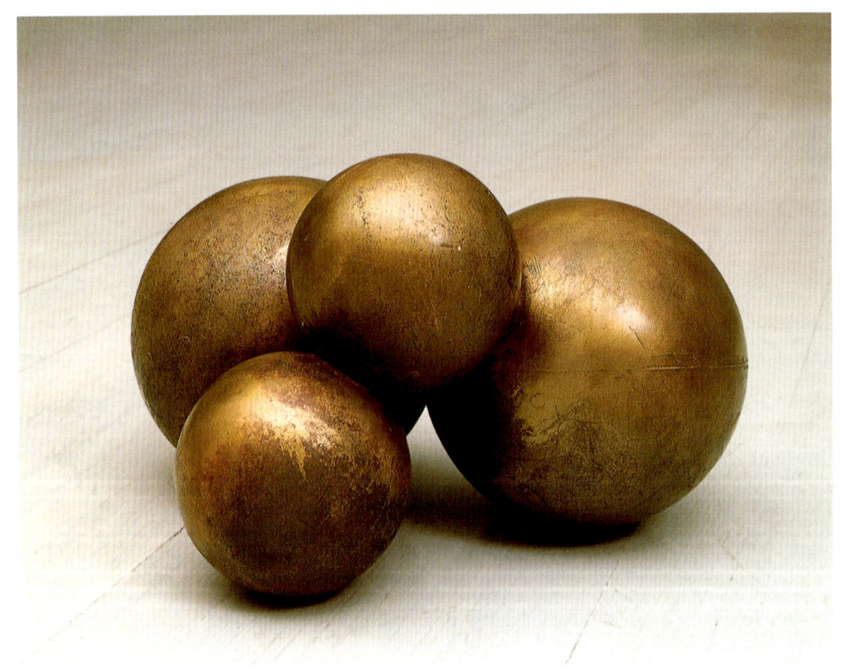

Trees (1973–93)

The idea of the tree as a symbol – of man and of the universe – dates from ancient times. It is central to the cosmologies of many cultures. In the Jewish Cabalistic tradition, for instance, the sacred tree is depicted sometimes as just that, a tree, and sometimes as a primal man.[35] Shapiro exploits a corresponding dual image, and one might say that in his work the tree grew into the figure. The tree appeared earlier than the figure. An untitled piece from 1973 (plate 222) is made simply of slivers of wood pinned on the wall. Its unpredictable way of extending itself across the wall implies the possibility of endless growth. Another wall piece, from 1975 (plate 223), more distinctly outlines a trunk and branches. This rigid relief, whose central axis and outward branching are echoed in a large drawing from the following year (plate 224), is built out from a strong vertical.

The figure-tree makes its first appearance in Shapiro's work in a bronze from 1976–77 (plate 225). This fallen form conveys in part Shapiro's reaction to his sister's suicide. The sculpture, with one leg lifeless and rigid, the other animated and bent, embodies two extremes. The animated limb would carry into future work; a similar sense of energy enlivens an extremely large drawing from 1981 that diagrams a figure-tree with blood-red pigment (plate 226). The drawn image seems ready to bloom.

A wall-mounted bronze from the same year (plate 227) resembles this drawing but renders the figure even more treelike. The segmented extensions reach out in every direction like branches capable of constant regeneration.

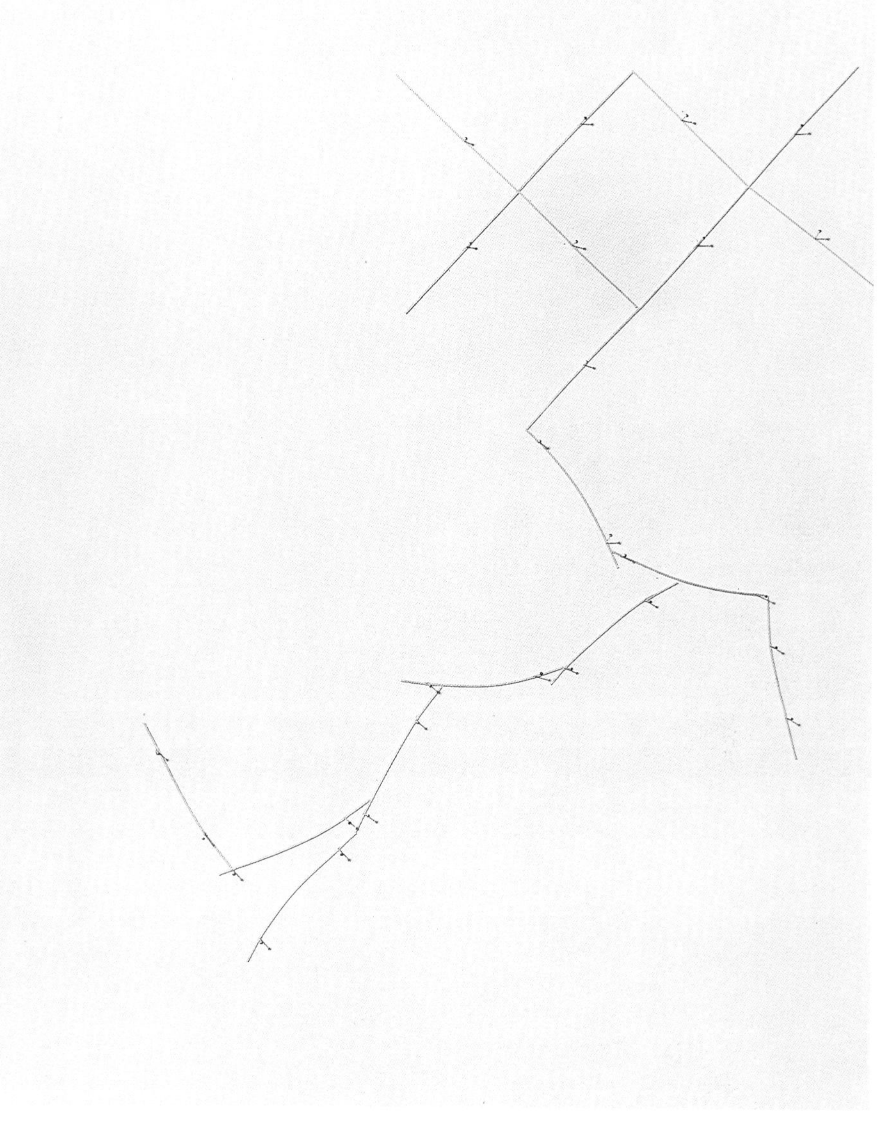

222 Untitled. 1973. Basswood and pins, 15¾ x 13½" (40 x 34.3 cm). Collection Paula Cooper

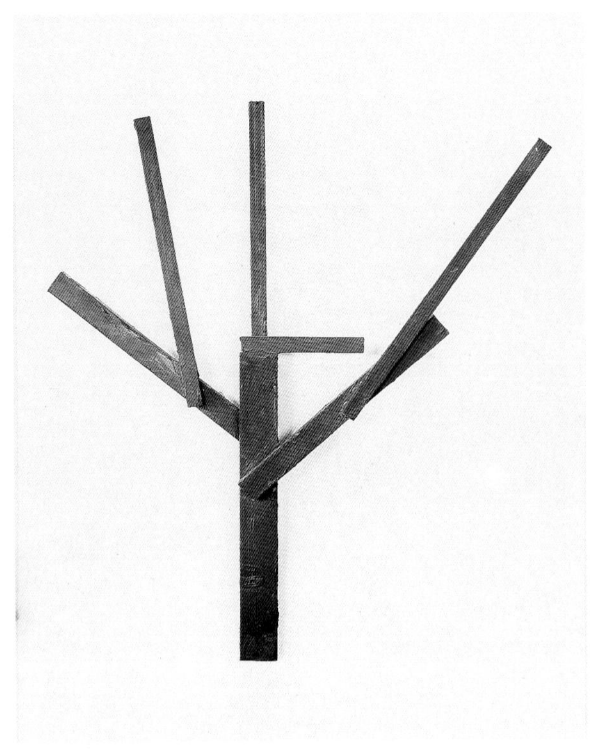

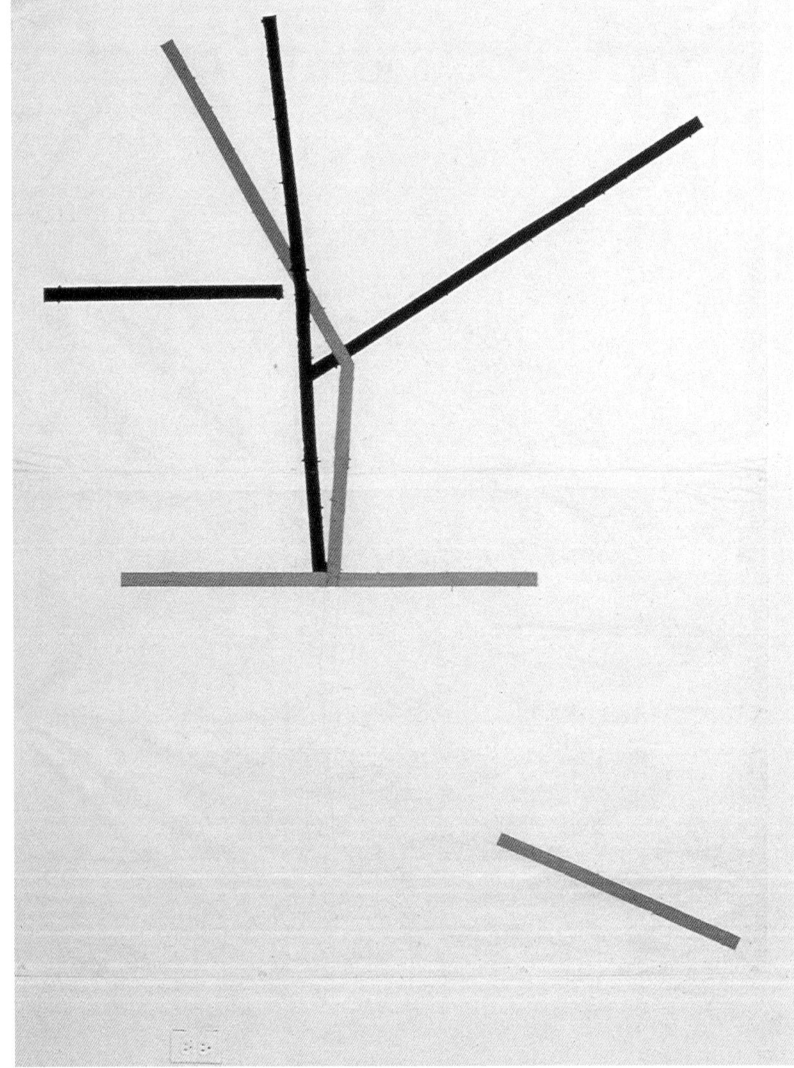

223 Untitled. 1975. Oil on wood, 26½ x 23½ x 3" (67.3 x 59.7 x 7.62 cm). Collection the artist

224 Untitled. 1976. Pencil and gouache on paper, 6'10" x 65½" (208.3 x 166.4 cm). Collection the artist

225 Untitled. 1976–77. Bronze, 4½ x 10⅛ x 5½" (10.8 x 25.7 x 14 cm). Modern Art Museum of Fort Worth. Museum Purchase with funds from the National Endowment for the Arts and the Benjamin J. Tillar Memorial Trust

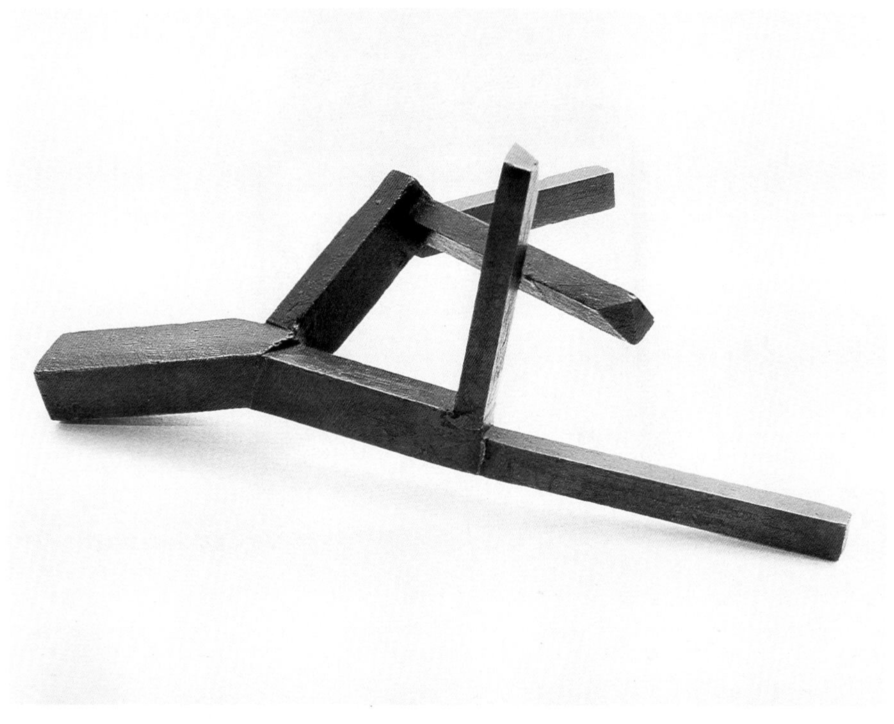

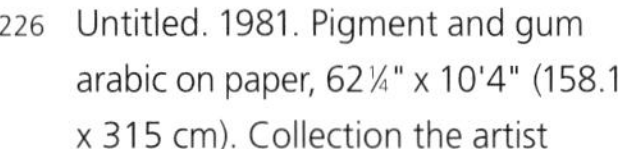

226 Untitled. 1981. Pigment and gum arabic on paper, 62¼" x 10'4" (158.1 x 315 cm). Collection the artist

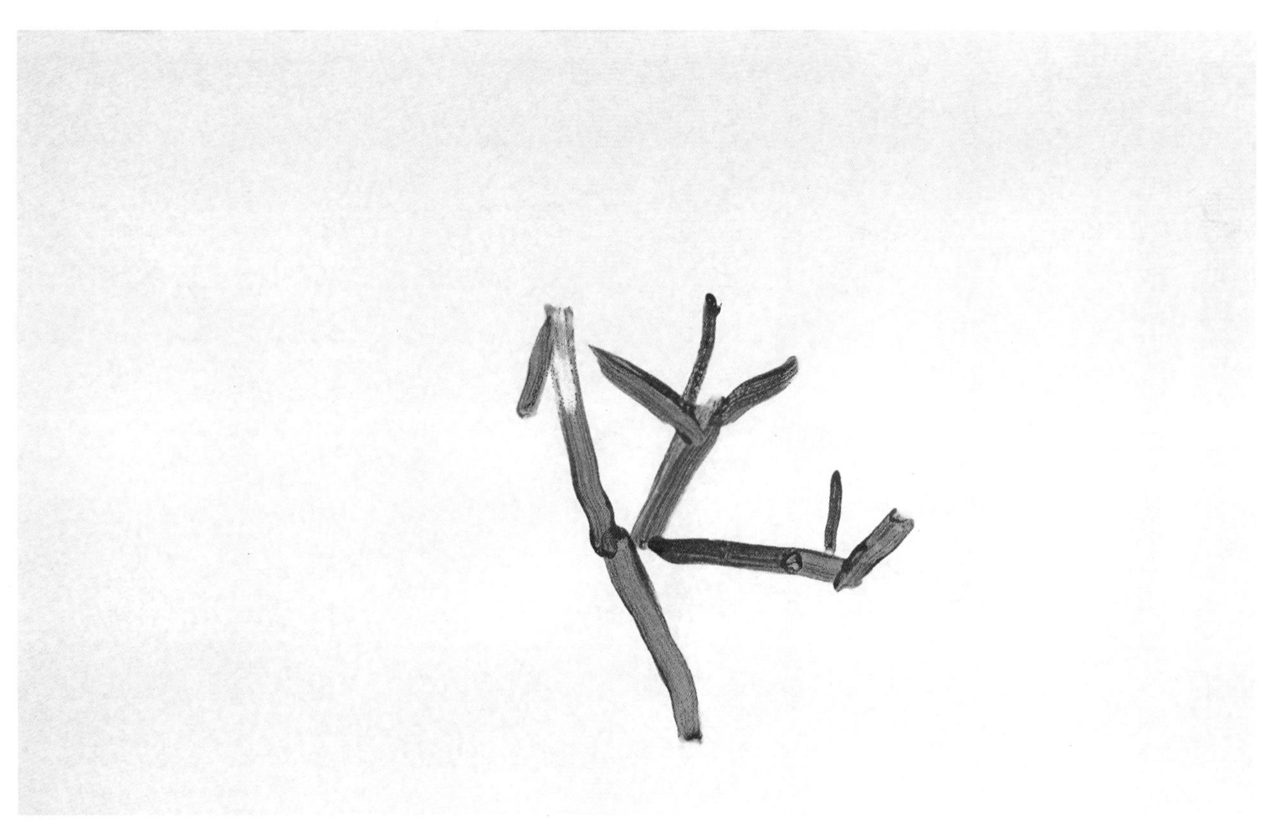

227 Untitled. 1981. Bronze, 5¼ x 15 x 8¼" (13.3 x 38.1 x 21 cm). Private collection

228 Untitled. 1981. Charcoal on paper, 22¼ x 10½" (55.5 x 26.5 cm). Collection Ann and Dan Feld

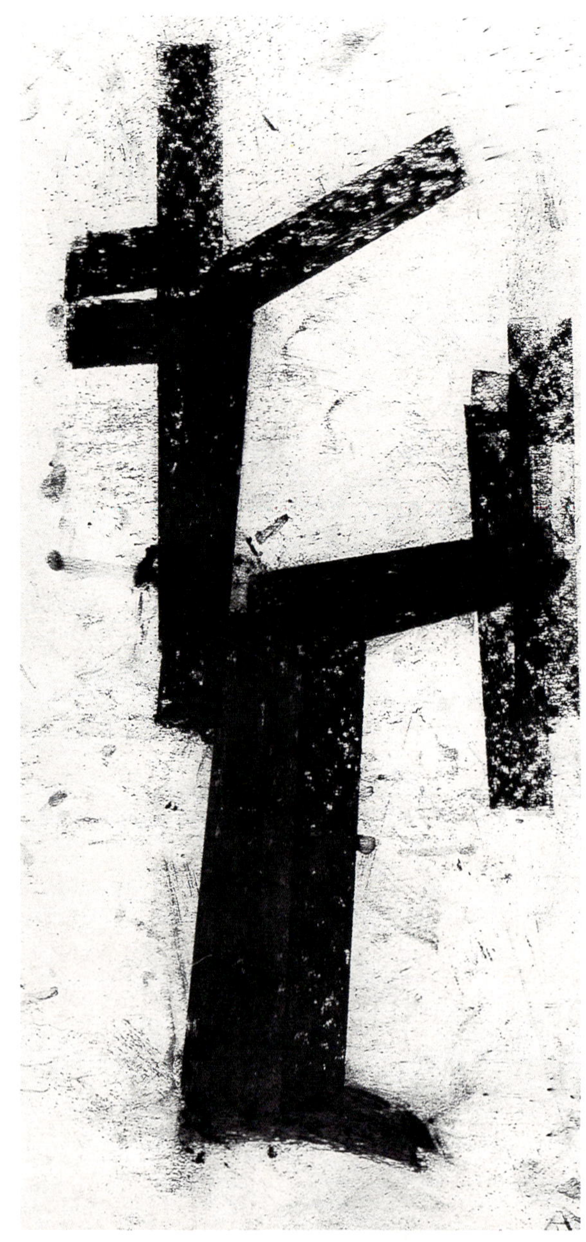

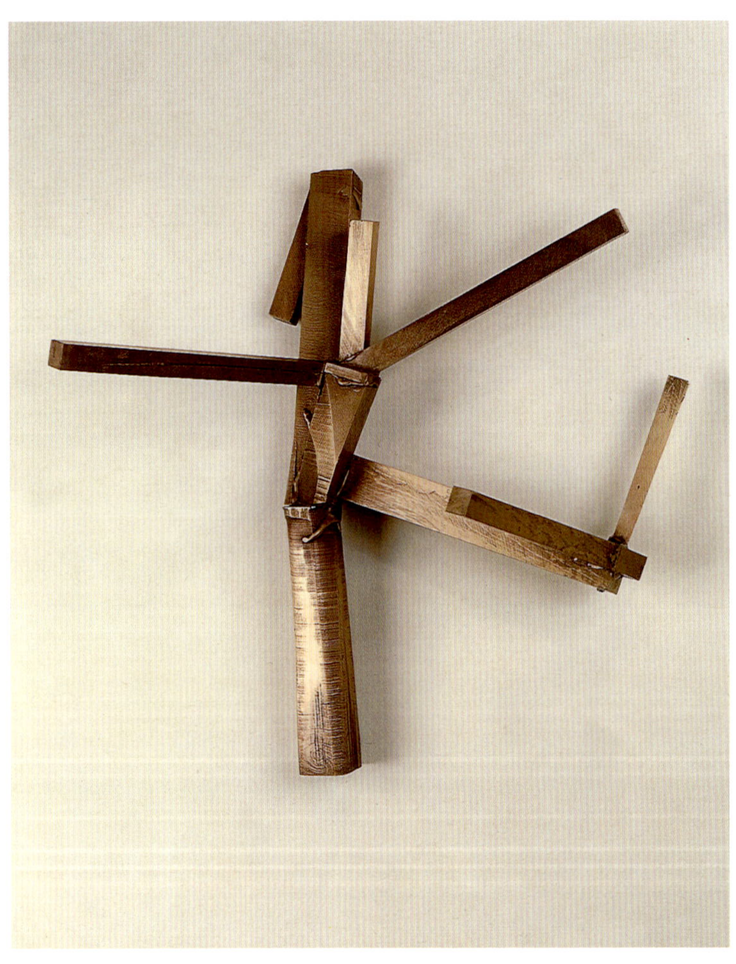

Another drawing from 1981 (plate 228) vacillates between figure and tree. From a rooted torso/trunk, two arms/branches stretch out. Their movement can be read as the gesturing of arms and hands or as the sprouting of new branches.

A decade later, the tree is the primary sign in a series of drawings and related sculptures. Shapiro confirms the close relationship between these drawings and the sculptures: "I was making drawings; then, looking at them, I decided they could function sculpturally." In linear drawings from 1992 (plates 229–31) that became the direct sources for sculptures, long, thin, branching lines invite us to read these forms as trees. The lines fill the paper freely; a strongly colored central axis supports profuse extensions highlighted with even brighter colors.

Wood studies from 1991 (plates 233, 234) are the intermediaries between these drawings and the related sculptures (plates 197, 232, 235), and openly convey the notion of constant rejuvenation.

The theme of unlimited growth in these works prompts comparison with Brancusi's monumental *Endless Column* (figure 19),[36] in which the vertical axis extends, in principle, to infinity. The soaring column rises by means of identical units stacked one on top of another. Shapiro's works, like Brancusi's column, grow into the open space of the sky. The difference between the works lies in their construction. Rarely do Shapiro's sculptures develop along a single axis. Instead, their growth is deliquescent, dividing off from the central axis and spreading in diverging directions.

The multiple trunks and branches evoke the tree more than the figure, and Shapiro underscores the tree reference by using wood rods. The large, linear extensions and the painted segments that give the trees shape suggest stages of growth. The lower elements are generally more solidly painted and darker in color. The outermost, thinnest branches display more vivid colors.

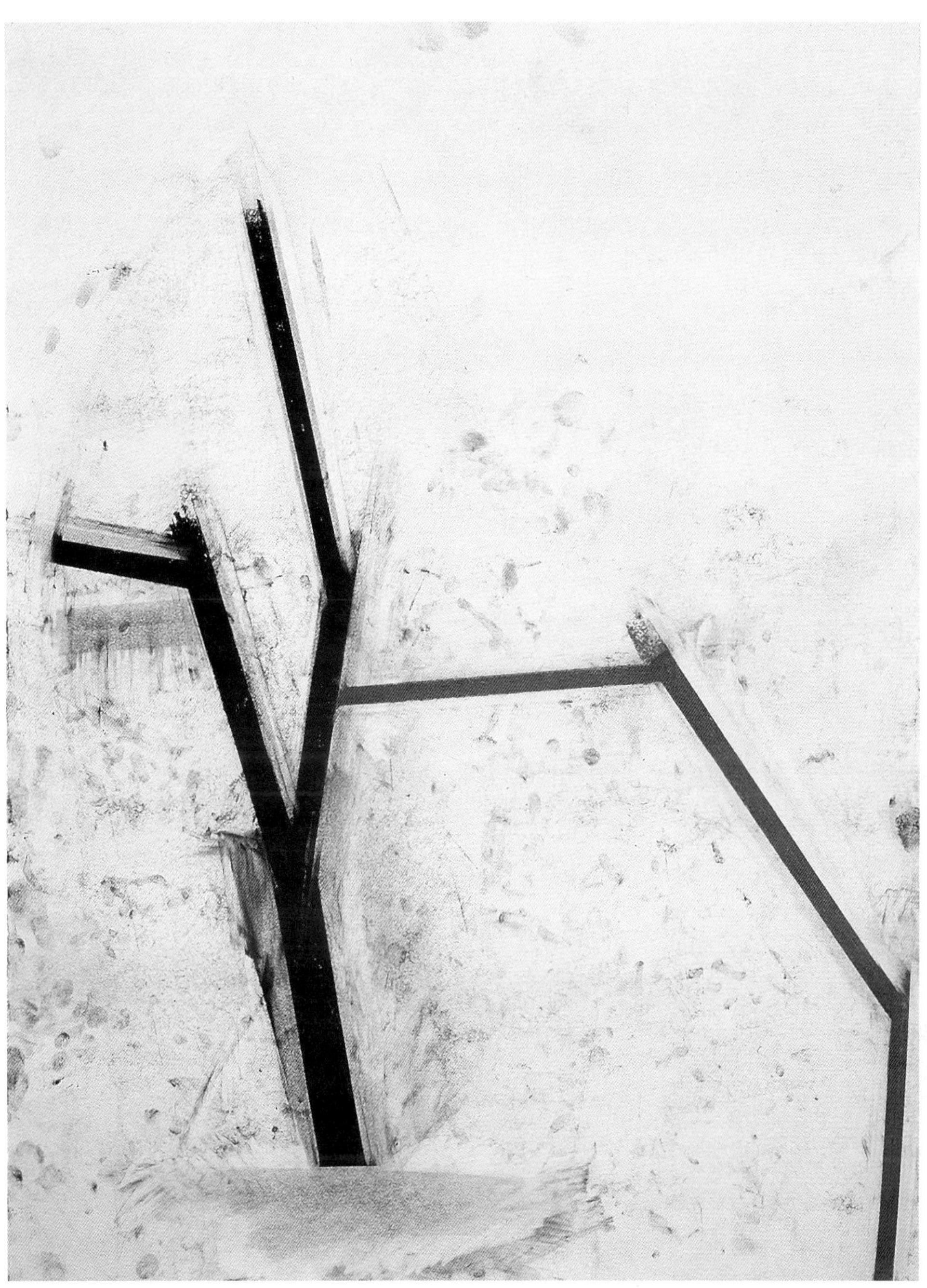

229 Untitled. 1992. Chalk, charcoal, and pastel on paper, 30 ½ x 23" (77.5 x 58.4 cm). Collection the Foundation for Contemporary Performance Arts, Inc.

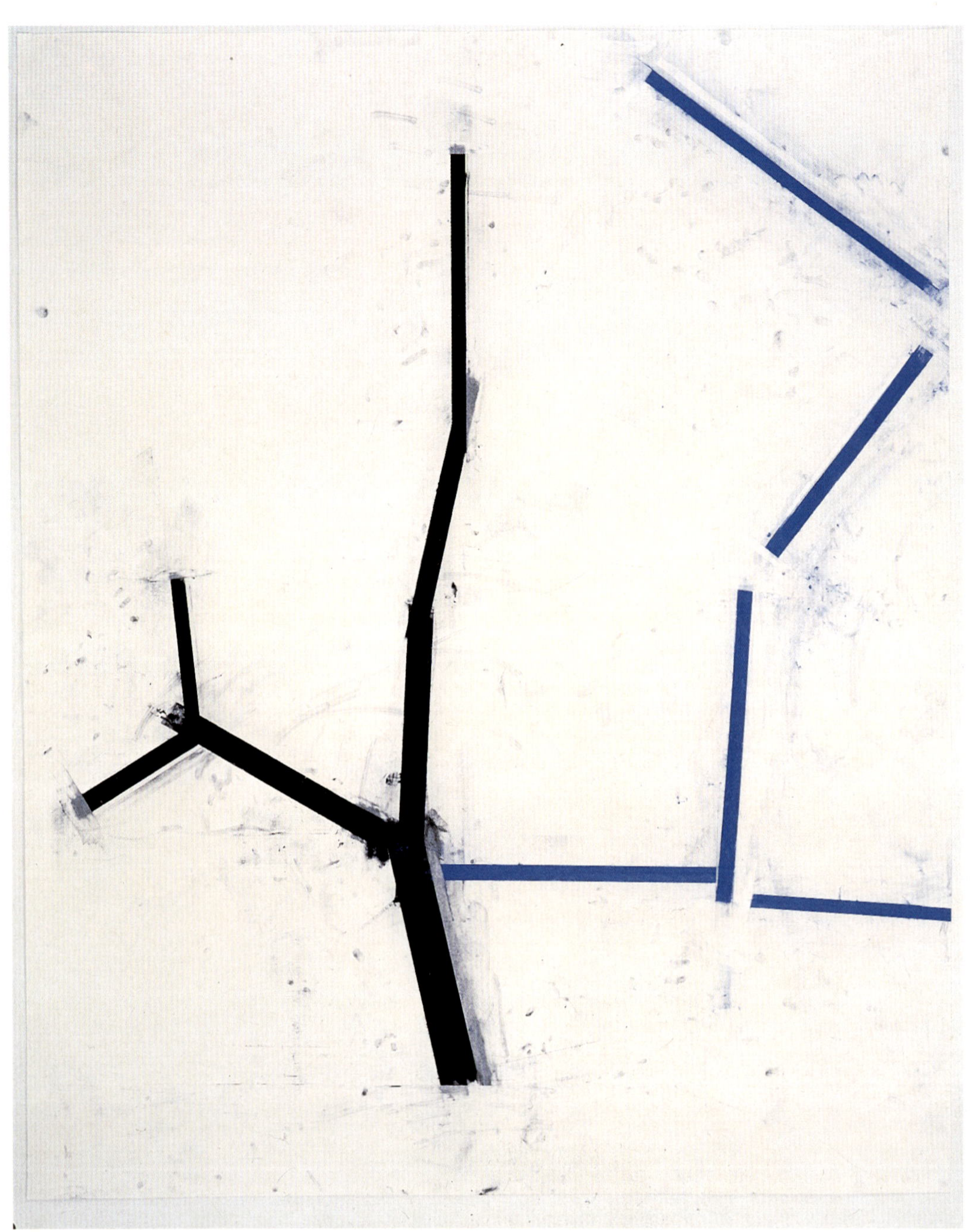

230 Untitled. 1992. Chalk, charcoal, and pastel on paper, 58 x 48" (147.3 x 121.9 cm). Collection the artist

OPPOSITE:

231 Untitled. 1992. Chalk, charcoal, and pastel on paper, 30½ x 23" (77.5 x 58.4 cm). Collection Hugh J. Freund

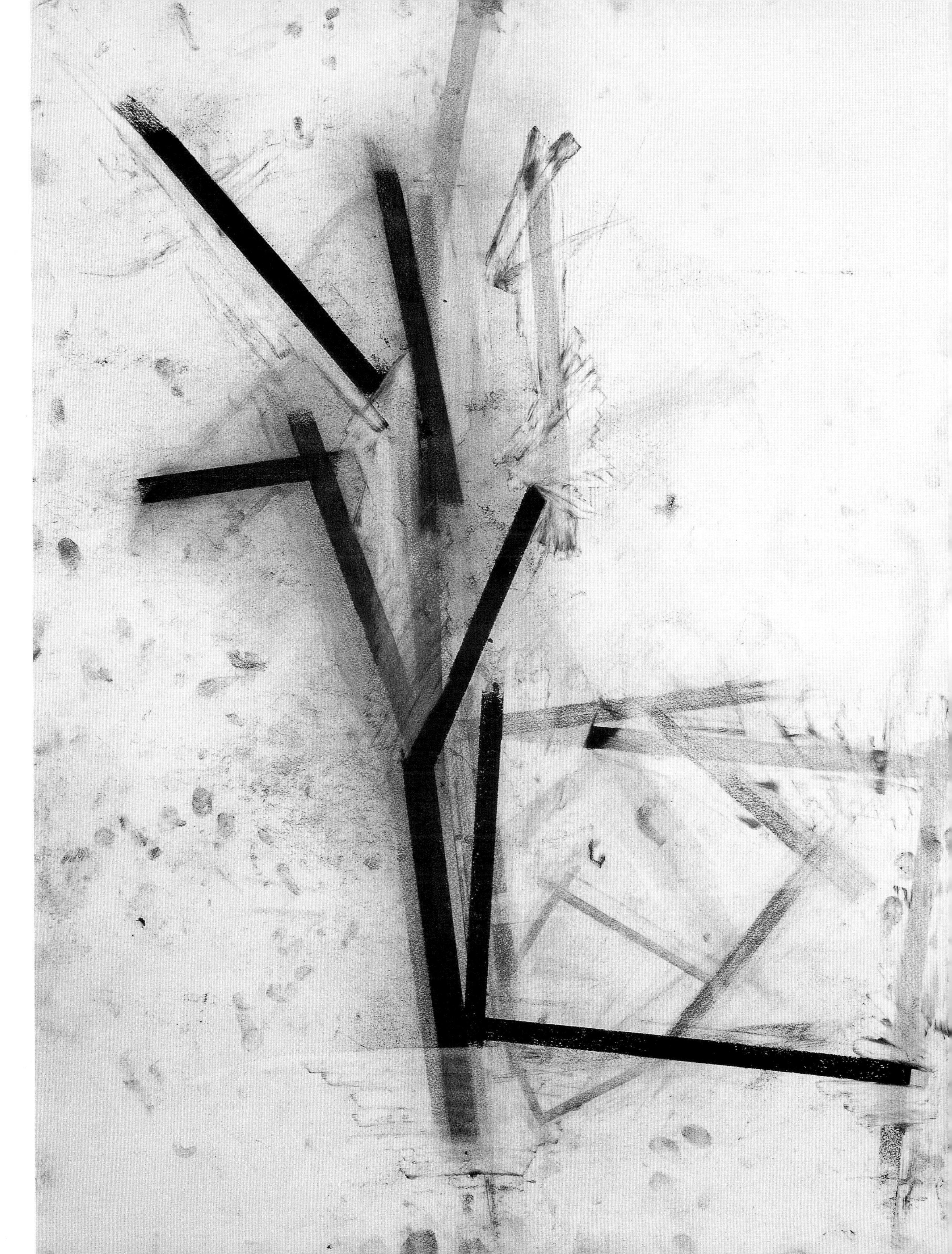

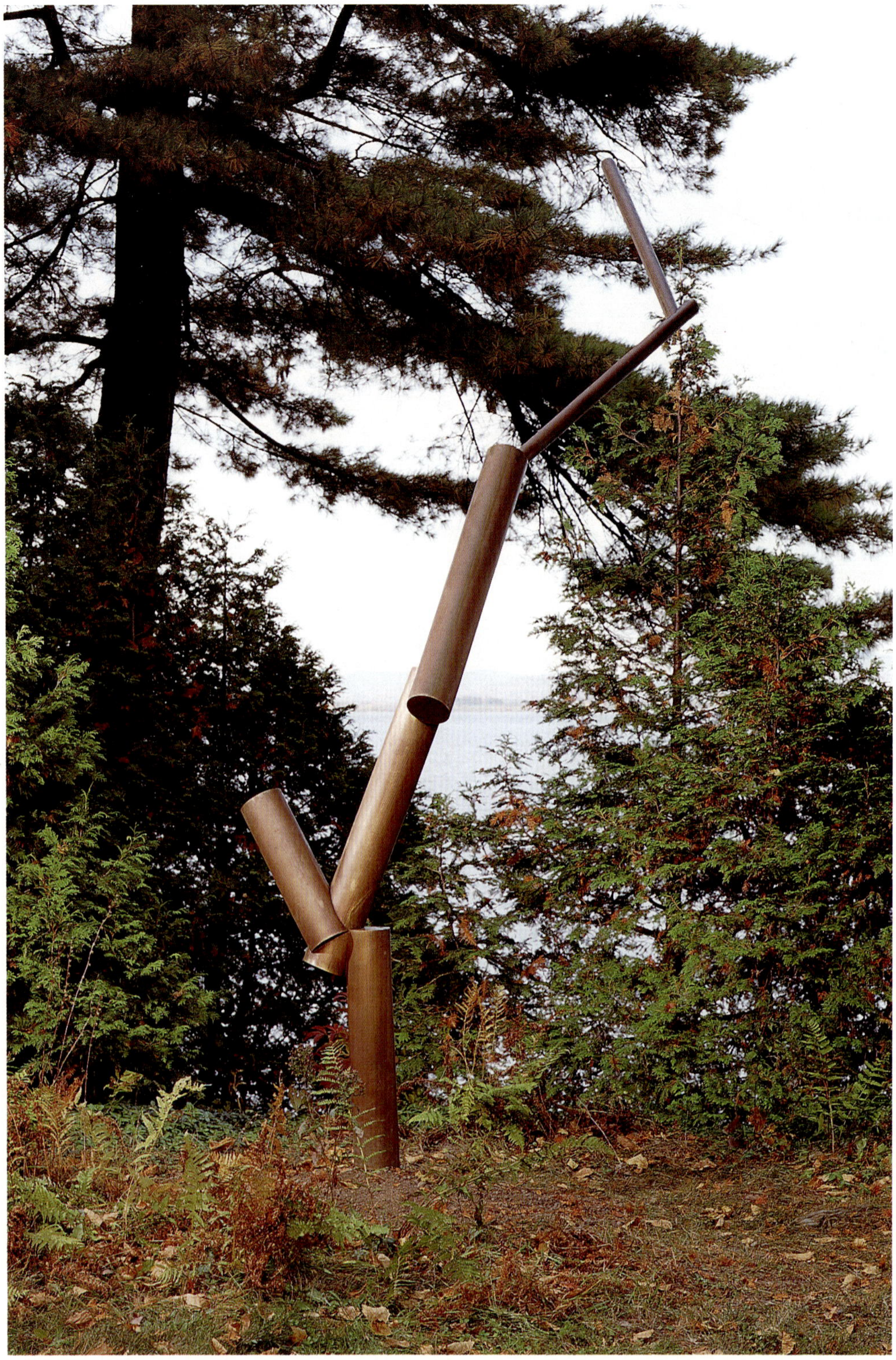

232 Untitled. 1992. Bronze (edition 0/3), 10'7¾" x 6'6¾" x 27" (324.5 x 199.9 x 68.6 cm). Collection the artist

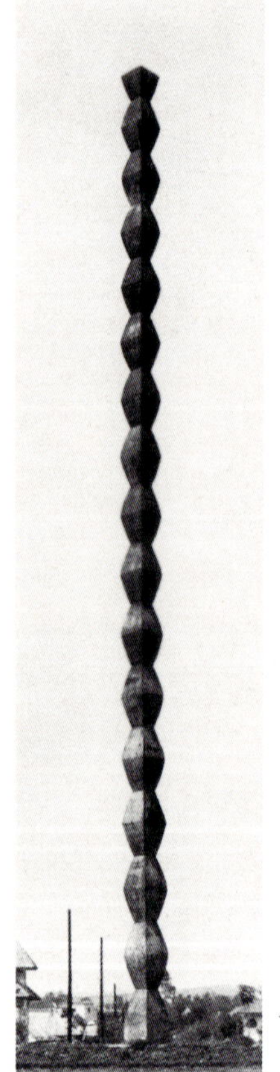

Fig. 19 Constantin Brancusi. *Endless Column*. 1937–38. Cast iron and copper, 98' (29.9 m) high. Tîrgu-Jiu, Romania

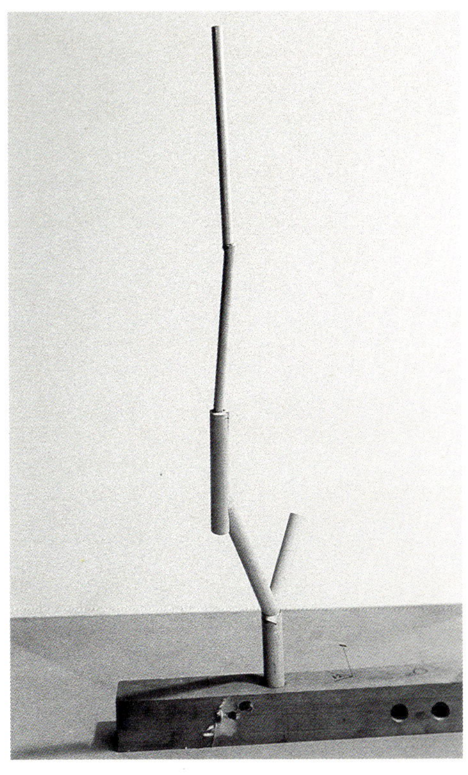

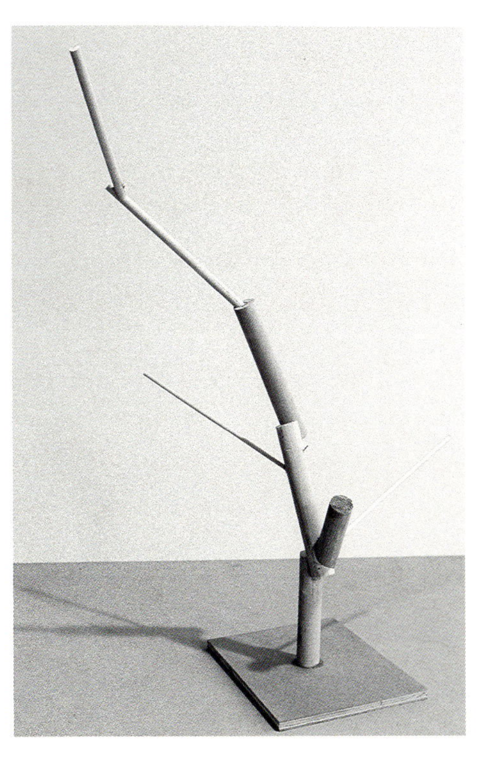

233 Study. 1991. Wood, 33½" (85.1 cm) high. Collection the artist

234 Study. 1991. Wood, 30½" (77.5 cm) high. Collection the artist

235 Untitled. 1993. Oil on wood, 7'8" x 36" x 9½" (233.7 x 91.4 x 24.1 cm). Courtesy PaceWildenstein

Open Space (1993–96)

By the early 1990s, Shapiro had arrived at a mature lexicon of forms upon which he could draw. He could now reach freely across thematic categories.

The contours of a low-lying plaster from 1993–94 (plates 236, 237) recall those of a coffin, an image long absent from Shapiro's work, and in that sense this sculpture is aberrant. Earlier, the coffin described an intimate metaphorical space; now, the vessel is bulky. Shapiro made four such coffins, each conceived as a complete work in itself. He has also exhibited several coffins together as an installation, with two coffins of nearly identical size set one atop the other and a bigger one at their side. Disturbingly matter-of-fact, they constitute an odd still life. These sarcophagi, open at one end, belie the etymology of that word: they do not devour flesh, but rather invite one to ponder the silent cavern within. Their thick, agitated, yet sensuous interiors contrast with the smooth outer walls.

From the stark whiteness of plaster, Shapiro turned to drawings and colorful painted sculptures. A series of painted wood sculptures is characterized by movements sweeping and daring on every level. A work from 1993 (plate 238) projects itself dramatically forward. Five raw beams, partly painted dark umber, extend down and across the floor from the tallest element, a freestanding, vertical plane. Linked by thin dowels, the beams point in various directions. Although this disrupted mass initially appears abstract, it soon reveals itself to be a falling figure.

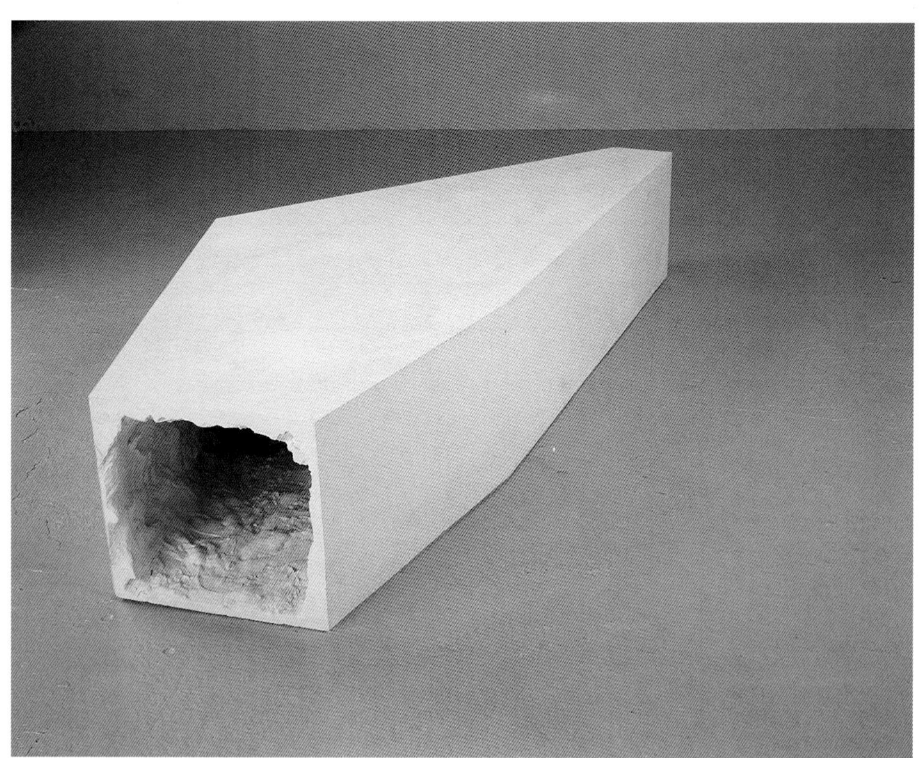

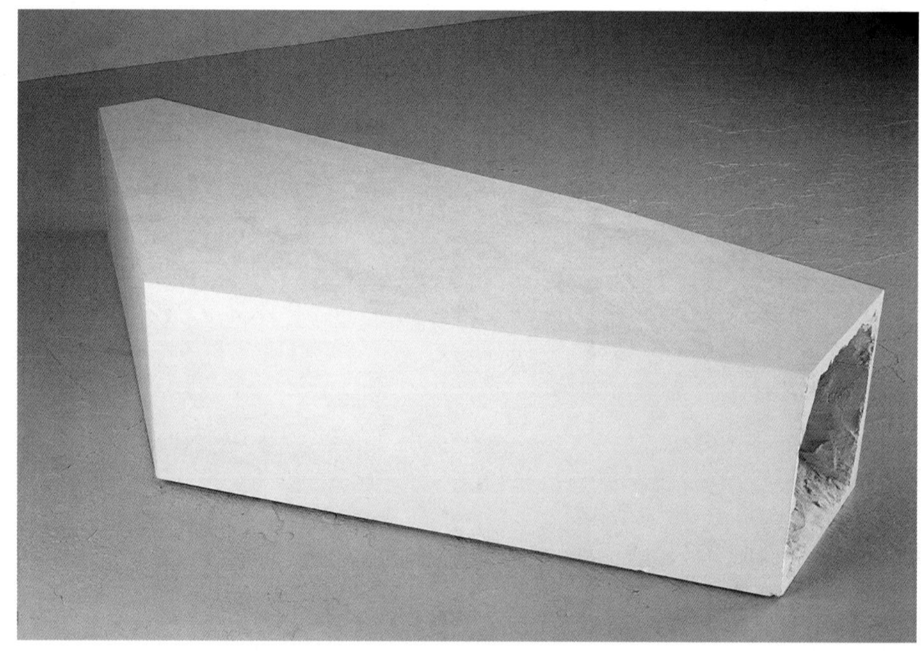

236, 237 Untitled. 1993–94. Plaster, 12¼ x 29½ x 69" (31.1 x 74.9 x 175.3 cm). Courtesy PaceWildenstein

Another piece, from 1993–94 (plates 239, 240), combines a falling figure with the familiar house form. This work is in turmoil. Two platforms on the ground are skewed against each other, one carrying a house tilted on its side and the other a figure, which falls against the house. Wood beams and poles serve as visual and/or structural support. Along with the platforms, they create an organizing framework for this complex construction. Expressive applications of yellow, red, and black paint help distinguish the major elements and chart their trajectory through space.

Color magnifies and unifies Shapiro's sculptural forms, as well as serving as a vehicle for expression. Two related sculptures from 1994–95 (plates 241, 242) tenderly evoke the reclining female figure. These similar configurations are each composed of four beams: a torso, a raised arm, and two legs lying one on top of the other. Paint in one work and plaster in the other caress the elongated torsos and divide the legs. The plaster platform of the smaller work cushions the figure and reinforces its horizontality.

The interplay between raw and painted wood in these later sculptures touches on both form and iconography. Shifts in weight and subtleties of joining give the viewer latitude for interpretation.

In contemporaneous large-scale drawings (plates 244, 246), color defines space and charges it emotionally. Shapiro layers chalk, charcoal, and pastel, and he models his forms through erasure. These soft, dry materials are friable; they leave a dusty trail of the artist's thought process.

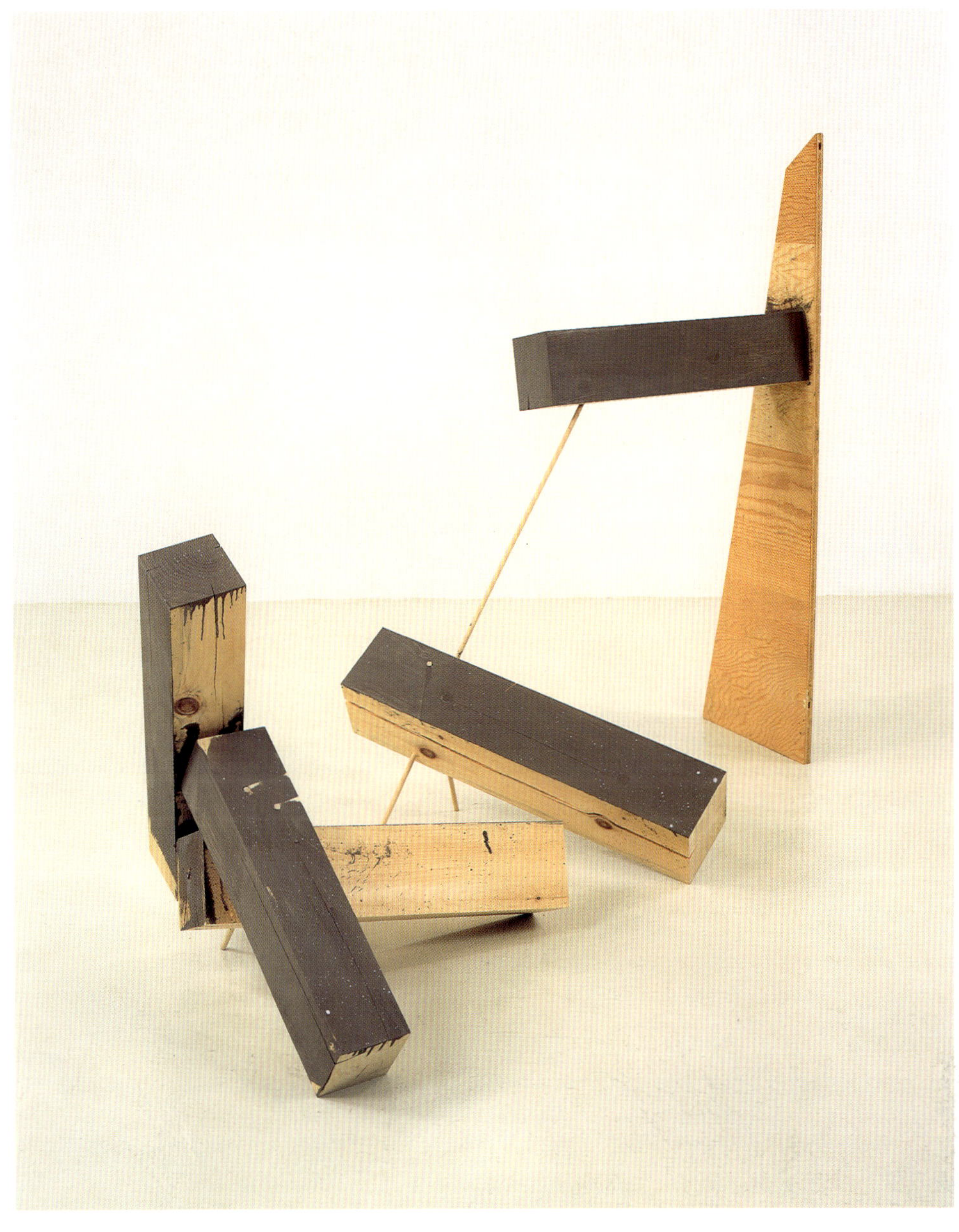

238 Untitled. 1993. Oil on wood, 47½ x 6'4" x 46" (120.6 x 193 x 116.8 cm). Courtesy PaceWildenstein

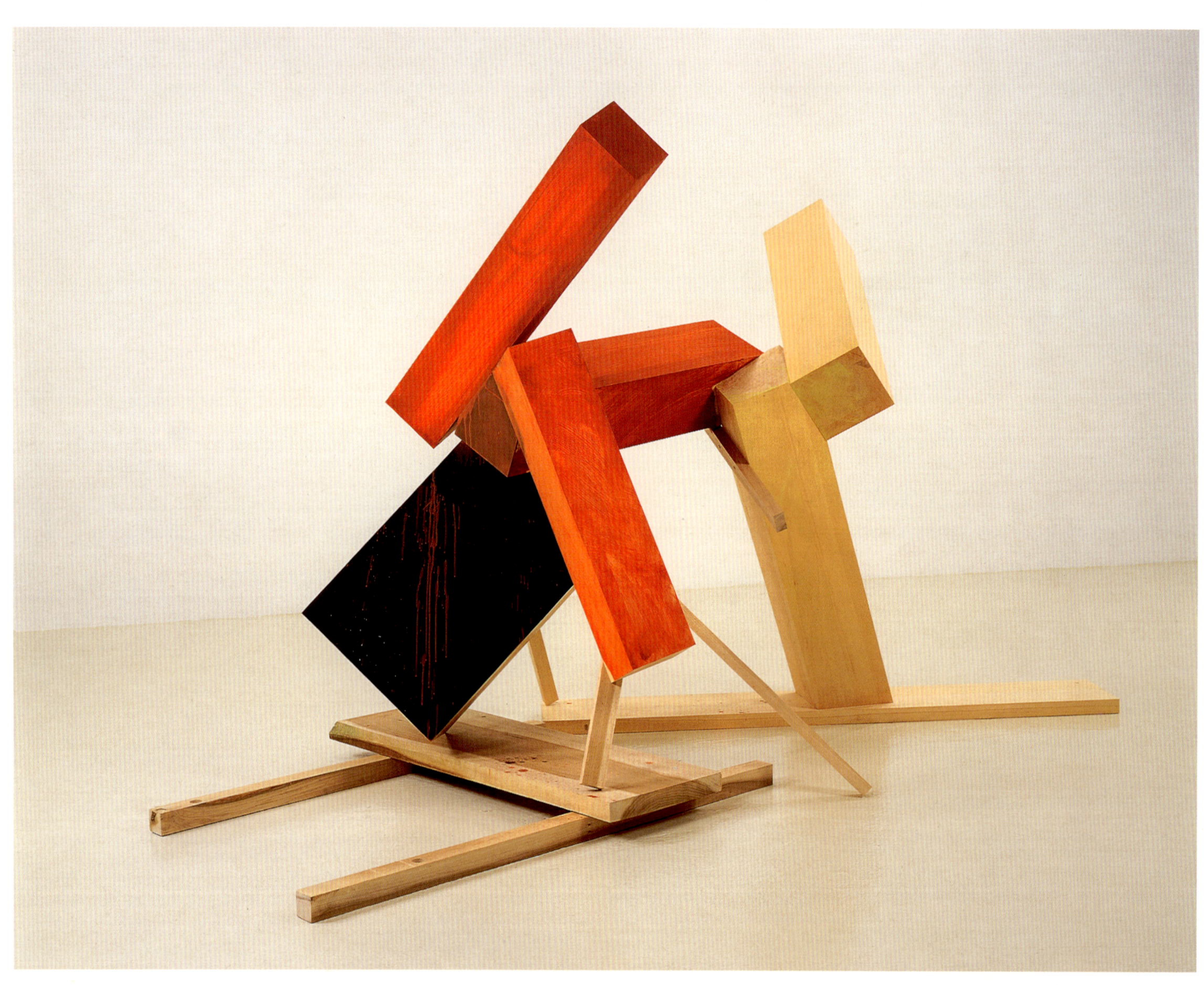

239, 240 Untitled. 1993–94. Oil on wood, 65" x 9'3" x 52" (165.1 x 281.9 x 132.1 cm). Courtesy PaceWildenstein

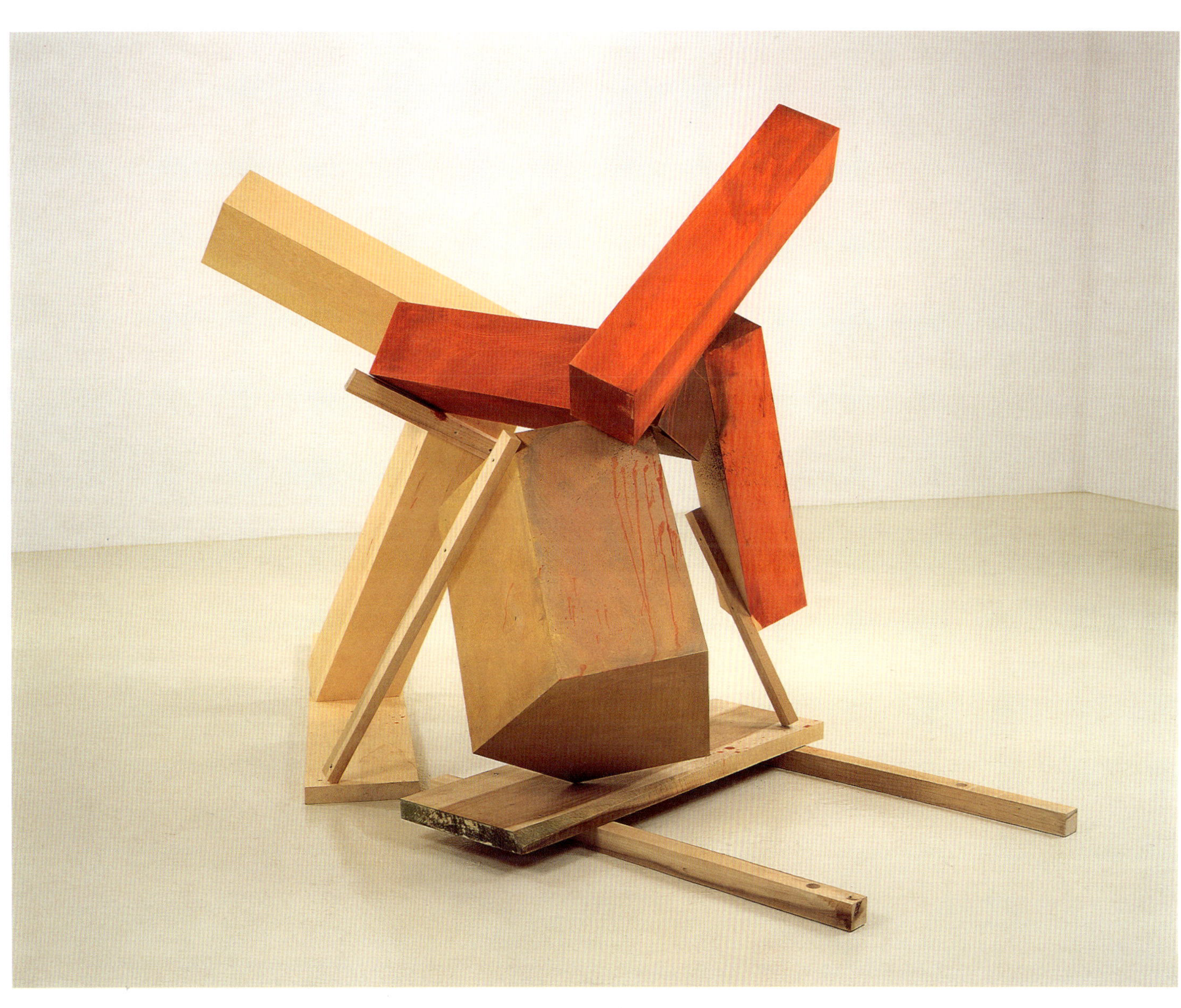

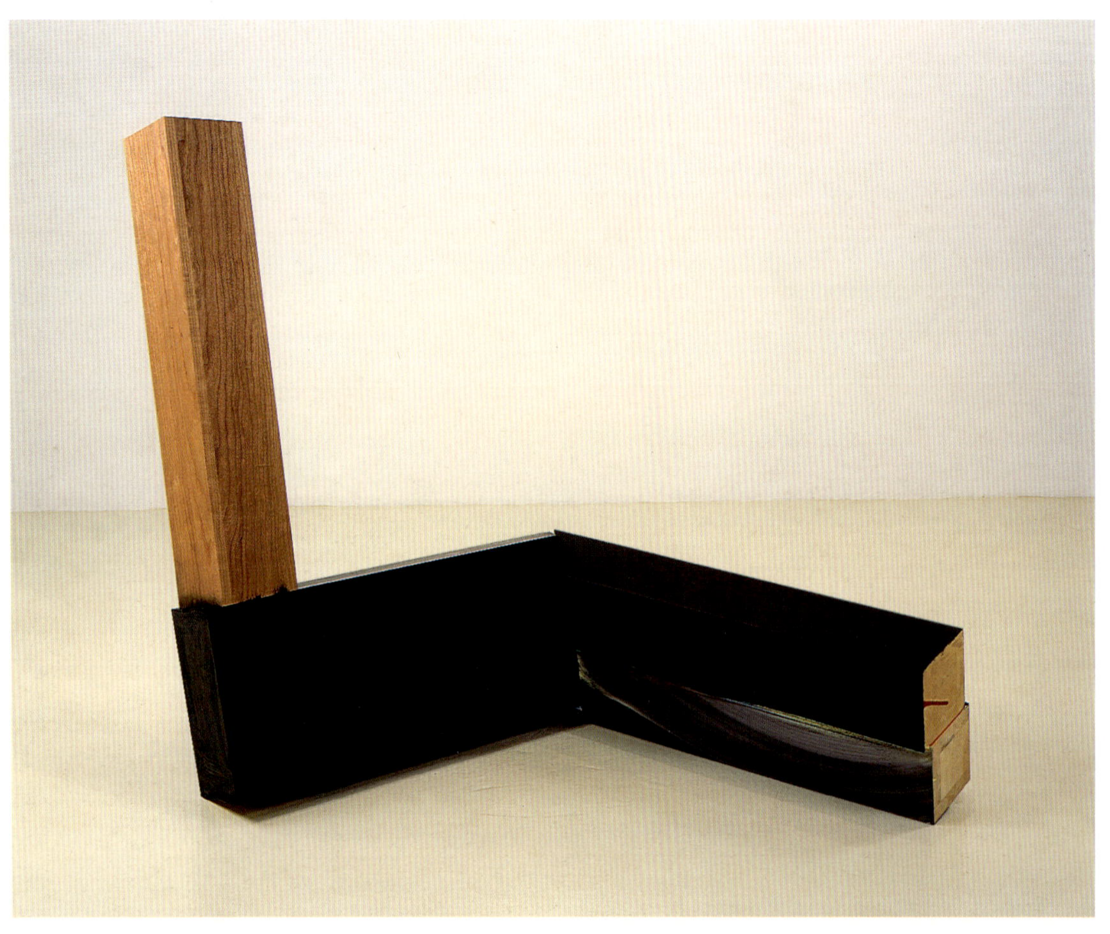

241 Untitled. 1994–95. Oil on wood, 46 x 60 x 32" (116.8 x 152.4 x 81.3 cm). Courtesy PaceWildenstein

242 Untitled. 1994–95. Plaster and wood, 11½ x 25½ x 18¼" (29.2 x 64.8 x 46.4 cm). Courtesy PaceWildenstein

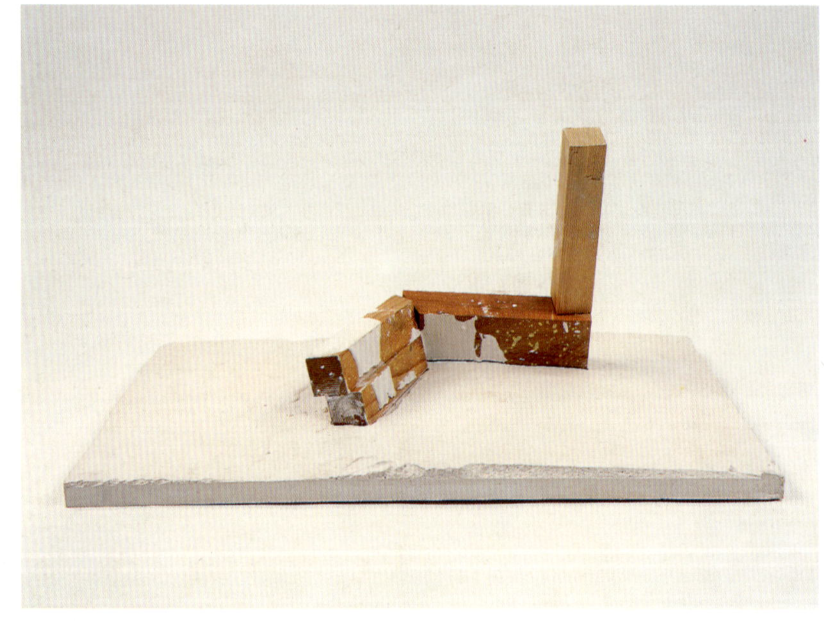

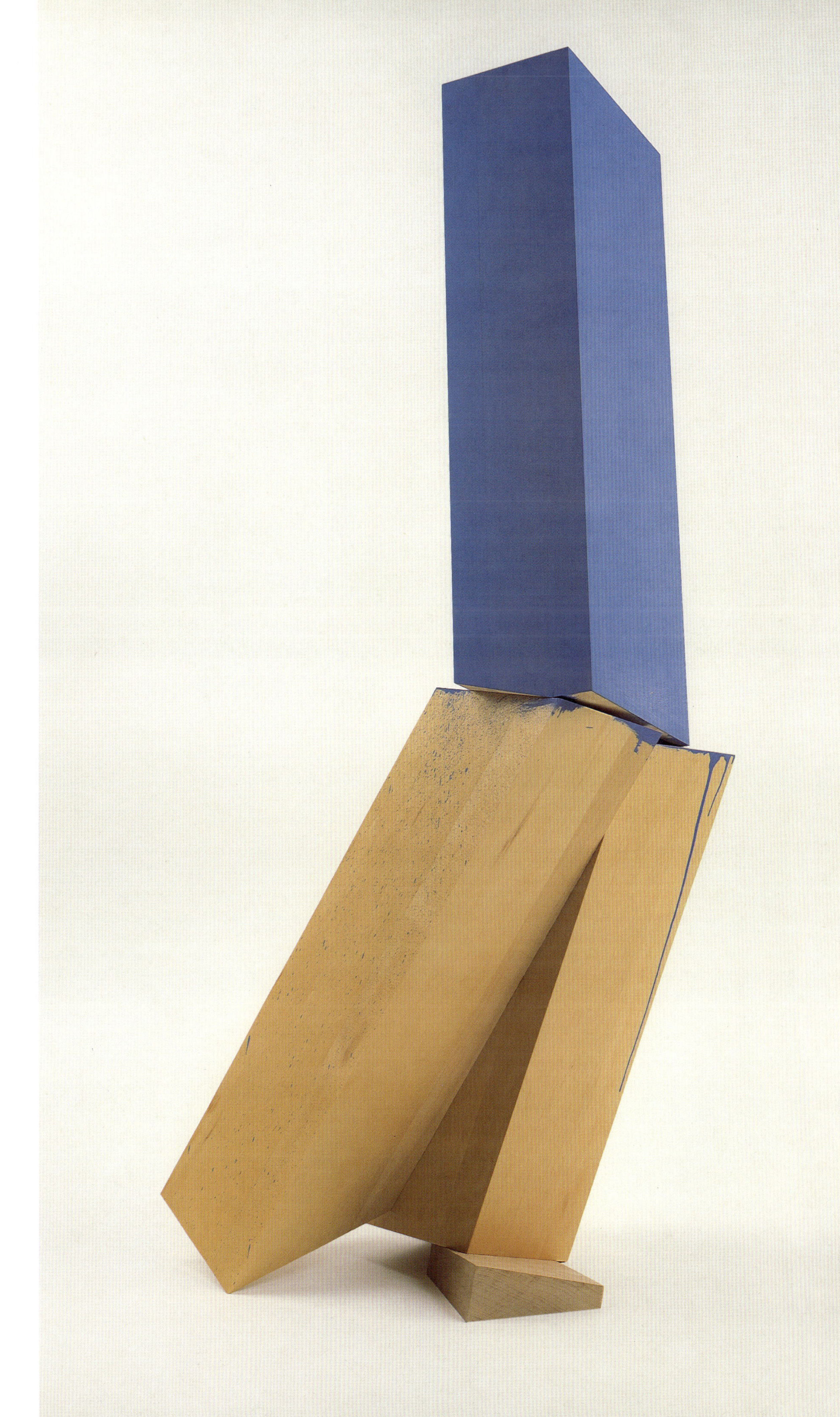

243 Untitled. 1994. Oil on wood, 47¾ x 28 x 18½" (121.3 x 71.1 x 47 cm). Collection Sony Europe

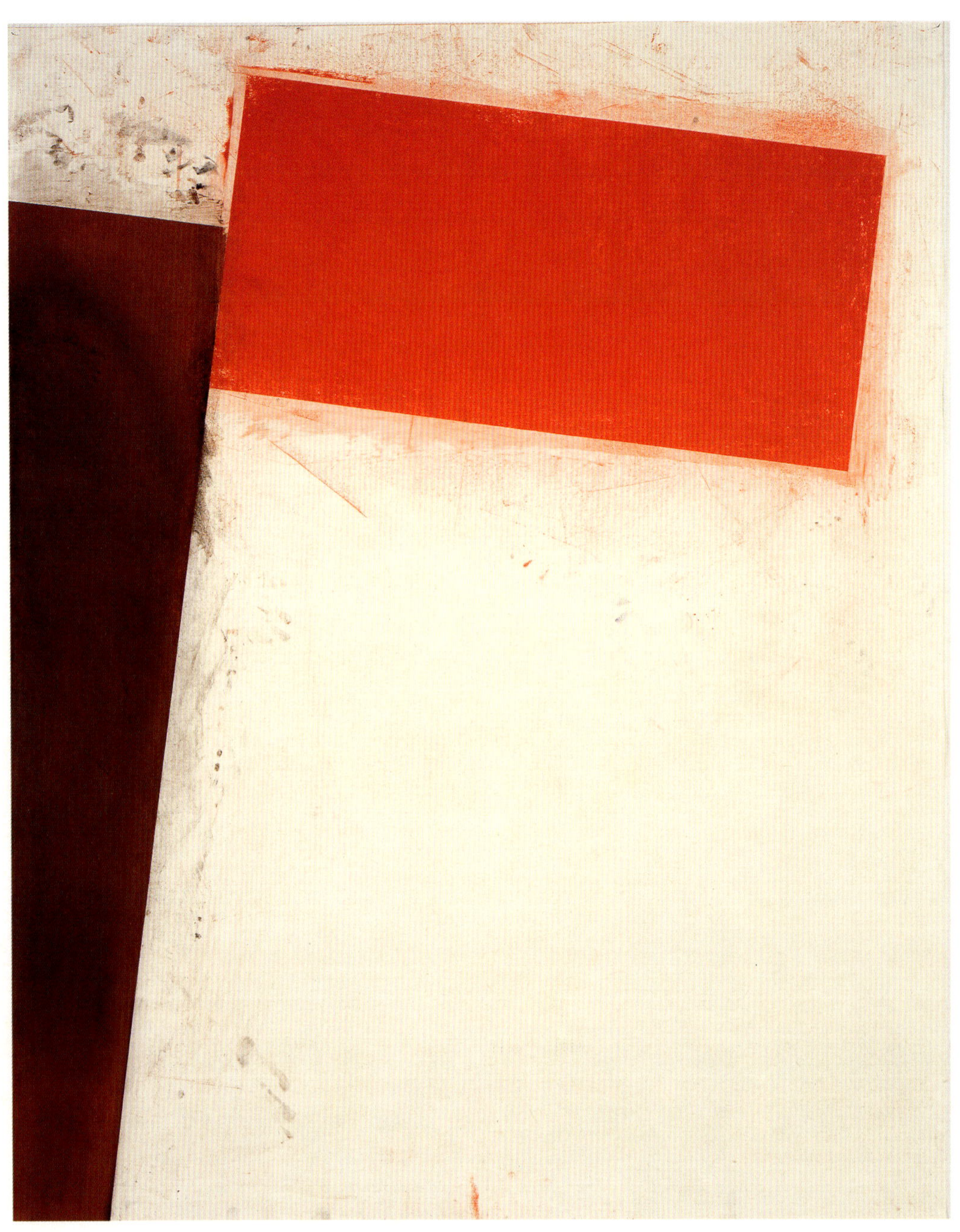

244 Untitled. 1994. Chalk, charcoal, and pastel on paper, 58 x 47" (147.3 x 119.4 cm). Private collection

OPPOSITE:

245 Untitled. 1994–95. Oil on wood, 67½ x 52½ x 32" (171.4 x 133.3 x 81.3 cm). Collection Antiss and Ronald Krueck

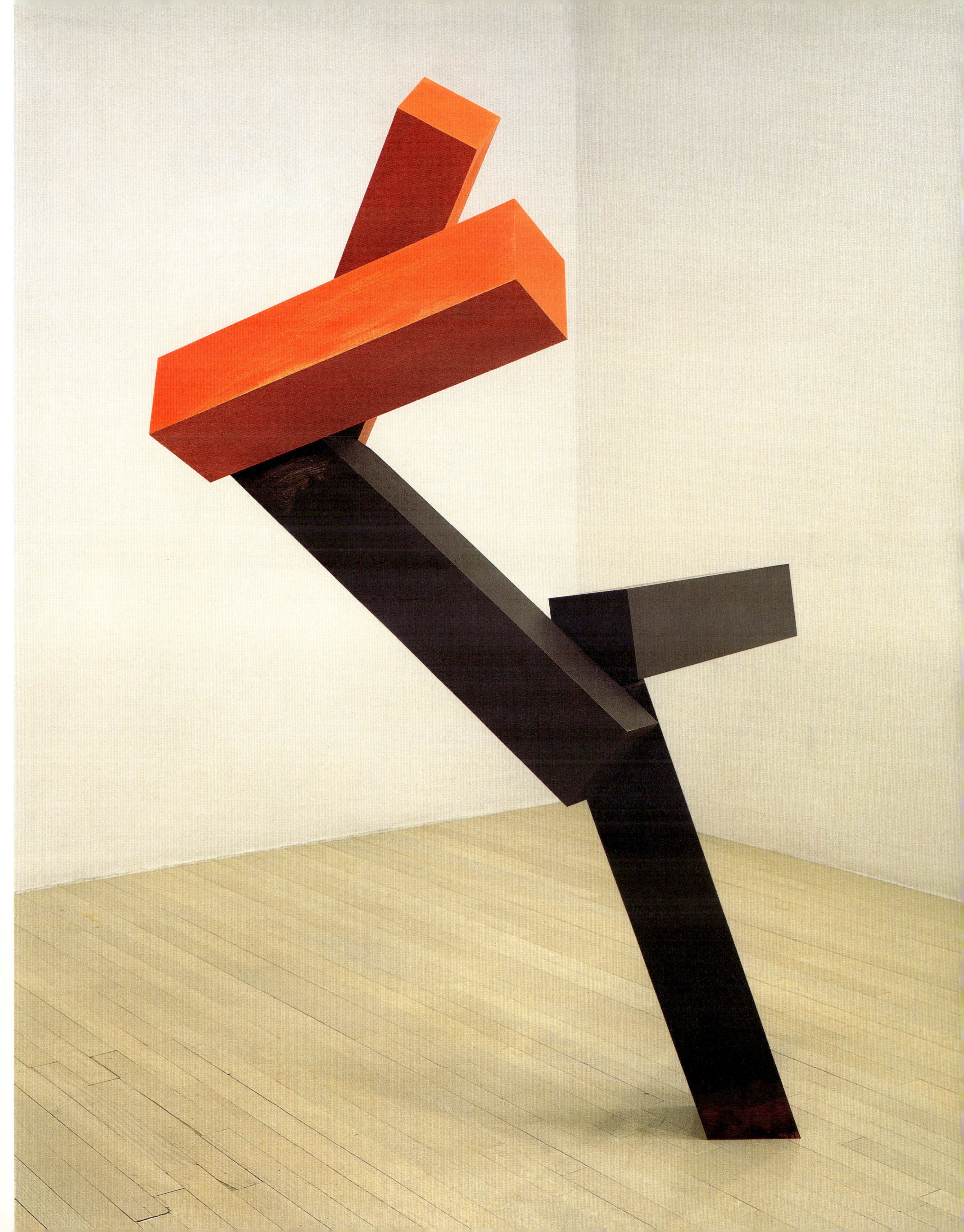

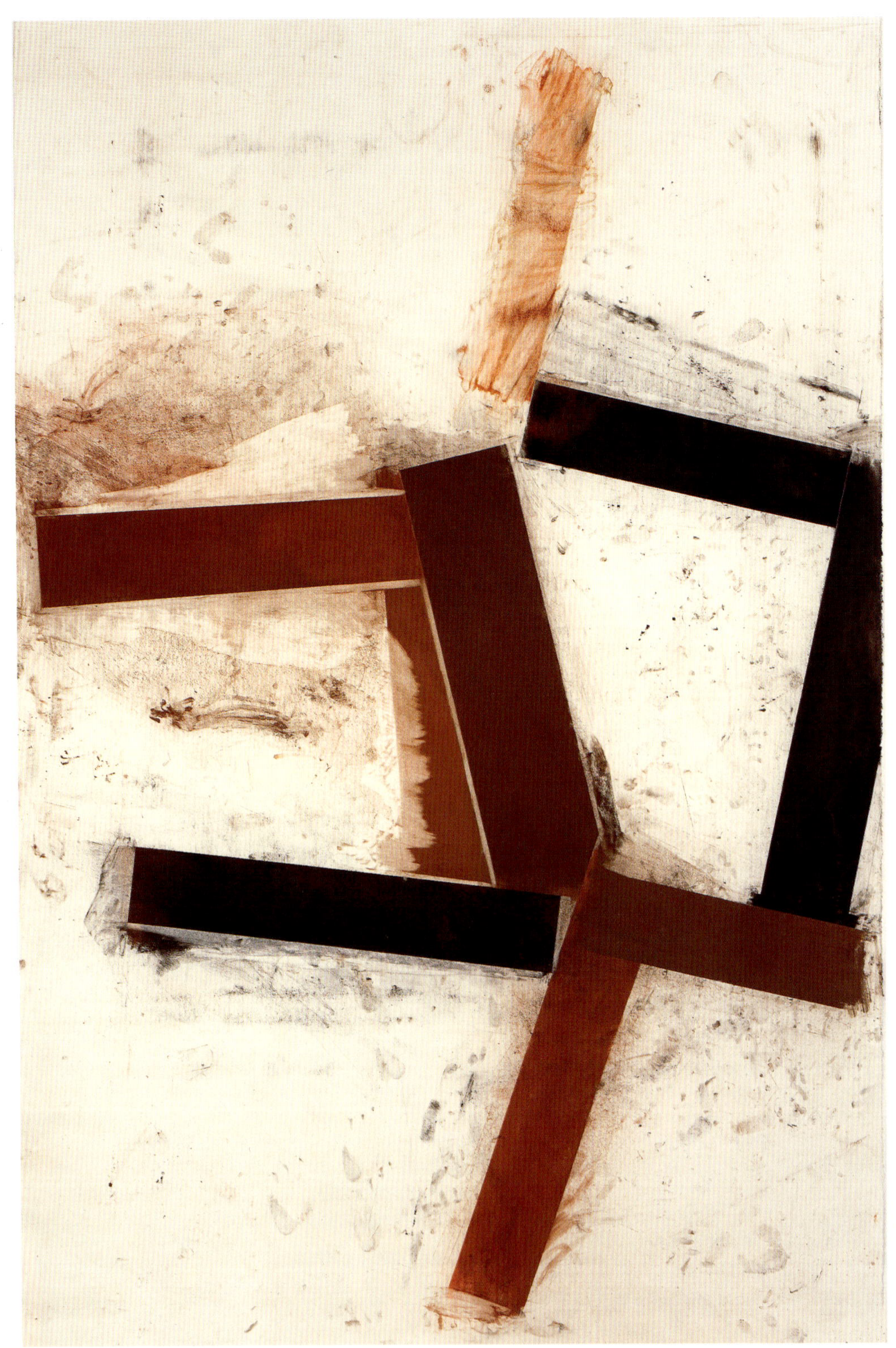

246 Untitled. 1994. Charcoal, chalk, and pastel on paper, 7'5" x 60¼" (229.2 x 153 cm). Collection Mr. and Mrs. Graham Gund

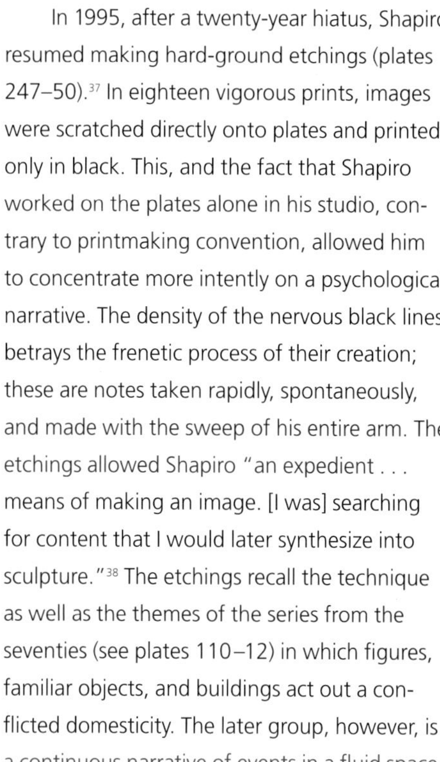

In 1995, after a twenty-year hiatus, Shapiro resumed making hard-ground etchings (plates 247–50).[37] In eighteen vigorous prints, images were scratched directly onto plates and printed only in black. This, and the fact that Shapiro worked on the plates alone in his studio, contrary to printmaking convention, allowed him to concentrate more intently on a psychological narrative. The density of the nervous black lines betrays the frenetic process of their creation; these are notes taken rapidly, spontaneously, and made with the sweep of his entire arm. The etchings allowed Shapiro "an expedient . . . means of making an image. [I was] searching for content that I would later synthesize into sculpture."[38] The etchings recall the technique as well as the themes of the series from the seventies (see plates 110–12) in which figures, familiar objects, and buildings act out a conflicted domesticity. The later group, however, is a continuous narrative of events in a fluid space.

There is no hierarchy in Shapiro's work with regard to medium. Etching, drawing, and sculpture are each used for their intrinsic qualities and their appropriateness to a particular subject. At the same time, they inform and influence each other.

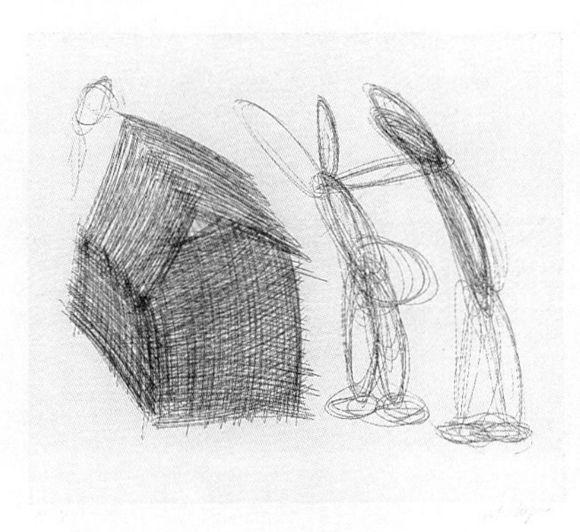

247 Untitled. 1995. Hard-ground etching, sheet: 18 x 19" (45.7 x 48.3 cm); image: 12 x 14" (30.5 x 35.6 cm). Published by the artist; printed by Maurice Payne, New York

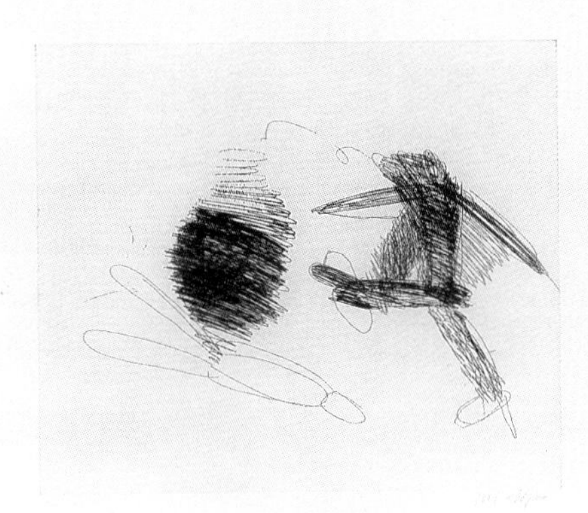

248 Untitled. 1995. Hard-ground etching, sheet: 18 x 19" (45.7 x 48.3 cm); image: 12 x 14" (30.5 x 35.6 cm). Published by the artist; printed by Maurice Payne, New York

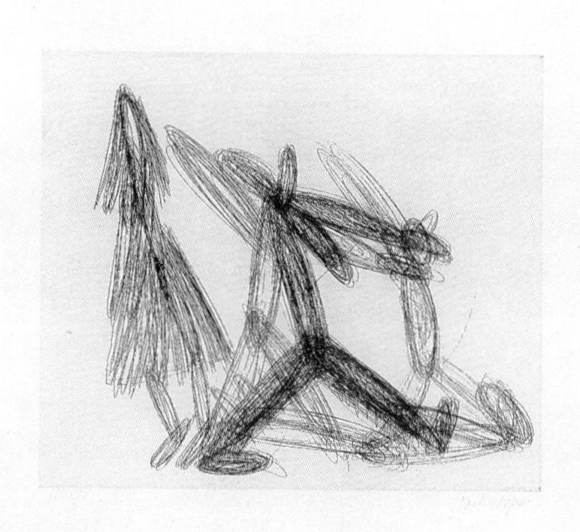

249 Untitled. 1995. Hard-ground etching, sheet: 17¾ x 19" (45.1 x 48.3 cm); image: 12 x 14" (30.5 x 35.6 cm). Published by the artist; printed by Maurice Payne, New York

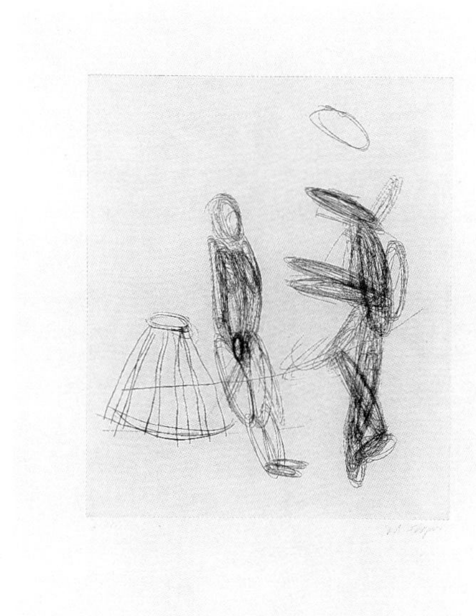

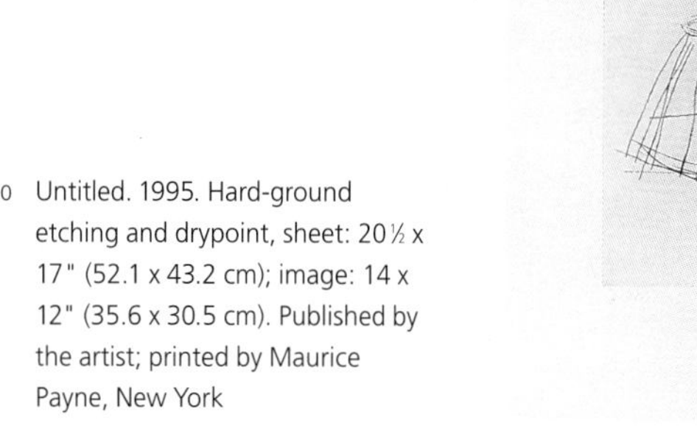

250 Untitled. 1995. Hard-ground etching and drypoint, sheet: 20½ x 17" (52.1 x 43.2 cm); image: 14 x 12" (35.6 x 30.5 cm). Published by the artist; printed by Maurice Payne, New York

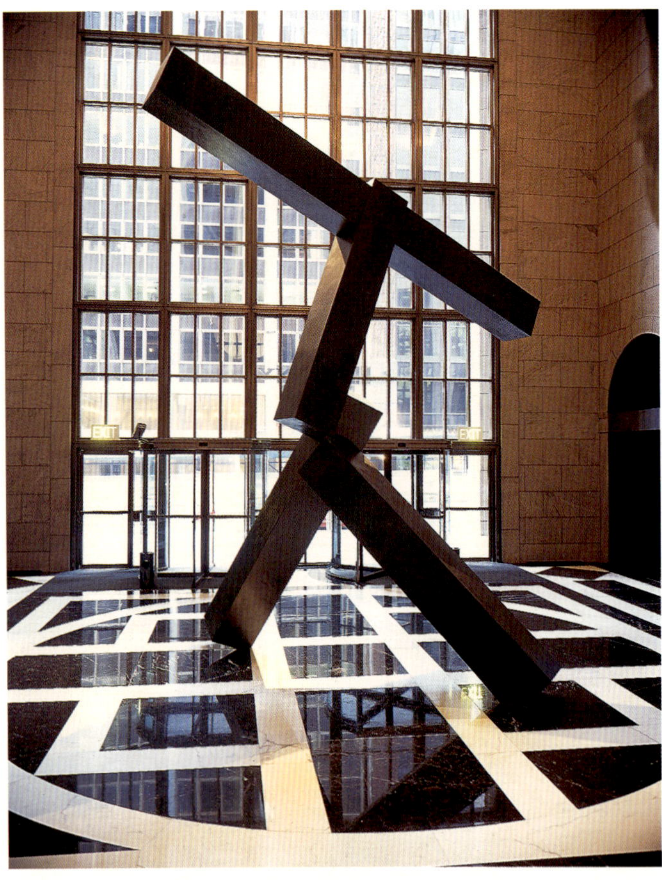

Two commissioned bronze sculptures from 1994 (plates 251, 252) – one installed in the atrium of the Sony building in New York City and the other at the entrance to a building on the Friedrichstadt-Passagen in Berlin – were conceived as responses to their respective urban environments.[39] These sculptures confront the surrounding architecture by opposing it with a human presence. This sometimes makes for exciting theater. In the Sony building, for instance, the figure takes charge of the corporate lobby, measuring itself against the limits of the space. Such friction between psychic and architectural space drives Shapiro's public works.

The central role of the figure has been perceptively described by Michael Brenson elsewhere in this volume: "Shapiro offers a vision of the human body as a physical and spiritual organism that changes so constantly and has so many sides that it can never be definitively categorized or controlled. Shifting identity is an essential part of its nature. So is movement. . . . Shapiro's figures are architectural building blocks that could be adjusted to any occasion: they are their own homes."[40]

251 Untitled. 1994. Bronze, 21' (640.1 cm) high. Collection Sony Music Entertainment Corporation

252 Untitled. 1994. Bronze, 14' x 9'3" x 18'6" (426.7 x 281.9 x 563.9 cm). Collection Tishman Speyer Berlin GmbH & Co.

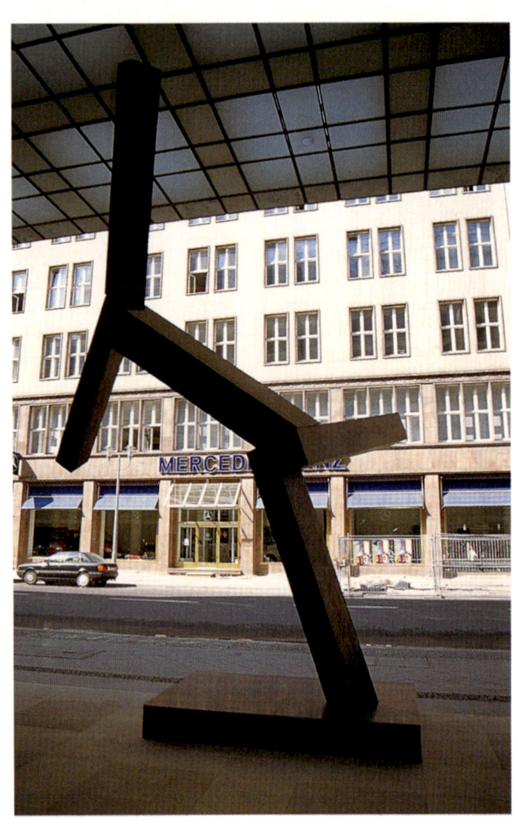

Shapiro accepted a major commission, for the Kansas City International Airport, that required him to place large sculptures in the open landscape. The group of sculptures titled *Three Figures/Fifteen Elements* (plates 253–56), situated along the highway leading to the airport, is among Shapiro's largest works in bronze, and its geometric configurations are stark against the undulating landscape. Given their roadside location, the sculptures are often viewed from passing cars. From close up they are therefore seen quickly, whether individually or as a group, as if themselves in motion, while from a distance they become an image of movement rather than an active embodiment of it.

Installing his work inside the confines of a conventional gallery affords Shapiro the opportunity to investigate the interaction of his independent sculptures. In an exhibition at the PaceWildenstein gallery in New York in 1996 (plate 257),[41] the precise choreographic placement of the individual works sets in motion a dance of similarities and differences. At work here is a complex manipulation of color, juxtaposition, weight, and scale, with a Baroque sweep through opposing spaces. Bronzes from 1994–96 (plates 258, 261–63) move ceaselessly; they spin and balance, contract and extend. Elements from one sculpture interact with other sculptures, creating unexpected configurations that animate the space.

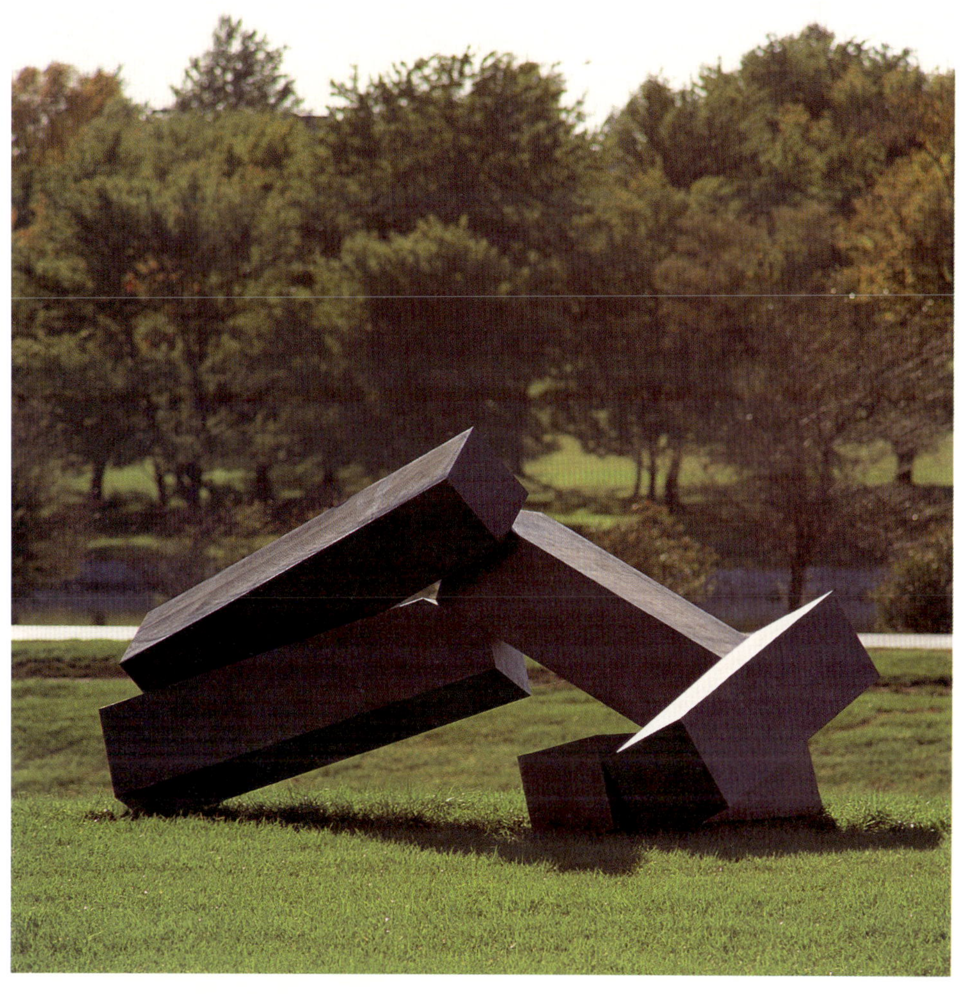

253 Component of *Three Figures/ Fifteen Elements*. 1994–96. Bronze, 8 x 21 x 9' (243.8 x 640.1 x 274.3 cm). One-Percent-for-Art Program, Kansas City, Missouri

FOLLOWING SPREAD:

254 Component of *Three Figures/ Fifteen Elements*. 1994–96. Bronze, 8 x 21 x 9' (243.8 x 640.1 x 274.3 cm). One-Percent-for-Art Program, Kansas City, Missouri. For the component at the right, see plate

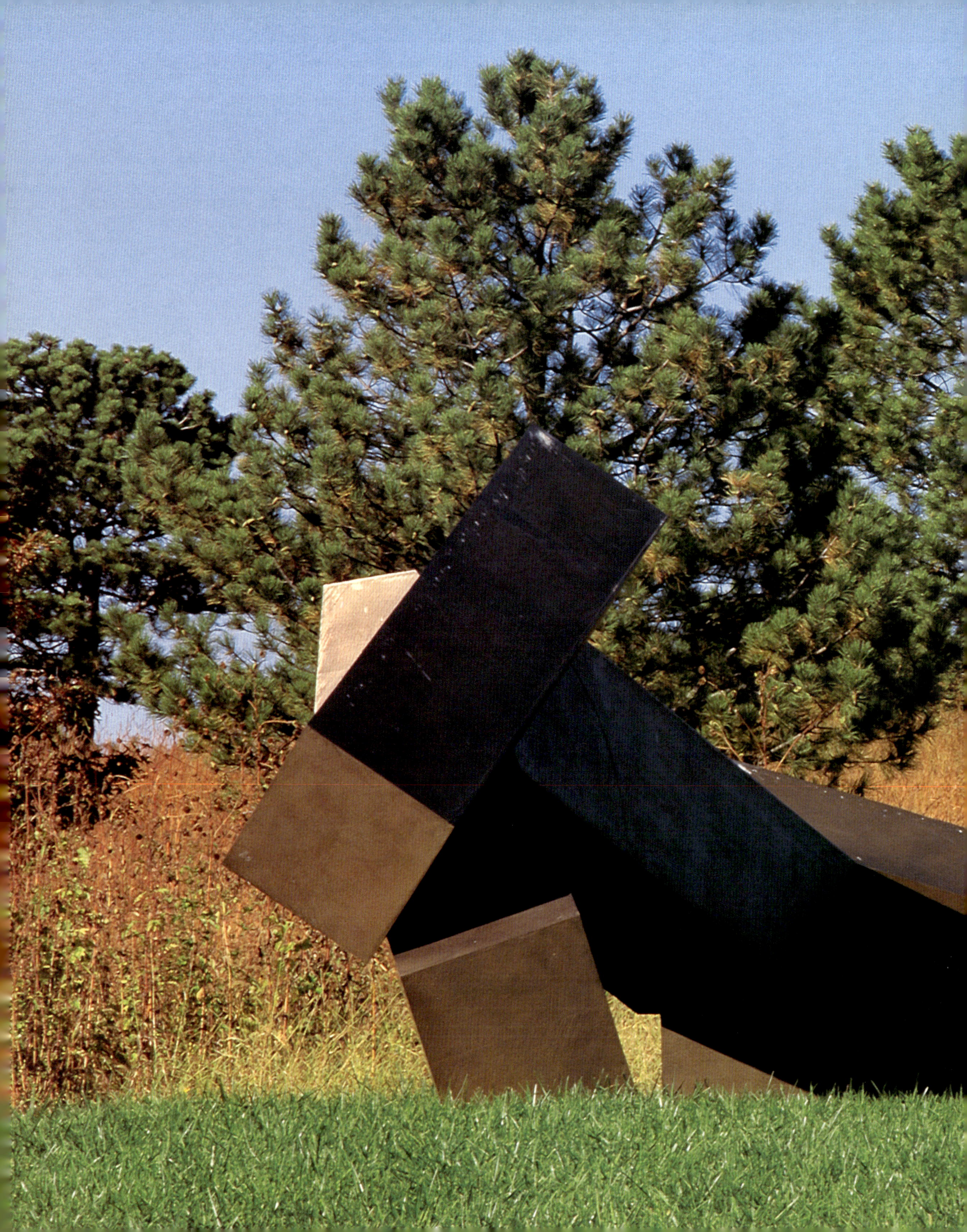

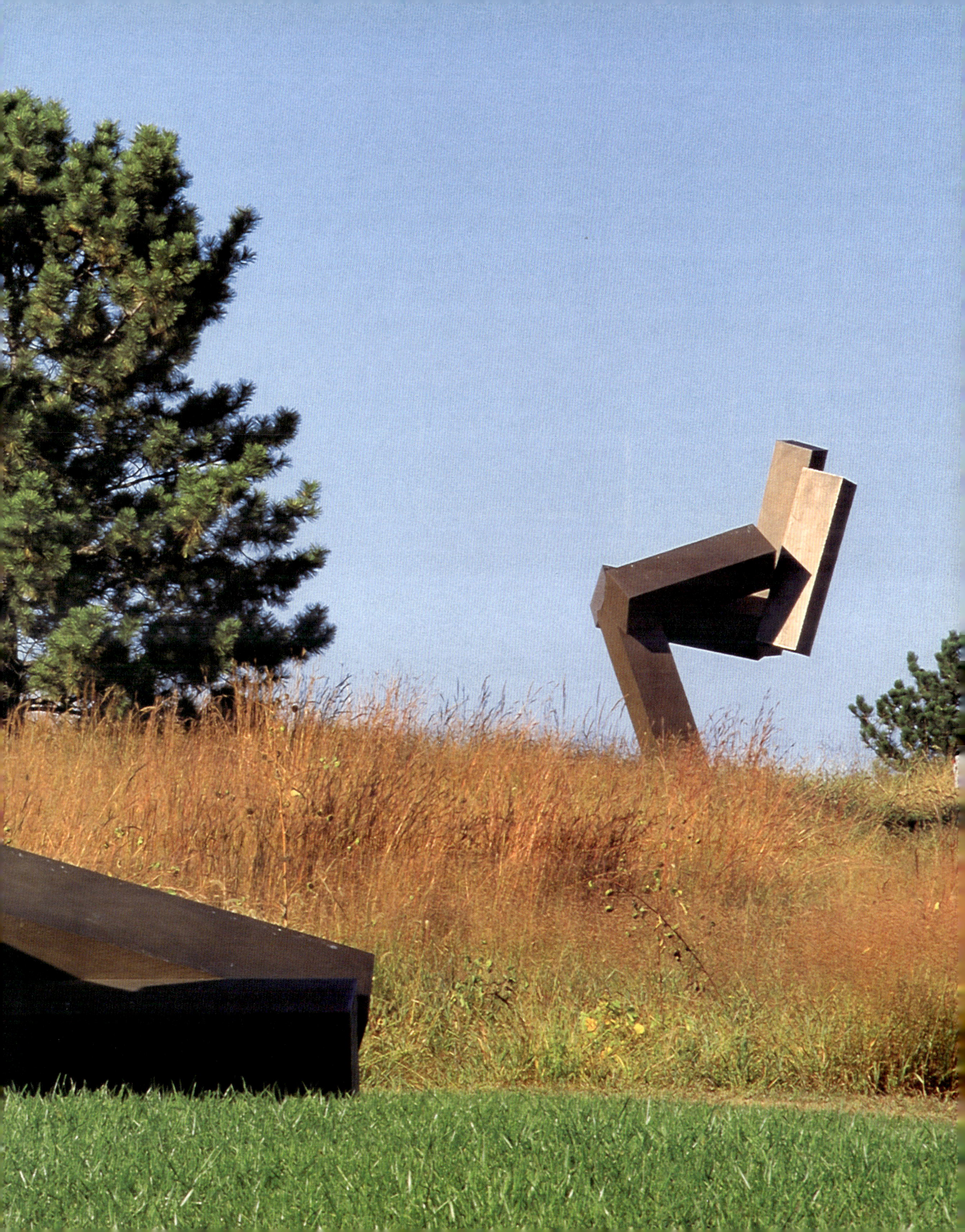

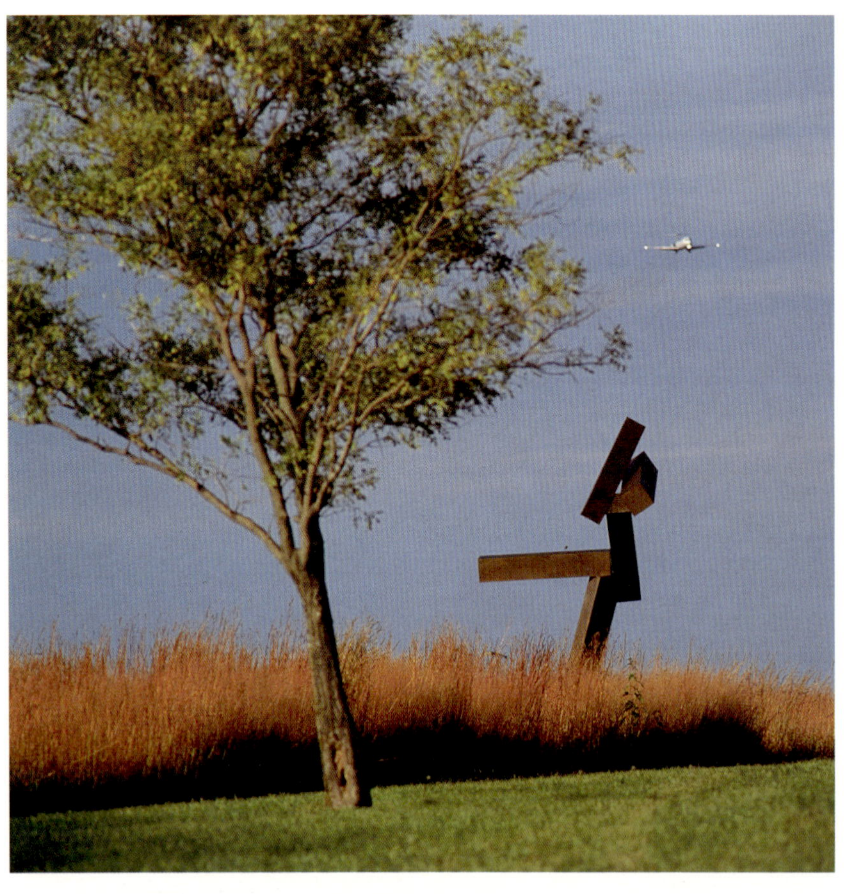

255 Component of *Three Figures/ Fifteen Elements*. 1994–96. Bronze, 22'6" x 18' x 10'6" (270 x 548.6 x 320 cm). One-Percent-for-Art Program, Kansas City, Missouri

256 Component of *Three Figures/ Fifteen Elements*. 1994–96. Bronze, 15' x 12'6" x 7'6" (457.2 x 381 x 228.6 cm). One-Percent-for-Art Program, Kansas City, Missouri

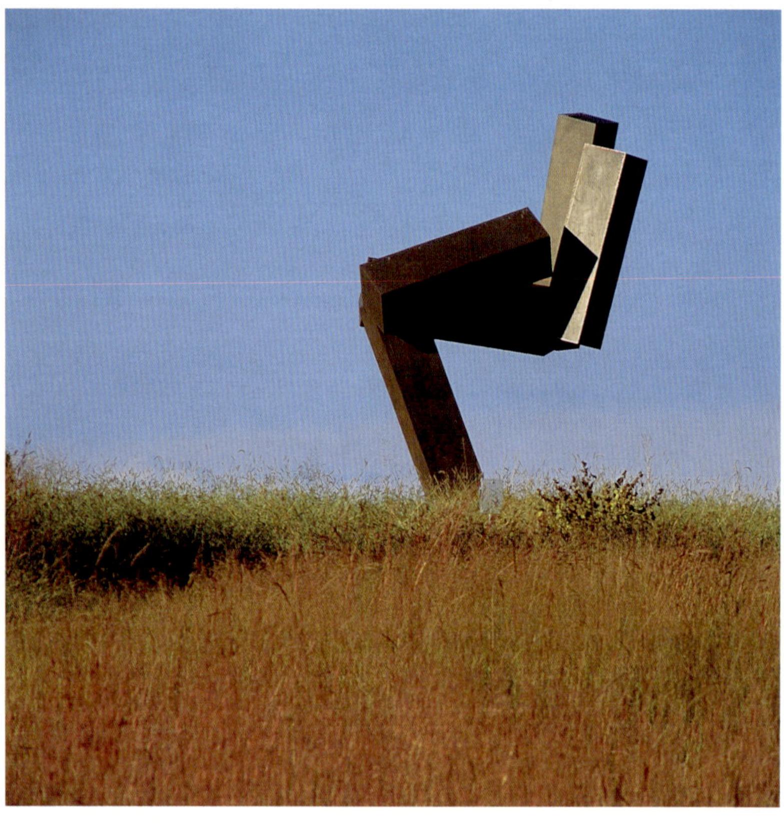

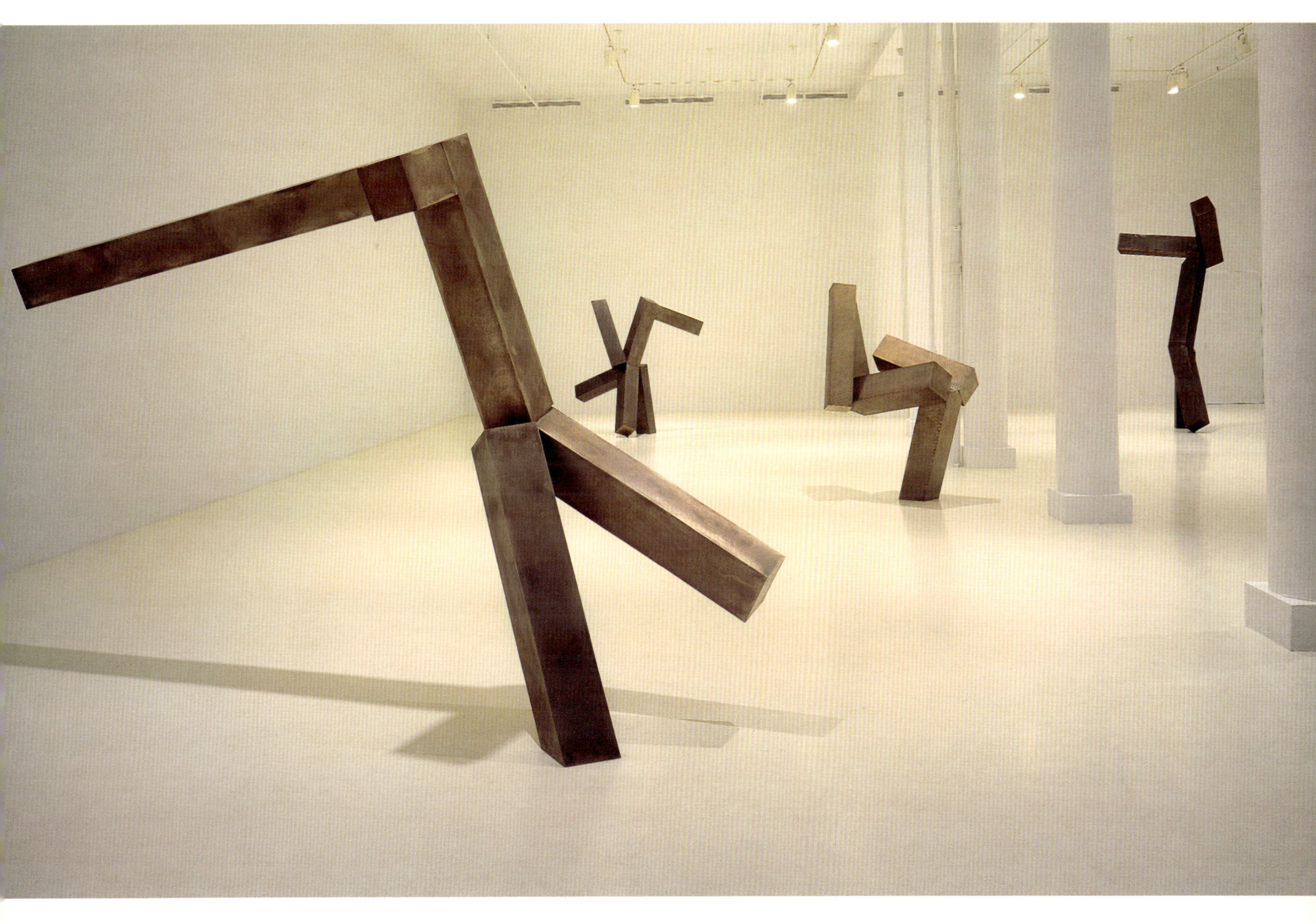

257 Installation view of the exhibition "Joel Shapiro: Recent Sculpture," PaceWildenstein, New York, 1996. Works shown here also appear in plates 258, 262, 263, 264.

A figure from 1996 with an unusually long arm (plate 264) performs Shapiro's characteristic balancing act between precision of form and ambiguity of meaning. One can follow his creative path in the numerous wood studies (plates 265–68) that preceded the final bronze, all marked by physical and emotional conflict – a struggle to keep intensely felt experience alive as concrete sculptural form. Joel Shapiro's thinking is rooted in the modernist figurative tradition. He is concerned with the investigation of form, through material and process, and this exploration is a way to locate meaning. In his work, meaning is fused into material. The physical facts of sculpture are made to resonate with human emotion.

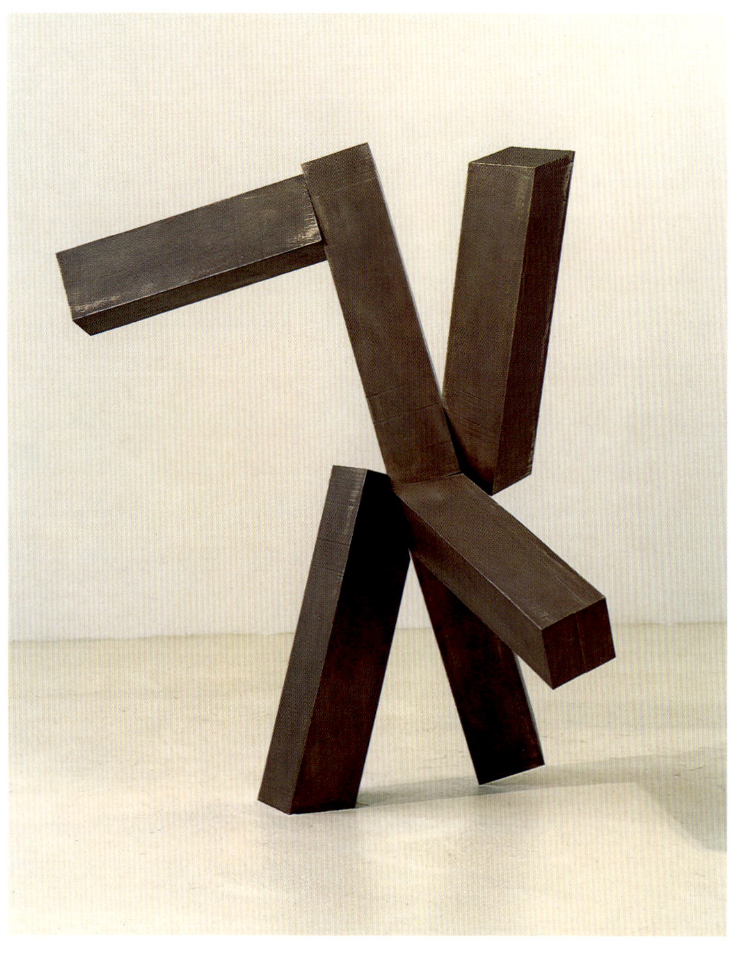

258 Untitled. 1995. Bronze (edition 1/4), 71 x 70 x 45" (180.3 x 177.8 x 114.3 cm). Courtesy PaceWildenstein

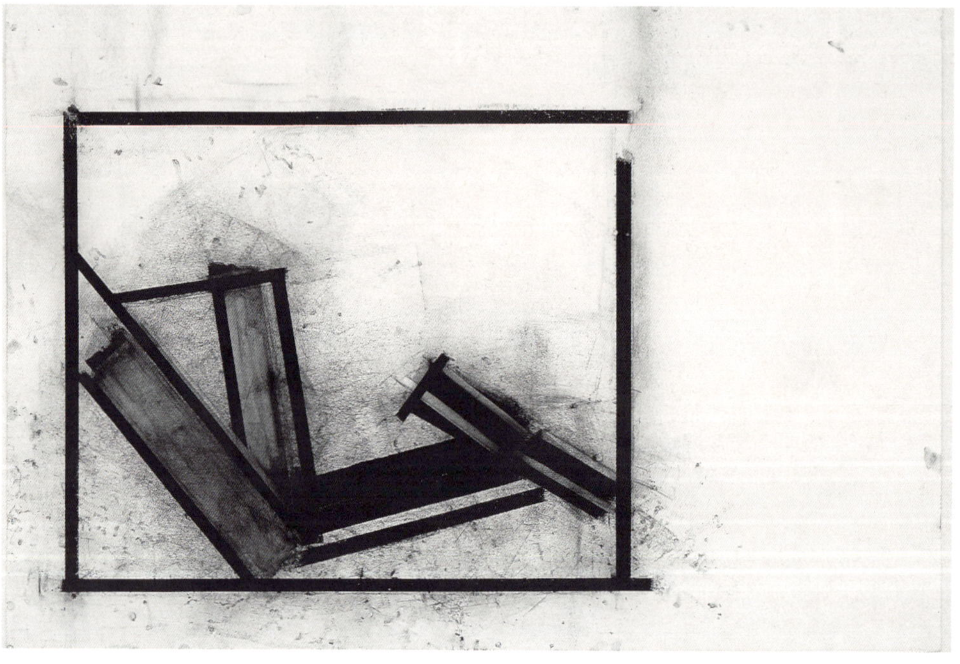

259 Untitled. 1996. Charcoal on paper, 40¼ x 59¾" (102.2 x 151 cm). Courtesy PaceWildenstein

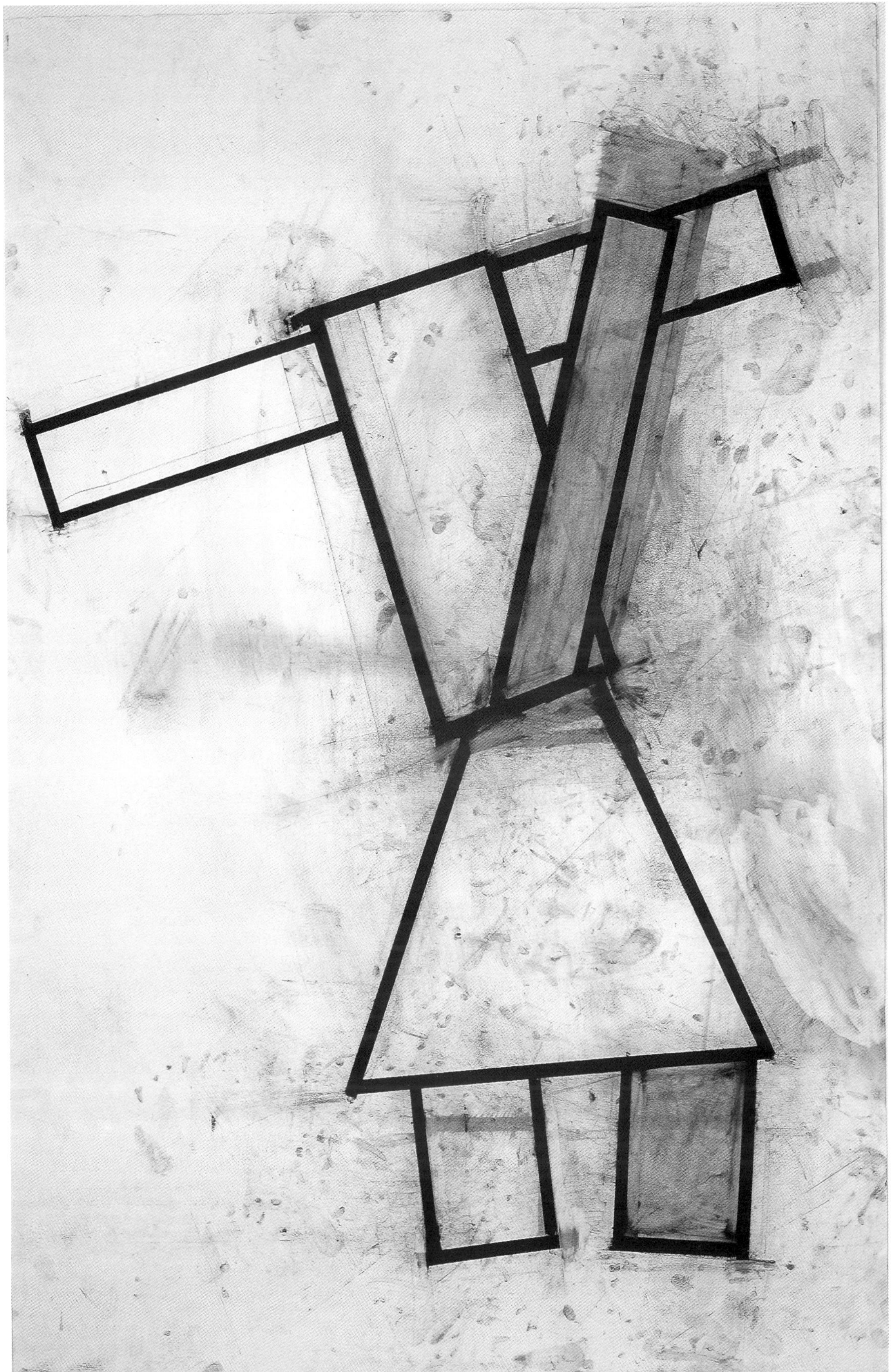

260 Untitled. 1996. Chalk and charcoal on paper, 60¼ x 40" (153 x 101.6 cm). Collection Ivy Shapiro

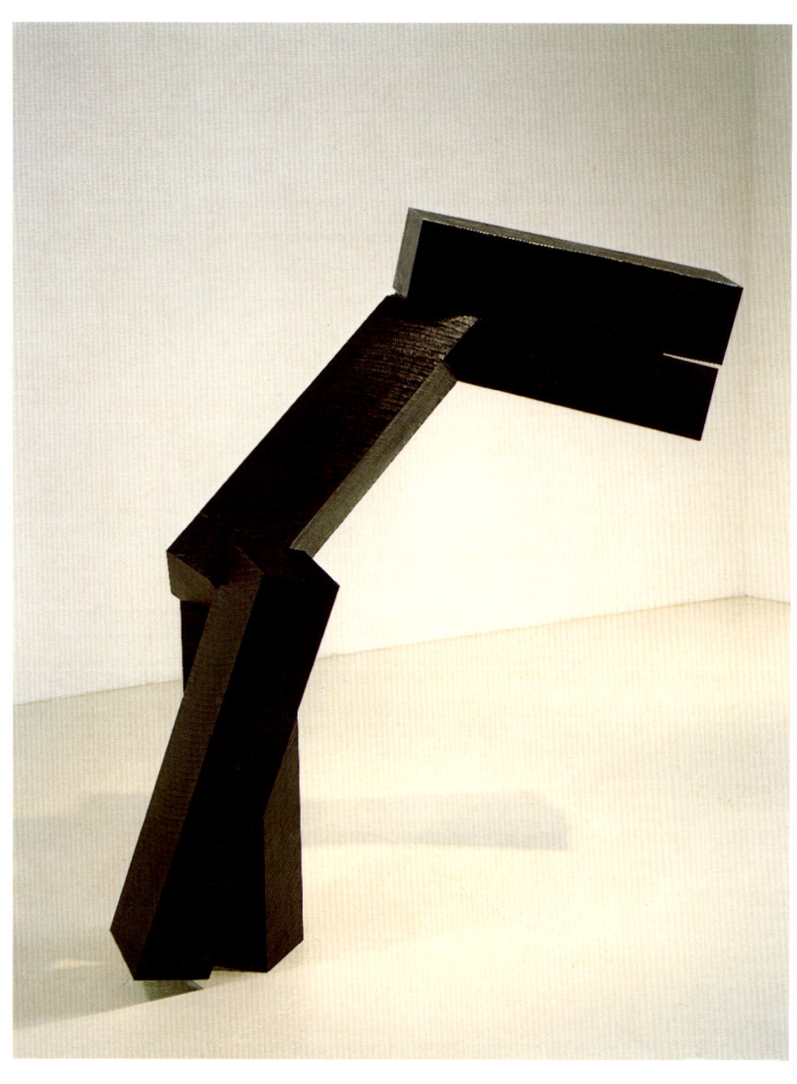

261 Untitled. 1995. Bronze (edition 1/2), 6'3" x 71" x 41" (218.4 x 180.3 x 104.1 cm). Courtesy PaceWildenstein

262 Untitled. 1995. Bronze (edition 1/3), 9'3¾" x 69" x 45" (283.9 x 175.3 x 114.3 cm). Collection Mr. and Mrs. William Mack

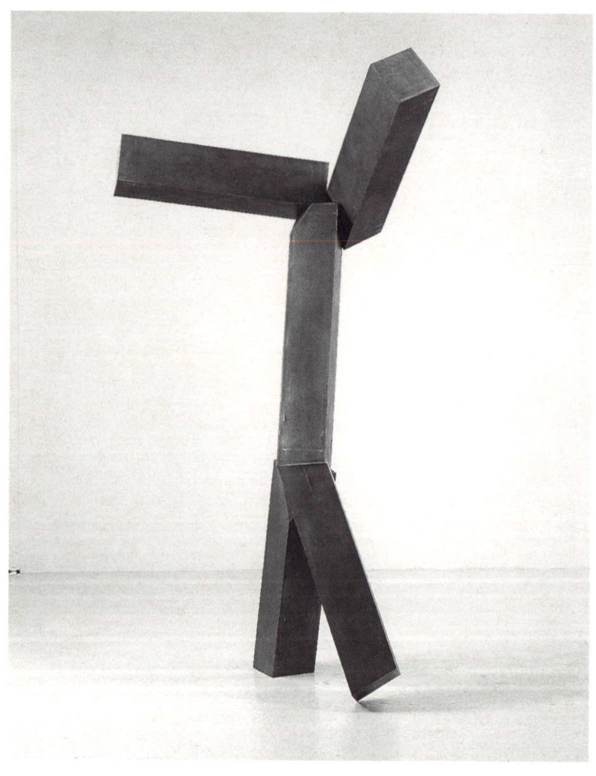

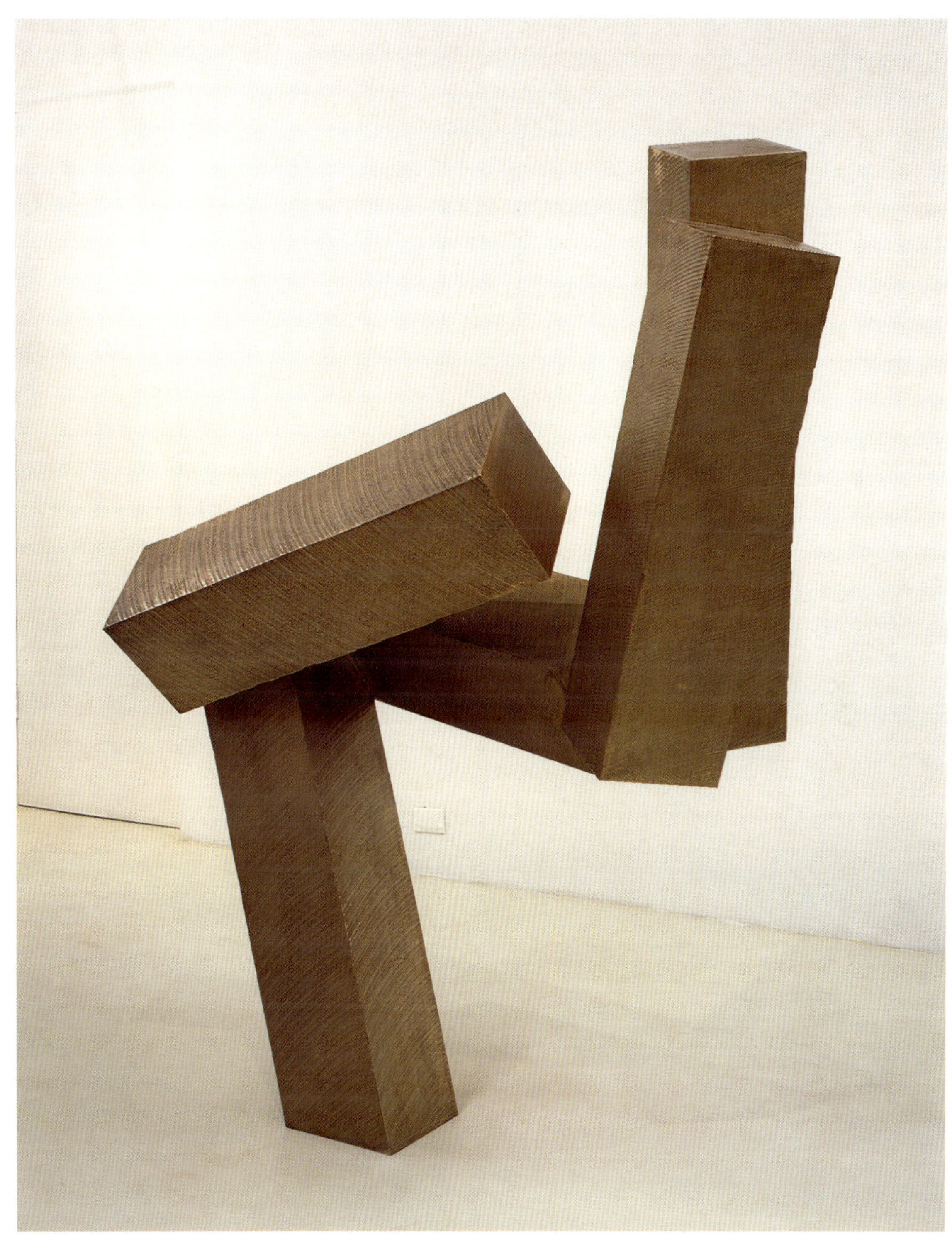

263 Untitled. 1994–95. Bronze (edition 1/3), 68¼ x 54 x 28½" (173.4 x 137.2 x 72.4 cm). Collection Robert F. and Patricia Ross Weis

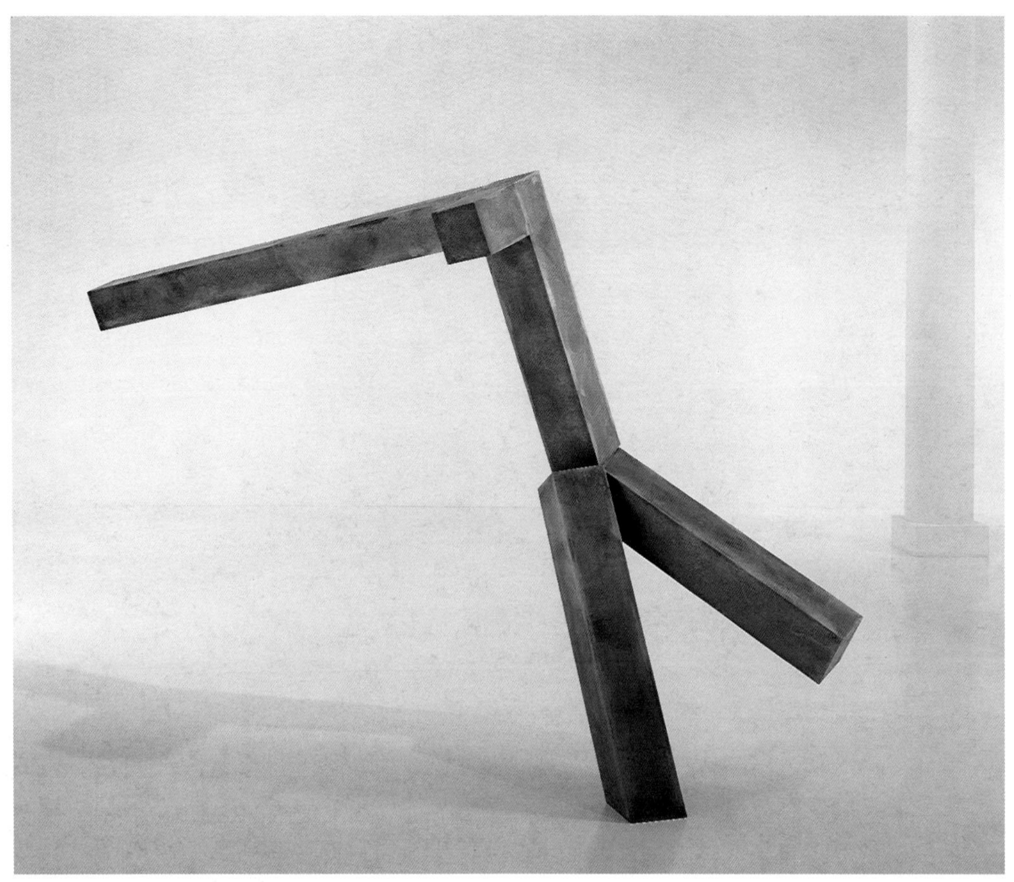

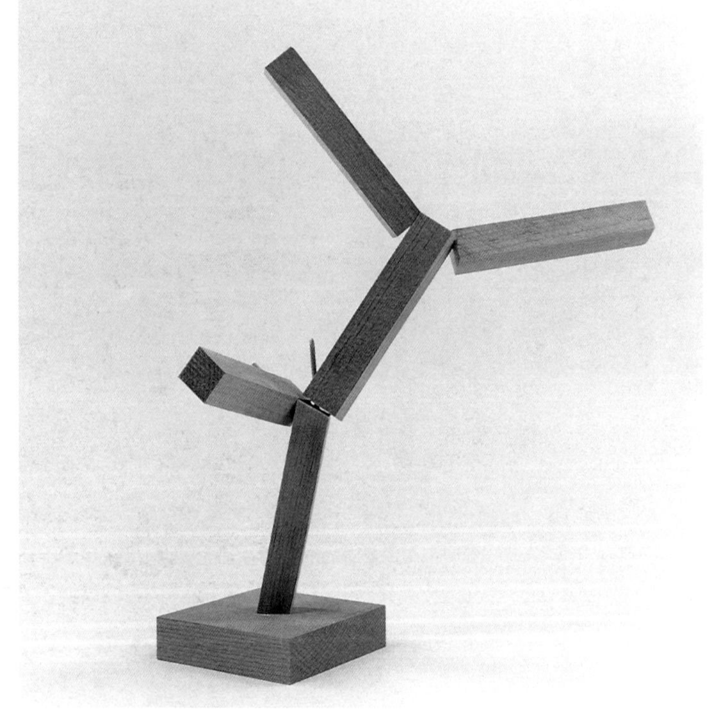

264 Untitled. 1996. Bronze (edition 1/4), 6'7¼" x 10'4" x 43" (201.3 x 315 x 109.2 cm). Courtesy PaceWildenstein

265 Study. 1995. Wood, 13¼ x 12¼ x 5" (33.7 x 31.1 x 12.7 cm). Collection the artist

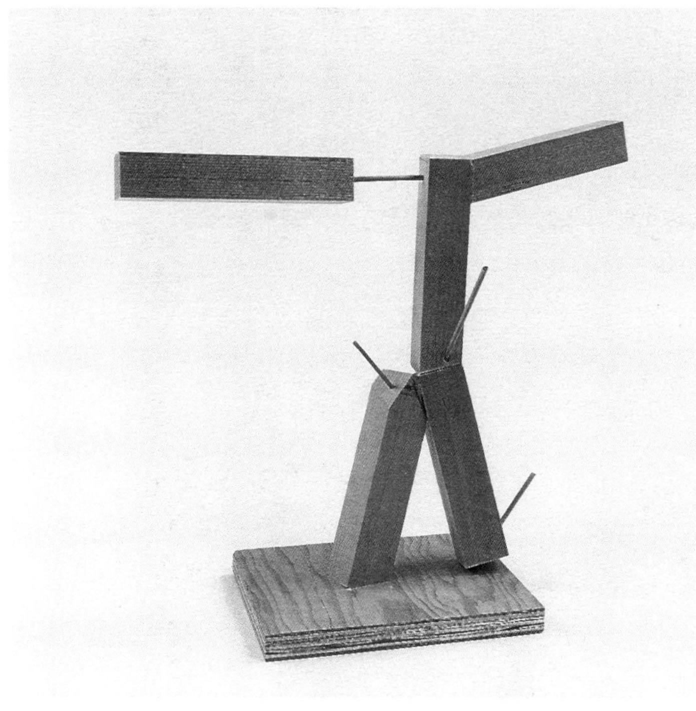

266 Study. 1995. Wood, 10 5/16 x 12 x 12 1/2" (26.2 x 30.5 x 31.8 cm). Collection the artist

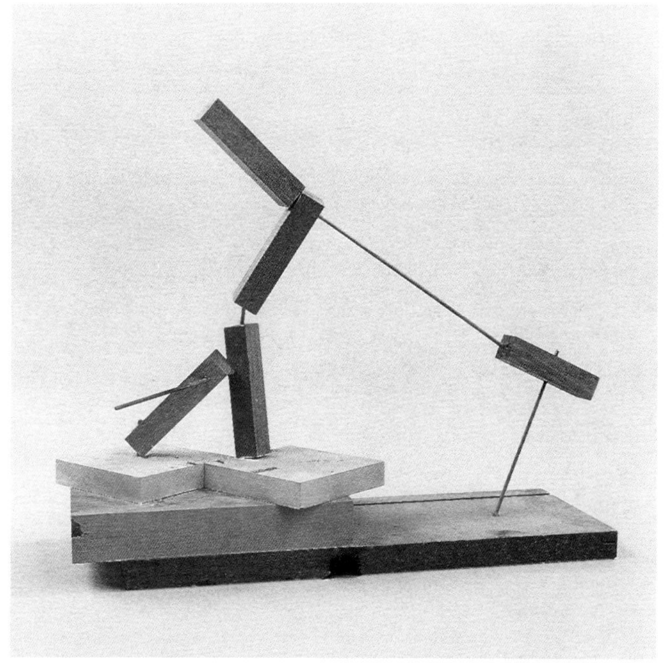

267 Study. 1995. Wood, 12 3/4 x 15 1/8 x 4" (32.4 x 38.4 x 10.2 cm). Collection the artist

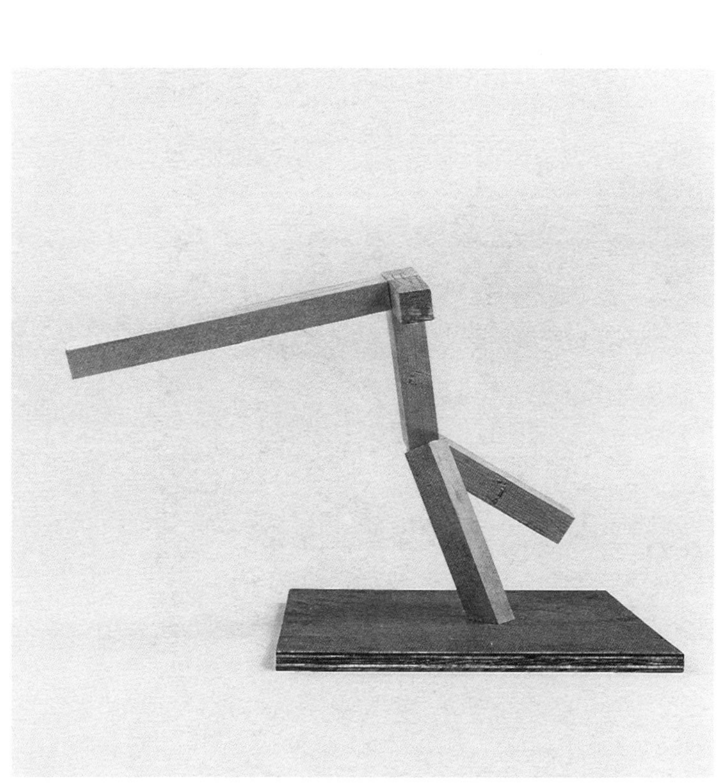

268 Study. 1995. Wood, 10 1/2 x 15 3/8 x 4 3/4" (26.7 x 39.1 x 12.1 cm). Collection the artist

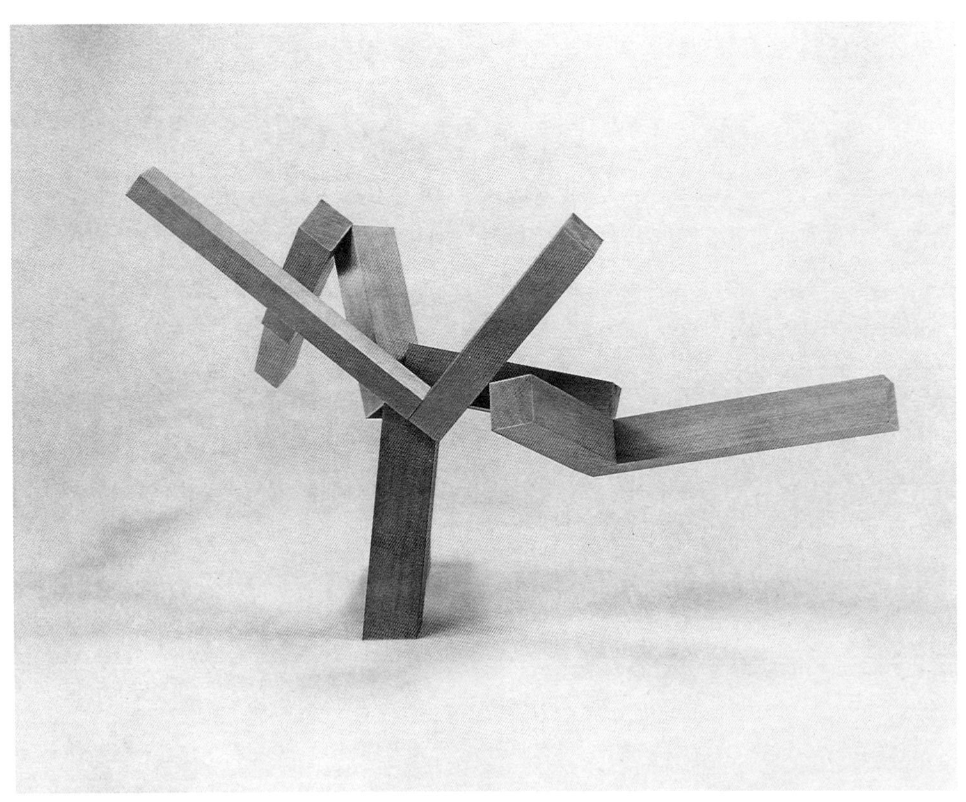

269 Study. 1997. Wood, 9 x 12¾ x 14" (22.4 x 32.4 x 35.6 cm). Collection the artist. Model for the sculpture shown in plate 270.

270 Untitled. 1997 (nearing completion at Tallix Foundry, Beacon, New York). Bronze, 10'6" x 21'6" x 9' (320 x 655.3 x 274.3 cm). Courtesy PaceWildenstein

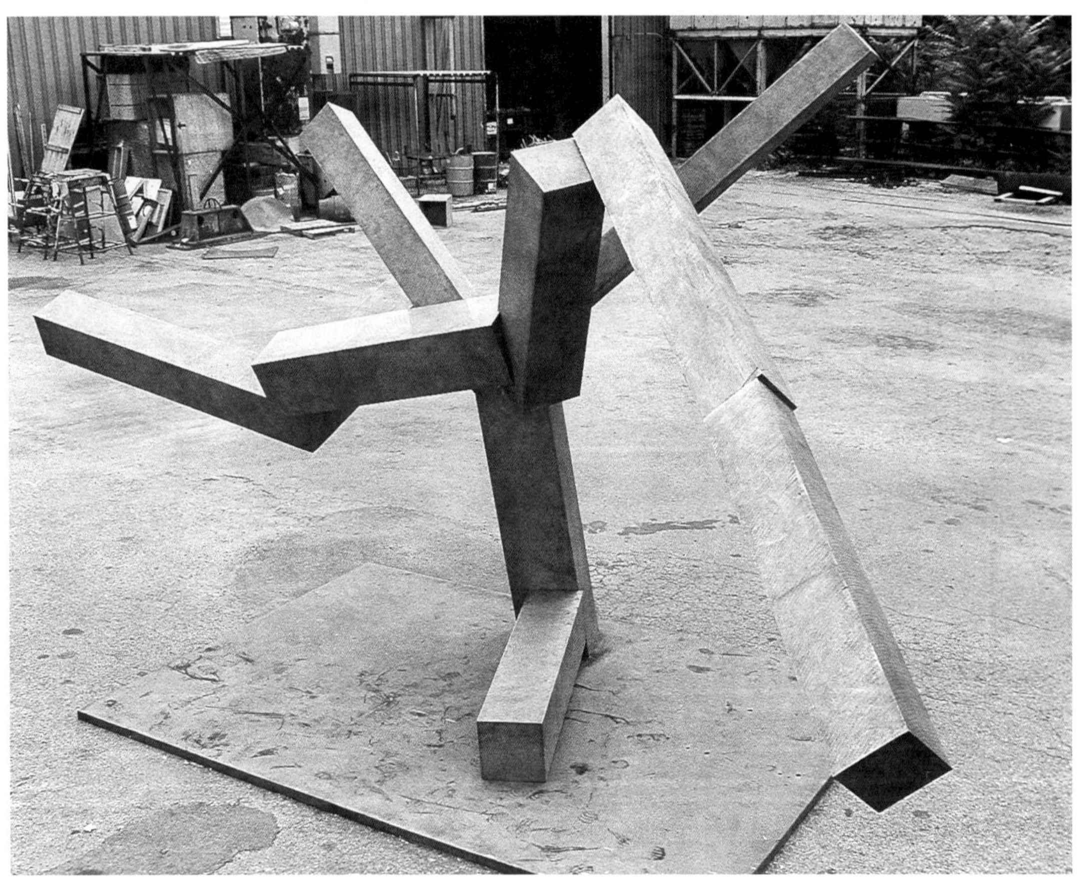

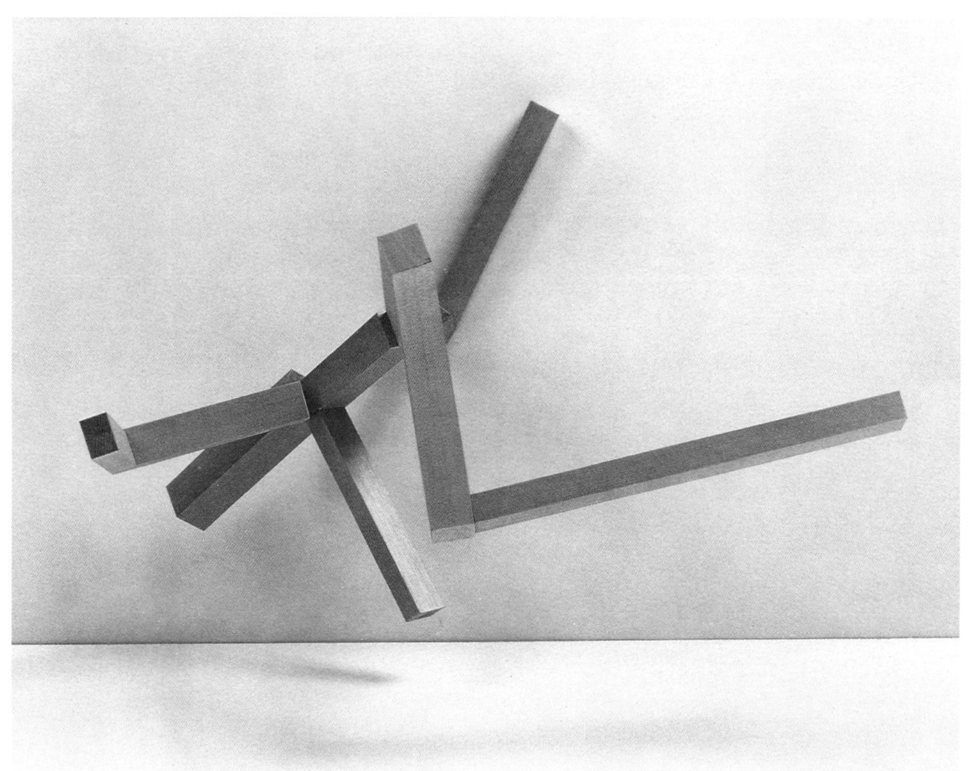

271 Study. 1997. Wood, 10¼ x 15½ x 10½" (26 x 39.4 x 26.7 cm). Collection the artist. A floor-mounted sculpture based on this wall-mounted study is shown in plate 272.

272 Untitled. 1997 (nearing completion at Tallix Foundry, Beacon, New York). Bronze, 8'6" x 12' x 10' (259.1 x 365.8 x 304.8 cm). Courtesy PaceWildenstein

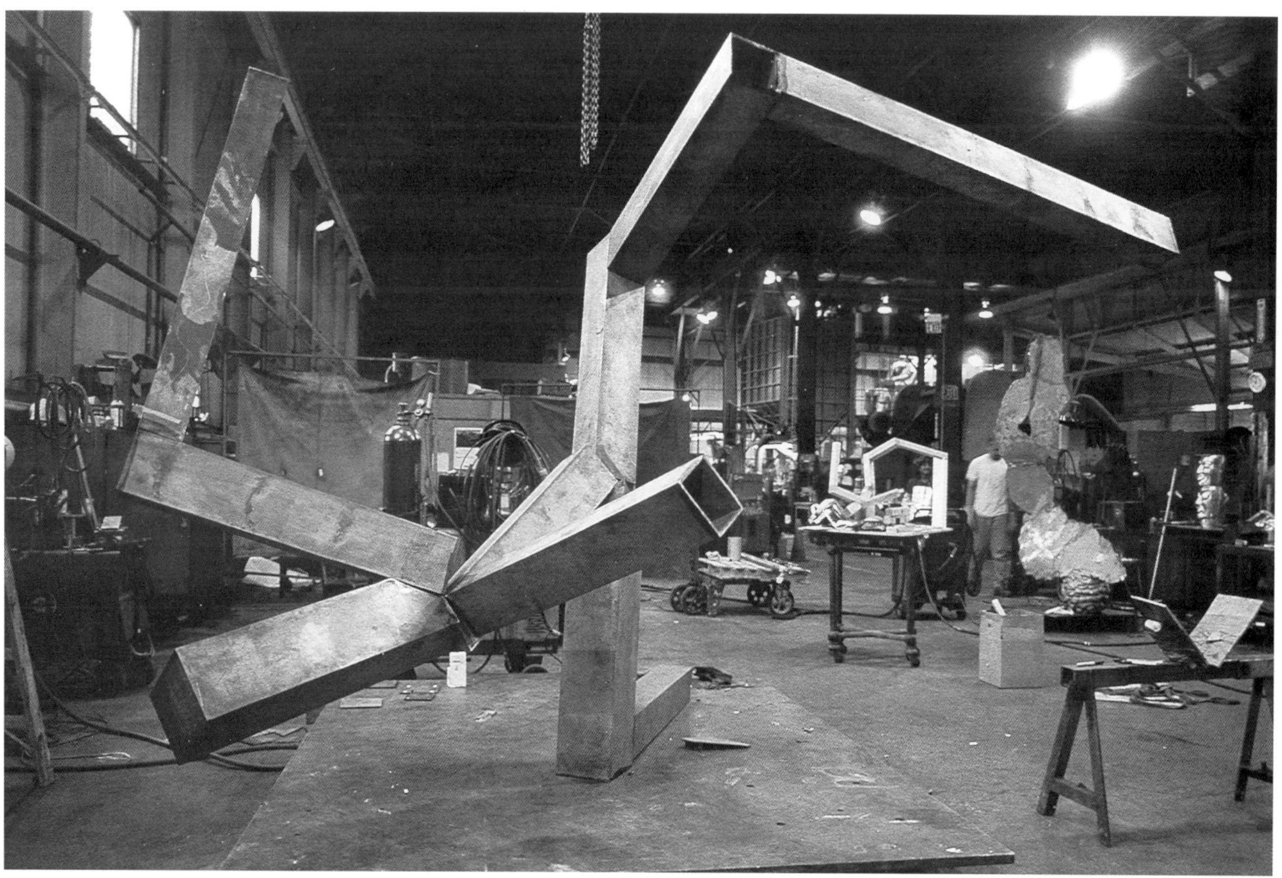

Notes to the Text

Unless otherwise indicated, quotations of Joel Shapiro in the text are from Hendel Teicher's interviews with the artist, August 1993 and May 1996.

1 Other works, commissioned for the interior of the memorial, all of them abstract, are by Ellsworth Kelly, Sol LeWitt, and Richard Serra. The works were selected by a jury composed of the following individuals (identified by the positions they held at the time): Ziva Amishai-Maisels, chairperson, Institute of Languages, Literature, and the Arts, Hebrew University, Jerusalem; Suzanne Delehanty, director, Contemporary Arts Museum, Houston; Howard Fox, curator of contemporary art, Los Angeles County Museum of Art; Gary Garrels, senior curator of painting and sculpture, Walker Art Center, Minneapolis; Raymond Nasher, founder, The Nasher Company, Dallas; Ned Rifkin, director, The High Museum of Art, Atlanta; Nancy Rosen, program administrator, Art for Public Spaces; Mark Rosenthal, adjunct curator, Solomon R. Guggenheim Museum, New York; and Nan Rosenthal, consultant to the Department of Twentieth-Century Art, The Metropolitan Museum of Art, New York.

2 This memorial was never realized. Jochen Gerz, Rebecca Horn, Oveis Saheb, and Micha Ullman were also invited to participate.

3 The application form was submitted to the Düsseldorf authorities in late 1989.

4 Joel Shapiro, "Commentaries," in Richard Marshall and Roberta Smith, *Joel Shapiro* (New York: Whitney Museum of American Art, 1982), p. 98.

5 Statements reported in Jean-Pierre Criqui, "Master of the Monumentalists," *Time,* October 13, 1967, p. 84; quoted in *Tony Smith* (Humlebaek, Denmark: Louisiana Museum for Moderne Kunst, 1995), n.p.

6 Letter from Barnett Newman to John de Menil, quoted in Harold Rosenberg, *Barnett Newman: Broken Obelisk and Other Sculptures* (Seattle: University of Washington Press, 1971), p. 13.

7 Ibid., p. 12.

8 Joel Shapiro, interviews with Lewis Kachur for the Archives of American Art, Smithsonian Institution; conducted in Westport, New York, July 15, 1988, and New York City, December 14, 1988.

9 Marcia Tucker, *Anti-Illusion: Procedures/Materials* (New York: Whitney Museum of American Art, 1969), p. 41.

10 Shapiro, interview with Kachur.

11 Ibid.

12 Ibid.

13 Pariscraft is the brand name of a commercial plaster.

14 Shapiro, interview with Kachur.

15 *Joel Shapiro* (Chicago: Museum of Contemporary Art, 1976), p. 6.

16 Shapiro, interview with Kachur.

17 Shapiro, "Commentaries," p. 96.

18 Ibid.

19 Roberta Smith, "Joel Shapiro," in Marshall and Smith, *Joel Shapiro,* p. 22.

20 On the critical dialogue between the two artists, see Phelan's interview with Shapiro in *Joel Shapiro: Painted Wood Sculpture and Drawings* (New York: The Pace Gallery, 1995). On Phelan's own work, see the texts by Richard Armstrong and Peter Schjeldahl in *Ellen Phelan: From the Lives of Dolls* (Amherst: University Gallery, University of Massachusetts, 1992), the catalogue of an exhibition organized by Marge Goldwater.

21 Gaston Bachelard, *The Poetics of Space,* trans. Maria Jolas (Boston: Beacon Press, 1969), p. 70.

22 Joel Shapiro, lecture delivered at the Museum of Modern Art, New York, March 30,1992.

23 Shapiro, "Commentaries," p. 98.

24 Ibid.

25 *Minotaure* (Paris), 1934 (no. 5), p. 42.

26 See *The Planar Dimension* (New York: Solomon R. Guggenheim Museum, 1979).

27 Published by Joel Shapiro and Catherine Mosley, New York, 1975.

28 Shapiro, "Commentaries," p. 101.

29 Ibid.

30 These figures remind one of another sculptor's fragmentation of the body, namely Rodin's, as described by Rainer Maria Rilke: "Each of these fragments possesses a coherence so exceptional and striking that it is indubitably so, and wants so little to be complete that one forgets that they are only parts. Suddenly one begins to suspect that to envision the body as a whole is more a matter for the scientist, and for the artist, starting from these elements, to create new relations and new entities, that are greater, more legitimate, more eternal." Quoted in *Le Corps en morceaux* (Paris: Musée d'Orsay, 1989).

31 Joel Shapiro, interview with Peter Boswell, in *Joel Shapiro: Outdoors* (Minneapolis: Walker Art Center; Kansas City, Mo.: Nelson-Atkins Museum of Art, 1995), p. 38.

32 Tony Smith, interview with Samuel Wagstaff, Jr., in Gregory Battcock, ed., *Minimal Art: A Critical Anthology* (Berkeley: University of California Press, 1995), p. 384.

33 Shapiro, interview with Boswell, p. 36.

34 Printed and published by Leslie Miller, The Grenfell Press, New York, 1990.

35 Gershom Scholem, *On the Mystical Shape of the Godhead* (New York: Schocken Books, 1991), p. 43.

36 The group of sculptures at Tîrgu-Jiu, near Hobitza, Romania, Brancusi's birthplace, includes *The Table of Silence, The Gate of the Kiss,* and *Endless Column.*

37 Etchings published by Joel Shapiro, printed by Maurice Payne, New York, 1995.

38 "Joel Shapiro on His Recent Prints: An Interview with James Cuno," *The Print Collector's Newsletter,* 27 (May–June 1996), p. 49.

39 Sculptures commissioned in 1994 by the Sony Music Entertainment Corporation, New York, and by Tishman Speyer, Berlin.

40 Michael Brenson, "Joel Shapiro and Figurative Sculpture," in the present volume, p.10.

41 Joel Shapiro joined The Pace Gallery in 1992.

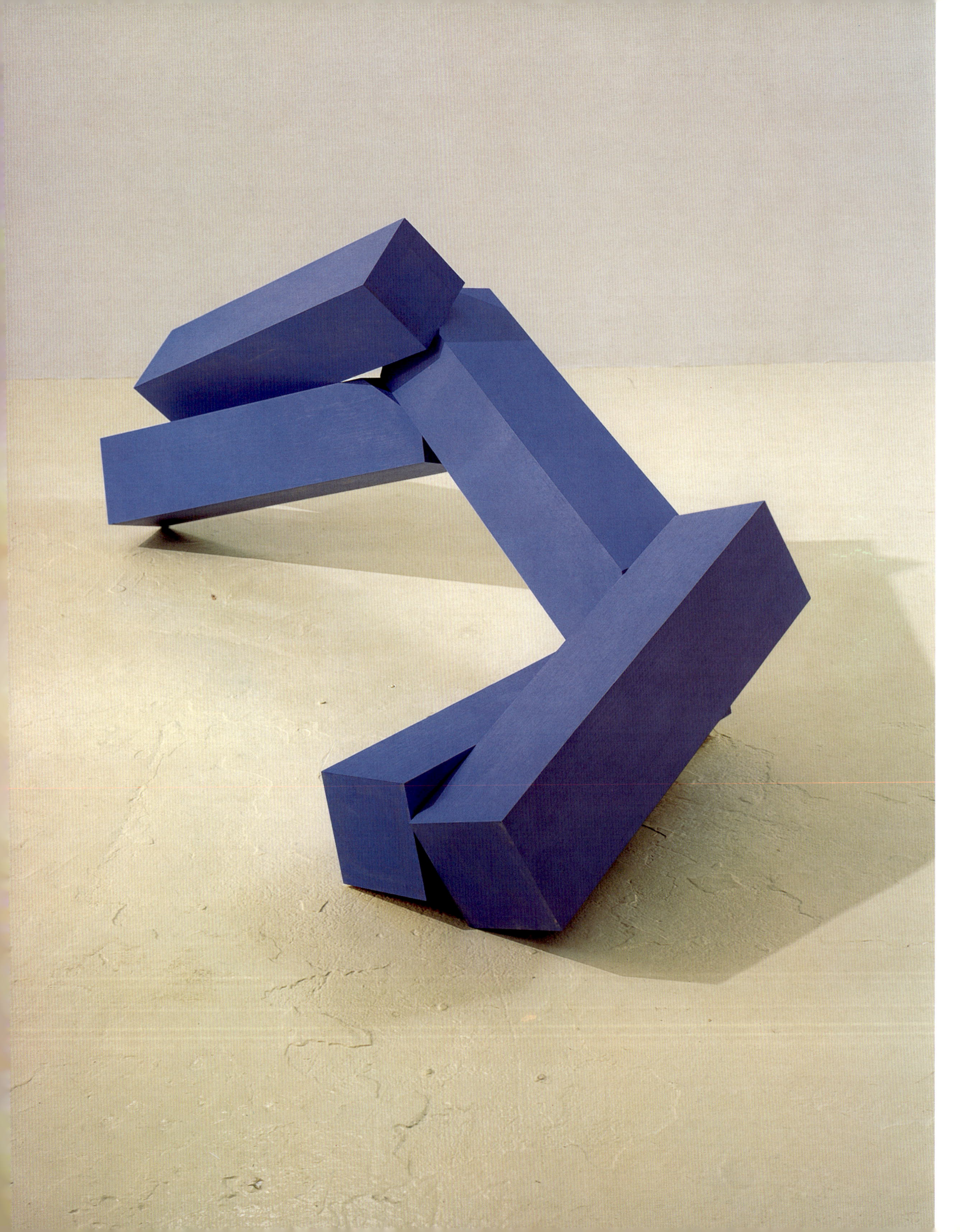

Biographical Chronology

OPPOSITE:
Untitled. 1997. Oil on wood, 29" x 6'7" x 32½" (73.7 x 200.7 x 82.6 cm). Courtesy PaceWildenstein

1941
September 27: Born, in New York, to Anna Lewis Shapiro and Joseph Shapiro.

1942–44
His father enlists in U.S. Army and is stationed at Camp Walters, Texas.

1945
Moves with his family to Sunnyside, Queens, New York.

1948–53
Attends Public School 150, Queens. Takes some painting and ceramics classes in the community.

1953–56
Attends junior high school.

1956–59
Attends Bayside High School in Queens (graduates 1959). Takes sculpture classes at the high school and painting classes at The Museum of Modern Art, New York.

1959–60
Attends the University of Colorado, Boulder, for two years.

1961
Having left the University of Colorado, moves back to New York. Works while taking classes at Queens College.

1962
Enrolls at New York University.

1962–64
Pursues pre-med studies at N.Y.U. (graduates 1964).

1965
Decides to join the Peace Corps.

Spring: Attends Peace Corps training program at the University of California, Davis.

1965–67
Spends nearly two years in southern India as a Peace Corps volunteer, conducting primary-school teacher-training institutes. Over the course of twenty-one months, works in four different villages in the state of Andhra Pradesh, traveling extensively between assignments. Lives first in Kurnool, on the Krishna River near the great historic site of Alampur. Then is relocated to Adilabad in the Deccan region, and often travels from there to the caves at Ellora and Ajanta. His third assignment is in the village of Guntur, near Amaravati, inland from the Bay of Bengal and close to the Orissa region. Finally, lives in Nellore, north of Madras.

1967
Winter: Returns to New York. Moves into a loft on lower Broadway and seriously begins to pursue a career as an artist.

Marries Amy Snider.

Summer: Accompanies Amy Snider to Baltimore for a program sponsored by the Whitney Museum of American Art for artists who teach art. Other participants include the Conceptualist Robert Barry. The faculty consists of Ron Clark and James Seawright. Barnett Newman, Harold Rosenberg, and Ad Reinhardt are among the visiting faculty members.

Fall: Enrolls in the N.Y.U. master's degree program in art, where he studies with James Wines.

1968
Makes early works that are divided between two extremes of his sensibility; some explore numerical systems, while others, less rigorously systematic, show a greater concern with expressivity.

In drawings, begins to emphasize elemental mark-making, using fingerprinting and dripped paint (plates 11, 19).

1968–69
Works at the Jewish Museum while a graduate student at N.Y.U.

1969
Makes a sculpture pairing pieces of magnesium and lead that have the same weight but different sizes (plate 24). Finding it impossible to get lead pieces of the required dimensions, he casts and then machines lead to his specifications.

Awarded M.A. degree from N.Y.U.

Robert Littman takes an interest in this work and shows it to Marcia Tucker. Shapiro is invited by Tucker and James Monte to participate in the group exhibition "Anti-Illusion: Procedures/Materials" at the Whitney Museum of American Art, the first public exhibition to include him.

Shapiro shows drawings to Brooke Alexander, who suggests that he contact Paula Cooper. Cooper includes one of his drawings in an exhibition.

Moves to new studio space on the second floor of an abandoned building at 54 Leonard Street.

November 13: Daughter, Ivy, is born.

1969–70
Teaches sculpture at Hofstra University, Hempstead, New York.

Makes drawings that consist of simple accumulated marks (plates 17, 18). Makes sculptures by using ordinary, repeated manual actions and rudimentary tools (plates 27, 28, 32, 34).

1970
Spring: Has his first solo exhibition, at the Paula Cooper Gallery, New York. Shows wall-mounted shelf pieces that employ a variety of different materials (plates 21, 22).

Spends the summer on the coast of Maine.

1971
Moves his studio to the top floor of the building at 54 Leonard Street. Destroys much of his two-dimensional work.

1971–72
Initiates a series of small, stylistically diverse oil paintings. Ultimately finds the process of painting too cumbersome for his needs, and gravitates toward drawing and the rapidity of charcoal and chalk.

1972
Is separated from Amy Snider. (They divorce in 1977.)

1972–73
Begins to cast work in iron at Bedi-Makky in Greenpoint, Brooklyn, a foundry that specializes in sand casting.

Winter: In a group show at the Paula Cooper Gallery, exhibits a four-part floor piece that introduces new imagery (plate 39).

1973
Spring: Exhibits a cast-iron bridge (plates 41, 42) in a solo show, the inaugural exhibition at The Clocktower, Institute for Art and Urban Resources, New York.

Summer: Travels with Bob Israel in Europe, visiting London, Paris, and Rome. His friend Max Gordon takes Shapiro to Capability Brown garden and to Stonehenge. In Rome, sees sculptures by Bernini.

Makes small images that have an architectural reference (plates 43, 57). Makes wall-mounted sculptures of a horse (plate 47) and a horse and rider (plate 49).

Meets his future wife, Ellen Phelan, a painter who has recently moved to New York from Detroit. The sustained critical dialogue between the two artists will become a factor in Shapiro's development.

1974
Winter: Exhibition of small works at the Paula Cooper Gallery.

Fall: Has his first show in Europe, the inaugural exhibition of the Salvatore Ala Gallery, Milan. In preparation for the exhibition, spends eight weeks in Milan working on sculpture that is then cast there.

Visiting artist at Princeton University. During the next several years, teaches sculpture at various universities in the New York area.

1975
Is awarded a Visual Arts Fellowship by the National Endowment for the Arts.

Begins to explore the possibility of employing figuration while executing a series of etchings with Catherine Mosley (plates 110–12).

Through the end of the decade, makes a series of wood reliefs, many of which are painted (plates 98–102).

1976
Spring: Has his first exhibition in Los Angeles, at Rico Mizuno's gallery space, which Paula Cooper rents for a short period of time. Shows small, reductive sculptures.

Fall: Has his first solo museum exhibition, at the Museum of Contemporary Art, Chicago, organized by Steven Prokopoff.

1976–79
Executes drawings that emphasize the function of lines as boundaries (plates 83–85).

1977
Through drawings and wall reliefs (plates 97, 103, 104), develops toward figurative sculpture (plates 113, 225).

His family begins to spend summers in the Adirondacks; rents houses on Loon Lake.

1978
Marries Ellen Phelan.

Spends a good deal of time in Los Angeles, through 1979, while Phelan teaches at the California Institute of the Arts.

1979
Fall: In New York, works on a large series of lithographs, with Maurice Sanchez, that is exhibited at the Brooke Alexander gallery the following fall.

Begins to cast his work at more modern foundries, which have abandoned the French sand technique for a more contemporary technique with bonded sand.

1979–early 1980s
Makes color gouaches that deal with single shapes found through drawing (plates 63, 106).

1980
Winter: Comprehensive exhibition of his sculpture and drawings at the Whitechapel Art Gallery, London, organized by Nicholas Serota. After the exhibition, begins to work on a larger scale.

Spring: Has his first exhibition in Japan. Visits Kyoto, Nara, and Tokyo.

Works with Patrick Strzelec, a sculptor and an employee of the Johnson Atelier, Princeton, New Jersey, in the casting of his sculptures.

Meets Ichiro Kato, a cabinetmaker who has worked with James Cooper. (Cooper frequently helps artists realize projects in wood.) Learns from Kato's skill with complicated joinery.

1981
Summer: In Jerusalem, works in cast plaster. These sculptures are exhibited at the Israel Museum later that summer.

1981–83
Continues to pursue figuration through fractionalized wood, bronze, and iron figures (plates 123–30). Also makes forays into abstraction.

1982
Fall: Retrospective exhibition at the Whitney Museum of American Art, New York, organized by Richard Marshall.

1983
Receives a commission from Douglas S. Cramer.

Receives a commission from the Cigna Corporation, Philadelphia, which provides the opportunity to do his largest sculpture up to this time.

1984
Spends summer in Amagansett, Long Island.

Autumn and early winter: Is at the American Academy in Rome with Ellen Phelan. Admires the work of Bernini, Boromini, and Caravaggio.

Begins to make works that reveal the hollow interior of a sculpture (see plate 152).

Receives the Brandeis University Creative Arts Award.

1985
His largest sculpture up to this time, fourteen feet high, is exhibited at the Seagram's Building, New York. The work is subsequently acquired by the Louisiana Museum for Moderne Kunst, Humlebaek, Denmark.

Fall: The Stedelijk Museum, Amsterdam, organizes an exhibition of his sculpture and drawings.

Acquires property in the Adirondacks on Lake Champlain. The site is a former camp that can accommodate studios. Begins spending three to five months a year there.

1985–86
Begins using thin rods that prop up the more substantial elements of the sculptures (plate 168).

1986
Is awarded the Skowhegan Medal for Sculpture.

1987
Works with Leslie Miller of Grenfell Press, New York, on a series of woodcuts, linoleum cuts, and pochoirs. The series continues until 1990, when the prints are exhibited at Pace Prints, New York.

1988
Receives commissions from the Fukuoka Sogo Bank, Fukuoka, Japan (plate 207), and from the Kawamura Memorial Museum of Art, Chiba, Japan.

1989
Dartmouth College commissions a sculpture from him for the Bedford Courtyard of its Hood Museum of Art (plate 208).

1989–90

Makes larger works that double certain elements of the figure (plates 176, 177).

Works with Aldo Crommelynck in Paris on a series of aquatints.

1990

The Des Moines Art Center organizes an exhibition that surveys the development of figuration in his work; the exhibition travels to The Baltimore Museum of Art and the Center for the Fine Arts, Miami. Concurrently, an exhibition organized by the IVAM Centre Julio González, Valencia, opens first at the Louisiana Museum for Moderne Kunst, Humlebaek, Denmark, and then travels to Valencia, Zurich, and Calais.

Is awarded the Merit Medal for Sculpture by the American Academy and Institute of Arts and Letters, New York.

Executes design for the National Book Award (through 1995).

1991

Is selected to create a sculpture for the United States Holocaust Memorial Museum, Washington, D.C.

1993

Spring: Has his first exhibition at The Pace Gallery, New York.

His outdoor sculpture for the United States Holocaust Memorial Museum is unveiled (plates 1, 6, 7, 9).

1994

Is elected to the Swedish Royal Academy of Art.

Executes a commission for Tishman Speyer Berlin GmbH & Co., Berlin, Germany (plate 252).

Executes a commission for Sony Plaza, New York (plate 251).

1994–96

Executes his largest sculpture to date, *Three Figures/Fifteen Elements* (plates 253–56), a work in three parts, for the Kansas City International Airport, commissioned by the Kansas City, Missouri, One-Percent-for-Art Program.

1995

An exhibition of his outdoor sculpture is organized by the Walker Art Center, Minneapolis, and the Nelson-Atkins Museum of Art, Kansas City, Missouri.

Begins spending time in Cambridge, Massachusetts, when Ellen Phelan accepts a professorship at Harvard University.

Makes a series of hard-ground etchings in his studio, printed by Maurice Payne (plates 247–50).

Spring: Exhibition at the PaceWildenstein gallery, New York, of his painted wood sculptures.

Executes design for the PEN/Newman's Own First Amendment Award

1996

Exhibition of his large, freestanding bronzes at PaceWildenstein in Los Angeles and at 142 Greene Street, New York.

Fall: Exhibition of his prints at the Gallery of Art, University of Missouri, Kansas City.

1997

Fall: Is appointed Artist-in-Residence at Phillips Academy. An exhibition of his sculpture from 1971–97 is held at the Addison Gallery of American Art, Phillips Academy, Andover, Massachusetts.

Exhibition of his recent work at the Haus der Kunst, Munich.

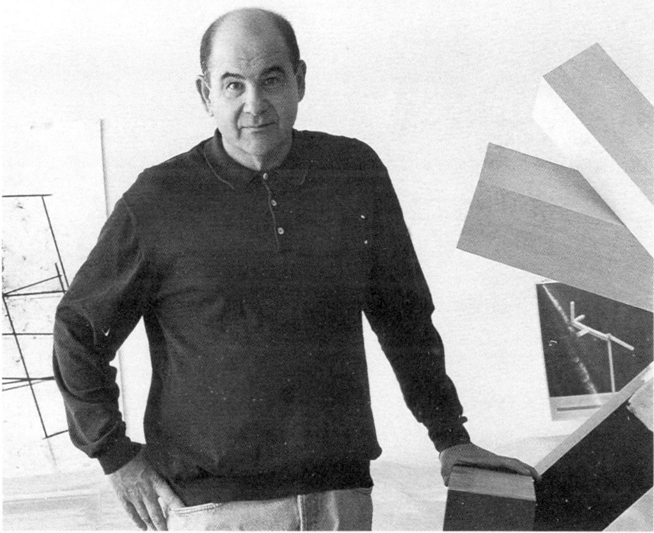

Joel Shapiro in his studio, 1997

Exhibition History

Compiled by Pamela Franks

SOLO EXHIBITIONS

1970

Paula Cooper Gallery, New York. "Joel Shapiro." March 8–April 1.

1972

Paula Cooper Gallery, New York. "Joel Shapiro." January 15–February 9.

1973

The Clocktower, Institute for Art and Urban Resources, New York. "Joel Shapiro." April 12–28.

1974

Paula Cooper Gallery, New York. "Joel Shapiro." February 9–March 6.

Galleria Salvatore Ala, Milan. "Works by Joel Shapiro." October 4–November 1.

1975

Paula Cooper Gallery, New York. "Joel Shapiro." October 11–November 5.

Walter Kelly Gallery, Chicago. "Joel Shapiro." Dates unavailable.

1976

Paula Cooper Gallery, Los Angeles. "Joel Shapiro." April 6–24.

Museum of Contemporary Art, Chicago. "Joel Shapiro." September 11–November 7.

1977

Max Protetch Gallery, Washington, D.C. "Joel Shapiro: Recent Sculpture." February 19–March 20.

Albright-Knox Art Gallery, Buffalo. "Joel Shapiro: Recent Work." March 26–April 17.

Susanne Hilberry Gallery, Birmingham, Michigan. "Recent Sculpture: Joel Shapiro." April 16–May 14.

Paula Cooper Gallery, New York. "Joel Shapiro." November 12–December 7.

Galerie Aronowitsch, Stockholm. "Joel Shapiro." November 19–December 15.

Galerie Nancy Gillespie–Elisabeth de Laage, Paris. "Joel Shapiro: Drawings." November 19–December 15.

1978

The Greenberg Gallery, St. Louis. "Joel Shapiro: New Sculptures." March 16–April 30.

Galerie m, Bochum, West Germany. "Joel Shapiro." Dates unavailable.

1979

Akron Art Institute. "Joel Shapiro Sculpture." February 3–March 18.

Galerie Mukai, Tokyo. "Joel Shapiro: Sculpture & Dessin." April 11–May 10.

Paula Cooper Gallery, New York. "Joel Shapiro." April 14–May 12.

Galerie Nancy Gillespie–Elisabeth de Laage, Paris. "Joel Shapiro." May 19–June 21.

The University Gallery, Ohio State University, Columbus. Spring.

1980

Whitechapel Art Gallery, London. "Joel Shapiro: Sculpture and Drawing." January 18–February 24. Traveled to Museum Haus Lange, Krefeld, West Germany, March 16–April 27; Moderna Museet, Stockholm, October 31–December 14.

Galerie Mukai, Tokyo. "Joel Shapiro." April 11–May 10.

Asher/Faure Gallery, Los Angeles. "Joel Shapiro." June 7–July 3.

Brooke Alexander, Inc., New York. "Joel Shapiro: Lithographs, 1979–1980." September 9–October 4. Traveled to Delahunty Gallery, Dallas, October 11–November 5.

Galerie Aronowitsch, Stockholm. "Joel Shapiro." November 8–25.

Paula Cooper Gallery, New York. "Joel Shapiro." November 19–December 13.

Bell Gallery, Brown University, Providence, Rhode Island. "Joel Shapiro." November 22–December 17. Traveled to Georgia State University, Atlanta, February 2–27, 1981; Contemporary Arts Center, Cincinnati, September 17–November 1, 1981.

1981

The Ackland Art Museum, University of North Carolina, Chapel Hill. "Facets I: Joel Shapiro." January 11–February 8.

John Stoller Gallery, Minneapolis. "Joel Shapiro: Sculpture, Drawings, Prints." April 10–June 28.

Daniel Weinberg Gallery, San Francisco. "Joel Shapiro: Recent Sculpture." May 5–June 6.

Israel Museum, Jerusalem. "Joel Shapiro." September–October.

Galerie Mukai, Tokyo. "Joel Shapiro: Sculpture." October 5–24.

Young Hoffman Gallery, Chicago. "Joel Shapiro: Sculptures and Drawings, 1975 through 1981." November 20–January 5, 1982.

1982

Paula Cooper Gallery, New York. "Joel Shapiro: Drawings." January 9–February 6.

Portland Center for the Visual Arts, Oregon. "Joel Shapiro." March 30–May 2.

Susanne Hilberry Gallery, Birmingham, Michigan. "Joel Shapiro: New Sculptures and Drawings." April 3–June 4.

Yarlow/Salzman Gallery, Toronto. "Joel Shapiro: Recent Sculptures and Drawings." April 6–May 1.

Whitney Museum of American Art, New York. "Joel Shapiro." October 21–January 2,1983. Traveled to Dallas Museum of Fine Arts, March 9–May 8, 1983; Art Gallery of Ontario, Toronto, August 13–May 8, 1983; La Jolla Museum of Contemporary Art, December 3–January 15, 1984.

1983

Galerie Aronowitsch, Stockholm. "Joel Shapiro." Opened May 5.

Paula Cooper Gallery, New York. "Joel Shapiro." May 5–June 4.

Asher/Faure Gallery, Los Angeles. "Joel Shapiro." November 19–December 24.

1984

Paula Cooper Gallery, New York. "Joel Shapiro: Gouaches." March 22–April 14.

Galerie Aronowitsch, Stockholm. "Joel Shapiro." April–May.

Paula Cooper Gallery, New York. "Joel Shapiro." November 1–29.

1985

Knoedler Kasmin, London. "Joel Shapiro." June 20–July.

Stedelijk Museum, Amsterdam. "Joel Shapiro." September 6–October 20. Traveled to Kunstmuseum, Düsseldorf, November 10–January 19, 1986; Staatliche Kunsthalle, Baden-Baden, February 1–March 31, 1986.

1986

Galerie Daniel Templon, Paris. "Joel Shapiro." March 9–May 3.

Seattle Art Museum. "Joel Shapiro." March 13–May 11.

Hal Bromm Gallery, New York. "Joel Shapiro." September 12–October 11.

The John and Mable Ringling Museum of Art, Sarasota, Florida. "Joel Shapiro." October 31–December 14.

Paula Cooper Gallery, New York. "Joel Shapiro." November 8–December 6.

Asher/Faure Gallery, Los Angeles. "Joel Shapiro." November 15–December 20.

1987

Donald Young Gallery, Chicago. "Joel Shapiro." April 3–May 2.

John Berggruen Gallery, San Francisco. "Joel Shapiro." September 30–November 28.

Hirshhorn Museum and Sculpture Garden, Smithsonian Institution, Washington, D.C. "Joel Shapiro: Painted Wood." December 2–February 28, 1988.

1988

Paula Cooper Gallery, New York. "Joel Shapiro." March 3–31.

Galerie Mukai, Tokyo. "Joel Shapiro." April 4–May 7.

Hans Strelow, Düsseldorf. "Joel Shapiro." April 29–June 4.

Susanne Hilberry Gallery, Birmingham, Michigan. "Joel Shapiro." May 21–June 22.

Galerie Daniel Templon, Paris. "Joel Shapiro." September 10–October 12.

The Cleveland Museum of Art. "Joel Shapiro: Recent Sculptures and Drawings." December 6–January 29, 1989.

1989

Asher/Faure Gallery, Los Angeles. "Joel Shapiro." January 14–February 11.

The Toledo Museum of Art, Ohio. "Playing with Human Geometry: Joel Shapiro's Sculpture." January 15–February 26.

Paula Cooper Gallery, New York. "Joel Shapiro." May 3–June 3.

Waddington Galleries, London. "Joel Shapiro." October 4–28.

1990

Pace Prints, New York. "Joel Shapiro." May 4–June 3.

The Greenberg Gallery, St. Louis. "Joel Shapiro." May 24–July 21.

Museet i Varberg, Varberg, Sweden. "Joel Shapiro: Skulptur & Grafik, 1985–1990." June 17–August 19.

Galerie Aronowitsch, Stockholm. "Joel Shapiro." September 1–29.

Louisiana Museum for Moderne Kunst, Humlebaek, Denmark. "Joel Shapiro." September 15–November 18. Traveled to IVAM Centre Julio González, Valencia, November 29–February 10, 1991; Kunsthalle, Zurich, March 23–May 26, 1991; Musée des Beaux-Arts, Calais, June 22–September 8, 1991.

Paula Cooper Gallery, New York. "Joel Shapiro." November 3–December 1.

Des Moines Art Center. "Joel Shapiro: Tracing the Figure." November 17–January 13, 1991. Traveled to The Baltimore Museum of Art, August 21–October 7; Center for the Fine Arts, Miami, April 6–June 2, 1991.

1991

Salon de Mars, Paris. "Joel Shapiro." March 20–25.

Center for the Fine Arts, Miami. "Joel Shapiro: Selected Drawings 1968–1990." April 6–June 2.

Asher/Faure Gallery, Los Angeles. "Joel Shapiro." April 20–May 18.

Galerie Mukai, Tokyo. "Joel Shapiro." May 10–June 8.

John Berggruen Gallery, San Francisco. "Recent Sculpture." October 30–November 30.

1993

The Pace Gallery (32 East Fifty-seventh Street), New York. "Joel Shapiro: Sculpture and Drawings." April 30–June 18.

The Pace Gallery (142 Greene Street), New York. "Joel Shapiro: Sculpture and Drawings." April 30–June 25.

Galerie Karsten Greve, Cologne. "Joel Shapiro: Skulpturen, Arbeiten auf Papier." September 23–January 6, 1994.

1994

Gallery Seomi, Seoul. "Joel Shapiro: Drawing and Sculpture." April 19–May 18.

Galleria Karsten Greve, Milan. "Joel Shapiro: Sculture e Disegni." September 8–November 8.

1995

Galerie Aronowitsch, Stockholm. "Joel Shapiro: Teckningar." February 11–March 15.

PaceWildenstein (32 East Fifty-seventh Street), New York. "Joel Shapiro: Painted Wood Sculpture and Drawings." March 24–April 22.

Galerie Karsten Greve, Paris. "Joel Shapiro Sculptures." May 4–August 31.

Sculpture Garden, Walker Art Center, Minneapolis. "Joel Shapiro: Outdoors." May 15–March 15, 1996. Traveled to Sculpture Park, Nelson-Atkins Museum of Art, Kansas City, Missouri, April 23–March 31, 1997.

Betsy Senior Gallery, New York. "Joel Shapiro: Etchings." October 26–December 22.

1996

Susanne Hilberry Gallery, Birmingham, Michigan. "Joel Shapiro: New Etchings and Painted Wood Sculptures." February 6–March 30.

Daniel Weinberg Gallery, San Francisco. "Joel Shapiro: Early Works." March 9–April 27.

PaceWildenstein, Los Angeles. "Joel Shapiro: Sculpture and Drawings." March 14–April 20.

Gallery of Art, University of Missouri, Kansas City. "Joel Shapiro: Selected Prints 1975–1995." September 7–October 25.

PaceWildenstein (142 Greene Street), New York. "Joel Shapiro: Recent Sculpture." September 26–November 2.

Gallery Seomi, Seoul. "Joel Shapiro: Recent Sculpture and Drawings." November 12–December 20.

1997

Galerie Jamileh Weber, Zurich. "Joel Shapiro." September 5–October 11.

Addison Gallery of American Art, Phillips Academy, Andover, Massachusetts. "Joel Shapiro: Sculpture in Clay, Plaster, Wood, Iron, and Bronze, 1971–1997." September 20–January 4, 1998.

Galerie Biedermann, Munich. "Joel Shapiro: Drawings." October 24–December 3.

Haus der Kunst, Munich. "Joel Shapiro: Skulpturen, 1993–1997." October 24–January 6, 1998.

SELECTED GROUP EXHIBITIONS

1969

Whitney Museum of American Art, New York. "Anti-Illusion: Procedures/Materials." May 19–July 6. Exhibition catalogue, texts by Marcia Tucker and James Monte.

Paula Cooper Gallery, New York. "Drawings." December 6–January 7, 1970.

Herter Gallery, University of Massachusetts, Amherst. "Recent Acquisitions." Winter.

1970

Emily Lowe Gallery, Hofstra University, Hempstead, New York. "Hanging/Leaning." February 2–27. Exhibition catalogue, Introduction by Robert R. Littman.

Akron Art Institute. "Drawings and Watercolors by Young Americans." September 30–October 15.

The Picker Art Gallery, Colgate University, Hamilton, New York. "Viewpoints 4: Kenneth Campbell, R. J. Kreznar, Ed O'Connell, Joel Shapiro, Gary Wojcik." October 21–November 15. Exhibition catalogue.

Weatherspoon Art Gallery, University of North Carolina, Greensboro. "Art on Paper." November 15–December 17.
The Museum of Modern Art, New York. "Paperworks." November 24–January 10, 1971.

Museum of Art, Rhode Island School of Design, Providence. "Art for Your Collection IX." December 9–January 7, 1971.

Whitney Museum of American Art, New York. "1970 Annual Exhibition: Contemporary American Sculpture." December 12–February 7, 1971. Exhibition catalogue, Foreword by John I. H. Baur.

Paula Cooper Gallery, New York. "Drawings." December 19–January 7, 1971.

1971

Van Deusen Galleries, Kent State University, Kent, Ohio. "Kent State University School of Art Annual Invitational Exhibition, Dedicated as a Memorial to May 4, 1970." April 4–15.

The Art Institute of Chicago. "The Society for Contemporary Art: Thirty-first Annual Exhibition." April 27–May 30.

Paula Cooper Gallery, New York. "Changing Group Exhibition." April–June.

Vassar College Art Gallery, Poughkeepsie, New York. "Twenty-six by Twenty-six." May 1–June 6. Exhibition catalogue, texts by Mary Delahoyd, Marguerite Klobe, Robin Brown, Nancy Cara Ackerman, and Stephen Martin.

Albright-Knox Art Gallery, Buffalo. "Kid Stuff?" July 25–September 6.

1972

The Aldrich Museum of Contemporary Art, Ridgefield, Connecticut. "Paintings on Paper." September 17–December 17.

Paula Cooper Gallery, New York. "Small Series." December 9–January 13, 1973.

1973

Paula Cooper Gallery, New York. "The Last Picture Show at 100 Prince Street." February 17–March 10.

Paula Cooper Gallery, New York. "Opening Group Exhibition." May 5–June 5.

Xerox Square Exhibition Center, Rochester, New York. "Art in Evolution." May 16–June 27. Exhibition catalogue, text by Anthony John Sorce.

Whitney Museum of American Art, New York. "American Drawings, 1963–1973." May 25–July 22. Exhibition catalogue, text by Elke M. Solomon.

Fogg Art Museum, Harvard University, Cambridge, Massachusetts. "New American Graphic Art." September 12–October 28.

Paula Cooper Gallery, New York. "Drawings and Other Work." December 15–January 9, 1974.

1974

The Clocktower, Institute for Art and Urban Resources, New York. "Figuratively Sculpting." Spring.

Indianapolis Museum of Art. "Painting and Sculpture Today, 1974." May 22–July 14. Traveled to The Taft Museum, Cincinnati, September 12–October 26. Exhibition catalogue.

The Art Institute of Chicago. "Seventy-first American Exhibition." June 15–August 11. Exhibition catalogue, Introduction by A. James Speyer.

Paula Cooper Gallery, New York. "Drawings and Other Work." December 7–January 8, 1975.

1975

The Garage, London. "Jennifer Bartlett and Joel Shapiro." April 23–May 17.

The Art Institute of Chicago. "The Small Scale in Contemporary Art." May 8–June 15. Exhibition catalogue, text by Peter Frank.

Paula Cooper Gallery, New York. "Spring Group Exhibition." June.

The Clocktower, Institute for Art and Urban Resources, New York. "Collectors of the Seventies, Part III: Milton Brutten and Helen Herrick." September 18–October 18.

Institute of Contemporary Art, University of Pennsylvania, Philadelphia. "Painting, Drawing, and Sculpture of the '60s and '70s from the Dorothy and Herbert Vogel Collection." October 7–November 18. Traveled to Contemporary Arts Center, Cincinnati, December 17–February 15, 1976.

Paula Cooper Gallery, New York."Fall Group Exhibition." December 6–January 7, 1976.

New Gallery, Cleveland. "Small Sculpture and Related Drawings." December 9–31.

1976

Johnson Gallery, Middlebury College, Middlebury, Vermont. "Recent Work." January 9–30.

Sales and Rental Gallery, The Baltimore Museum of Art. "Drawings." February.

Fine Arts Center Gallery, University of Massachusetts, Amherst. "Critical Perspectives in American Art." April 10–May 9. Traveled to United States Pavilion, 37th Venice Biennale, July 18–October 10. Exhibition catalogue, Introduction by Hugh M. Davies, texts by Sam Hunter, Rosalind Krauss, and Marcia Tucker.

Fine Arts Building, New York. "Roelof Louw, Marvin Torfield, Joel Shapiro: New Sculpture, Plans, and Projects." May 1–11.

The Renaissance Society at the University of Chicago. "Ideas on Paper, 1970–1976." May 2–June 6.

Paula Cooper Gallery, New York. "Group Exhibition." May 29–June 26.

37th Venice Biennale. "International Events, '72–'76." July 18–October 10. Exhibition catalogue: *Environments, Participation, Cultural Structures,* vol. 2.

Grey Art Gallery and Study Center, New York University. "Project Rebuild." August 11–27.

Akademie der Künste, West Berlin. "New York: Downtown Manhattan – SoHo." September 5–October 17.

Art Gallery of New South Wales, Sydney. "Biennale of Sydney: Recent International Forms in Art." November 13–December 19. Exhibition catalogue.

Susanne Hilberry Gallery, Birmingham, Michigan. "Opening Exhibition." December 10–January 31, 1977.

1977

Willard Gallery, New York. "Abstract Images." January 4–February 3.

Moore College of Art, Philadelphia. "Collection in Progress: 200 or So Selections from the Collection of Milton Brutten and Helen Herrick." January 14–February 11. Exhibition catalogue, text by Dianne Perry Vanderlip.

Galerie Nancy Gillespie–Elisabeth de Laage, Paris. "Dessins contemporains: Europeans et Americains." January 29–February 24.

Whitney Museum of American Art, New York. "1977 Biennial Exhibition: Contemporary American Art." February 15–April 3. Exhibition catalogue, Foreword by Tom Armstrong, Introduction by Barbara Haskell, Marcia Tucker, and Patterson Sims.

Institute of Contemporary Art, University of Pennsylvania, Philadelphia. "Improbable Furniture." March 10–April 10. Traveled to La Jolla Museum of Contemporary Art, California, May 20–July 6. Exhibition catalogue, texts by Suzanne Delehanty and Robert Pincus-Witten.

Visual Arts Museum, School of Visual Arts, New York. "A Question of Scale." April 4–22.

The Renaissance Society at the University of Chicago. "Ideas in Sculpture, 1965–

1977." May 1–June 11. Exhibition catalogue, text by Anne Rorimer.

Kassel, West Germany. "Documenta 6." June 24–October 2. Exhibition catalogue: *Malerei, Plastik, Performance,* vol. 1.

Paula Cooper Gallery, New York. "Group Show." September 10–October 12.

Museum of Contemporary Art, Chicago. "Ten Years: A View of a Decade." September 10–November 10. Exhibition catalogue, Introduction by Stephen Prokopoff, texts by Martin Friedman, Robert Pincus-Witten, and Peter Gay.

Walker Art Center, Minneapolis. "Scale and Environment: 10 Sculptors." October 2–November 27. Exhibition catalogue, Introduction by Martin Friedman, texts by Michael R. Klein, Laurence Shopmaker, Lisa Lyons, and Judith Hoos Fox.

Whitney Museum of American Art, Downtown Branch, New York. "Small Objects." November 3–December 7. Exhibition brochure.

The New Museum of Contemporary Art, New York. "Early Work by Five Contemporary Artists: Ron Gorchov, Elizabeth Murray, Dennis Oppenheim, Dorothea Rockburne, Joel Shapiro." November 11–December 30. Exhibition catalogue, Introduction by Marcia Tucker, interviews by Susan Logan, Allan Schwartzman, and Marcia Tucker.

1978

BlumHelman Gallery, New York. "Jenney, Nauman, Serra, Shapiro." February–March.

Protetch-McIntosh Gallery, Washington, D.C. "Minimal Image." March 1–30.

Vassar College Art Gallery, Poughkeepsie, New York. "Hunt, Jenney, Lane, Rothenberg, Shapiro." April 9–June 4. Exhibition catalogue, edited by Peter Morrin.

Whitney Museum of American Art, New York. "American Art: 1950 to the Present." May 3–September 10.

P.S. 1, Institute for Art and Urban Resources, Long Island City, New York. "Indoor/ Outdoor." May 16–21.

Thomas Segal Gallery, Boston. "Sculpture." June 3–July 7.

Hal Bromm Gallery, New York. "Sculpture." September 5–30.

Paula Cooper Gallery, New York. "Tenth Anniversary Show." September 9–October 4.

Stedelijk Museum, Amsterdam. "Made by Sculptors." September 14–November 5. Exhibition catalogue, texts by Rini Dippel and Geert van Beijeren.

Whitney Museum of American Art, Downtown Branch, New York. "Architectural Analogues." September 20–October 25. Exhibition brochure, text by Lisa Phillips.

Stamford Museum, Connecticut. "100 Drawings of the 1970s from the Collection of Richard Brown Baker." October 8–December 10. Exhibition catalogue.

Institute of Contemporary Art, University of Pennsylvania, Philadelphia. "Dwellings." October 20–November 25. Traveled to Neuberger Museum, State University of New York, Purchase. Exhibition catalogue, Acknowledgments by Suzanne Delahunty, text by Lucy R. Lippard.

The University of Michigan Museum of Art, Ann Arbor. "Works from the Collection of Dorothy and Herbert Vogel." November 11– January 1, 1979. Exhibition catalogue.

Paula Cooper Gallery, New York. "Group Exhibition." December 12–January 10, 1979.

1979

The Ackland Art Museum, University of North Carolina, Chapel Hill. "Drawings About Drawing: New Directions in the Medium, 1968–1978." January 28–March 11. Exhibition catalogue, text by Innis W. Shoemaker.

The Katonah Gallery, Katonah, New York. "Removed Realities: New Sculpture." January 28–March 4.

Adler Gallery, Los Angeles. "Drawings and Sculpture." February 3–March 17.

Whitney Museum of American Art, New York. "1979 Biennial Exhibition." February 6–April 8. Exhibition catalogue, Preface by Tom Armstrong, Foreword by John G. Hanhardt, Barbara Haskell, Richard Marshall, Mark Segal, and Patterson Sims.

UCSB Art Museum, University of California, Santa Barbara. "Sculptural Perspectives: An Exhibition of Small Sculpture of the 70s." February 14–March 25. Exhibition catalogue, text by Phyllis Plous.

University Gallery of Fine Art, Ohio State University, Columbus. "Acquisitions, 1976–78." March 27–April 29. Exhibition catalogue, Introduction by Betty Collings.

The Aldrich Museum of Contemporary Art, Ridgefield, Connecticut. "The Minimal Tradition." April 29–September 2. Exhibition catalogue, Preface by Richard E. Anderson, Introduction by Dorothy Mayhall.

The Museum of Modern Art, New York. "Contemporary Sculpture: Selections from the Collection of the Museum of Modern Art." May 18–August 7. Exhibition catalogue.

Whitney Museum of American Art, New York. "Decade in Review: Selections from the 70s." June 19–September 2.

Yarlow/Salzman Gallery, Toronto. "Five Sculptors: Sculpture, Prints, Drawings." July 7–August 3.

La Jolla Museum of Contemporary Art, California. "Selections from the Permanent Collection." July 18–August 19.

Texas Gallery, Houston. "From Allan to Zucker." August 17–September 28.

The Metropolitan Museum of Art, New York. "Recent Acquisitions, 1979." October 16–December 28.

Weatherspoon Art Gallery, University of North Carolina, Greensboro. "Art on Paper." November 11–December 16.

1980

Whitney Museum of American Art, Downtown Branch, New York. "Painting in Relief." January 30–March 5. Exhibition brochure, text by Lisa Phillips.

Bell Gallery, Brown University, Providence, Rhode Island. "Invitational." February 1–24.

Galerie Yvon Lambert, Paris. "Paula Cooper at Yvon Lambert." February 17–March 15.

Kulturhistorisches Museum, Bielefeld, West Germany. "Zeitgenössische Plastik." April 20–June 15. Exhibition catalogue, texts by Erick Franz, Annelie Pohlen, Ann Lauterbach, and Alain Kirili.

Institute of Contemporary Art, Boston. "Drawings/Structures." May 7–June 29. Exhibition catalogue, text by Stephen Prokopoff.

Hayward Gallery, London. "Pier + Ocean: Construction in the Art of the Seventies." May 8–June 22. Traveled to Rijksmuseum Kröller-Müller, Otterlo, July 13–September 8. Exhibition catalogue, Introduction by Gerhard von Gravenitz.

Werkenpark, Basel. "Skulptur im 20. Jahrhundert." May 10–September 14. Exhibition catalogue, text by Dr. Reinhold Hohl.

Landmark Gallery, New York. "Drawings 1980." May 19–June 11.

United States Pavilion, 39th Venice Biennale. "Drawings: The Pluralist Decade." June 1–September 30. Traveled to Institute of Contemporary Art, University of Pennsylvania, Philadelphia, October 4– November 9; Museum of Contemporary Art, Chicago, May 29–June 26, 1981. Exhibition catalogue, Introduction by Janet Kardon, texts by John Hallmark Neff, Rosalind Krauss, Richard Lorber, Edit deAk, John Perrault, Howard N. Fox, and Nancy Foote.

Westfälisches Landesmuseum für Kunst and Kulturgeschichte, Münster. "Reliefs, Formprobleme zwischen Malerei und Skulptur im 20. Jahrhundert." June 1–August 3. Traveled to Kunsthaus, Zurich, August 28–November 2. Exhibition catalogue.

Grey Art Gallery and Study Center, New York University. "Perceiving Modern Sculpture: Selections for the Sighted and Non-Sighted." July 8–August 22. Exhibition catalogue, text by Robert R. Littman.

Thomas Segal Gallery, Boston. "Paintings, Sculpture, Drawings, Prints and Photographs." September 13–October 8.

Los Angeles Institute of Contemporary Art. "Architectural Sculpture." September 30–November 21. Exhibition catalogue, Foreword by Robert L. Smith, Introduction by Debra Burchett, texts by Susan C. Larsen, Lucy R. Lippard, and Melinda Wortz.

Galerie Schellmann & Klüser, Munich. "Interior Sculpture." October–November.

1981

Max Hutchinson Gallery, New York. "Sculptors' Drawings and Maquettes." January 13–February 14.

Whitney Museum of American Art, New York. "1981 Biennial Exhibition." February 4–April 19. Exhibition catalogue, Foreword by Tom Armstrong, Preface by John G. Hanhardt, Barbara Haskell, Richard Marshall, and Patterson Sims.

Galerie Gillespie-Laage-Salomon, Paris. "Trois Dimensions: Sept Americains." March 28–June 2.

Visual Arts Museum, School of Visual Arts, New York. "Sculptural Density." March 30–April 24.

The Detroit Institute of Arts. "Constructivism and the Geometric Tradition: Selections from the McCrory Corporation Collection." April 22–June 21.

The Aldrich Museum of Contemporary Art, Ridgefield, Connecticut. "New Dimensions in Drawing." May 2–September 6.

Galerie m, Bochum, West Germany. "Bestandsaufrahme, Tätig Keitsberight einer Galerie." May 27–September 27.

Margo Leavin Gallery, Los Angeles. "Cast, Carved and Constructed: An Exhibition of American Sculpture." August 1–September 19.

Louisiana Museum of Moderne Kunst, Humlebaek, Denmark. "Amerikanische Zeichnungen der Siebziger Jahre." August 15–September 20. Traveled to Kunsthalle, Basel, October 4–November 18; Städtische Galerie im Lenbachhaus, Munich, February 16–April 11; Wilhelm-Hack-Museum, Ludwigshafen, West Germany, September–October 1982. Exhibition catalogue, texts by Richard Armstrong, Alfred Kren, Carter Ratcliff, and Peter Schjeldahl.

Galerie Mukai, Tokyo. "Drawing: Joel Shapiro, Jennifer Bartlett, Elizabeth Murray." August 24–September 22.

Akron Art Museum. "The Image in American Painting and Sculpture, 1950–1980." September 12–November 8. Exhibition catalogue, Foreword by Tom Armstrong, text by Paul Cummings.

Contemporary Arts Center, Cincinnati. "Alex Katz and Joel Shapiro." September 17–November 1.

Whitney Museum of American Art, New York. "Drawing Acquisitions, 1978–1981." September 17–November 15. Traveled to Whitney Museum of American Art–Fairfield County, Stamford, Connecticut, December 18–February 3, 1982. Exhibition catalogue, Foreword by Tom Armstrong, text by Paul Cummings.

Paula Cooper Gallery, New York. "Benefit Exhibition for The Kitchen." September 19–26.

P.S. 1, Institute for Art and Urban Resources, Long Island City, New York. "Figuratively Sculpting." October–December 13.

Sewall Art Gallery, Rice University, Houston. "Variants: Drawings by Contemporary Sculptors." November 2–December 12. Traveled to Art Museum of South Texas, Corpus Christi, December 31–January 28, 1982; The High Museum of Art, Atlanta, March 26–May 2, 1982. Exhibition catalogue, text by Esther de Vécsey.

Hayden Gallery, Massachusetts Institute of Technology, Cambridge. "Body Language: Figurative Aspects of Recent Art." November 21–December 24. Exhibition catalogue.

Albright-Knox Art Gallery, CEPA Gallery, and Hallwalls, Buffalo. "Figures: Forms and Expressions." November 21–January 3, 1982. Exhibition catalogue, texts by Carlotta Kotik, Susan Krane, Robert Cottington, Biff Henrich, William Currie, and G. Roger Denson.

1982

Milwaukee Art Museum. "American Prints: 1960–1980." February 5–March 21. Exhibition catalogue.

Whitney Museum of American Art, New York. "Selected Prints and Sculpture Acquired Since 1978." February 9–April 4.

Whitney Museum of American Art–Fairfield County, Stamford, Connecticut. "Surveying the Seventies: Selections from the Permanent Collection." February 12–March 31. Exhibition catalogue, text by Lisa Phillips.

USF Art Galleries, Tampa, and Jacksonville Art Museum. "Currents: A New Mannerism." Part I: February 12–March 23; Part II: May 14–June 17.

Hayden Gallery, Massachusetts Institute of Technology, Cambridge. "Great Big Drawings." April 3–May 2.

Whitney Museum of American Art, New York. "Abstract Drawings 1911–1981: Selections from the Permanent Collection." May 5–July 11. Exhibition brochure, text by Paul Cummings.

Yale University Art Gallery, New Haven, Connecticut. "Prints by Contemporary Sculptors." May 18–August 31. Exhibition catalogue.

The Art Institute of Chicago. "Seventy-fourth American Exhibition." June 12–August 1. Exhibition catalogue, Preface by A. James Speyer, text by Anne Rorimer.

Kassel, West Germany. "Documenta 7." June 19–September 29.

Contemporary Arts Center, Cincinnati. "Drawings from the Collection of Agnes Gund Saalfield." July 9–August 28.

Margo Leavin Gallery, Los Angeles. "Works in Wood." July 10–September 11.

San Francisco Museum of Modern Art. "Twenty American Artists: Sculpture 1982." July 22–September 19. Exhibition catalogue, Foreword by Henry T. Hopkins, Introduction by George W. Neubert.

Brainerd Art Gallery, State University College, Potsdam, New York. "Directions in Metal: Work Produced at The Johnson Atelier Technical Institution of Sculpture." September 1–22. Exhibition catalogue, text by Georgia Coopersmith.

Brooke Alexander Gallery, New York. "Selected Prints III." September 7–October 2. Exhibition catalogue.

Paula Cooper Gallery, New York. "Changing Group Exhibition." September 11–October 21.

The Aldrich Museum of Contemporary Art, Ridgefield, Connecticut. "Post-MINIMALism." September 19–December 19. Exhibition catalogue.

Whitney Museum of American Art at Philip Morris, New York. "Twentieth-Century Sculpture: Statements of Form." October 21–January 2, 1983. Exhibition catalogue.

Palacio de las Alhajas, Madrid. "Correspondencias: 5 Arquitectos, 5 Escultores." October–November. Traveled to Málaga and Bilbao, Spain. Exhibition catalogue, texts by Carmen Giménez and Juan Muñoz.

1983

Daniel Weinberg Gallery, Los Angeles and San Francisco. "Drawing Conclusions: A Survey of American Drawings, 1958–1983." January 29–February 26.

Whitney Museum of American Art–Fairfield County, Stamford, Connecticut. "Entering the Eighties: Selections from the Permanent Collection." February 11–April 13.

Galerie Aronowitsch, Stockholm. "Sol LeWitt and Joel Shapiro." Opened February 26.

School of Visual Arts, New York. "BIG American Figure Drawings." March 7–24.

SVC/Fine Arts Gallery, University of South Florida, Tampa. "Objects, Structures, Artifice: American Sculpture 1970–1982." April 9–May 30. Exhibition catalogue.

McIntosh/Drysdale Gallery, Houston. "Small Bronzes: A Survey." April 12–May 14.

The Renaissance Society at the University of Chicago. "The Sixth Day: A Survey of Recent Developments in Figurative Sculpture." May 8–June 15. Exhibition catalogue.

Moderna Museet, Stockholm. "Moderna Museet, 1958–1983" (twenty-fifth-anniversary exhibition). Opened May. Exhibition catalogue.

Whitney Museum of American Art, New York. "Minimalism to Expressionism: Painting and Sculpture Since 1965 from the Permanent Collection." June 2–December 14.

Bonnier Gallery, New York. "Chia, Gorchov, Judd, Mangold, Marden, Ryman, Shapiro, Stella, True, Twombly." June 4–July 2.

Margo Leavin Gallery, Los Angeles. "Black and White." June 25–August 13.

Thomas Segal Gallery, Boston. "Sculpture as Architecture." July 6–August 19.

Daniel Weinberg Gallery, Los Angeles. "Season's Greetings." September 10–October 8.

Des Moines Art Center. "Director's Choice." September 13–November 13. Exhibition catalogue, Introduction by James T. Demetrion.

Jersey City Museum, Jersey City, New Jersey. "Selected Drawings: An Exhibition of Works by Sixteen Contemporary Artists." September 14–October 15.

Tate Gallery, London. "New Art." September 14–October 23. Exhibition catalogue, text by Michael Compton.

The New Museum of Contemporary Art, New York. "Language, Drama, Source and Vision." September 23–November 9.

School of Art, Yale University, New Haven, Connecticut. "Student Choice Exhibition." October 3–14.

Delahunty Gallery, Dallas. "Contemporary Drawings." October 8–November 9.

Nassau County Museum of Fine Art, Roslyn Harbor, New York. "Sculpture: The Tradition in Steel." October 9–January 22, 1984. Exhibition catalogue, text by Janice Parente and Phyllis Stigliano.

Ateneum, Helsinki. "ARS '83: Helsinki." October 14–December 11. Exhibition catalogue.

The Brooklyn Museum, New York. "The American Artist as Printmaker: Twenty-third National Print Exhibition." October 28–January 22, 1984. Exhibition catalogue.

The Main Art Gallery, Visual Arts Center, California State University, Fullerton. "The House That Art Built." October 28–December 7. Exhibition catalogue, essays by Dextra Frankel, Jan Butterfield, and Michael H. Smith.

Galerie Maeght-Lelong, New York. "Sculpture on a Small Scale." November 1–December 9.

The Museum of Contemporary Art, Los Angeles. "The First Show: Painting and Sculpture from Eight Collections 1940–1980." Opened November 18. Exhibition catalogue.

Klein Gallery, Chicago. "Habitats." December.

1984

Paula Cooper Gallery and Leo Castelli Gallery, New York. "Artists Call – Against U.S. Intervention in Central America Benefit Exhibition." January 14–28.

Bernice Steinbaum Gallery, New York. "1 + 1 = 2." January 24–February 18. Traveled to Brentwood Gallery, St. Louis; University of California, Irvine; University of Northern Iowa Gallery of Art, Cedar Falls. Exhibition catalogue.

University Center Gallery, Bucknell University, Lewisburg, Pennsylvania. "Parasol and Simca: Two Presses/Two Processes." February 3–April 4. Traveled to Sordoni Art Gallery, Wilkes College, Wilkes-Barre, Pennsylvania. Exhibition catalogue, Introduction by Joseph Jacobs, text by Lizbeth Marano.

Hirshhorn Museum and Sculpture Garden, Smithsonian Institution, Washington, D.C. "Drawings 1974–1984." March 15–May 13. Exhibition catalogue, text by Frank Gettings.

The Renaissance Society at the University of Chicago. "The Meditative Surface." April 1–May 16. Exhibition catalogue.

Neuberger Museum, State University of New York, Purchase. "The Private Eye: Twentieth-Century Art from New York and Connecticut Collections." April 8–June 10.

Donald Young Gallery, Chicago. "American Sculpture." Opened April 28.

Williams College Museum of Art, Williamstown, Massachusetts, and Museum of Fine Arts, Boston. "The Modern Art of the Print: Selections from the Collection of Lois and Michael Torf." Williams, May 5–July 16; MFA, August 1–October 14. Exhibition catalogue, texts by Clifford S. Ackley, Thomas Krens, and Deborah Menaker.

The Museum of Modern Art, New York. "An International Survey of Recent Painting and Sculpture." May 17–August 19. Exhibition catalogue.

Fuller Goldeen Gallery, San Francisco. "50 Artists, 50 States." July 11–August 25.

Margo Leavin Gallery, Los Angeles. "American Sculpture." July 17–September 15.

The Parrish Art Museum, Southampton, New York. "Forming." July 29–September 23. Exhibition catalogue, text by Klaus Kertess.

The Guinness Hop Store, Dublin. "ROSC '84." August 19–November 17.

Barbara Krakow Gallery, Boston. "Universal Limited Art Editions: Recent Publications." September 7–October 2. Exhibition brochure.

The Bruce Museum, Greenwich, Connecticut. "Sculpture: The Language of Scale." September 15–December 1. Exhibition catalogue.

Neuberger Museum, State University of New York, Purchase. "Hidden Desires: Six American Sculptors." September 30–December 23.

The Newark Museum. "American Bronze Sculpture: 1850 to the Present." October 18–February 3, 1985. Exhibition catalogue, text by Gary A. Reynolds.

Margo Leavin Gallery, Los Angeles. "Eccentric Image(s)." October 20–November 24.

Seattle Art Museum. "American Sculpture: Three Decades." November 15–January 27, 1985.

The Contemporary Art Gallery, Tokyo. "Eight Artists from Paula Cooper Gallery." December 7–31.

Cable Gallery, New York. "Sex." Opened December 8.

1985

The Hudson River Museum, Yonkers, New York. "A New Beginning: 1968–1978." February 3–May 5. Exhibition catalogue, Introduction by Ted Greenwald, text by Mary Delahoyd.

Emily Lowe Gallery, Hofstra University, Hempstead, New York. "The Art Heritage at Hofstra." February 3–March 3. Exhibition catalogue.

Marilyn Pearl Gallery, New York. "Between Abstraction and Reality." February 6–March 2.

Daniel Weinberg Gallery, Los Angeles. "Drawings." February 20–March 16.

Hayden Gallery, Massachusetts Institute of Technology, Cambridge. "Giacometti to Johns: The Albert and Vera List Family Collection." March 1–April 27.

Paula Cooper Gallery, New York. "Sculptors' Drawings." March 7–30.

Museum of Contemporary Art, Chicago. "Selections from the William J. Hokin Collection." April 20–June 26. Exhibition catalogue.

Paula Cooper Gallery, New York. "Sculpture." May 4–June 1.

Mary Boone Gallery, New York. "Brooklyn Academy of Music Benefit." June 1–29.

Whitney Museum of American Art–Fairfield County, Stamford, Connecticut. "Affiliations: Recent Sculpture and Its Antecedents." June 28–August 24. Exhibition catalogue. Text by Joshua Decter and David Lurie.

Museo Rufino Tamayo, Mexico City. "Imagenes en Cajas." July 18–September 8.

Contemporary Arts Center, Cincinnati. "Body and Soul: Aspects of Recent Figurative Sculpture." September 6–October 12. Exhibition catalogue, text by Sarah Rogers-Lafferty.

Fine Arts Gallery, California State University, Los Angeles. "Black and White Drawings from the David Nellis Collection." September 23–October 18.

The Museum of Modern Art, New York. "Twentieth Anniversary of the National Endowment for the Arts." September 23–October 29.

The Brooklyn Museum. "Contemporary American Prints Recent Acquisitions, Louis Comfort Tiffany Foundation Purchases." September 27–December 30. Exhibition brochure, text by Barry Walker.

The Bronx Museum of the Arts, New York. "Geometric Abstraction: A Decade of Selections, 1975–1986." October 3–December 28.

Janie C. Lee Gallery, Houston. "Charcoal Drawings, 1880–1985." October–November. Exhibition catalogue.

Daniel Weinberg Gallery, Los Angeles. "AIDS Benefit Exhibition: A Selection of Works on Paper." November 9–20.

Krannert Art Museum, University of Illinois, Urbana–Champaign. "Three Sculptors: John Duff, Joel Shapiro, Richard Tuttle." November 9–December 22. Exhibition catalogue, text by Kenneth Baker.

Edward Thorp Gallery, New York. "Stone." November 16–December 16.

The Art Museum, Princeton University, Princeton, New Jersey. "A Decade of Visual Arts at Princeton: Faculty, 1975–1985." November 17–January 12, 1986. Exhibition catalogue.

Sotheby's, New York. "A Benefit Auction for Gay Men's Health Crisis." November 18–20.

Sheldon Memorial Art Gallery, University of Nebraska, Lincoln. "Contemporary Bronze: Six in the Figurative Tradition." November 19–January 19, 1986. Traveled to Kansas City Art Institute, Kansas City, Missouri, February 13–March 20, 1986; Des Moines Art Center, Des Moines, Iowa, April 8–June 1, 1986. Exhibition catalogue, Introduction by George W. Neubert, artist biographies by Vivian Kiechel.

The Museum of Modern Art, New York. "Contemporary Works from the Collection of The Museum of Modern Art." November 21–April 1, 1986.

Solomon R. Guggenheim Museum, New York. "Transformations in Sculpture." November 22–February 16, 1986. Exhibition catalogue, text by Diane Waldman.

Paula Cooper Gallery, New York. "Changing Sculpture Exhibition." November 23–January 4, 1986.

The Museum of Modern Art, New York. "Big Drawings." November 25–March 4, 1986.

Barbara Toll Fine Arts, New York. "Drawings!" December 7–January 4, 1986.

Larry Gagosian Gallery, New York. "Sculpture." December 10–January 25, 1986.

Knight Gallery, Charlotte, North Carolina. "Drawings." December 20–February 7, 1986.

1986

Tony Shafrazi Gallery, New York. "Sculpture." January 11–February 8.

Fort Lauderdale Museum of Art, Florida. "American Renaissance: Painting and Sculpture Since 1940." January 12–March 30. Exhibition catalogue, edited with Introduction by Sam Hunter, texts by Malcolm R. Daniel, Harry F. Gaugh, Sam Hunter, Karen Koehler, Kim Levin, Robert C. Morgan, and Richard Sarnoff.

City Gallery, New York. "1986: A Celebration of the Arts Apprenticeship Program." January 29–March 15.

The Brooklyn Museum, New York. "Public and Private: American Prints Today – The Twenty-fifth National Print Exhibition." February 7–May 5. Traveled to Flint Institute of Arts, Flint, Michigan, July 28–September 7; Rhode Island School of Design, Providence, September 29–November 9; Museum of Art, Carnegie Institute, Pittsburgh, December 1–January 11, 1987; Walker Art Center, Minneapolis, February 1–March 22, 1987. Exhibition catalogue, text by Barry Walker.

Whitney Museum of American Art at Equitable Center, New York. "Figure as Subject: The Last Decade. Selections from the Permanent Collection of the Whitney Museum of American Art." February 13–June 4. Exhibition catalogue, text by Patterson Sims.

Susanne Hilberry Gallery, Birmingham, Michigan. "Sculpture." March 1–April 1.

The Corcoran Gallery of Art, Washington, D.C. "Spectrum: The Generic Figure." March 8–April 20. Exhibition catalogue.

Whitney Museum of American Art at Phillip Morris, New York. "Sculpture Court Installation." March–August.

The Arkansas Arts Center, Little Rock. "National Drawing Invitational." May 9–June 29. Exhibition catalogue, Introduction and essay by Townsend Wolfe.

Gemini G.E.L. and Margo Leavin Gallery, Los Angeles. "1986 Museum of Contemporary Art Benefit Auction." May 10–13.

Palacio de Velázquez, Madrid. "Between Geometry and Gesture: American Sculpture, 1965–1975." May 13–July 20. Exhibition catalogue, Introduction by Richard Armstrong and Richard Marshall, texts by Carmen Giménez, Richard Armstrong, Marga Paz, text on Joel Shapiro by James Collins.

Arnold Herstand & Company, New York. "American Sculpture: A Selection." June 4–July 31.

Galleria Bonomo, Bari, Italy. "Inaugurazione." Opened June 6.

The Museum of Contemporary Art, Los Angeles. "The Barry Lowen Collection." June 16–August 10. Exhibition catalogue, text by Christopher Knight.

Contemporary Sculpture Center, Tokyo. "New Trends, New Technique Advances in World Sculpture." June–October.

Frankfurter Kunstverein, Schirn Kunstalle Frankfurt. "Prospect '86." September 9–November 2. Exhibition catalogue, Introduction by Peter Weiermair, text on Joel Shapiro by Manfred Schneckenburger.

Hal Bromm, New York. "Non Objective." September 12–October 12.

Galerie Gabrielle Maubrie, Paris. "Dessins de sculptures." September 24–October 24.

Galerie Aronowitsch, Stockholm. "En Subjektiv Historia." Opened September 27.

Phoenix Art Museum. "Focus on the Image: Selections from the Rivendell Collection." October 5–February 7, 1987. Traveled to Museum of Art, Norman, Oklahoma, April 25–August 30, 1987; Munson-Williams-Proctor Institute Museum of Art, Utica, New York, September 27, 1987–March 20, 1988; University of South Florida Art Galleries, Tampa, April 17–September 10, 1988; Lakeview Museum of Art and Sciences, Lakeview, Illinois, October 1, 1988–January 2, 1989; University Art Museum, California State University, Long Beach, January 30–May 28, 1989; Laguna Gloria Art Museum, Austin, June 25, 1989–January 2, 1990. Exhibition catalogue, texts by Nina Felshin and Thomas McEvilley.

Janie C. Lee Gallery, Houston. "Twentieth Century Drawings and Sculptures." Opened October 9.

John Berggruen Gallery, San Francisco. "Sculpture and Works in Relief." October 15–November 15.

John Berggruen Gallery, San Francisco. "Works from the Paula Cooper Gallery." October 15–November 15. Exhibition catalogue.

Museum of Fine Arts, Boston. "'70s into '80s: Printmaking Now." October 22–February 8, 1987. Exhibition catalogue, text by Clifford S. Ackley.

The Wellesley College Museum, Wellesley, Massachusetts. "1976–1986: Ten Years of Collecting Contemporary Art – Selections from the Edward Downe, Jr., Collection." November 13–January 18, 1987. Exhibition catalogue, texts by Patterson Sims and Suzanne Stroh.

American Academy and Institute of Arts and Letters, New York. "Thirty-eighth Annual Academy-Institute Purchase Exhibition." November 17–December 14.

Marian Locks Gallery, Philadelphia. "The Purist Image." November. Exhibition catalogue, Foreword by Marian Locks and Lenore Malen, text by Robert Storr.

The Museum of Contemporary Art, Los Angeles. "Individuals: A Selected History of Contemporary Art 1945–1986." December 6–January 10, 1987. Exhibition catalogue.

Barbara Toll Fine Arts, New York. "Drawings: 60's–80's." December 6– January 10, 1987.

Brooke Alexander Gallery, New York. "Benefit for The Kitchen." December 10–23.

Paula Cooper Gallery, New York. "Group Exhibition." December 10–January 15, 1987.

1987

Daniel Weinberg Gallery, Los Angeles. "Changing Group Exhibition." January 17–February 14.

Gallery of Art, University of Missouri, Kansas City. "Cast in Bronze." January 25–February 22.

John Berggruen Gallery, San Francisco. "New Acquisitions." January 27–March 28.

Sylvia Cordish Fine Arts, Baltimore. "Drawings." March 5–28.

Wadsworth Atheneum, Hartford. "From the Collection of Sol LeWitt." March 12–May 24.

Galeria EMI–Valentim de Carvalho, Lisbon. "Artists from the Paula Cooper Gallery." March 20–May 24. Exhibition catalogue.

Dallas Museum of Art. "A Century of Modern Sculpture: The Patsy and Raymond

Nasher Collection." April 5–May 31. Traveled to National Gallery of Art, Washington, D.C., June 28–January 3, 1988. Exhibition catalogue, texts by Elizabeth Frank, Steven A. Nash, Nan Rosenthal, and Robert Rosenblum.

Paula Cooper Gallery, New York. "Art Against AIDS: A Benefit Exhibition." June 4–July 4. Exhibition catalogue, text by Robert Rosenblum.

Thomas Segal Gallery, Boston. "Drawing for Sculpture." June 10–September 10.

The Greenberg Gallery, St. Louis. June 20–August 1.

Paula Cooper Gallery, New York. "Changing Group Exhibition." Summer 1987.

Holly Solomon Gallery, New York. "Early Concepts of the Last Decade." September 10–26.

Carnegie-Mellon University Art Gallery, Pittsburgh. "Drawings from the Eighties." September 13–November 8.

James Goodman Gallery, New York. "Strong Statements in Black and White." October 6–31.

Marc Richards Gallery, Los Angeles. "Drawings." October 29–November 31.

Ushimado, Japan. "The Fourth Japan Ushimado International Art Festival." November 1–3. Exhibition catalogue.

Paula Cooper Gallery, New York. "Changing Group Exhibition." December 2–January 30, 1988.

Hirschl & Adler Gallery, New York. "Lead." December 3–January 16, 1988.

Lannan Museum, Lake Worth, Florida. "Abstract Expressions: Recent Sculpture." December 18–May 10, 1988. Exhibition catalogue, text by Bonnie Clearwater.

1988

John Berggruen Gallery, San Francisco. "Selected Sculpture." January 16–February 27.

Kent Fine Art, New York. "Artschwager, Shapiro, Byars." February 4–March 5.

Genovese Graphics, Boston. "Black in the Light." February 6–March 5.

Williams College Museum of Art, Williamstown, Massachusetts. "Big Little Sculpture." February 13–April 17. Traveled to Plymouth State College Art Gallery, Plymouth, New Hampshire, October 12–November 5; The New Britain Museum of American Art, New Britain, Connecticut, November 13–January 5, 1989; Johnson Gallery, Middlebury College, Middlebury, Vermont, January 15–February 26, 1989; St. Paul's School, Art Center in Hargate, Concord, New Hampshire, April 4–May 20, 1989. Exhibition catalogue, text by Phyllis Tuchman.

Lawrence Oliver Gallery, Philadelphia. "John Chamberlain, Donald Judd, Richard Serra, Joel Shapiro." March 10– April 9.

John C. Stoller & Co., Minneapolis. "Painting in Relief, Sculpture on the Wall." Opened March 11.

La Jolla Museum of Contemporary Art, California. "Selections from the Permanent Collection: Part II." Opened March 18.

Whitney Museum of American Art, New York. "Twentieth-Century American Art: Highlights from the Permanent Collection of the Whitney Museum of American Art." Traveled to Robert Hull Fleming Museum, University of Vermont, Burlington, March 25–May 22; Hunter Museum of Art, Chattanooga, Tennessee, June 12–August 7; Phoenix Art Museum, August 26–October 2. Exhibition catalogue, text by Patterson Sims.

Whitney Museum of American Art, New York. "Figure as Subject: The Revival of Figuration Since 1975 – Selections from the Permanent Collection of the Whitney Museum of American Art." Traveled to Erwin A. Ulrich Museum of Art, Wichita State University, Wichita, Kansas, April 6–June 12, 1988; The Arkansas Arts Center, Little Rock, June 24–August 21, 1988; Amarillo Art Center, Amarillo, Texas, September 10–October 22, 1988; Utah Museum of Fine Arts, University of Utah, Salt Lake City, November 13, 1988–January 15, 1989; Madison Art Center, Wisconsin, February 4–March 26, 1989. Exhibition catalogue, text by Patterson Sims.

Philadelphia Museum of Art. "New Art on Paper: The Hunt Manufacturing Co. Collection." April 16–July 3. Exhibition catalogue, texts by Ellen S. Jacobwitz and Ann Percy.

The Saatchi Collection, London. "Philip Guston, Joel Shapiro, Leon Golub, Sigmar Polke." April 29–September. Exhibition catalogue, text by Peter Schjeldahl.

Milwaukee Art Museum. "1988: The World of Art Today." May 6–August 28. Exhibition catalogue, text by Russell Bowman.

Brattleboro Museum and Art Center, Brattleboro, Vermont. "Embodiments." May 14–August 16. Exhibition catalogue.

Mayor Rowan Gallery, London. "Eleven Artists from Paula Cooper." May 20–June 22.

John Berggruen Gallery, San Francisco. "Selected Acquisitions." July 16–September 3.

Whitney Museum of American Art at Equitable Center, New York. "Sculpture Since the Sixties from the Permanent Collection of the Whitney Museum of American Art." August 18–August 9, 1989. Exhibition catalogue, Introduction by Susan Lubowsky, text by Patterson Sims and Susan Lubowsky.

John Davis Gallery, New York. "Unpainted Metal." September 6–October 1.

John Berggruen Gallery, San Francisco. "Works on Paper." September 8–October 8.

The Aldrich Museum of Contemporary Art, Ridgefield, Connecticut. "Innovations in Sculpture." September 24–December 31.

The Carnegie Museum of Art, Pittsburgh. "Carnegie International." November 5–January 22, 1989. Exhibition catalogue, essays by Thomas McEvilley, Lynne Cooke, Milena Kalinovska, text on Joel Shapiro by Kellie Jones.

Duke University Museum of Art, Durham, North Carolina. "SoHo at Duke." November 11–December 28.

Instituto de Estudios Norteamericanos, Barcelona. "Sightings: Drawing with Color." November 16–December 16. Traveled to Casa Revilla, Valladolid, Spain, December 27–January 20, 1989; Museo Barjola, Gijón, Spain, February 1–28, 1989; Museu Calouste Gulbenkian, Lisbon, March 6–April 7, 1989; Pratt Manhattan Gallery, New York, April 24–May 20, 1989; Rubelle and Norman Scuffler Gallery, Pratt Institute, Brooklyn, New York, June 12–July 7, 1989. Exhibition catalogue, text by Donald Kuspit.

Leo Castelli Gallery, New York, and Brooke Alexander Gallery, New York. "Twenty-fifth Anniversary Exhibition for the Benefit of the Foundation for Contemporary Performance Arts, Inc." December 8–30.

Museum of Contemporary Art, Chicago. "Three Decades: The Oliver-Hoffman Collection." December 17–February 5, 1989. Exhibition catalogue, texts by Camille Oliver-Hoffman, I. Michael Danoff, Phyllis Tuchman, Lynne Warren, and Bruce Guenther.

1989

Institut Néerlandais, Paris. "Amsterdam/Art: Regards – Dessins contemporains." January 19–March 5. Exhibition catalogue, text by Ad Petersen.

The Arkansas Arts Center, Little Rock. "Revelations: Drawing/America." January 19–March 26. Previously traveled to Umjetnička Galerija Bosne i Hercegovine, Sarajevo, Yugoslavia, June 7–28, 1988; Moderna Galerija, Ljubljana, Yugoslavia, July 5– August 5, 1988; Galerija Josip Bepo Benkovič, Herceg-Novi, Yugoslavia, August 11–25, 1988. Museo de Arte Contemporaneo, Seville, October 3–21, 1988; Washington Irving Center, Madrid, November 3–22, 1988; Festival International du Dessin Contemporain, Grand Palais, Paris, December 14–31, 1988. Exhibition catalogue, Introduction and text by Townsend Wolfe.

The John and Mable Ringling Museum of Art, Sarasota, Florida. "Contemporary Perspectives 1: Abstraction in Question." January 20–April 2. Traveled to Center for the Fine Arts, Miami, May 20–July 23. Exhibition catalogue, texts by Roberta Smith, Joan Simon, and Bruce W. Ferguson.

Kunsthalle, Recklinghausen, West Germany. "Niemandsland." January 29–March 5. Exhibition catalogue, text by Kornelia von Berswordt-Wallrabe.

Pratt Manhattan Gallery, New York. "Sightings: Drawing with Color." April 24–May 20. Exhibition catalogue, text by Donald Kuspit.

Marisa del Re Gallery, New York. "The Linear Image: American Master Works on Paper." April 25–May 27. Exhibition catalogue.

Whitney Museum of American Art, New York. "1989 Biennial Exhibition." April 27–July 9. Exhibition catalogue.

John C. Stoller & Co., Minneapolis. "Seven Sculptures by Seven Sculptors." May 5–July 9.

"Art Against AIDS San Francisco." May 18–June 18. Exhibition catalogue.

Fundació Joan Miró, Barcelona. "La Triennal de dibuix Joan Miró." June 15–September 10.

Yokohama Museum of Art, Japan. "Contemporary Art from New York: The Collection of the Chase Manhattan Bank." June 18–October 1. Exhibition catalogue.

Whitney Museum of American Art, New York. "Art in Place: Fifteen Years of Acquisitions." July 7–October 29. Exhibition catalogue, texts by Tom Armstrong and Susan C. Larsen.

Fondation Daniel Templon, Musée Temporaire, Fréjus, France. "Exposition inaugurale." July 11–September 10. Exhibition catalogue.

Daniel Weinberg Gallery, Los Angeles. "A Decade of American Drawing, 1980–1989." July 15–August 26.

John Berggruen Gallery, San Francisco. "Sculpture." July 19–September 2.

The Brooklyn Museum, New York. "Projects and Portfolios: The Twenty-fifth National Print Exhibition." October 6–December 31. Exhibition catalogue, text by Barry Walker.

John C. Stoller & Co., Minneapolis. "Sculptor's Drawings." Opened October 20.

Janie C. Lee Master Drawings, New York. "Master Drawings 1859–1989." October–November. Exhibition catalogue.

American Academy and Institute of Arts and Letters, New York. "Forty-first Annual Academy-Institute Purchase Exhibition." November 13–December 10.
Paula Cooper Gallery, New York. "Group Exhibition." December 2–23.

Jersey City Museum, Jersey City, New Jersey. "Contemporary Woodblock Prints." December 6–March 3, 1990. Exhibition catalogue, text by Susan Tallman.

BlumHelman Gallery, New York. "Drawing Portfolios." December 12–22.

Fabian Carlsson Gallery. "American Masters." December 15–February 6, 1990.

National Gallery of Art, Washington, D.C. "The 1980's: Prints from the Collection of Joshua P. Smith." December 17–April 8, 1990. Exhibition catalogue, interview with Joshua P. Smith by Ruth E. Fine.

1990

John Berggruen Gallery, San Francisco. "Recent Acquisitions." February 14–March 17.

Gagosian Gallery, New York. "Major Sculpture." February 17–March 17.

Galerie Ressle, Stockholm. "Minimalism." February 24–March 17.

Whitney Museum of American Art, New York. "The New Sculpture 1965–75: Between Geometry and Gesture." March 2–June 3. Exhibition catalogue, texts by Richard Armstrong, John G. Hanhardt, Robert Pincus-Witten et al.

Paula Cooper Gallery, New York. "Trisha Brown Company Benefit Art Sale." April 11–21.

The Contemporary Art Gallery, Tokyo. "Minimal Art." April 13–May 23.

Kunstnernes Hus, Oslo. "The Art of Drawing." May 5–June 1. Exhibition catalogue, text by Reidar M. Kraugerud.

The Art Institute of Chicago. "Affinities and Intuitions: The Gerald S. Elliot Collection of Contemporary Art." May 12–July 29.

Curt Marcus Gallery and Castelli Graphics, New York. "The Kitchen Art Benefit." May 31–June 6.

BlumHelman Gallery, New York. "Artists for Amnesty." June 6–16.

Paula Cooper Gallery, New York. "Group Exhibitions." June 7–15.

Daniel Weinberg Gallery, Santa Monica, California. "Sculpture." June 9–July 14.

Brooke Alexander Editions, New York. "Selected Publications 1969–1989." June 21–August 3.

John Berggruen Gallery, San Francisco. "Selected Paintings, Drawings and Sculpture." July 5–September 8.

John C. Stoller & Co., Minneapolis. "For Summer: Some Recent Acquisitions." July 6–September 8.

Galerie Thaddaeus Ropac, Salzburg. "Group Exhibition." July 27–August 31.

Nippon Convention Center, Tokyo. "Pharmakon '90." July 28–August 20. Exhibition catalogue, texts by Jan Avgikos, Achille Bonito Oliva and Motoaki Shinaohara.

Pace Prints, New York. "Group Exhibition." September 7–October 6.

Museum of Fine Arts, Boston. "The Unique Print: '70s into '90s." September 15–December 16.

Palace of Exhibitions, Budapest. "Eighth International Small Sculpture Triennial of Budapest." September 27–October 8. Exhibition catalogue.

Hood Museum of Art, Dartmouth College, Hanover, New Hampshire. "Minimalism and Post-Minimalism: Drawing Distinctions." October 27–December 16. Traveled to Parrish Art Museum, Southampton, New York, September 22–November 17, 1991. Exhibition catalogue, text by James Cuno.

Angles Gallery, Santa Monica, California. "Group Exhibition." November 2–26.

Gallery Yamaguchi, Osaka. "Minimal and . . ." November 5–22.

Asher/Faure, Los Angeles. "Home." November 17–December 22. Exhibition catalogue.

Paula Cooper Gallery, New York. "Act Up Auction for Action." November 27–30.

American Academy and Institute of Arts and Letters, New York. "Forty-second Annual Academy-Institute Purchase Exhibition." November.

1991

John C. Stroller & Co., Minneapolis. "Face and Figure/Figure and Face." January 10–February.

Margo Leavin Gallery, Los Angeles. "Twentieth-Century Collage." January 12–February 16. Traveled to Centro Cultural Arte Contemporáneo, Mexico City, June 13–August 13; Musée d'Art Contemporain, Nice, September 27–November 11.

BlumHelman Gallery, New York. "Masterworks." January 16–February 23.

Whitney Museum of American Art, New York. "The 1980s: A Selected View from the Permanent Collection." January 16–March 3.

The Museum of Contemporary Art, Los Angeles. "Recent Work/Recent Acquisitions." January 19–February 17.

Wexner Center for the Arts, Ohio State University, Columbus. "Selection from the Permanent Collection." January 26–February 24.

Asher/Faure, Los Angeles. "Not on Canvas." February 16–March 23.

John Berggruen Gallery, Los Angeles. "Large Scale Works on Paper." February 21–March 16. Exhibition catalogue.

FAE/Musée d'Art Contemporain, Pully, Switzerland. "Sélection." April 10–October 13. Exhibition catalogue, text by Charles A. Riley II.

The Gallery at Bristol-Myers Squibb, Princeton, New Jersey. "Watercolor Across the Ages." April 13–May 27.

The Platt Gallery, Los Angeles. "Works from Private Collections: Contemporary Figurative Sculpture." May 2–29.

Museum of Contemporary Art, San Diego. "On the Road: Selections from the Permanent Collection." June 8–August 4. Previously traveled to Duke University Museum of Art, Durham, North Carolina, September 7–November 4, 1990; J. B. Speed Art Museum, Louisville, Kentucky, December 4, 1990–January 27, 1991; Museum of Fine Arts, Springfield, Massachusetts, March 3–May 19, 1991; subsequently traveled to Memorial Art Gallery, University of Rochester, Rochester, New York, September 28–November 17, 1991; Utah Museum of Fine Arts, University of Utah, Salt Lake City, May 18–June 28, 1992; The Philbrook Museum of Art, Tulsa, Oklahoma, July 17–September 1,

1992. Exhibition catalogue, essay by Ronald J. Onorato.

Galerie Pierre Huber, Geneva. "Sol LeWitt, David Rabinowitch, Joel Shapiro, Tony Smith." June 14–July 27.

John Berggruen Gallery, San Francisco. "Small Format Works on Paper." June 26–August 3.

Courthouse Gallery, Lake George, New York. "Summer Studios." June 27–September 6. Exhibition catalogue, text by James Goss.

Pfizer Inc., New York. "Geometric Perspectives." June 27–September 27.

Fondation Daniel Templon, Musée Temporaire, Fréjus, France. "La Sculpture contemporaine après 1970." July 4–September 29. Exhibition catalogue, Introduction by Caroline Smulders, texts by Carter Ratcliffe, Pierre Cabanne, Daniel Dobbels, Siegfried Gohr, and Demetrio Paparoni.

American Fine Arts, New York. "Vito Acconci, Jeff Koons, Joel Shapiro." September 14–October 12.

The Museum of Contemporary Art at The Temporary Contemporary, Los Angeles. "Selections from the Permanent Collection, 1975–1991." September 14–December 15.

Betsy Senior Contemporary Prints, New York. "Antony Gormley, Joel Shapiro, Judith Shea." September 17–November 5.

American Academy and Institute of Arts and Letters, New York. "American Academy and Institute of Arts and Letters: Forty-third Annual Purchase Exhibition." November 11–December 8.

Galerie Gmurzynska, Cologne. "Vision von Raum: Kunst und Architektur von 1910 bis 1990." November 15–January 31, 1992. Exhibition catalogue.

Paula Cooper Gallery and Matthew Marks Gallery, New York. "Act-Up Benefit Exhibition." December 5–21.

Eliot Smith Contemporary, St. Louis. "Sam Fentress, Gary Passanise, Joel Shapiro." December 6–February 2, 1992.

Tony Shafrazi Gallery, New York. "A Passion for Art: Watercolors and Works on Paper." December 7–January 25, 1992.

1992

Museum of Art, Fort Lauderdale. "Stars in Florida." February 7–March 22. Exhibition catalogue, Introduction by Dr. Kenworth W. Moffett.

Rubin Spangle Gallery, New York. "Group Exhibition." February 15–March 14.

The Museum of Modern Art, New York. "Allegories of Modernism: Contemporary Drawing." February 16–May 5.

San Jose Museum of Art, San Jose, California. "Drawing Redux." March 22–June 21. Exhibition catalogue, text by Phyllis Tuchman.

The New Museum of Contemporary Art, New York. "XV Benefit." May 3.

Rhona Hoffman Gallery, Chicago. "Fifteenth Anniversary Exhibition." May 8–June 13.

BlumHelman Gallery, New York. "The Figure." June 3–July 25.

The Pace Gallery, New York. "Summer Group Exhibition." June 5–September 11.

Johnson Atelier, Mercerville, New Jersey. "Grounds for Sculpture." June 6–August 31.

Nieuwe Kerk, Amsterdam. "Century in Sculpture." Summer 1992.

Vivian Horan Fine Art, New York. "Pitched Black." November 5–December 19.

Weatherspoon Art Gallery, University of North Carolina, Greensboro. "Twenty-eighth Annual Exhibition of Art on Paper." November 24–January 6, 1993. Exhibition catalogue.

1993

The Pace Gallery, New York. "Sculpture and Color." January 15–February 6.

The Carnegie Museum of Art, Pittsburgh. "Pittsburgh Collects." February 20–April 25.

Weatherspoon Art Gallery, University of North Carolina, Greensboro. "In Search of Form: Drawings by Fifteen Sculptors." March 14–May 9.

Takashimaya, Tokyo. "Manhattan Breeze: Five Contemporary Artists." April 22–27. Traveled to Takashimaya, Osaka, April 29–May 4; Kyoto, May 13–18; Yokohama, June 10–15. Exhibition catalogue, text by Tadao Ogura.

The Newark Museum. "The Director's Anniversary, 1968–1993: A Legacy and a Mandate." April 28–September 5.

Le Domaine de Kerguéhennec, Centre d'Art, Locminé, France. "De la main à la tête: L'Objet théorique." May 1–September 19. Exhibition brochure.

Grounds for Sculpture, Hamilton, New Jersey. "Spring/Summer Exhibition." May 22–September 30.

Paula Cooper Gallery, New York. "Group Show." Summer 1993.

45th Venice Biennale, Peggy Guggenheim Collection, Venice. "Drawing the Line Against AIDS," exhibition in conjunction with "Art Against AIDS Venezia." June 8–13. Exhibition catalogue.

The Pace Gallery (142 Greene Street), New York. "Wall and Floor." July 6–September 10.

The Utsukushi-ga-hara Open-Air Museum, Nagano-ken, Japan. "Fujisankei Biennale." July 16–October 31.

IVAM Centre del Darme (sponsored by IVAM Centre Julio González, Valencia). "Postminimal Sculptures at the Collection of IVAM." September–December.

Whitney Museum of American Art, New York. "In a Classical Vein: Works from the Permanent Collection." October 21–April 3, 1994.

Paula Cooper Gallery, New York. "25 Years, Part I." October 23–November 27.

Margaret Lipworth Fine Art, Boca Raton, Florida. "Masters of American Print." November 4–December 1.

1994

The Pace Gallery, New York. "Sculptors' Maquettes." January 14–February 12.

Nina Freudenheim Gallery, Buffalo. "Sculpture." January 22–March 2.

Transamerica Pyramid Lobby, San Francisco. "The Figure in Sculpture." February 2–April 13.

Friesen Gallery, Seattle. "Twenty-six Artists: A Selection of Works from John Berggruen Gallery." February 8–March 20.

Whitney Museum of American Art, New York. "Ideas for Objects: Selected Sculptures and Drawings from the Permanent Collection." March 31–September 4.

Galleri Nord, Stockholm. "Grafik: Jonathan Borofsky, David Hockney, Howard Hodgkin, Joel Shapiro." April 29–May 21.

The InterArt Center, New York. "Gift." May 13–June 25.

The Aldrich Museum of Contemporary Art, Ridgefield, Connecticut. "Thirty Years: Art in the Present Tense – The Aldrich's Curatorial History, 1964–1994." May 15–September 17.

PaceWildenstein, New York. "White Works." July 8–September 9.

Academy of Art College, San Francisco. "Academy of Art College Sculpture Exhibition." August 4–21.

Daniel Weinberg Gallery, San Francisco. "Selected Works." September–October 1.

Newport Harbor Art Museum, Newport Beach, California. "The Essential Gesture." October 15–December 31. Exhibition catalogue, text by Bruce Guenther.

Anthony Slayter-Ralph, Santa Barbara. "Fine Lines." October 20–December 11.

Barbara Mathes Gallery, New York. "Sculpture: The Figure Transformed." October 26–December 30.

1995

The Museum of Modern Art, New York. "American Sculptors in the 1960s: Selected Drawings from the Collection." February 16–June 13.

The Denver Art Museum. "Options: Selections from the Modern and Contemporary Permanent Collection." February 23–June 18.

Neuberger Museum, State University of New York, Purchase. "Crossing State Lines: Twentieth-Century Art from Private Collections in Westchester and Fairfield Counties." March 26–June 18.

Lannan Foundation, Los Angeles. "Floored: Sculpture from the Lannan Foundation Collection." April 8–August 13.

PaceWildenstein (142 Greene Street), New York. "Group Show." Summer.

Paula Cooper Gallery, New York. "Cornered." June 9–July 28.

The Museum of Modern Art, New York. "Sculpture from the Collection." June 17–August 20.

PaceWildenstein, New York. "Summer 1995." June 28–August 31.

Aspen Art Museum, Aspen, Colorado. "Contemporary Drawing: Exploring the Territory." July 27–September 24. Exhibition catalogue, text by Mark Rosenthal.

Anne Reed Gallery, Ketchum, Indiana. "Group Show." August 1–31.

The Metropolitan Museum of Art, New York. "Sculptors' Drawings, 1945–90." August 22–January 7, 1996.

The Century Association, New York. "Drawings from the Collection of Agnes Gund." October 3–November 16.

The White House, Washington, D.C. "Twentieth-Century American Sculpture at The White House: Exhibition III." October 6–March 15, 1996. Curated by Alison de Lima Greene.

Fundação Cultural de Curitiba, Curitiba, Brazil. "XI Mostra da Gravura Cidade de Curitiba, Mostra America (Brazil)." October 23–December 23. Exhibition catalogue, text by Deborah Panek.

Tel Aviv Museum of Art. "A Passion for the New: New Art in Tel Aviv Collections." October 30–January 27, 1996. Exhibition catalogue, text by Nehama Guralnik.

Waddington Galleries, London. "Of the Human Form." Opened December 22.

1996

C. Grimaldis Gallery, Baltimore. "Drawings by Sculptors." January 4–27.

Barbara Mathes Gallery, New York. "The House Transformed." January–March 2.

Gagosian Gallery, New York. "The Human Body in Contemporary American Sculpture." February 1–March 2.

Museum of Contemporary Art, San Diego. "Continuity and Contradiction." March 10–August 31. Traveled to Center for the Fine Arts, Miami Beach, December 19–February 23, 1997.

National Gallery of Art, Washington, D.C. "The Robert and Jane Meyerhoff Collection." March 31–July 21. Exhibition catalogue.

National Museum of American Art, Smithsonian Institution, Washington, D.C. "Contemporary Printmaking in America: Collaborative Prints and Presses." May 10–August 4.

National Gallery, Alexandros Soutzos Museum, Athens. "Art at the End of the Twentieth Century: Selections from the Whitney Museum of American Art." June 10–September 30. Traveled as "Multiple Identity: American Art, 1975–1995, from the Whitney Museum of American Art" to Museu d'Art Contemporani, Barcelona, December 18–April 6, 1997; Kunstmuseum, Bonn, June–September 1997.

The Museum of Modern Art, New York. "Thinking Print: Books to Billboards, 1980–95." June 20–September 26. Exhibition catalogue, text by Deborah Wye.

Frith Street Gallery and Karsten Schubert Gallery, London. "From Figure to Object: A Century of Sculptors' Drawings." September 13–November 2. Exhibition catalogue, text by Richard Shone.

Richard Gray Gallery, Chicago. "Figuration." October 4–November 11.

Pace Prints, New York. "Golden Oldies and New Delights." October 4–19.

The White House, Washington, D.C. "Twentieth-Century American Sculpture at The White House: Exhibition V." October 8–April 1997. Curated by Earl A. Powell III.

Fine Arts Museums of San Francisco, California Palace of the Legion of Honor. "Masterworks of Modern Sculpture: The Nasher Collection." October–January 1997. Traveled as "A Century of Sculpture: The Nasher Collection" to Solomon R. Guggenheim Museum, New York, February–April 1997. Exhibition catalogue, Introduction by Carmen Giménez, interview with Raymond Nasher by Steven A. Nash, text by Michael Brenson.

Paula Cooper Gallery, New York. "Group Show." November 29–January 5, 1997.

1997

Barbara Mathes Gallery, New York. "Gallery Selections." January.

The Corcoran Gallery of Art, Washington, D.C. "Proof Positive, 1957–1987." February 15–June 30. Traveled to Armand Hammer Museum of Art and Cultural Center, UCLA, Los Angeles, October 27, 1997–January 4, 1998. Exhibition catalogue.

A/D, New York. "Wood Not Wood/Work Not Work." March 22–May 3.

The Queens Museum of Art, New York. "Queens Artists: Highlights of the Twentieth Century." March 26–July 6.

Joseph Helman Gallery, New York. "Allegory." May 6–June 21. Exhibition catalogue, texts by Frederic Tuten and Diane Waldman.

Margaret Woodson Fisher Sculpture Gallery, Leigh Yawkey Woodson Art Museum, Wasau, Wisconsin. "Contemporary Sculpture: The Figurative Tradition." June–May 1998.

Addison Gallery of American Art, Phillips Academy, Andover, Massachusetts. "The Serial Attitude." September 20–January 4, 1998.

Galerie Jamileh Weber, Zurich. "Masters of Contemporary Sculpture." October 14–November 13.

Public Collections

The Ackland Art Museum, University of North Carolina, Chapel Hill

Addison Gallery of American Art, Phillips Academy, Andover, Massachusetts

Albright-Knox Art Gallery, Buffalo

Art Gallery of Ontario, Toronto

The Art Institute of Chicago

Art Museum of South Texas, Corpus Christi

Australian National Gallery, Canberra

The Baltimore Museum of Art

British Museum, London

Eli Broad Foundation, Los Angeles

The Brooklyn Museum of Art, New York

Cincinnati Art Museum

The Cleveland Museum of Art

Colby College Museum of Art, Waterville, Maine

The Corcoran Gallery of Art, Washington, D.C.

Douglas S. Cramer Foundation, Los Angeles

Dallas Museum of Art

The Denver Art Museum

Des Moines Art Center

The Detroit Institute of Arts

Fine Arts Museums of San Francisco

Fogg Art Museum, Harvard University, Cambridge, Massachusetts

Grand Rapids Art Museum

Hakone Open-Air Museum, Hakone-machi, Japan

The High Museum of Art, Atlanta

Hirshhorn Museum and Sculpture Garden, Smithsonian Institution, Washington, D.C.

Hood Museum of Art, Dartmouth College, Hanover, New Hampshire

Instituto Valenciano de Arte Moderno, Valencia

Israel Museum, Jerusalem

IVAM Centre Julio González, Valencia

Kawamura Memorial Museum of Art, Chiba, Japan

Kunsthaus, Zurich

Lannan Foundation, Los Angeles

Los Angeles County Museum of Art

Louisiana Museum for Moderne Kunst, Humlebaek, Denmark

The Menil Collection, Houston

The Metropolitan Museum of Art, New York

Milwaukee Art Museum

Modern Art Museum of Fort Worth

Moderna Museet, Stockholm

Musée National d'Art Moderne, Centre Georges Pompidou, Paris

Museum of Contemporary Art, Chicago

The Museum of Contemporary Art, Los Angeles

Museum of Contemporary Art, San Diego

Museum of Fine Arts, Boston

The Museum of Fine Arts, Houston

The Museum of Modern Art, New York

Museum Overholland, Amsterdam

National Gallery of Art, Washington, D.C.

The Newark Museum

North Carolina Museum of Art, Raleigh

The Parrish Art Museum, Southampton, New York

Philadelphia Museum of Art

The Picker Art Gallery, Colgate University, Hamilton, New York

The John and Mable Ringling Museum of Art, Sarasota, Florida

Rose Art Museum, Brandeis University, Waltham, Massachusetts

The Saint Louis Art Museum

Sheldon Memorial Art Gallery and Sculpture Garden, University of Nebraska, Lincoln

Stedelijk Museum, Amsterdam

Tate Gallery, London

Tel Aviv Museum of Art

The Toledo Museum of Art, Ohio

United States Holocaust Memorial Museum, Washington, D.C.

University of Massachusetts, Amherst

Walker Art Center, Minneapolis

Weatherspoon Art Gallery, University of North Carolina at Greensboro

Wexner Center for the Arts, Ohio State University, Columbus

Whitney Museum of American Art, New York

Commissions and Publicly Sited Works

1983–84

Cigna Corporation, Philadelphia. Architect: Kohn, Pederson, & Fox

1985–86

Louisiana Museum for Moderne Kunst, Humlebaek, Denmark

1988

Fukuoka Sogo Bank, Fukuoka, Japan. Architect: Arata Isozaki

1988–89

Creative Artists Agency, Los Angeles. Architect: I. M. Pei & Partners

Kawamura Memorial Museum of Art, Chiba, Japan. Architect: I. Ebihara

1988–90

General Services Administration, Los Angeles. Architect: Ellerbe Becket

1989–90

Hood Museum of Art, Dartmouth College, Hanover, New Hampshire. Architect: Centerbrook, Charles Moore

1991–93

United States Holocaust Memorial Museum, Washington, D.C. Architect: James Ingo Freed; Pei, Cobb, Freed & Partners

1994

Tishman Speyer Berlin GmbH & Co., Berlin, Germany. Architect: Professor O. M. Ungers

1994–95

Sony Plaza, New York. Architect: Philip Johnson; Gwathmey Siegel & Associates Architects

Friedrichstadt-Passagen, Berlin, Germany. Architect: O. M. Ungers

1994–96

Kansas City International Airport, Kansas City, Missouri

Bibliography

Compiled by Pamela Franks

Group-exhibition catalogues are cited within the exhibition listings.

MONOGRAPHS AND SOLO-EXHIBITION CATALOGUES

Joel Shapiro. Text by Rosalind Krauss. Chicago: Museum of Contemporary Art, 1976.

Joel Shapiro. Text by Linda Cathcart. Buffalo: Albright-Knox Art Gallery, 1977.

Joel Shapiro: Lithographs, 1979–1980. New York: Brooke Alexander, Inc., and Paula Cooper Gallery, 1980.

Joel Shapiro: Sculpture and Drawing. Text by Roberta Smith. London: Whitechapel Art Gallery, 1980.

Joel Shapiro. Text by Stephanie Rachum. Jerusalem: Israel Museum, 1981.

Joel Shapiro. Text by William Jordy. Providence, R.I.: Bell Gallery, Brown University, 1981.

Joel Shapiro: Sculpture. Text by Toshiaki Minamura. Tokyo: Galerie Mukai, 1981.

Joel Shapiro. Text by Richard Marshall and Roberta Smith. New York: Whitney Museum of American Art, 1982.

Joel Shapiro. Text by Marja Bloem and Karel Schampers. Amsterdam: Stedelijk Museum, 1985.

Joel Shapiro: Sculptures and Drawings, 1981–85. Text by Mark Ormond. Sarasota, Fla.: The John and Mable Ringling Museum of Art, 1986.

Joel Shapiro: Painted Wood (brochure). Text by Ned Rifkin. Washington, D.C.: Hirshhorn Museum and Sculpture Garden, Smithsonian Institution, 1987.

Joel Shapiro. Text by Lynne Cooke. Tokyo: Galerie Mukai, 1988.

Joel Shapiro. Text by Lynne Cooke. London: Waddington Galleries, 1989.

Joel Shapiro. Text by Nancy Princenthal and Rosalind Krauss. Humlebaek, Denmark: Louisiana Museum for Moderne Kunst; Valencia: IVAM Centre Julio González, 1990.

Joel Shapiro: Skulptur & Grafik, 1985–1990. Text by Staffan Schmidt. Varberg, Sweden: Museet i Varberg, 1990.

Joel Shapiro: Tracing the Figure. Text by Donald Kuspit, interview by Deborah Leveton. Des Moines: Des Moines Art Center, 1990.

Joel Shapiro. Text by Hanna Hummeltenberg. Munich: WB Verlag, Künstler Kritisches Lexikon der Gegenwartskunst, 1991.

Joel Shapiro: Sculptures – Wood, Bronze. Tokyo: Galerie Mukai, 1991.

Joel Shapiro: Selected Drawings, 1968–1990. Text by Mark Ormond and Paul Cummings. Miami: Center for the Fine Arts, 1991.

Joel Shapiro: Sculpture and Drawings. Text by Peter Schjeldahl. New York: The Pace Gallery, 1993.

Joel Shapiro: Drawing and Sculpture (brochure). Text by Choi Insu. Seoul: Gallery Seomi, 1994.

Joel Shapiro: Outdoors. Text by Deborah Emont Scott and Peter Boswell. Minneapolis: Walker Art Center; Kansas City, Mo.: Nelson-Atkins Museum of Art, 1995.

Joel Shapiro: Painted Wood Sculpture and Drawings. Interview by Ellen Phelan. New York: The Pace Gallery, 1995.

Geometric Order of Energy: Joel Shapiro. Text by Sung Hee Kim. Seoul: Gallery Seomi, 1996.

Joel Shapiro: Sculpture and Drawings. Text by Michael Brenson. Los Angeles: PaceWildenstein, 1996.

Joel Shapiro: Skulpturen, 1993–1997. Text by Donald Kuspit. Munich: Haus der Kunst, 1997.

SELECTED ARTICLES AND REVIEWS

1969

Glueck, Grace. "Air, Hay and Money." *New York Times,* May 25, 1969.

Kramer, Hilton. "Art: Melting Ice, Hay, Dog Food, Etc." *New York Times,* May 24, 1969.

Schjeldahl, Peter. "To Experience Art as It Is Evolving." *New York Times,* December 28, 1969.

Wasserman, Emily. "Reviews." *Artforum,* 8 (September 1969), p. 57.

1970

Paris, Jeanne. "Hanging/Leaning." *Long Island Press,* February 8, 1970.

Pincus-Witten, Robert. "Reviews: New York." *Artforum,* 8 (May 1970), pp. 74–81.

Ratcliff, Carter. "New York Letter." *Art International,* 14 (May 1970), pp. 76–86.

———. "Reviews and Previews." *Art News,* 69 (May 1970), pp. 20–28.

1972

Borden, Lizzie. "Reviews: New York." *Artforum,* 10 (April 1972), pp. 81–89.

de Jong, Constance. "New York Miscellaneous." *Attitudes,* 4 (February 1972).

Ratcliff, Carter. "New York Letter." *Art International,* 16 (March 1972), pp. 28–36.

Wolmer, Denise. "In the Galleries." *Arts Magazine,* 46 (March 1972), pp. 57–59.

1973

Crimp, Douglas. "New York Letter." *Art International,* 17 (March 1973), pp. 40–42.

———. "New York Letter." *Art International,* 17 (Summer 1973), pp. 88–90.

———. "Reviews and Previews." *Art News,* 72 (Summer 1973), pp. 100–101.

Gilbert-Rolfe, Jeremy. "Joel Shapiro Works in Progress." *Artforum,* 12 (December 1973), pp. 73–74.

Smith, Roberta. "Reviews: Joel Shapiro." *Artforum,* 11 (June 1973), pp. 85–88.

1974

Collins, James. "Reviews." *Artforum,* 12 (May 1974), pp. 73–74.

Lubell, Ellen. "Arts Review: Joel Shapiro." *Arts Magazine,* 48 (April 1974), pp. 67–69.

1975

Béar, Liza. "Joel Shapiro Torquing: A Dialogue with Liza Béar." *Avalanche,* 11 (Summer 1975), pp. 15–19.

Kramer, Hilton. "Art: Joel Shapiro." *New York Times,* November 1, 1975.

Lubell, Ellen. "Arts Review: Joel Shapiro." *Arts Magazine,* 50 (December 1975), p. 20.

Morris, Robert. "Aligned with Nazca." *Artforum,* 14 (October 1975), pp. 26–39.

1976

Bruner, Louise. "Frogs, Frogs Everywhere in Chicago Contemporary Show." *The Blade* (Toledo, Ohio), October 3, 1976.

Floroni, Giosetta. "New York Strizza L'occhio a Morandi." *Tempo,* April 1976, p. 19.

Glueck, Grace. "Bringing Back the Biennale." *New York Times,* May 2, 1976.

Kramer, Hilton. "Our Venice Offering – More a Syllabus Than a Show." *New York Times,* May 2, 1976.

"Museum and Dealer's Catalogues." *The Print Collector's Newsletter,* 7 (November–December 1976), pp. 151–52.

"Prints and Photographs Published." *The Print Collector's Newsletter,* 6 (January–February 1976), pp. 160–62.

Ratcliff, Carter. "Notes on Small Sculpture." *Artforum,* 14 (April 1976), pp. 35–42.

Schwartz, Sanford. "Little Big Sculpture." *Art in America,* 64 (March–April 1976), pp. 53–55.

Seldis, Henry J., and William Wilson. "Art Walk." *Los Angeles Times,* April 16, 1976.

Siegel, Jeanne. "Abstraction and Representation Made Visible." *Arts Magazine,* 51 (November 1976), pp. 70–73.

Smith, Roberta. "Review: New York – Joel Shapiro." *Artforum,* 14 (February 1976), pp. 64–65.

1977

Bannon, Anthony. "Sculpture by Shapiro Demands Awareness." *Buffalo Evening News,* March 29, 1977.

Bruner, Louise. " 'Improbable Furniture' Exhibit Is Far Out – and Very Hilarious." *The Blade* (Toledo, Ohio), August 14, 1977.

Cheney, Helen. "Feature Interview: Joel Shapiro." *Detroit Artists Monthly,* 2 (May 1977), pp. 1, 3–4.

Clark, Susan. "Shapiro's 'Aggressive' Geometry Shapes Space into Solid Forms." *Buffalo Evening News,* March 25, 1977.

Colby, Joy Hakanson. "Three Exhibits Bring Breath of Fresh Air." *Detroit Sunday News,* April 24, 1977.

Glueck, Grace. "Art People." *New York Times,* March 4, 1977.

Hess, Thomas B. "Art: Ceremonies of Measurement." *New York,* 10 (March 21, 1977), pp. 60–62.

"Improbable Furniture." *Philadelphia Arts Exchange,* May–June 1977, p. 38.

Kramer, Hilton. "Art: Joel Shapiro." *New York Times,* December 2, 1977.

Lewis, Jo Ann. "Galleries." *Washington Post,* March 12, 1977.

Masheck, Joseph. "Cruciformality." *Artforum,* 15 (Summer 1977), pp. 56–63.

Miro, Marsha. "Two Radical Artists: A Londoner's Photos, Shapiro's Sculpture." *Detroit Free Press,* May 8, 1977.

Russell, John. "Art: The New Museum Where Small Is Beautiful." *New York Times,* November 11, 1977.

Shapiro, David. "A View of Kassel." *Artforum,* 16 (September 1977), p. 61.

Smith, Roberta. "The 1970s at the Whitney." *Art in America,* 65 (May–June 1977), pp. 91–93.

1978

Field, Marc. "On Joel Shapiro's Sculptures and Drawings." *Artforum,* 16 (Summer 1978), pp. 31–37.

Foster, Hal. "Review." *Artforum,* 16 (February 1978), pp. 67–68.

Henry, Gerrit. "New York Reviews: Joel Shapiro." *Art News,* 77 (February 1978), pp. 149–51.

Hess, Thomas B. "Where Have All the ISMS Gone?" *New York,* 11 (February 13, 1978), pp. 69–79.

Lipkin, Joan. "Art in Review." *Saint Louis Literary Supplement,* June 1978, p. 13.

Lubell, Ellen. "Reviews: Joel Shapiro." *Arts Magazine,* 52 (February 1978), pp. 35–36.

Pincus-Witten, Robert. "Strategies Worth Pondering: Bochner, Shapiro, Reise, LeWitt." *Arts Magazine,* 52 (April 1978), pp. 142–45.

Quigley, Michael A. "Challenging Our Standard Perspectives." *Daily Pennsylvanian* (Philadelphia), November 16, 1978.

Ratcliff, Carter. "Joel Shapiro's Drawings." *The Print Collector's Newsletter,* 9 (March–April 1978), pp. 1–4.

———. "New York Letter." *Art International,* 22 (January 1978), pp. 85–92.

1979

Blakeney, Rae. "The Significance of Small." *Artweek,* March 10, 1979, p. 5.

Coplans, John. "Joel Shapiro: An Interview." *Dialogue,* 1 (January–February 1979), pp. 7–9.

Kramer, Hilton. "Art: Joel Shapiro." *New York Times,* April 27, 1979.

Lecombre, Sylvain. "Joel Shapiro: Couper l'espace." *Art Press International,* July–August 1979, p. 41.

Lubell, Ellen. "Art: Joel Shapiro." *Soho Weekly News,* May 10, 1979, p. 46.

Russell, John. "Minimal Art in Ridgefield." *New York Times,* July 20, 1979.

Schjeldahl, Peter. "Reviews: New York – Joel Shapiro." *Artforum,* 17 (Summer 1979), pp. 63–65.

Stevens, Mark. "The Dizzy Decade." *Newsweek,* March 26, 1979, pp. 88–94.

"What's News, What's Coming." *Vogue,* August 1979, p. 30.

1980

Baker, Kenneth. "Sculpture from the Ground Up." *Boston Phoenix,* December 9, 1980.

Foster, Hal. "Reviews: New York." *Artforum,* 19 (November 1980), pp. 84–85.

Hess, Elizabeth. "Art: Figuratively Speaking." *The Village Voice,* December 10, 1980, p. 105.

Hicks, Bill. "Gallery Explorations." *The London Times* (Educational Supplement), February 2, 1980.

Isozaki, Arata. "Joel Shapiro at Galerie Mukai." *Yomiuri Shinbun* (Tokyo), May 8, 1980.

Januszczak, Waldemar. "Mario Merz, Joel Shapiro." *The Guardian* (London), February 19, 1980.

"Joel Shapiro." *Asahi Evening News* (Tokyo), April 25, 1980.

Larson, Kay. "Review." *New York,* 13 (December 8, 1980), p. 78.

Nakahara, Yusuke. "Small and Big Sculpture by Joel Shapiro: Interview with the Artist." *Bijutso Techo,* 32 (June 1980), pp. 180–201.

"Prints and Photographs Published: Joel Shapiro." *The Print Collector's Newsletter,* 11 (September–October 1980), pp. 132–33.

Russell, John. "Art: Joel Shapiro." *New York Times,* December 12, 1980.

———. "Art: The Zeitgeist Signals Just Downstairs on 73rd Street." *New York Times,* November 7, 1980.

Saunders, Wade. "Hot Metal." *Art in America,* 68 (Summer 1980), pp. 86–95.

Sozanski, Edward. "Shapiro's Sculpture Is Perceptual Experience." *Providence Sunday Journal,* November 30, 1980.

Vaizey, Marina. "Art." *The Times* (London), January 27, 1980.

Welch, Douglas. "Reviews: Joel Shapiro." *Arts Magazine,* 55 (November 1980), p. 35.

Wohlfert, Lee. "Art: Young Artists New

Yorkers Are Talking About." *Town and Country,* September 1980, pp. 199–207.

1981

Artner, Alan. "Large or Small, Shapiro Sculptures Scaled to Please." *Chicago Tribune,* November 29, 1981.

Carr, Carolyn Kinder. "Akron Art Museum: The Image in American Painting and Sculpture, 1950–1980." *Dialogue,* 4 (September–October 1981), pp. 36–37.

Crossley, Mimi. "In the Galleries: Reviews." *Houston Post,* November 27, 1981.

Foreman, B. J. "Awkward Art at Center's Opener." *Cincinnati Post,* September 21, 1981.

"Group Show at John Weber." *Art News,* 80 (September 1981), pp. 233–34.

Johnson, Patricia C. "The Image of the House Through the Artists' Eyes." *Houston Chronicle,* November 15, 1981.

"Katz/Shapiro Exhibitions Open Contemporary Arts Center's Season." *Cincinnati Enquirer,* September 23, 1981.

Payant, René. "Les Formes complexes de Joel Shapiro." *Art Press,* 46 (March 1981), p. 23.

Phillips, Deborah C. "Reviews: Joel Shapiro." *Arts Magazine,* 55 (January 1981), pp. 29–30.

Rickey, Carrie. "Curatorial Conceptions: The Whitney's Latest Sampler." *Artforum,* 19 (April 1981), pp. 52–57.

Ronnen, Meir. "Small Is Beautiful." *Jerusalem Post Magazine,* September 11, 1981.

Schall, Jan. "Visiting Artist: Joel Shapiro." *Southeast Art Papers,* March–April 1981, p. 17.

Smith, Roberta. "Biennial Blues." *Art in America,* 69 (April 1981), pp. 93, 95.

"The Seated Muse: Chairs by Artists." *Réalités,* March–April 1981, p. 98.

Stearns, Robert. "Joel Shapiro." *Dialogues,* September–October 1981, pp. 30–31.

1982

Baker, Kenneth. "The Saying and the Seeing." *Christian Science Monitor,* March 18, 1982.

———. "Drawing Conclusions." *Boston Phoenix,* April 20, 1982.

———. "Joel Shapiro." *Christian Science Monitor,* September 8, 1982.

Bonet, Juan Manuel. "Escultores y Arquitectos juntos en Madrid La Sencillez Creadora." *Tiempo,* November 15–22, 1982, p. 101.

Brenson, Michael. "Sculpture Takes On a Fresh Prominence." *New York Times,* September 12, 1982.

Caldwell, John. "Two Shows: Photos and Drawings." *New York Times,* January 31, 1982.

Coffin, Anne. "Corporate Collecting: State of the Art." *Downtown,* October 1982, pp. 1, 4.

"Drawings from the Collection of Agnes Gund Saalfield." *Dialogue,* July–August 1982, p. 29.

Gedo, Mary Matthews. "Art Institute of Chicago Exhibition." *Arts Magazine,* 57 (September 1982), p. 20.

Glueck, Grace. "Art After Two Years: 'Selected Prints III.' " *New York Times,* September 24, 1982.

Jordy, William H. "The Sculpture of Joel Shapiro." *The New Criterion,* 1 (December 1982), pp. 54–57.

Knight, Christopher. "Joel Shapiro's Work Tugs at Our Heartstrings." *Los Angeles Herald Examiner,* November 7, 1982.

Larson, Kay. "Ways with Wit." *New York,* 15 (November 15, 1982), p. 98.

Lawson, Thomas. "Too Good to Be True." *LAICA Journal,* Summer 1982, pp. 42–45.

Phillips, Deborah C. "Joel Shapiro." *Art News,* 81 (May 1982), pp. 162–63.

"Preview, 1982–83." *Art in America: Annual, 1982,* pp. 19–21.

Price, Aimée Brown. "The Collectors: Contemporary Focus." *Architectural Digest,* 39 (October 1982), pp. 116–23.

Russell, John. "Drawings by Joel Shapiro." *New York Times,* January 22, 1982.

———. "Sculpture: Joel Shapiro in Whitney Exhibition." *New York Times,* October 22, 1982.

Schjeldahl, Peter. "Clemente to Marden to Kiefer." *The Village Voice,* October 12, 1982, p. 83.

Sutinen, Paul. "Joel Shapiro at Portland Center for Visual Arts." *Williamette Week* (Portland, Ore.), April 28, 1982.

Taylor, Robert. "Great Big Drawings: Sometimes They Work." *Boston Globe,* April 18, 1982.

Tomkins, Calvin. "Looking for the Zeitgeist." *The New Yorker,* 58 (December 6, 1982), pp. 150–53.

Wolff, Theodore F. "Is Modernism Dead? No – But Maybe Too Ingrown." *Christian Science Monitor,* November 9, 1982.

"The World of Joel Shapiro." *Axis* (Japan), October 1982, pp. 64–67.

1983

Anderson, Alexandra. "The New Bronze Age." *Portfolio,* 5 (March–April 1983), pp. 79–83.

Armstrong, Richard. "Reviews." *Artforum,* 22 (October 1983), p. 77.

Artner, Alan G. "The Return of the Human Touch: Figurative Sculpture Is Really Back in Vogue." *Chicago Tribune,* May 15, 1983.

Clark, James. "Joel Shapiro: Art Gallery of Ontario." *Vanguard,* 12 (November 1983), p. 49.

Damsker, Matt. "Sculptor's Forms Question Nature of Sculpture." *Los Angeles Times,* December 9, 1983.

"The Galleries, La Cienega Area." *Los Angeles Times,* November 25, 1983.

Kidder, Gayle. "House Is Not a Home to Joel Shapiro." *San Diego Union,* December 2, 1983.

Klein, Michael. "New York Reviews." *Art News,* 82 (February 1983), p. 147.

Knight, Christopher. "Joel Shapiro Is a Master of 'Monumental Intimacy.' " *Los Angeles Herald Examiner,* December 11, 1983.

Kuspit, Donald. "Manifest Densities." *Art in America,* 71 (May 1983), pp. 148–52.

Kutner, Janet. "Explorations of Space: Shapiro's Sculptures Offer Eccentric Points of View." *Dallas Morning News,* March 14, 1983.

Levin, Kim. "Top Forms." *The Village Voice,* May 24, 1983, pp. 84–85.

Linker, Kate. "Reviews, New York." *Artforum,* 21 (January–February 1983), p. 79.

Lloyd, Robert. "Why So Gloomy, Gus?" *Los Angeles Herald Examiner,* November 25, 1983.

Lowe, Ron. "DMFA Stages Major Show of Joel Shapiro's Sculpture." *Texas Star Telegram* (Fort Worth), March 6, 1983.

Lugo, Mark-Elliot. "It's a Perfect Exhibit to Trip Up Lovers of Art." *San Diego Tribune,* December 16, 1983.

Marvel, Bill. "Minimal and More: Is That Little Thing Really a Work of Art?" *Dallas Times Herald,* April 3, 1983.

Moser, Charlotte. "Renaissance Show Surveys Ten Years of Using Human Forms in Sculpture." *Chicago Sun-Times*, May 29, 1983.

Muchnic, Suzanne. "Exhibiting a World of Difference." *Los Angeles Times,* December 20, 1983.

Ondrechen, Jana. "Shapiro's Size Is Small in Size, Big on Warmth." *La Jolla Light,* December 3, 1983.

Raynor, Vivien. "The Spirit of the '80s." *New York Times,* March 27, 1983.

———. "Art: Neo-Expressionists or Neo-Surrealists?" *New York Times,* May 13, 1983.

Rose, Barbara. "Americans: Two Shows Contrast Then . . . and Now." *Vogue,* 173 (August 1983), pp. 116, 120.

Russell, John. "Art: New New Museum." *New York Times,* October 7, 1983.

———. "Sculpture on a Small Scale." *New York Times,* November 11, 1983.

"Sculpture and Fiction." *Bomb,* 6 (1983), p. 38.

Shapiro, Michael. "Four Sculptors on Bronze Casting: Nancy Graves, Bryan Hunt, Joel Shapiro, Herk Van Tongeren." *Arts Magazine,* 58 (December 1983), pp. 111–17.

Tomkins, Calvin. "The Art World: Season's End." *The New Yorker,* July 18, 1983, pp. 80–83.

"Weekend Guide, Art: Adding to the Slate." *Los Angeles Times,* November 18, 1983.

1984

Baker, Kenneth. "Artist's Dialogue: The Art of Joel Shapiro." *Architectural Digest,* 41 (June 1984), pp. 170–77.

Berger, Maurice. "Joel Shapiro: War Games." *Re-Dact: An Anthology of Art Criticism,* 1 (1984), pp. 16–21.

Braff, Phyllis. "From the Studio." *East Hampton (N.Y.) Star,* August 2, 1984.

Brenson, Michael. "A Living Artists Show at the Modern Museum." *New York Times,* April 21, 1984.

Fukaya, Tetsu. "Neo y Chromosome." *Brutus,* 85 (April 1, 1984), pp. 132–133.

"A Gallery of Art from American Corporations." *Art and Auction,* 7 (October 1984), pp. 135–44.

Glueck, Grace. "Bronze in the Hands of American Sculptors." *New York Times,* December 23, 1984.

Gordon, Alastair. "Letters to the Editor." *New York Times Magazine,* August 19, 1984.

"Hidden Desires: Six American Sculptors." *Neuberger Museum Fall 1984 Calendar,* p. 1.

Knight, Christopher. "Cal State Long Beach Show Looks Sentimentally at Artists as Heroes." *Los Angeles Herald Examiner,* April 11, 1984.

McGill, Douglas. "Art People: SoHo Thefts – The Outcome." *New York Times,* November 23, 1984.

Murray, Mary. "Toledo Alive." *Dialogue,* September–October 1984, p. 22.

Pincus, Robert L. "A Transformer of Minimalism." *Los Angeles Times,* November 5, 1984.

Russell, John. "Street Life by Mark Tobey – And a Decade of Drawings." *New York Times,* April 1, 1984.

———. "Art: Just the Show for Summer in Hamptons." *New York Times,* August 3, 1984.

Shirey, David L. "Bronzes at Newark Museum." *New York Times,* November 4, 1984.

Smith, Roberta. "Exercises for the Figure." *The Village Voice,* November 20, 1984, pp. 107–8.

1985

Brenson, Michael. "Changing Sculpture Exhibition." *New York Times,* December 20, 1985.

Conrady, Helene. "Poesie aus Holz und Eisen." *Neue Rhein Zeitung* (Düsseldorf), November 13, 1985.

Cooke, Lynne. "Exhibition Reviews: Joel Shapiro, Sculptures and Drawings at Knoedler, London." *The Burlington Magazine,* 127 (September 1985), pp. 635–36.

"Douglas Cramer: One of the Most Powerful Producers in Hollywood Talks About His Collection of Contemporary Art." *Art and Antiques,* November 1985, pp. 46–47.

Friedrichs, Yvonne. "Balken im Raum." *Rheinisches Post,* November 13, 1985.

Gibson, Eric. "The Minimal and the Magical." *The New Criterion,* 3 (January 1985), pp. 42–44.

———. "Thinking About the Seventies." *The New Criterion,* May 1985, pp. 45–48.

Hayward, Brooke. "High Art in the Valley." *House and Garden,* 157 (November 1985), pp. 154–158, 262, 266, 269.

Hernandez, Celestino-Celso. "ARCO '85 de la Escultura." *Hartisimo,* March–May 1985, p. 24.

Maister, Helga. "Minimales und Magisches." *Westdeutsche Allegmeine Zeitung,* November 28, 1985.

Ratcliff, Carter. "The Collectors: Contemporary Cast." *Architectural Digest,* 42 (February 1985), pp. 118–25.

Roskam, Mathilde. "Emoties in compacte vormen." *Parool* (Amsterdam), September 9, 1985.

Russell, John. "Art Breathes Freely at M.I.T.'s New Center." *New York Times,* April 28, 1985.

Saunders, Wade. "Talking Objects: Interviews with Ten Younger Sculptors." *Art in America,* 73 (November 1985), pp. 110–37.

Schneckenburger, Manfred. "Process and Konstruktion." *NKIE,* 9 (1985), p. 29.

"Sculpture: Language of Scale Opening September 15 at Bruce Museum." *Greenwich Time,* September 4, 1985.

Sill, Gertrude Grace. "Sculpture: 'Language of Scale' at the Bruce." *Fairfield (Conn.) Citizen News,* October 16, 1985.

Simon, Joan. "Interview with Joel Shapiro." In *Gordon Matta-Clark.* Chicago: The Museum of Contemporary Art, 1985.

Sorkin, Michael. "A Light in the Forest." *House and Garden,* 157 (January 1985), pp. 87–101.

Stiemer, Flora. "Spelen met bewigingen." *Algemeen Dahblad* (Amsterdam), September 21, 1985.

Tuchman, Phyllis. "Bryan Hunt's Balancing Act." *Art News,* 84 (October 1985), pp. 65–73.

"Von Galerie zu Galerie: Skulpturen als Balance-Akte." *Düsseldorf Hefte,* 24 (Fall 1985), p. 14.

Wesseling, Janneke. "Shapiro's 'miniaturen' in monumentaliteit onovertroffen." *NRC Handelsblad* (Amsterdam), September 21, 1985.

Wolff, Theodore. "Sculpture, Old and New." *Christian Science Monitor,* February 11, 1985.

———. "Today's Landscape Painting – Large, Bold, Unsentimental." *Christian Science Monitor,* February 11, 1985.

Zimmer, William. "The Big and Little of Sculpture." *New York Times,* October 13, 1985.

1986

"Album: Joel Shapiro." *Arts Magazine,* 61 (November 1986), pp. 114–15.

Altabe, Joan. "Art in the Balance." *Sarasota (Fla.) Herald-Tribune,* October 26, 1986.

———. "Shapiro's Work Mirrors Man's Evolution." *Sarasota (Fla.) Herald-Tribune,* November 3, 1986.

Arnoux, Brigitta. "Kühne Formen im weiten Raum." *Badische Nueste Nachrichten* (Karlsruhe), February 4, 1986.

Auffermann, Verena. "Gegenwart ist Summe des Vergangenen." *Frankfurter Rundschau,* September 15, 1986.

Baker, Kenneth. "Newer Art in Small Doses." *San Francisco Chronicle,* March 21, 1986.

Braxmaier, Rainer. "Ein aussergwöhnlich vielseitiger Künstler lässt manchem Zweifel Raum." *Badisches Tagblatt* (Baden-Baden), February 3, 1986.

Brenson, Michael. "Art." *New York Times,* August 3, 1986.

———. "Joel Shapiro." *New York Times,* November 14, 1986.

———. "Sculpture Breaks the Mold of Minimalism." *New York Times,* November 23, 1986.

Cohen, Ronny. "A New Look at Big Drawing." *Drawing,* 8 (September–October 1986), pp. 52–57.

Cooke, Lynne. "Joel Shapiro at the Stedelijk Museum." *Artscribe,* June–July 1986, pp. 83–84.

———. "What Is Modern Sculpture?" *Artscribe,* November–December 1986, pp. 56–58.

Dagen, Philippe. "Joel Shapiro: Exercices de sculpture moderne" (interview). *Art Press,* 109 (December 1986), pp. 38–40.

———. "Joel Shapiro: Fantaisies géometriques." *Le Monde* (Paris), April 23, 1986.

———. "Joel Shapiro: Galerie Daniel Templon." *Art Press,* 104 (June 1986), p. 77.

Drohojowska, Hunter. "MOCA Exhibit a Tribute to Barry Lowen's 'Eye' for Art." *Los Angeles Herald Examiner,* July 6, 1986.

Gibson, Eric. "Two Sculptors." *The New Criterion,* 4 (January 1986), pp. 57–60.

Hejny, Mathias. "Ein Abgesang auf den wilden Kampfgeist." *Allgemeine Zeitung Mainz,* September 19, 1986.

"Joel Shapiro." *L'Autre Journal* (Paris), April 16, 1986.

"Joel Shapiro: Ohne Titel." *Lahrer Anzeiger* (Lahr), February 13, 1986.

La Palma, Marina. "A Cryptic Lyricism." *Artweek,* 17 (December 6, 1986), p. 1.

Larson, Kay. "The Shrinking Spiral." *New York,* 19 (January 13, 1986), p. 58.

———. "Body and Soul." *New York,* 19 (February 10, 1986), pp. 72–73.

Malone, Maggie. "A Museum of One's Own?" *Manhattan, Inc.,* April 1986, pp. 159–61.

McGill, Douglas C. "New Midtown Branch for the Whitney." *New York Times,* January 27, 1986.

———. "Art People," *New York Times,* October 31, 1986.

Merkel, Ursula. "Joel Shapiro." *Kunstforum,* 84 (June–August 1986), pp. 274–75.

Monteil, Annemarie. "Listiges Spiel mit dem Minimalen." *Basler Zeitung* (Basel), March 5, 1986.

Muller, Gerald. "Kultur-Nachrichten." *Ortsgespräch,* 49 (February 15–28, 1986), pp. 4–5.

Neubert, George. "Small Scale." *International Sculpture,* 5 (November–December 1986), pp. 9–13.

Richard, Paul. "Upbeat Creature Feature at the Corcoran." *Washington Post,* March 15, 1986.

Saunders, Wade. "At Critical Mass." *Art in America,* 74 (October 1986), pp. 152–55.

Schwartz, Sanford. "The Saatchi Collection, or A Generation Comes into Focus." *The New Criterion,* 4 (March 1986), pp. 22–37.

Sischy, Ingrid. "On Location: Joel Shapiro." *Artforum,* 25 (November 1986), pp. 4–5.

Sozanski, Edward J. "A Focus on Work of Six Minimalists." *Philadelphia Inquirer,* November 20, 1986.

Tuchman, Phyllis. "Shapiro: Redirecting Sculpture's Shapes." *Newsday* (New York), November 28, 1986.

———. "70s Imagery Tells How We Got to Where We Are Today." *Newsday* (New York), December 14, 1986.

University Art Museum Calendar (Berkeley), February 1986, p. 12.

Von Berswordt, Kornelia. "Joel Shapiro." *NKIE,* 12 (March–April 1986), p. 40. Reprinted in *Arte Factum,* 2 (February–March 1986), pp. 52–53.

Wilson, William. "A MOCA Show to Hold Your Breath By." *Los Angeles Times,* June 22, 1986.

Winter, Peter. "Der menschliche Winkel." *Frankfurter Allgemeine Zeitung* (Frankfurt), February 21, 1986.

Wurster, Reinhold. "Schräg gegen die schöne Ordnung." *Schwäbisches Tagblatt* (Tübingen), February 14, 1986.

1987

Baker, Kenneth. "Shapiro Has It Figured Out." *San Francisco Chronicle,* October 21, 1987.

Bass, Ruth. "Minimalism Made Human." *Art News,* 86 (March 1987), pp. 94–101.

Berman, Ann E. "Sculptors-in-Progress." *Town and Country,* 141 (September 1987), pp. 269–72.

Brenson, Michael. "Images That Express Human Emotions." *New York Times,* July 26, 1987.

Christon, Lawrence. "Art and the Alien Social Picture." *Los Angeles Times/ Calendar,* December 20, 1987.

Clothier, Peter. "Douglas Cramer: Passionate Perfectionist." *Art News,* 86 (Summer 1987), pp. 146–50.

Glueck, Grace. "The Fine Art of Collecting Collectors." *New York Times,* May 3, 1987.

Hedglon, Mary. "Tons of Art Roll into Storm King Show." *Times Herald Record* (Middletown, N.Y.), May 15, 1987.

Kratt, Mary. "Risk-Free Art?" *Charlotte (N.C.) Observer,* November 30, 1987.

Lewis, Jo Ann. "At the Hirshhorn, the Joys of the New." *Washington Post,* December 2, 1987.

Maschal, Richard. "Art for Coliseum: $400,000 Project." *Charlotte (N.C.) Observer,* August 28, 1987.

———. "The Man Behind 'Gumby': Shapiro Talks About His Work." *Charlotte (N.C.) Observer*, September 11, 1987.

———. "How Do You Make the Choice of Art a Democratic One?" *Charlotte (N.C.) Observer,* December 18, 1987.

Neisser, Judith. "A Magnificent Obsession: Gerald Elliot, a Compulsive Collector." *Art and Auction,* 10 (December 1987), pp. 108, 113.

"Ornament the Season." *Harper's Bazaar,* 120 (December 1987), pp. 98, 100, 185.
"Pressing On." *The Print Collector's Newsletter,* 18 (May–June 1987), p. 59.

Princenthal, Nancy. "Joel Shapiro at Paula Cooper." *Art in America,* 75 (February 1987), pp. 141–42.

Rubinstein, Meyer R., and Daniel Weiner. "Joel Shapiro." *Arts Magazine,* 61 (March 1987), p. 97.

Wolff, Millie. "Sculptures at Lannan Provoke Viewer's Intellect." *Palm Beach (Fla.) Daily News,* December 22, 1987.

1988

Bass, Ruth. "Joel Shapiro." *Art News,* 87 (Summer 1988), pp. 171–72.

Beaumont, Mary Rose. "Eleven Artists from Paula Cooper." *Arts Review,* 40 (June 3, 1988).

Bouisset, Maiten. "Constructions de Joel Shapiro." *Beaux Arts,* 59 (September 1988), p. 94.

Brenson, Michael. "Human Figures Enshrined by the Early Greeks." *New York Times,* February 14, 1988.

Dagen, Philippe. "Constructions, Reconstructions." *Le Monde* (Paris), September 14, 1988.

Dorment, Richard. "Looking Death in the Face." *Daily Telegraph* (London), May 5, 1988.

Feaver, William. "Monsters in Jeans." *The Observer* (London), May 8, 1988.

Greenberg, Jeanne. "Dialogue with Joel Shapiro." *Splash Magazine,* Winter 1988, pp. 12–15.

Johnson, Ken. "Joel Shapiro at Paula Cooper." *Art in America,* 76 (July 1988), p. 133.

Kent, Sarah. "Saatchi's Showcase." *Time Out* (London), May 8, 1988.

Kohen, Helen. "Emphasis Kept on Art at Lannan." *Miami Herald,* March 27, 1988.

Le Chevallier, Isabelle. "Quatre Artistes a la Saatchi." *Beaux Arts,* 59 (July–August 1988), p. 101.

Lee, David. "Violence Viewed on Canvas." *The Times* (London), April 29, 1988.
McClintic, Miranda. "Sculpture Today." *Art and Auction,* 10 (May 1988), pp. 162–63, 167.

Packer, William. "Figuratively Speaking." *The Financial Times* (London), May 10, 1988.

Raynor, Vivien. "Small Scale Sculpture on View in New Britain." *New York Times,* December 11, 1988.

Selinsky, Debbie. "Art History Major Gets Chance to Organize Duke Exhibition." *Durham Morning Herald,* November 5, 1988.

Silva, Arturo. "French Frames, American Grains." *Daily Yomiuri* (Tokyo), April 14, 1988.

Sozanski, Edward, J. "Works of Four Prominent Sculptors." *Philadelphia Inquirer,* March 17, 1988.

"Stepping Out." *Art and Antiques,* 10 (May 1988), pp. 35–36.

Thornton, Gene. "Art That Requires an Act of Faith." *Raleigh (N.C.) News and Observer,* December 4, 1988.

Wilson, Christopher. "Saatchi Good Show." *Sunday Telegraph Magazine* (London), May 1, 1988.

1989

Baker, Kenneth. "Reference to Breakdown: Joel Shapiro's Sculptures of the 80s." *Artforum,* 27 (February 1989), pp. 102–6.

Brenson, Michael. "The Whitney Today: Fashionable to a Fault." *New York Times,* January 1, 1989.

———. "A Sculptor Who Rejects Nothing." *New York Times,* May 21, 1989.

Burr, James. "Triumph and Tragedy." *Apollo,* n.s. 130 (October 1989), pp. 282–84.

Christy, George. "The Great Life." *Hollywood Reporter,* January 19, 1989.

Cullinan, Helen. "Sorting Through 'Untitled' Art." *Cleveland Plain Dealer,* January 12, 1989.

Gibson, Eric. "Donald Judd: The End of Sculpture." *The New Criterion,* 7 (April 1989), p. 55.

Glueck, Grace. "A 'Yellow Brick Road' Brightens a Museum." *New York Times,* November 12, 1989.

Goldberger, Paul. "Refined Modernism Makes a Splash in the Land of Glitz." *New York Times,* December 17, 1989.

Greenberg, Jeanne. "Dialogue with Joel Shapiro." *Splash Magazine,* Winter 1989, pp. 12–15.

Greenspan, Stuart. "Previews." *Art and Auction,* 12 (November 1989), p. 260.

Grimes, Nancy. "Whitney Biennial." *Tema Celeste,* 7 (July–September 1989), pp. 66–68.

Kachur, Lewis. "Sculpture's Unbounded Range." *Art International,* 8 (Autumn 1989), pp. 57–58.

Kastor, Elizabeth. "Three New Sculptures at NGA." *Washington Post,* November 23, 1989.

Kent, Sarah. "Joel Shapiro." *Time Out* (London), October 25, 1989.

Kimmelman, Michael. "Helms Bill, Whatever Its Outcome, Could Leave Mark on Arts Grants." *New York Times,* July 30, 1989.

Knight, Christopher. "Mortal Yearnings." *Los Angeles Herald Examiner,* January 27, 1989.

Kramer, Hilton. "The Whitney's '89 Biennial Exhibition: Bourse for Marketing Reputation." *New York Observer,* 3 (May 15, 1989), pp. 1, 13.

Larson, Kay. "The Children's Hour." *New York,* 22 (May 8, 1989), p. 95.

———. "The Whitney Biennial." *Galeries Magazine,* 8 (June–July 1989), p. 66.

Marcus, Liz. "Joel Shapiro." *Sculpture,* September–October 1989, pp. 83–84.

"Minimalist with a Human Touch." *The American* (London), September 22, 1989.

Morgan, Robert C. "Letter from Europe." *Arts,* 63 (January 1989), p. 110.

Princenthal, Nancy. "Against the Grain: Joel Shapiro's Prints." *The Print Collector's Newsletter,* 20 (September–October 1989), pp. 121–24.

Schjeldahl, Peter. "The Muses on Strike." *Seven Days* (New York), 2 (May 17, 1989), p. 67.

Sherman, Mary. "Excellent Exhibit Draws on Contemporary Artists." *Chicago Sun-Times,* June 9, 1989.

Smith, Roberta. "More Women and Unknowns in the Whitney Biennial." *New York Times,* April 28, 1989.

Tuchman, Phyllis. "Sculpture Parks: A New Collecting Trend Becomes an American Institution." *The Journal of Art,* 2 (September–October 1989), p. 23.

Yau, John. "Official Policy." *Arts,* 64 (September 1989), p. 54.

1990

Alton, Peder. "Skulptural Cirkus." *Dagens Nyheter* (Stockholm), September 14, 1990.

Anfam, David. "Evaluating a Radical Decade." *Art International,* 12 (Autumn 1990), pp. 94–95.

Ashton, Dore. "The New Sculpture." *Contemporanea,* 3 (Summer 1990), p. 106.

"Balancekunst." *Dagbladet* (Oslo), September 15, 1990.

Benezra, Neal. "Gerald S. Elliot." *Galeries Magazine,* June–July 1990, pp. 118–29.

Brenson, Michael. "The State of the City as Sculptors See It." *New York Times,* July 27, 1990.

———. "Joel Shapiro." *New York Times,* November 23, 1990.

Clothier, Peter. "Living with Art: Jay Chiat." *Art News,* 89 (May 1990), pp. 113–16.

Danto, Arthur C. "Postminimalist Sculpture." *The Nation,* 250 (May 14, 1990), pp. 680–84.

Degener, Patricia. "Subject Matter Confers Appeal upon Cool, Cerebral Works." *St. Louis Post-Dispatch,* June 17, 1990.

Dorsey, John. "Figures Without Features." *Baltimore Sun,* August 21, 1990.

———. "Sculptors' Drawings Complement Shapiro Show" and "Shapiro Shows Minimalism Isn't a Dead End." *Baltimore Sun,* August 19, 1990.

Gibson, Eric. "Sculptor Joel Shapiro: From Abstraction to Representation." *Washington Times,* August 29, 1990.

Giuliano, Mike. "BMA Exhibit Examines Sculptor's Human Allusions." *Baltimore Evening Sun,* August 23, 1990.

Gralnick, Herbert. "Energy Marks Sculptor Joel Shapiro's New Work on Exhibit." *St. Louis Jewish Light,* May 16, 1990.

Hall, James. "World Chronicle." *Art International,* 10 (Spring 1990), p. 68.

Hughes, Robert. "Sculpture of the Absurd." *Time,* 136 (October 1, 1990), pp. 100–102.

"Interview: Joel Shapiro Talks with Paul Cummings." *Drawing,* 12 (July–August 1990), pp. 31–35.

Jimenez, Pablo. "Joel Shapiro: psicologia del signo." *ABC de las artes,* November 29, 1990.

"Joel Shapiro: Tracing the Figure." *Wall Street Journal,* August 21, 1990.

Landecker, Heidi. "Garden Allegory." *Architecture,* 79 (December 1990), pp. 60–65.

Levinson, Joan. "Maximum from the Minimum." *Riverfront Times* (St. Louis), June 27–July 3, 1990, p. 44.

Nusbaum, Eliot. "Twenty-five Shapiro Works on View Here." *Des Moines Sunday Register,* November 25, 1990.

Obiol, Maria Jose. "Joel Shapiro expone sus esculturas se las emociones en Valencia." *El Pais* (Madrid), November 29, 1990.

Pohl, Eva. "Mennesket i bevaegelse." *Berlingske Tidende* (Copenhagen), October 11, 1990.

Princenthal, Nancy. "The New Sculpture, 1965–1975: Between Geometry and Gesture." *Sculpture,* 9 (July–August 1990), pp. 40–45.

"Prints and Photographs Published." *The Print Collector's Newsletter,* 21 (July–August 1990), p. 111.

Richard, Paul. "The Sculptor's Energetic Life Forms." *Washington Post,* August 25, 1990.

"Rumfang." *Politiken* (Copenhagen), October 5, 1990.

Russell, John. "Adding Up the Costs of Changes at the Top." *New York Times,* March 18, 1990.

Shortal, Helen. "Joel Shapiro's Bronze Ages." *City Paper* (Baltimore), August 31, 1990.

Smith, Roberta. "Sculpture at the Whitney: The Radical Years." *New York Times,* March 9, 1990.

Sozanski, Edward J. "Sculptor's Humanism Comes Through." *Philadelphia Enquirer,* September 2, 1990.

"Space Cases." *Elle,* 5 (November 1990), p. 230.

Steinbach, Alice. "Drawing Out the Giggles of Youth." *Baltimore Sun,* September 24, 1990.

"Una selection de obras de Joel Shapiro muestra en el IVAM el futuro de la escultura actual." *Diaro 16* (Madrid), November 29, 1990.

1991

Bonetti, David. "Ten Who Shaped Their World." *San Francisco Examiner,* March 20, 1991.

"Borofsky, Otterness and Shapiro Create Figures for the Los Angeles Federal Building." *GSA Arts,* Summer 1991, pp. 1, 3–4.

Bosetti, Petra. "Figuren in der Schwebe." *Art: Das Kunstmagazin,* April 1991, p. 4.

Braff, Phyllis. "Defining the Minimalist Directions from the Sixties to the Present." *New York Times,* November 10, 1991.

Brockman, Linda. "Tracing the Figure." *Palm Beach (Fla.) Jewish World,* April 12–18, 1991.

Clothier, Peter. "Living with Art: The Gershes Bringing Home the Bacon." *Art News,* 90 (December 1991), p. 59.

Cotter, Holland. "Joel Shapiro at Paula Cooper." *Art in America,* 79 (July 1991), p. 125.

Cummings, Mary. "The 'Art' of Collecting." *Southampton (N.Y.) Press,* September 26, 1991.

Cutajar, Mario. "An Acquiescent Dignity." *Artweek,* 22 (April 11, 1991), pp. 1, 16.

Decker, Andrew. "Best Bids: From Major to Minor." *New York,* 24 (February 4, 1991), p. 32.

Dobbels, Daniel. "Joel Shapiro au bord de la chute." *Libération,* July 29, 1991.

Greenstein, M. A. " 'My Awe and Wonder of That Moment Remained . . .' " *Artweek,* 22 (April 11, 1991), pp. 15, 20.

Faust, Gretchen. "Joel Shapiro." *Arts Magazine,* 65 (February 1991), p. 102.

"Hauser der Erinnerung und Ballet Mecanique." *Neue Zurcher Zeitung* (Zurich), April 8, 1991.

Hergott, Fabrice, and Jerome Saglio. "Du Nord à La Bretagne." *Galeries Magazine,* August–September 1991, pp. 80–85.

Jaunin, Françoise. "Parcours en Helvetie." *Galeries Magazine,* August–September 1991, pp. 64–67.

"Joel Shapiro choisit le Musée des Beaux-Arts de Calais." *Nord Littoral,* June 28, 1991.

Knight, Christopher. "MOCA's New Scupture a Fine Match of Work, Space." *Los Angeles Times,* February 20, 1991.

Kohen, Helen. "Shapiro's Layered Works Dominate Space at CFA." *Miami Herald,* April 21, 1991.

Perez, David. "Joel Shapiro." *Lapiz,* 75 (February 1991), p. 94.

Perl, Jed. "Mostly Minimal: Joel Shapiro." *Art and Antiques,* 8 (February 1991), p. 91.

Pincus, Robert L. "An Ambitious Survey of Contemporary Sculpture." *San Diego Union,* April 7, 1991.

Rolet, Fernand. "Choregraphies immobiles de Joel Shapiro." *La Voix du Nord,* August 2, 1991.

Russo, Alex. "Mystery of Minimalism." *Hampton Chronicle-News,* October 31, 1991.

———. "Two Shows at Parrish." *Southampton (N.Y.) Press,* November 14, 1991.

Schneider, Greg. "Joel Shapiro." *Artweek,* 22 (May 16, 1991), p. 13.

Seager, Susan. "Judges Flay, Praise Federal Building's Art." *Los Angeles Daily Journal,* November 22, 1991.

Shinn, Jerry. "Son of Gumby." *Charlotte (N.C.) Observer,* February 25, 1991.

Slivka, Rose C.S. "From the Studio." *East Hampton (N.Y.) Star,* October 31, 1991.

Smulders, Caroline. "Joel Shapiro, L'Espace Métamorphique." *Art Press,* 159 (June 1991), pp. 23–27.

1992

"Art for Art's Sake." *The Print Collector's Newsletter,* 23 (March–April 1992), p. 18.

Baker, Kenneth. "Big-City Art Doesn't Know Way in San Jose." *San Jose Chronicle,* May 24, 1992.

Bigham, Elizabeth French. "Joel Shapiro." *Tema Celeste,* 36 (Summer 1992), pp. 82–83.

Bonetti, David. "Drawing Show Draws on Mainstream Successes." *San Francisco Examiner,* June 12, 1992.

Burkhart, Dorothy. "A Fine Line: Drawing from the 80s." *San Jose Mercury News,* March 1992.

Dance Ink, 3 (Fall 1992), p. 29 (reproduction of drawing by Shapiro: Untitled, 1988).

Decker, Andrew. "Collector's Lawsuit Reveals Absence of Secondary Market." *Atelier,* July 1992, p. 60.

"Drawing Redux." *San Jose Mercury News,* March 20, 1992.

"Drawings on Exhibition." *Drawing,* 13 (March–April 1992), p. 132.

Gardner, Paul. "Waking Up and Warming Up." *Art News,* 91 (October 1992), pp. 114–17.

Gimelson, Deborah. "Newhouse's Koons from Gagosian: $1 Million, Maybe." *New York Observer,* March 16, 1992.

Kertess, Klaus. "Cast in Bronze." *Elle Decor,* 22 (April–May 1992), pp. 17–21.

Kimmelman, Michael. "Just What Is a Drawing? Definitions, Definitions," *New York Times,* February 21, 1992.

"1991 in Review: Public Art." *Art in America Annual, 1992* (August 1992), pp. 34–35.

Ramljak, Suzanne. "Collectors: Joseph Helman." *Sculpture,* 11 (November–December 1992), pp. 24–25.

Raynor, Vivien. "Outdoor Home for Sculpture." *New York Times* (New Jersey edition), July 12, 1992.

Saltz, Jerry, and Robert Gober. "Paula Cooper." *Galeries Magazine,* June–July 1992, pp. 99–103, 126–27.

Sherman, Ann Elliott. "Paper Views." *Metro,* March 26–April 1, 1992, p. 33.

Sozanski, Edward J. "A Sculpture Park Is Taking Root at Johnson Atelier near Trenton." *Philadelphia Inquirer,* July 9, 1992.

Vogel, Carol. "The Art Market." *New York Times,* January 10, 1992.

1993

"Art and Politics . . . Again." *Mirabella,* April 1993, pp. 80–82.

"Art Slated for Holocaust Memorial." *Art in America,* 81 (February 1993), p. 29.

Campbell, Robert. "Wellesley's Work of Art: College's New Museum Is a Triumph of Design Inside a Boring Container." *Boston Sunday Globe,* October 10, 1993.

Cotter, Holland. "Art in Review: Joel Shapiro." *New York Times,* May 21, 1993.

"Cronica de Exposiciones." *ARTE: Revista de las artes visuales,* 7 (November–December 1993), pp. 53–54.

"El IVAM Centre del Carme inaugura con dos muestras." *Diario 16* (Madrid), October 1, 1993, p. 47.

Forgey, Benjamin. "A Powerful Testament." *Art News,* 92 (April 1993), pp. 40–42.

Gill, Brendan. "The Holocaust Museum: An Unquiet Sanctuary." *The New Yorker,* 59 (April 19, 1993).

Glueck, Grace. "Witnesses to the Making of a Most Glamorous Borough." *New York Observer,* May 31, 1993.

"Goings On about Town: Art." *The New Yorker,* May 31, 1993, p. 17.

Iranzo, Amador. "Laurens Mol y la escultura postminimal abren temporada en el Centre del Carmen." *El Mercantil Valenciano* (Valencia), October 1, 1993.

Jarque, Vicente. "Más allá del minimalismo." *El Guia,* September 1993, pp. 54–55.

Johnson, Ken. "Art and Memory." *Art in America,* 81 (November 1993), pp. 90–99.

Kimmelman, Michael. "Making Art of the Holocaust: New Museum, New Works." *New York Times,* April 23, 1993.

Kuspit, Donald. "Joel Shapiro, Pace Gallery." *Artforum,* 32 (November 1993), p. 103.

Larson, Kay. "Where Does It End?" *New York,* 26 (May 10, 1993), pp. 66–68.

"Las esculturas post-minimal del IVAM." *Diario 16* (Madrid), September 26, 1993, p. 45.

MacAdam, Barbara. "Joel Shapiro, Pace." *Art News,* 92 (October 1993), p. 160.

Maschal, Richard. "Our Public Image." *Charlotte (N.C.) Observer,* June 19, 1993.

Padon, Thomas. "Reviews." *Sculpture,* 12 (November–December 1993), p. 54.

Pinchbeck, Daniel. "Openings." *Art and Antiques,* 15 (May 1993), p. 21.

Princenthal, Nancy. "Joel Shapiro at Pace." *Art in America,* 81 (September 1993), p. 109.

Richard, Paul. "Obscene Pleasure: Art among the Corpses." *Washington Post,* April 18, 1993.

Rivelles, Rafael Prats. "Una aproximación a la escultura post-minimal." *Que y Donde,* October 11–17, 1993, p. 7.

Schemo, Diana Jean. "Holocaust Memorial Hailed as Sacred Debt to Dead." *New York Times,* April 23, 1993.

———. "Museum Opens with Firm Grip on the Emotions." *New York Times,* April 27, 1993.

Smith, Roberta. "Art in Review: '25 Years, Part I.' " *New York Times,* November 26, 1993.

Veroli, Patrizia. "New York: Joel Shapiro, The Pace Gallery." *Terzo Occhio,* 19 (September 1993).

Villaescusa Blanca, José V. "Exposiciones: La escultura post-minimal en las colecciones del IVAM." *Tendencias,* 1 (November 1993), p. 32.

1994

Gibson, Eric. "The Figure Reconsidered." *Sculpture,* 13 (May–June 1994), p. 10.

Goodrow, Gérard A. "Joel Shapiro, Karsten Greve." *Art News,* 93 (February 1994), p. 150.

Kang, Tae Hee. "The Artworld of Joel Shapiro." *Space,* May 1994.

Litt, Steven. "Eugene Stevens: The Gallery in Pepper Pike." *Art News,* 93 (January 1994), pp. 99–101.

Thorson, Alice. "Artist Now at Work on Airport Sculpture." *Kansas City Star,* April 10, 1994.

1995

Auer, James. "Art Museum Exhibit Embraces Pluralism." *Milwaukee Journal Sentinel,* September 10, 1995.

Castenfors, Marten. "Balansakt med volymer." *Svenska Dagbladet* (Stockholm), February 18, 1995.

Chandler, Mary Voelz. "Exhibit of Drawings Outlines Method's Frontiers." *Rocky Mountain News*, August 13, 1995.

Dagen, Philippe. "Dans les galeries." *Le Monde* (Paris), May 15, 1995.

Jenkins, Loren. "Drawing: The Wellspring of Art." *Aspen Times Gazette*, Summer 1995, p. 5.

Landi, Ann. "Kiss and Tell." *Art News,* 94 (February 1995), pp. 116–19.

"Museums and Dealer Catalogues." *The Print Collector's Newsletter,* 26 (May–June 1995), p. 69.

Smith, Roberta. "Joel Shapiro Looks Back, Differently." *New York Times,* March 31, 1995.

Suchère, Eric. "Joel Shapiro: Galerie Karsten Greve." *Art Press,* 204 (July–August 1995), p. 81.

Vogel, Carol. "Second Night of Caution at Auction." *New York Times,* May 4, 1995.

Wilson, Jane. "Primal Drawing." *Aspen Times*, July 29 and 30, 1995, pp. 1B, 20B.

1996

Adhikari, Sara. "American Art to Celebrate Indian Freedom." *Sunday Times* (New Delhi), March 10, 1996.

Avilia, Oscar. "Two Sculptures Installed at KCI." *Kansas City Star,* May 2, 1996.

Baker, Kenneth. "Minimalism and More by Shapiro." *San Francisco Chronicle,* April 2, 1996.

Bevan, Roger. "Contemporary Art Sales, London." *The Art Newspaper,* January 1996, pp. 29–30.

Conroy, Sarah Booth. "The White House's New Scene." *Washington Post,* January 8, 1996.

Cuno, James. "Joel Shapiro on His Recent Prints: An Interview." *The Print Collector's Newsletter,* 27 (May–June 1996), pp. 46–50.

Gear, Josephine. "The Old Is New Again: Joel Shapiro at PaceWildenstein." *Review Art,* 2 (October 15, 1996), p. 1.

Jin-Hi, Lee. "Joel Shapiro at Gallery Seomi." *Space: Arts and Architecture—Environment,* December 1996, pp. 40–47.

MacAdam, Barbara A. "Joel Shapiro: Punch and Judy." *Art News,* 95 (January 1996), p. 83.

Pagel, David. "Joel Shapiro's Sculptures Embody Joy of Movement." *Los Angeles Times,* March 28, 1996.

Peebles, Debra. "New Public Gardens." *Pitch Weekly,* May 23, 1996, p. 48.
Selby, Holly. "Exhibit of a Lifetime." *Baltimore Sun,* March 31, 1996.

Slesin, Suzanne. "Prairie Home Companions." *House and Garden,* 165 (November 1996), pp. 196–203.

Smith, Roberta. "Celebrating Size and Rough Simplicity. Still." *New York Times,* July 26, 1996.

Solomon, Deborah. "Windy City's Cool New Museum." *Wall Street Journal,* June 24, 1996.

Thorson, Alice. "Building Blocks . . . Just for Fun." *Kansas City Star,* May 18, 1996.

———. "Something Special on the Ground." *Kansas City Star,* May 20, 1996.

1997

Adams, Brooks. "Art World Diva." *Elle Decor,* 7 (February 1997), pp. 128–33.

Landi, Ann. "Queens Bounty." *Newsday* (New York), April 4, 1997.

"Preview: Joel Shapiro, Haus der Kunst." *Artforum,* 36 (September 1997), p. 69.

Vogel, Carol. "Inside Art." *New York Times,* March 21, 1997.

Acknowledgments

The preparation of this book has involved the goodwill, talent, and energy of many people, and to each of them I owe a profound debt of gratitude. I thank Annie Lefevre, whose insightful comments on my original French text were indispensable; Charles Ruas and Molly Stevens, for their hard work in translating the text into English; and Anna Jardine, for her careful reading of the translation.

At Joel Shapiro's studio, I received invaluable assistance from Lindsay Walt and Pamela Franks, who gathered research materials on the works as well as biographical and bibliographical data. Patrick Strzelec and Ichiro Kato generously supplied information about Shapiro's working methods.

My thanks to Paula Cooper, Julian Lethbridge, Elizabeth Murray, Ellen Phelan, and Anna and Ivy Shapiro for their many observations about the artist. Critical contributions to the project were made by the staff of the Paula Cooper Gallery, especially Natasha Sigmund, who helped with research in the gallery's archive and in collecting photographs. Likewise, the assistance of the PaceWildenstein gallery and its staff, particularly Douglas Baxter, has been essential.

I am deeply grateful to Coosje van Bruggen and Terry Winters, who have supported this project from its inception.

Finally, it has been a pleasure and an honor to work with Joel Shapiro. Without his commitment and collaboration, this book would not have been possible.

H. T.

Photograph Credits

Unless otherwise indicated, a page number refers to all of the illustrations on that page.

Shigeo Anzai: pages 123 upper right, 124, 129 upper left, 150 upper left

© 1998 Artists Rights Society (ARS), New York/ADAGP, Paris: pages 44 bottom, 49 bottom, 70 lower right, 79 lower left, 157 upper left, 170 bottom

Courtesy Asher/Faure: page 128

Peter Bellamy, courtesy Paula Cooper Gallery, New York: page 133

Geoffrey Clements, courtesy Paula Cooper Gallery, New York: 28 upper left, 28, 31 upper right, 32 lower right, 33 top, 38, 42 upper left, 43 upper left, 48 lower right, 51 upper left, 54 lower right, 55, 56, 57, 62 upper right, 71 lower right, 83, 87 upper left, 89 upper left, 92, 93 upper left, 94, 96 upper right, 98 lower left, 99, 104 upper right, 107 upper left, 111, 112 upper left, 115 lower left, 116 lower right, 119 upper left, 119 lower right, 125 lower left, 131 lower right, 137 lower right, 144 upper right, 151, 163

Giorgio Columbo: page 58

Courtesy Paula Cooper Gallery, New York: pages 32 upper left, 40 lower right, 42 middle right, 44 upper left, 47 upper left, 48 upper left, 61 upper left, 63 lower right, 64, 85, 86, 97 upper right, 98 upper left, 101, 153, 155, 166

Bevan Davies, courtesy Paula Cooper Gallery, New York: page 93 lower right

James Dee: pages 18 upper left, 19, 127 lower right, 181 middle left, 181 lower left; courtesy Paula Cooper Gallery, New York: pages 35 upper center, 53 lower right, 69 lower right, 95, 107 lower right, 115 upper right, 118 upper left, 120 lower right, 125 upper right, 127 upper left, 157 lower right, 158 upper left; courtesy Betsy Senior Gallery, New York: 181 upper left, 181 lower right

eeva-inkeri, courtesy Paula Cooper Gallery, New York: pages 73–75, 90–91, 105 upper right, 164 upper left

Susan Einstein: page 42 bottom

© 1998 Courtesy the Estate of Eva Hesse: page 42 bottom

© 1998 Estate of David Smith/Licensed by VAGA, New York: page 109 lower right

Janice Felgar: page 110 upper left

David Finn: page 144 lower left

Larry Fuchsman, courtesy Paula Cooper Gallery, New York: page 67 upper left

Bill Jacobson, courtesy PaceWildenstein, New York: page 162 lower right

Balthazar Korab, Troy, Michigan, © 1998 Barnett Newman Foundation/Artists Rights Society (ARS), New York: page 22 top

Dan Lenore, courtesy Paula Cooper Gallery, New York: page 33 lower right

Judy Linn: page 117 lower left

Robert E. Mates and Paul Katz, courtesy Paula Cooper Gallery, New York: page 46

©1998 Succession H. Matisse/Artists Rights Society (ARS), New York: pages 10, 11

©1997 Diana Michener: page 201

©1998 Moderna Museet, Stockholm: page 103 lower right

Andrew Moore, courtesy Paula Cooper Gallery, New York: pages 39, 59 lower right, 137 upper right, 150 lower right

Andre Morain: pages 112 lower right, 113 upper right, 116 upper right, 122 upper left

©1998 The Museum of Modern Art, New York: pages 10, 11, 13, 44 lower right, 49 lower right, 132

Wojtek Naczas: pages 2–3, 59 upper left, 66 lower left, 67 lower right, 68, 80, 81, 108, 121 lower left, 131 upper left, 134, 139, 152 upper left, 170; courtesy PaceWildenstein, New York: pages 16, 22 lower left, 23, 148, 149

© The Nelson Gallery Foundation: page 142

Courtesy PaceWildenstein, New York: page 20

© 1998 Pollock-Krasner Foundation/ Artists Rights Society (ARS), New York: page 129 lower right

Nathan Rabin: page 29 upper right; courtesy Paula Cooper Gallery, New York: page 30

©1998 Réunion des Musées Nationaux, Paris: page 96 lower right

Walter Russell, © 1998 Carl Andre/ Licensed by VAGA, New York: page 34 bottom

E. G. Schempf: pages 152 lower right, 183–86

Joel Shapiro: pages 21, 34 upper left, 35 lower right, 36, 37 lower right, 49 top, 53 upper left, 76, 156 center left, 162 center left, 171 upper left, 171 lower left, 194 lower right, 195 lower right

Jerry L. Thompson: page 104 lower left; courtesy Paula Cooper Gallery, New York: page 103 upper left; ©1996: Whitney Museum of American Art, New York: pages 65, 100

©1998 Whitney Museum of American Art: page 121 upper right

Ellen Page Wilson, courtesy PaceWildenstein, New York: pages 4–5, 8, 37 upper right, 40 upper left, 54 upper left, 60, 69 upper right, 72, 140 lower left, 140 lower right, 141 lower left, 141 upper right, 146–47, 160 lower left, 160 upper right, 161, 162 upper right, 167–69, 171 upper right, 172–80, 182 upper left, 187–93, 194 upper left, 195 upper left, 198